I0763129

TAPESTRY TALKING

UNDERSTANDING THE LANGUAGE OF HANDWOVEN ART
WITH 326 WORKS FROM AROUND THE WORLD

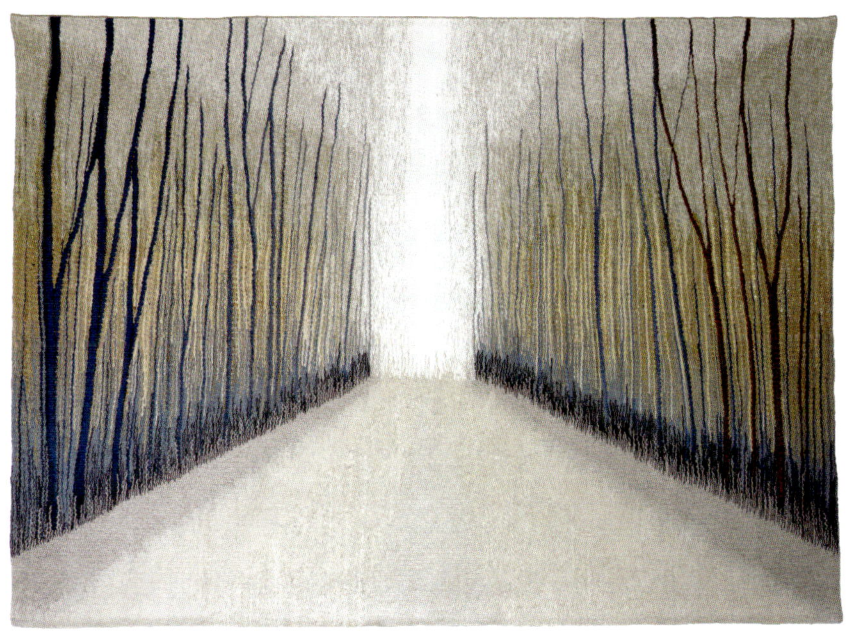

MICALA SIDORE

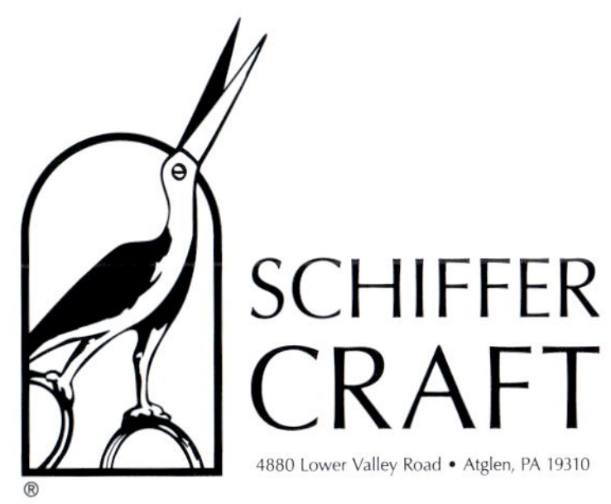
SCHIFFER CRAFT
4880 Lower Valley Road • Atglen, PA 19310

Other Schiffer Craft Books by the Author:

The Art Is the Cloth: How to Look at and Understand Tapestries, foreword by Charissa Bremer-David, ISBN 978-0-7643-5992-7

Other Schiffer Craft Books on Related Subjects:

Anatomy of a Tapestry: Techniques, Materials, Care, Jean Pierre Larochette & Yadin Larochette, illustrations by Yael Lurie, ISBN 978-0-7643-5933-0

Fiber Craft Heritage: Easy-to-Learn Textile Techniques from the Stone Age to Today, with 52 Try-It Projects, Doris Fischer, ISBN 978-0-7643-6962-9

Dimensional Cloth: Sculpture by Contemporary Textile Artists, Andra F. Stanton, foreword by Josephine Stealey, ISBN 978-0-7643-5536-3

Library of Congress Control Number: 2025939857

Pages 12, 13, 67, 99: Samplers woven by Micala Sidore.
Interior and back cover design by Lori Malkin Ehrlich
Front cover design by Lindsay Hess
Front cover image: Melanie Cros, *Al Mamzar Beach, Dubai*, 2023 (see page 105)
Back cover images: *(L top)* Andra Dirina, *Light Dawned*, 2022 (see page 124). *(L center)* Åse Pedersen, *Energikilde*, 1982, photo: Annar Bjørgli (see page 178). *(L bottom)* Louise Oppenheimer, *Birches*, 2008 (see page 142). *(R center)* Louise Martin, *Two Blues*, 2019 (see page 79).
Title page image: Uisce A. Jakubczyk, *Runaway*, 2017 (see page 136)
Type set in Ten Oldstyle / Gibson

ISBN: 978-0-7643-7141-7
ePub: 978-1-5073-0699-4
Printed in China

10 9 8 7 6 5 4 3 2 1

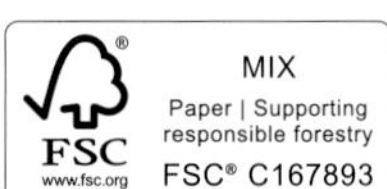

Published by Schiffer Craft
An imprint of Schiffer Publishing, Ltd.
4880 Lower Valley Road
Atglen, PA 19310
Phone: (610) 593-1777; Fax: (610) 593-2002
Email: Info@schifferbooks.com
Web: www.schifferbooks.com

To the community of tapestry weavers who have provided me so much to look at, think about, and consider. The work they share with me, both their tapestries and their thoughts, continues to excite and move me. I remain constantly grateful for their generosity.

To Jean Claude Lagrange (1947–2025).

And to my lovely Bill Oram, all day every day, all night every night—and whatever other time there might be. You are always present; you are always ready and able to help.

Sense of touch is the most emotional of our senses. To touch and be touched has a central meaning in human development. Working with your hands develops creativity and problem-solving abilities. Working with different materials benefits three-dimensional understanding. To handle includes the word hand. There is a connection between thinking and making things by hand. As well as materials and working with my hands, my works contain thought, emotions, sitting still, intuition, and intensity.

—Aino Kajaniemi

In 2020 Sarah Swett began to weave small tapestries of four-letter words. She has now woven at least a hundred, including the ones shown here. (At my request, she wove a few specifically for this book.) The caption details her wide range of materials.

Each of these pieces names a chapter ahead—except for *hand*, which is included among them as a reminder: The work here is made by hand.

The 99 Noun Project (details), Sarah Swett

Materials noted in this format:
warp / ground weft / letter weft (dye stuff)

yarn: wool/silk, coffee filter paper, wool
woad: wool/silk, linen, wool (indigo)
warp: wool, wool, wool
weft: wool, wool, wool
seed: wool, coffee filter paper, wool (madder/cochineal)
sett: wool, coffee filter paper, wool
line: wool, wool, wool
slit: silk, linen, wool
grid: wool, wool, wool
size: silk, linen, wool
mark: silk, linen, wool
time: silk, linen, wool
text: silk, linen, wool
hand: silk, linen, wool

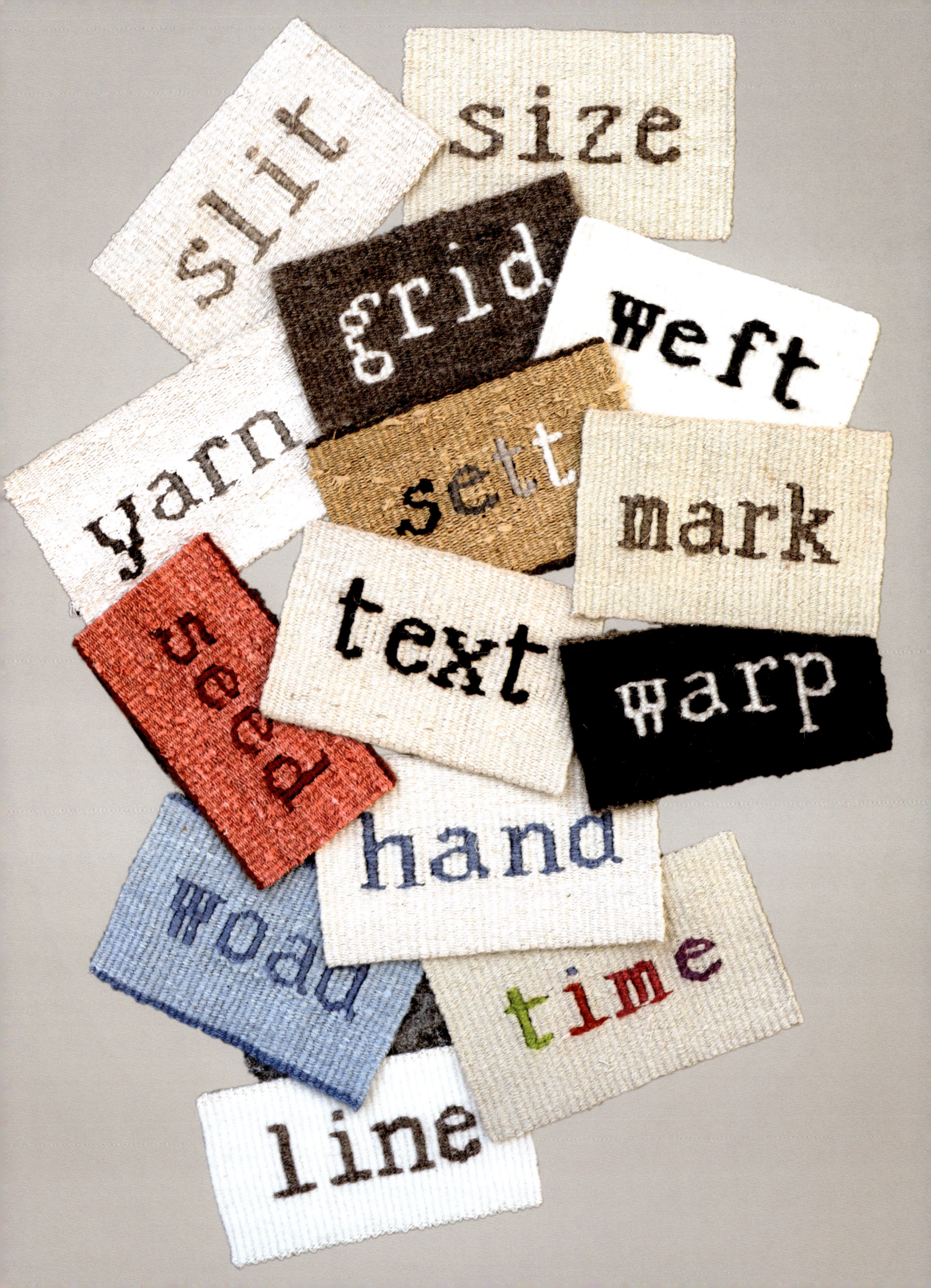

slit
size
grid
weft
yarn
sett
mark
seed
text
warp
hand
woad
time
line

The delight of the visual image [in a tapestry] is inseparable from the way the image was constructed.

—Lyman Pittman, *Pueblo Chieftain* review of 1992 *International Tapestry Network: Exhibit One*

All Navajo weavings could be described as Tale Tellers. Each uniquely reflected its creator and the time of its creation.

—Anne Hillerman, *The Tale Teller*

OPPOSITE: *States + Moods,* details (see page 22)
Shula Litan
1990s | 36" × 36" | handmade paper

CONTENTS

ACKNOWLEDGMENTS

I have had the amazing good luck to work with a team of friends, people who know what they are doing and help me so well.

First and foremost, the following four:

Stan Sherer, the photographer, who knows how to make images work, how to make them conform to the color profile for printing. Who always plays close attention to what he sees and listens to what I can tell him. His work is unfailingly excellent. (If you have a problem with an image, blame me.)

My beloved Brigitte Hogan exchanged thoughts, ideas, and reactions with me almost every day. She made endless phone calls all over Europe and befriended bureaucrats at government institutions, museums, and galleries. Brigitte knows how to get results. She is composed of capability, compassion—and humor.

Anna Slezak, whom I described in every email in which I introduced her as my helper and colleague. Anna reached out with permission needs. She offered to answer questions and showed unfailing sweetness and good will. She organized it all very well. Anna loves textiles.

My editor Sandra Korinchak, who has always been ready to help, answer my questions, reassure me, and just, in general, be immensely kind and understanding when I might otherwise have melted down.

My local angels, the friends who have cheered me on: Beth Beede, Lisa d'Errico, James Emery, Andrea Hairston, Pan Morigan, Dennie Pinardi, Nancy and Bern Reinke, and Robin Stolk. And the angels who live farther afield: Corlis Carroll, Tanya DeMarsh-Dodson, Louis Dorsey, Stephen Foster, Catherine Gourdin, Joan Harlow, Patrick McCay, Pam Pier, Naomi Machado. My sister, Sara Mae, and my brother, Ralph. My sister-in-law, Kate.

To Ludmilla Egorova, Andrew Schneider, and Anastasia Schneider, organizers of Scythia Biennial Symposium on Textile and Fiber Art, in Ukraine, who provided me with endless information and images (as well as Andrew's and Anastasia's tapestries!).

Andra Dirina of the Latvian Textile Art Association for her help in reaching out to various members (as well as providing me with her own piece!).

Karlos Meeuws (and his wife, Darlene), who, during his regular visit to his good Zapotec friends in Teotitlán del Valle, Mexico, collected signatures for my permission forms—and showed me the work he was loving. Nifty.

Ulrikka Mokdad, in Denmark, and Laçi Valy, in Hungary, both did research for me, gave me contact information, answered questions—all with immense good will.

Marta Figlerowicz, who wrote and translated emails for me in Polish.

Alice Bernadac at the Cité Internationale de la Tapisserie (Aubusson, France) welcomed me when I visited her institution, introduced me to other local tapestry weavers, and helped without hesitation when I requested particular images.

Harry Ree at the Powerhouse Museum in Sydney, Australia, was cheerful about every request I made, every question I raised. He also sought to help me locate certain weavers in their collection whom I wished to include.

To the people who are the spouses, colleagues, children (and so on) of tapestry weavers who speak no English, or who have died, or who do not like fiddling with computers, etc.: You helped me with permission to use their work and so made my task easier.

And to all the contributors to my version of crowdsourcing. You helped me pay the various fees at museums and other institutions.

3e Gigue (3rd jig), details (see page 166)
Micheline Beauchemin
1972 | 83.5" × 112.2" | wool
Musée National des Beaux-Arts du Québec
Photographer: Julie Bouffard

PREFACE

In my first book (*The Art Is the Cloth*), and in this one, I have chosen to do one thing: to invite the reader to see what there is to see in handwoven tapestries. But my first book and this one do the job differently. The first provided examples of how tapestries reflect on their identity as a piece of cloth. By investigating them by theme, such as trompe l'oeil or directionality, I sought to inform readers about the field, and the traditions and visual effects it draws on.

The book you're holding now reveals tapestries differently, grouping them by thirteen weaving techniques to show what can result from each. Four-letter words are used partly for fun and partly to stress how basic and how accessible these techniques are. Each chapter is named with a four-letter word—warp, weft, sett, and so on. The images within the chapter fill out its meaning. As in my first book, many of the tapestries in one chapter might also appear in another. I've made my choices here so that each work will illuminate a particular process.

This book is also meant for two kinds of readers: weavers and nonweavers. For those who do not weave, I hope that understanding these thirteen techniques of tapestry will enrich awareness of what is going on. For the makers, I hope that by illustrating how other weavers have explored these techniques, this book will help you develop your own visual language.

I draw on what I learned during my own tapestry education. In the 1980s, I became an intern at la Manufacture Nationale des Gobelins, the French government's tapestry studio. My studio head would say, "*Que ça soit joli*" ("It has to be beautiful"). And then I had to learn what that meant. The more than two years I spent in that studio deeply influenced the way in which I think—as this book will attest.

I have since that time traveled widely in many countries, meeting scores of tapestry weavers and viewing many hundreds of tapestries. I have talked with everyone I could. Along the way, I have looked beyond the formal definition of tapestry that I learned during my internships: “flat, mural, and without perspective.” Some of what I have discovered—an assortment of work that makers from various weaving cultures have created—is in these pages.

This is not, however, a “how to” book (there are already many good ones), but a “why” or a “why not” book—an attempt to consider how and especially why weavers do what they do. What effects can various techniques create? How do these techniques work together? What themes that appear regularly in historical work continue to inspire today’s tapestry weavers? In what ways can a piece composed of yarn work? Interlacing threads produces cloth, of which tapestry is one kind. Like any art, the field of tapestry is rich with possibilities. The results can work as photographic or impressionistic or dimensional or—whatever. Tapestry covers a massive range.

I have felt passionate about tapestry since I wove my first over forty years ago. I knew then that this was what mattered to me: It was my work. It is still.

If you like looking at and/or weaving things and are ready to get some hints that might deepen and enrich the experience, this book is meant for you. What works for you, either as a weaver, or as a viewer? I hope this book will tickle the imagination—what is possible in a tapestry?

P and P Horned Toad and Lightning Twill, details (see page 79)
Venancio Aragón
2023 | 24" × 29" | wool, mohair; wool warp; natural and synthetic dyes

HOW WEAVING WORKS

Here are six basic terms. Each deals with an aspect of weaving. Feel free to refer back to these if you come across technical mentions that you are unfamiliar with.

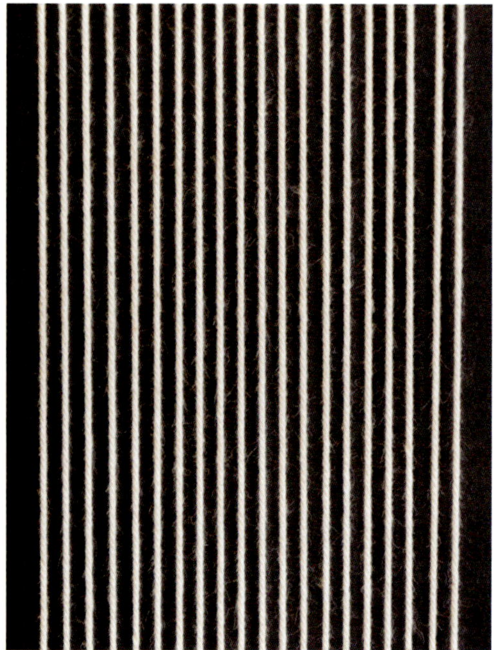

◀ **warp**
On the loom, the warp looks like this before the weaver begins to weave: parallel threads, under tension.

▶ **warp and weft**
The horizontal weft threads here go over and under the warp. You can discern a very basic grid.

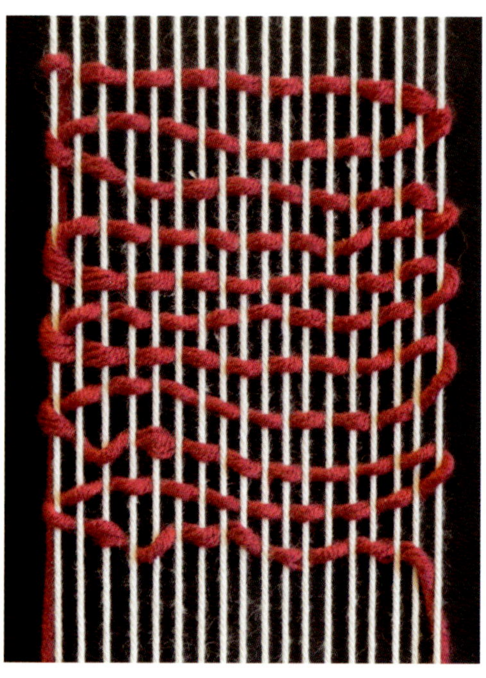

◀ **plain weave**
Individual weft goes over and under individual warps. Both elements are equally visible.

▶ **weft-faced plain weave**
If the weaver tamps the weft down in among the warp threads, it covers the warp, making the cloth weft-faced. No warp is visible except as vertical ridges.

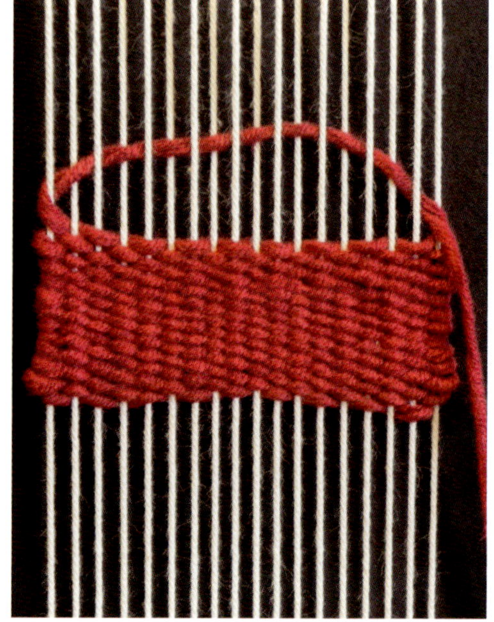

▲ **sett**

Covering alternating warp threads produces plain weave. Here you see a bottom section consisting of one weft over one warp. In the next section up, the weft covers pairs of warp, then three warps, then four warps, then six. The surface texture changes with each changed sett.

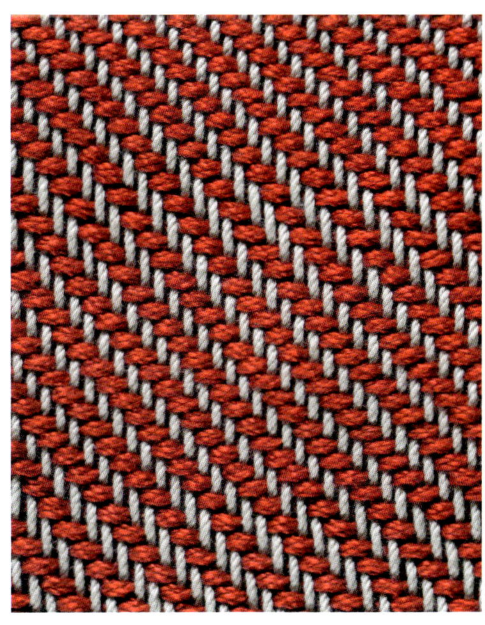

▲ **twill**

The diagonal lines here are twill, the result of a particular weaving pattern. Look at your blue jeans—you will see the diagonal twill line there too.

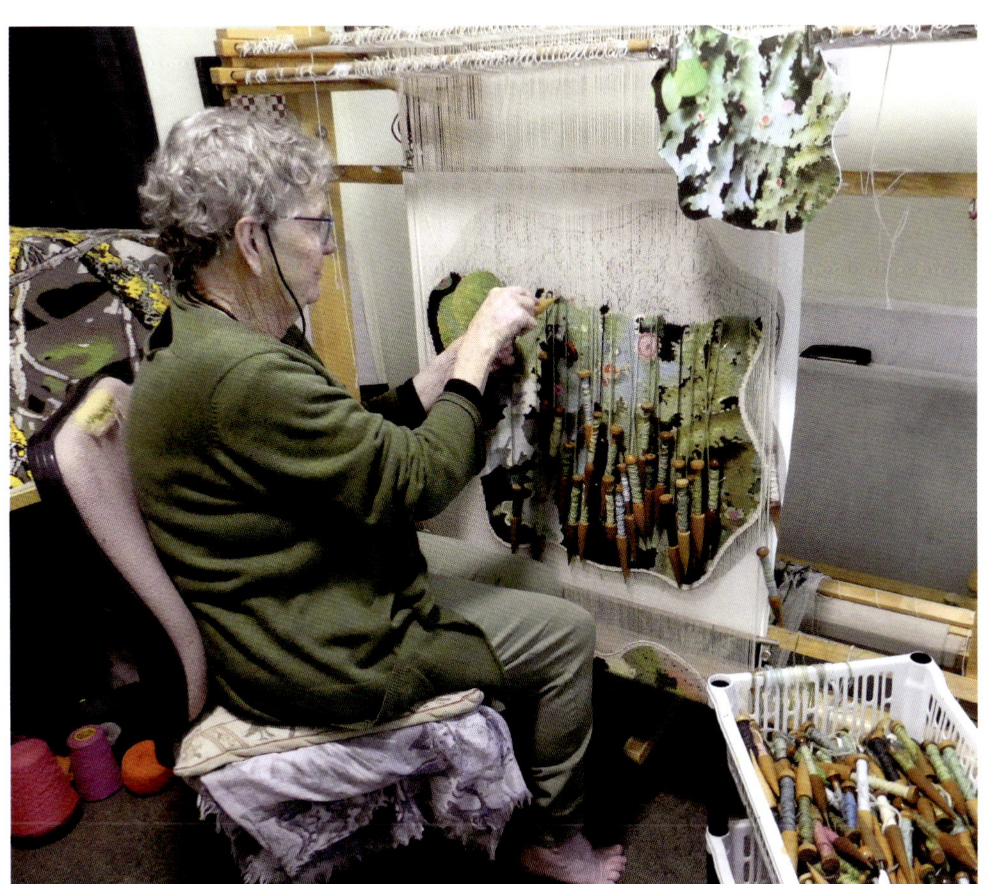

How it looks when a weaver is at the loom and weaving. Marilyn Rea-Menzies working on her series about lichen (see page 199). Bobbins, spools of yarn, and a cartoon (to the right above her head) are visible. *Photo: Bruce Roberts*

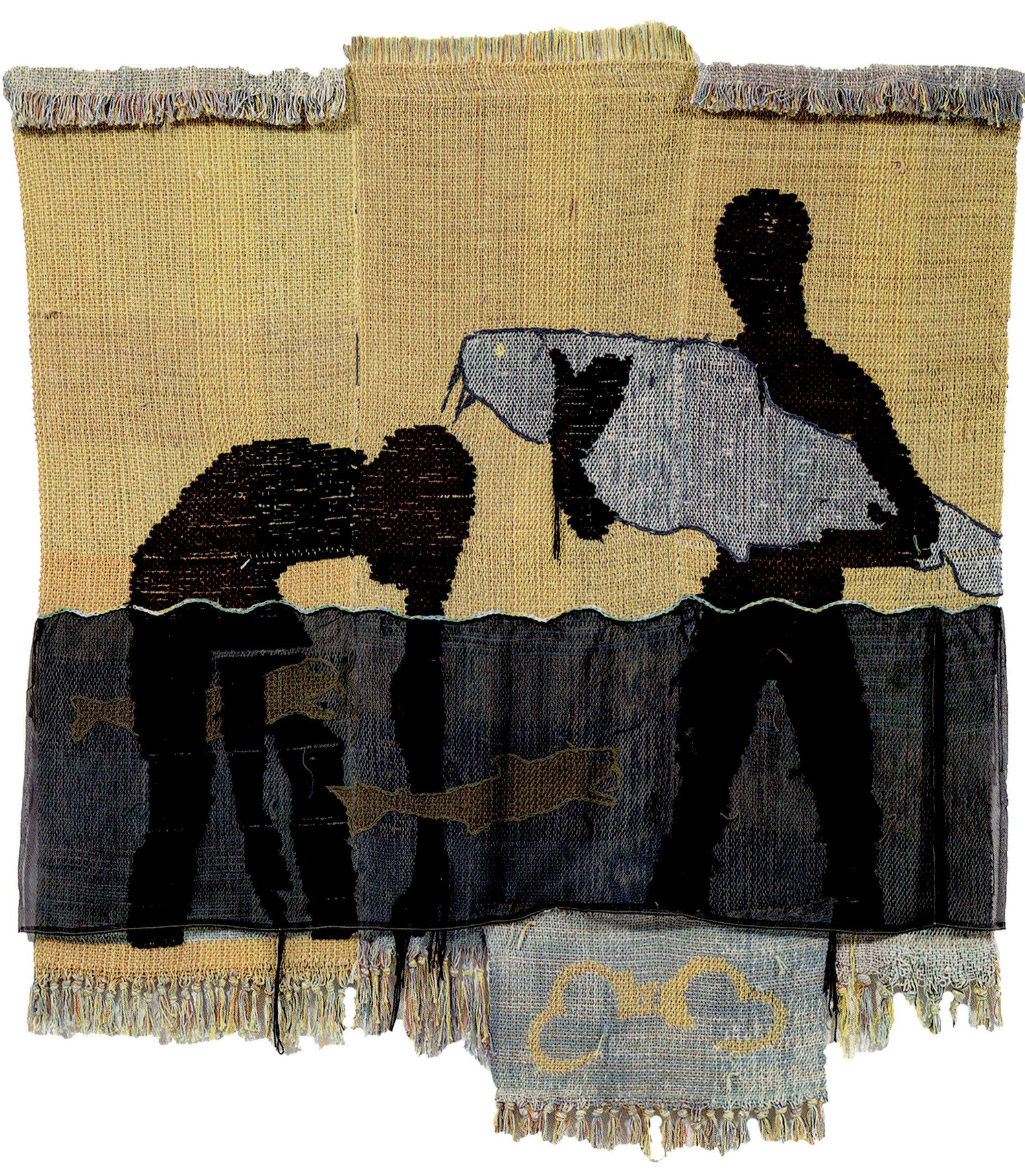

yarn

Weavers choose the yarns they use, looking for what will best interpret their ideas. The first section of this chapter gives examples of the more conventional yarns and, for some, unexpected backstories.

The second section shows unconventional materials. With these, we have to ask how they add to what we see.

The final section (**oh my!**) moves us into even stranger places. We notice what the weaver can do that opens up new territory.

cotton

Tapestry weavers often use cotton seine twine for their warps. Diedrick Brackens, an African American living in Southern California, uses cotton exclusively for both warp and weft. Cotton provides the starting point: It is "the primary material because it is a very easy material to manipulate, it takes color beautifully, and its historical significance in the United States relative to enslavement, violence, and subjugation has had lasting effects on Black bodies." He draws his inspiration in part from other textiles of his culture, including quilts and overshot bedspreads. His pieces often retell horrifying stories from African American history. Brackens's grandmother taught him to sew. He took classes in weaving at college, where, after his first week in the studio, he fell in love with its "spellbinding" looms.

In this piece the black and gray silhouettes stand out against the varied gold and brown of the ground, and through the gray of the water. One of Brackens's major figures holds a huge catfish, and the other reaches down for more.

Bitter Attendance, Drown Jubilee
Diedrick Brackens
2018 | 72" × 72" | cotton, acrylic, silk organza
Courtesy of the artist and Jack Shaiman Gallery

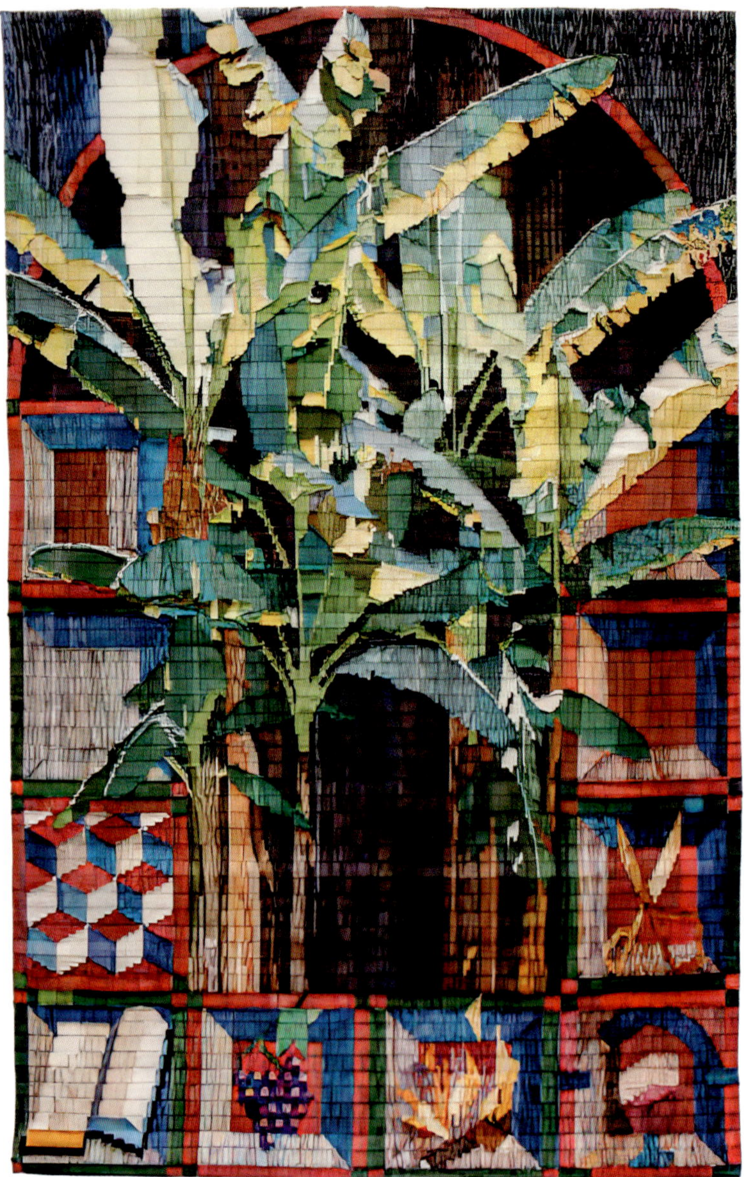

linen

Judith Poxson Fawkes worked with linen exclusively. It had what she wanted in her work: good color, strength, consistency in results. By using a multiple-shaft loom, she could emphasize the straight edges of her rows of thread and build up shapes systematically. Her earlier pieces emphasize line and geometry, and then, in time, her images developed more curves, which here play against the straight lines.

LEFT: *Roman Banana*
Judith Poxson Fawkes
1993 | 70" × 46" | linen
Courtesy of Russo Gallery (Portland, Oregon) and Tom Fawkes

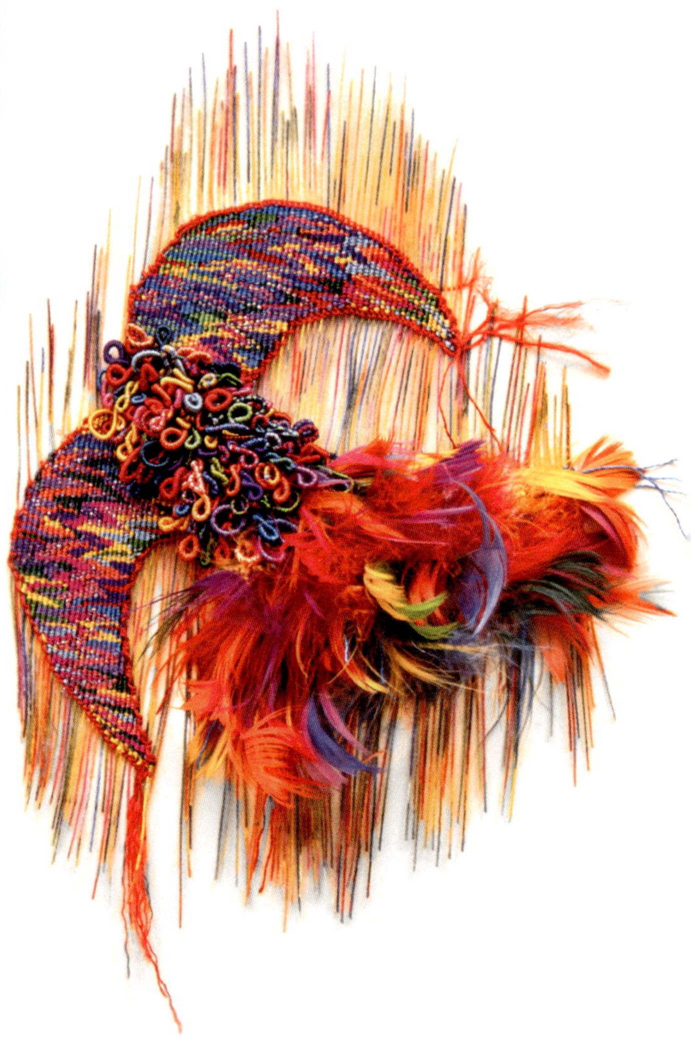

rayon

Anita Berman said that rayon offered a sheen that she imagined existed only in the realm of silk. But as she discovered, rayon shines as silk does not. Because she loved opera, she dedicated this piece to the Italian tenor Bonaventura Bottone, whom she admired endlessly. How else to do justice to his exceptional voice except with lustrous thread and a complex bird-shaped construction further embellished with feathers?

wool

Each breed of sheep has wool with specific properties and characteristics. The users of the wool can often tell you the origin story of the source, whether the fleece comes from sheep or some other animal, the feel of the thread, the structure of the fiber, the length of the staple, the way the wool reflects light. Sometimes tapestry weavers choose to work with certain breeds exclusively.

Sasha Stoyanov has chosen Awassi, a breed local to the Middle East (where she lives). She likes the feel of the yarn and likes the range of its natural colors, which remind her of her local landscape. Here she lets its long strands drift over her portraits as though we see these people through a curtain.

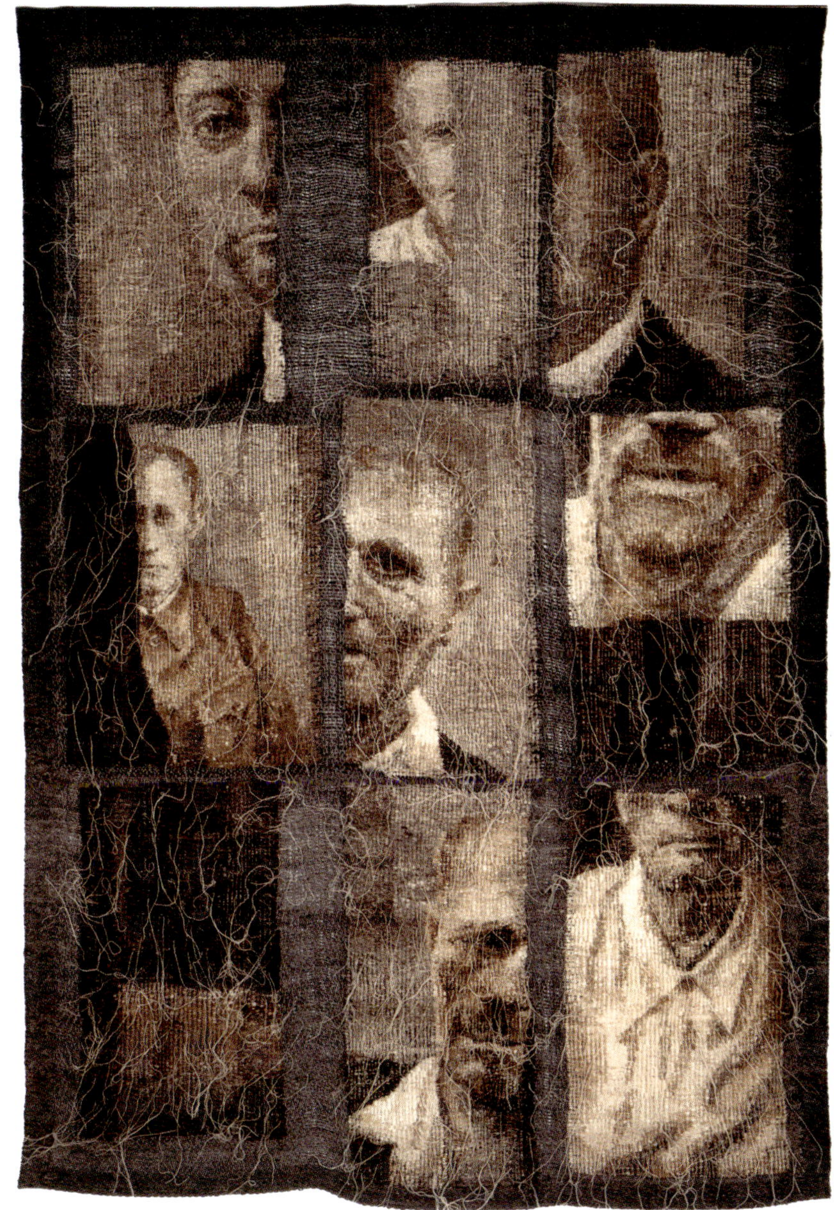

RIGHT: *Judges*
Sasha Stoyanov
1998 | 91" × 60" | Awassi wool, sisal

OPPOSITE: *Homage to Bonaventura. Songbird*
Anita Berman
1993 | 8" × 6" | rayon

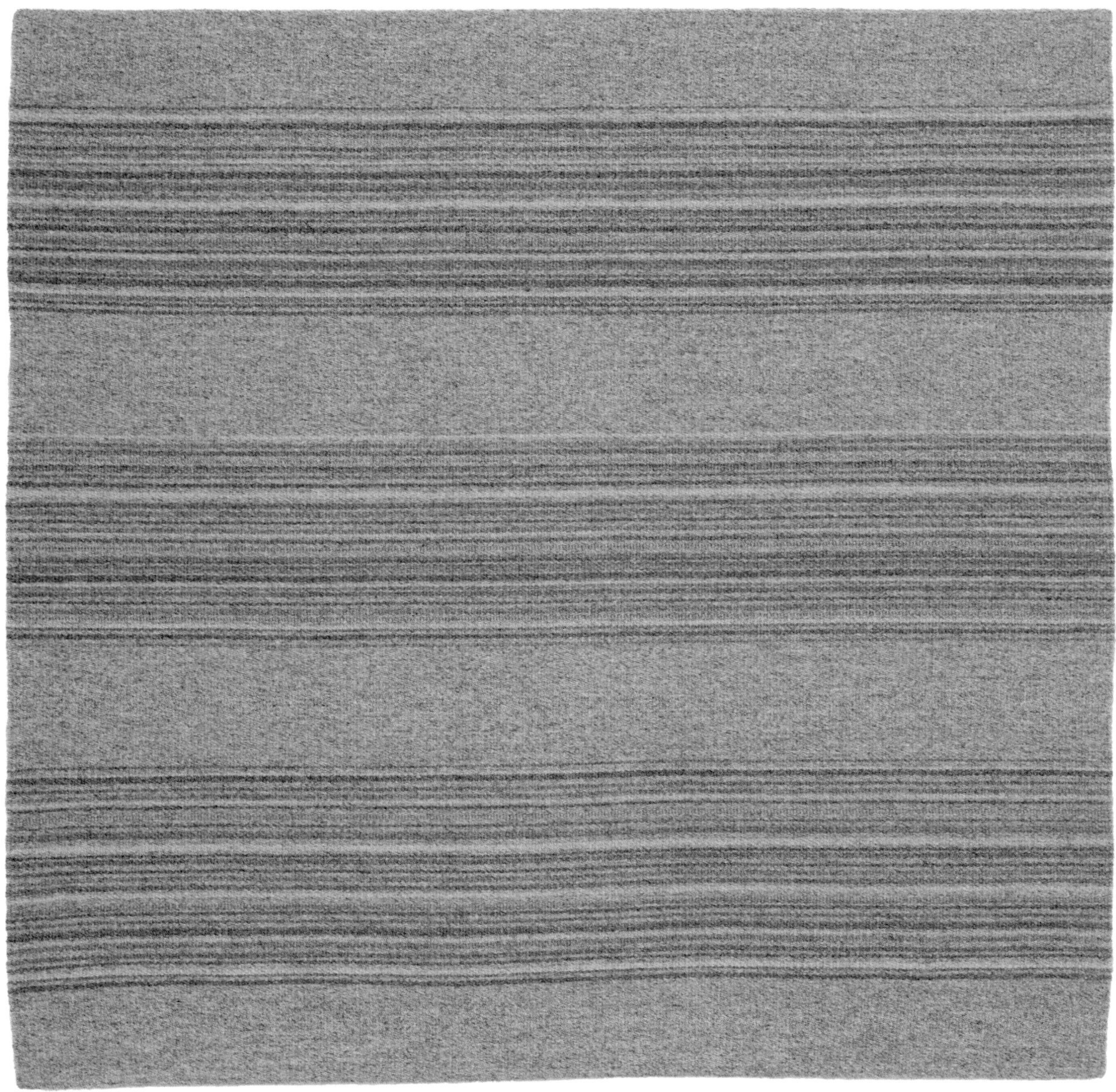

For years, Cornelia Theimer Gardella has played with line. This piece, a byproduct of when she lived in the Southwest of the United States, comes from a series using churro yarn. Churro sheep, the first domesticated sheep introduced into North America, were imported from southern Spain in the sixteenth century and became an essential component of Southwest American culture. Native Americans used them both for food and clothing. In the mid-1800s, Kit Carson and other settlers began systematically to exterminate Navajo livestock; the Navajo were forced off their traditional lands. Even after the exile ended, the federal government continued the policy of herd destruction. That finally ended during the second half of the twentieth century, and the breed has begun to recover. It is still considered "rare."

The sheep remain integral to the culture and are highly valued. The fleece produces a yarn that is rough and difficult to spin. Gardella says that the subject of her work is the churro itself. She loves its range of natural colors and uses the thickest spun version.

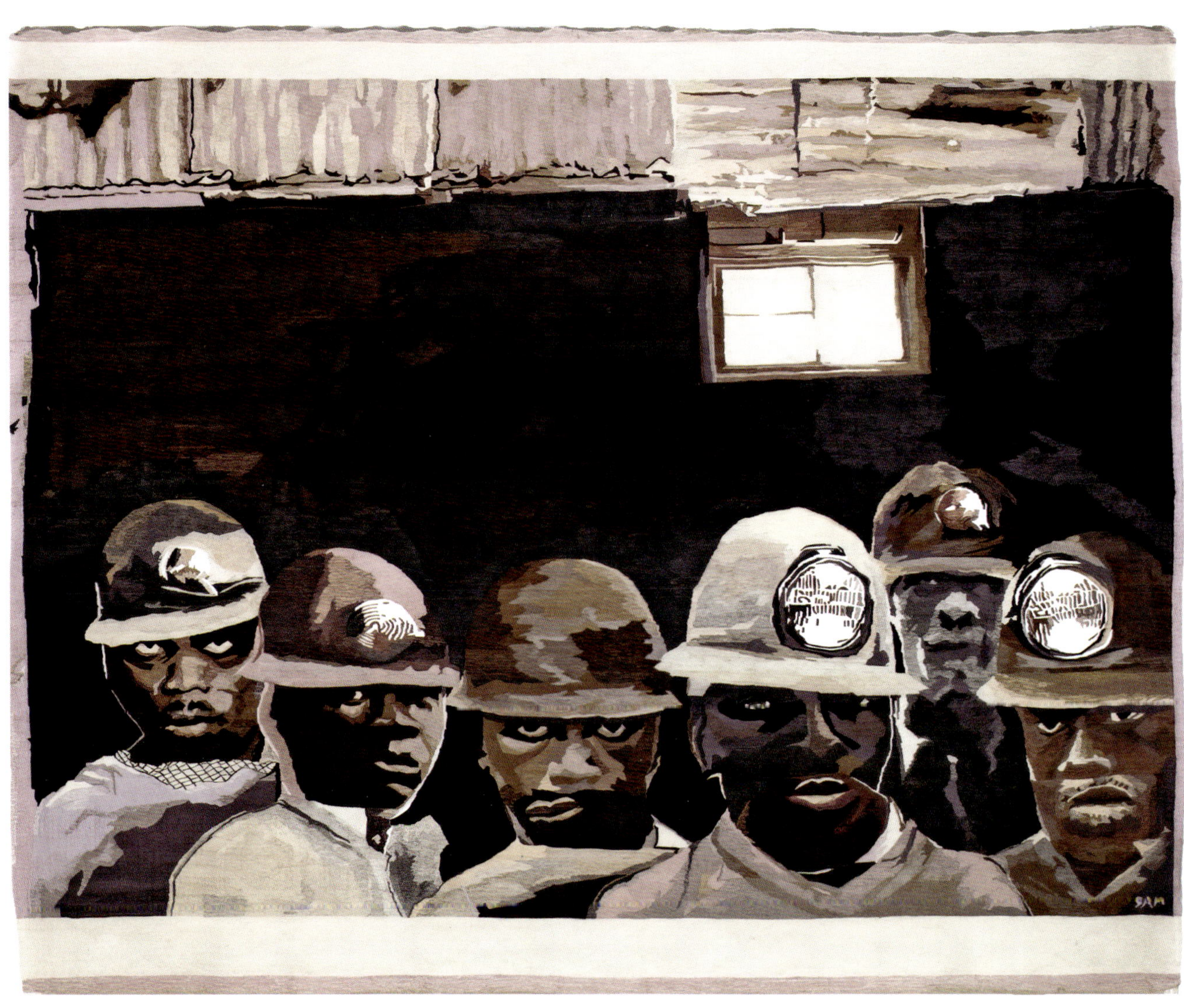

Night Shift
designed by Sam Nhlengethwa,
woven at Stephens Tapestry Studio
2006 | 8'4.5" × 9'9.5" | mohair

OPPOSITE: *Untitled Grays*, part of the *New Mexico churro* series
Cornelia Theimer Gardella
2017–21 | 43.3" × 41.3" | undyed New Mexico churro, hand-dyed silk; cotton warp

mohair

Mohair (from goats) is a mainstay of the Stephens Tapestry Studio, located now in South Africa, the world's largest producer of mohair. Sam Nhlengethwa's miners have helmets with lights—which display the reflective qualities of the mohair itself.

gold

Gold appears in tapestries from many historical periods. Because of its costliness and shine, it tends to bring with it a sense of grandeur.

In the first piece here, woven in the Low Countries and representing the Spanish/Habsburg Empire of the sixteenth century, Atlas bears the weight of a global sphere. In the second, woven in Paris during its occupation by the Third Reich, a godlike figure drives a chariot pulled by bulls.

The designers of these tapestries are important historically. Bernard van Orley served as an official artist for the Habsburg court, and the design works as a statement of empire. Werner Peiner served as one of the official artists of the Third Reich; he was a favorite of Hermann Göring. The Nazis believed that the epic qualities of the tapestry medium were a perfect symbol for the ambitions of the regime.

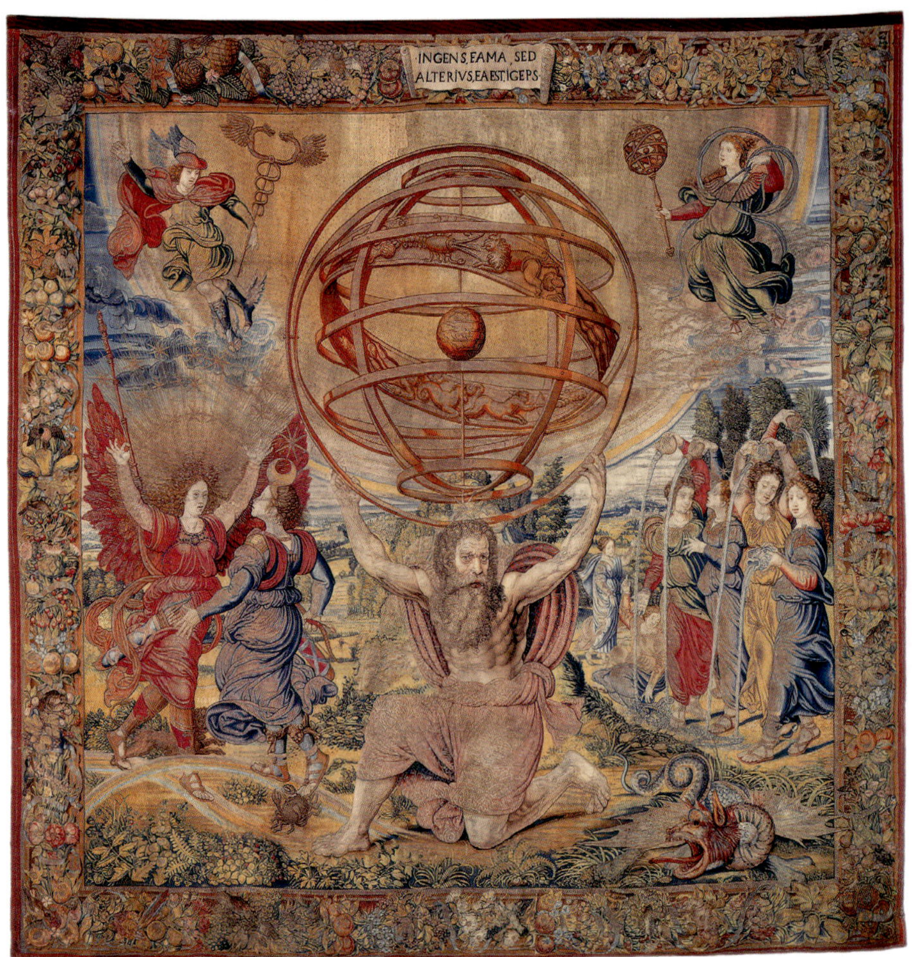

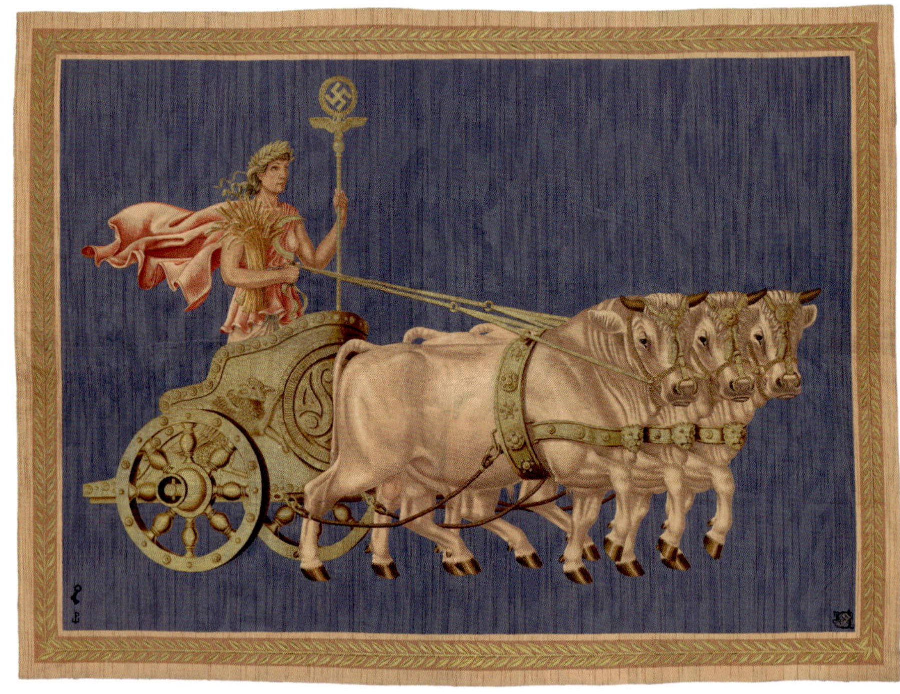

TOP: *Atlas Supporting the Armillary Sphere* (*The Spheres* series, 2nd tapestry)
Ordered by Georg Wezeler, design attributed to Bernard van Orley
before 1543 | 11'2" × 11'4" | gold, silver, silk, wool
Courtesy of the government of Spain, El Palacio Real, Madrid, Spain

BOTTOM: *Le Char des Tauraux, ou Cèrés* (The Chariot of Bulls, or Ceres)
Designed by Werner Peiner, woven at Manufacture Nationale des Gobelins
1941–44 | 11'10" × 16'5" | wool, silk, silk covered with gold

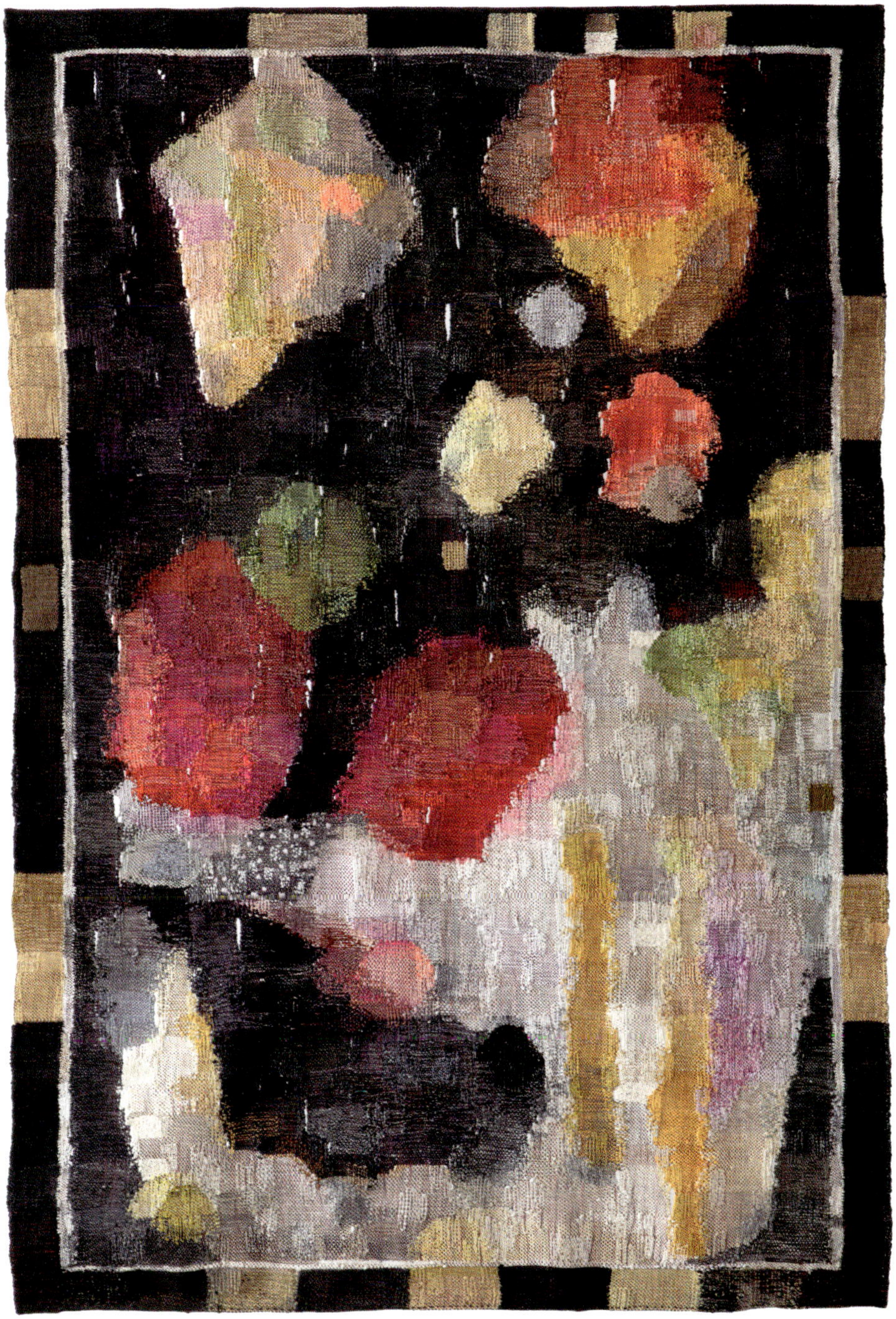

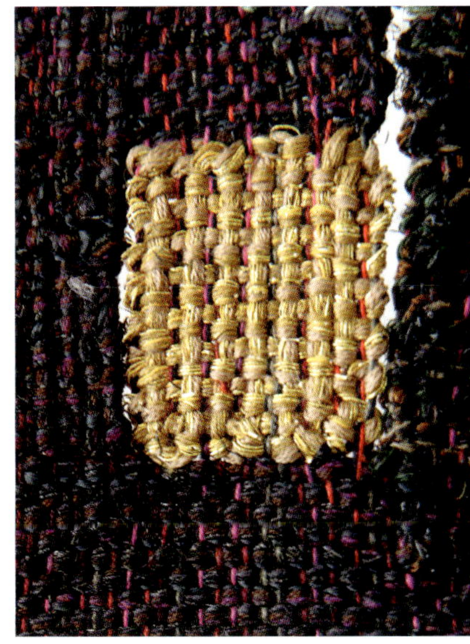

By looking down, I see upward and detail
Inka Kivalo
2023 | 67.75" × 45.7" | cotton, linen, silk, gold from epaulet factory

While both of these tapestries contain gold—indeed, *Le Char des Tauraux* contains almost 9 pounds of it—none of these countries (Low Countries, Spain, France, Germany) had gold mines to produce local supplies. But Spain was extracting gold from its conquests in the New World; the Nazis may well have stripped gold from victims of gas chambers. Speculations, the first probable, the second quite possible.

On the other hand, Inka Kivalo acquired her gold thread in her native Finland, at a factory that produces epaulets for uniforms. She likes incorporating it regularly into her work and uses it as one color among many.

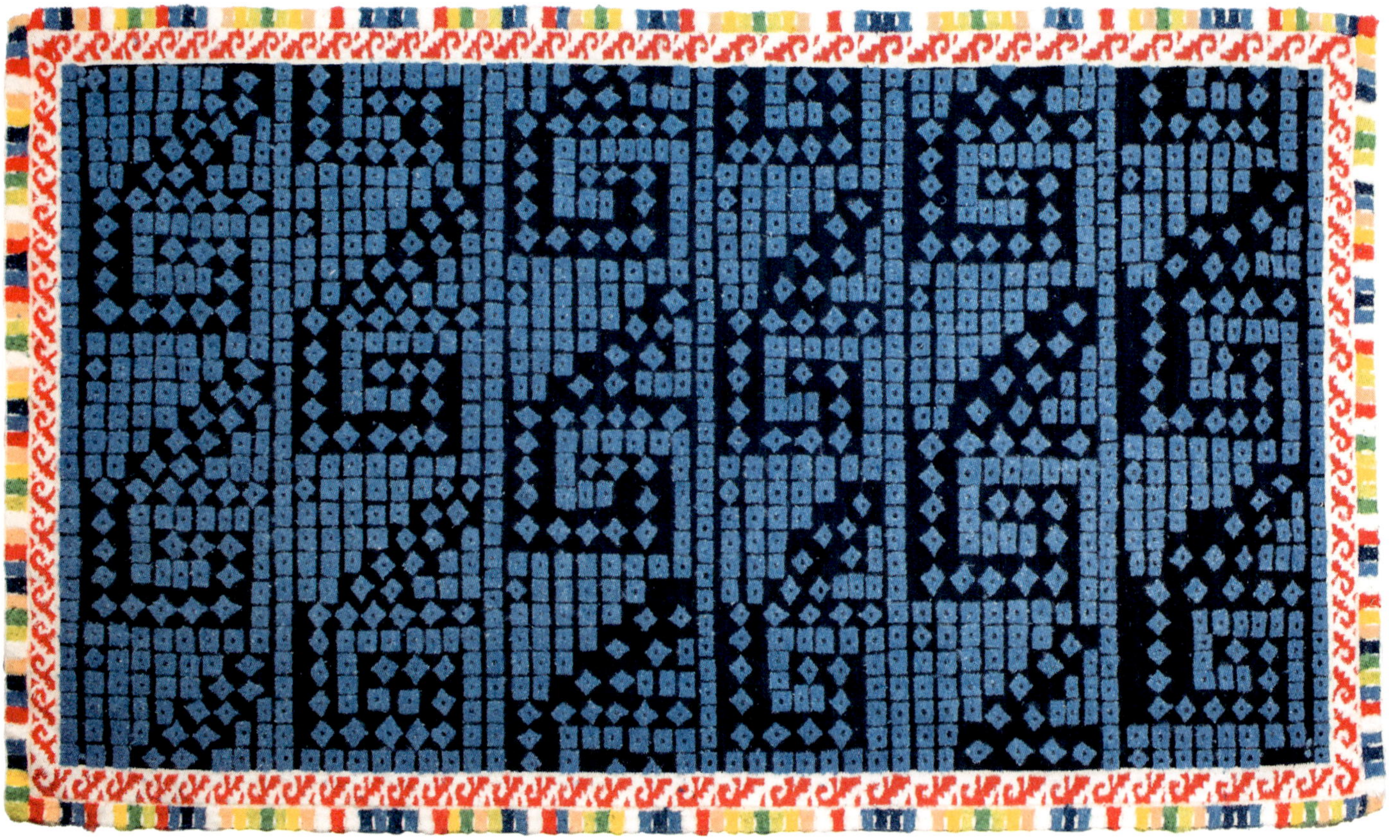

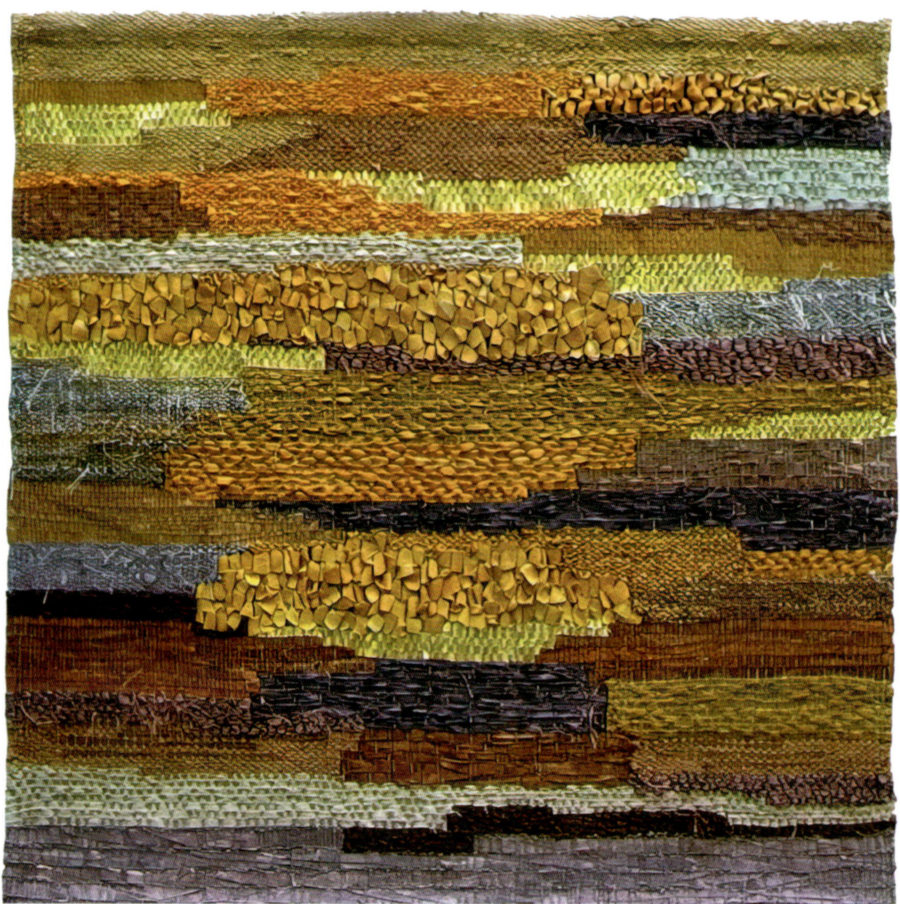

ABOVE: *Tilma* (Feather cape)
Roman Gutierrez
2020 | 47.25" × 66.75" |
duck down, cotton
Courtesy of the Houston
Museum of Natural Sciences

LEFT: *States + Moods*
Shula Litan
1990s | 36" × 36" | handmade paper

unexpected materials

In the small town of Teotitlán del Valle, near Oaxaca, Mexico, lives a capable community of Zapotec tapestry weavers. One of them, Roman Gutierrez, decided to see if he could learn how to include materials he had seen in historical tapestries from the area. Here he works with duck down spun into thread.

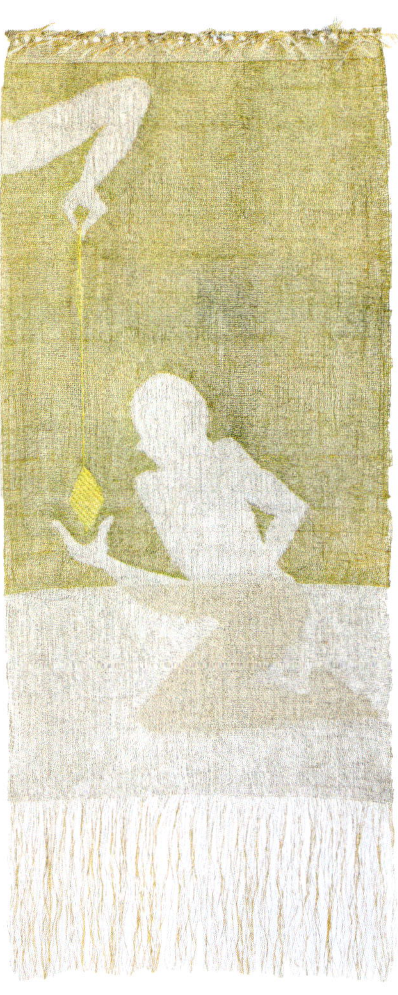

Shula Litan lived in Israel for many years after her family escaped Poland just before the Nazi invasion. She worked with a variety of textiles and textile techniques and devoted her last years to paper. She made it and incorporated it, in various forms, into the rest of her work, as with the weft of this tapestry. The paper creates an interesting surface of layers and bumps, and it absorbs the dyes brilliantly. The piece suggests the landscape where she came to live.

Lin Qiqing's piece radiates brightness. She works with various papers in colors that suggest floating in the air. Her paper is less substantial than Litan's; her paler figures compare in interesting ways to Brackens's (on page 14).

Seduction
Lin Qiqing
2023 | 80" × 65" |
handspun book yarn, Japanese paper yarn, wool, cotton dyed with marigold and indigo

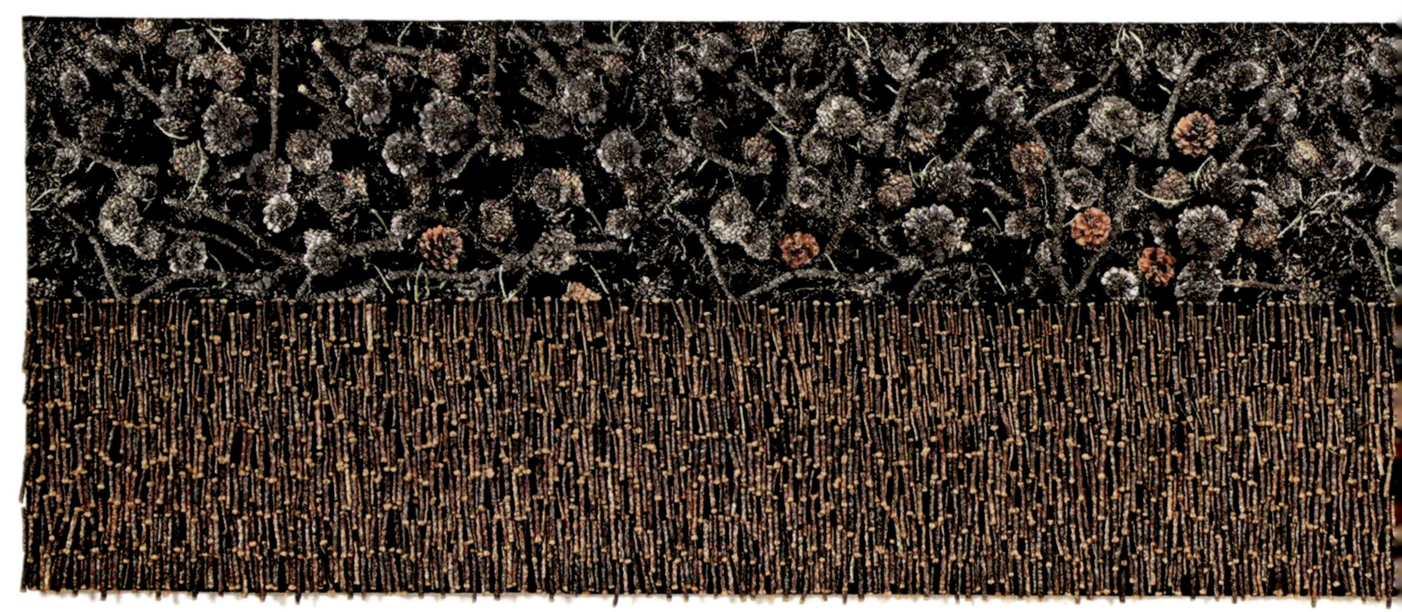

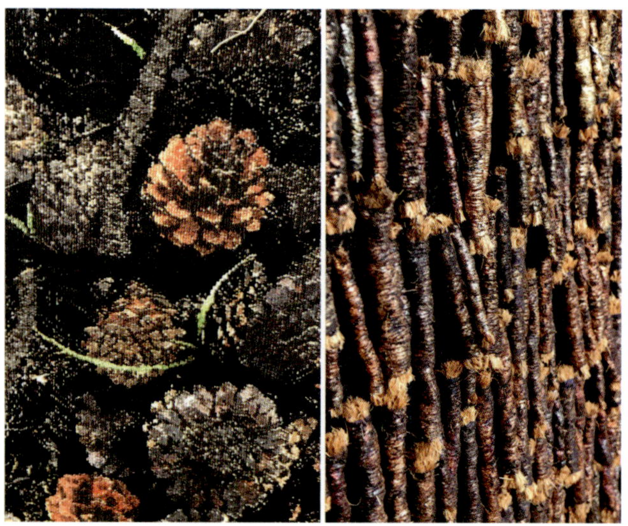

The Forest Floor
Ann Naustdal
2021 | 35.5" × 10'6" | linen, coco rope, oxidized silver leaf
Photographer: Kim Müller

Ann Naustdal regularly uses very textured materials (coco rope in the bottom half), which contrasts with a traditional Gobelins tapestry technique (the top section). The piece invites touch. In 2014, Naustdal earned the very first Ian Rankin Cordis Prize, an international award in the field of tapestry.

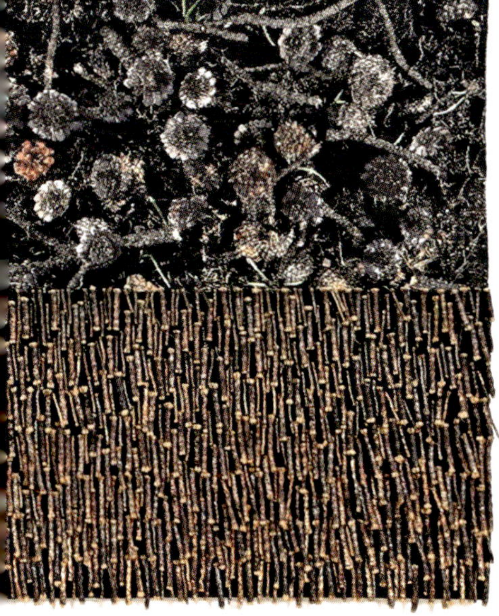

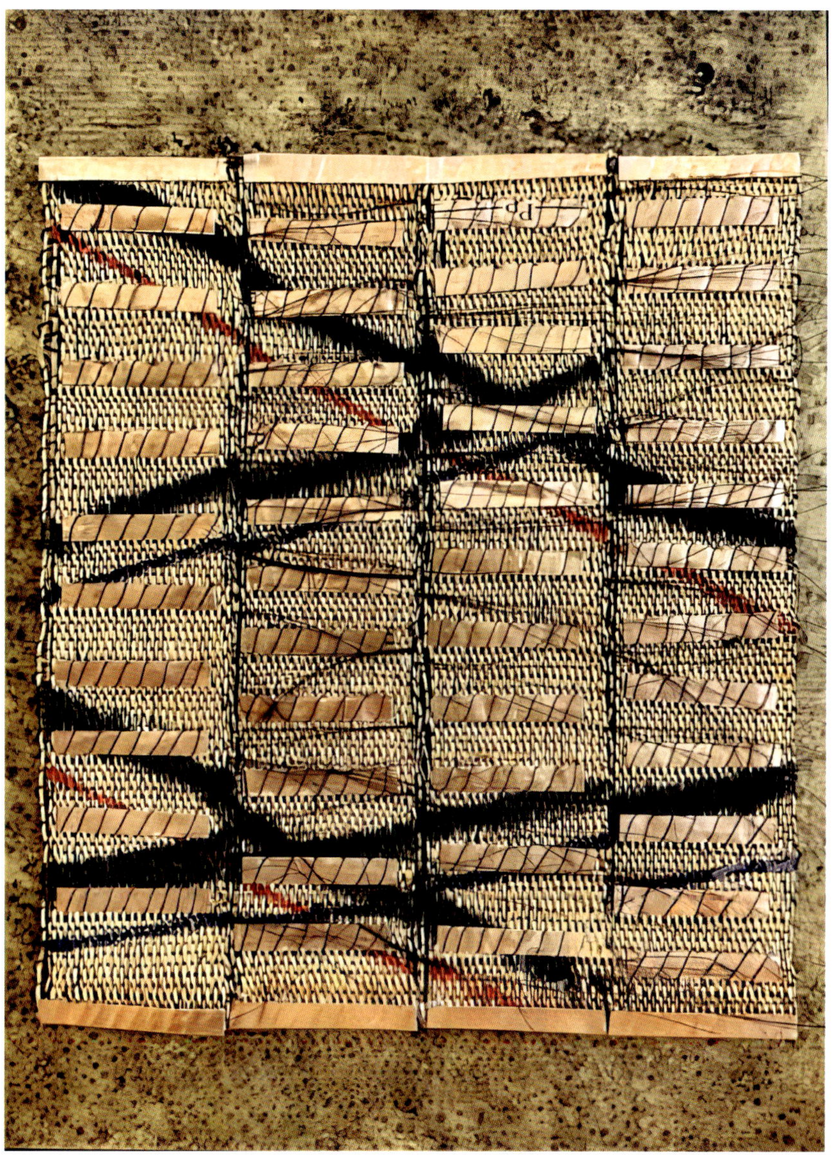

Red and Gold
Adela Akers
2022 | 12" × 9" | linen, horsehair, acrylic paint, metal foil (from around the tops of wine bottles)

Adela Akers's service in the Peace Corps in Peru and travels to Mexico introduced her to an exciting range of textile possibilities. She liked to combine unexpected materials—the examples here being horsehair and the metal foil from the tops of wine bottles (the horizontal golden bands). She has mounted the woven section on top of a painted surface, contrasting the two media.

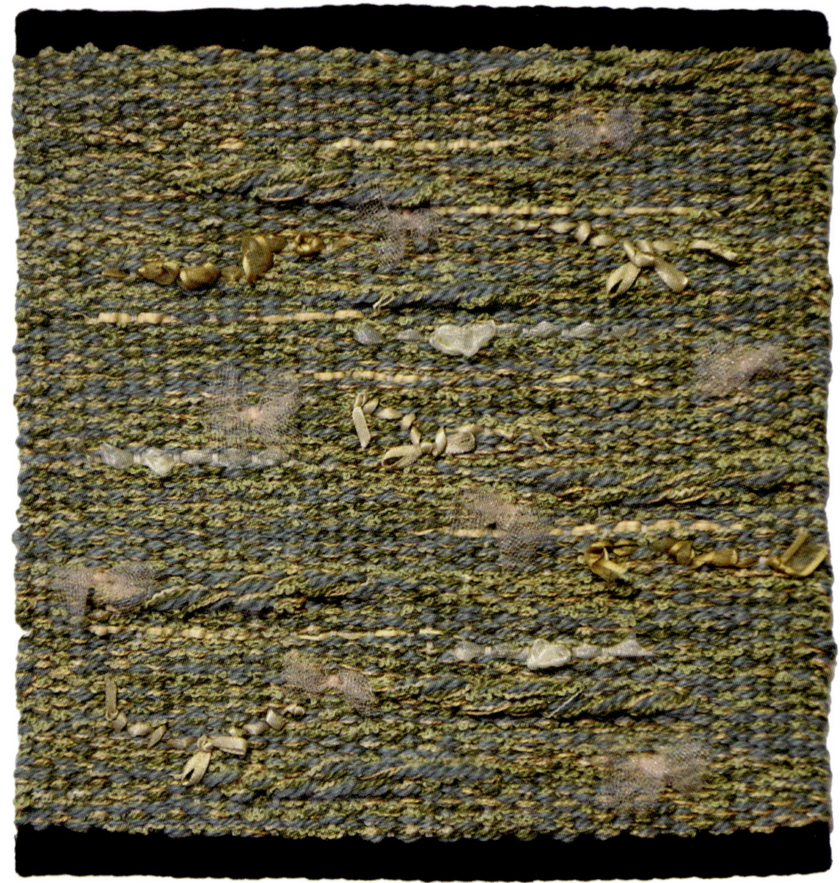

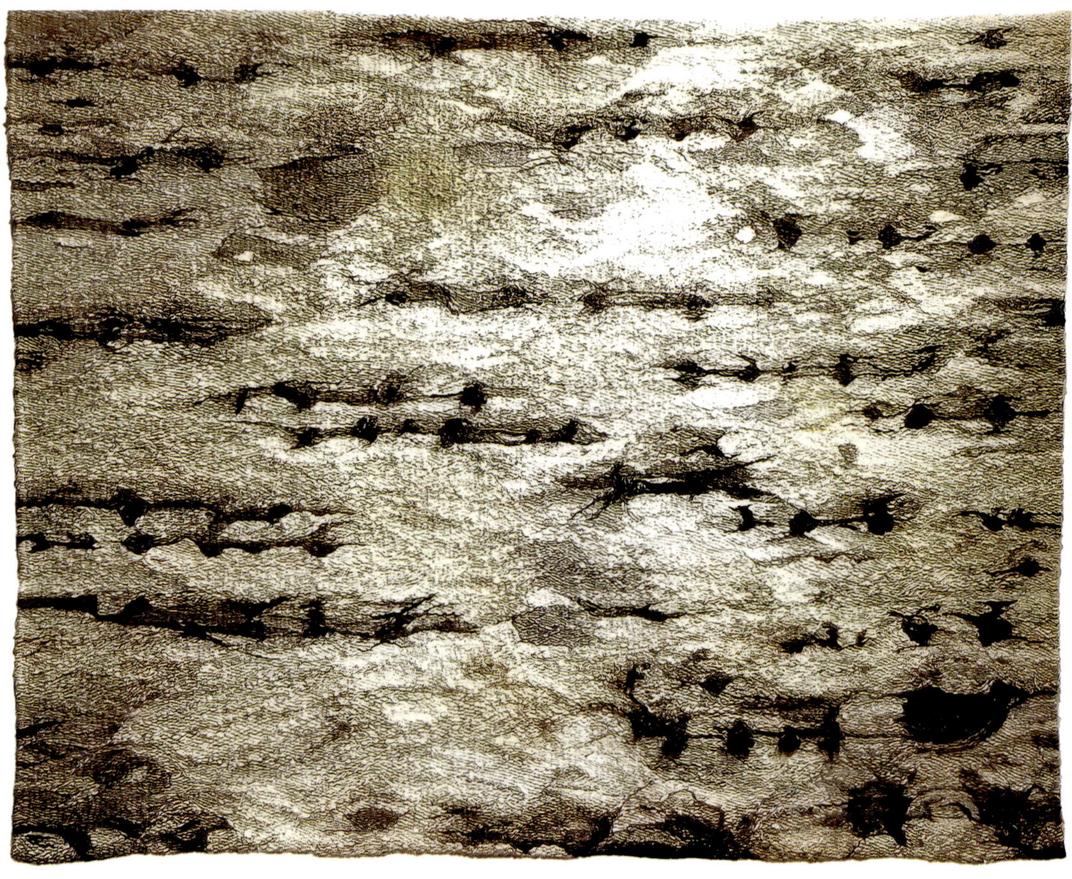

LEFT: *Spring Hills*
Sue Weil
2014 | 10" × 10" | cotton, wool, rayon ribbon, tulle, raffia; cotton warp

BELOW: *Triptych: Lockdown* (middle section)
Ixchel Suarez
2020–23 | 31.5" × 43.3" | cotton, wool, silk, linen, bamboo fiber, metallic thread

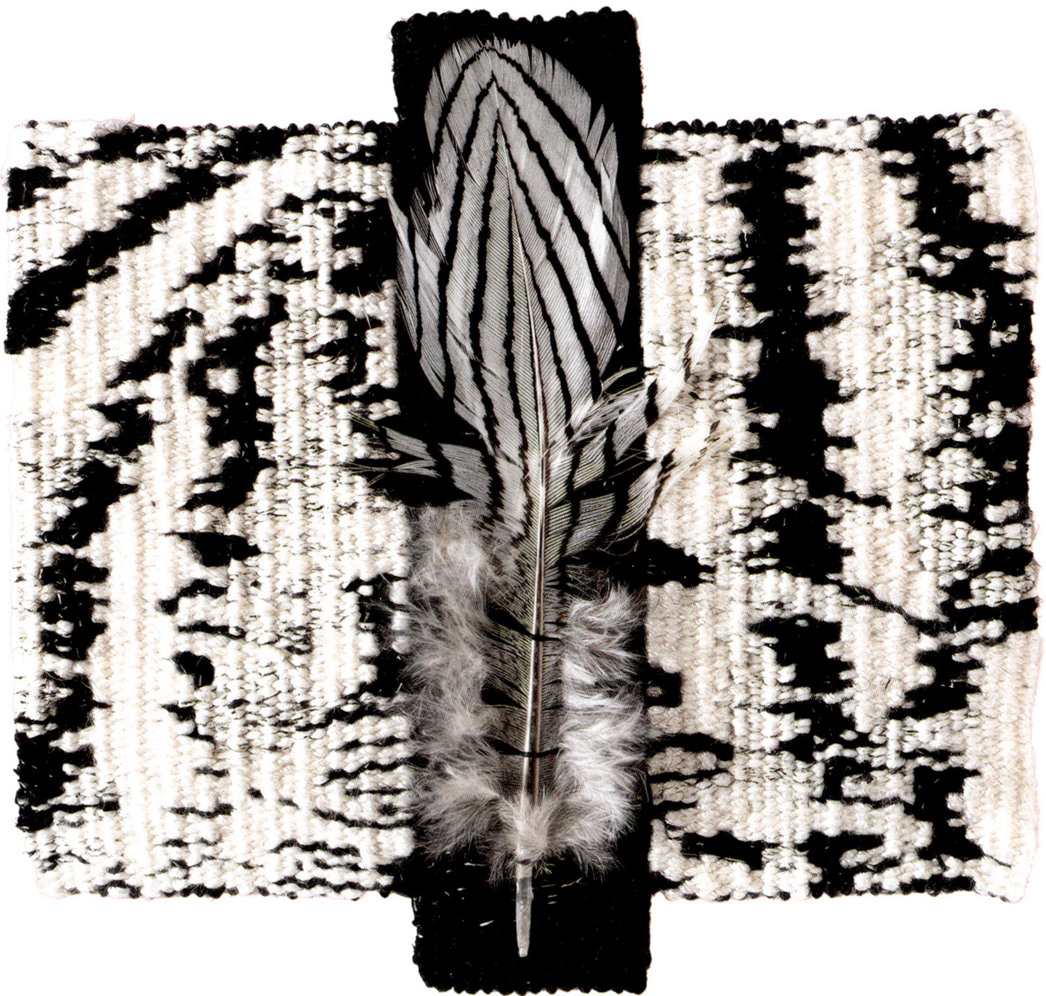

Like Akers's, Sue Weil's combination of materials contrasts. Here are lovely textures and colors, more conventional materials embellished with other materials, like raffia. The surface shows subtle movement, with shifts between wefts that cover one warp—and wefts that cover more than one.

ABOVE: *Flight Pattern*
Ellen Ramsey
2019 | 5" × 6" | wool, silk, paper, pheasant feather
Photographer: Bret Corrington

Ixchel Suarez worked her way through the COVID-19 pandemic by weaving, for instance, a triptych, of which this is the central section. She has limited her palette to grays and blacks, and the surface looks soft, even puffy, as though you could insert your hand into the surface. Yet, the metallic thread might indicate thorns.

Ellen Ramsey's image echoes the feather she has set in the middle of her tapestry, but these echoes emphasize how different the tapestry medium is. The image shows the sharpest contrast imaginable between the blacks and whites.

Joanna Foslien's piece needs to be seen in close-up, when those dots and dashes in white resolve themselves into the tea bag material they were. She had collected the paper of tea bags for a long time before she began to weave. The black and red contrasts with the papers, which now and again show a hint of tannin.

Anne Jackson established her reputation with a large series on the subject of witches. But she has never abandoned her wild sense of humor, as in this piece, where the batteries emphasize how silly hens seem to be. What makes a hen go?

The beads with which Jane Freear-Wyld decorates her tapestry feel cold. They suggest the irregularities of ice thickening over the deep blue of water.

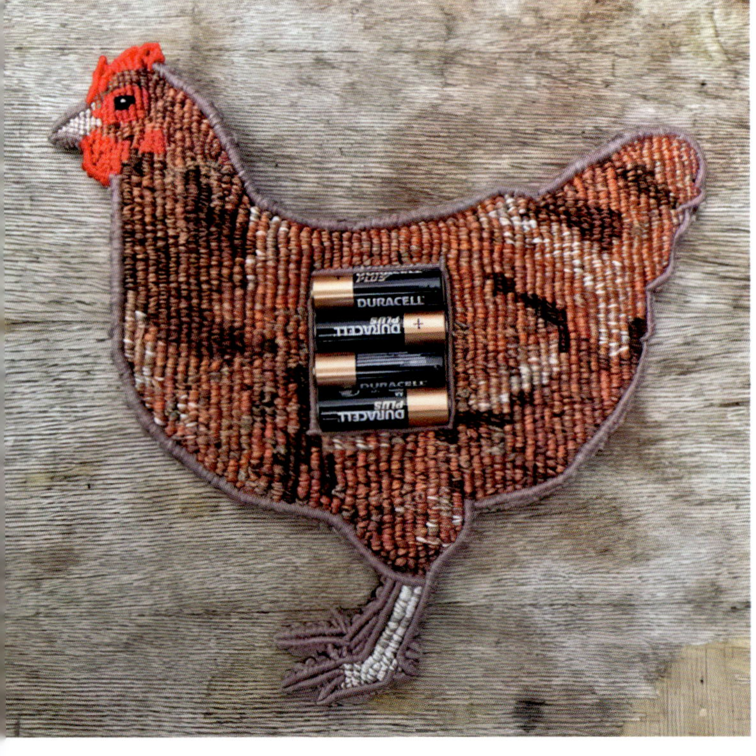

ABOVE: *Untitled*
Joanna Foslien
2012 | 57" × 30" | tea bags, wool; cotton seine twine warp

LEFT: *Battery Hen*
Anne Jackson
ca. 2000 | 11.7" × 8.3" | cotton, linen, synthetics, AAA batteries

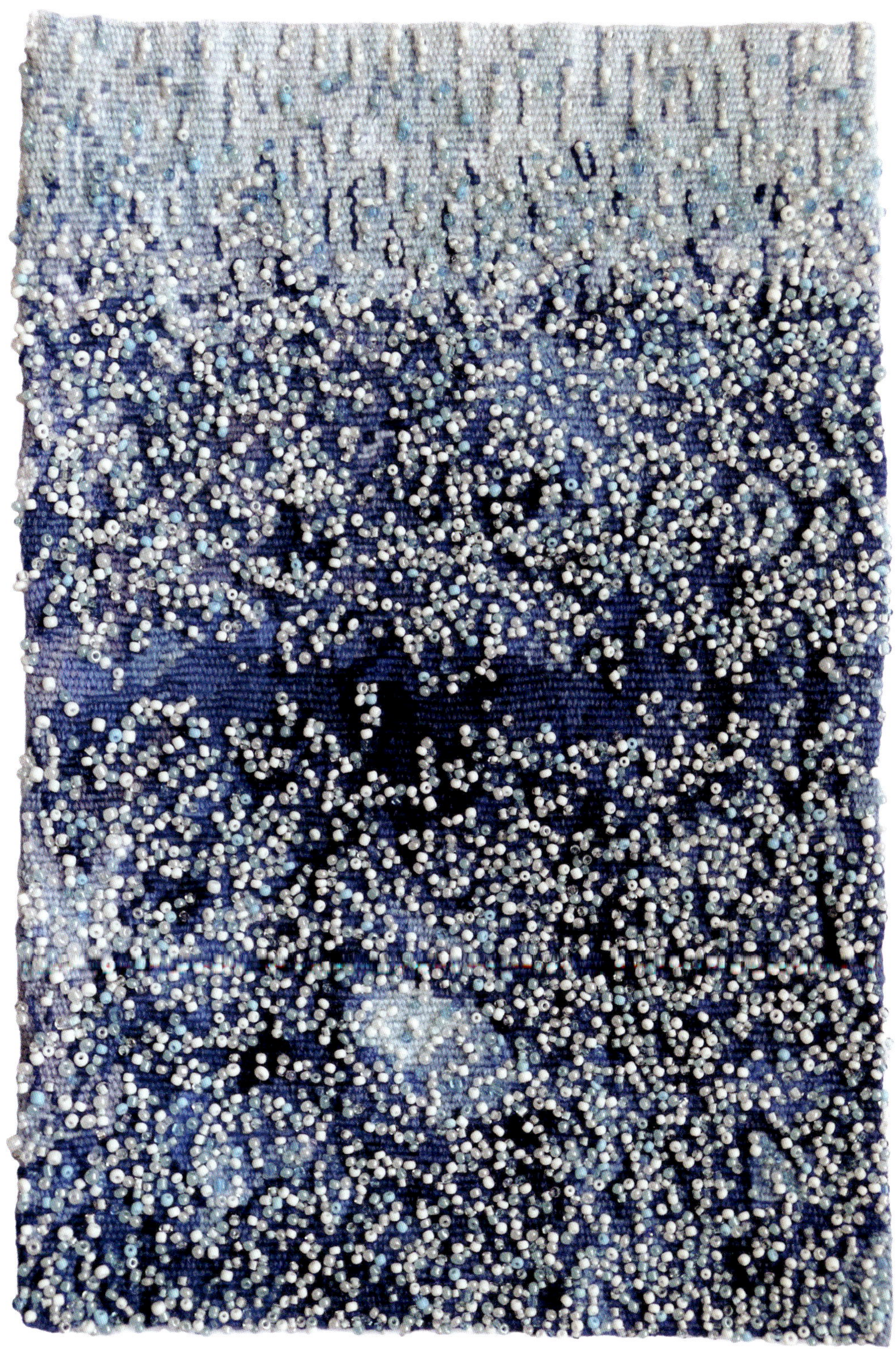

Ice 2
Jane Freear-Wyld
2024 | 11.8" × 7.9" | monofilament, cotton, glass beads; cotton warp

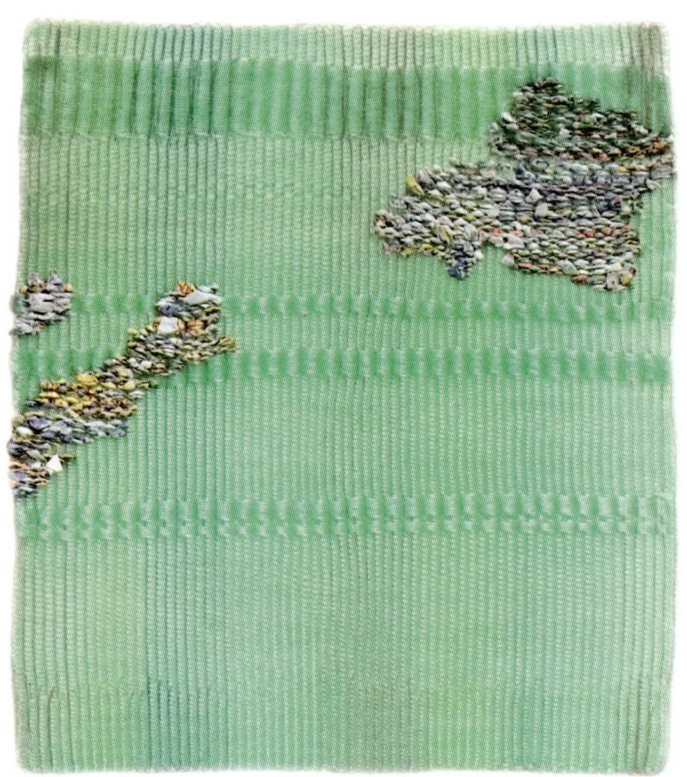

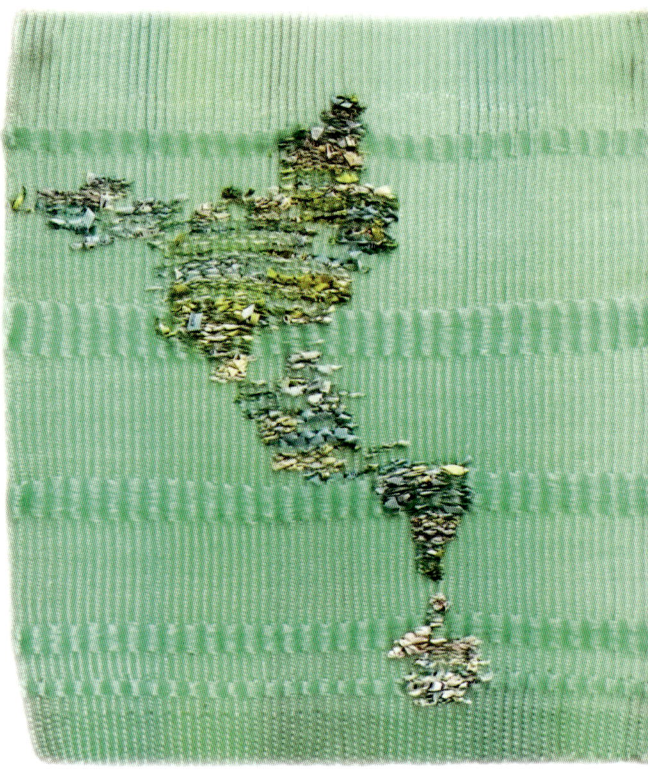

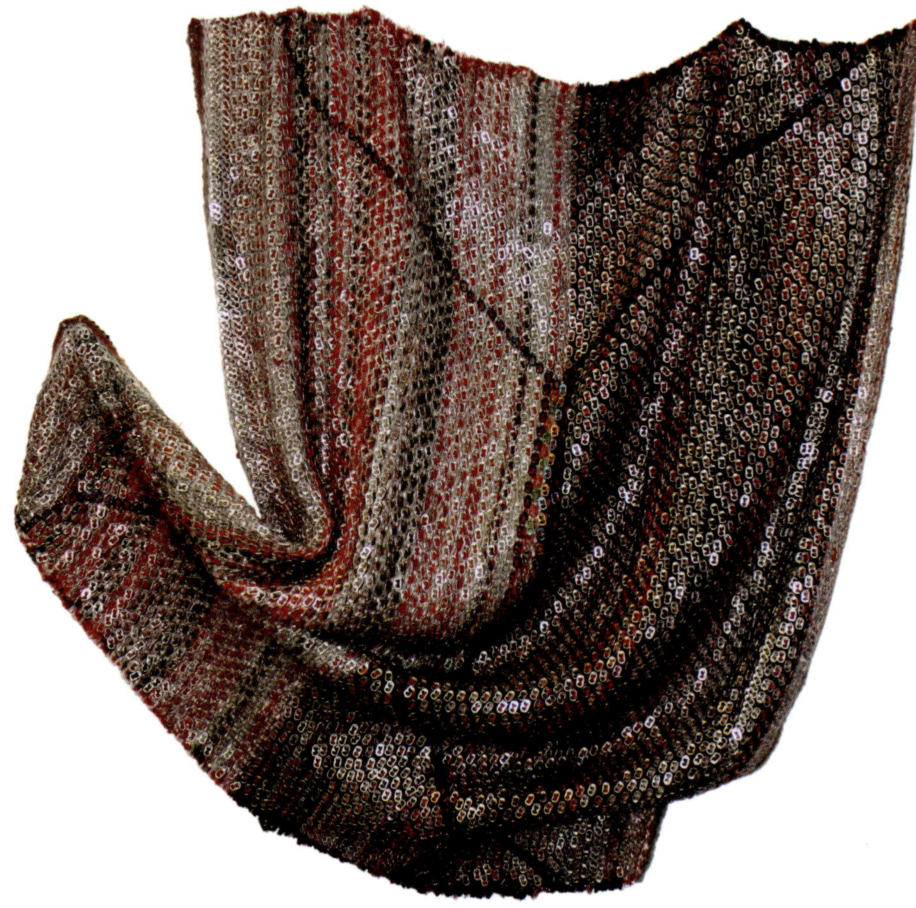

TOP: *Finding Center*
Mary Babcock
2008 | each section 9" × 8.25" | vintage fishing line, international, USA national and Hawaiian Island maps
As described by the weaver: "*Left*: Oahu, Molokai, Lanai woven from continental maps; *center*: continents woven from maps of Hawaiian archipelago; *right*: self-portrait woven from road maps of places I have lived."
Photographer: Hal Lu

LEFT: *Touch of a Dragon*
Krystyna Sadej
2024 | 73.6" × 78.7" × 7.8" | recycled transparent and black plastic, synthetic yarn, pop tabs

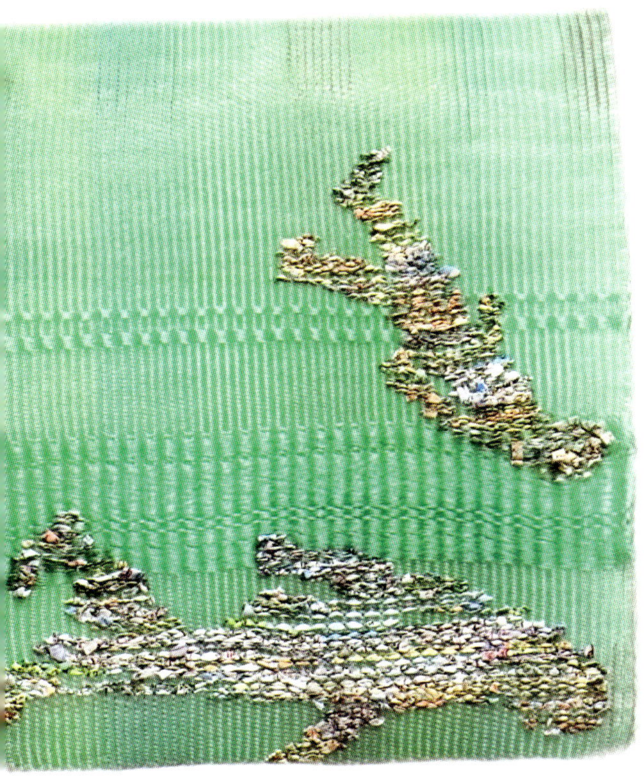

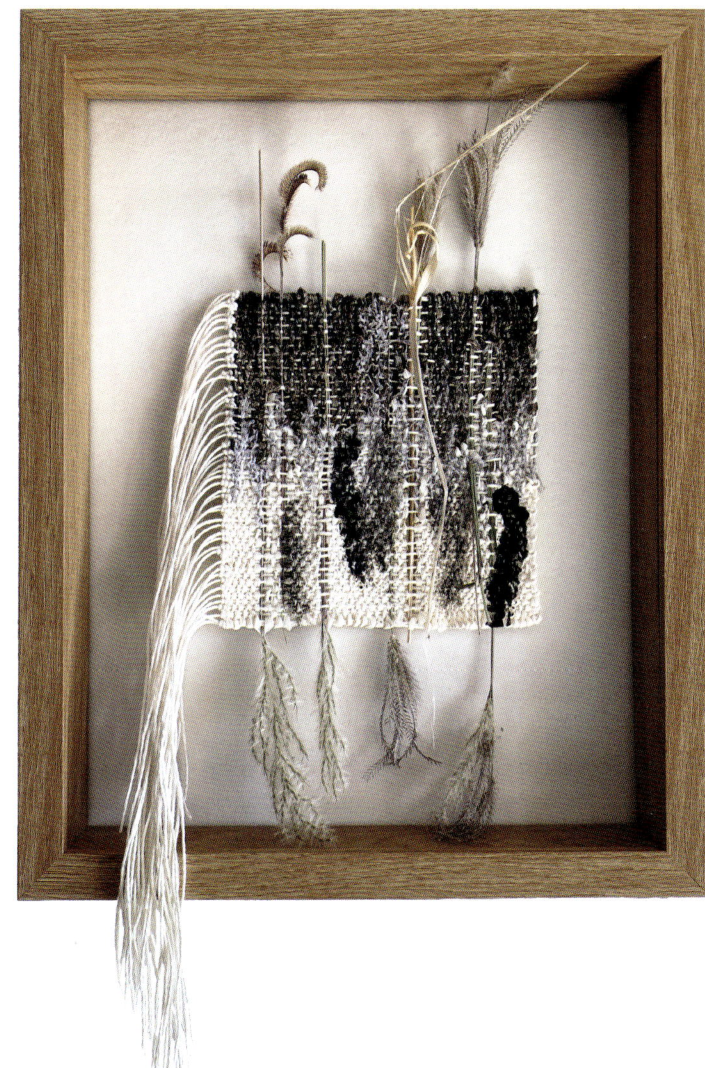

ABOVE: *Ashfall*
Molly Elkind
2022 | 18.5" × 12" × 3" | linen, paper, matte medium, blue grama, Chinese silver beard, feathertop rhodes, and needle-and-thread grasses, printed with ashes

Mary Babcock's decision to include maps spun into thread seems especially useful for a piece about a group of islands in the middle of the vast Pacific. She refers to the third section as a self-portrait, suggesting that she herself still inhabits the places she has lived.

I think that unexpected textures serve as a key to Krystyna Sadej's *Touch of a Dragon*. After all, why wouldn't a dragon feel like this—plastic, synthetics, pop tabs? Tapestry attracts the senses—the maker here takes full advantage of that impulse to touch these glittering scales.

Molly Elkind used many grasses here in the weft, and her ashes discolor the surface. The linen warp provides a traditional structure until she uses it unconventionally, letting it flow off the left side.

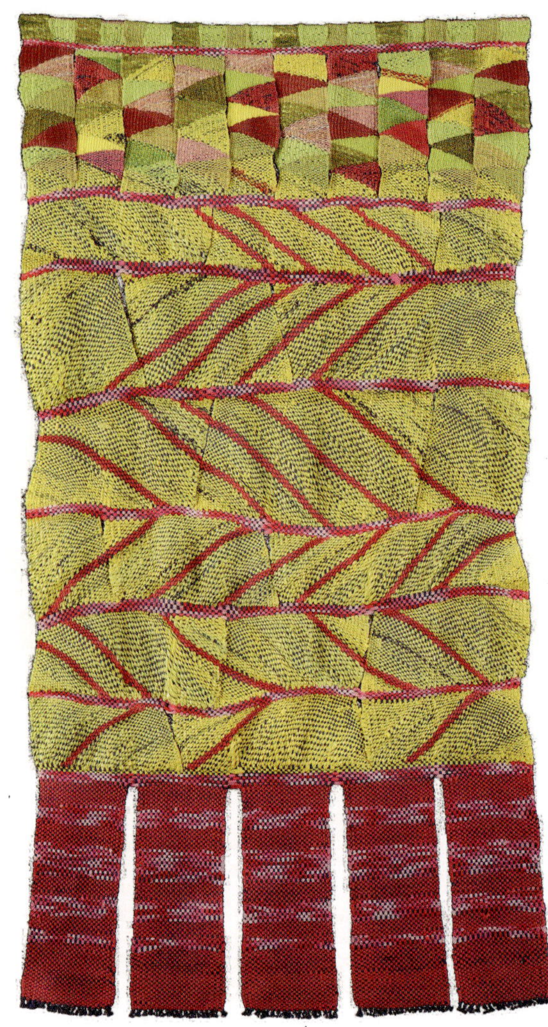

Super Bloom
Deborah Corsini
2023 | 53" × 29" | plastic bags, soy silk, rayon ribbon, linen, raffia, cotton, plastic yarn

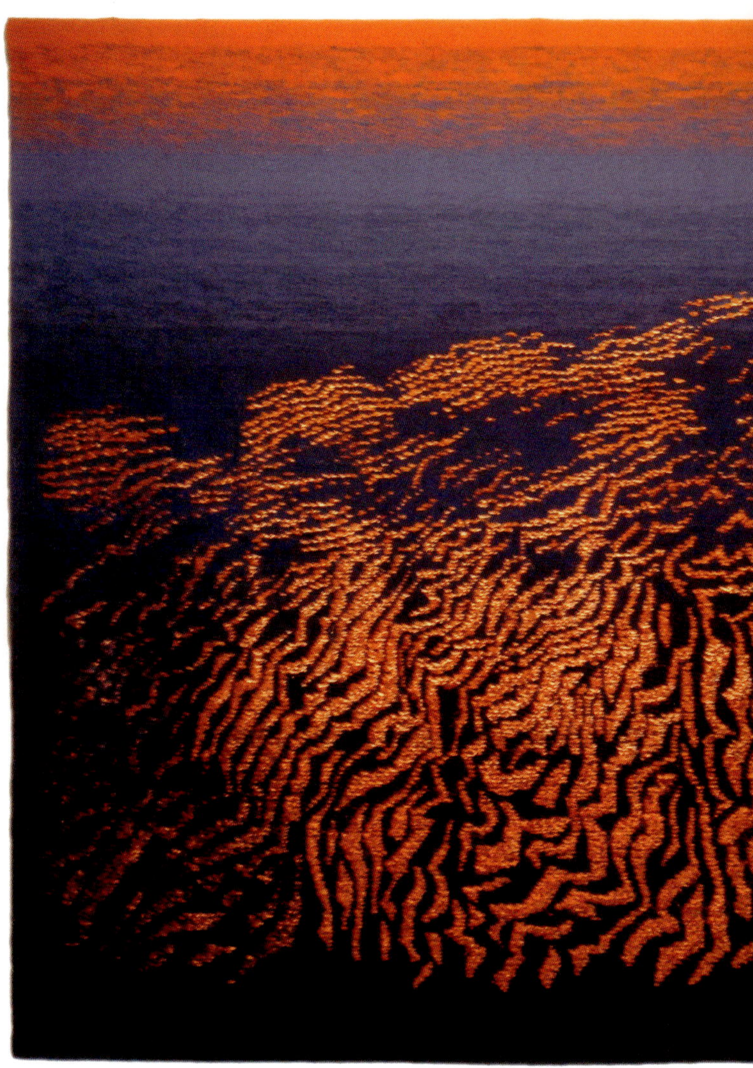

Signs in the Sand, Sunset
Egils Rozenbergs
2009 | 90.5" × 98.4" | wool, linen, copper

Deborah Corsini has explored wedge weave for years—a technique that produces the angles in this image (see introduction to chapter 3, page 55). She has also been collecting plastic bags in a studio drawer, and, of late, she has begun to raid that store, pairing like colors, in the ironically titled *Super Bloom*. Her statement illuminates the horrors of a material that will not decompose. The result catches the light; it is unexpectedly lovely, but the immutable plastic remains.

Egils Rozenbergs's inclusion of copper does good work in this very large piece (measuring around 7.5 × 8 feet). Its shine, creating a woven pattern, adds to the impression of an ocean at sunset.

Joyce Crain has worked for years with netting, iridescent film, and plastic ribbon to construct her city maps. These radiate more color than any city ever could. She fulfills commissions for people who love to recognize their own urban environment.

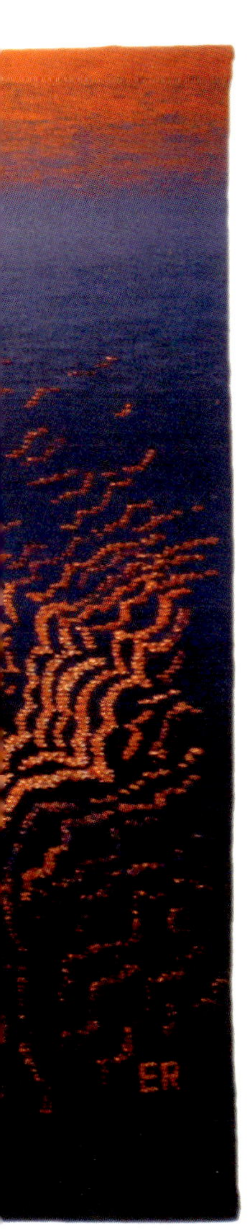

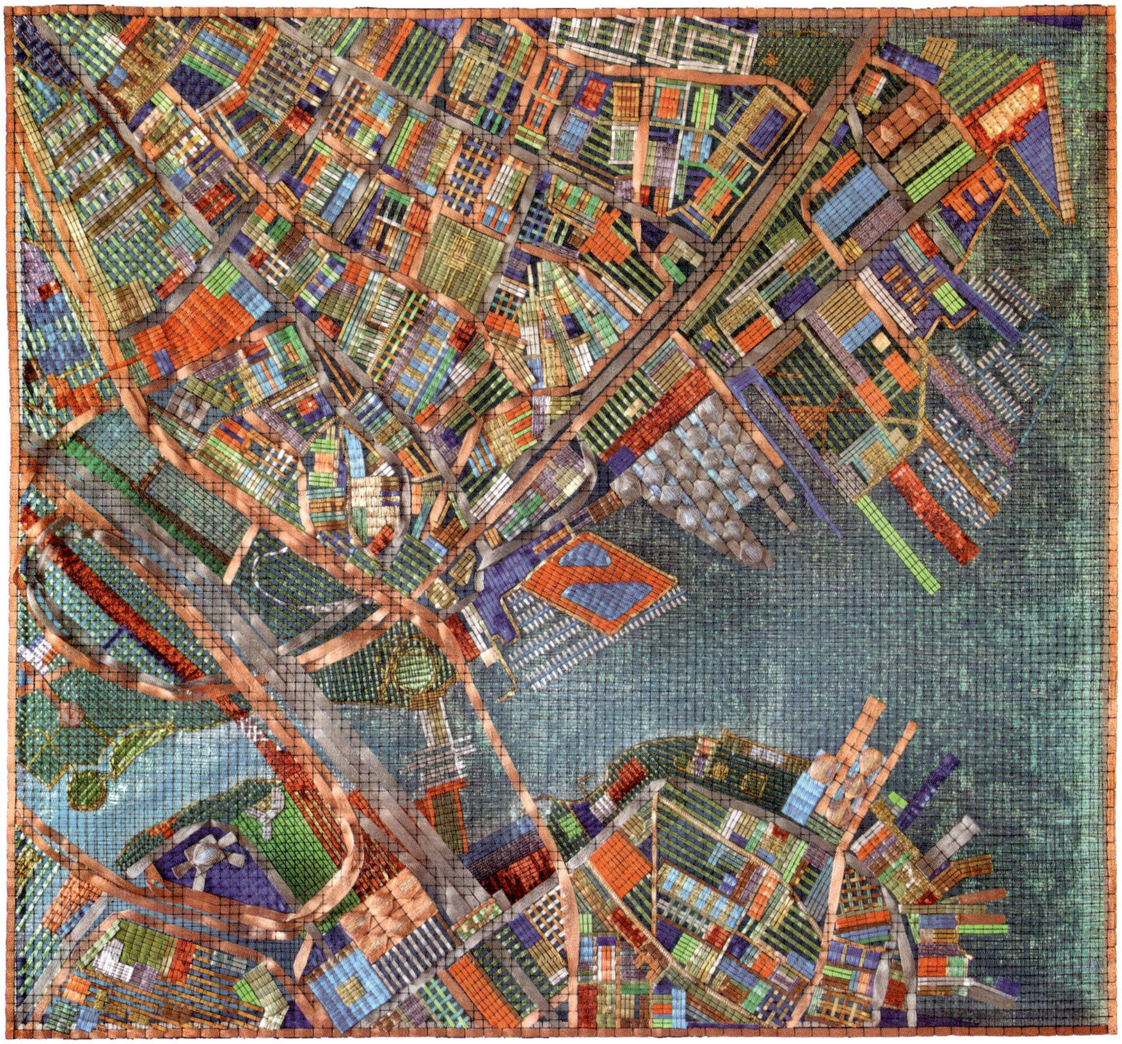

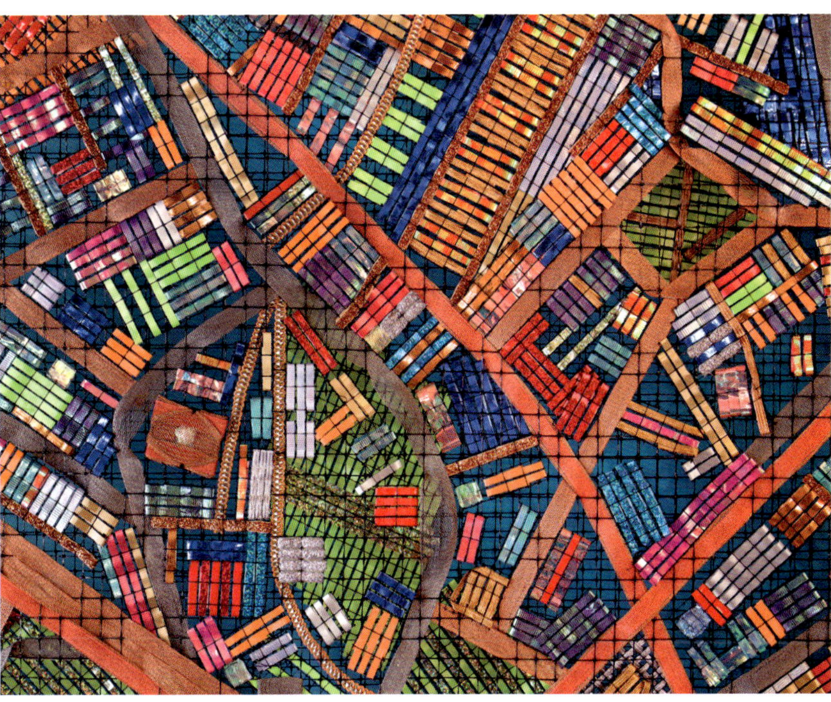

Boston
Joyce Crain
2019 | 48" × 48" |
plastic netting, metallic braids, iridescent film, fabric, plastic ribbon
Commissioned by Home Base, Charlestown, Massachusetts
Photographer: Carl Philabaum

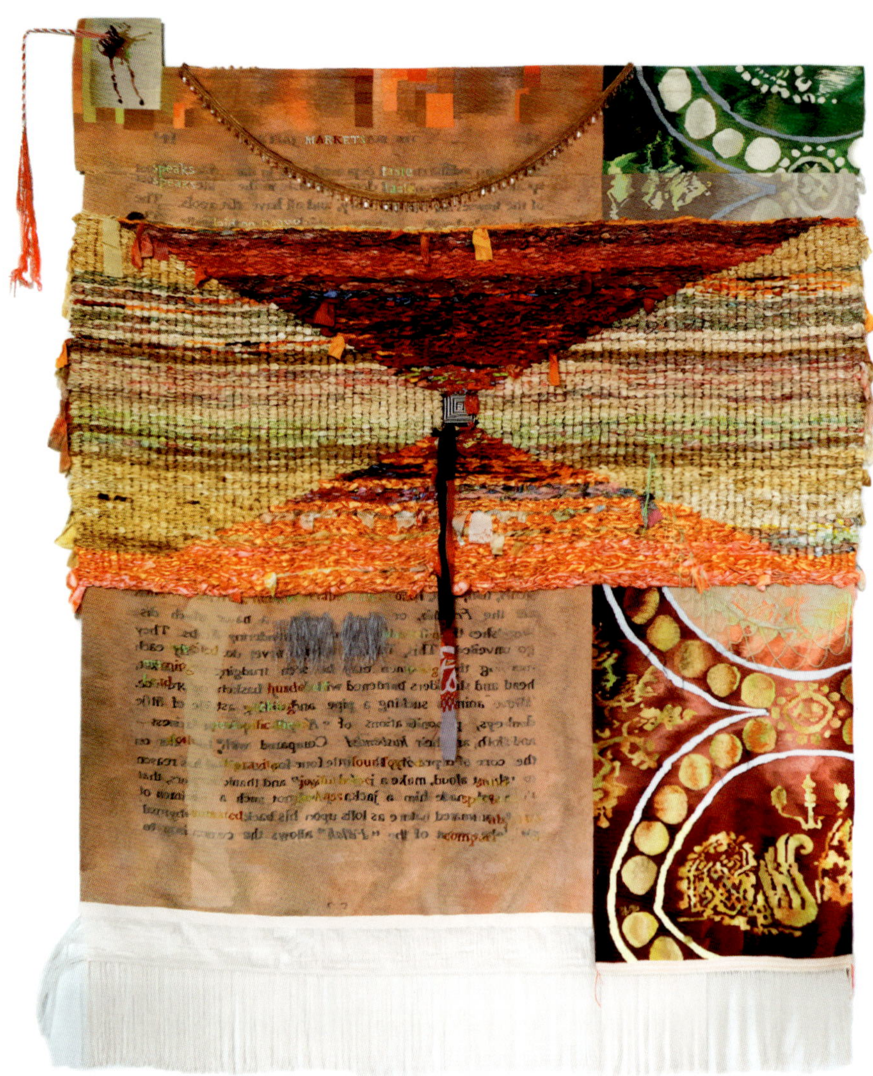

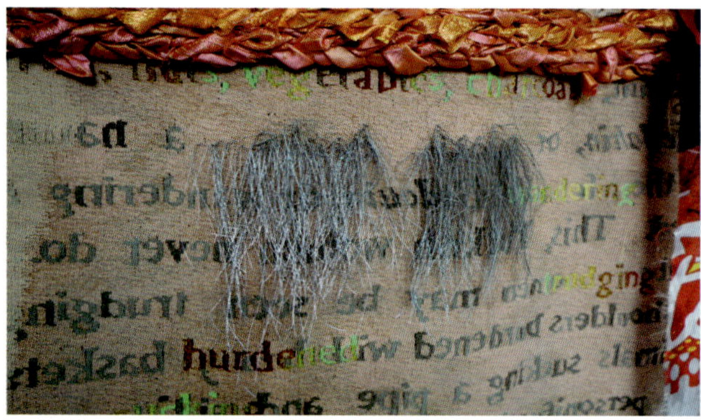

Shelley Socolofsky created this entire tapestry by weaving it of radically different materials, including using strips of cloth from such things as a sari and a sleeping bag, even a text from a travelogue, woven backward. She includes fringe, and the tapestry's other side (she means it to be seen from both sides) shows a complex surface of knots and braids. Thus, she is emphasizing qualities in her piece that highlight its textile identity.

ABOVE: *Concubine*
Shelley Socolofsky
2020 | 112" × 94" × 1.5" | cotton, wool, silk, plastic, reflective glass, thread, deconstructed woman's sari, child's Disney *High School Musical Two* sleeping bag, scarves, silk stained with onion skins and berries, mason twine, survivalist's twine, nylon rope, Kevlar, glass beads, trim, nylon thread, packing plastic
Design: digital collage incorporating vintage imperialist travel log documenting a food market in Jaffa, Middle Eastern textile design, artist's drawings

OPPOSITE: *Totems*
Włodzimierz Cygan
2022 | 3 elements, 11.8" × 27.5" each | wool, sisal, fiber optic cable

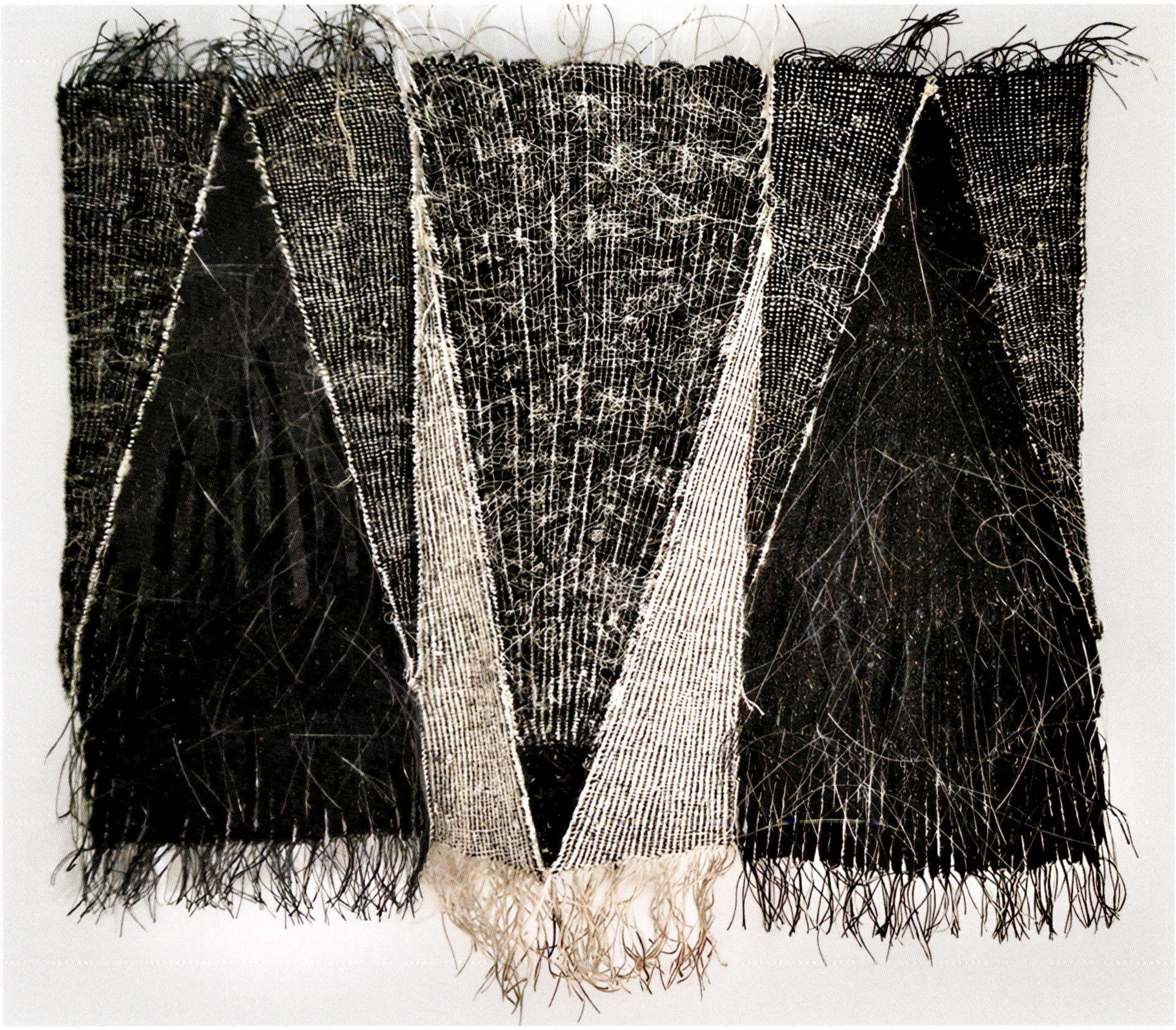

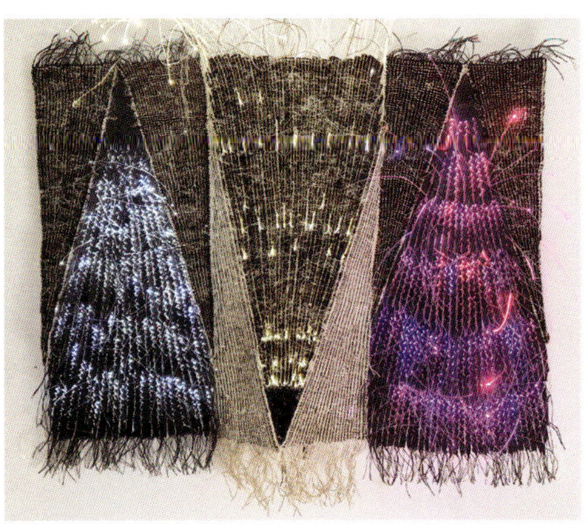

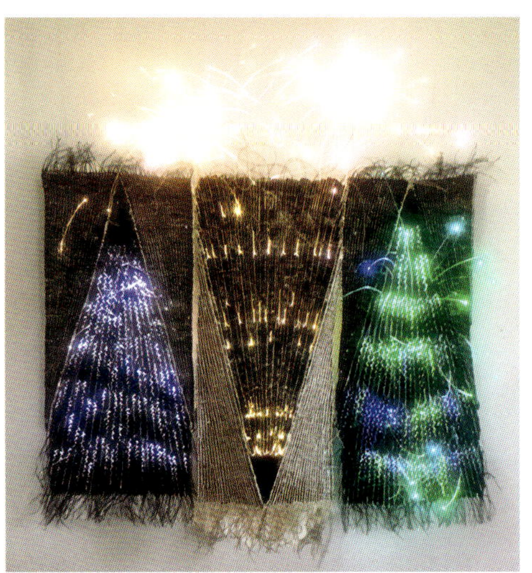

oh my!

This part of the chapter is devoted to the materials and processes that are especially unusual.

Włodzimierz Cygan's fiber optic cable changes color as you walk by. It offers an image that won't remain static.

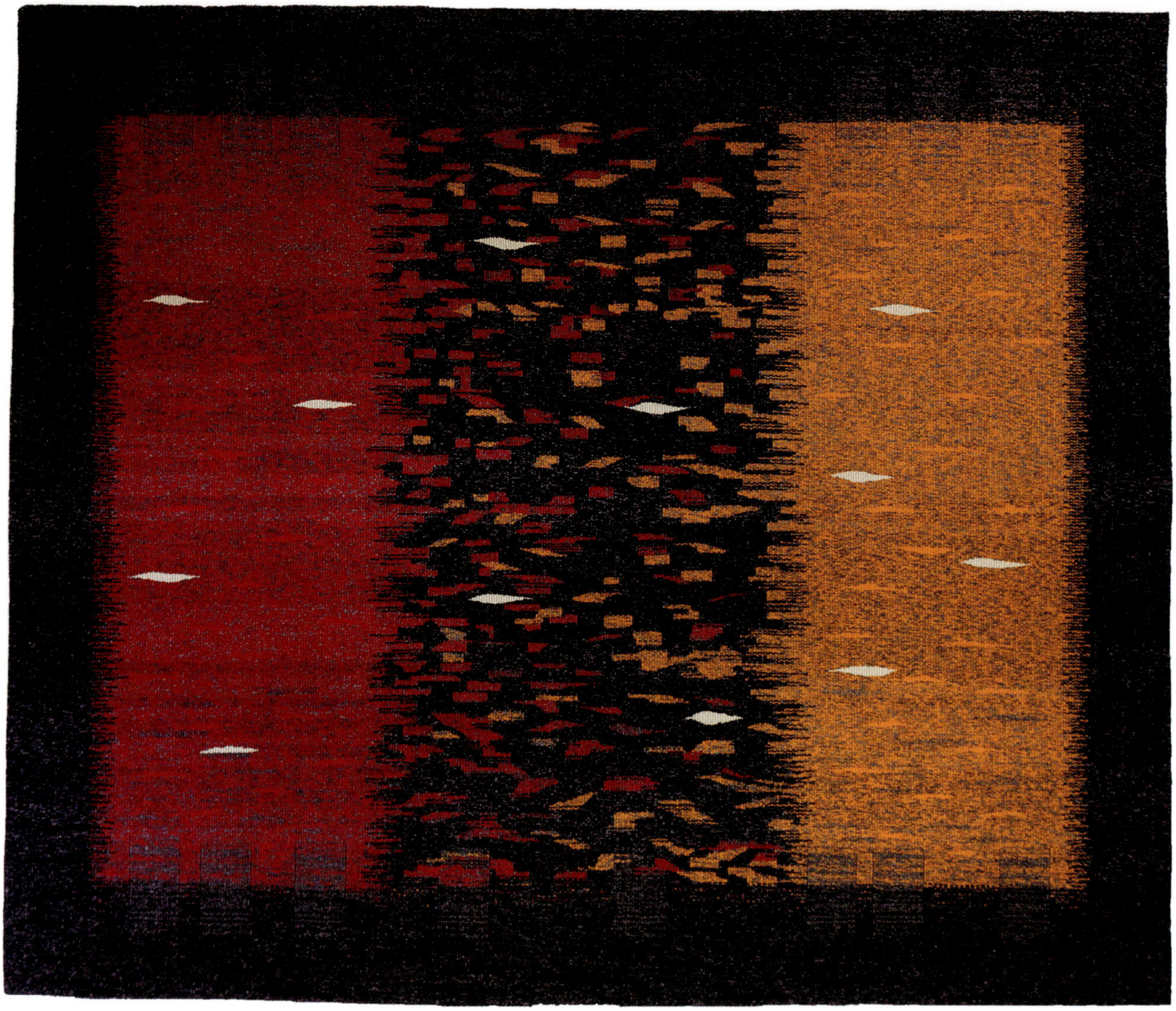

Metamorphosis
Alastair Duncan
2018–19 | 59" × 59" | wool, conductive thread; cotton warp
Audio: alastairduncan.bandcamp.com

Alastair Duncan works conductive thread and interactive audio into his tapestries. He has long appreciated the rhythmic aspects of the weaving process. He has found a way to enlarge the flat woven field into an extra dimension. Use the QR code to listen.

A number of years ago, Dorothy Clews began to bury some of her tapestries, recalling that one claim of the tapestry medium is that they last a long time. She decided to test the endurance of what she made. Her materials list includes some things that are less substantial than thread but produce visible results.

When Paola Moreno began this piece, she was thinking about how the Inca apparently burned a number of their weavings as a way of keeping them out of the hands of the Spanish conquistadors. Her tapestry has a partially charred surface. Part of this image results from digital manipulation: The left and right sides at the bottom show front and back.

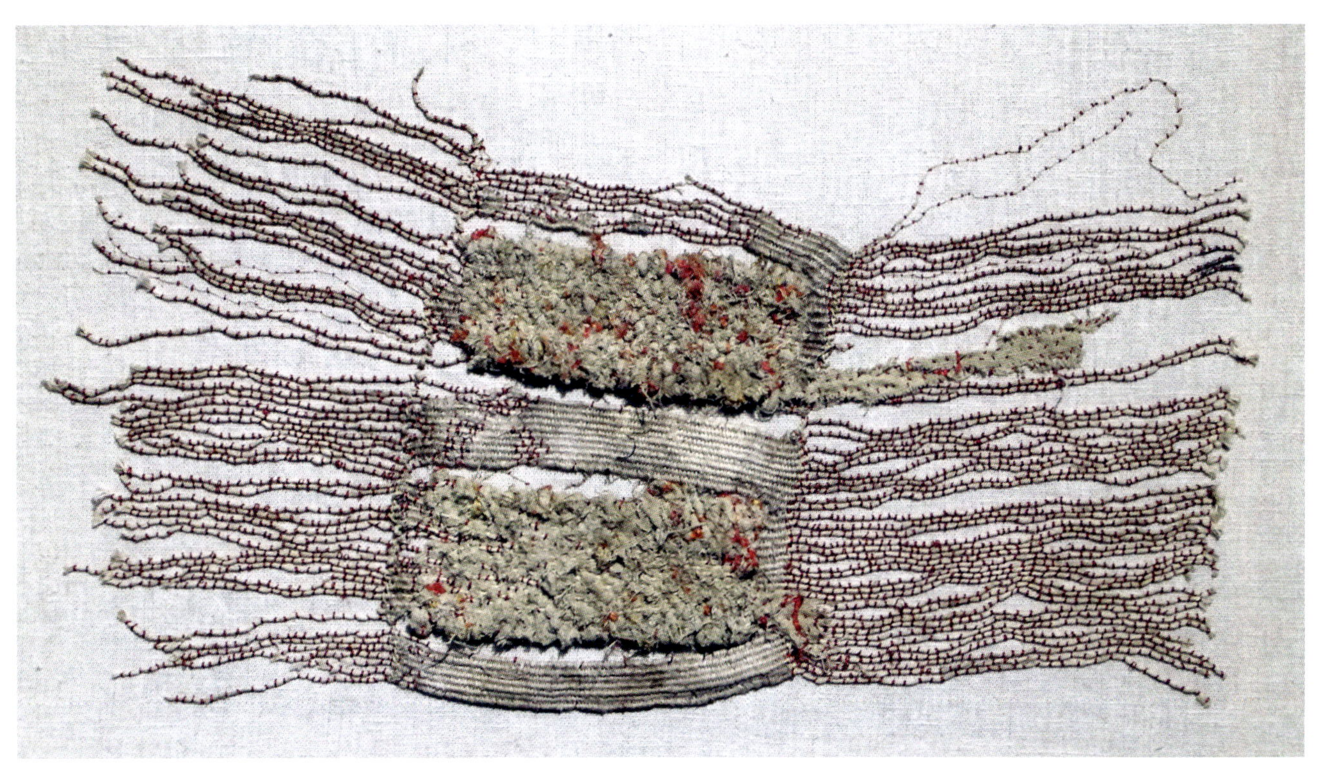

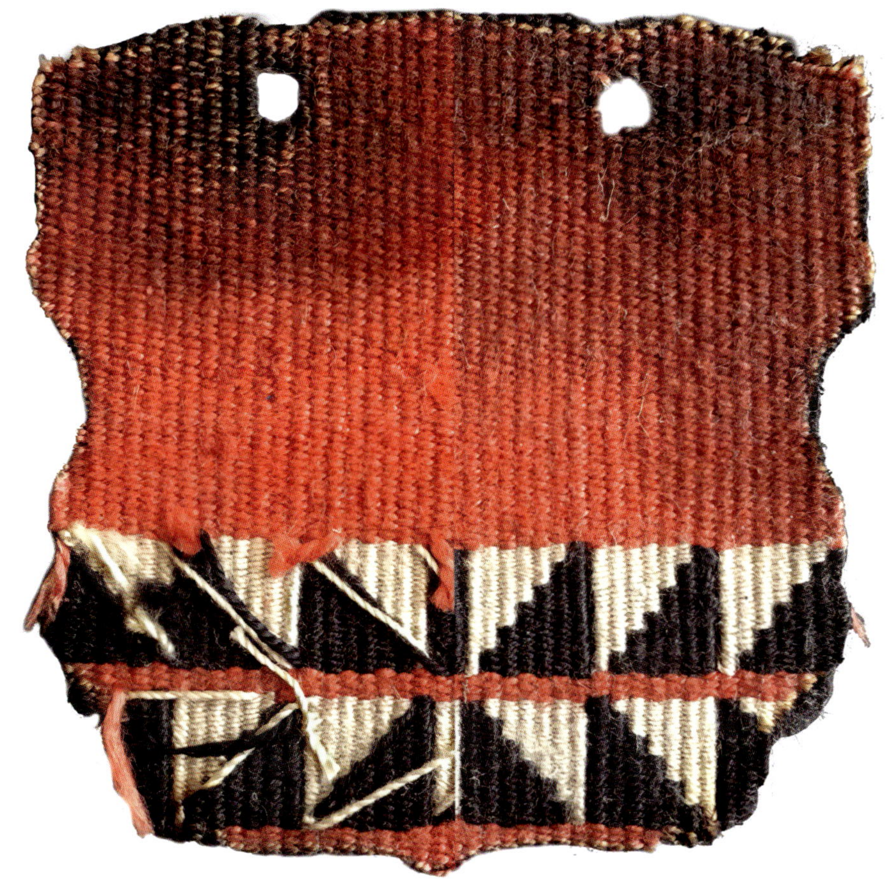

ABOVE: *Losing the thread, not checkmate, but stalemate*
Dorothy Clews
2014 | 11" × 14.2" | decomposition, sun, rain, earth, microorganisms, time, cotton seine twine, linen, cotton

RIGHT:
Memories of Inca Textiles
Paola Moreno
2002 | 3.1" × 3.5" | cotton, threads, fire, digital manipulation

woad

Woad is a plant from ancient times. Properly prepared—dried, powdered, and fermented—it can be used as a dyestuff. During the Middle Ages, it became the single most reliable source for blue, a staple among dyes in Europe—and the basis for fortunes in the southwest of France. That area is still known for woad ("pastel" in French). Woad is in part indigo, but when pure indigo began to arrive reliably in Europe—more colorfast, the color stronger and less labor intensive to work with—woad fell out of favor. Tourist offices still advertise *la route de la pastel* (should it be called "Woad Road" in English?), though the fortunes it created have dissipated.

This chapter is named woad (a good four-letter word)—but we are actually looking at all the various ways that weavers employ color.

During the 1980s I interned at the French national tapestry studio, les Gobelins. On the floor above the studio where we interns worked was *le magasin*, the store, where weavers went to pore through drawers of spools of yarns and weave at small looms to try out their choices for their samplers.

Choosing a color was not self-evident. We were instructed to unwind the threads from the spool into a figure eight, which we laid flat on our palms and then held up to the natural light. Subsequently we wove what we had found into a small sampler and looked at it again, next to other colors that we might choose. The look of the yarn color on the spool differs from yarn color flat in your hand, which differs from the yarn color when woven. It was always a challenge. (I was once convinced that I had found a suitable yellow—and the professional weavers pronounced it too "acid.")

The range of yarn colors at les Gobelins is immense, undoubtedly larger than that at any other studio in the world. In its first approximately 160 years, colors were simply added to its stores as the need arose. This changed in 1824, when a chemist named Eugène Chevreul became the director of the dyeing studio, and he subsequently undertook to organize it all. He began with the color wheel (devised by Sir Isaac Newton in 1666) and decided that each hue should have 200 variations of light

and dark. Circles are divided into 360 degrees, and Chevreul divided the colors into 5-degree increments. This results in 14,400 colors.

Issues arise, such as how long any color lasts. Over time, green disappears, and purple is notoriously unstable. Nonweavers have sometimes thought that only red and blue are the "correct" tapestry colors.

When I was there, les Gobelins was reorganizing their stocks of color, and, beginning in the 1990s, using a computer program (which cannot differentiate color as well as the human eye). Regular changes in the programming meant that one organizational system after another had to be abandoned.

After I announced my plans for this book, many weavers emailed me comments about the importance of color. This chapter shares some of what I have seen, pieces where the colors speak clearly and with delight.

Jo Barker fills sketchbooks with washes of color and shapes. She specifies the importance of light. This piece has its roots in a visit she made to Egypt, where she was "fascinated by the effects of light and shadows through the screens on many buildings."

Cobalt Haze
Jo Barker
2009 | 14.5" × 33.5" | wool, cotton, linen, embroidery threads

Mary Farmer made many tapestries with a highly reduced palette and a remarkably even surface. This particular piece marked a breakthrough. She wrote, "Areas of black and yellow should be seen as solid colour but, because they are built up from a mixture of colour, more fluctuations should be produced by variations in light, than is the case with flat colour." The picture here shows one result of the photographer's lighting, but from different angles or in different lighting, the piece looks lighter or darker.

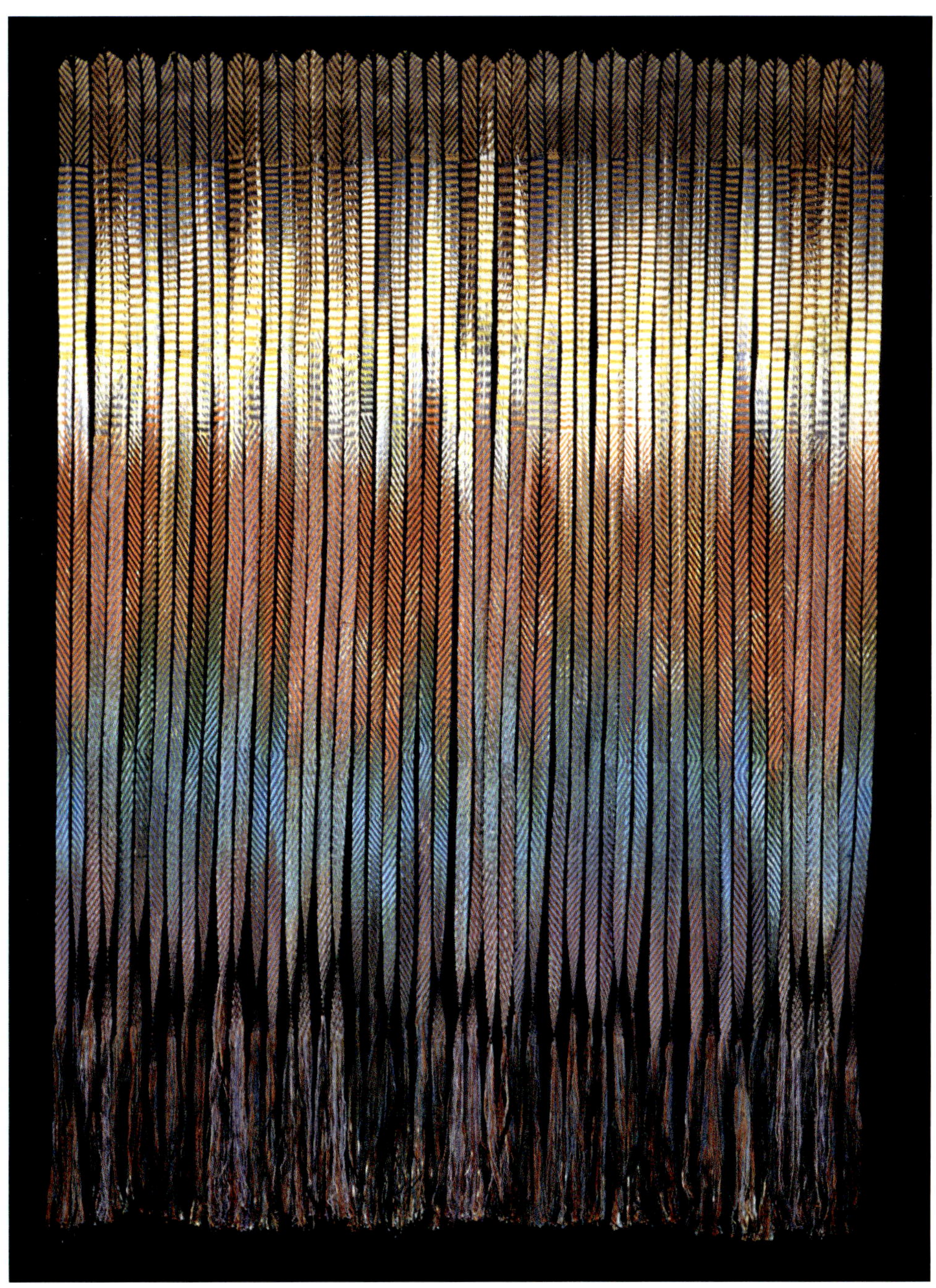

Candace Crockett weaves bands and then sees how they work with each other. Hung as a unit here, their shimmering movement radiates joy.

OPPOSITE: *Bright Side*
Mary Farmer
1979 | 59" × 44.5" | cheviot wool; cotton warp

ABOVE: *Light*
Candace Crockett
2000 | 45" × 40" | cotton, linen, rayon

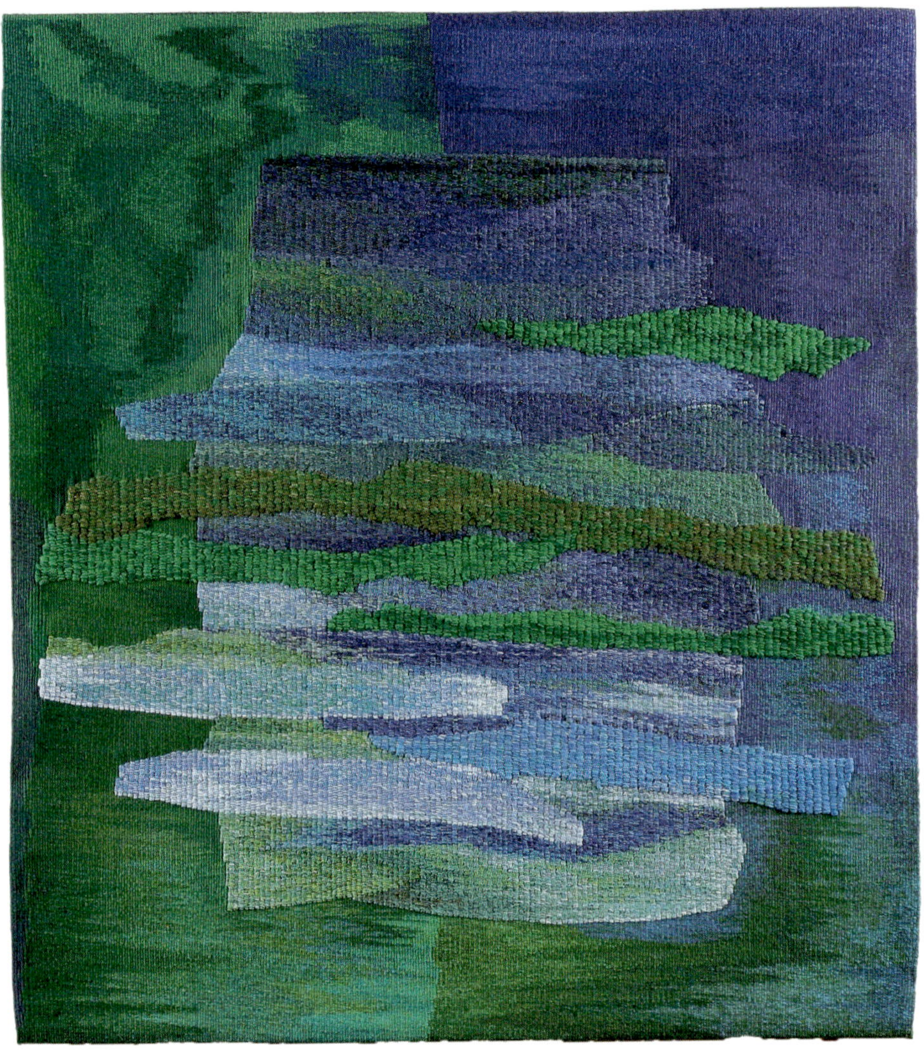

Mireille Guerin's use of blue and green make a visual puzzle. Is that central section part of the flat of the tapestry—or is it set in at a distance from the field around it?

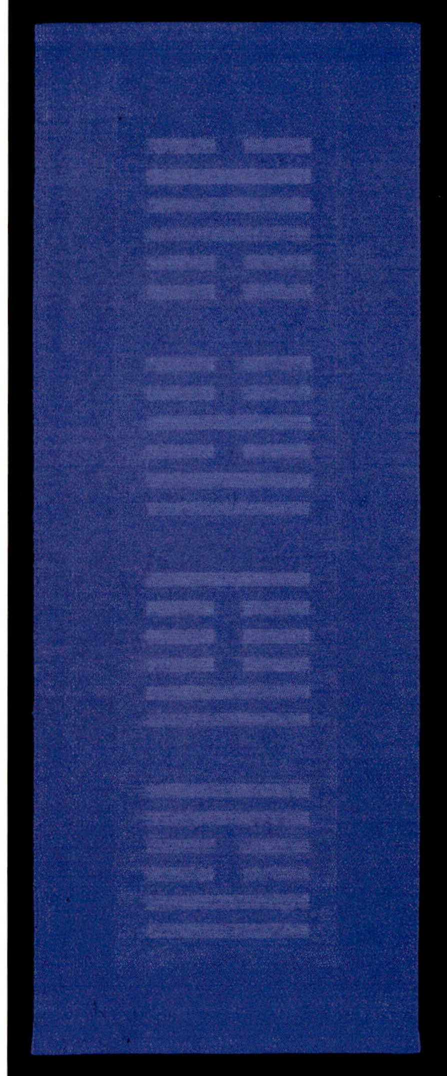

Blues and black dominate James Koehler's palette in this piece; he dyed his own yarn. His series of Koans began in the 1990s; here his immensely disciplined use of blues creates an I Ching hexagram. The tapestry communicates stillness. A koan is a kind of Zen paradox, which he has translated into cloth.

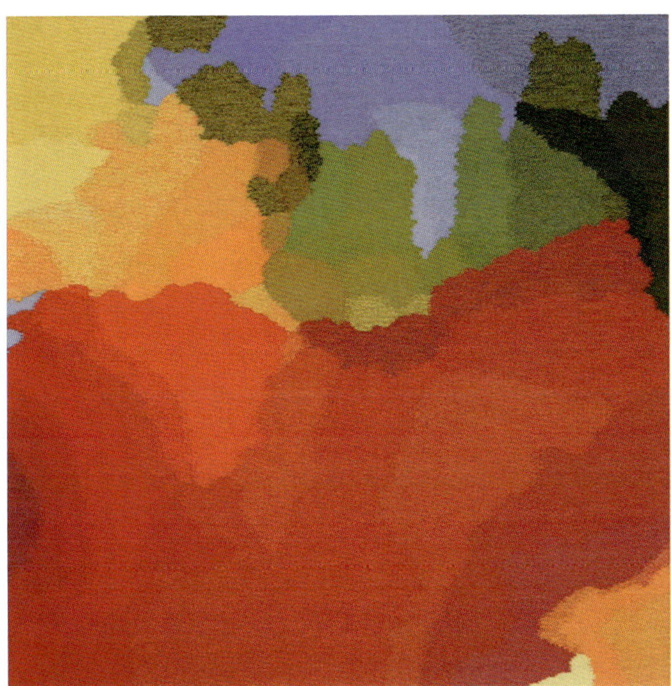
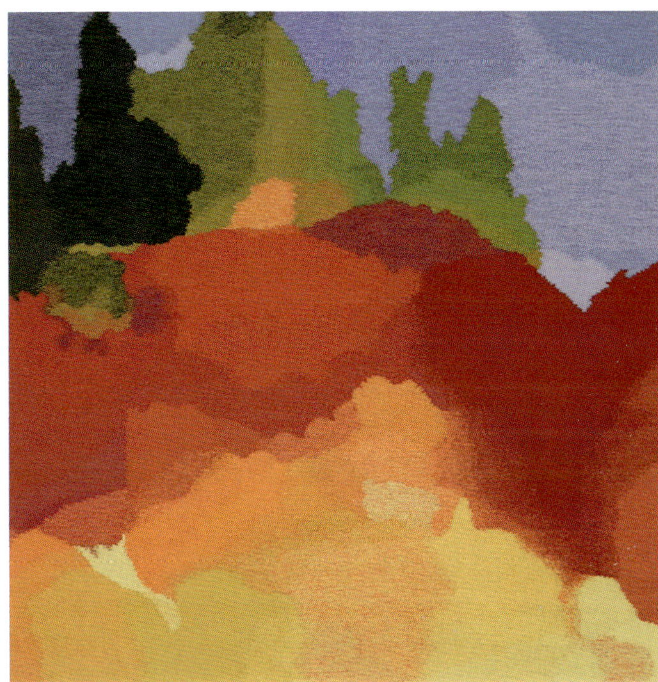

Ramona Sakiestewa has created dramatic shapes that look like clouds or, from the title, clusters of star systems. It is hard to believe that each piece is only 20 inches square. The reds dominate and seem to spill over the other colors, asserting authority.

OPPOSITE, TOP: *Passage*
Mireille Guerin
2012 | 51.2" × 45.3" × 2" | wool, cotton, linen, rayon

LEFT: *Koan/Dialog I*
James Koehler
hand-dyed wool; cotton seine twine warp

ABOVE: *Nebula 22, Nebula 23*
Ramona Sakiestewa
2009 | 20" × 20" | dyed wool weft; wool warp
Collection of Carl and Marilynn Thoma

The foreground of Katia Paroczi's eerie landscape feels like water and the irregular surfaces stirred up by the wind. Thicker bands give way to thinner bands. Red gulls fly against dark-blue mountains under sky where the blue darkens as the eye moves up.

DY Begay also uses varying bands, which swell and contract—perhaps an abstraction of Southwestern US landscape. Begay has earned her worldwide reputation in part for the colors she uses. From her land in Arizona, she collects dyestuffs for her yarns. This piece uses what she found: alkanet, aniline, logwood, madder roots, gray yarn dyed with madder.

Fiona Hutchison's strength here comes partly from the power of size—the tapestry is roughly 6 by 8 feet; again, like Paroczi, she emphasizes red and blue. She creates an impression of texture. I want to visit this place and sail my way through that narrow passage in between two pieces of land. Or are they cliffs?

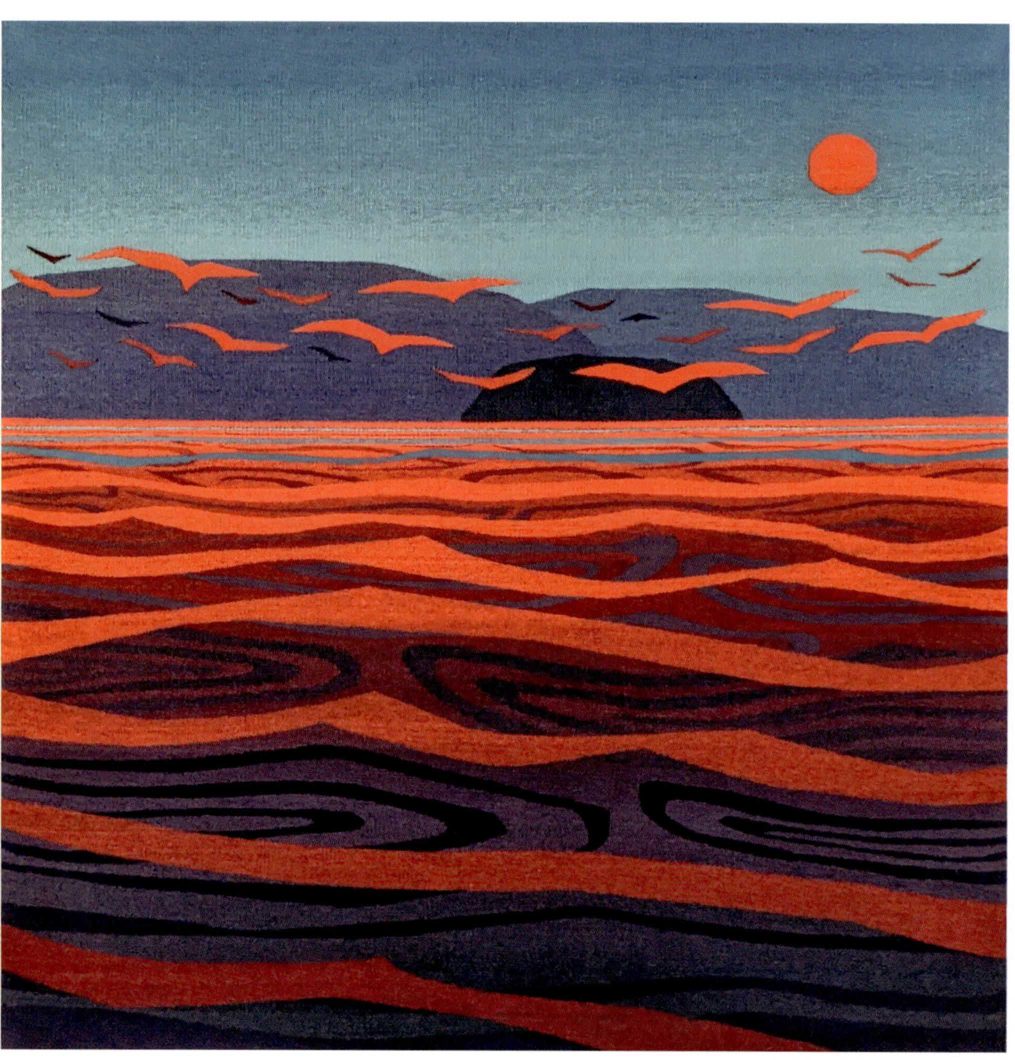

LEFT: *Bay Impressions II*
Katia Paroczi
2017 | 40" × 40" | handspun wool; cotton warp

OPPOSITE, TOP: *Red Earth*
DY Begay
2007 | 19" × 37.5" | wool
Collection of Augustana College Art Museum
Photographer: Jim Marshall

OPPOSITE, BOTTOM: *Harbor Wall*
Fiona Hutchison
1998 | 74.5" × 95.5" | wool, some cotton and linen; black mohair warp

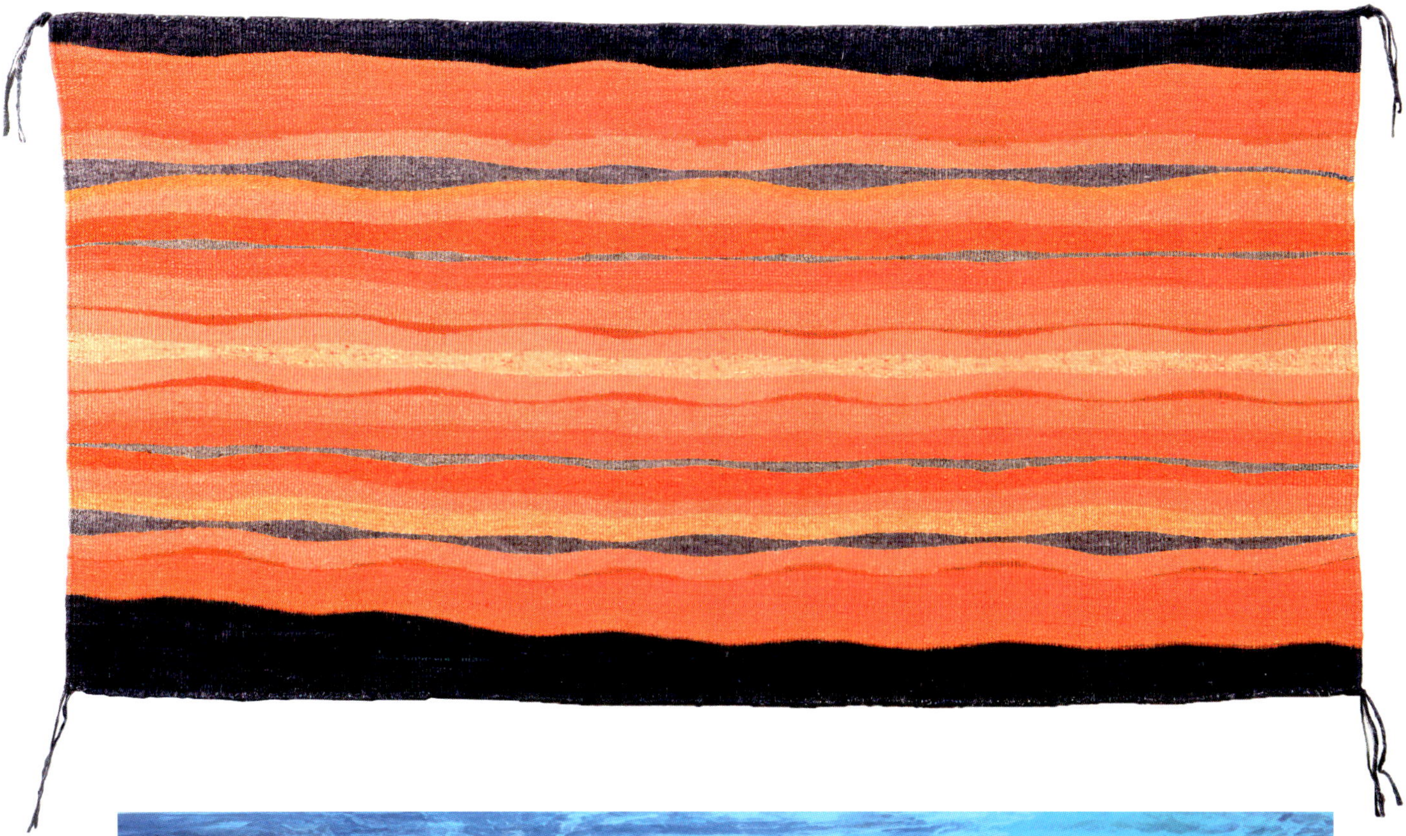

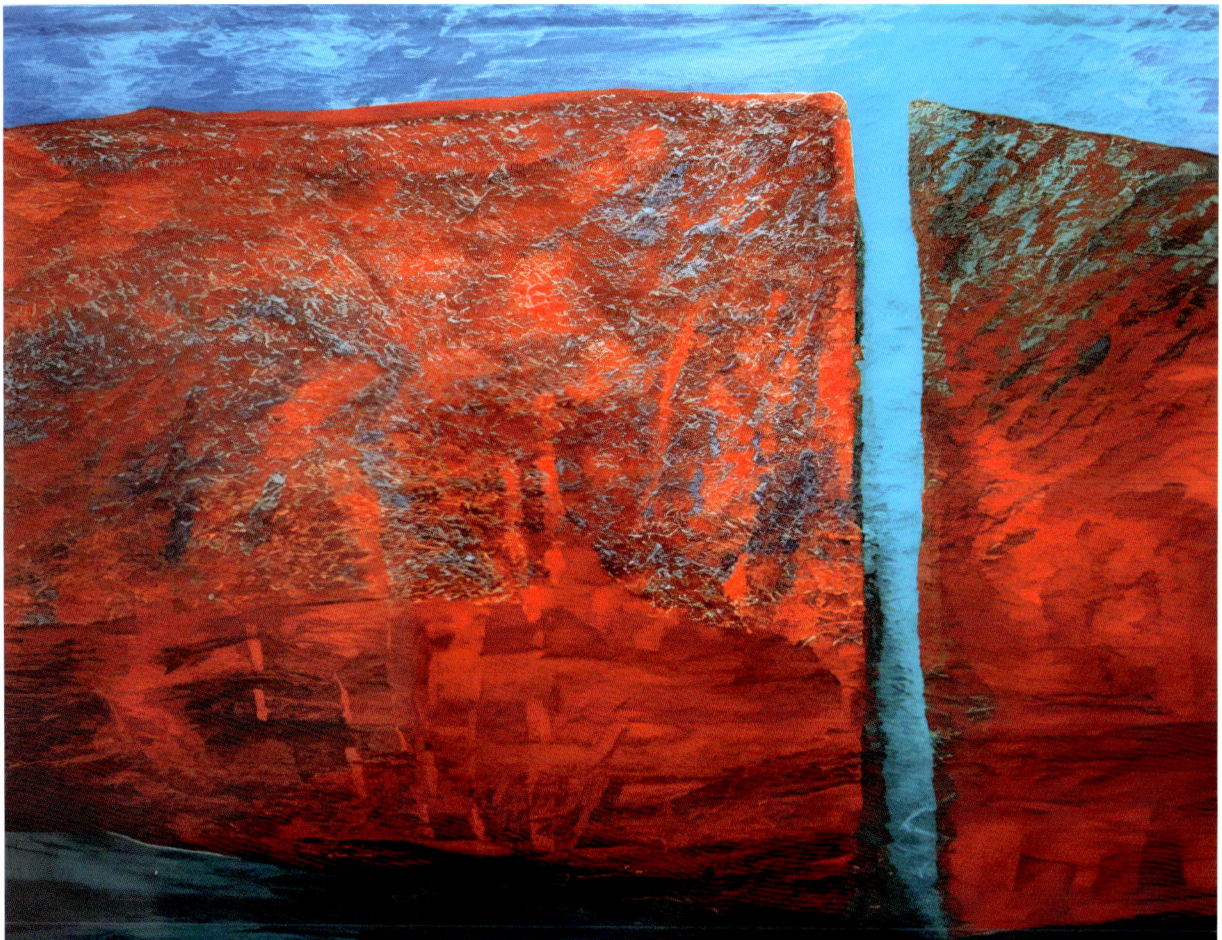

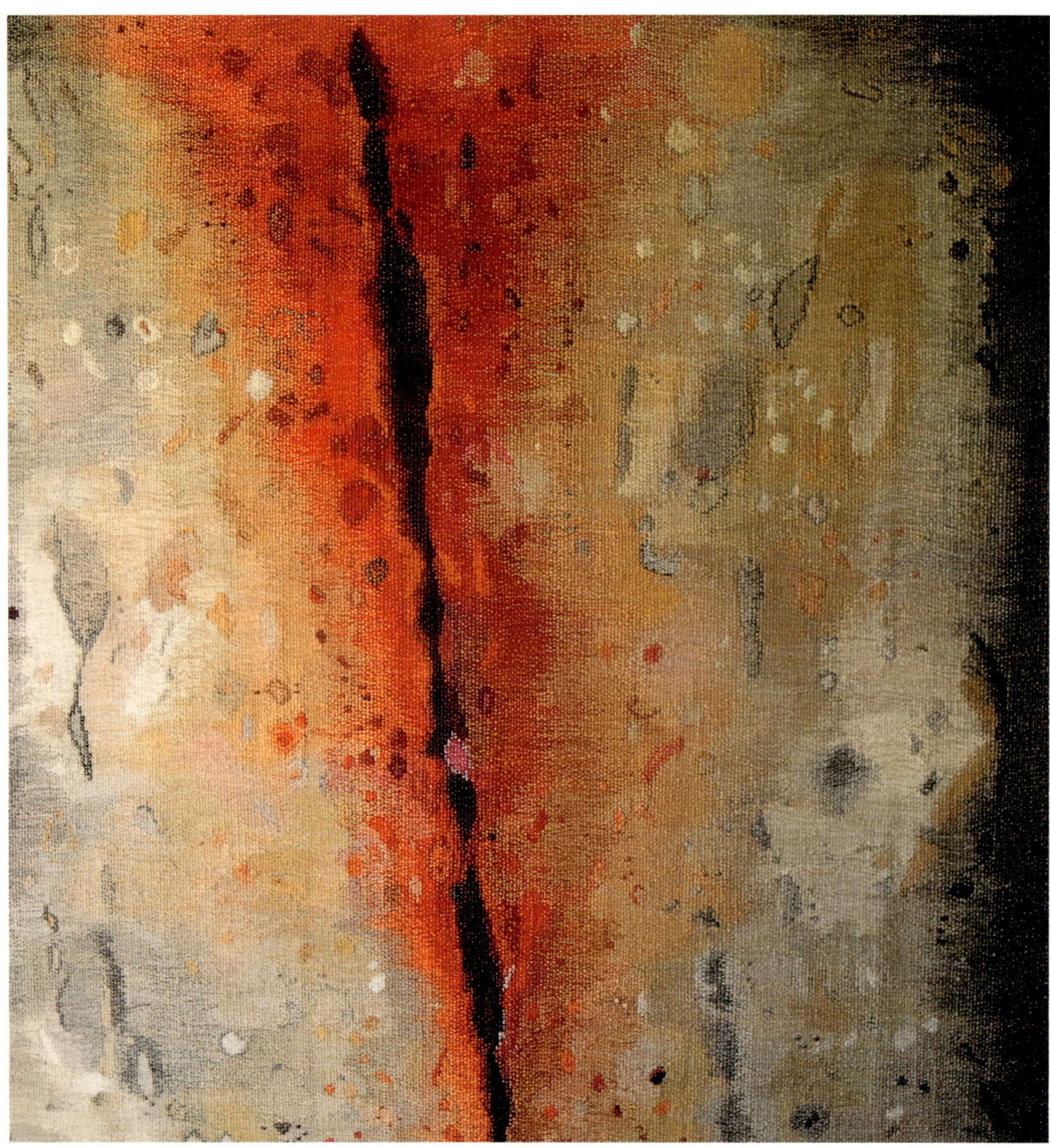

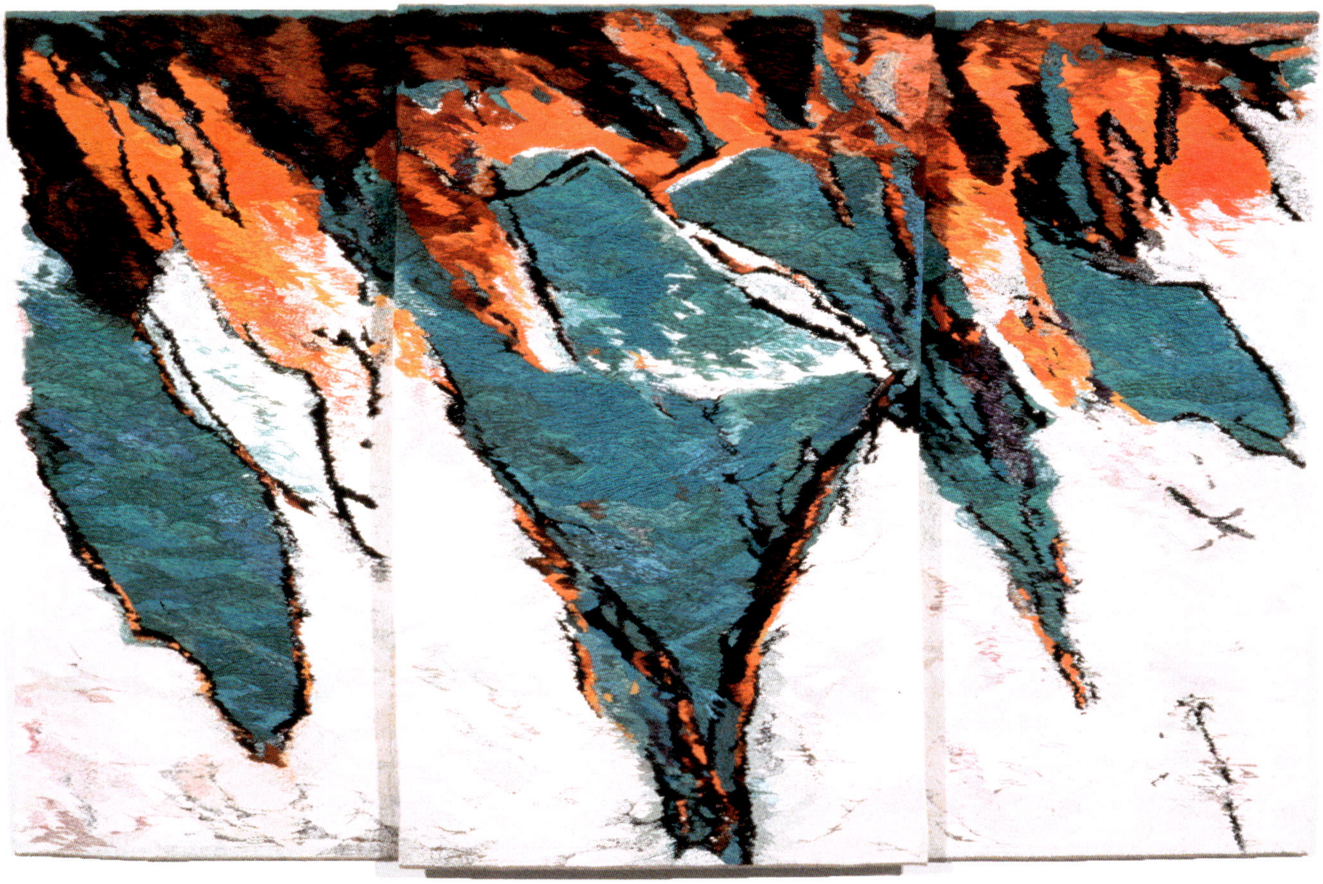

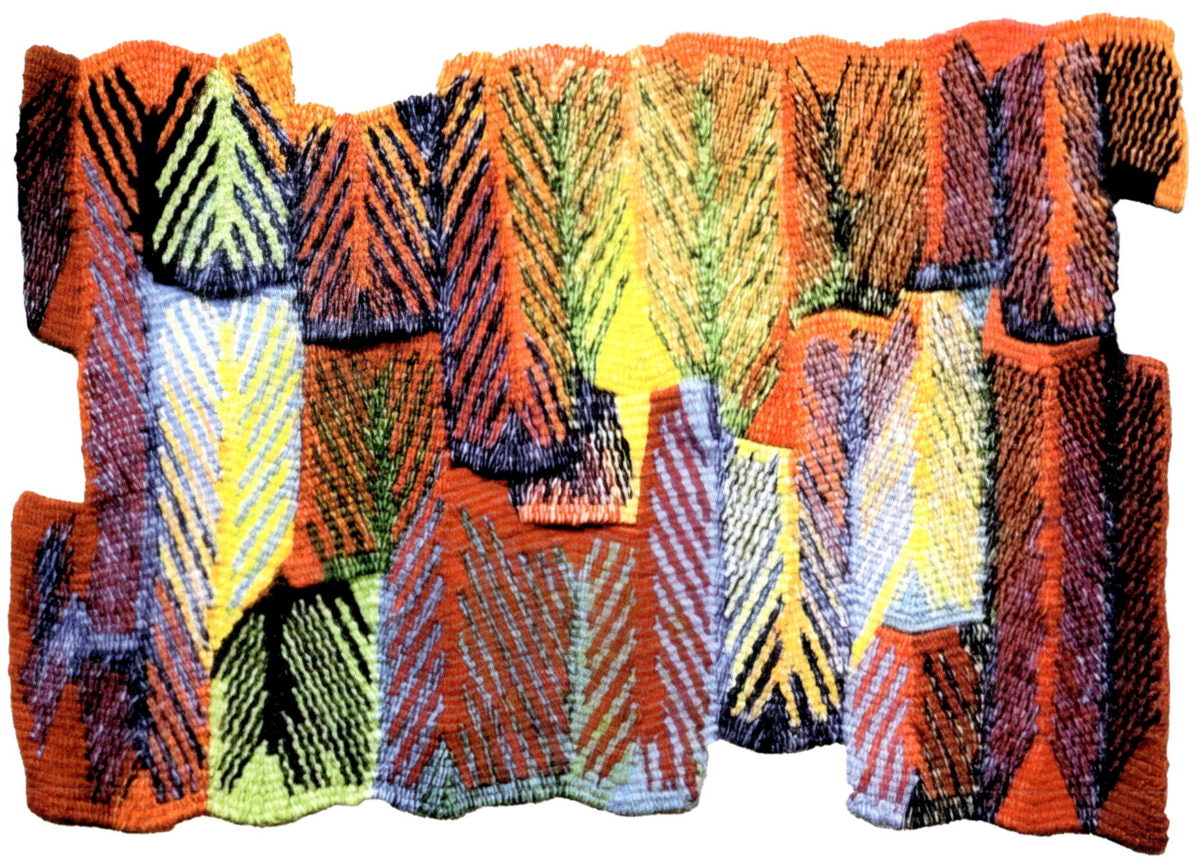

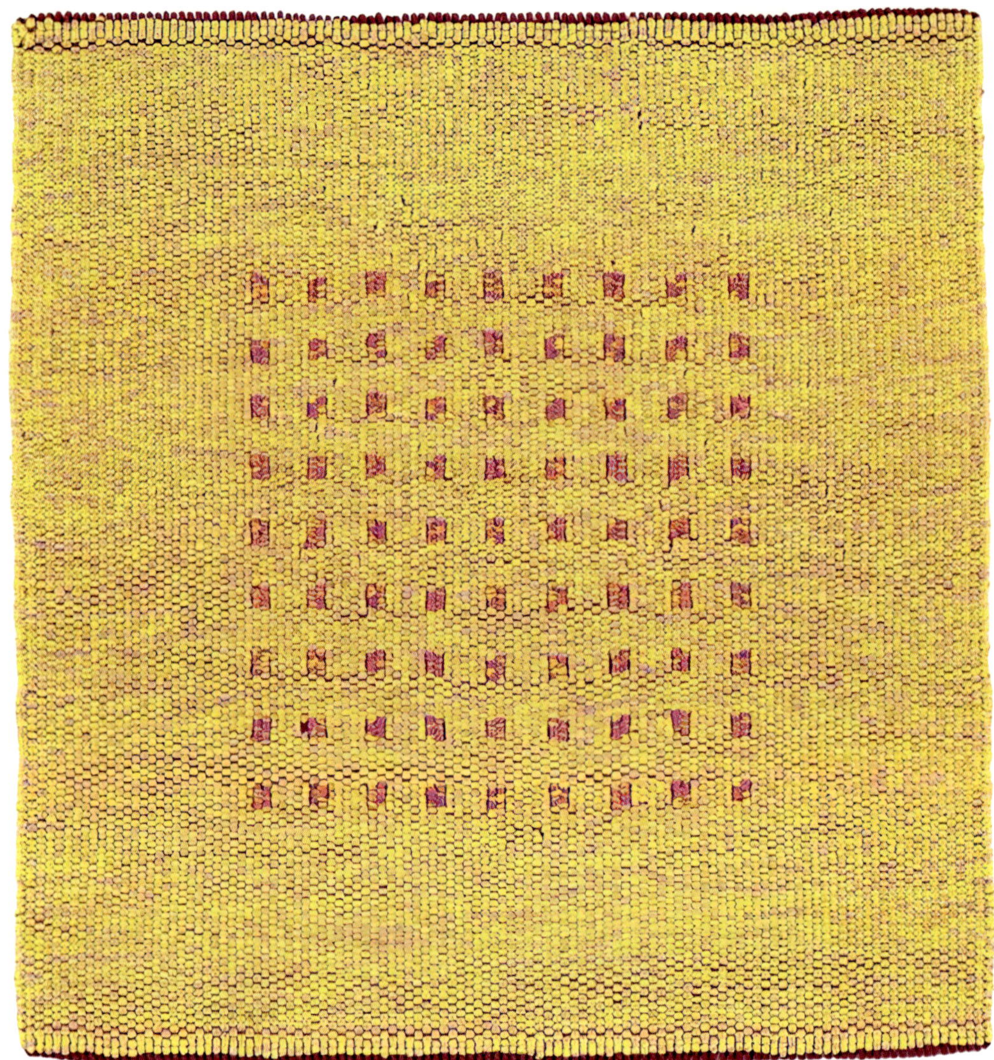

Cheryl Thornton has woven something small, red, and yellow—7 by 7 inches. The red of the warp shows up insistently in the small squares, forming a grid pattern in the middle, but also irregularly elsewhere, as though bleeding into the yellow field.

Inka Kivalo's so-called miniature is not small—nearly 6 feet on either side. Golds, purples, yellows, off-white, and black work almost like pools of spilled inks. On the page, the tapestry will look small; in a room, it would dominate.

Ingunn Skogholt may be weaving the pattern of a wooden plank where we see the grain with its knots. She has translated this pattern into oranges, golds and grays.

Sicily Gold
Cheryl Thornton
2018 | 7" × 7" | cotton, viscose; red warp

OPPOSITE, TOP: *Wood Divided I*
Ingunn Skogholt
2005 | 75" × 73" | wool, linen, synthetics; cotton warp

OPPOSITE, BOTTOM: *Big Miniature*
Inka Kivalo
2008 | 69" × 71" | cotton, linen, silk
Photographer: Johnny Korkman

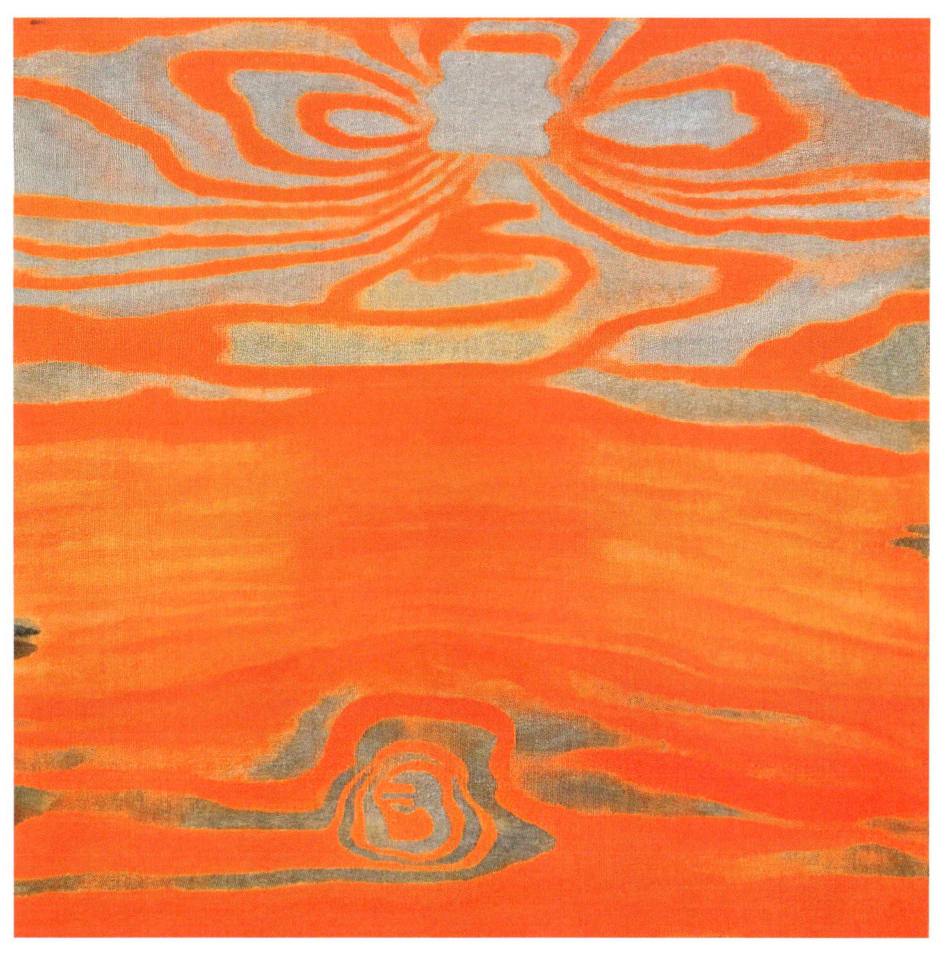

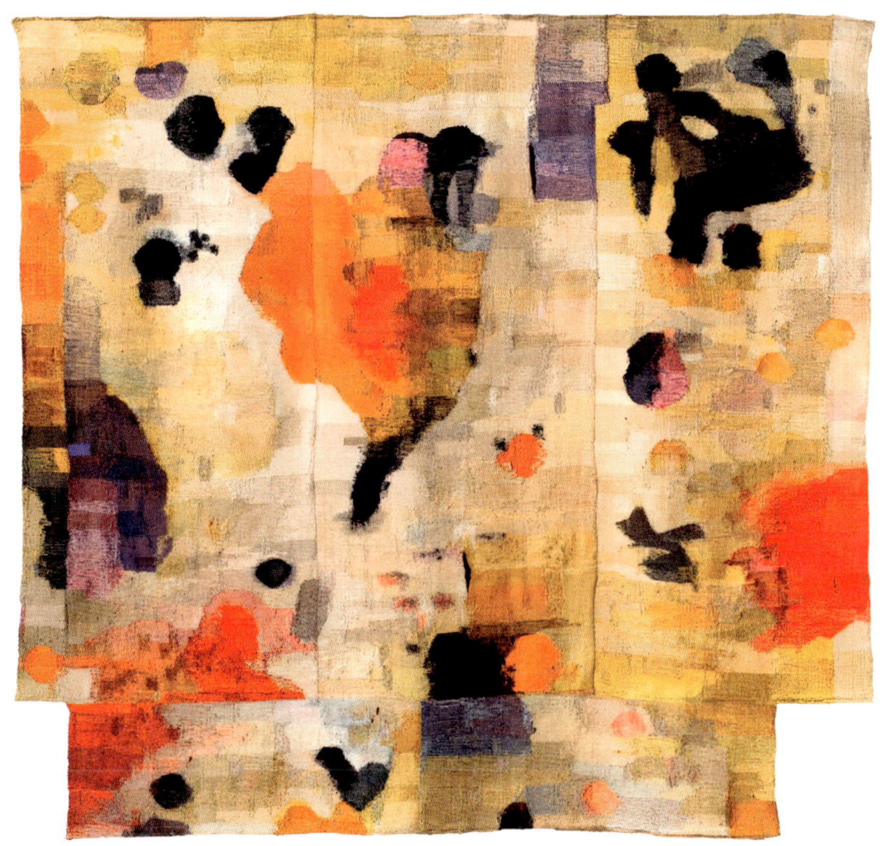

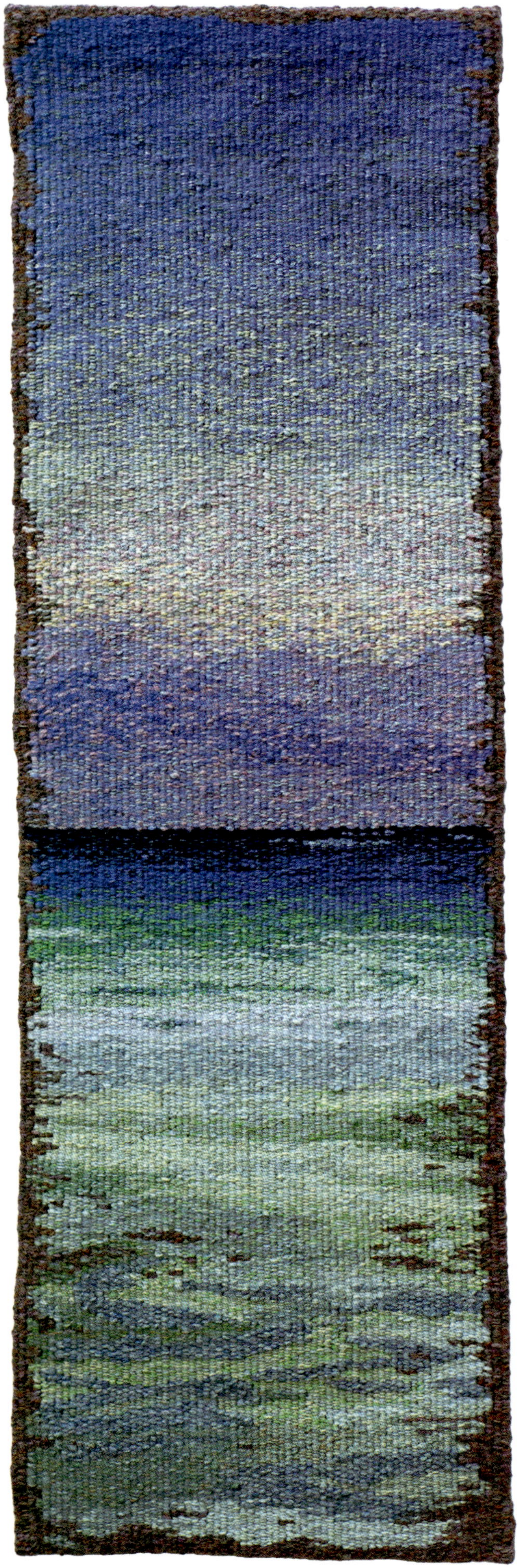

The Thomsons, mother Leila (now deceased) and daughter Jo, run an art studio in the Orkney Islands. When I visited, I asked about the dominance of blue in their production. "Look around you." The door to my right had a central glass panel, and, looking out, I saw sea and sky. Blue. The two women often discussed which blues belonged in their environment and which did not. It mattered since they sought to make work that embodied their sense of place. The daughter's tapestry is radiantly still, the sea reflecting and not reflecting the sky. The mother's is constantly dynamic, with its turning birds and invasive waters. Blue.

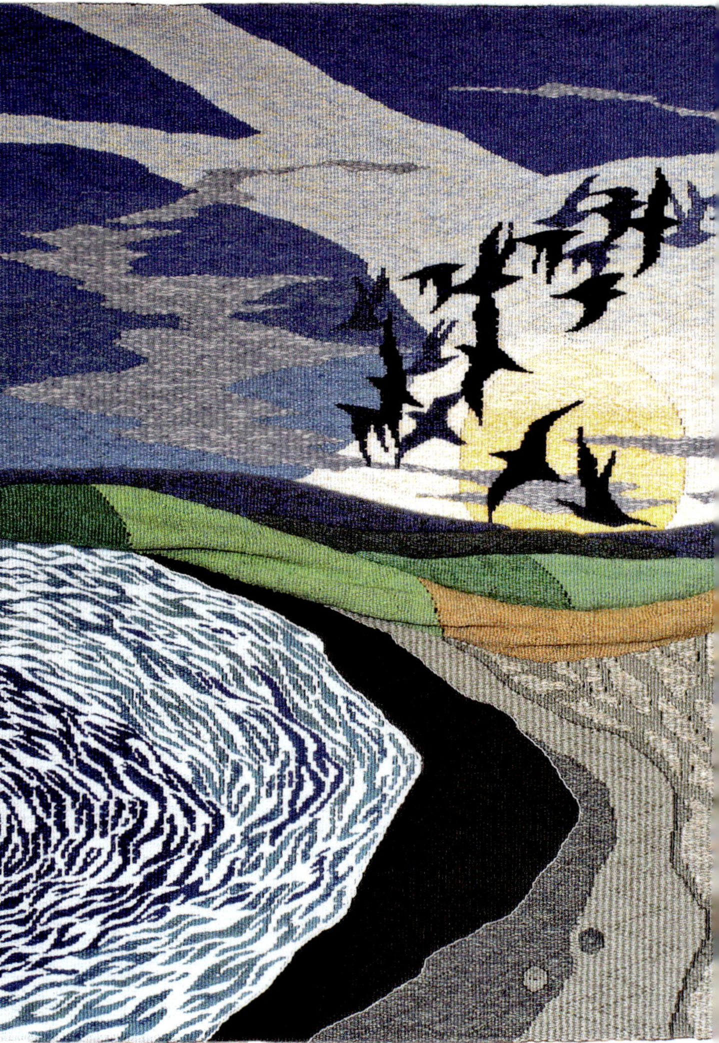

OPPOSITE: *Beyond the Horizon*
Jo Thomson
2020 | 28" × 9" | cotton, rayon, wool, a tiny bit of linen; cotton warp

BELOW: *In Search of Solace*
Leila Thomson
2006 | 3' × 4' | cotton, linen, rayon, wool; cotton warp

RIGHT: *A Trio of New Horizons*
Cresside Collette
2011 | 12.2" × 25.6" (each) | wool, cotton, synthetic; cotton warp

Both Cresside Collette and Kay Lawrence live in Australia, where the memorable landscape exerts immense influence. For Collette, who spent her first years in Ceylon (now Sri Lanka), Australia is a radical change from the tropical environment she knew. About 70% of Australia consists of desert. She has tried to combine these life experiences and see how they interact. Three times she varies the opposition of pink and green, near complements. Is it morning? Are the green fields Australian? Collette comments on how "soft green vegetation [gives] way to a harsher, more architectural skyline."

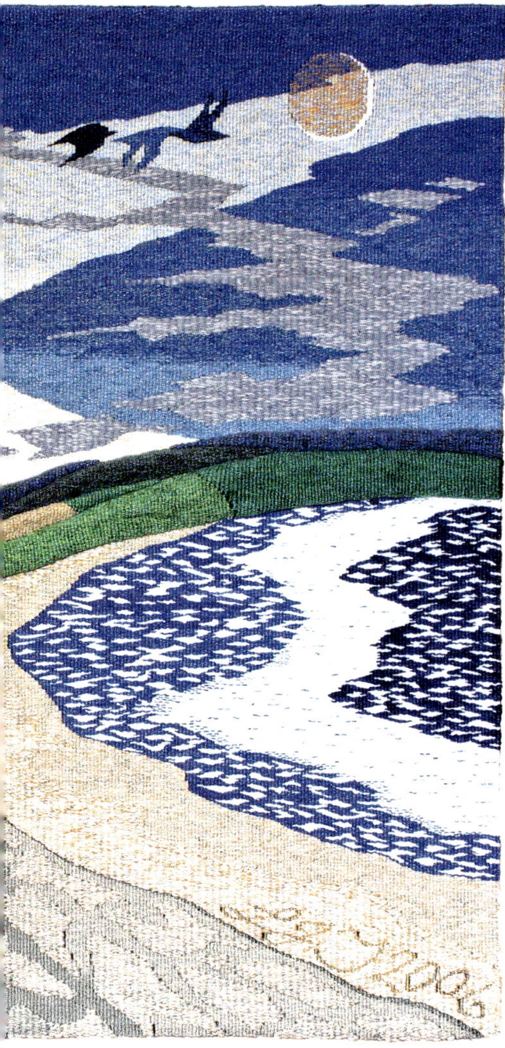

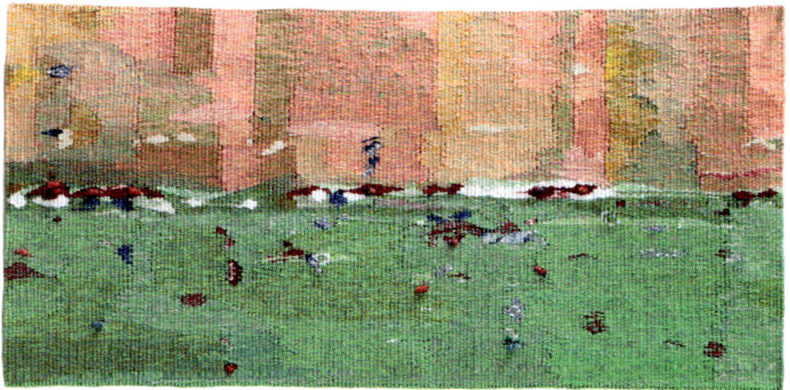

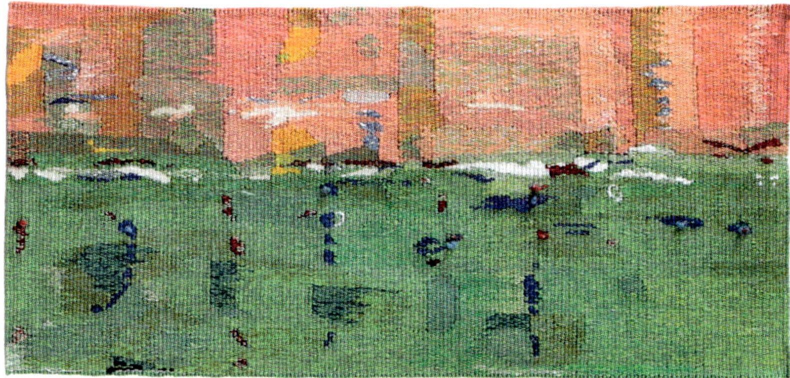

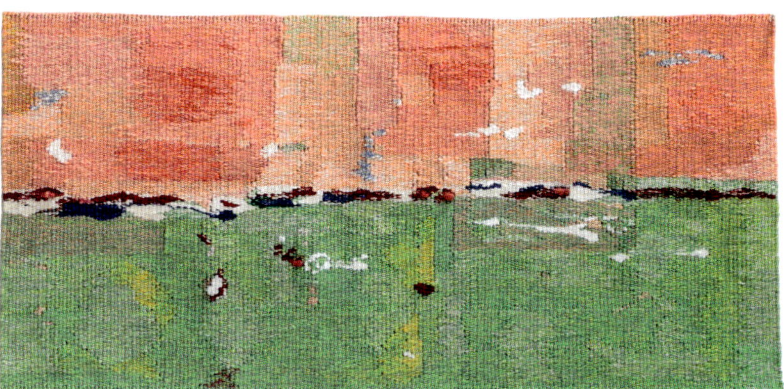

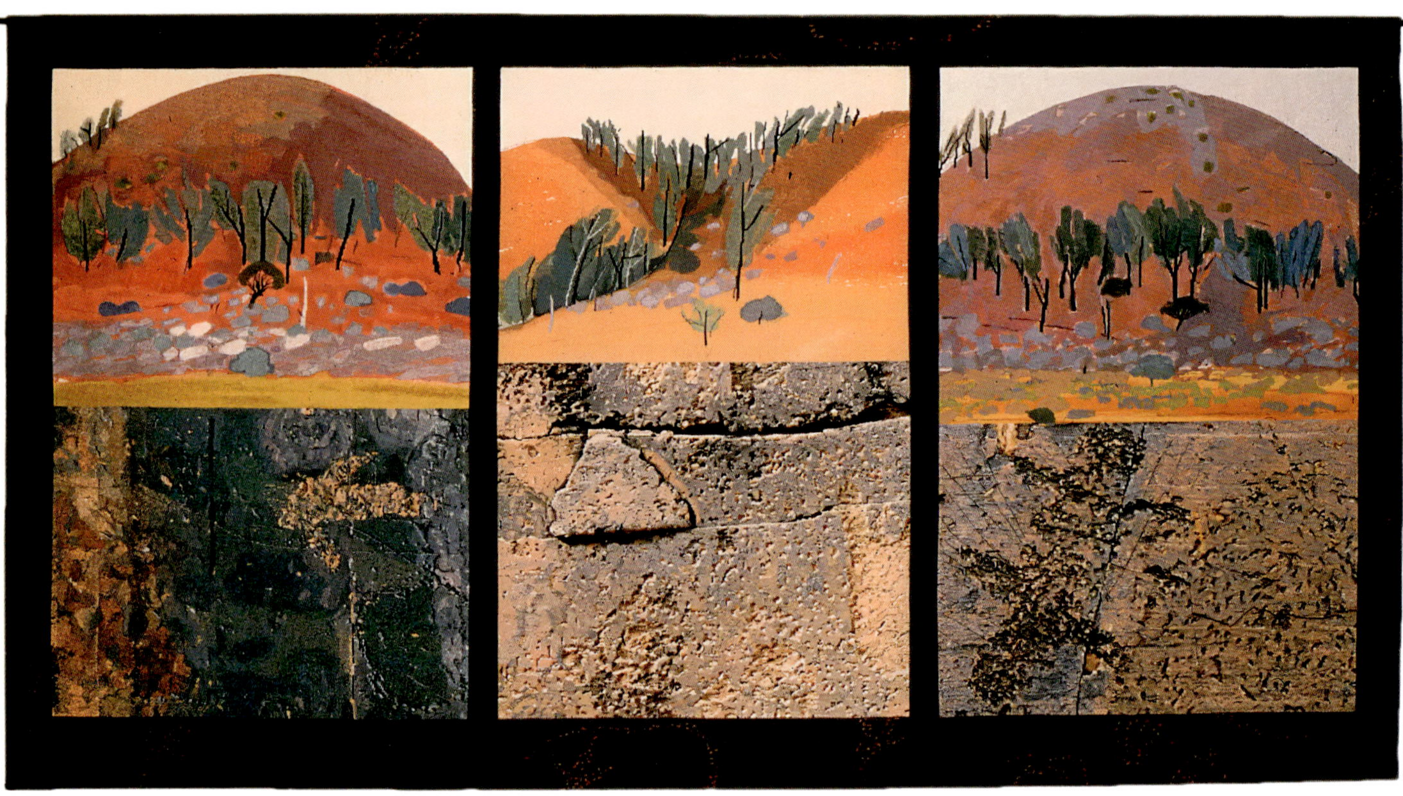

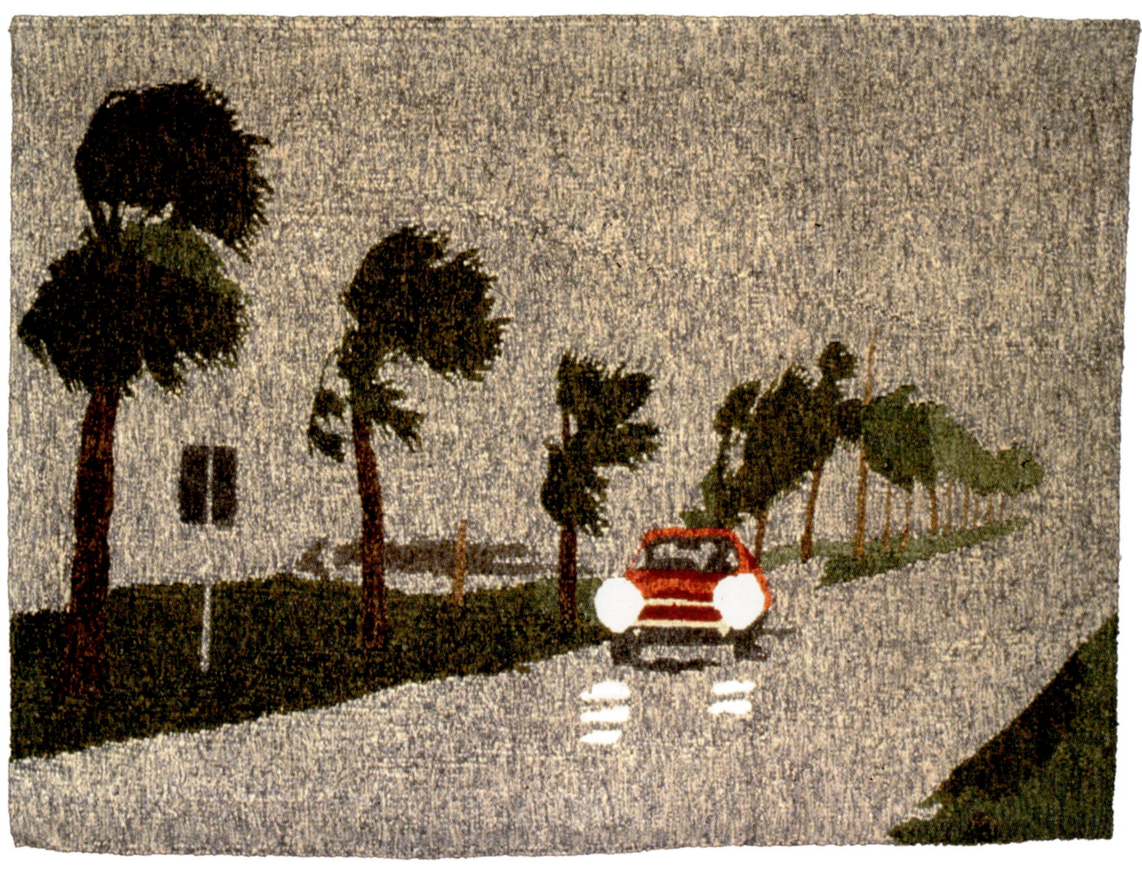

Lawrence's work captures the country in all its variety. In the bottom half, she has emphasized the textures of rock at Red Gorge, a place of the Adnyamathanha and petroglyphs. Above, with stylized tree shapes, almost like a Fred Williams painting, she helps the viewer imagine vastly different sensory experiences, the red/gray, rounded hills to right and left frame the yellow valley between them. Commissioned by Parliament House, the tapestry hangs in the prime minister's dining room.

Martha Matthews's piece has long been a favorite of mine. Consider the limited palette and all she accomplishes. Looking at it carefully, you might feel that the wind is blowing and that the rain is soaking you. I love the car, red, with its headlights reflecting in pools of water as it speeds towards us.

Maria Robinson's *Against All Odds* may serve us especially well when we stand in front of it. From close-up or from a distance, the birch trees contrast with the nearby orange-and-yellow forest. She comments that the tapestry "was inspired by birch trees that we almost lost from heavy rain and following frost."

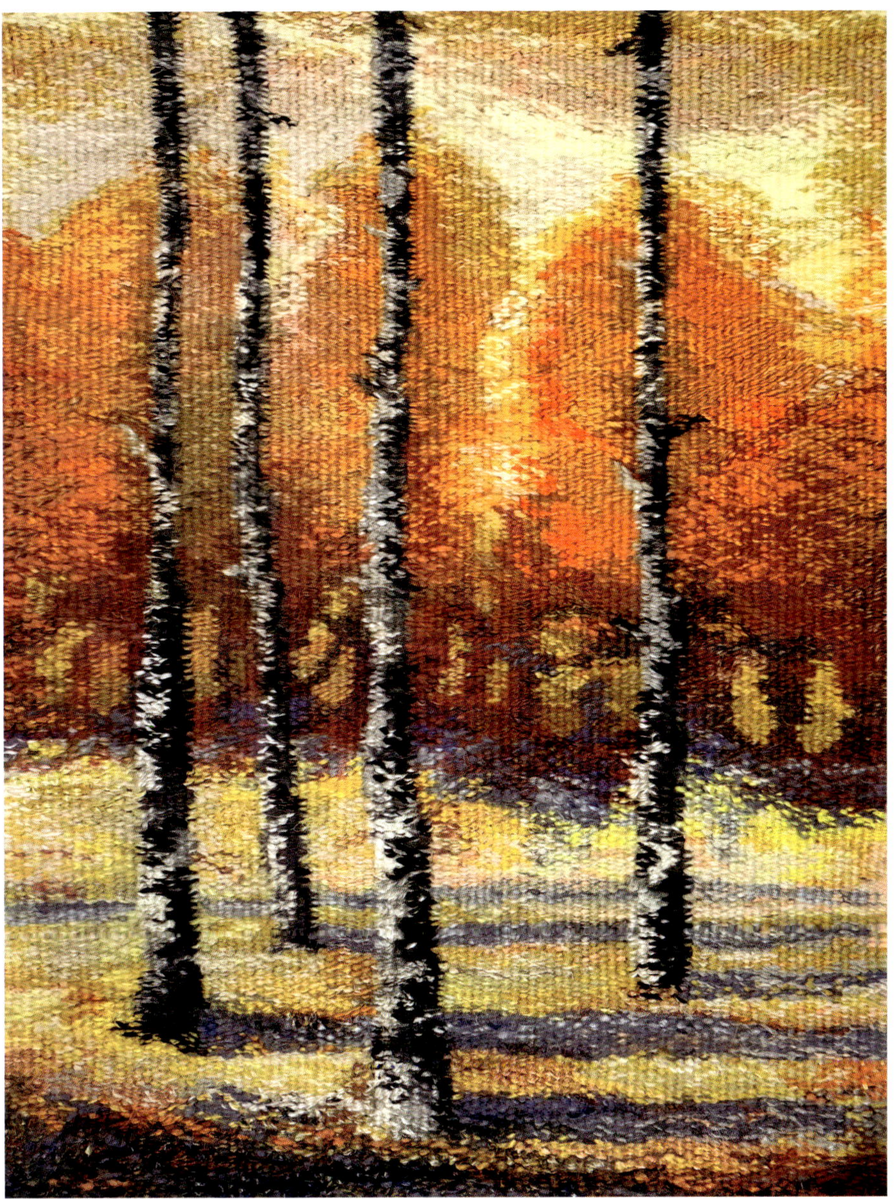

OPPOSITE, TOP: *Red Gorge, Two Views*
Kay Lawrence
1987–88 | 6.33' × 11.77' | wool, cotton, linen; cotton warp
Weavers: Kay Lawrence,
Shirley Benlow, Chris Cochius, Jude Stewart
Commissioned by Parliament House Construction Authority

OPPOSITE, BOTTOM: *Rain Storm*
Martha Matthews
36" × 48"

ABOVE: *Against All Odds*
Maria Robinson
2019 | 30" × 23" | wool, synthetic yarns; polyester rope warp

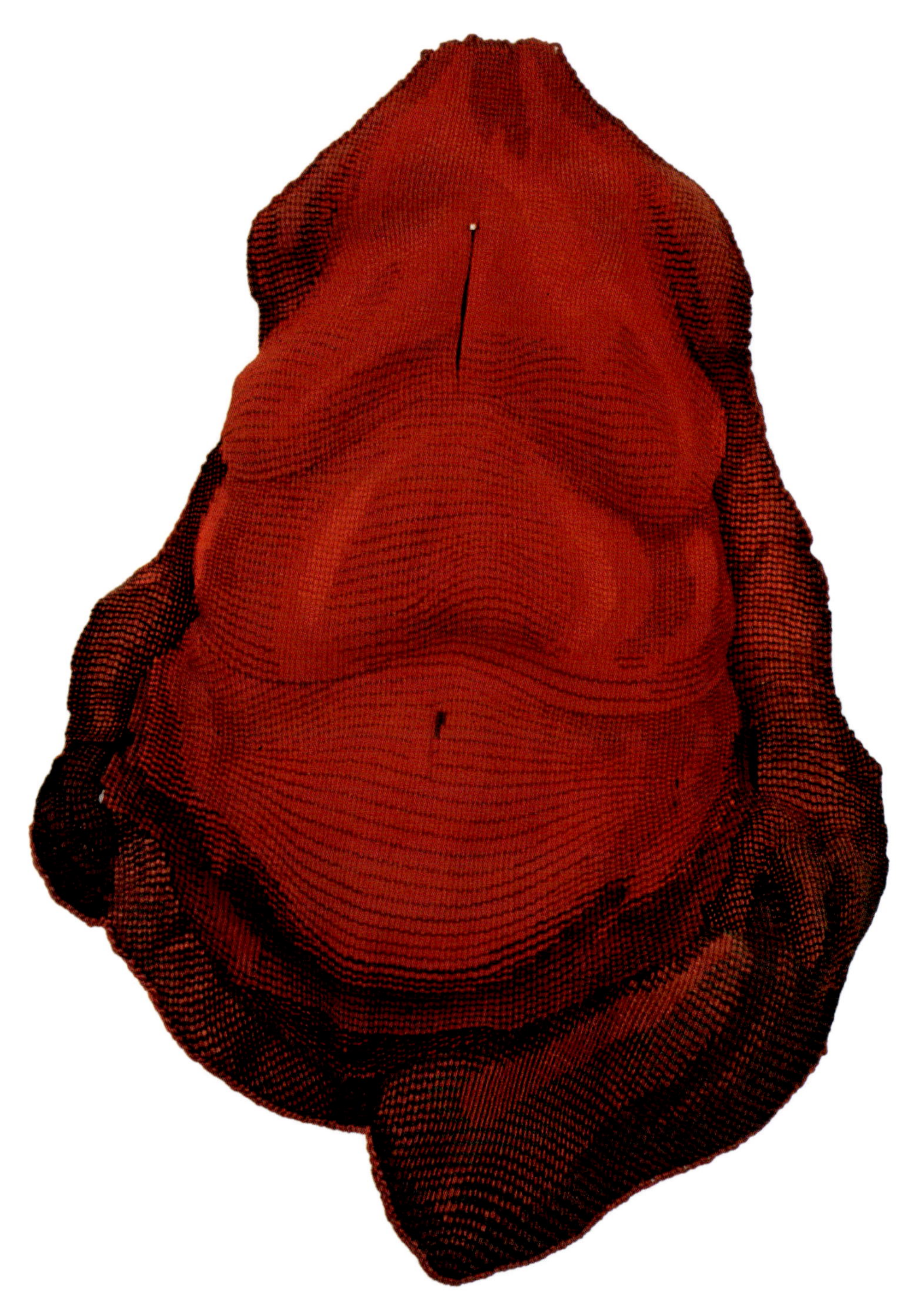

warp

Before a weaver can begin to weave, they must do several things. First, they must measure their warp, a group of threads organized to be parallel and under tension between two fixed beams on the loom. Warp awaits the interlacing of the weft, which will create the tapestry.

Often in a traditional tapestry, the backbone (the warp) will disappear behind the weft, that which develops the pattern and design. (This is why tapestry is often labeled *weft-faced*.)

A careful look at the cloth that defines tapestry reveals the ribs created by the warps. Sometimes, tracing those lines can inform you, the viewer, in which direction the weaver wove. Typically, historical large European tapestries hang so that the warp is horizontal. This decision keeps the yarn, which can weigh quite a lot, from slipping downward along the warp.

This chapter offers other ways to consider warp.

Rule of thumb: If you weave the weft thread at right angles to the warp, standard practice, you produce a flat surface. If you weave the weft other than at right angles to the warp, the weft pulls the warp out of plumb. The Navajo began to employ this technique in the nineteenth century, calling it a wedge weave. Other names for this technique include "pulled warp" and "eccentric weft." Well-known tapestry weaver Silvia Heyden used it almost constantly. The results can include a dramatic dimensionality with which both Christine Laffer and Susan Iverson have experimented.

A Warm Resistance
Christine Laffer
1994 | 20" × 14" × 2" | cotton, linen, rayon, wool
Collection of (and photo by) Barbara Heller

Among the several pieces where Laffer used this technique, producing work that bulges and bloats, this is a good example. She includes lines that emphasize the shape and a warm red in the expanding center.

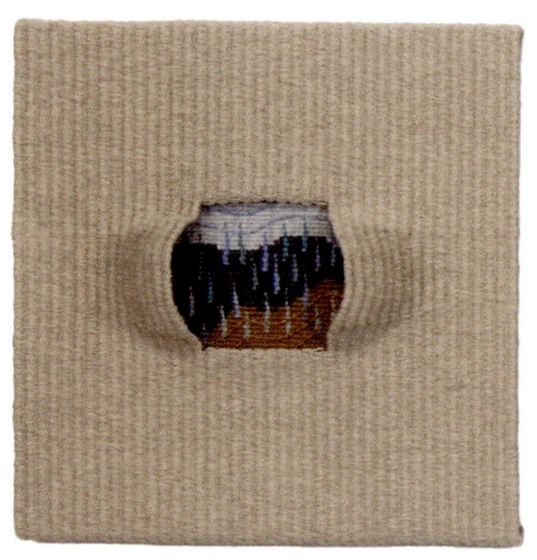
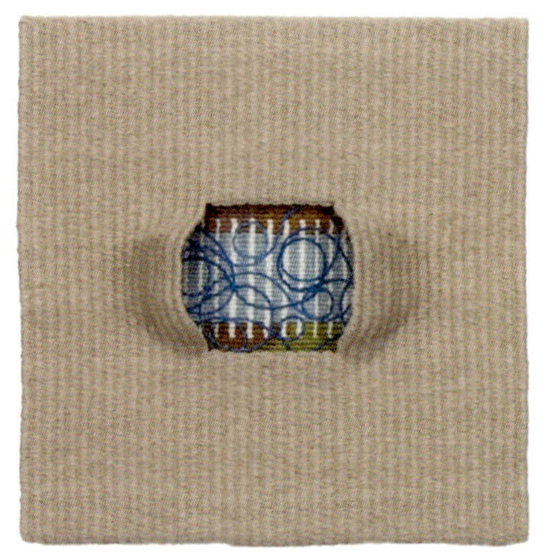
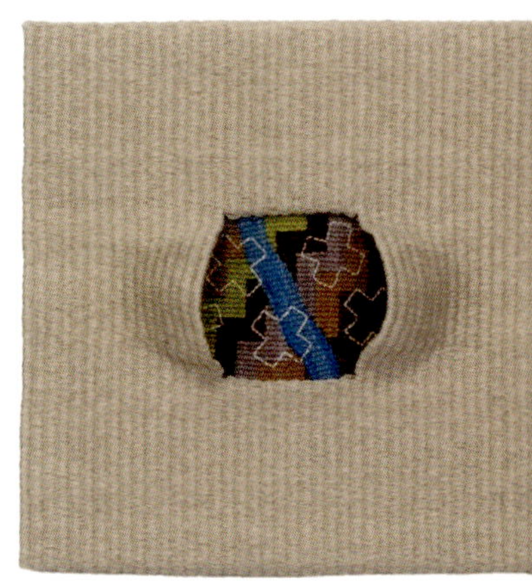

Iverson, originally inspired by Herman Scholten's work, has for years sought ways to work with pulled warp (she has even written a book on its possibilities). The first picture here shows a straight-on look at four pieces; the look from the side shows the dramatic results of her pulled warp.

ABOVE AND BELOW:
The Pond (from the front and from the side)
Susan Iverson
2009 | each piece 13.5" × 13.5" × 3.75" | linen, silk; linen warp
Pulled warp and embroidery
Photographer: Taylor Dabney

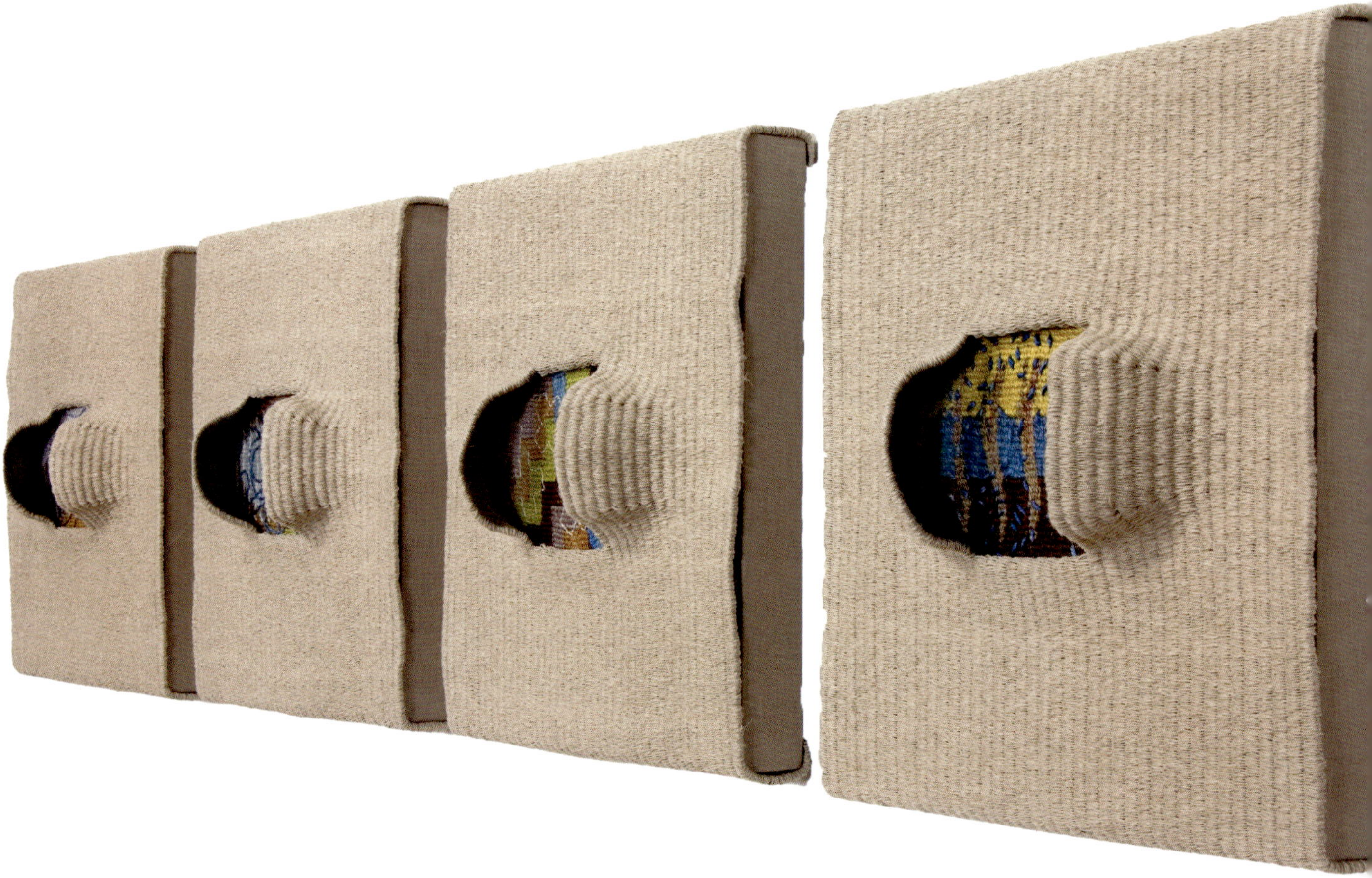

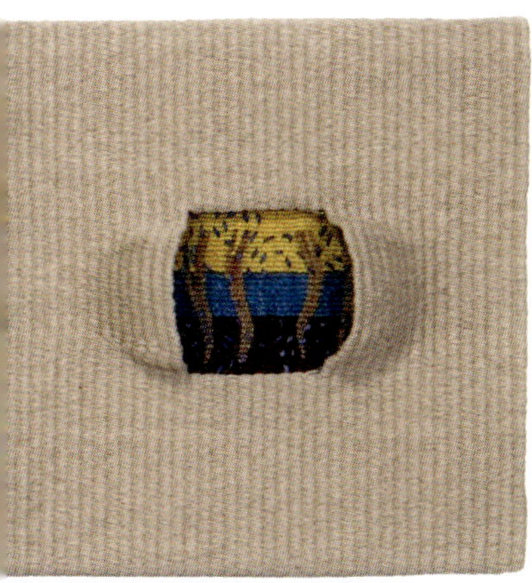

works including visible warp

Marianna Ortega's knitter looks almost like a marionette. Like many tapestry designs, this work is self-reflective—a piece of cloth showing someone manipulating yarn to make a piece of cloth.

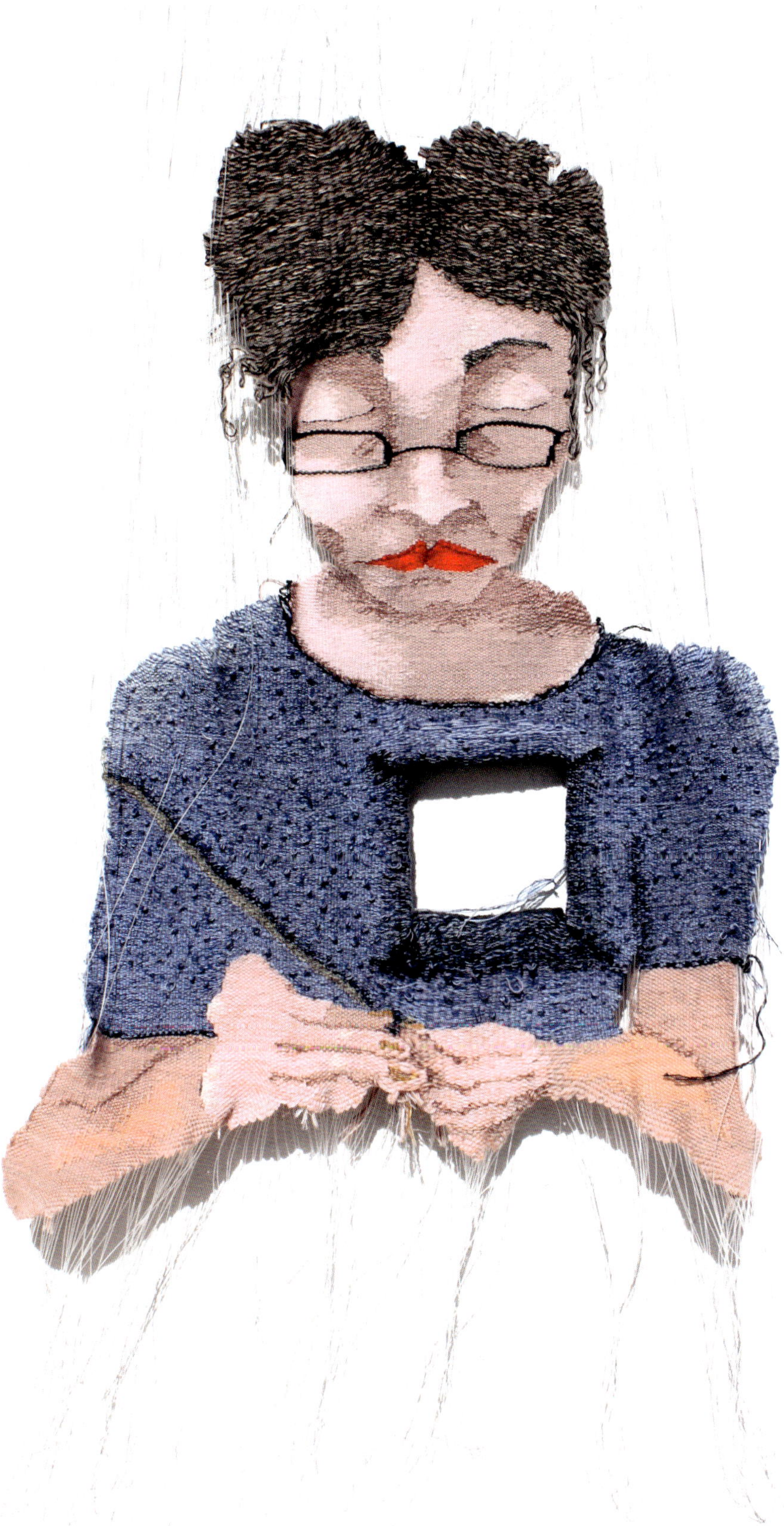

Memory Weaver
Marianna Ortega
2016 | 46.5" × 21.25" | cotton; nylon fishing-line warp

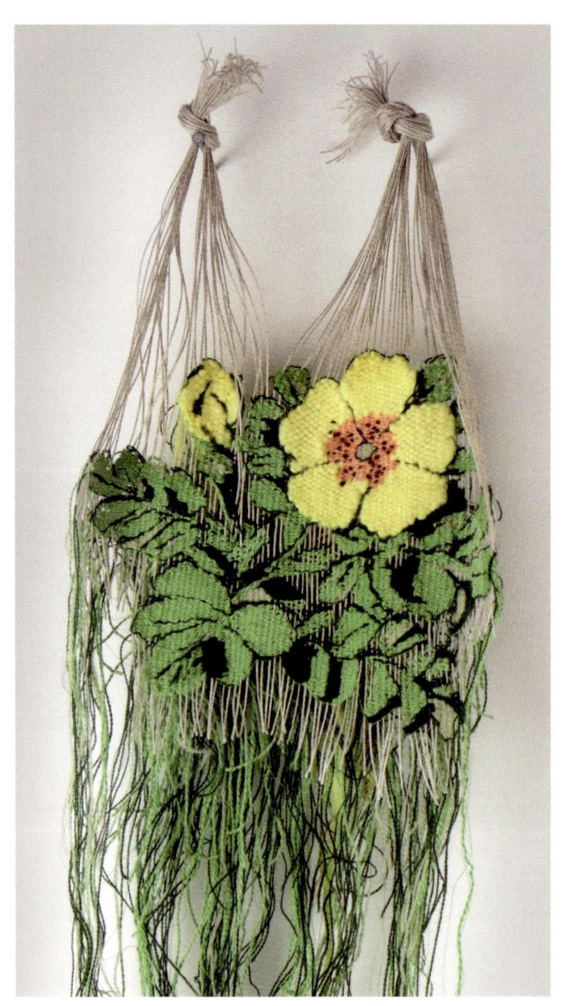

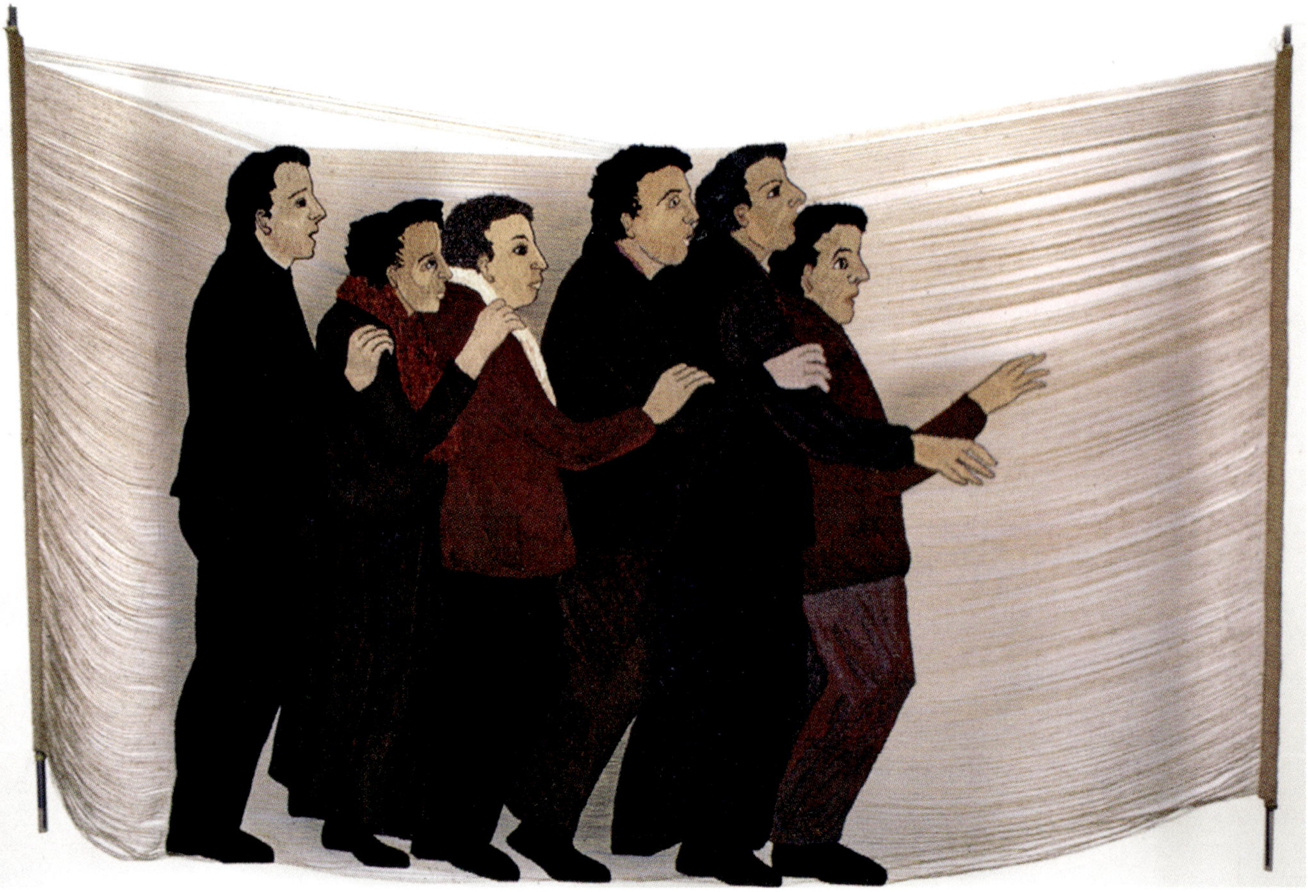

Tonje Høydahl Sørli's flowers speak of a pot, hanging in the window, with spare threads of warp and green yarn that suggest vines.

Claire Rado is showing us a crowd of half a dozen figures who are held together by the visible warp, as though Rado is alerting us to the human network.

The variations in the surface of Justine Randall's *Night Sky* are not a photographer's mistake. She has given us visible warp threads (the white vertical lines), crossed systematically by dark weft, to reshape the opposition of darkness and light.

OPPOSITE, TOP: *Chasing Reality Lately*
Tonje Høydahl Sørli
2022 | 42" × 10.5" × 2" | linen, Spælsau wool, cotton, worsted yarn

OPPOSITE, BOTTOM: *Être Humain* (Human Being)
Claire Rado
1998 | 63" × 90.5"

ABOVE: *The Night Sky: 10 pm Moonlight*
Justine Randall
2016 | 63" × 64.2" | wool, exposed cotton warp

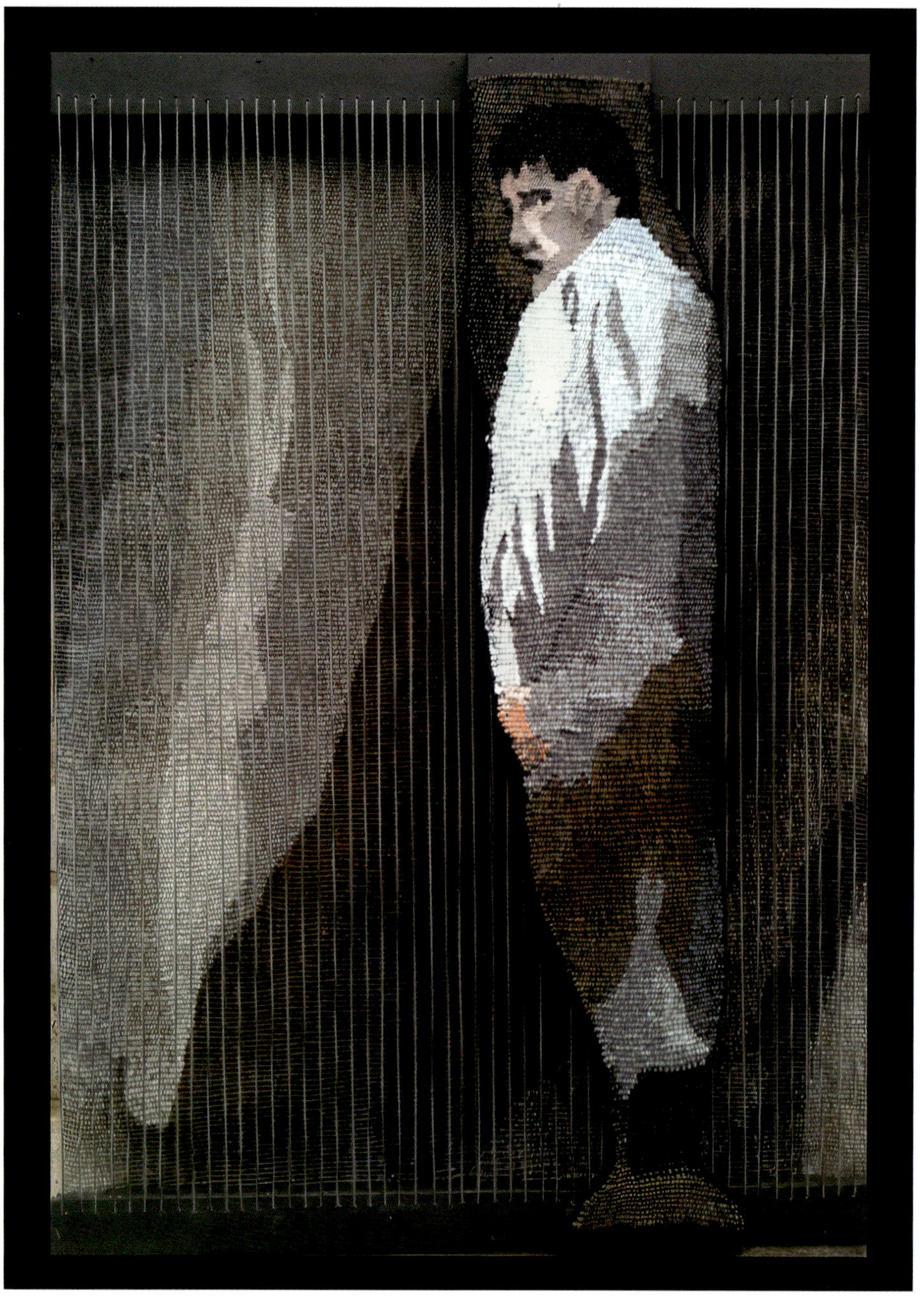

The Lost Boy
Matty Smith
2010 | 28.75" × 21.25" × 2" | wool; cotton warp

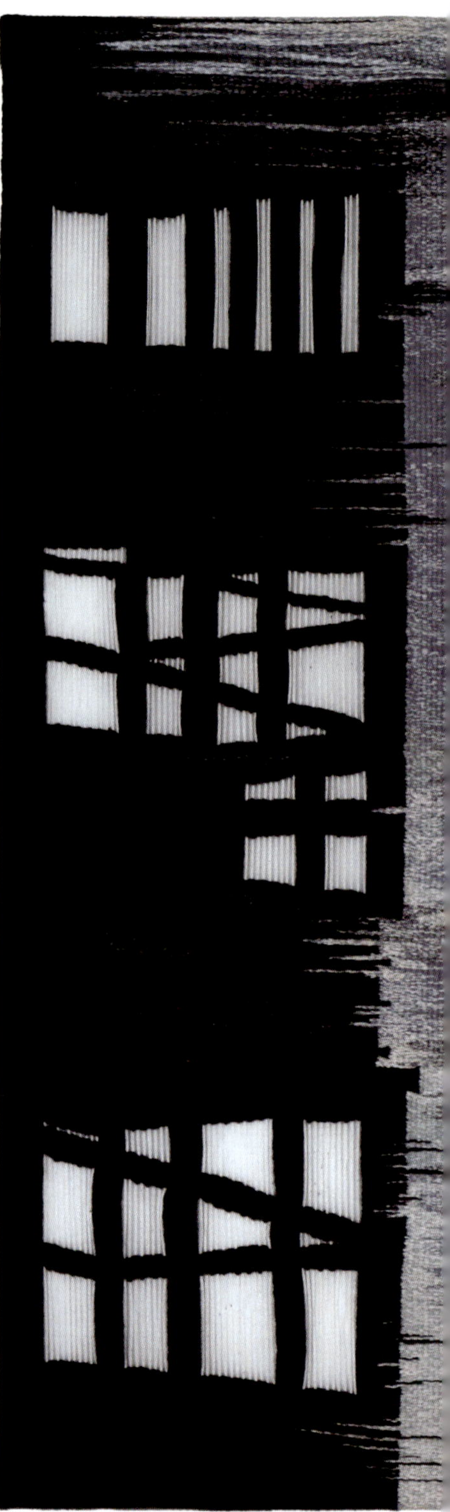

Two Sides of One Life
Oleksandr Federenko
2018 | 44.8" × 30.7" | wool, cotton

Matty Smith has woven three layers to give us *The Lost Boy*. The background of simple weaving (visible on the left, abstract grays), vertical lines (warp) like a jail cell, or confinement—or even frightening emptiness?—and the image of the boy, more realistically rendered.

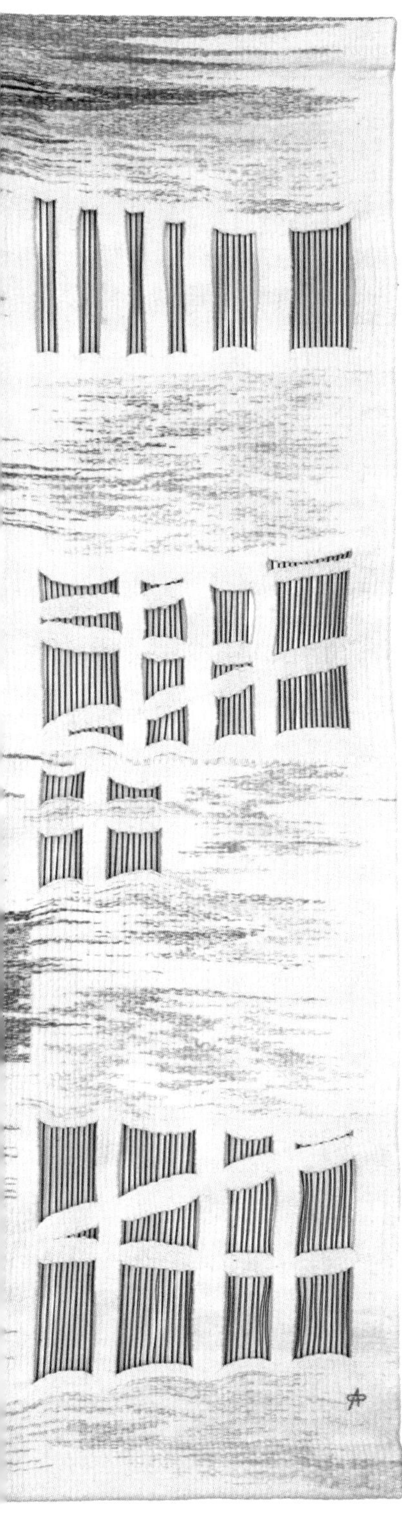

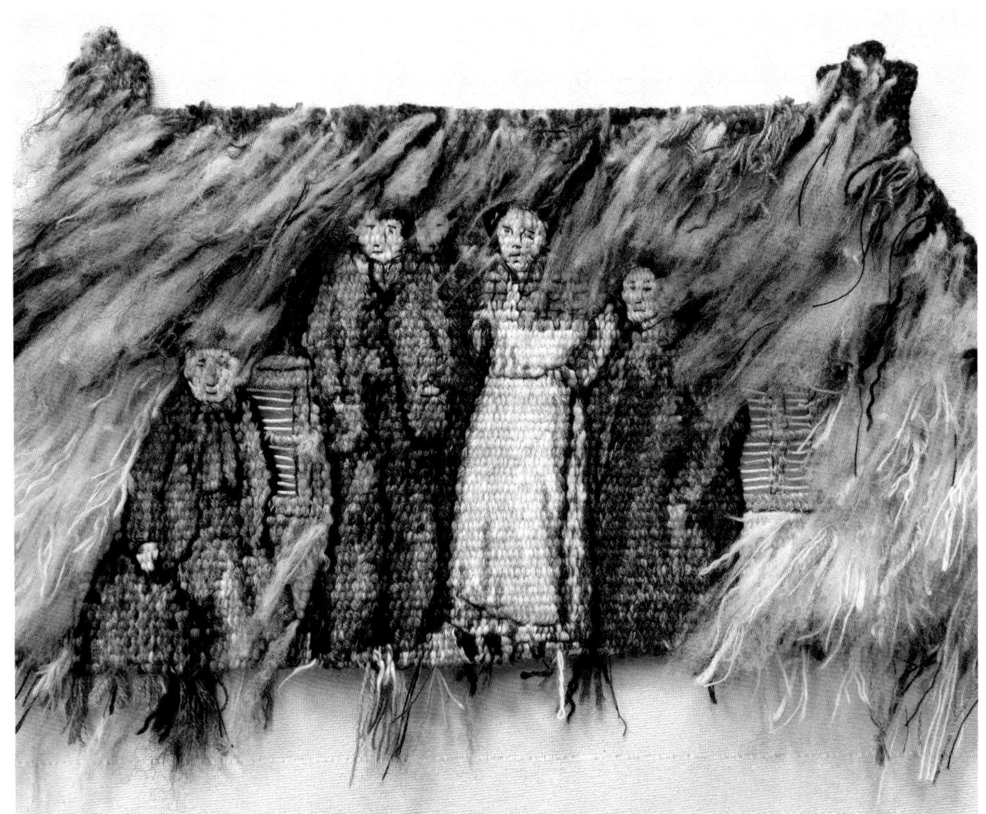

Traces
Valerie Kirk
2024 | 11" × 15.75" | wool, cotton, mixed fibers

Oleksandr Federenko has created a mirror image, one black and the other white, with visible warps within each window frame. We may all feel like this—on the one hand, on the other hand. The central section encroaches on and then connects the two halves.

Valerie Kirk's scenario centers on a cottage that might represent the crofts of her native Scotland, many of which are now empty and abandoned. Openings in the walls show the skeleton of the structure without any protective layer; the visible horizontal threads are warp. The fleecy parts of the wool also suggest the disintegration of what might have been a whole, even as the wind blows. The figures look distressed and yet immobile, as though there is nothing to be done. The black/white palette adds to the bleakness.

Karine Pinet's kitten makes me laugh as the claws reveal the warp. It is as if the kitten is real enough to destroy the weaving.

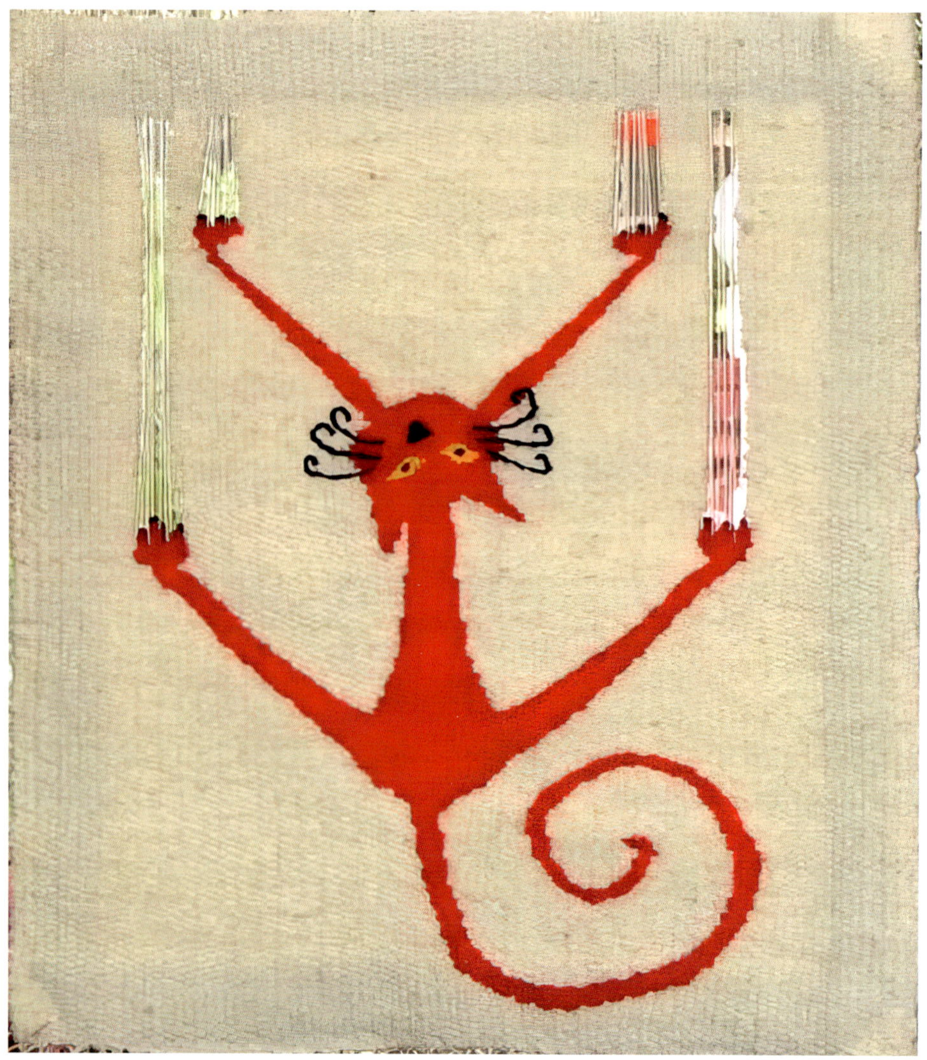

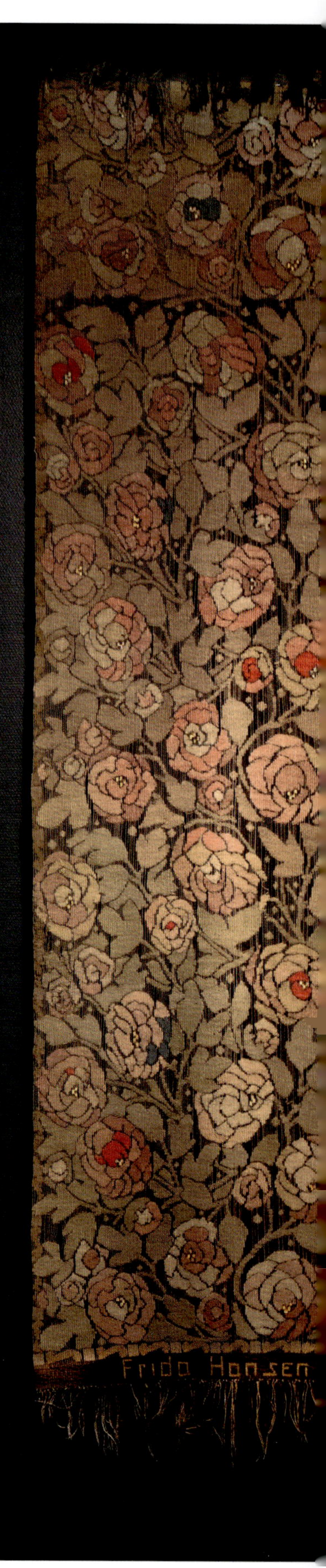

Frida Hansen, of late-nineteenth- and early-twentieth-century Norway, developed a system of weaving known as "transparent tapestries" and included gaps in the woven surface (here, black gaps, with visible warp, between the flowers). Although her warp is vertical and thus might permit downward slippage of the weft, the wool is also especially fuzzy and clings to what is woven across it.

ABOVE: *Mistigri*
Karine Pinet
2019–20 | 15.75" × 11.8" | wool, synthetics; cotton warp

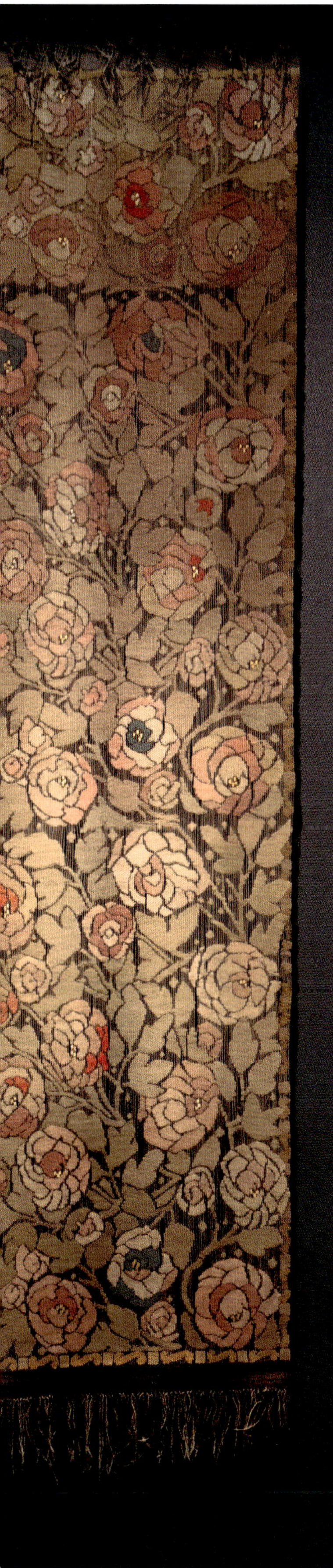

LEFT: *Peoner* (Peonies)
Frida Hansen
ca. 1928 | each section
8'9" × 27.15" | wool, silk
Stavanger Art Museum

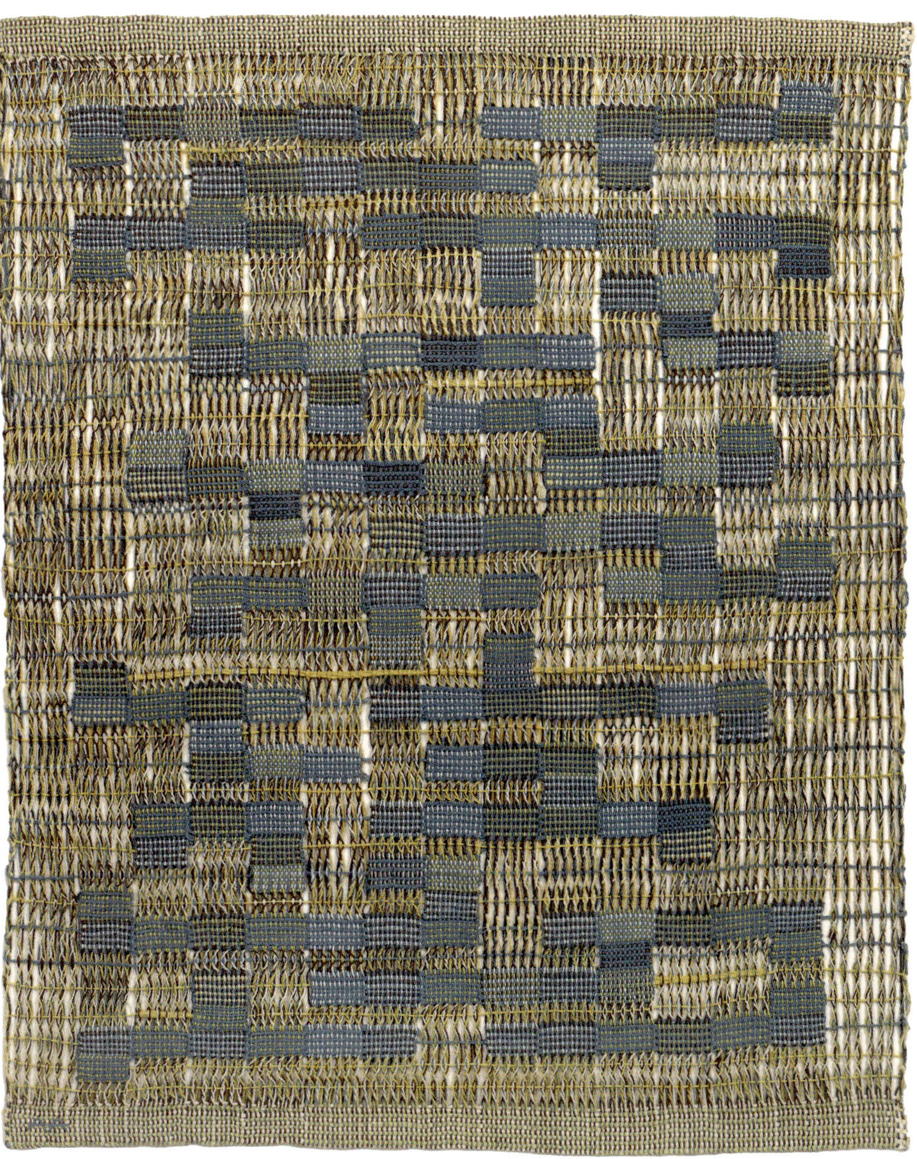

ABOVE: *Tikal*
Anni Albers
1958 | 30" × 23" | cotton
Museum of Arts and Design

At the Bauhaus, a German design school (1919–33), Anni Albers began her studies and subsequently spent her life experimenting in weaving and graphic design, and writing books about them. *Tikal* takes the name of a Mayan temple complex in Guatemala: the tapestry includes uneven surfaces, like walls and rocks of various sizes (or perhaps a ground plan), and includes patches of bare warp.

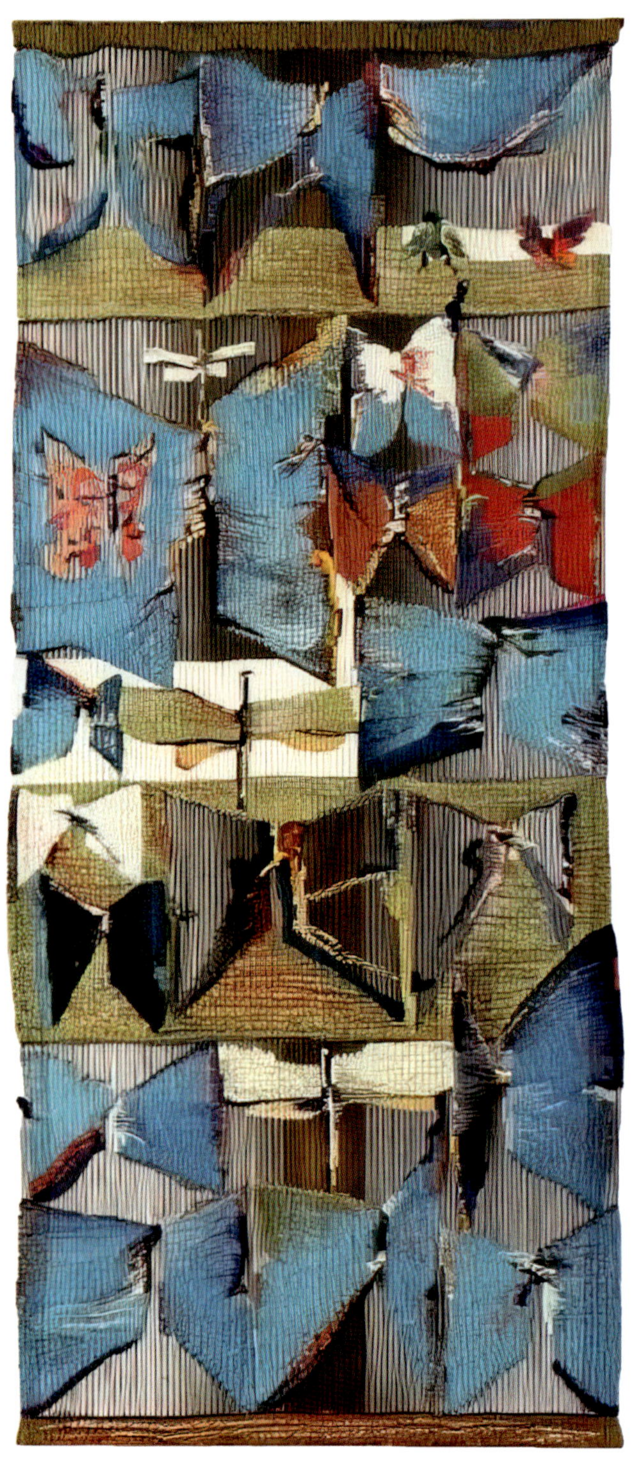

Butterflies
Hédi Tarján
1978–82 | 58.5" × 22.8" | wool
Museum of Applied Arts, Budapest

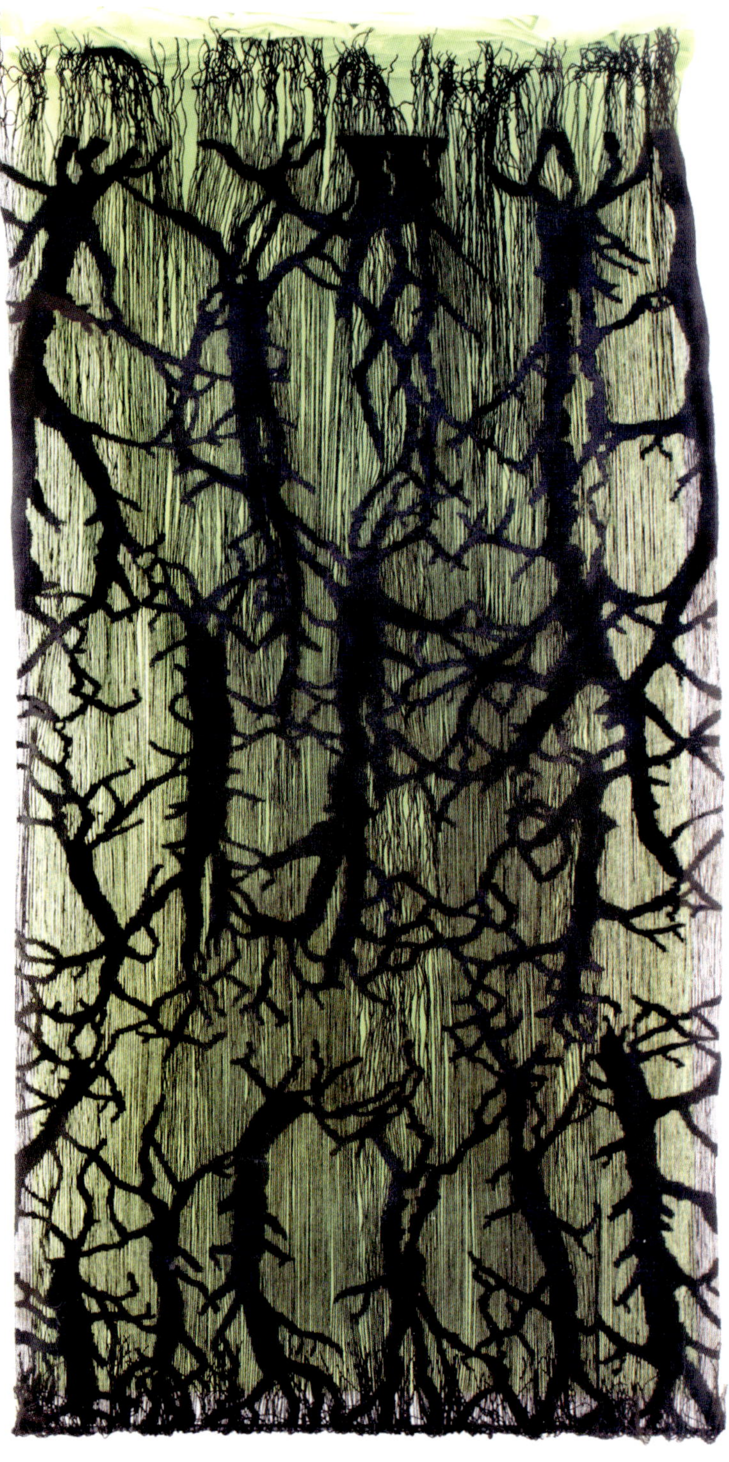

Poisonous Web
Unn Sonju
2015 | 78.75" × 59" | wool, linen, polyester and acetate backdrop

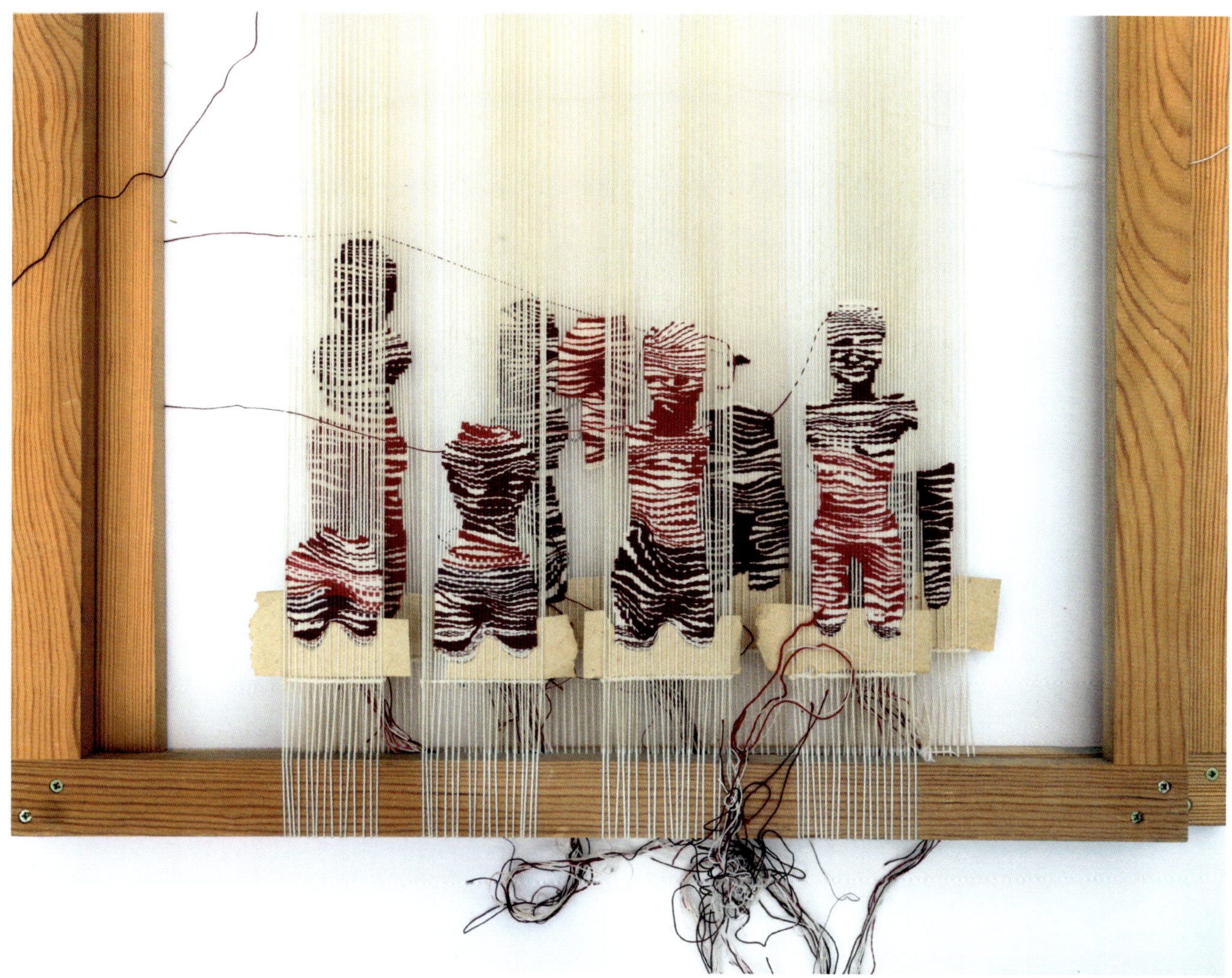

Mute
Patricia Taylor
2005 | 26" × 19" | silk; cotton warp

The unwoven sections of Hédi Tarján's *Butterflies* emphasize the shape of the wings, the warp standing in for air. Perhaps they are settling in for the night.

Unn Sonju includes that sickly green backcloth as a separate layer behind her trees, reinforcing the sense of poison.

Pat Taylor has wrapped a continuous warp around her loom—and proceeds to construct shapes, heads, body parts, both in front and in back of the frame. Notice the heads with mouths blocked off, truly mute.

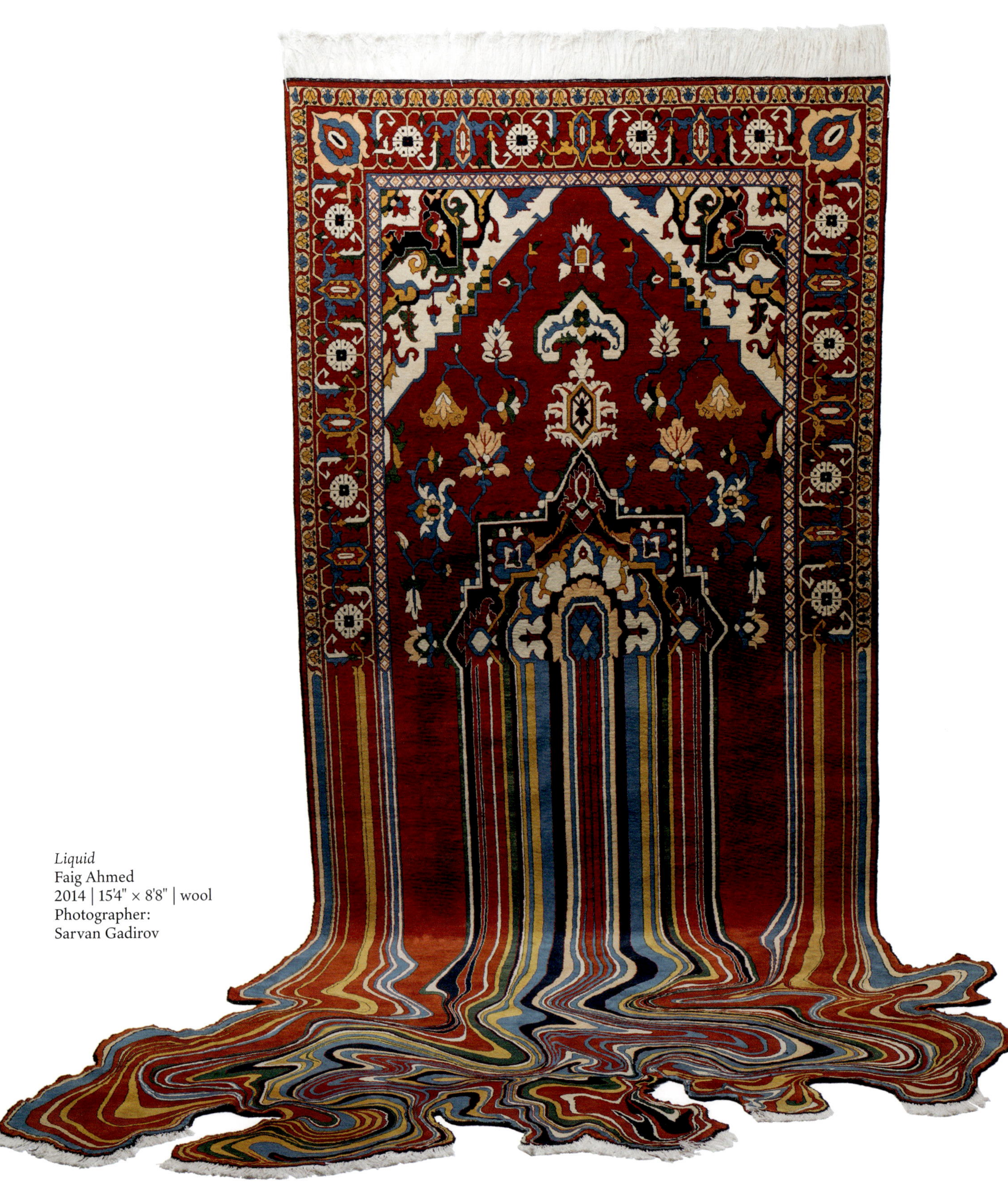

Liquid
Faig Ahmed
2014 | 15'4" × 8'8" | wool
Photographer:
Sarvan Gadirov

CHAPTER 4

weft

The horizontal weft interlaces the vertical warp. It goes over and under in one direction—and then under and over in the opposite direction. In traditional tapestry, both European and Native American, the weft takes the dominant role. The warp disappears except for leaving vertical ridges in the body of the cloth. This is called weft-faced plain weave. My teacher in France, Jacques Postel, once explained that the warp should not move; the weft is doing all the work.

Some tapestry weavers use techniques in highly visible interactions that bring the weft to life in ways that are atypical for traditional tapestry. There are many weaving patterns, many ways to interlace warp and weft. That is the subject of this chapter—weft doing the unexpected.

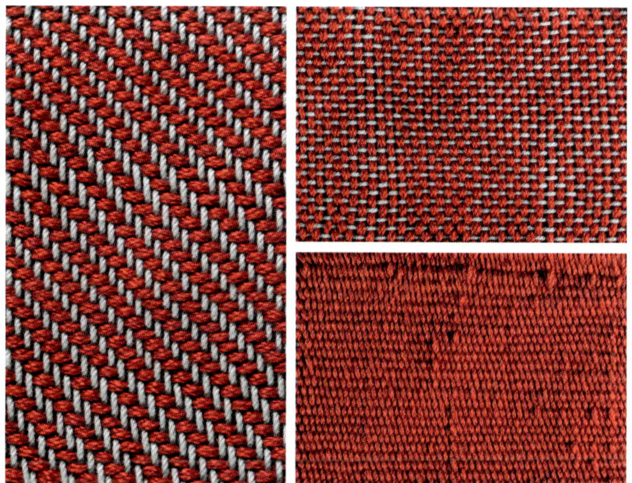

These nontraditional tapestry weavers play with the interaction of the two elements—with the patterns, with the colors, with the way it feels—in order to produce what they are seeking to make.

Faig Ahmed's pieces take you aback. They might even make you laugh: Have you ever imagined that a pile rug could look like this? (Which room in the house could cope?) The threads that compose at least half the piece look as though they might be in free fall, becoming liquid. They are very carefully integrated into the whole. Ahmed's decision to challenge our assumptions about what a rug should look like is thrilling.

LEFT: A sampler
On the left: twill
On the right: plain weave (*above*), weft-faced plain weave (*below*)

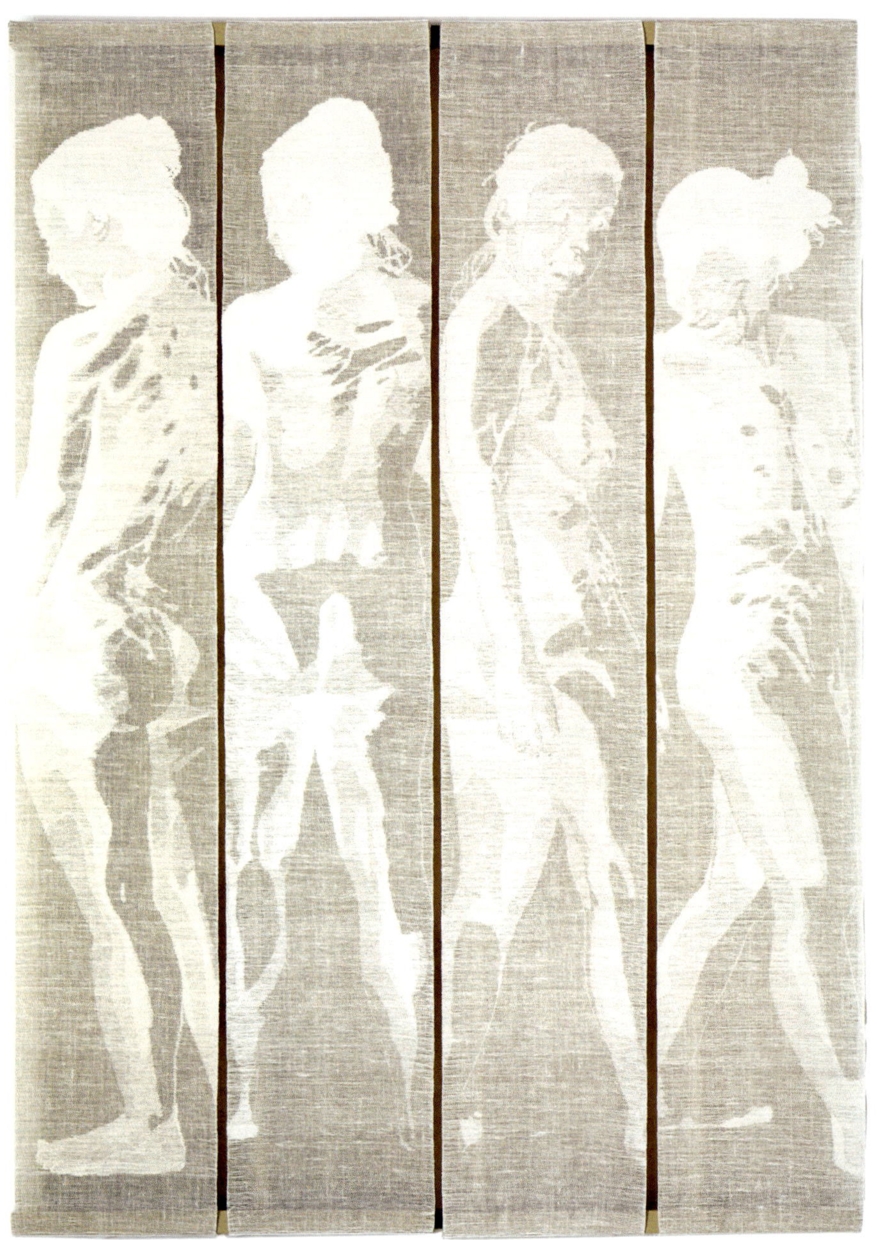

Luminosities
Cyndy Barbone
2014 | 82" × 60" (each section is 14.5" wide) | linen

Cyndy Barbone's people might be standing still or walking. They might be the same figure seen in several poses. Looking at the piece up close, you can see both the weft and warp, and the fineness of the thread, leaving an almost ghostly impression.

Ann Booth has made a series of ten pieces to honor ten women of Ba'hai faith who have been executed by the Iranian regime. Here she has combined plain weave with soumak, a technique that leaves an irregular ridge, alternating with the flat of plain weave. The ridge is harder to see in a photograph. But you can see the two techniques in the alternating lines of dark (plain weave) and light (soumak).

Sitthichai Smanchat also combines these two weave structures and uses jute, a material often used for burlap, as though his portrait of "Guru Dev" might be a sketch. The matted surfaces emphasize all the more how very woven the rest looks.

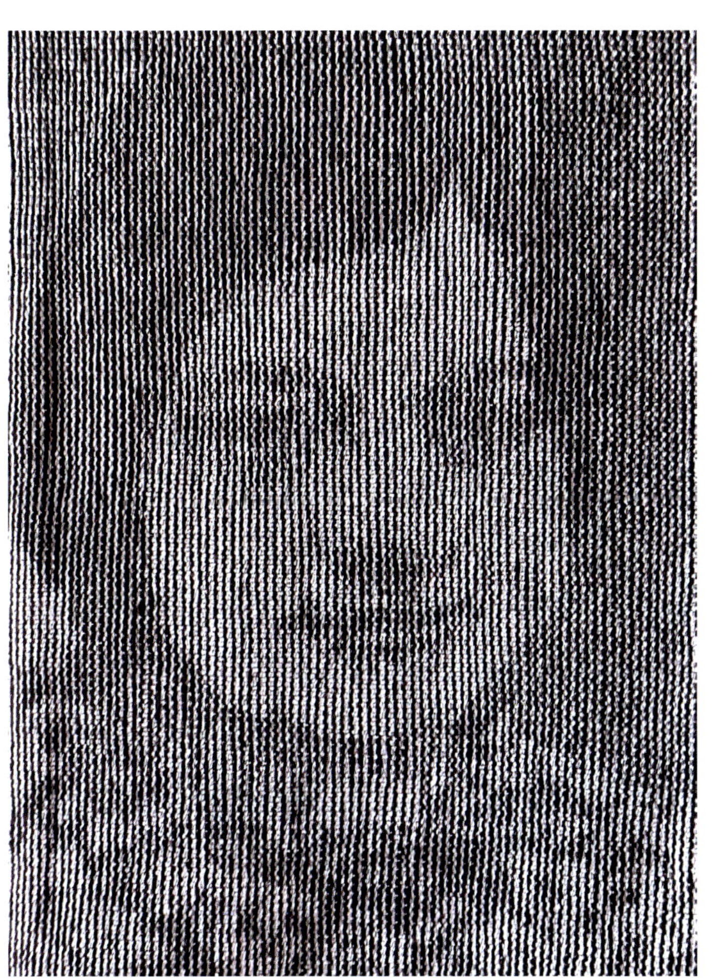

Masiud Nirumand
Ann Booth
2022 | 31" × 20" | wool

Guru Dev (Rabindranath Tagore)
Sitthichai Smanchat
2007 | 21.6" × 11.8" | bleached jute
Collection of Nandan Gallery, Kala Bhavanya, Visva-Bharati University

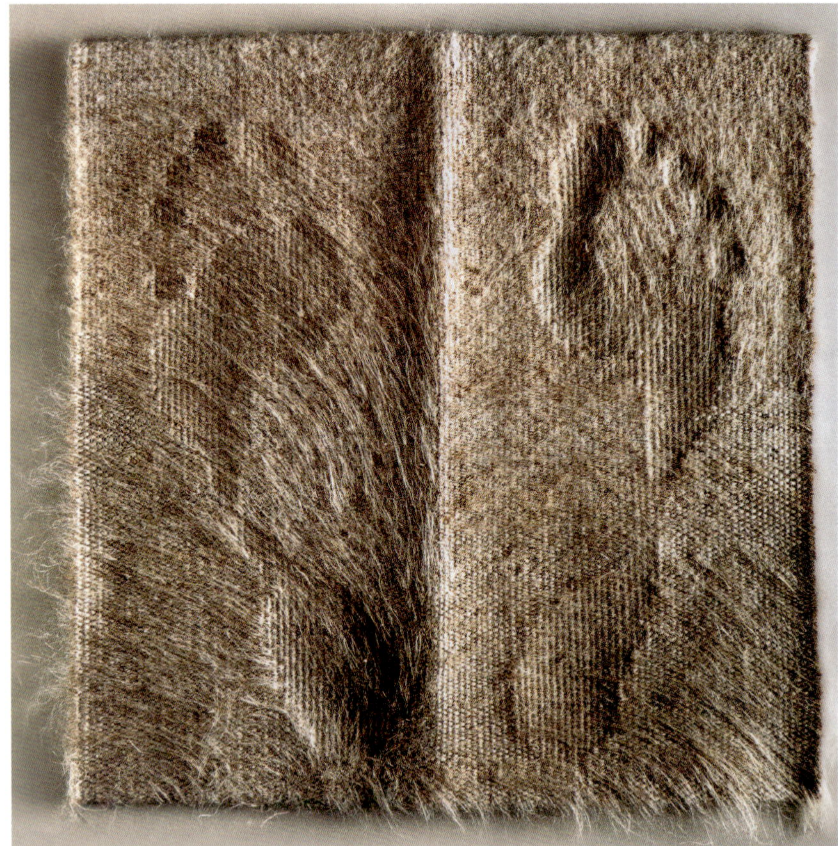

Emilia Domanska has combined several techniques (and materials). Traditional tapestry is already labor intensive, but Domanska's piece is even more so. (She says that it took her two weeks to weave—and it is about a foot square.) She explains, "The difference in the thickness of the threads that expand the warp differently made the surface naturally carved, creating the impression of an imprint on the ground. It took meticulous precise work to create the shape of the bare feet." She was then able to comb out threads, which play on the surface.

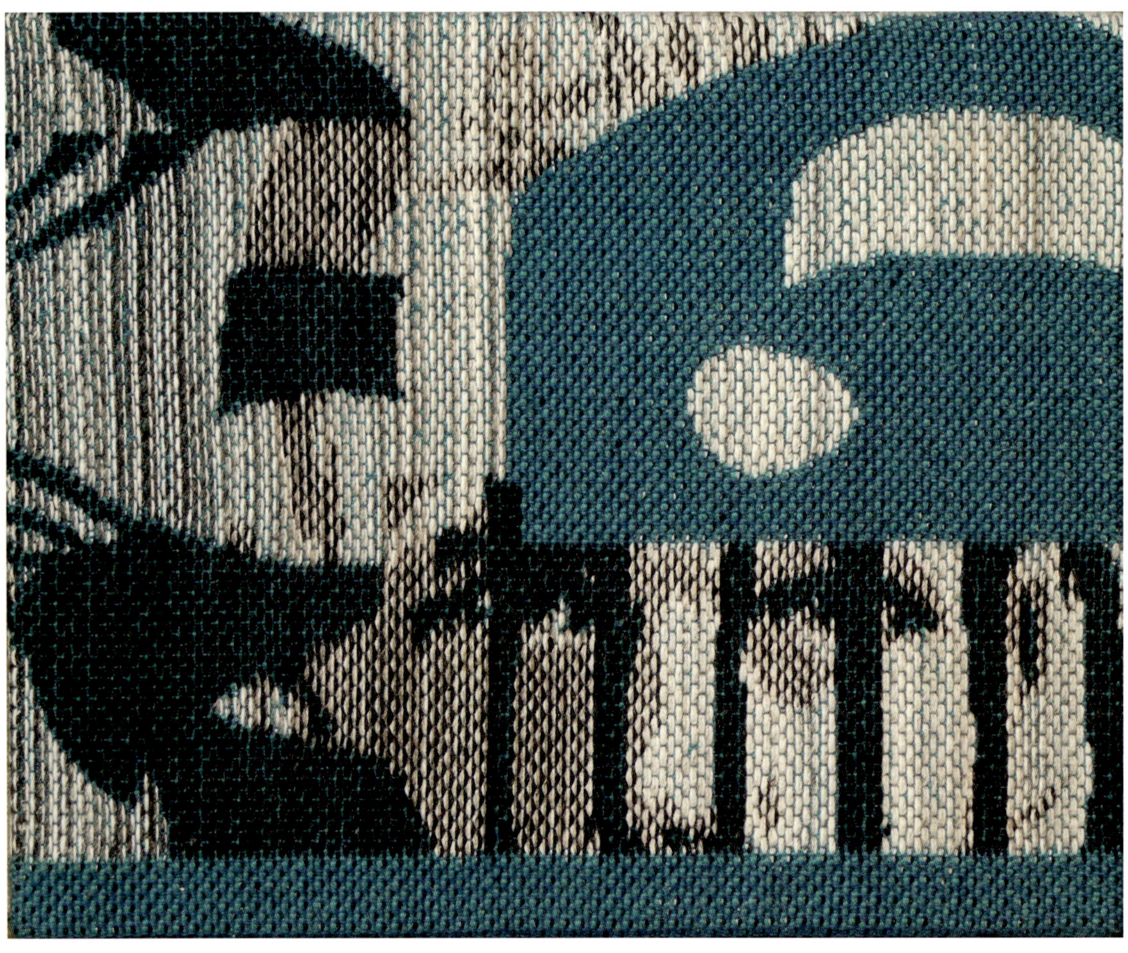

OPPOSITE, TOP: *Terra II*
Emilia Domanska
2001 | 11.8" × 11.8" | linen, hemp

OPPOSITE, BOTTOM: *Cryptic Chronicle*
(summer and winter weaves)
Deborah Silver
2021 | 16" × 20" | wool, cotton, rayon, silk

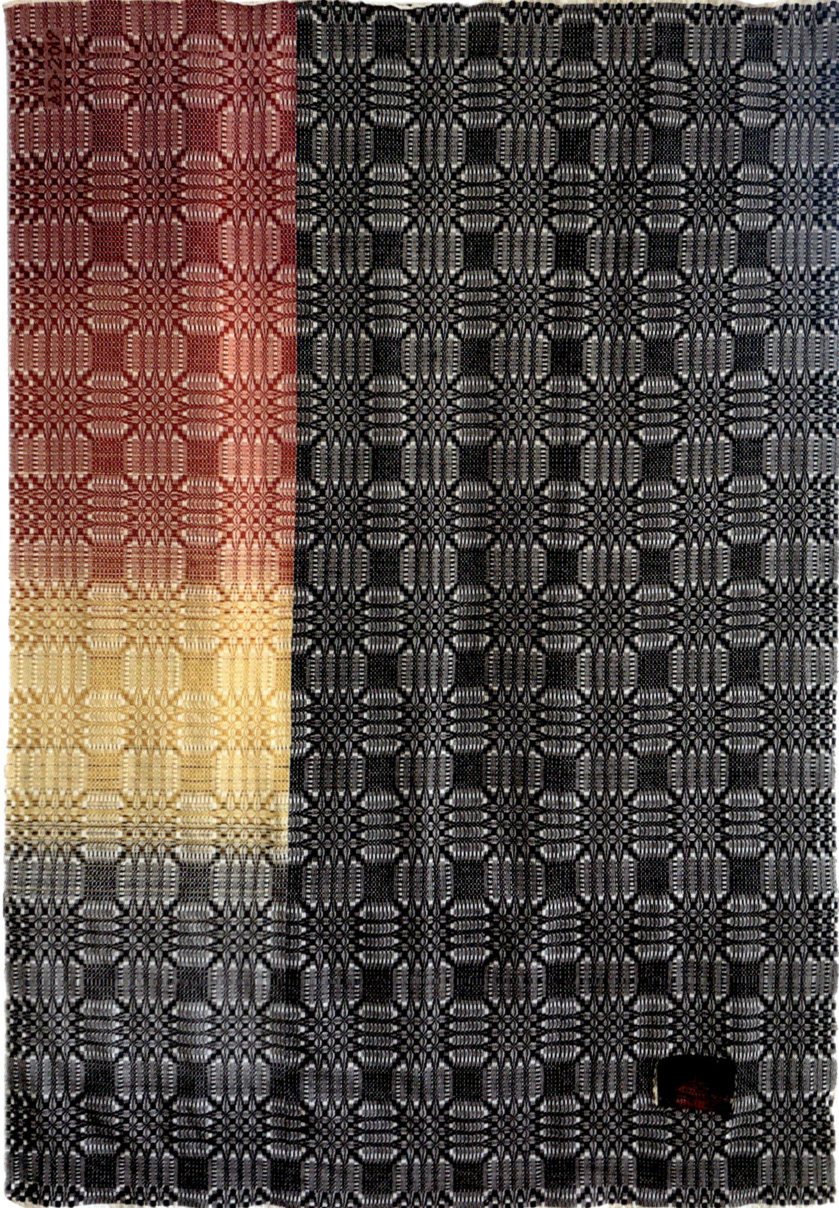

Deborah Silver has written a book about her work with multiple-shaft looms and the imagery she achieves. She chose a "summer and winter" pattern for this piece. Often, Silver gets her inspiration from historical pieces, as here, where the iconography of historic Huari weavings has triggered her imagination.

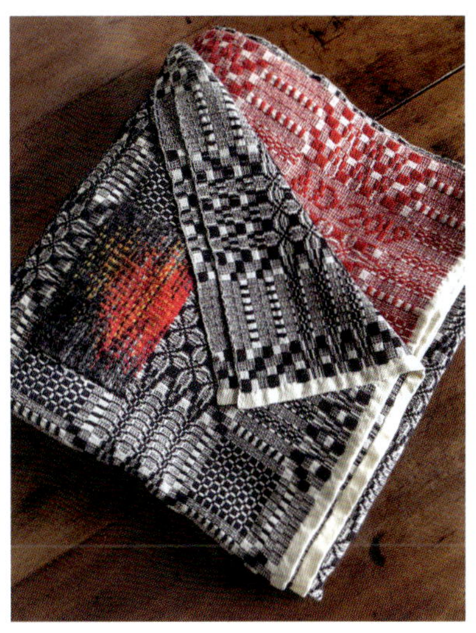

Keep Me Warm
(pine cone bloom draft)
Allie Dudley
2019 | 102" × 72" | wool, cotton

Weavers often use one of the most traditional weaving patterns, overshot (a kind of twill-based weaving structure), to make bedspreads. (Dorothy Burnham wrote a highly appreciated guide to some of these, *Keep Me Warm One Night—Early Handweaving in Eastern Canada.*) Allie Dudley has inserted a lovely little tapestry detail in the bottom right corner of her larger spread (as well as her initials, and the year she wove it). It makes me laugh.

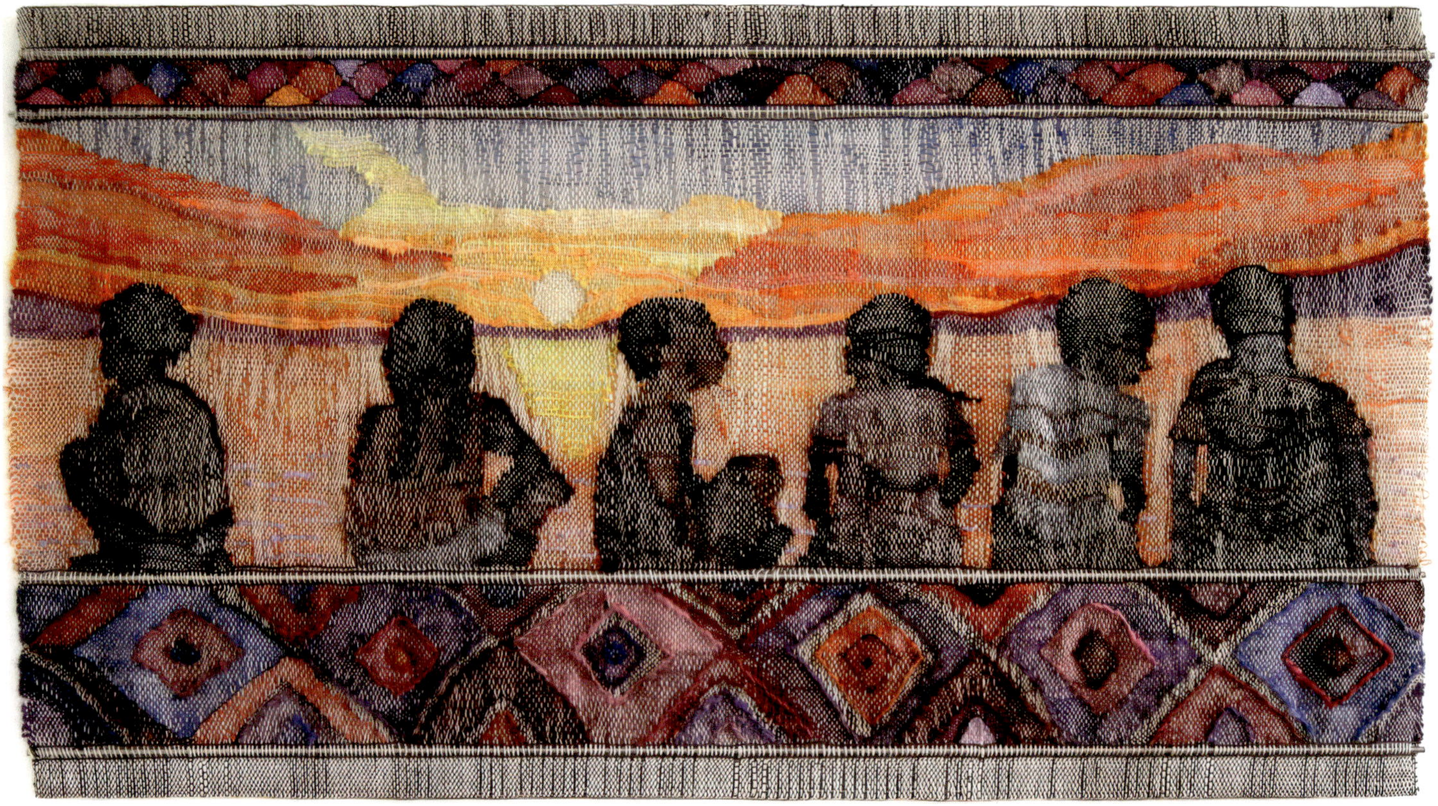

Both Inge Kronblad Thorning (emphasizing vertical threads) and Dorthe Herup (horizontal threads) weave people embedded in the crossed warp and weft. Thorning's children are characterized by bodily posture and separated from the fiery ground by their darker coloration, while the elaborate frame emphasizes the presence of the weave structure into which they fit. Herup's men have greater detail, almost photographic, but they are seen through a transparent screen of the finely colored weft.

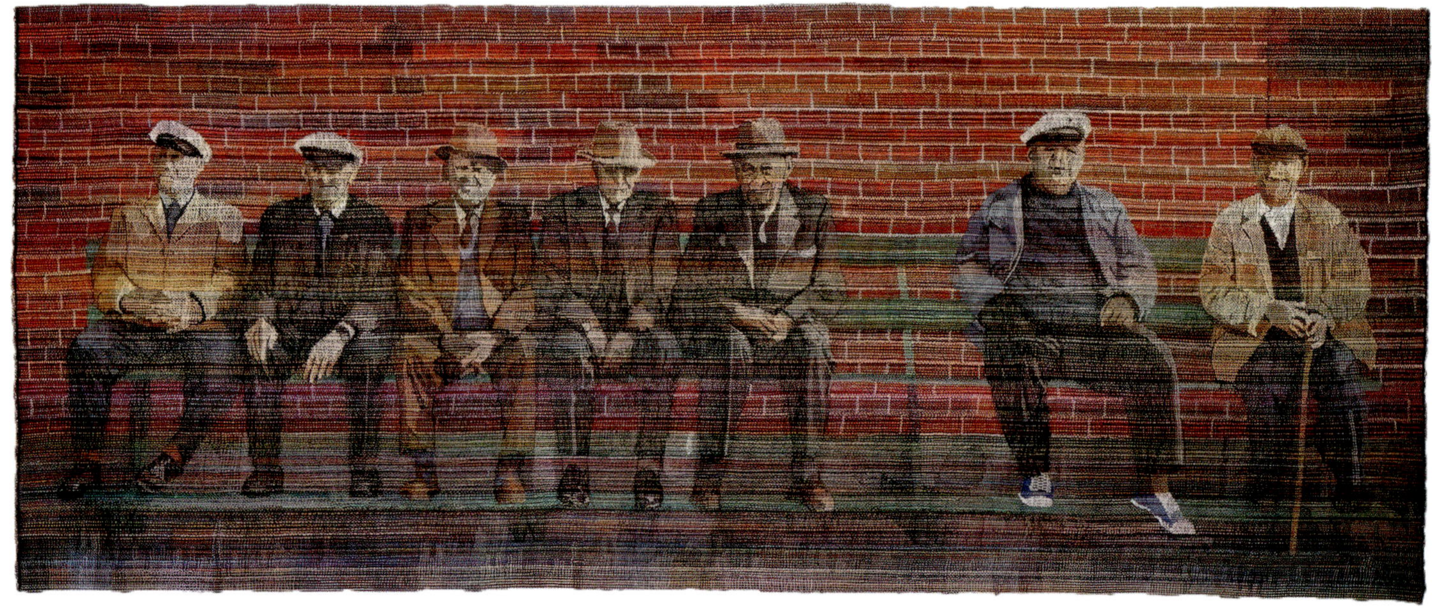

OPPOSITE, TOP: *Children at Sunset*
Inge Kronblad Thorning
2012 | 27.15" × 51.2" | handspun wool, dyed horsehair

OPPOSITE, BOTTOM: *The Bench*
Dorthe Herup
2018 | 70.9" × 14'8" | wool, hair, cotton
Photographer: Tomas Moss

RIGHT: *Black Bird House*
Barbara Eckhardt
1987 | 47" × 28" | cotton, linen, ramie

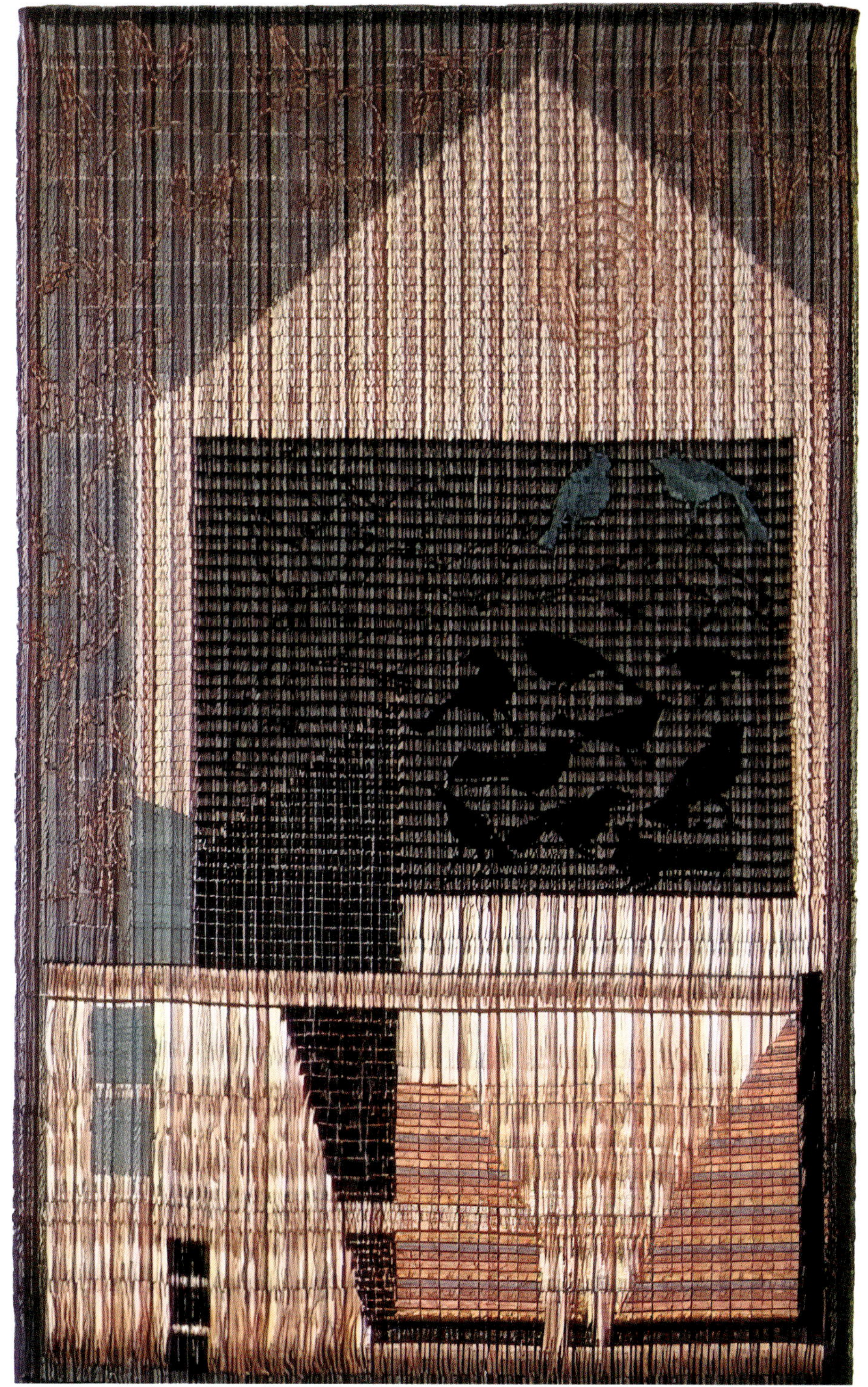

Barbara Eckhardt worked at a twelve-shaft loom, using a third of the shafts for each of three layers that produced different kinds of fabric in this single piece. (A vast number of weave structures can be woven with four shafts.) She made thick layers and thin layers—layers where the details were easier to achieve. She loved weaving architecture; she loved birds even more.

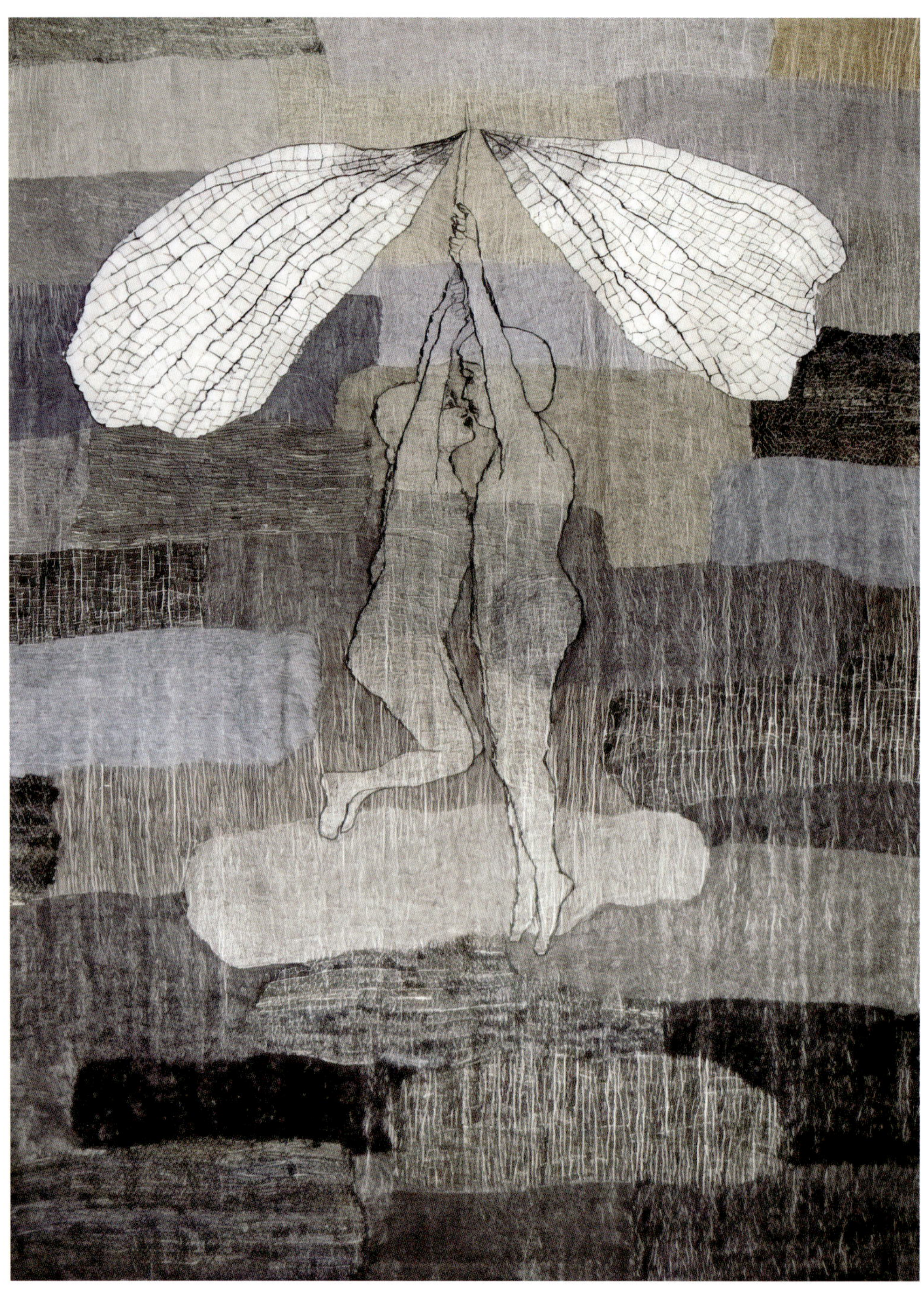

Confidence
Aino Kajaniemi
2014 | 7'1" × 5'3" | linen, cotton, wool, viscose, jute, sisal, fishing line

Aino Kajaniemi learned her tapestry technique, where both warp and weft are visible, during her studies in Finland. In that regard, her work resembles that of her some of her fellow Finnish weavers. Her personal style includes both whimsy and powerful feeling, as in this large dreamlike piece, in which she has captured a moment of surrealistic intensity.

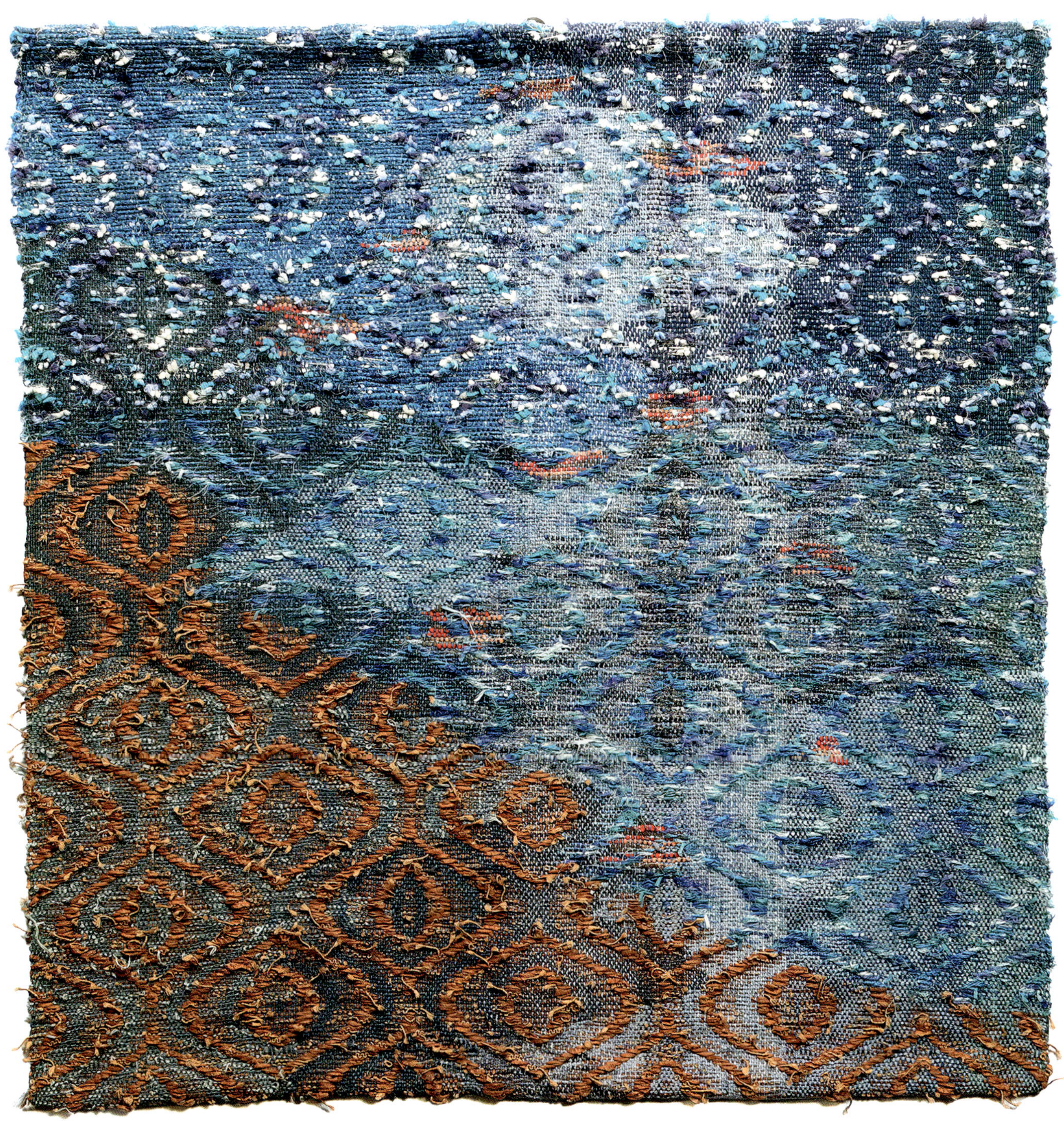

Beach/Texture in Nature
Doerte Weber
2019 | 33" × 33" | cotton, polyester, ribbon, recycled jeans

Doerte Weber (German, by the way, for "weaver") takes advantage of texture to get what she wants, using unexpected and casual materials such as recycled blue jeans. We can see woven shapes on the surface, where she explored the "rose path" technique, easiest to see in the patterns of the brown/red area.

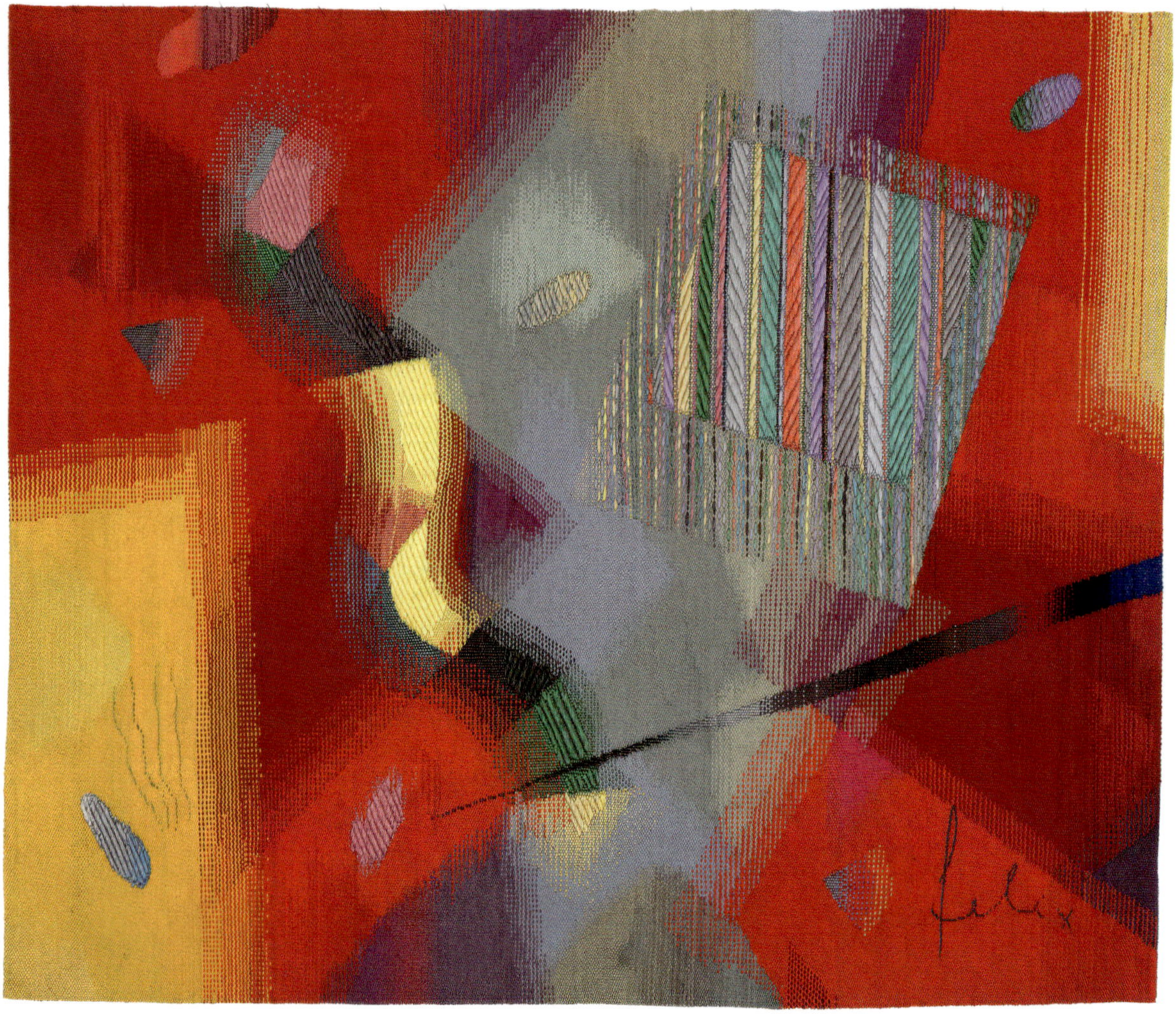

ABOVE: *Flaming Gothic*
Feliksas Jakubauskas
2019 | 51.2" × 60.25" | wool, viscose, silk

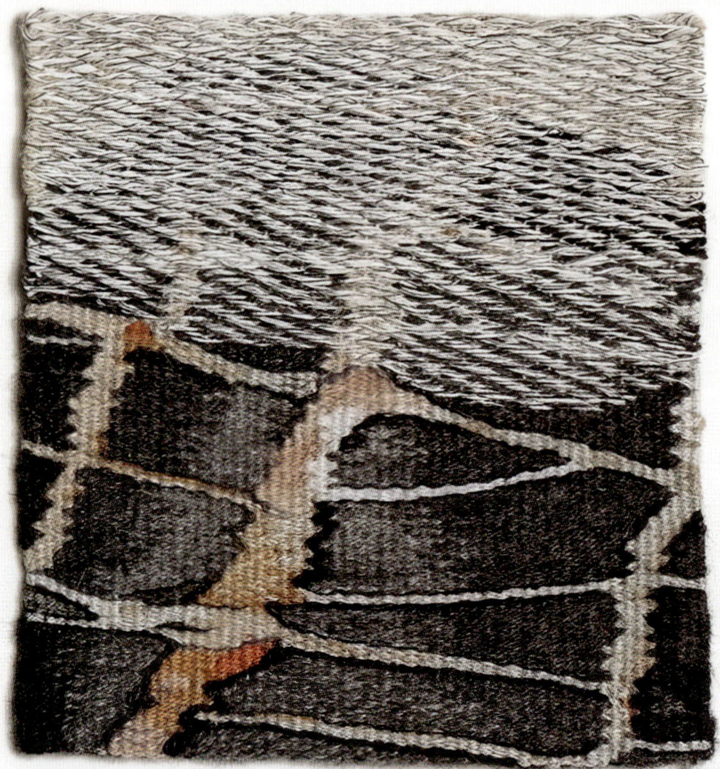

LEFT: *A Misty Hill*
Mette Lise Rössing
2008 | 6.7" × 6.3"

OPPOSITE: *Sun Trees*
Henry Easterwood
1970 | 29" × 32.5" | wool
Memphis Brooks Museum
Gift of the estate of Herbert and Arlene Goldman

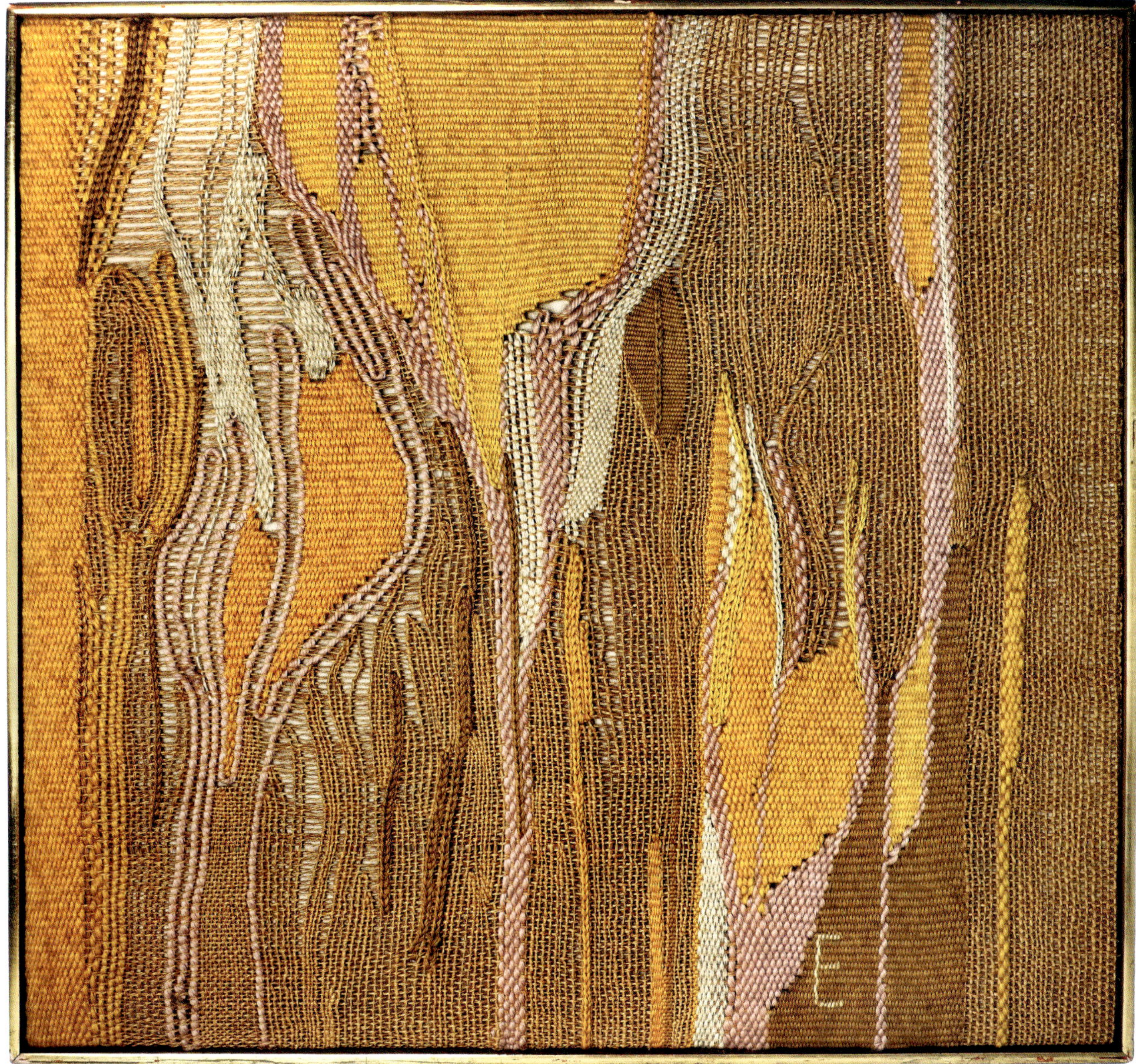

Feliksas Jakubauskas embellishes his surface with a weave he calls "diagonal," primarily in the square and rectangle in the upper right: a basic twill. The result looks as though he has woven several layers (clear and in focus)—but it is a single layer.

Mette Lise Rössing combines weave structures in this small piece. This might be a glimpse of roads crossing in the bottom (standard weft-faced tapestry)—while the lacy effect (twill) at the top of the piece might be fog. Or they could be land and sea.

Henry Easterwood's piece has a lovely rhythm and gentle colors. The surface includes flat areas of weft-faced plain weave (the apricot color) and ridges (soumak) in browns, tans, pale pinks, and off-white. Easterwood served as the resident teacher of weaving at the Memphis College of Art. Over his forty years there, he developed a highly respected textile department.

Nicole Bunting has made an idiosyncratic piece, with various weave structures and different weft weights. One of her materials is "journaled cotton fabric": strips of cotton fabric on which she had written—and which she then tore into strips and wove.

Venancio Aragón has, according to his own explanation, "hybridized twill." Among Navajo elders, he explains, the result is "sometimes referred to as Horned Toad Twill due to the diamond shapes resembling horned toads moving in opposite directions. This may not be understood by some Navajo people and non-Navajo people."

Louise Martin has long been devising unusual ways to weave tapestries—and this three-part shaped piece shows one. Her threads crisscross in unexpected ways, not looking as systematic as plain weave, for instance, would. The bright happy greens, blues, and mustards cozy up to each other. You want to touch them, run your hand over them. Martin has also, among other accomplishments, won the prestigious Cordis Prize.

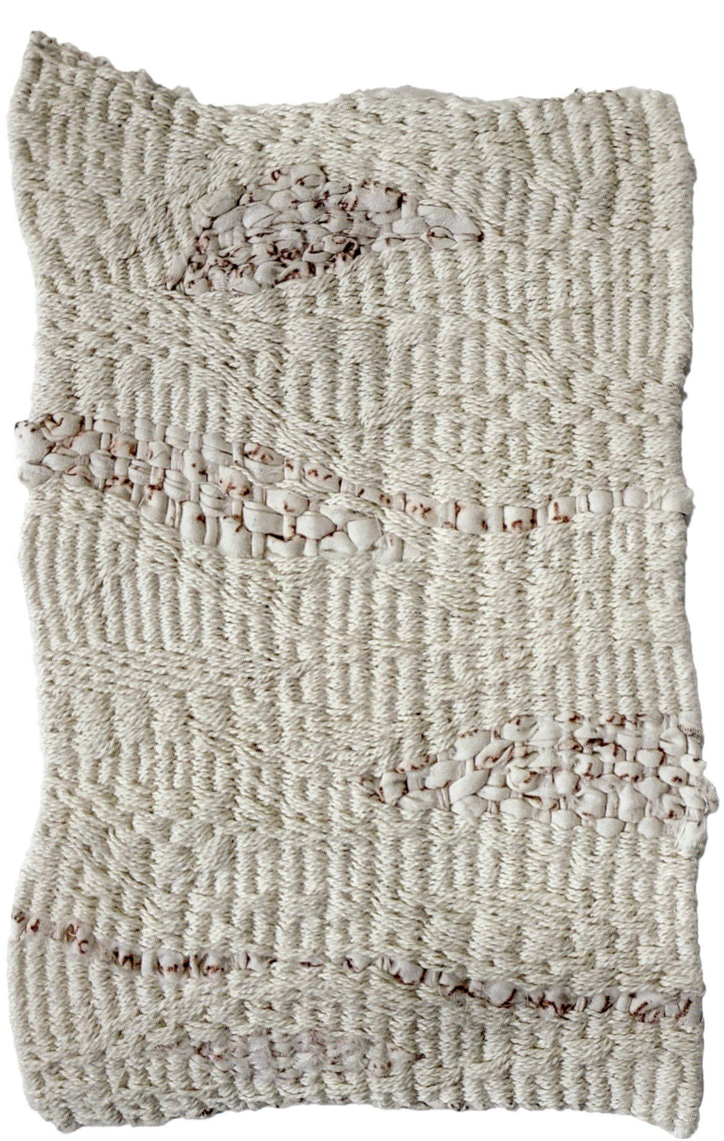

Who, What, Where
Nicole Bunting
2016 | 12.5" × 8" | journaled cotton fabric, cotton yarn; cotton fabric warp

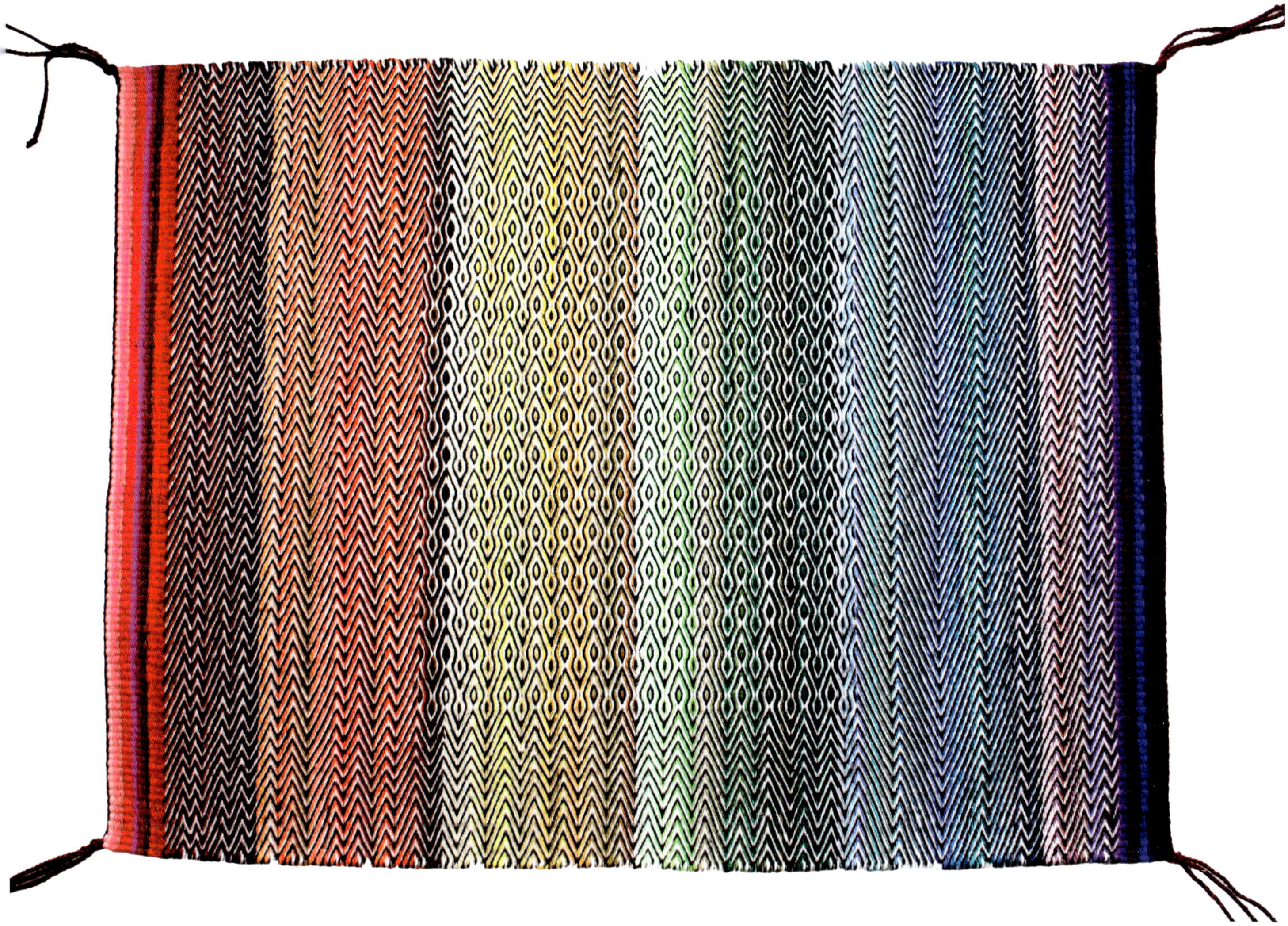

ABOVE: *P and P Horned Toad and Lightning Twill*
Venancio Aragón
2023 | 24" × 29" | wool, mohair; wool warp; natural and synthetic dyes

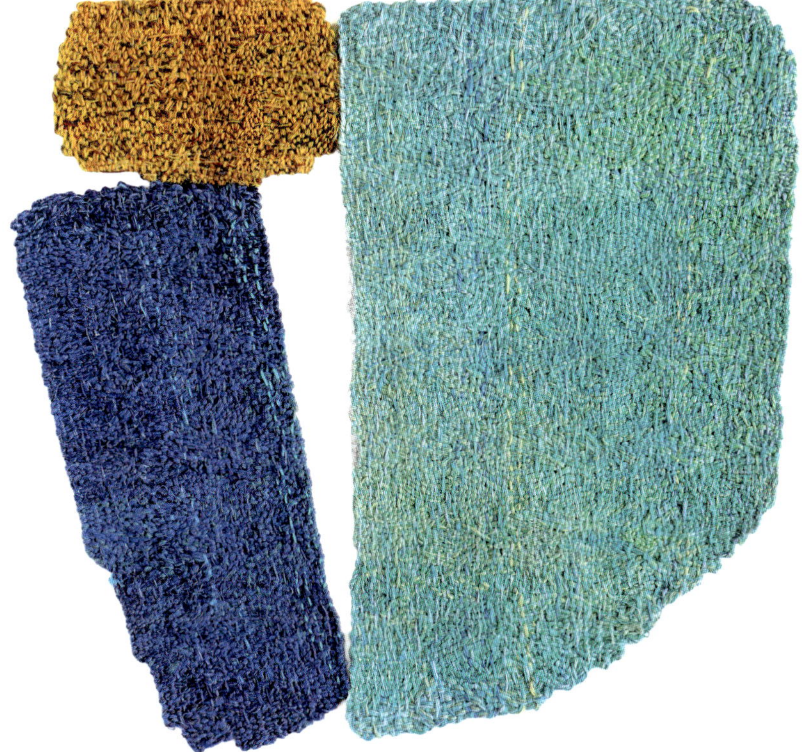

RIGHT: *Two Blues*
Louise Martin
2019 | 10.4" × 11" | cotton, wire, linen, wool, silk

CHAPTER 5

seed

In tapestry, a line occurs when the weaver lays a weft thread across several warp threads—and then goes back again. A seed occurs when the weaver lays a single weft thread over a single warp thread. The seed color contrasts with the field around it, composed of other colors. Several seeds in a row produce a dotted line, a specific characteristic of tapestry weaving.

In one of his several essays about tapestry, Michael Crompton enlarges on this point: "The weaver has the ability to utilise a single colour from one side of the weave to create a dotted regular line. The artist [e.g., a painter] would make a continuous line. In order to inform the viewer that my tapestries are designed and woven by a weaver, I utilise this woven dotted line in all my work. This creates a strong visual effect and combines well with blocks of colour, highlights the perimeters of shapes and makes for interesting surface manipulations." Only a weaver can create this systematic proof that the surface is woven.

That seeds communicate the nature of the medium is only one thing that they can accomplish; they also create certain visual effects.

The Line
Elżbieta Kędzia
1980 | 94.5" × 67" | wool, linen

Elżbieta Kędzia makes a whole dark cloth with a title of *The Line*, but, with a few exceptions of actual continuous lines, she has filled her cloth with seeds that, at a distance, seem like lines.

Annick Top's design plays with the look of early computer printouts. Two Gobelins weavers worked on either side of this tapestry—one to weave and the other to advise whether they had woven across the right warp. Precision was essential.

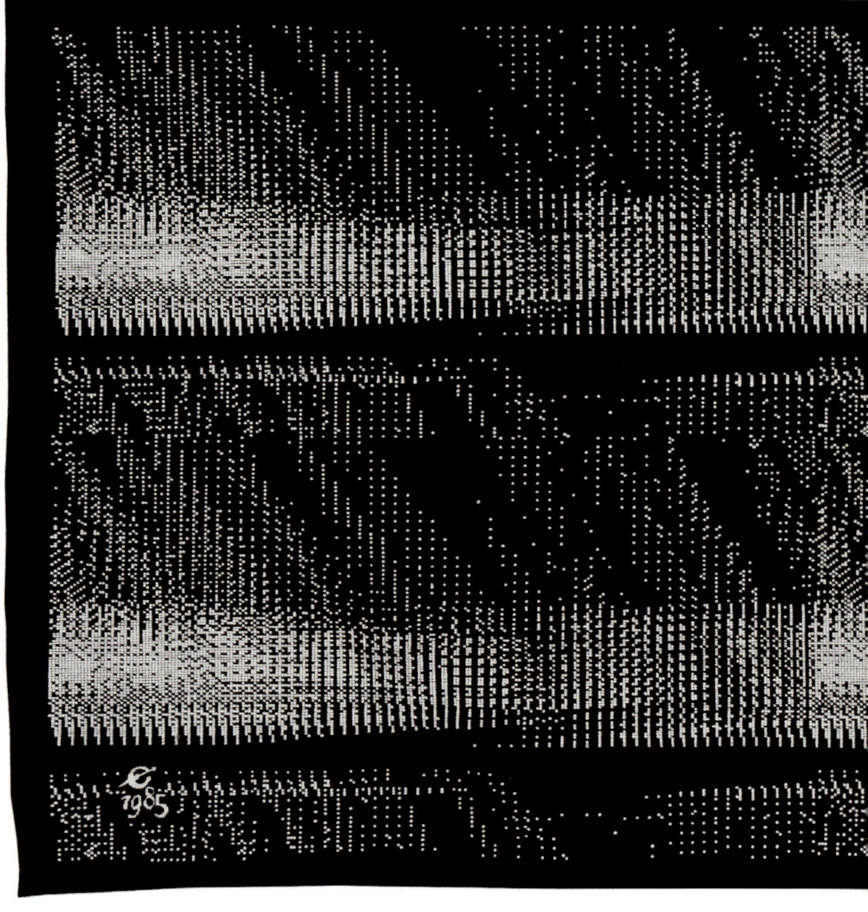

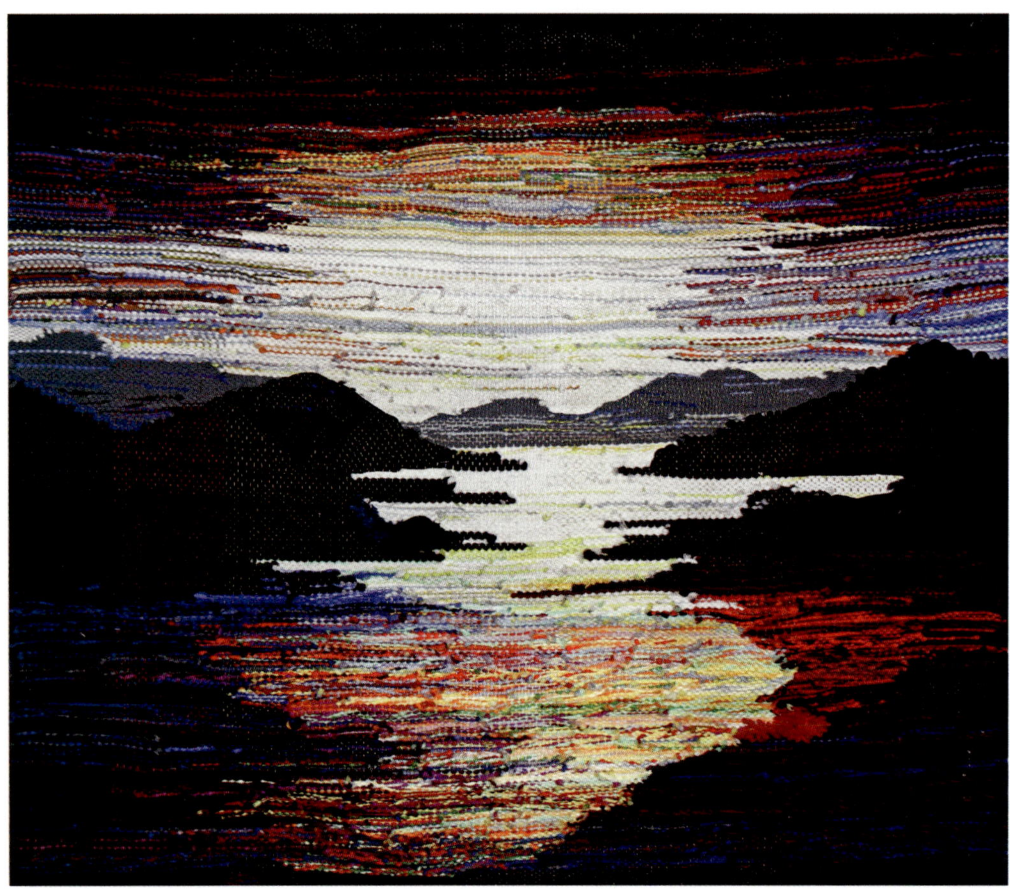

Morning Light
Bhatu Bhamare
2015 | 20" × 24" | wool; cotton warp

Givre Astral (Astral frost)
Annick Top
1986 | 6'5" × 8'5"
La Manufacture Nationale des Gobelins; weavers: Annie Asselinou and André de Marzi

Bhatu Bhamare centers his morning light over water, with brilliant-colored seeds in the sky and water. As we look at this dawn, we realize that Bhamare achieves this prismatic visual affect by laying down single wefts in color after color after color.

Michael Crompton's *Inversnaid* is both landscape and an excellent example of what he wrote about, with the dotted lines defining water and hills.

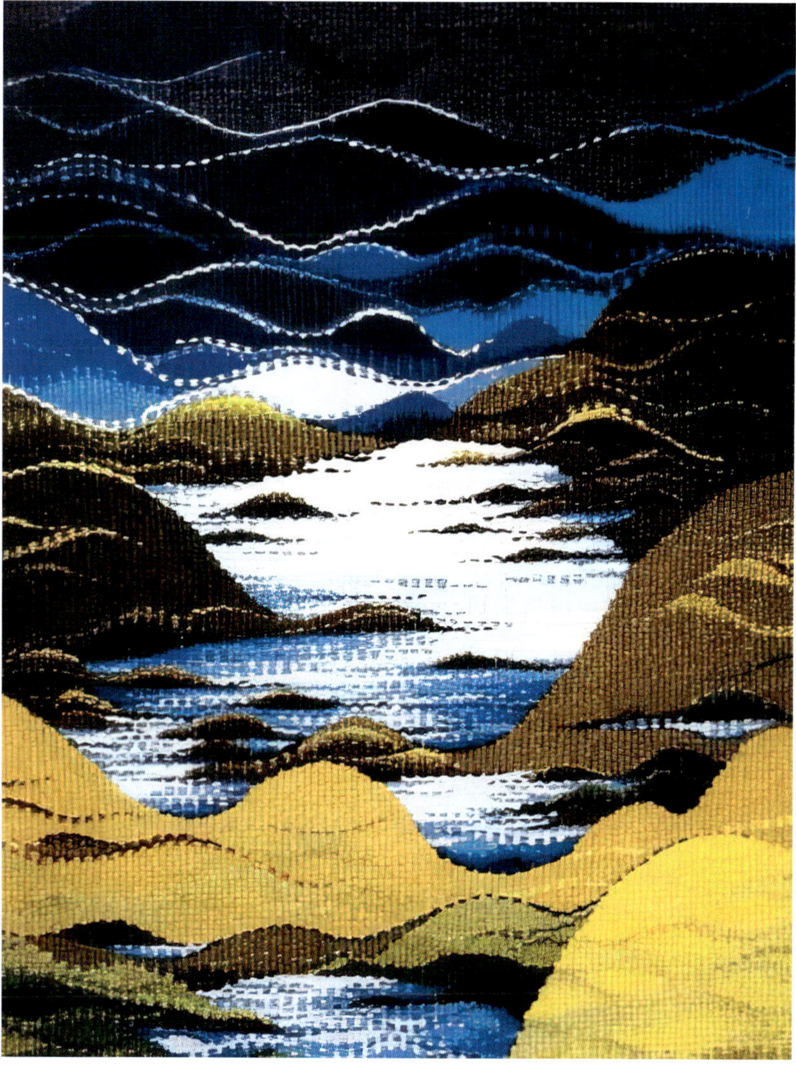

Inversnaid
Michael Crompton
2001 | 34" × 24.4" | wool, man-made fibers

Jan Austin's trees and lake are visible through what might be windows, but the white dots feel like snow. These results feel like a paradox—are we outside or inside?

On the facing page, Lynn Cornelius weaves a narrow white path from which blues and whites shoot off. The seeds make the path a center of energy. She names her piece *Point of Departure*, but it is not clear where we are going. Is the trail actually a rocket we are riding?

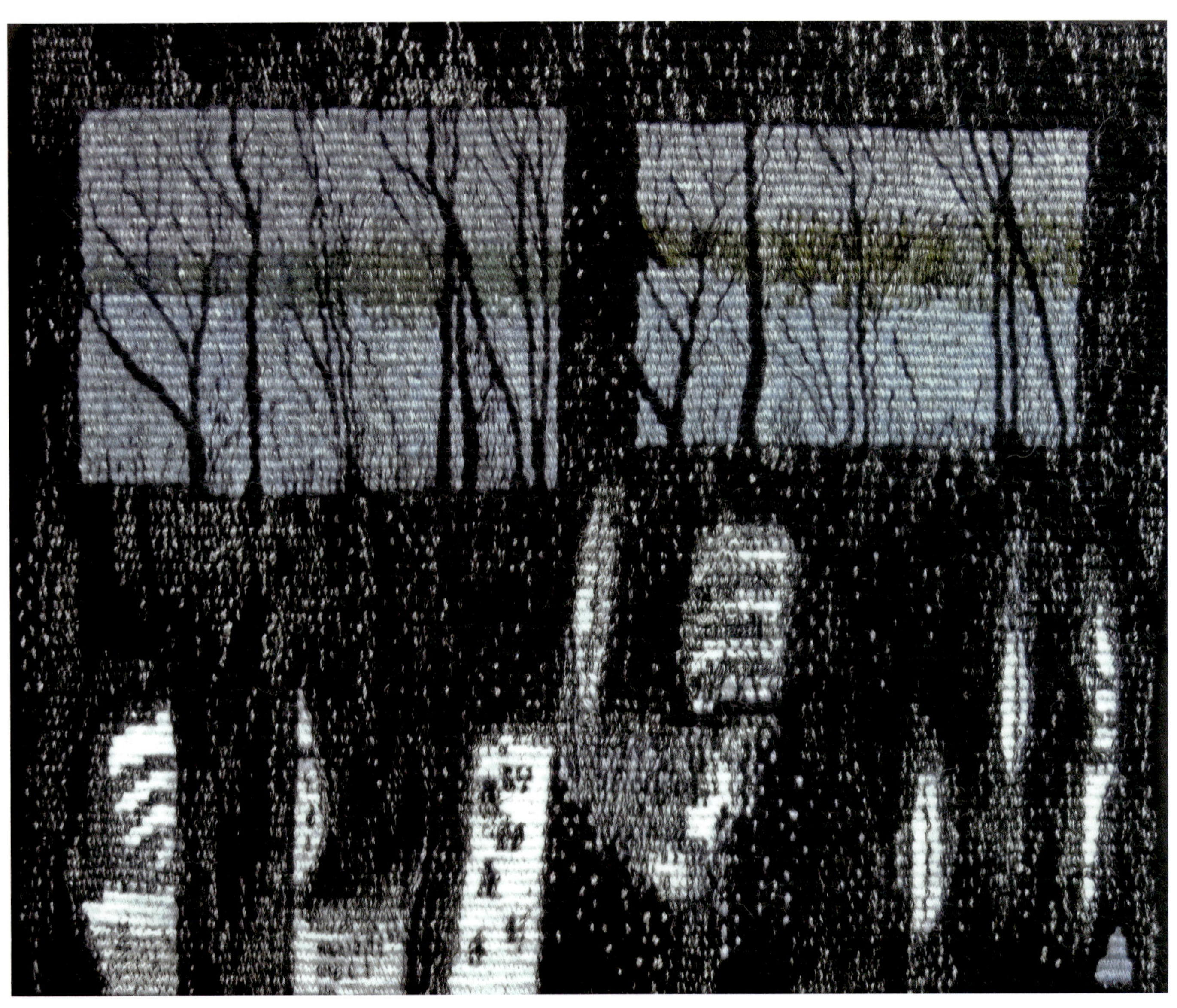

Another Forest Through the Trees
Jan Austin
2016 | 8" × 10" | wool, rayon, silk, cotton, linen; cotton warp

In part because of the color scheme, Penny Howe's seeds seem like falling rain. Her single figure walks away from us. The surrounding landscape has a tree and a path, but the rest remains indistinct.

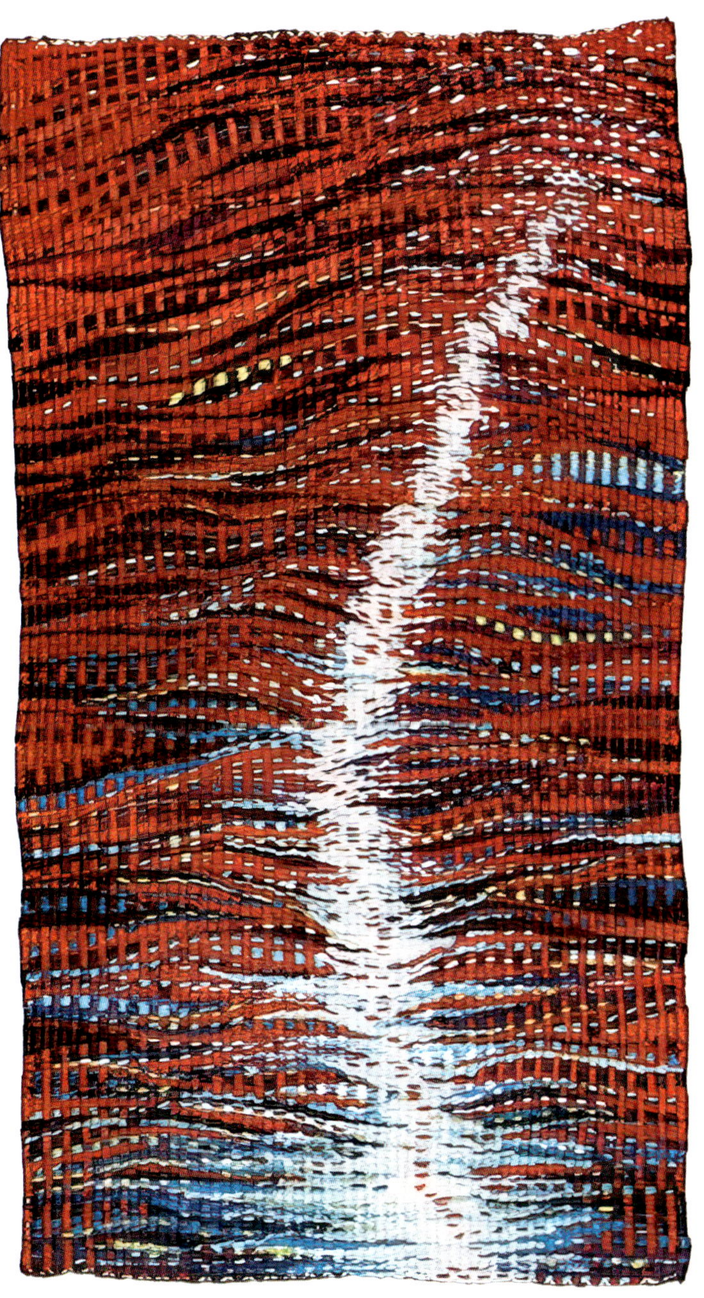

Point of Departure
Lynn Cornelius
2005 | 13" × 7" | dyed cotton, rayon, silk

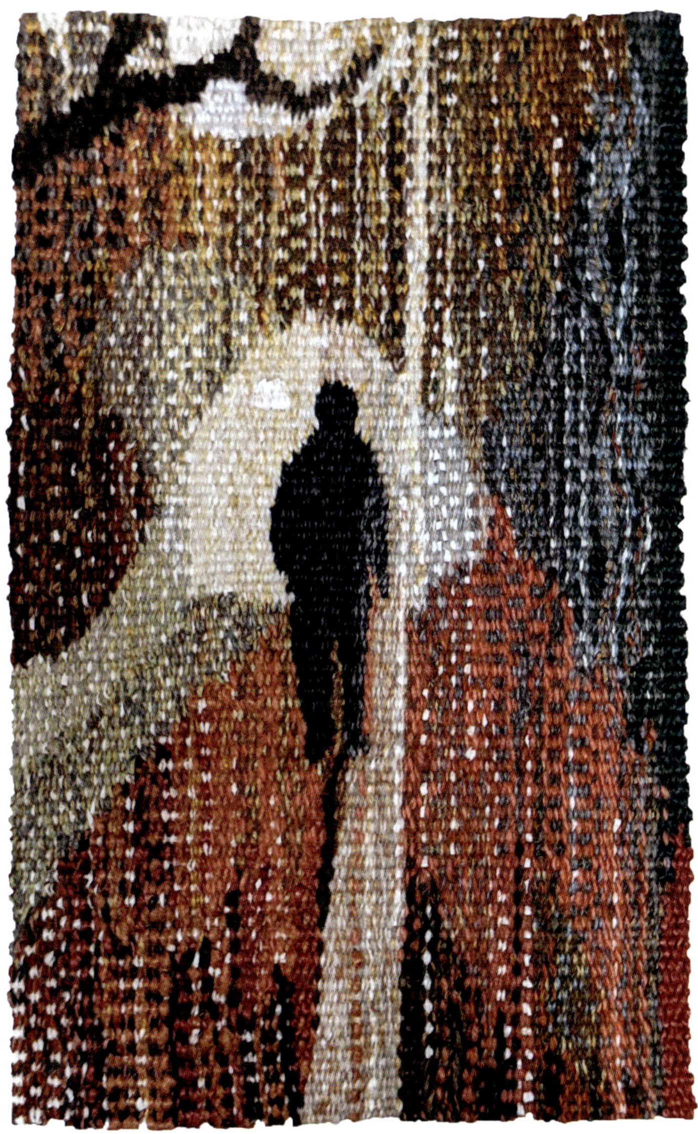

Unknown Path
Penny Howes
2021 | 16.15" × 10.6" | wool, wool/silk, silk, paper, linen, bamboo, jute; cotton warp

Marie Thumette-Brichard's field of blues, so rich you might dive in, includes white seeds that skate over the surface.

Kay Lawrence constructed a series of funnels and sieves, thinking of the symbolic value of each—males and females. You see here one of the sieves. By alternating one row of gray with two rows of white, she gives the impression of holes.

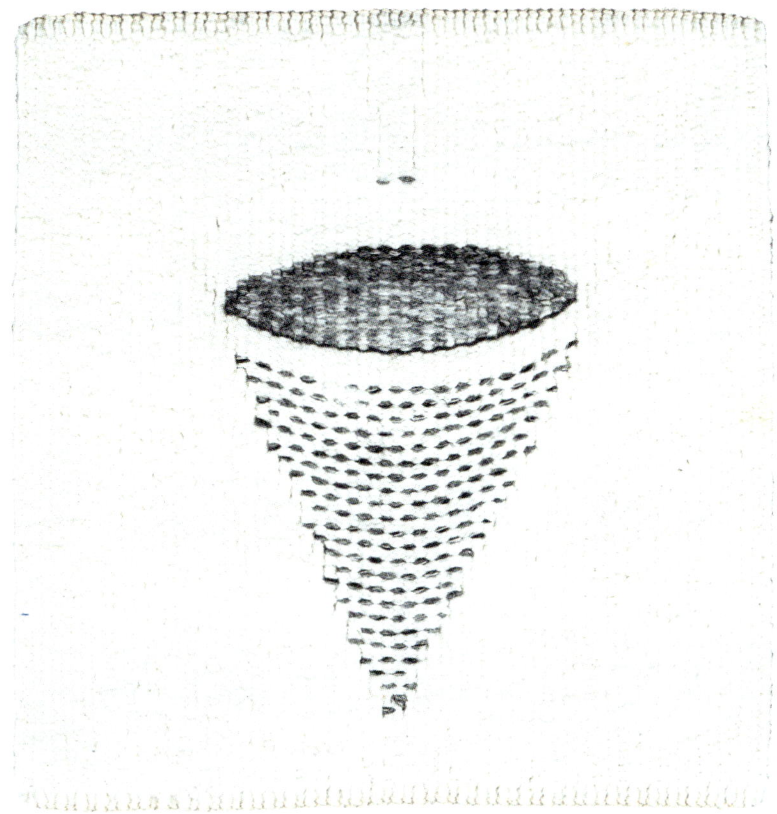

Margaret Jones goes from dark red to green, through seeds of black.

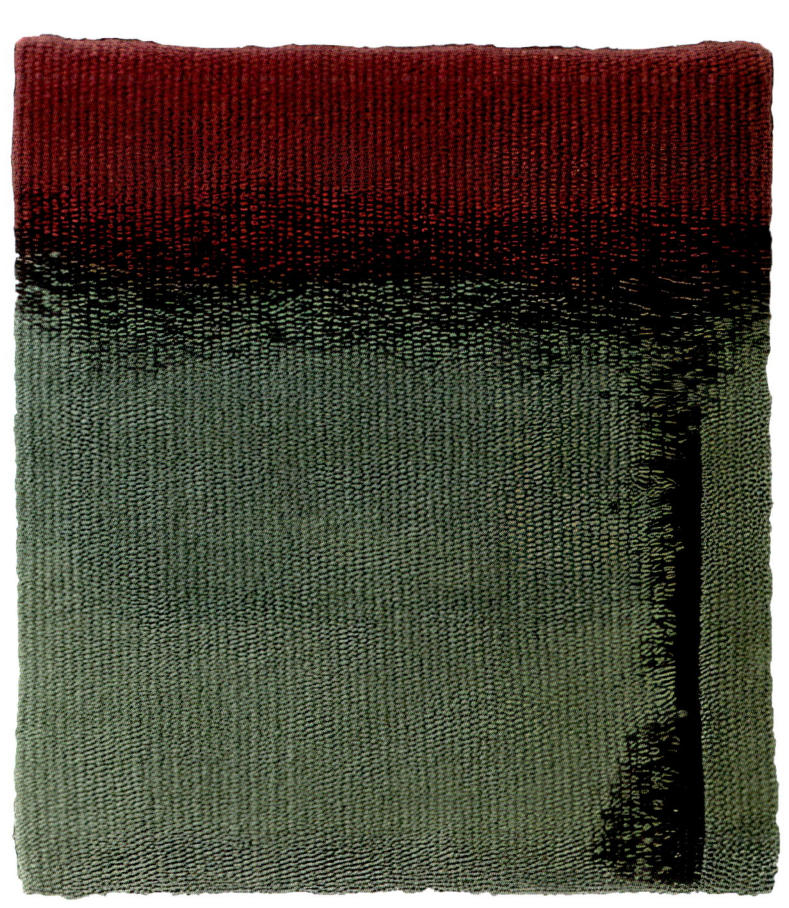

OPPOSITE: *Bleu* (Blue)
Marie Thumette-Brichard
2015 | 9.8" × 9.8" | wool, metallic

ABOVE: *Spill*
Kay Lawrence
1998 | 7" × 7" | linen, wool, cotton; cotton warp

RIGHT: *Field of Dreams*
Margaret Jones
2022 | 8.25" × 8" | wool; cotton warp

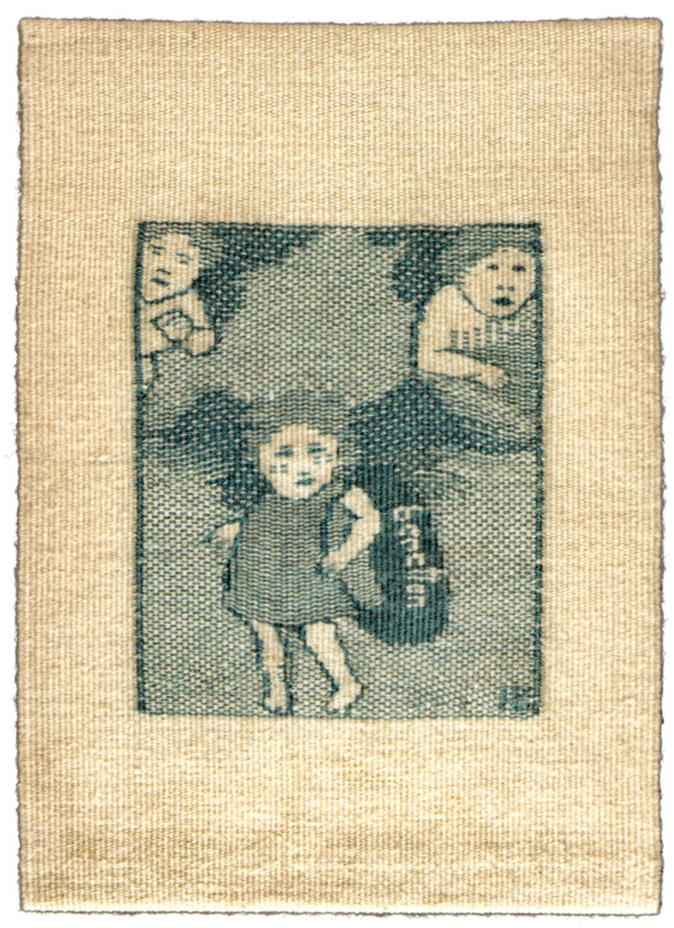

Benetton's Angel
Beata Hauser
Second half of 20th century | 11.2" × 8.5" | wool

Beata Hauser's children are blue and white. Almost the whole of the ground is composed of seeds. The children, though, have white skin, clothing woven with lines. The name Benetton might refer to the clothing company, which produced controversial advertisements with political and social content.

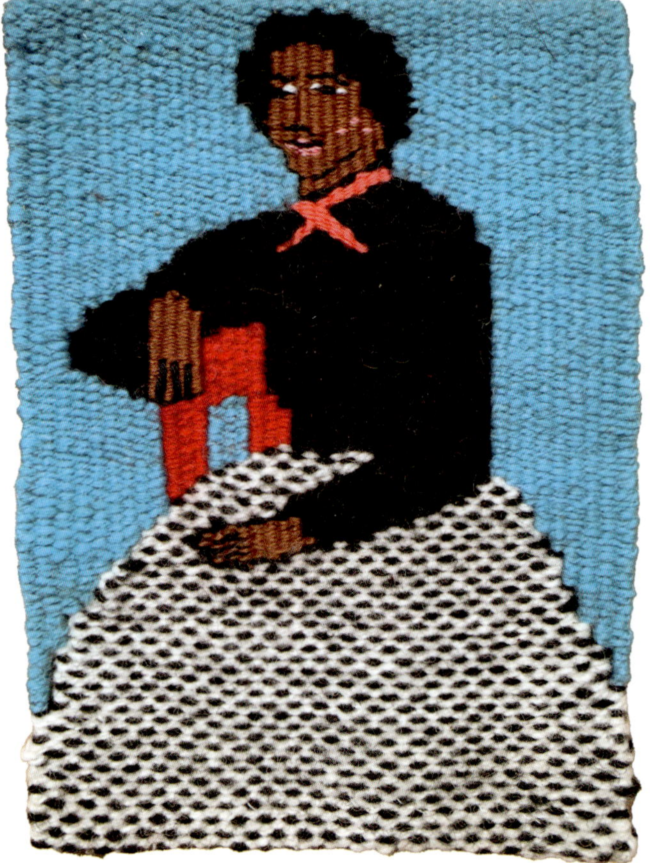

Amy Belgan began with a cartoon from a photograph of a woman in a chair. Her seeds, woven like Lawrence's, make skirt fabric.

Woman in Red Chair
Amy Belgan
2021 | 7" × 5" | wool, acrylic, embroidery floss

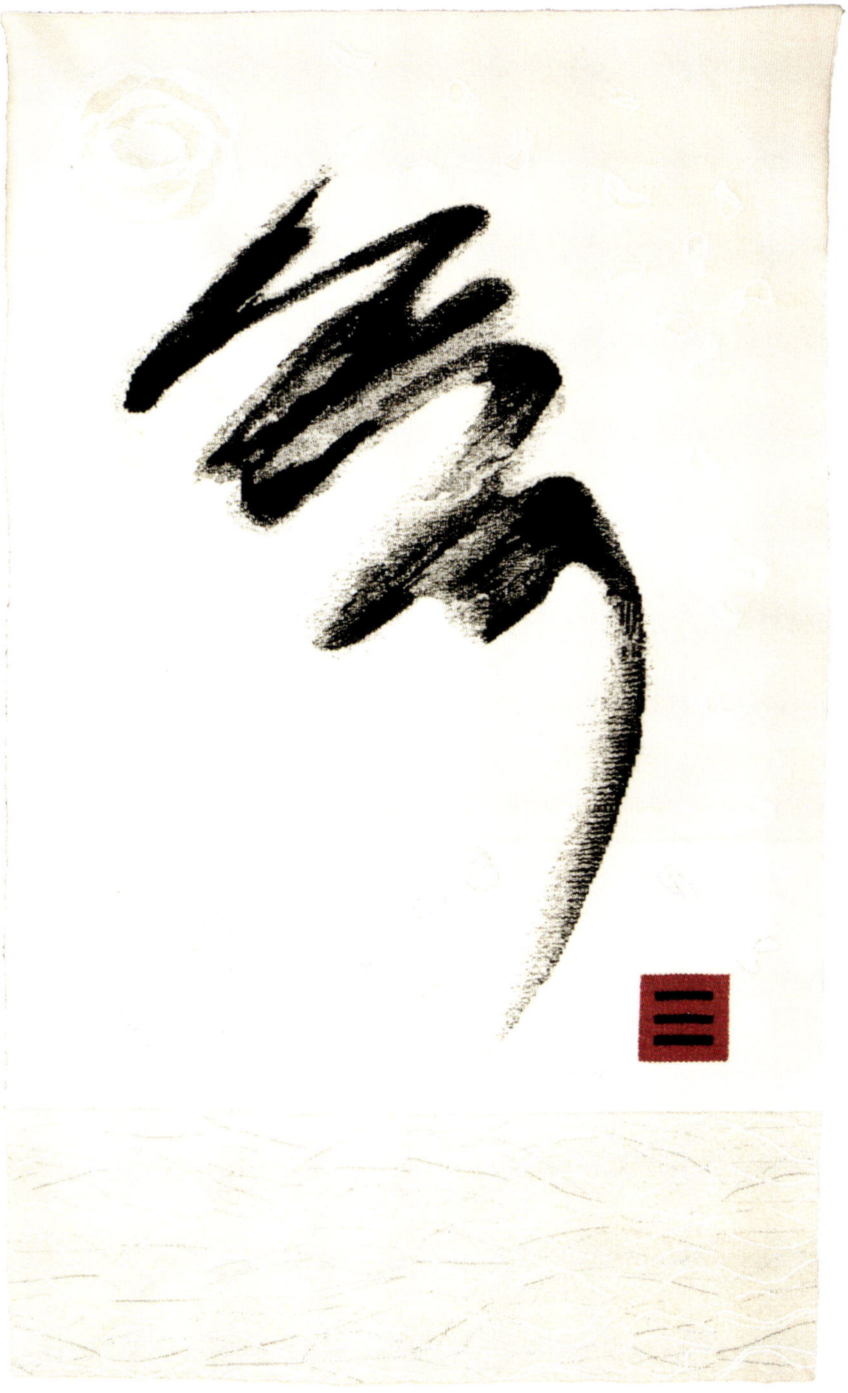

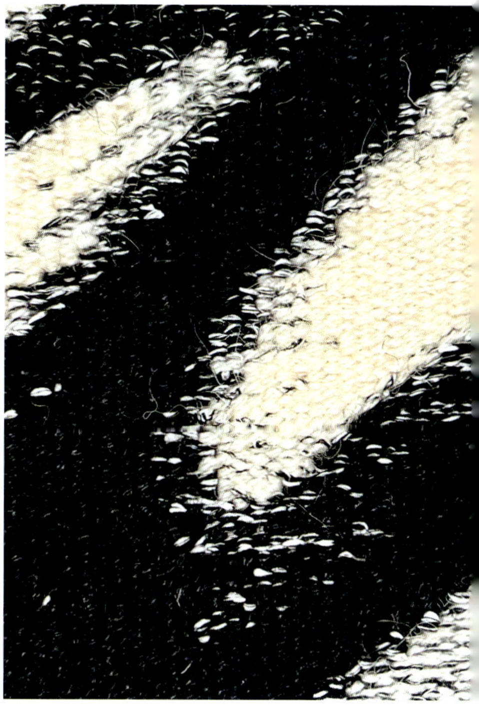

Awakening
Ellen Ramsey
2012 | 60" × 36" | wool, silk, rayon, chenille, viscose, retro reflective ribbon; cotton warp

Ellen Ramsey's looping curving shape over an ocean adds seeds, which leave the impression that she used a fountain pen—and was running out of ink.

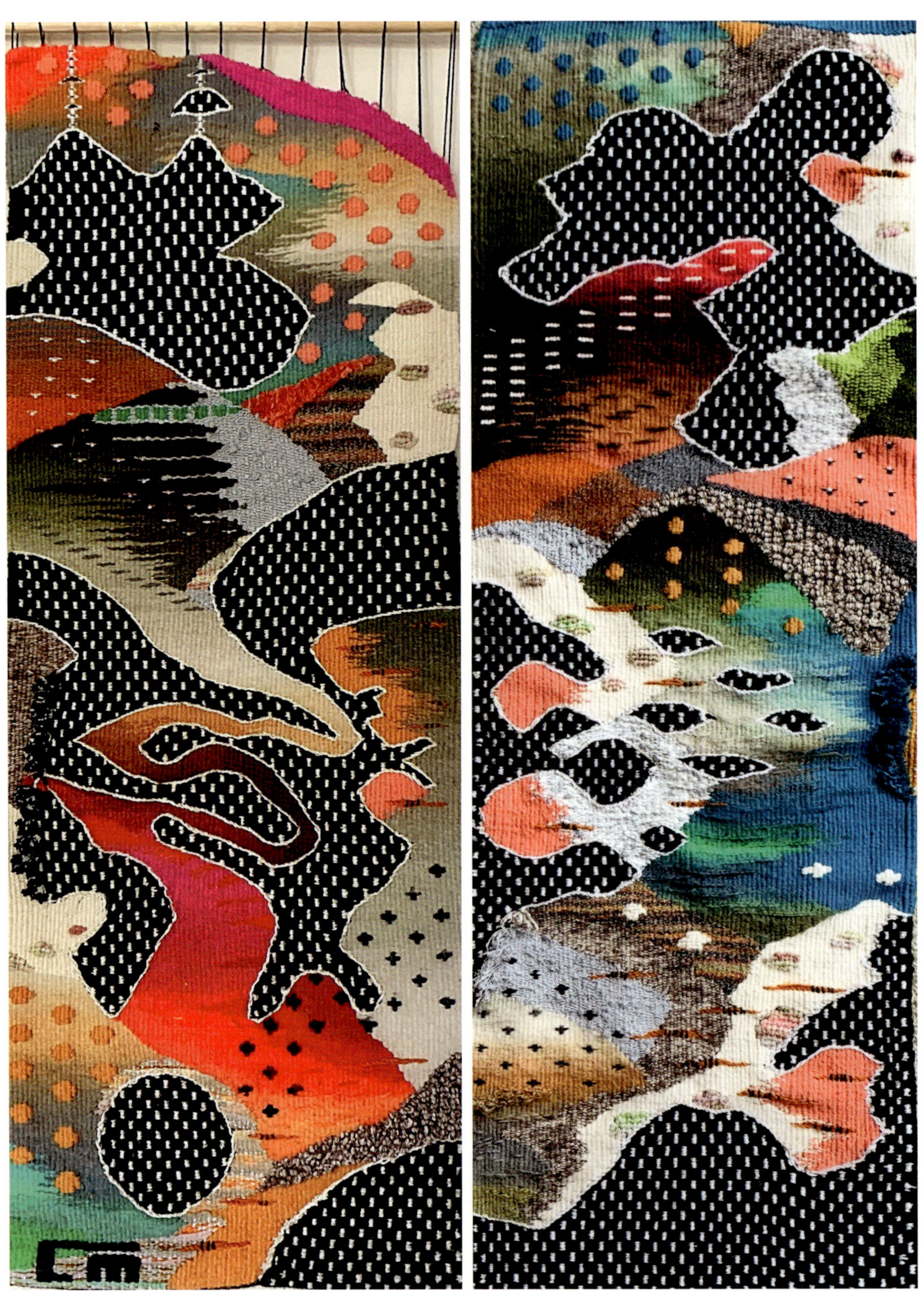

OPPOSITE: *The Joy of Two*
Carol Macdonald
2022 | 30" × 12" (each) | wools, cottons

The seeds in Carol Macdonald's *The Joy of Two* are more complex than they look. Each elongated white mark in the black fields is composed of three white seeds, woven one above the other. The uniformity of the seeds battles it out with the remainder of each piece, with its groups of textured, brightly colored areas.

The lines in Ann Roth's *Letting Go* are like incomplete sentences, or even a set of stairs going down and up. The irregular edges make lively what might otherwise be static.

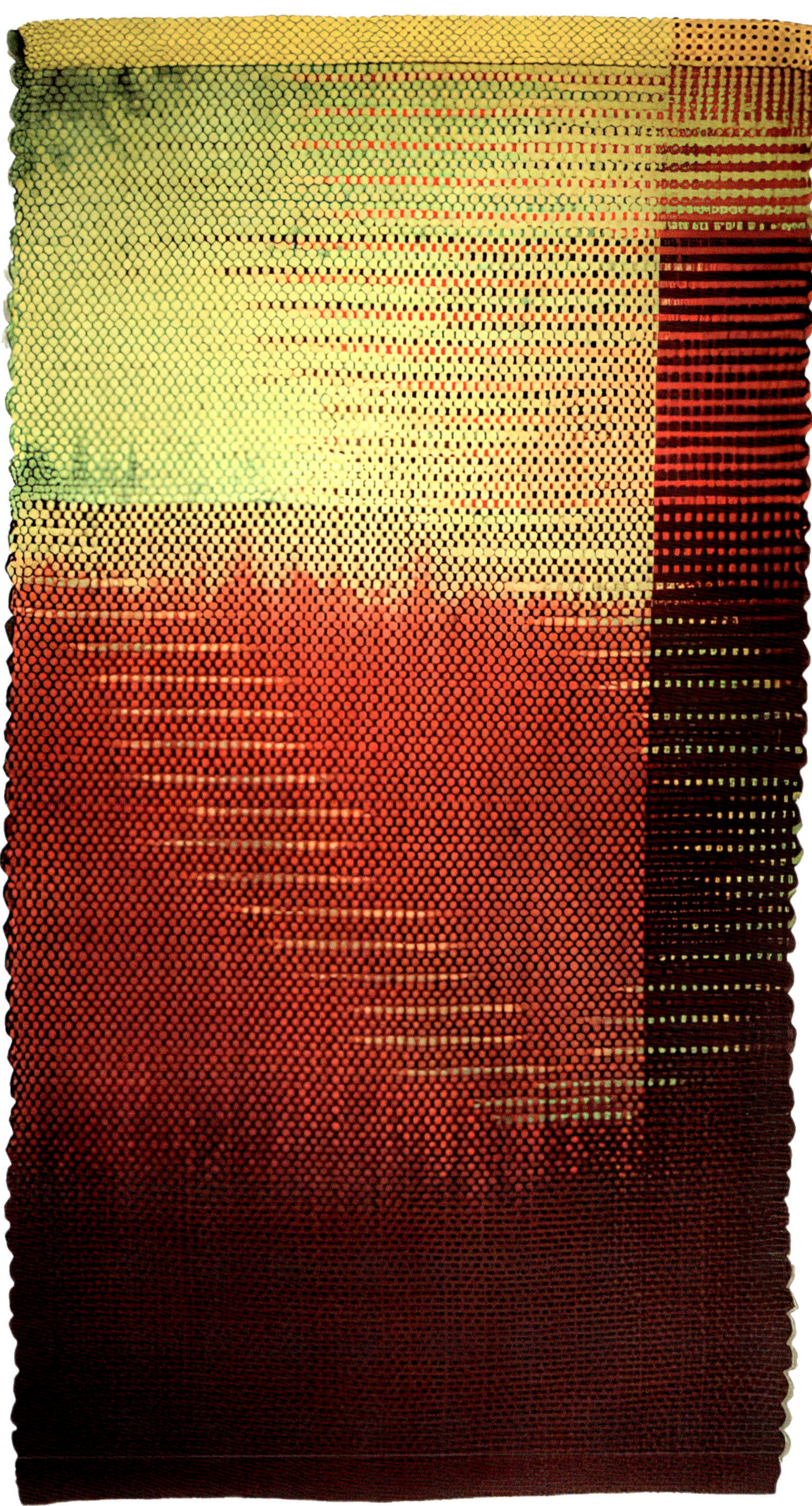

Letting Go
Ann Roth
2008 | 62" × 35" | cotton
hand-dyed warp and weft ikats

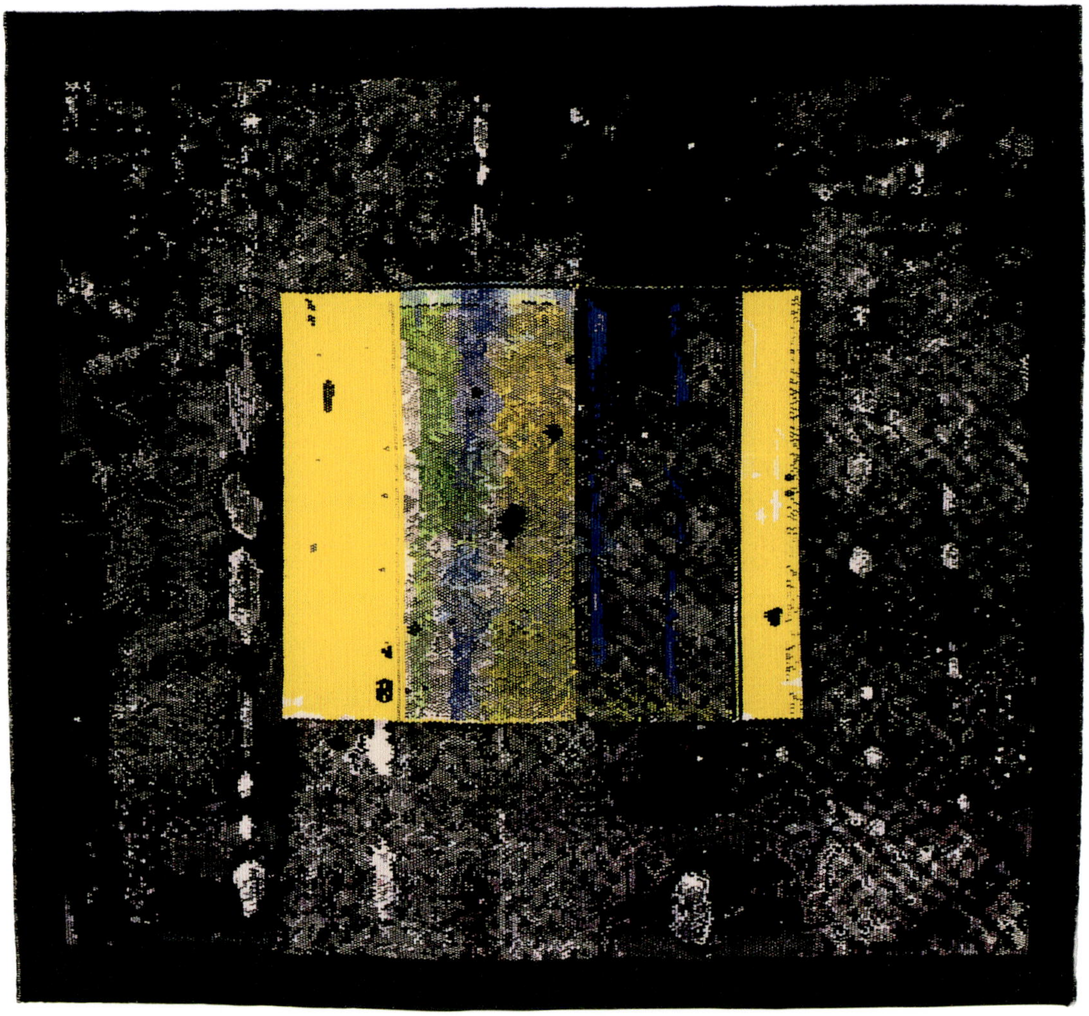

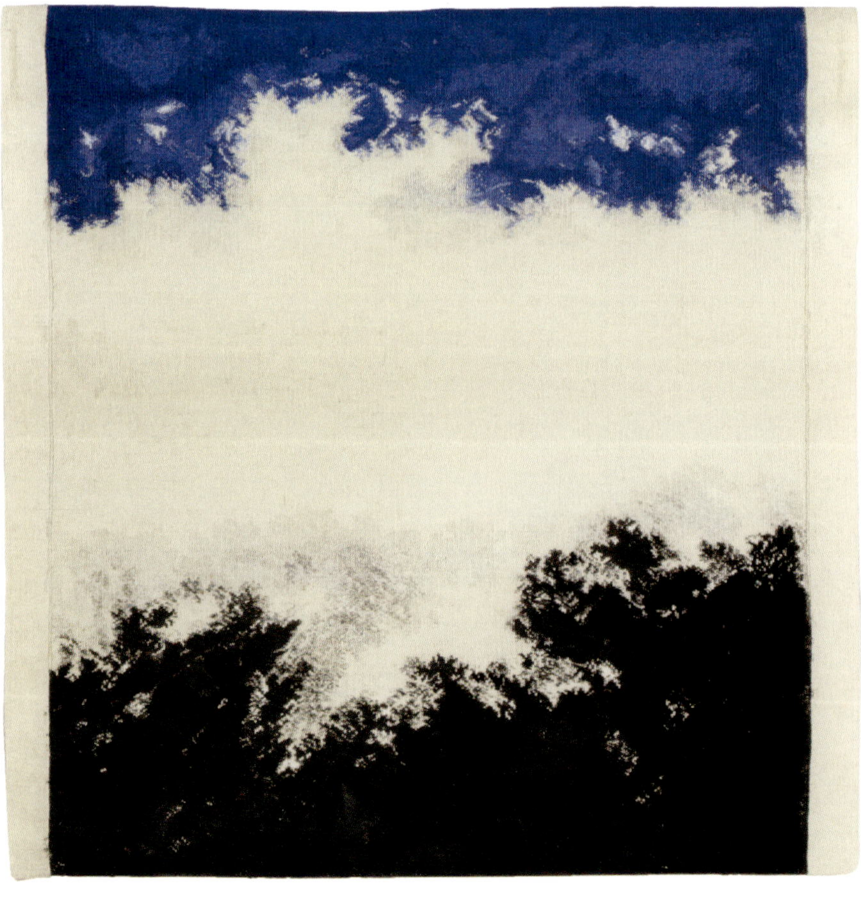

ABOVE: *Scene No. 3*
Marcel Marois
2000–2002 | 37.4" × 40.3" | wool, cotton

LEFT: *Broken White Bands with New Blue*
Sara Brennan
2010 | 45.5" × 45.5" | wool, cotton, cottolin

seeds adding special effects and moods

With his usual meticulousness, placing his threads with immense care, Marcel Marois makes solid rectangular shapes play against the solid black and white seeds and spots. Does the title—*Scene No. 3*—suggest drama? Is the yellow a door? Or is the scene simply abstract scenery?

Sara Brennan restricts her palette to blue, white, and black. The seeds add atmosphere, extending something like a shadow or dust that augments the shapes we see. That bottom black shape might indicate trees; the white might be clouds, with the blue breaking through above. Or it might be pure play with color.

Trish Armour has employed seeds to make the lace and the veil the bride wears. Yet, we can see her face clearly, as well as the rest of the flowers that surround her.

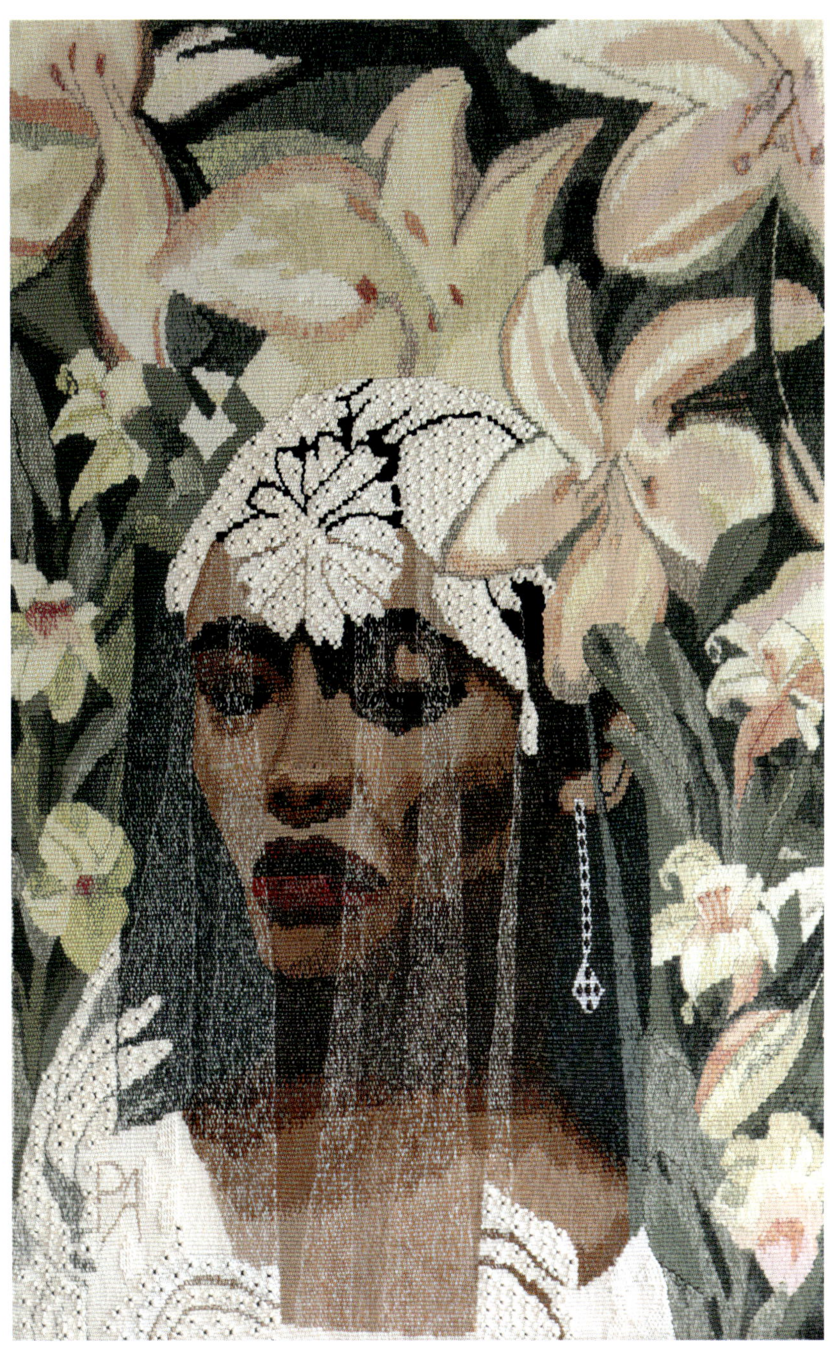

The Bride
Trish Armour
2021 | 38.5" × 25.5" | wool, Tencel, rayon, acrylic; cotton warp

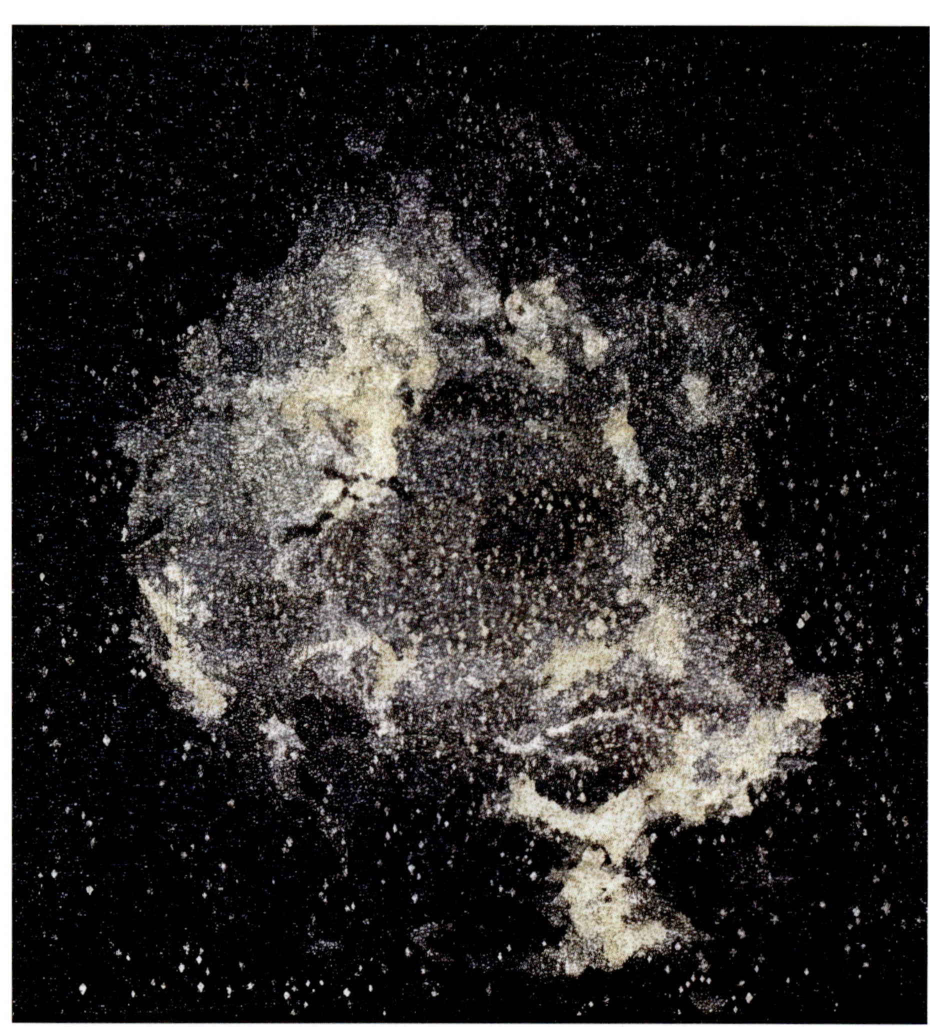

LEFT: *Galaxy II*
Ibolya Hegyi
1995 | 43.3" × 43.3" | wool, metallic yarn

BELOW: *Awelye No. 1*
Gloria Petyarre/Pitjara
1993 | 6.5' × 9' | wool, cotton
Australian Tapestry Workshop
Weavers: Grażyna Bleja, Irja West, Barbara Mauro

OPPOSITE: *Pièta for World War I*
Thomas Bayrie (designer)
2016–17 | 15.17' × 14.6' | wool, cotton, silk
Atelier Patrick Guillot, with weavers Patrick Guillot and Olivier Baude

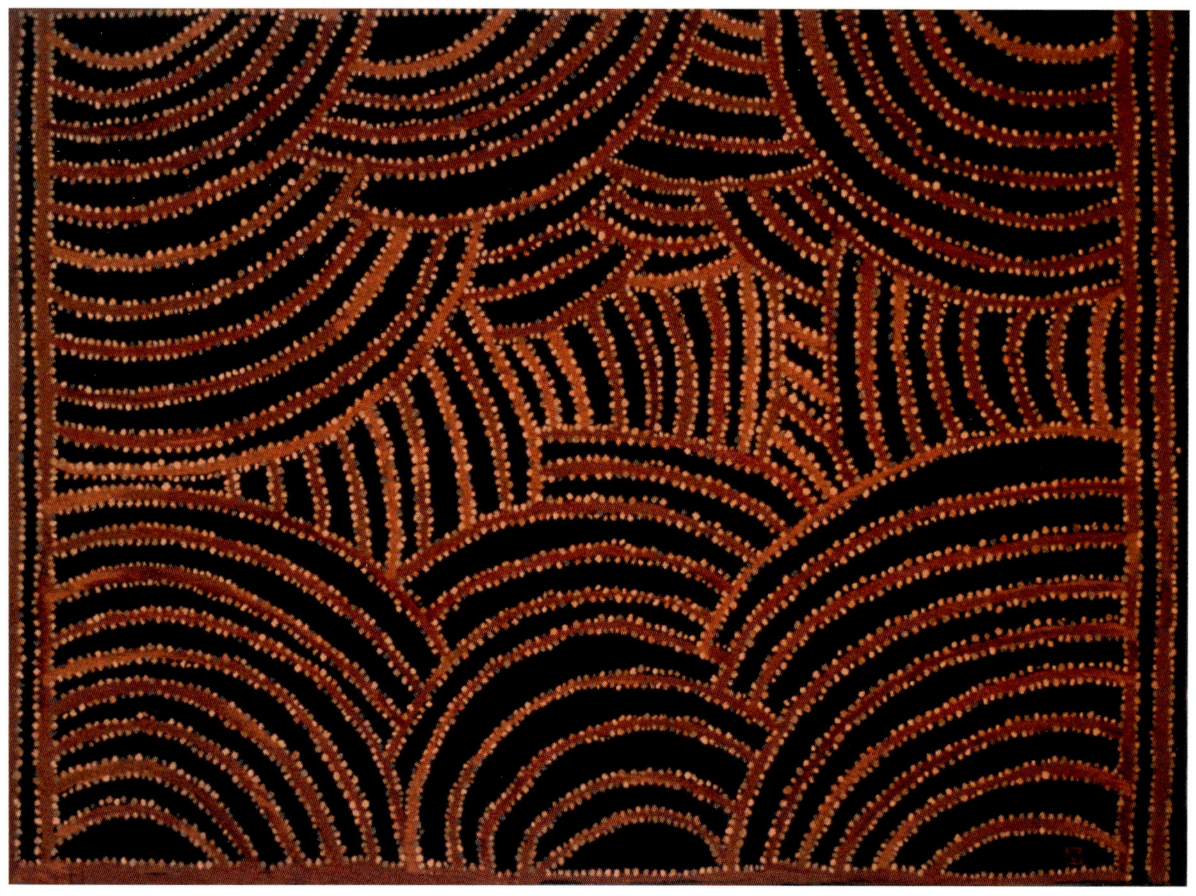

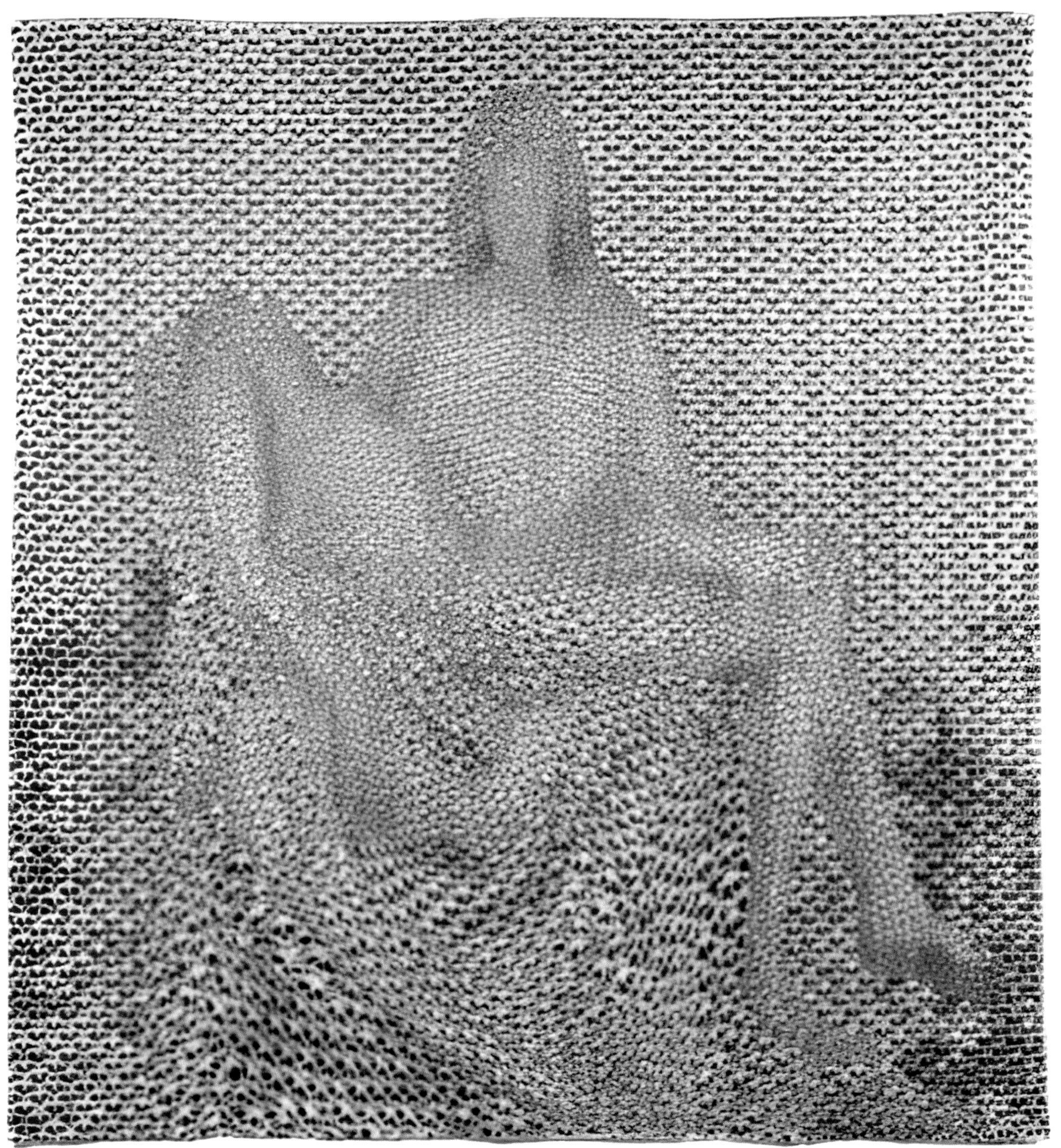

Ibolya Hegyi used seeds in an extremely sophisticated fashion as she envisions the night sky, infused with patterns of light, and gives us a vast repetition of stars. Her galaxy almost looks like a human skull.

Some cultures rely on dots in their art—like Aboriginal dreamings. The cartoon for this tapestry, a design by Gloria Petyarre (also spelled Pitjara), imitates these visual effects with great orange and gold curves, outlined by dots in a field of black. The Australian Tapestry Workshop has rendered the design brilliantly.

Thomas Bayrie's chain mail, filling the entire woven field as it does, creates complex variations of repeated motifs. The seeds give a sense of volume.

Lise Froelund has massed a wild collection of seeds to make a child, both in a variety of whites, yellows, blues, and reds, and again, in the upper left, something more like a photographic negative. The effect recalls pointillism, although the weaver is certainly not painting. Froelund had the right tool for this work, a digital Jacquard handloom.

Mathieu Mercier's rope looks photographically real—and huge: It measures 10 feet square. You must approach it and stand very close before the illusion breaks down into its dots (*see detail*). Digital photographers understand pixels; weavers understand seeds.

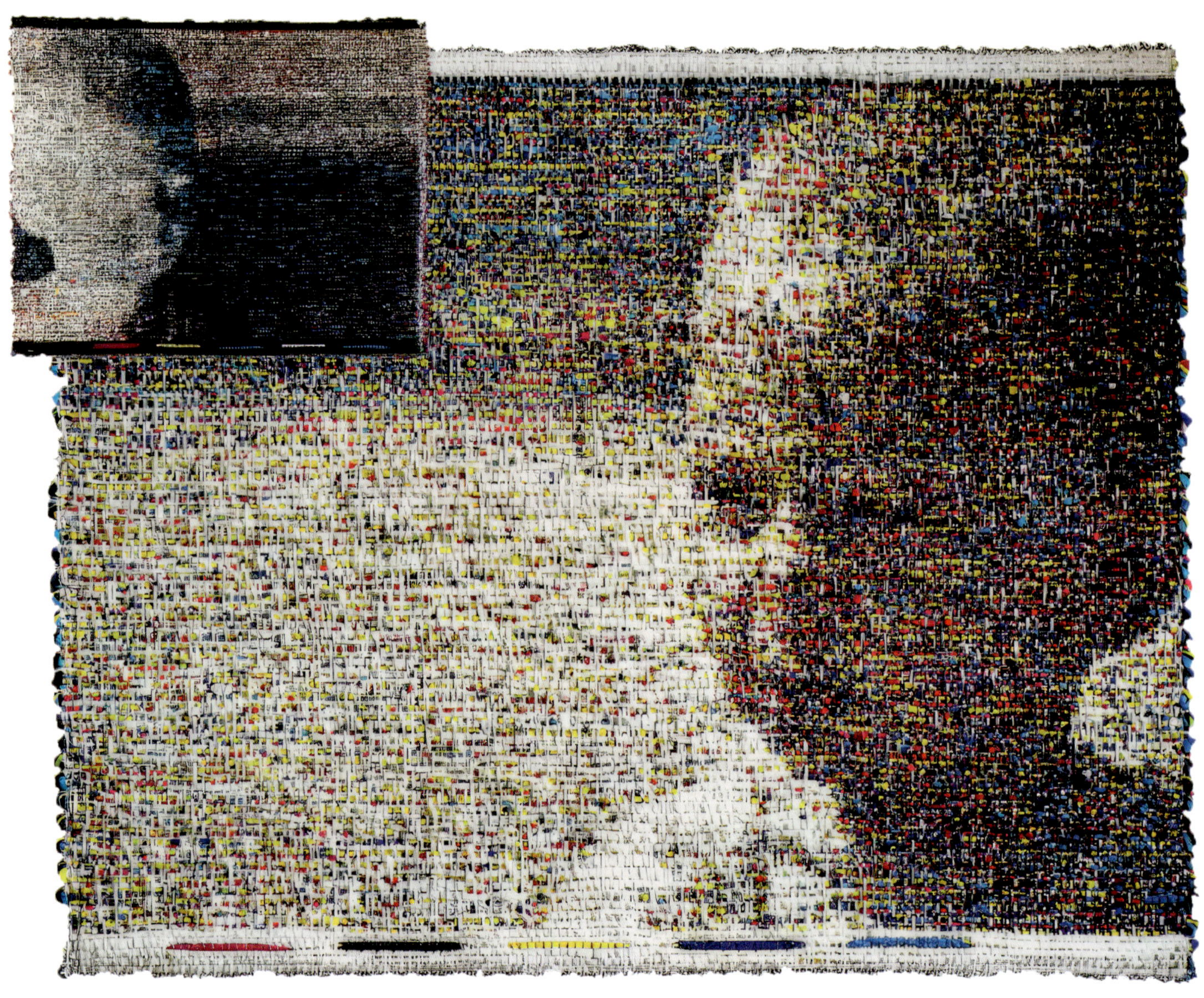

Child
Lise Froelund
2016 | 43.3" × 55.1" | polyester, viscose, paper
Photographer: Anette Fuglsang

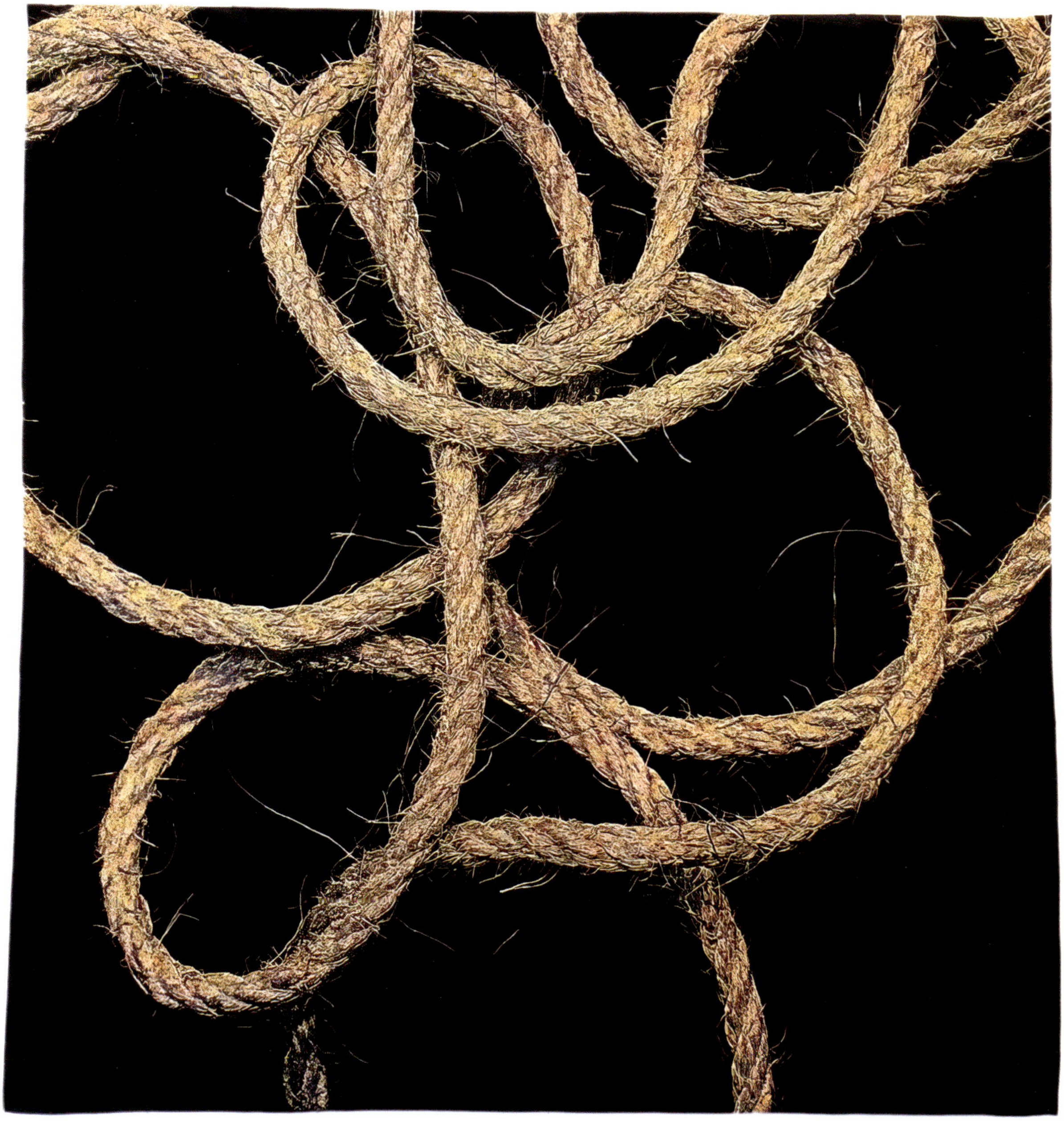

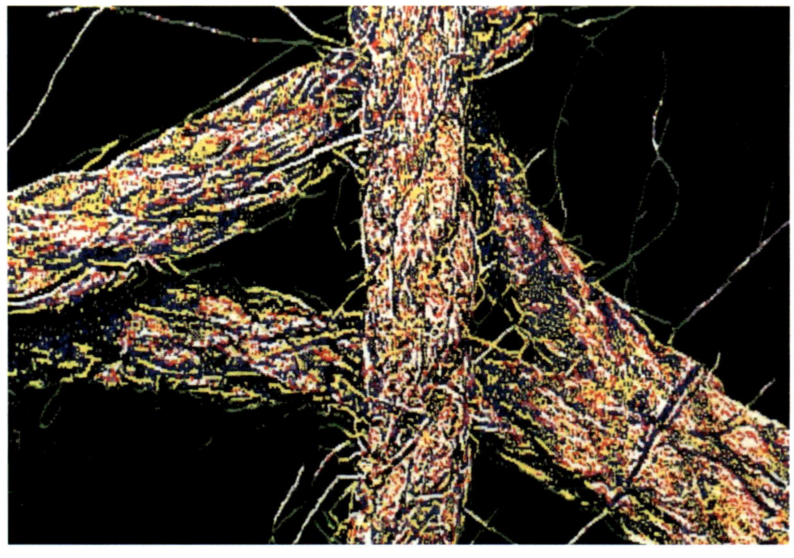

Sans Titre—Corde Pixel
(Untitled—pixelated rope)
Mathieu Mercier
2014 | 10'6" × 10'6" | wool, metalized polyester
Atelier Legouiex; weavers: Daniel Bayle, Agnes-Mare Durieux

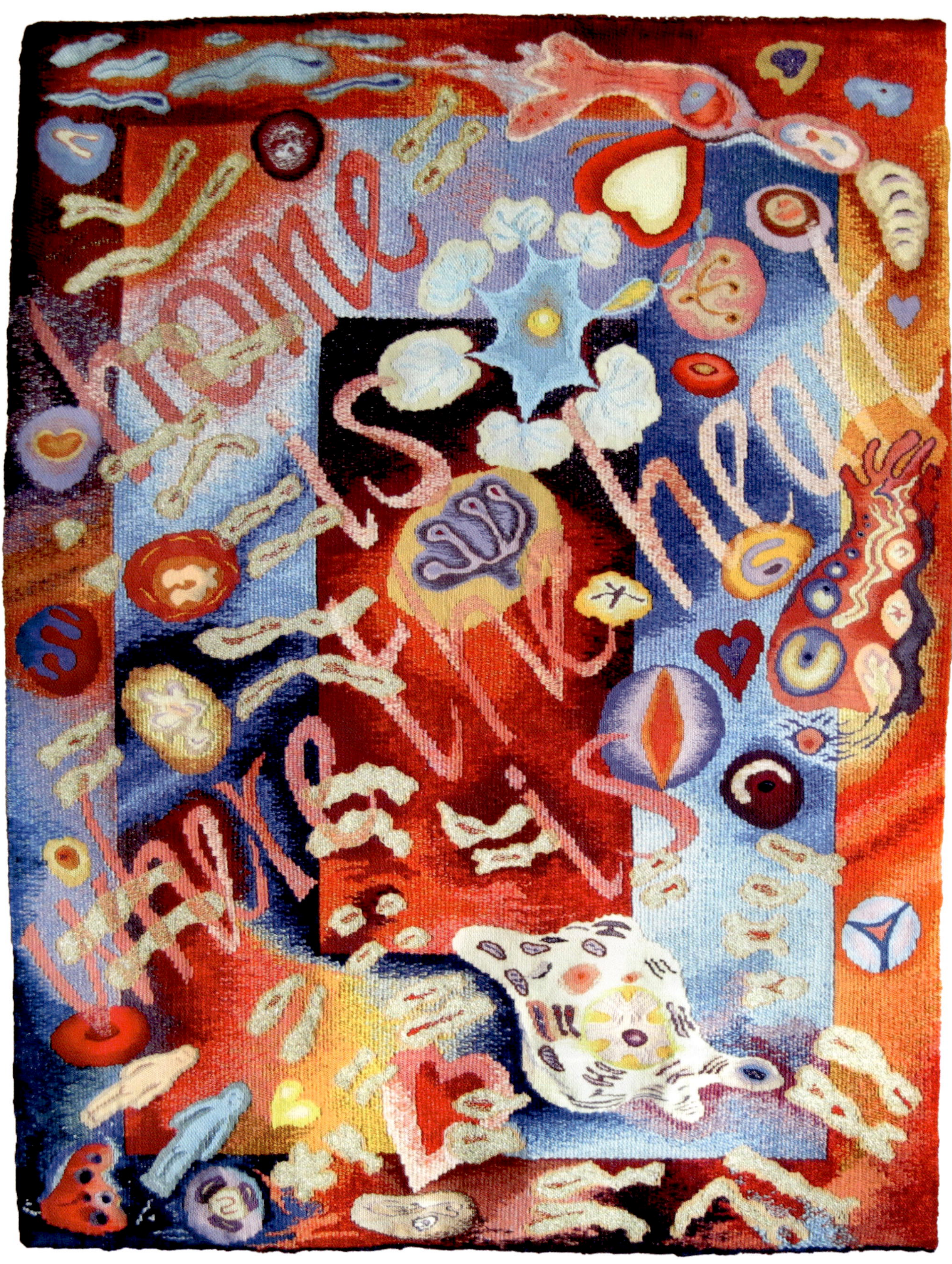
home
heart

CHAPTER 6

sett

Traditional European and North American tapestry consists of plain weave—which entails one weft thread covering alternate warp threads. Covering is basic. The idea is to alternate (over and under) single warp threads. But weavers can also cover warp threads in a different pattern. If the weft, for instance, covers alternate pairs of threads (this is known as a basket weave), the surface changes.

A weaver can vary the sett, creating a variety of surfaces. The result is a shift in what we see. This chapter shows the results of this play with sett, which makes for a constantly changing texture.

Christine Sawyer combined different setts within the same piece. For objects, a finer sett permits greater detail. A circle's curves are smoother with a finer sett.

OPPOSITE:
Home is where the heart is
Christine Sawyer
2004 | 47.25" × 37.4" | wool, cotton, metallic yarns

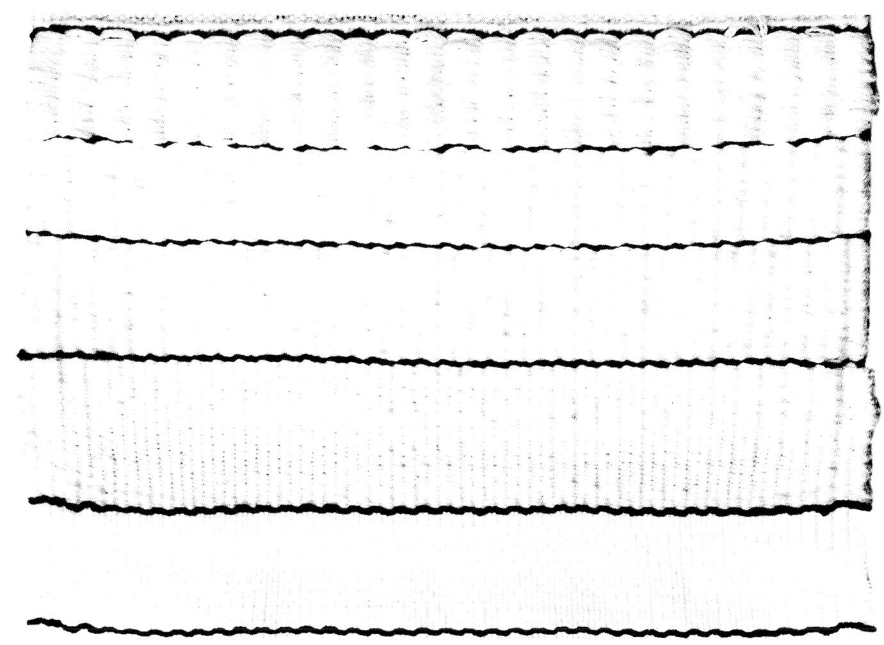

RIGHT: Sett sampler

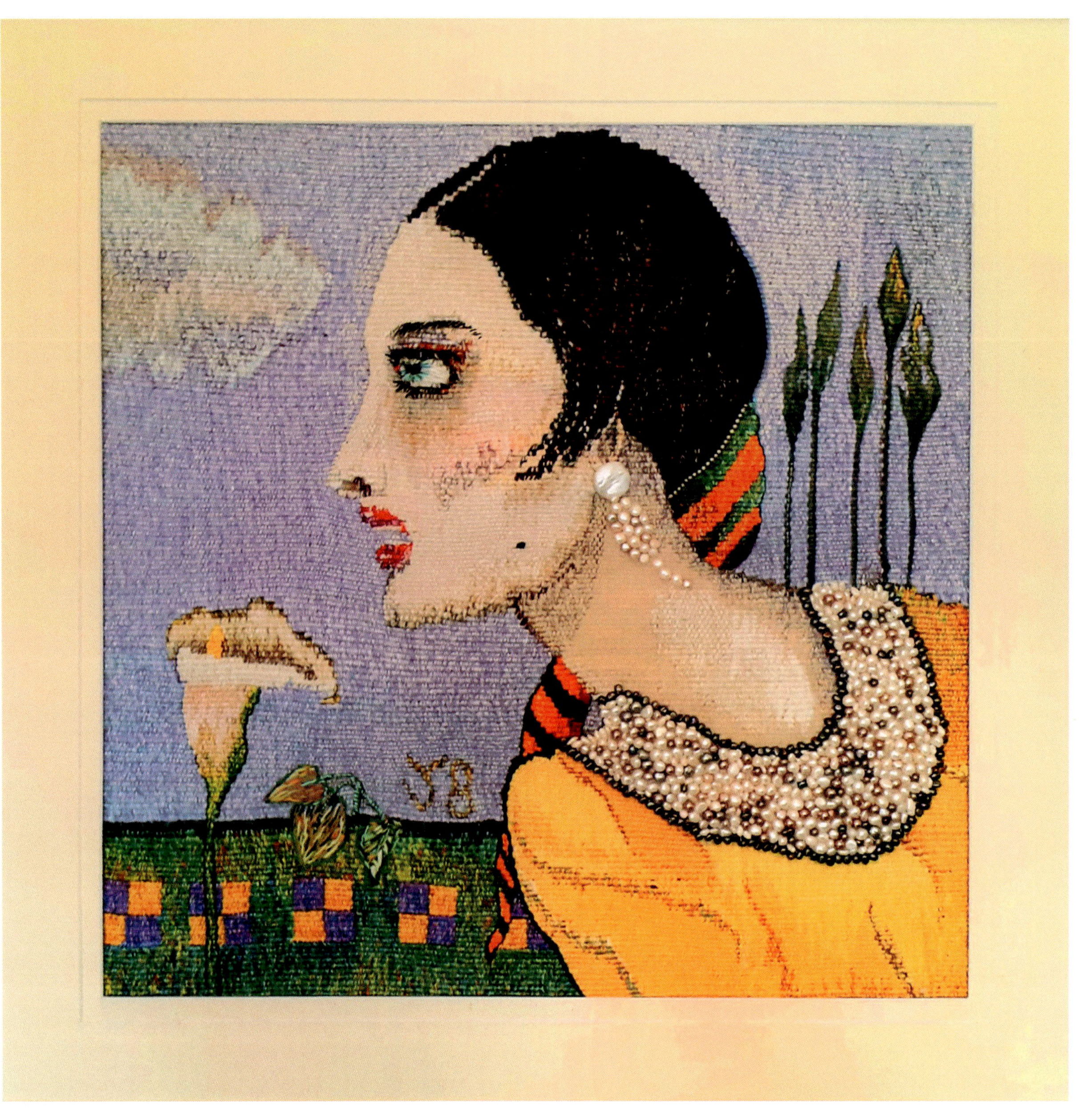

Good morning, Minerva (10 epi)
John Brennan
2014 | 28" × 28", framed; 19" × 19", unframed | cotton, silk, rayon, linen, wool, gold, silver, freshwater pearls, mother-of-pearl, metallic beads

John Brennan decided to see if a change in the sett (8 ends per inch [epi] in one piece, 10 epi in the other) would make a difference in the time he spent to weave each tapestry. While he changed some colors, the portraits differ only slightly (look at the eyes). The lack of difference between the two speaks to the meticulousness of Brennan's weaving. In the end, the time he took was not noticeably different.

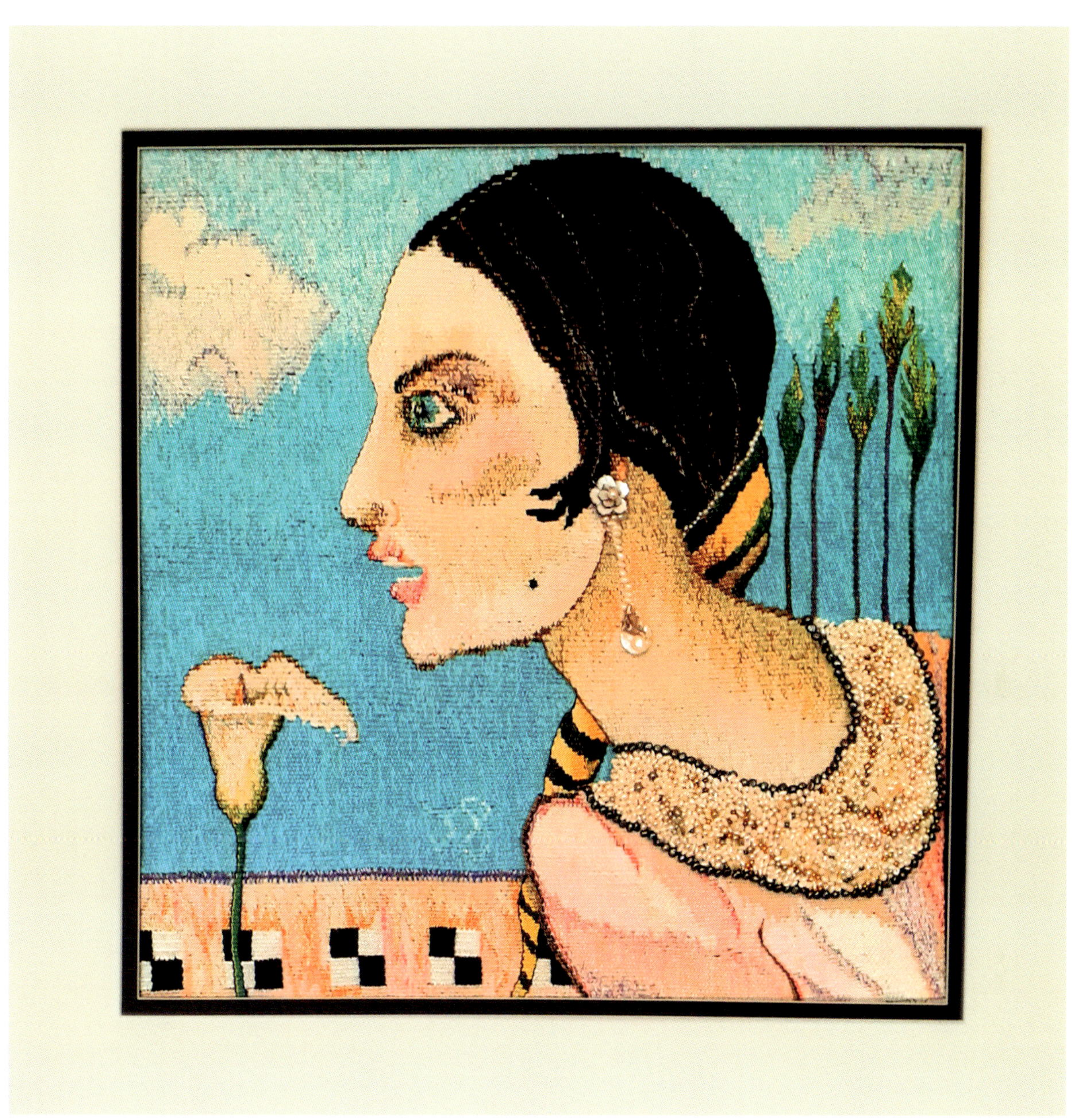

Minerva, good morning again (8 epi)
John Brennan
2014 | 30" × 30", framed; 19.5" × 19.5", unframed | cotton, silk, rayon, linen, wool, gold, silver, freshwater pearls, mother-of-pearl, metallic beads

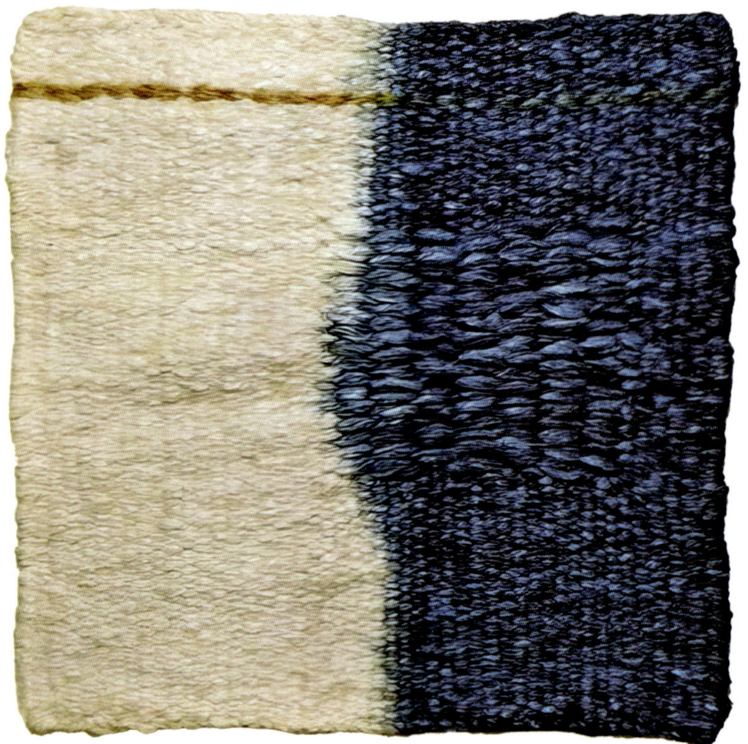

Lyn Hart wove this small piece and then dipped it into an indigo dye bath. The differences in the setts she has used (look along the center of the blue) are further emphasized by that almost feathery quality between the dyed and undyed parts.

Marta Gașienica-Szostak made this small piece with cotton. The white yarn makes it easier to see the shifts in the surface. Notice the effect of the dimensional bulges, on the right at the middle.

Indigo Monsoon
Lyn Hart
2017 | 9.5" × 10" | mixed fibers

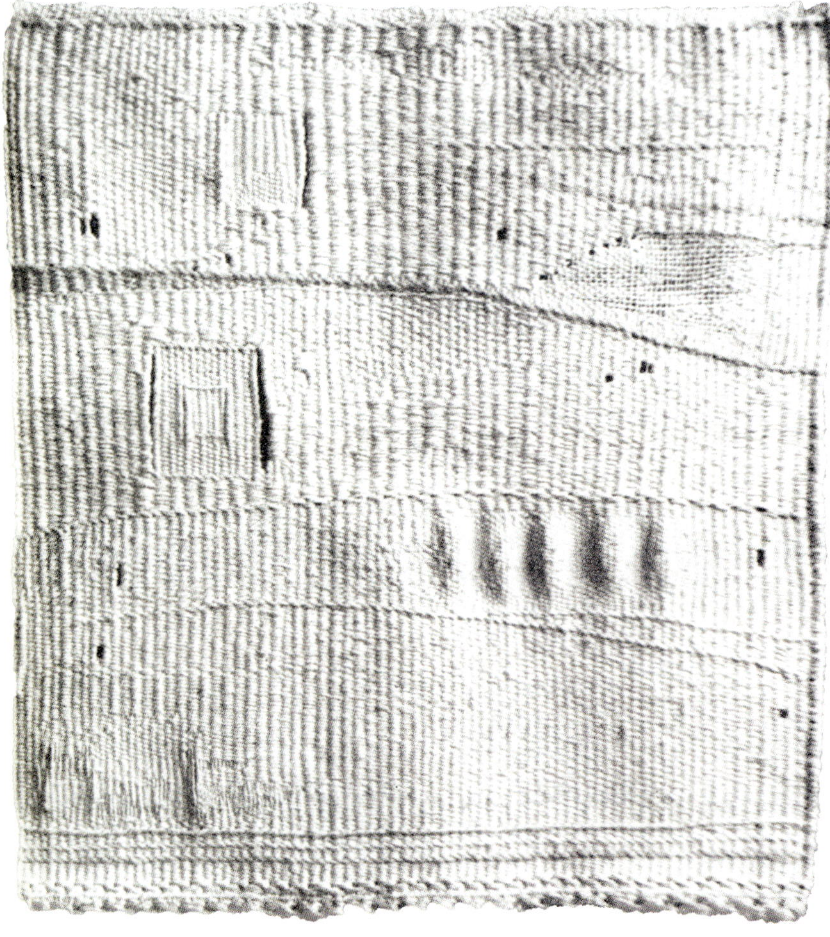

Monolog II
Marta Gașienica-Szostak

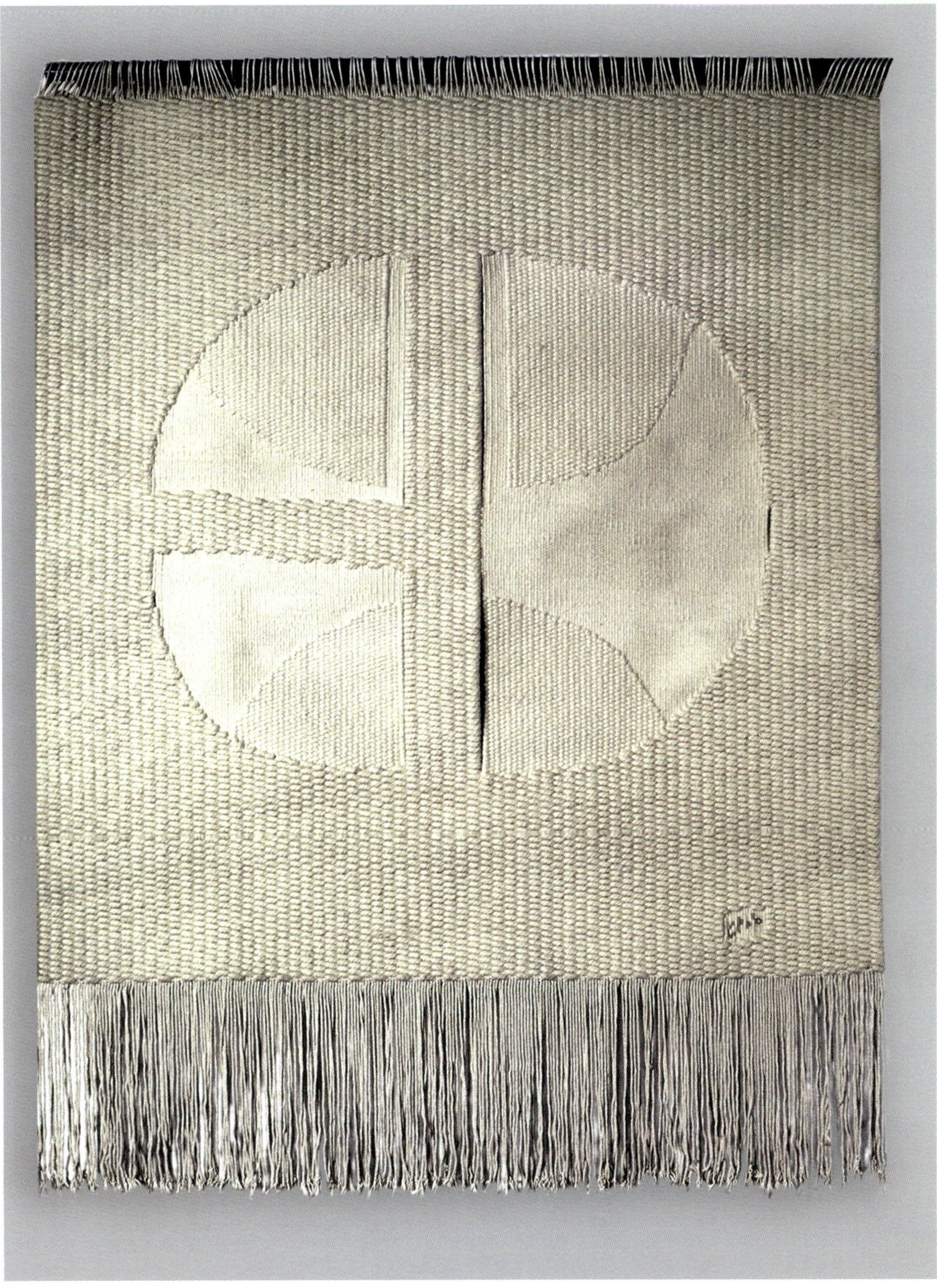

Thomas Gleb devoted his tapestry work to sett changes. He found heavier and finer materials to use as weft, using white/off-white almost exclusively. In this sizable tapestry, the sett moves between greater and fewer—and is very fine at the center. His signature (*bottom right*) is especially visible, in a small bubble that differs from what is around it.

La Coupe d'Eliahou (Eliahou's cut)
Thomas Gleb
1978 | 67.7" × 65" | cotton, wool
Atelier Lagoueix

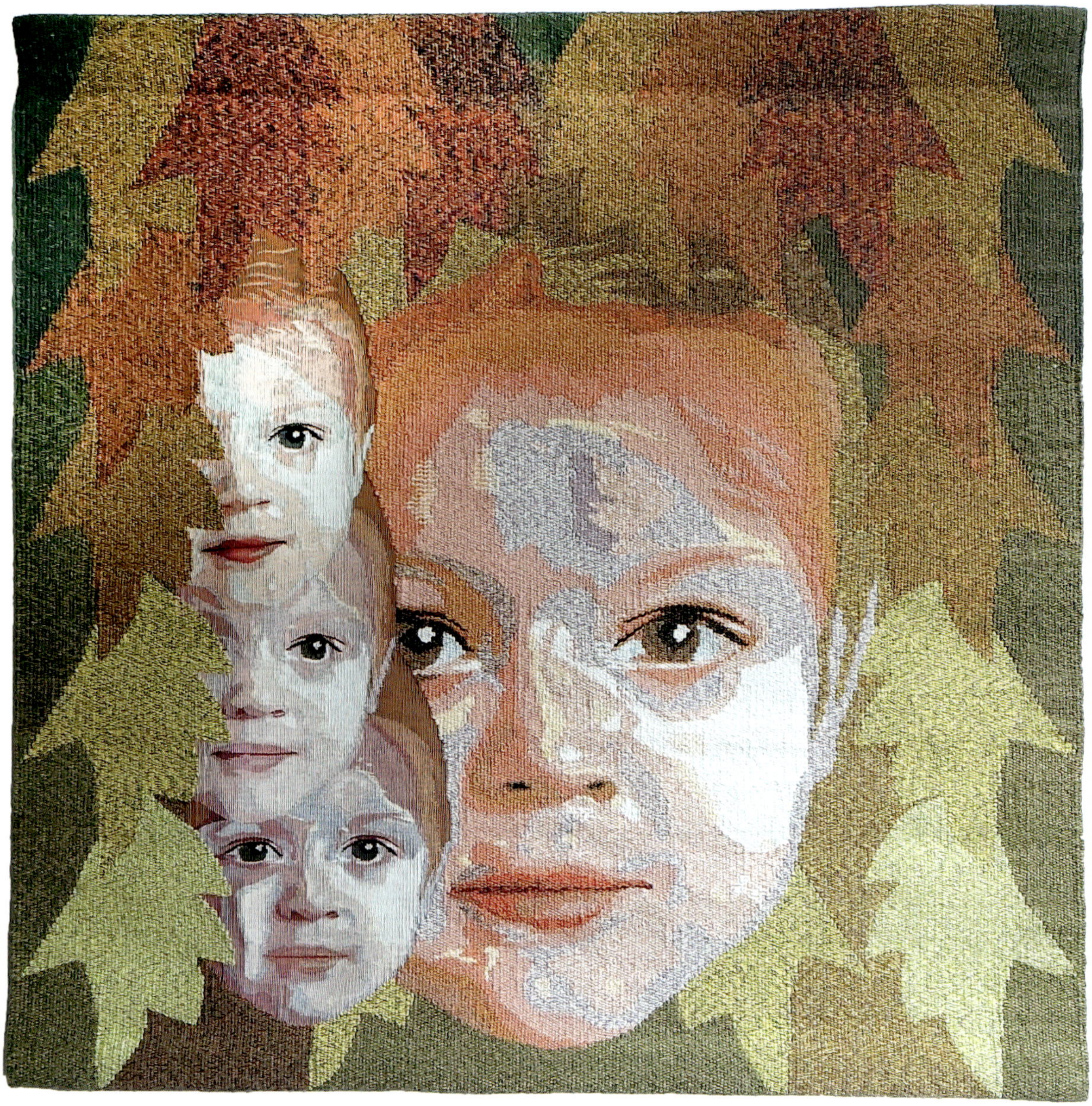

Thin Skin
Elke Hülse
2020 | 39.4" × 39.4" | cotton, acrylic, wool, linen

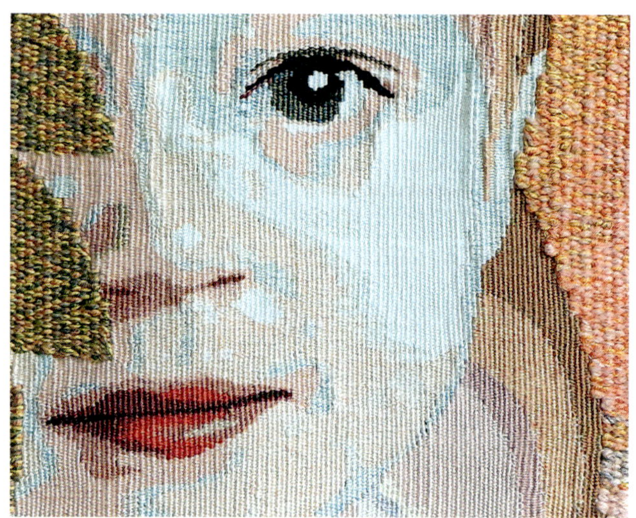

Elke Hülse gives us faces. Compare the tapestry with the close-up. In the left side of the detail, it is very difficult to see the actual sett (except that it is very fine).

Melanie Cros uses sett to present differences between textures in the seas and the sands. Note the small areas of pile.

Al Mamzar Beach, Dubai
Melanie Cros
2023 | 27.5" × 27.5" | wool, linen, lurex, cotton

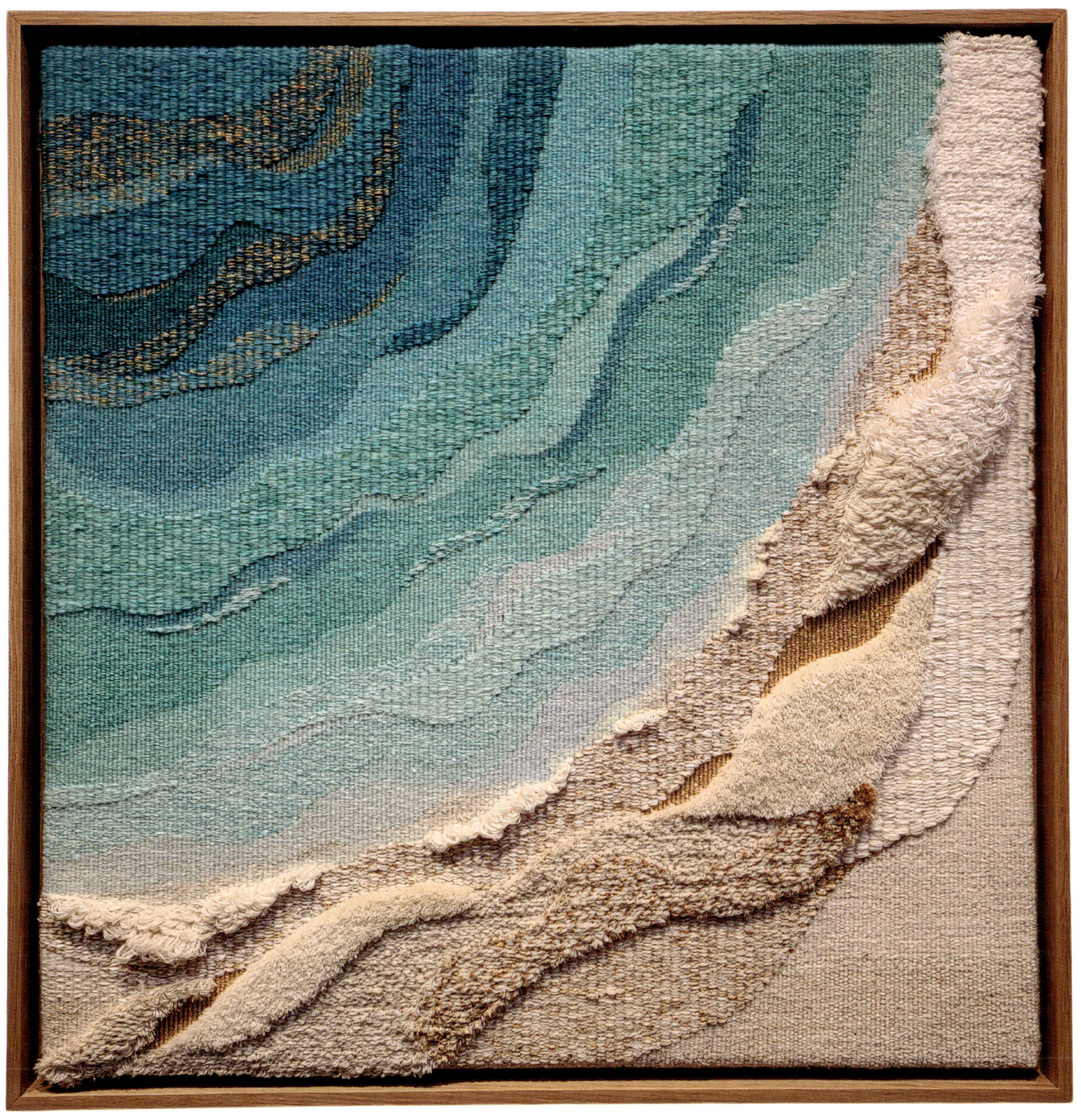

Haeseung Kang made this tapestry early in her career. The surface is both disciplined and elegant, moving among several setts, which make for thicker and thinner vertical lines.

Katarzyna Lavocat, trained in the art of the mural (the tapestry is 7 by 6.5 feet), has combined a variety of setts. In the detail, for instance, you can see how in using a lighter blue, she makes the weft jump many warps, as if protecting an area of potential vulnerability.

Light and Shadow
Haeseung Kang
94.5" × 74.8" | wool, cotton

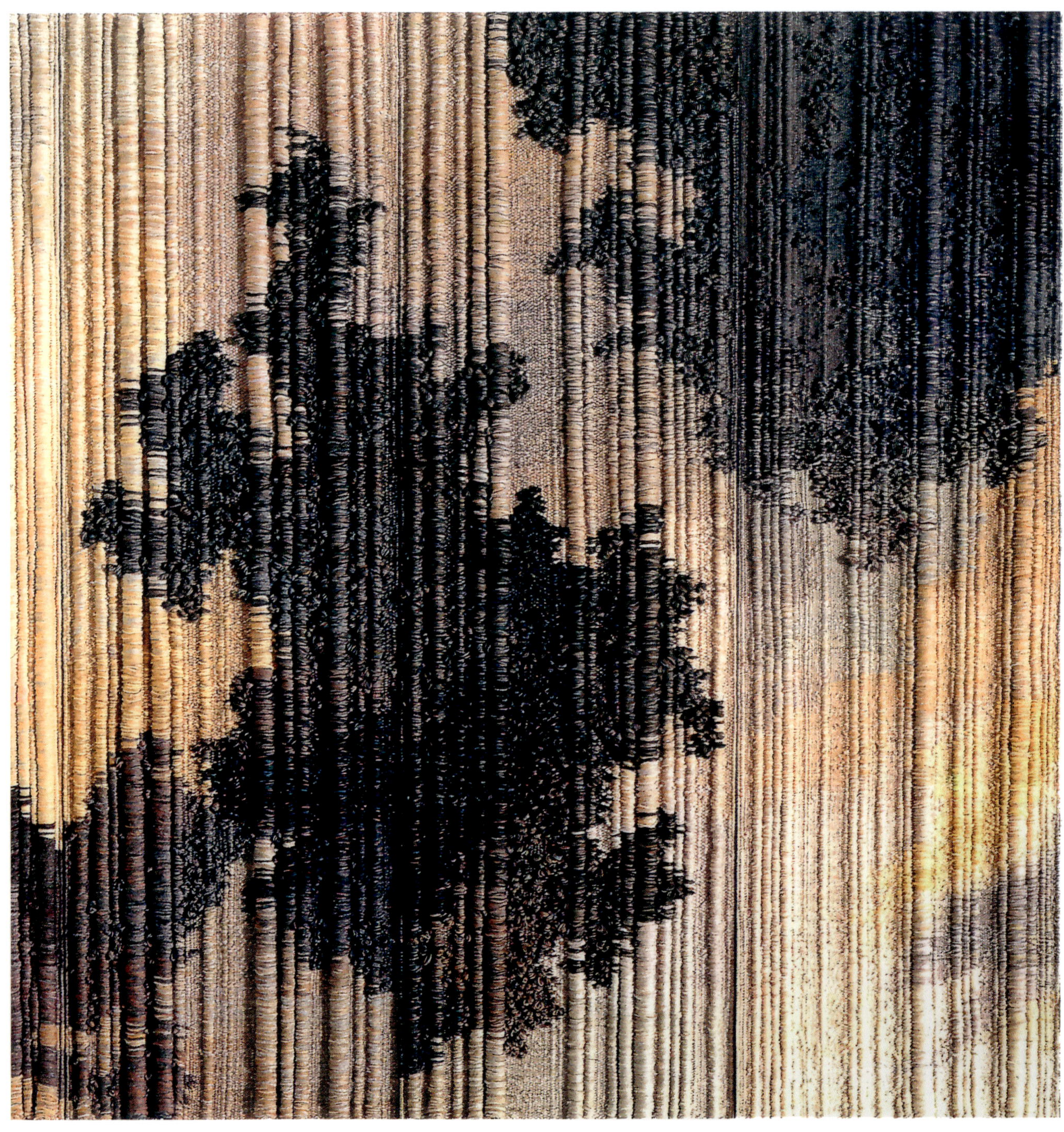

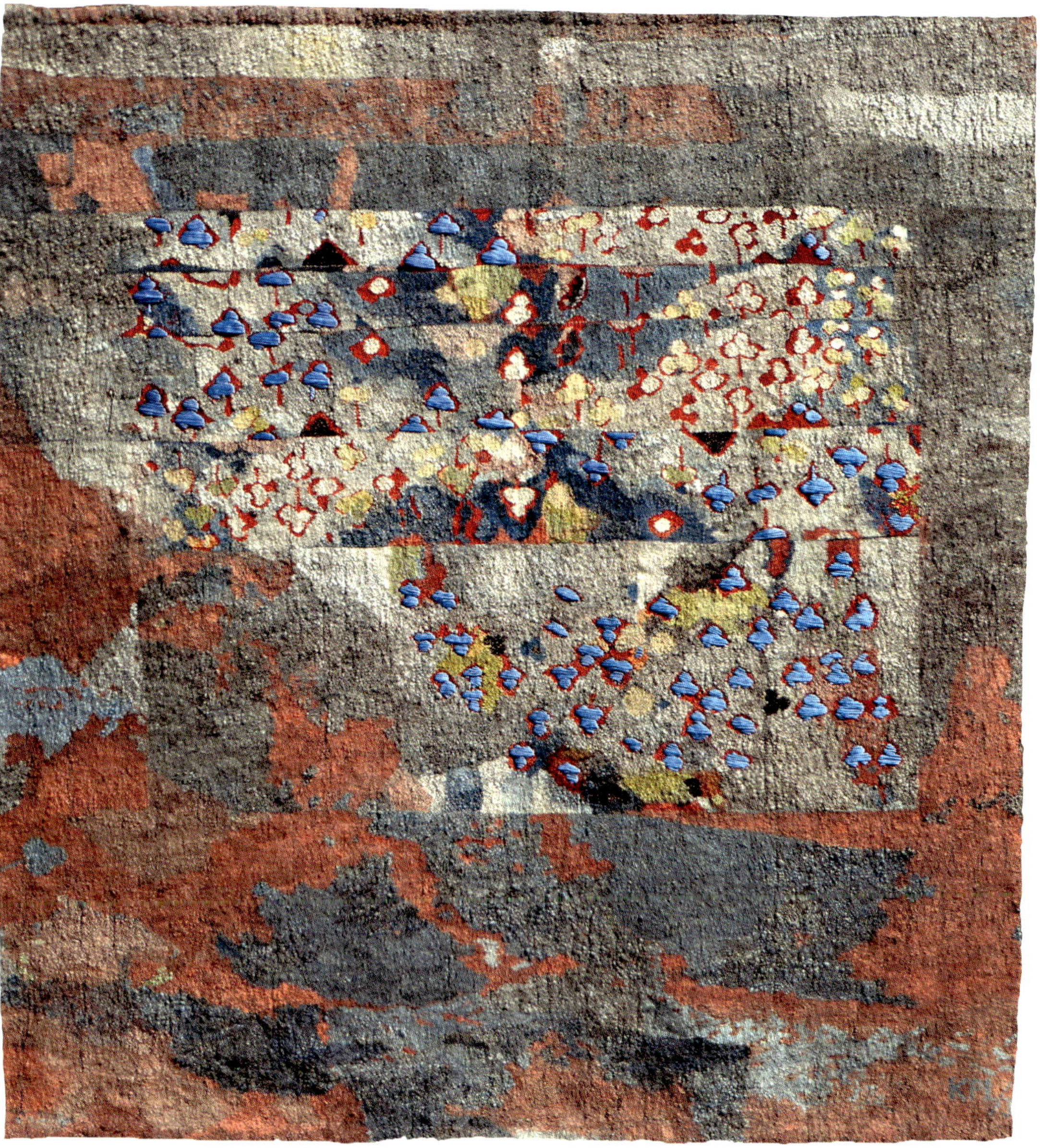

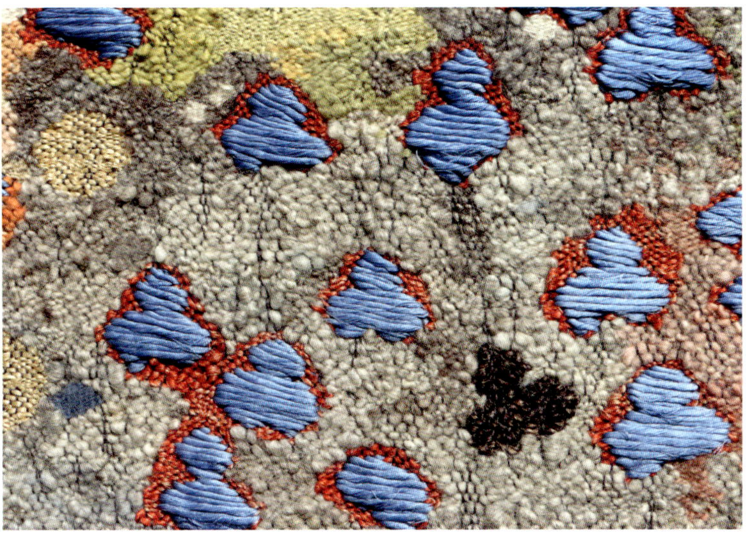

Promenade à Giverny
(Walk at Giverny)
Katarzyna Lavocat
2010–12 | 84" × 78.75"
| flax, handspun wool,
sisal, silk
dye stuffs: indigo, madder,
cochineal, reseda (weld)

line

Weaving is the process of interlacing threads. Every time weavers pass the weft yarn through the warp, first in one direction and then back again, they have created a line. This process is basic to all weaving. In time, lines of the same color produce a cloth of a single color. If the weaver alternates color a and color b and continues in this vein, they create vertical lines (known as "pick and pick"); if they go back and forth with color a, then back and forth with color b, and continue in this vein, they create horizontal lines (each of which is called a "pass").

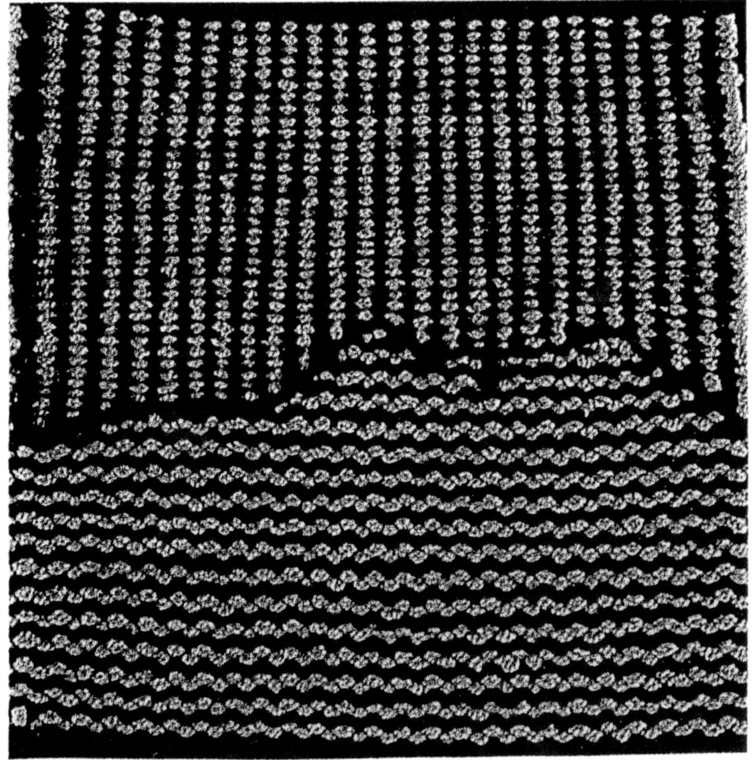

A caveat: While a weaver's passes make horizontal lines, and pick and pick make vertical lines, these lines may not appear as horizontal and vertical when the viewer sees them. If the weaver begins the tapestry at the bottom, what gets woven horizontally will appear horizontal, and so on. But perhaps the weaver may choose to weave their piece from what will be the side. When the piece is complete, the weaver will then turn the tapestry so that the side is now the bottom. Then, passes will

LEFT: From the side, as the weaver wove it

OPPOSITE: From straight on, as the viewer sees it
Untitled
Patricia McArthur
1988 | 8" × 8"

appear vertical and pick and pick will appear horizontal. It all depends on whether you weave from the bottom or from the side.

Often the weaver chooses to weave in the direction where there are more horizontal lines; these are simpler to weave. Human bodies and letters, for instance, are composed more of verticals than of horizontals and thus are easier to weave from the side.

Here are two images of Patricia McArthur's piece. On the left, you see how she wove it, from bottom to top. On the right, you see how it looks once finished, and then turned—what was the bottom is now the left side. To accomplish what she did, McArthur chose two basic techniques. In the image on the left, she wove alternating black and white passes (on the bottom), then wove black and then white, and then black and then white (and so on) pick and pick (on top). Now look at the piece once turned. McArthur has produced a profile.

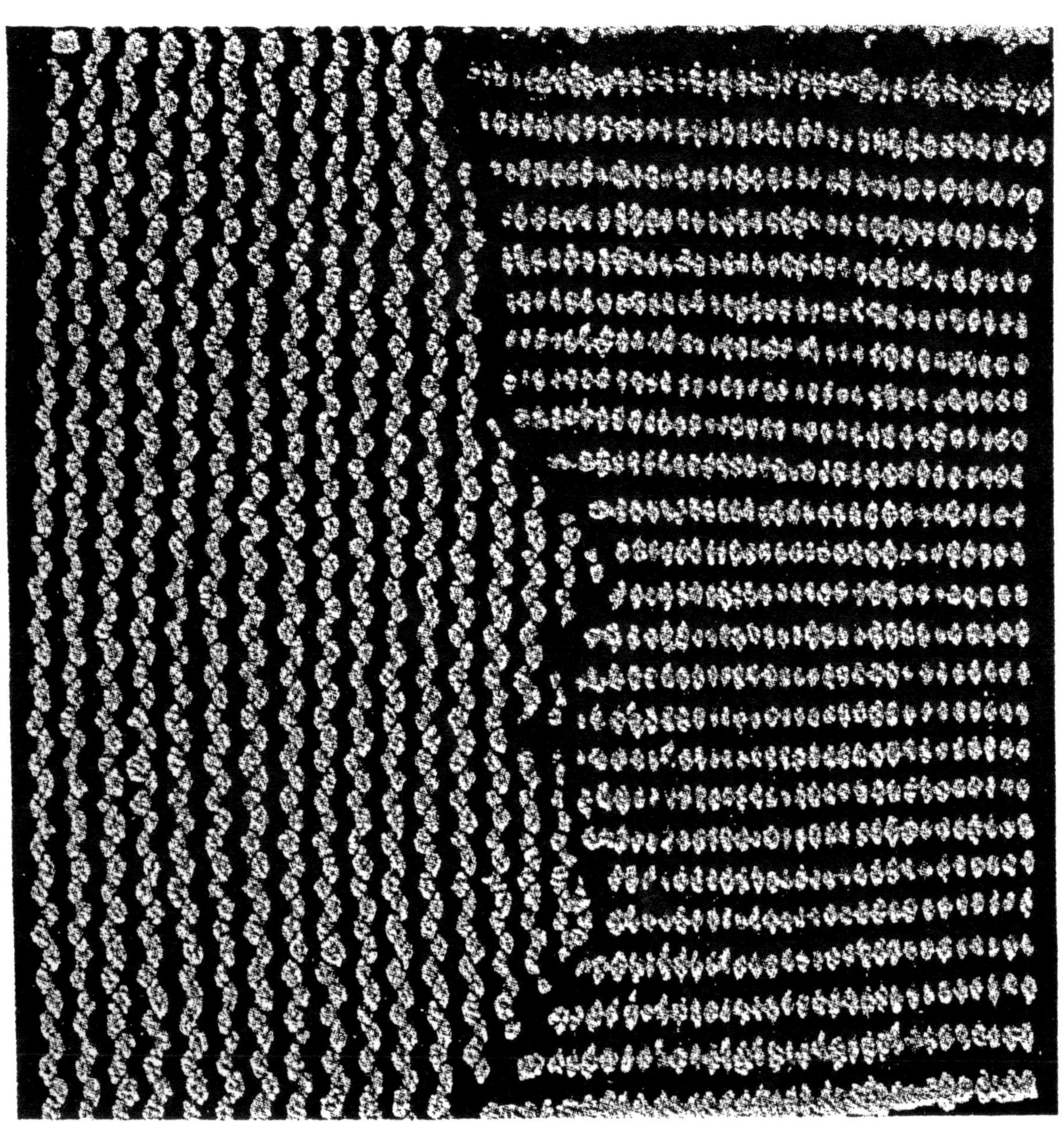

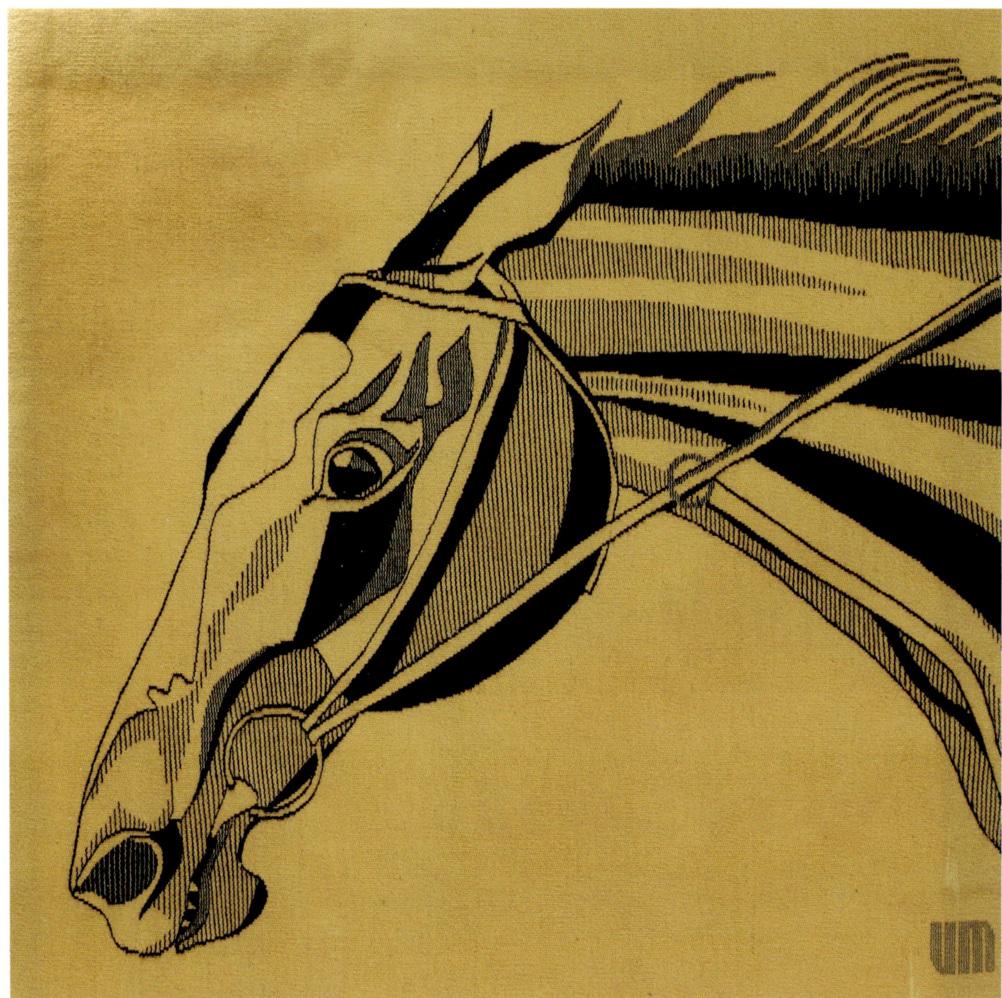

Flying without Wings
Ulrikka Mokdad
2009 | 33" × 33" | Norwegian Spælsau wool; linen warp

Ulrikka Mokdad's elegant and precise horse has a pattern of passes to emphasize movement and shadow. She began to weave from what is now the side. Note, for instance, the fine lines in the horse's cheeks and around his mouth.

Pat Dozier has woven her piece of pottery from the bottom and included large sections of horizontal black and white lines (the black sections are composed entirely of black weft). It was thought that pottery predated weaving—until researchers realized that pottery patterns came directly from the models of woven cloth. Her *dreamings* have jagged designs, a pot with lightning bolts.

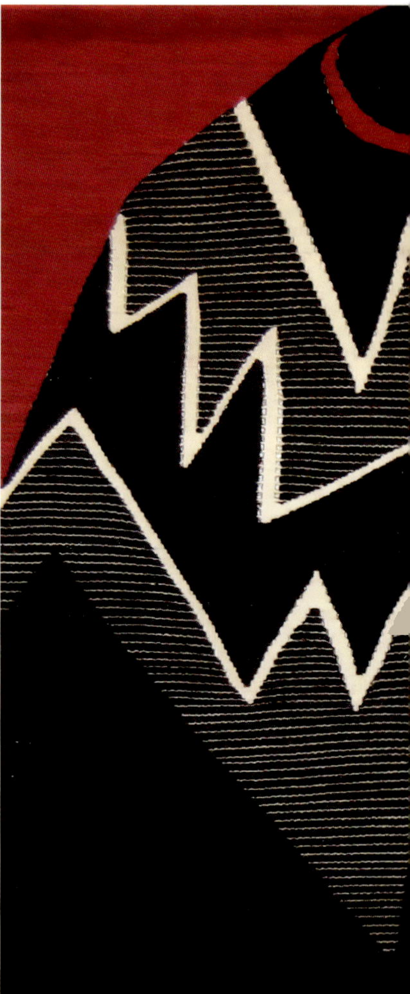

Pottery Dreamings
Pat Dozier
2007 | 36" × 36" | hand-dyed wool

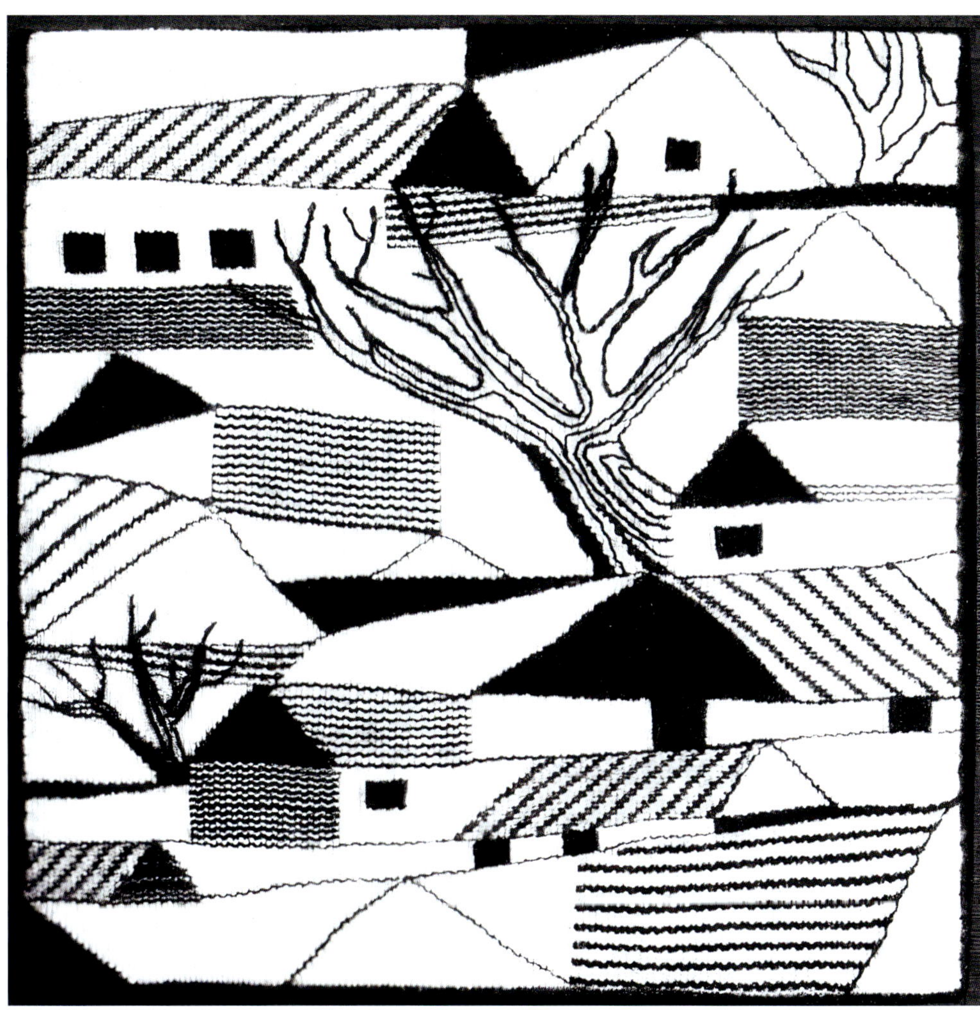

Winter's Silence
Becky Stevens
2016 | 15" × 15" | wool

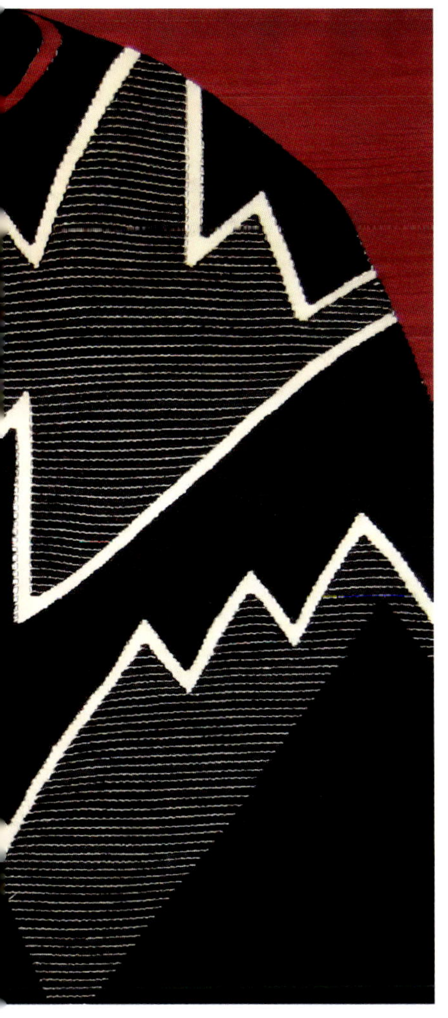

Becky Stevens limits her colors to black and white to show us buildings in winter, where a center tree dominates. Lines embellish roofs and trees. There is a quiet feeling to the image, in keeping with the title.

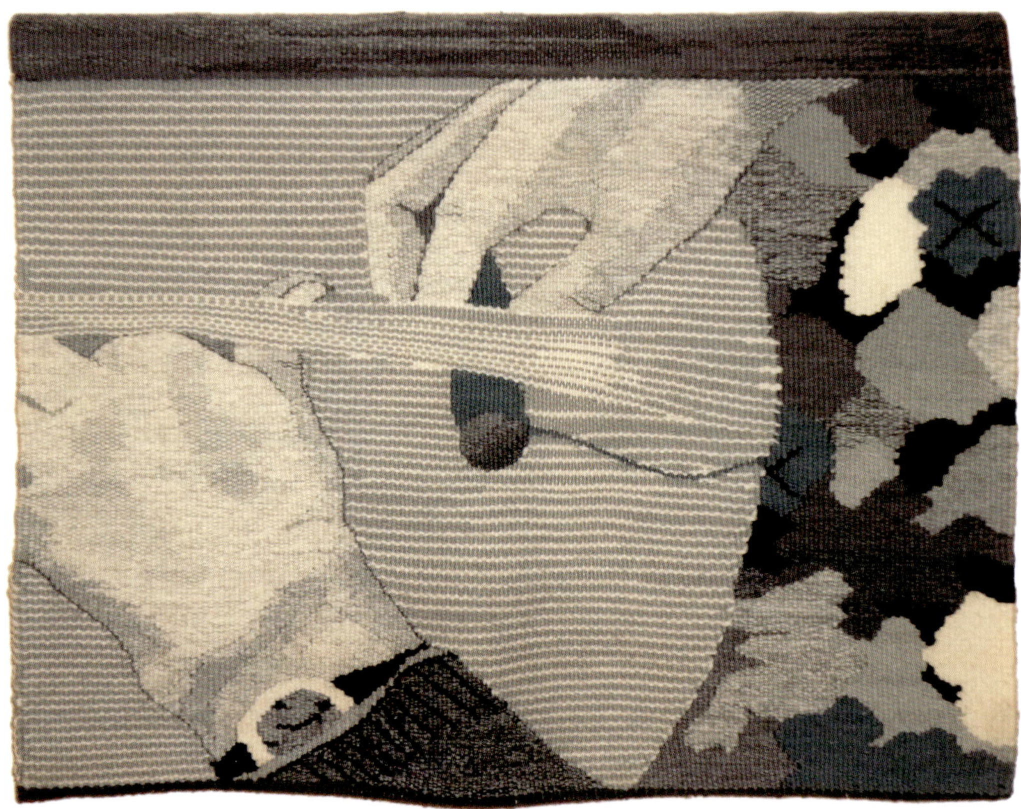

LEFT: *Weaving Hands*
Alison Jones
1995 | 21.6" × 27.5" |
wool

BELOW: *Grass II*
Ewa Latkowska-Żychska
1980 | 47.25" × 60.6" |
linen, cotton

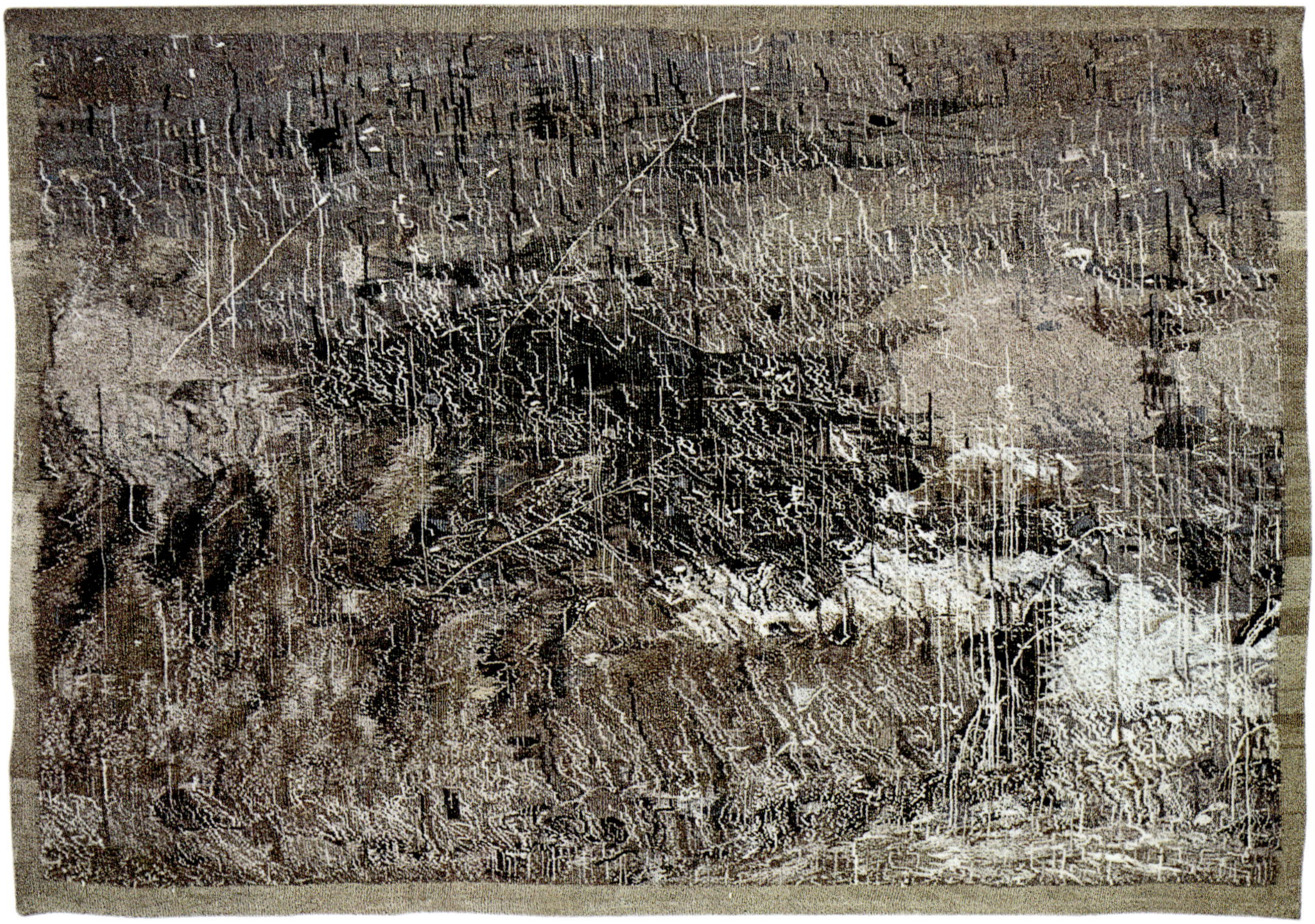

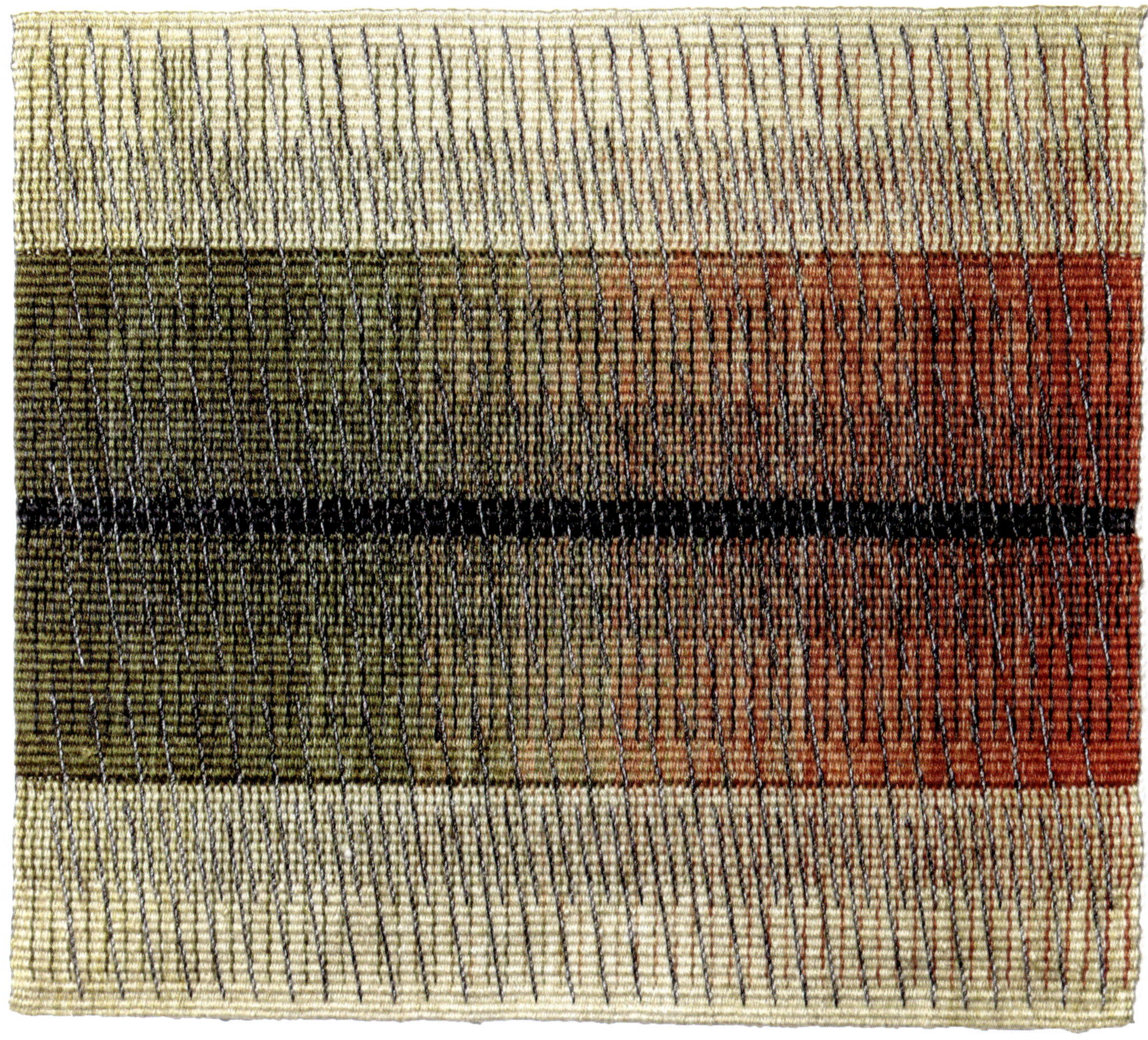

Essence #2, Red Flower Tree
Joyce Hayes
2021 | 7.5" × 8.75" | silk, rayon; linen warp
natural dyes

Alison Jones gives us her hands weaving and shows us how they manipulate some of the lines representing warp. A number of tapestry weavers have found the self-reference inherent in such work a perfect subject for their own tapestries.

Ewa Latkowska-Żychska's *Grasses* displays the tangle in a field, where each blade, each line, goes in another direction, including straight up.

Joyce Hayes has for years used very fine threads. Here she creates horizontal bands. The more you study it, the more you recognize the tapestry's complexity: Its lines are very straight, though not always vertical.

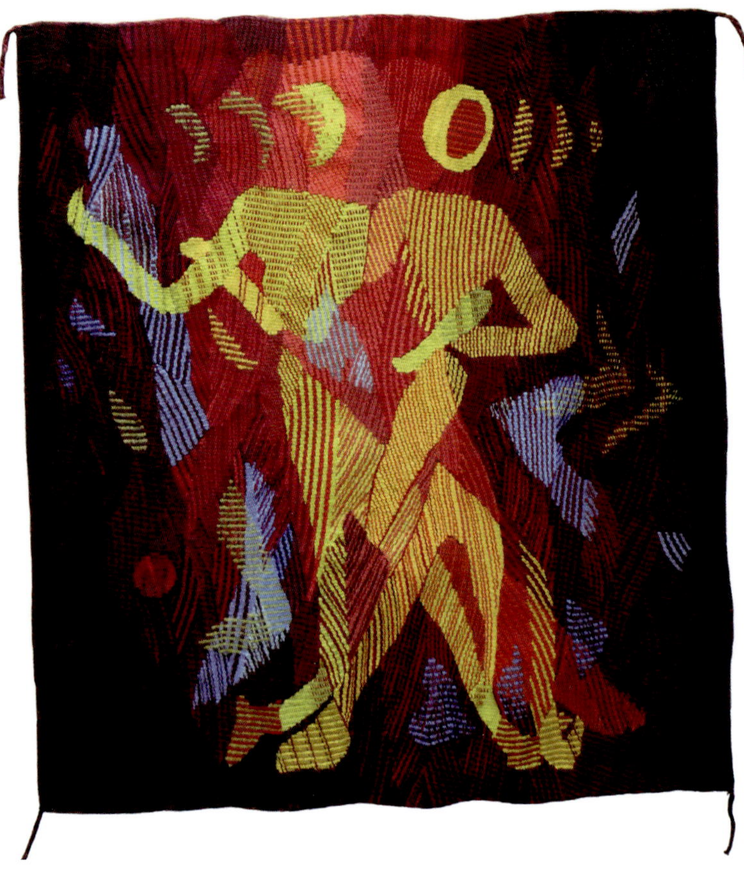

LEFT:
On a Dark Winter Night, Dancing the Blues
Stephanie Hoppe
2018 | 41" × 37"–38" | churro, borgmattgarn, yarn from Silvia Heyden's stash (a present from Silvia's daughter after Silvia's death)

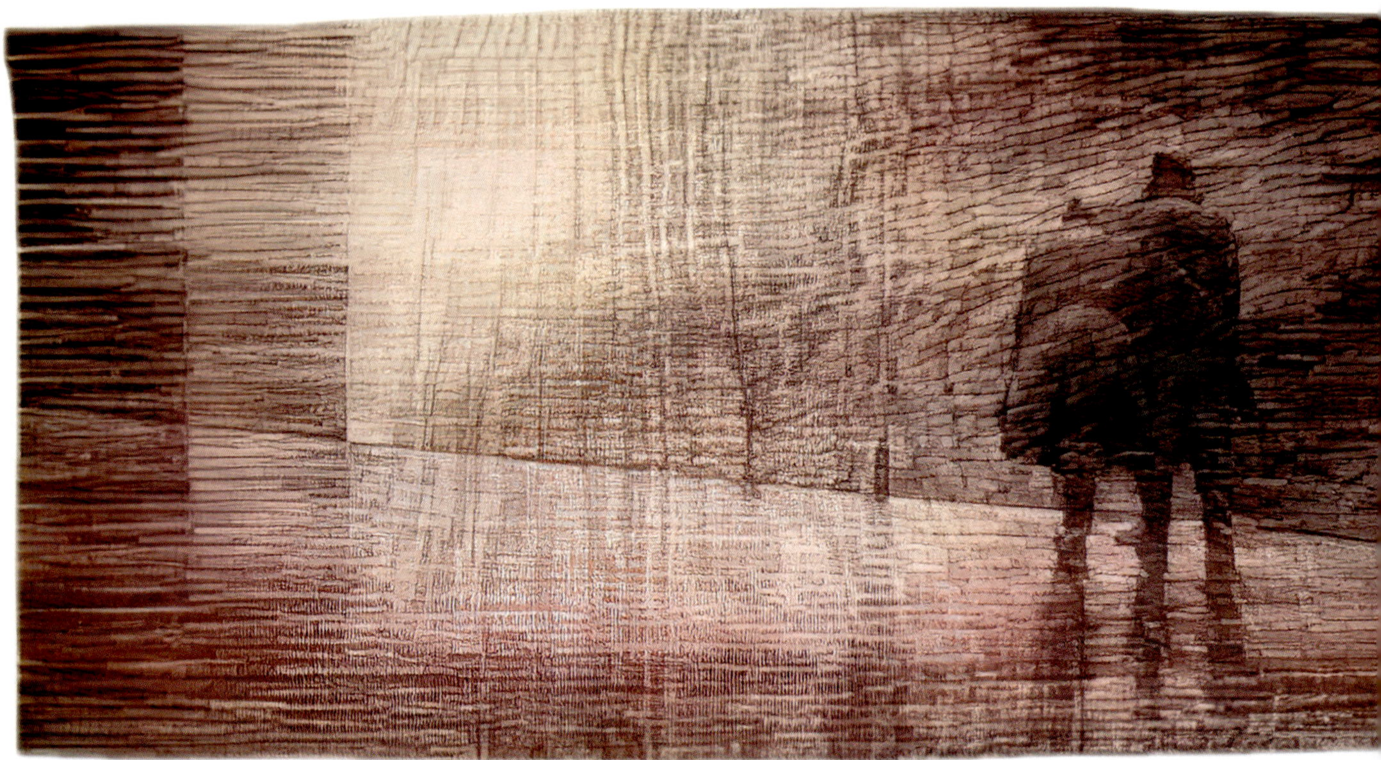

ABOVE: *Freedom*
Rosza Polgar
1999 | 31.9" × 78.75" | cotton, silk, wool

Stephanie Hoppe's bright figures, composed of diagonal lines, dance across the tapestry.

Rosza Polgar composed *Freedom* almost entirely of horizontal lines. The two figures move away from us into a dark unknown, to the side of a section where she has incorporated light, looking almost like a gauze curtain. The palette is otherwise restricted to a range of browns.

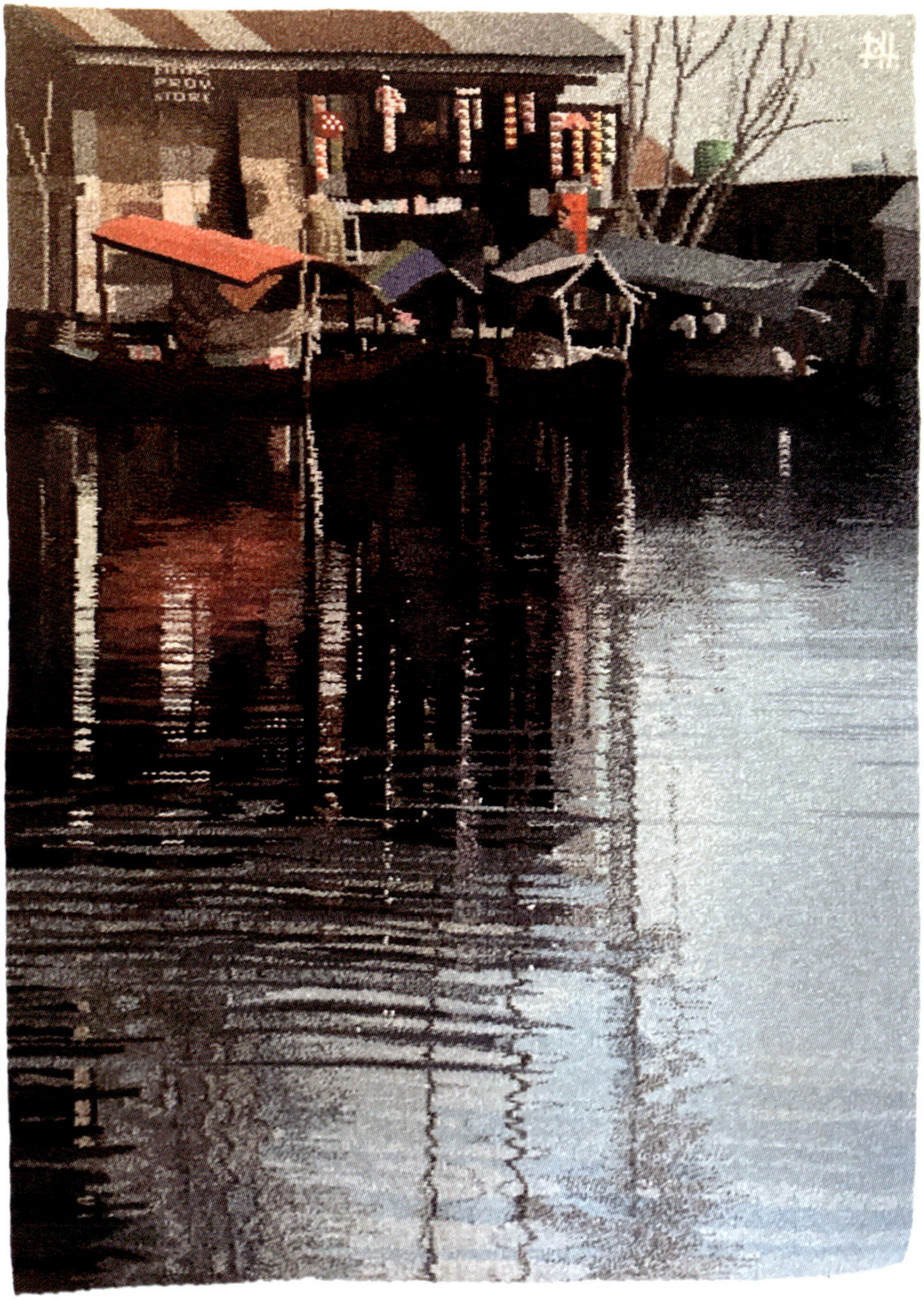

Srinagar Waterside
Peter Harris
2019 | 60" × 45" | wool; linen warp

A body of water often includes lines showing the effects of wind and tides. Peter Harris has included all of these and, more quietly, lines in the packets of snack food that hang vertically from the structure near the boats, and horizontal ripples that play against the vertical reflections.

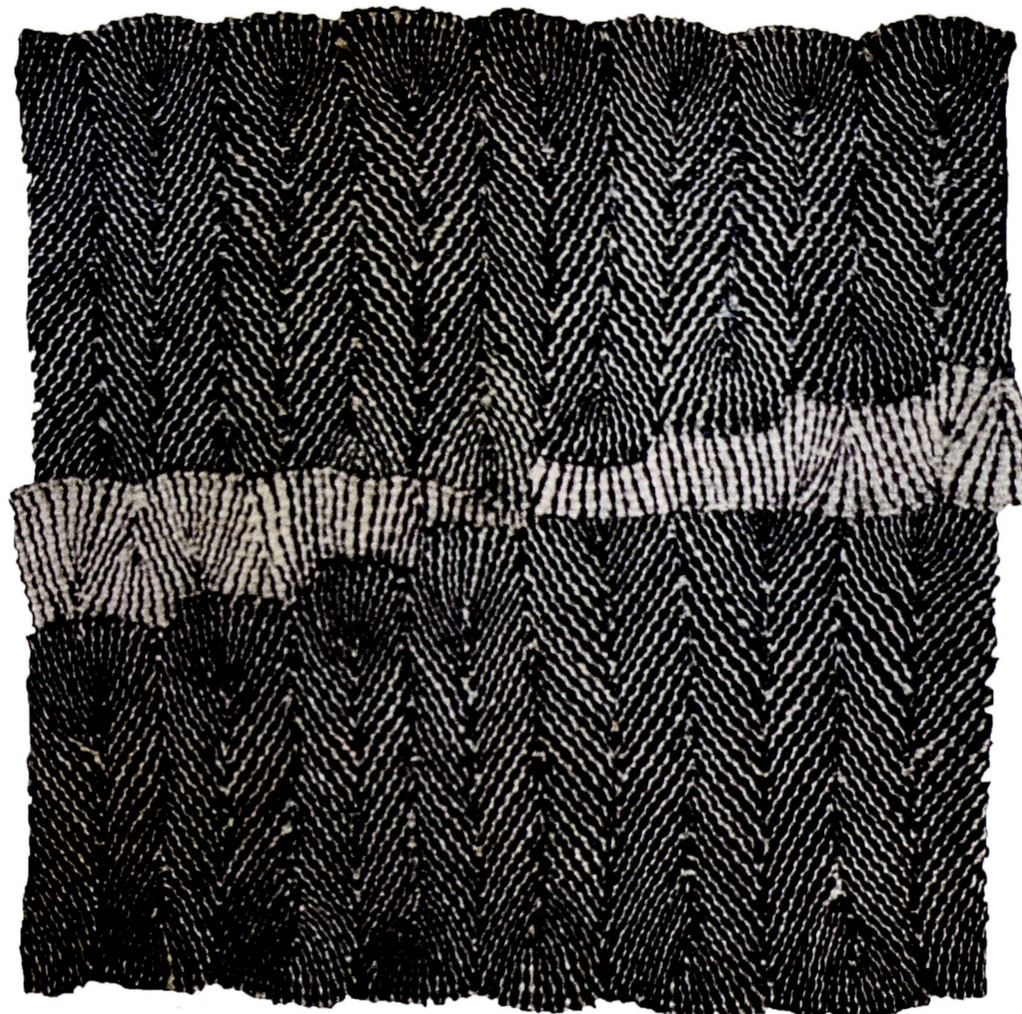

LEFT: *Reversion*
Silvia Heyden
1994 | 23.6" × 24.4" | linen, cotton; linen warp

BELOW: *Lineas Convergentes* (Converging lines)
Pamela Abad
2022 | 14.6" × 10.6" | Ecuadoran wool, cotton

During her long career, Silvia Heyden wove more than 500 tapestries. She also wrote a book about what she had learned, now a classic (*The Making of Modern Tapestry*). She has here woven alternating lines of white and black, at an angle, almost like feathers. This pure play, as she explores the relationship between warp and weft, somewhat resembles wedge weave. Heyden felt that each of her threads knew how to follow the lead of each of the others, even more than she knew how to make them do something. She did not worry about enforcing straight sides; she wanted the yarn to tell its own story. In some cases, the lines above continue movement from the lines below; in others, they reverse it.

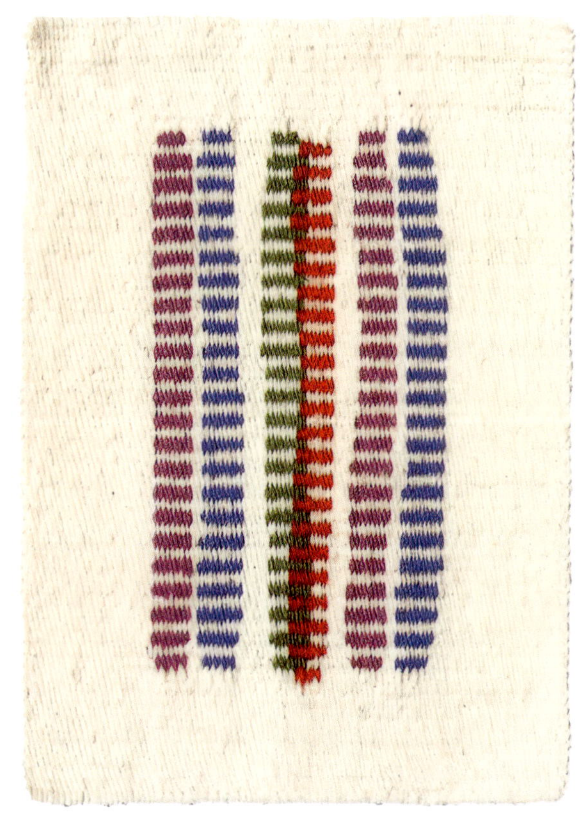

Emergence
Su Egen
2024 | 51.5" × 49.5" |
nötargarn; linen warp

Pamela Abad explores alternating picks, where groups of colored lines have an organic feel. Each set of color displays a slight but definite curve, with the central two meeting and seeming to embrace.

Su Egen achieves visual trompe l'oeil by careful weaving. She has long used highly organized bands of color in her work.

Patricia Williams incorporates areas with dark blue and white lines that work almost as though her bus has hair blowing in the wind. The dark blue and white sections contrast with the bright palette of the rest of the tapestry.

Lines build up a series of curves: Inga Skujina's figure lies along the slope of a mound. Nearby birds and insects fly. Each mound contains alternating vertical lines (pick and pick) to give variation to the ground. Her title (*Between*) cues us to see earth and sky or maybe even past and future.

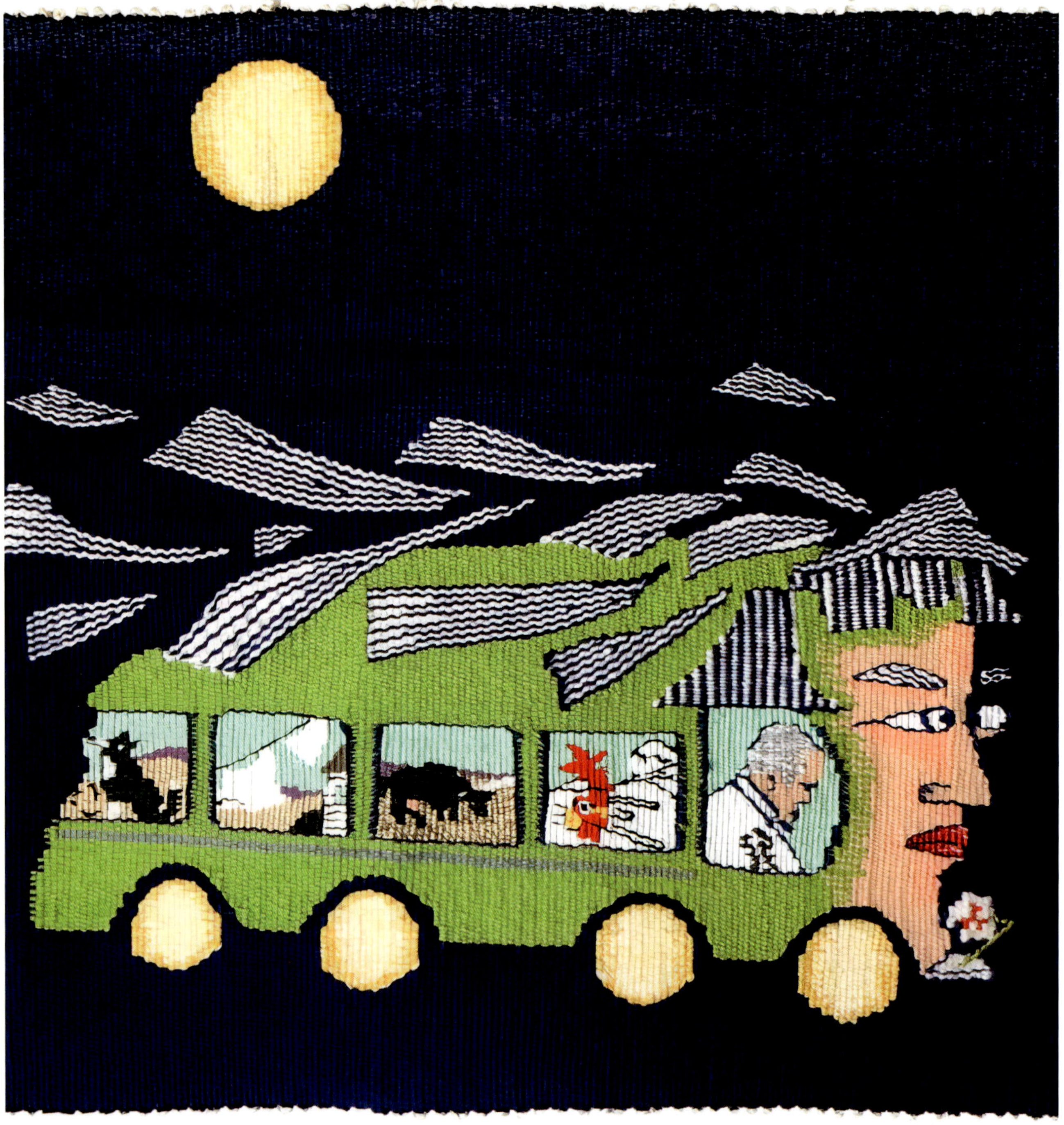

The Full Moon of July 1, 2015
Patricia Williams
2020 | 20" × 20" | wool; cotton seine twine warp
Photographer: Patricia Quinn Williams

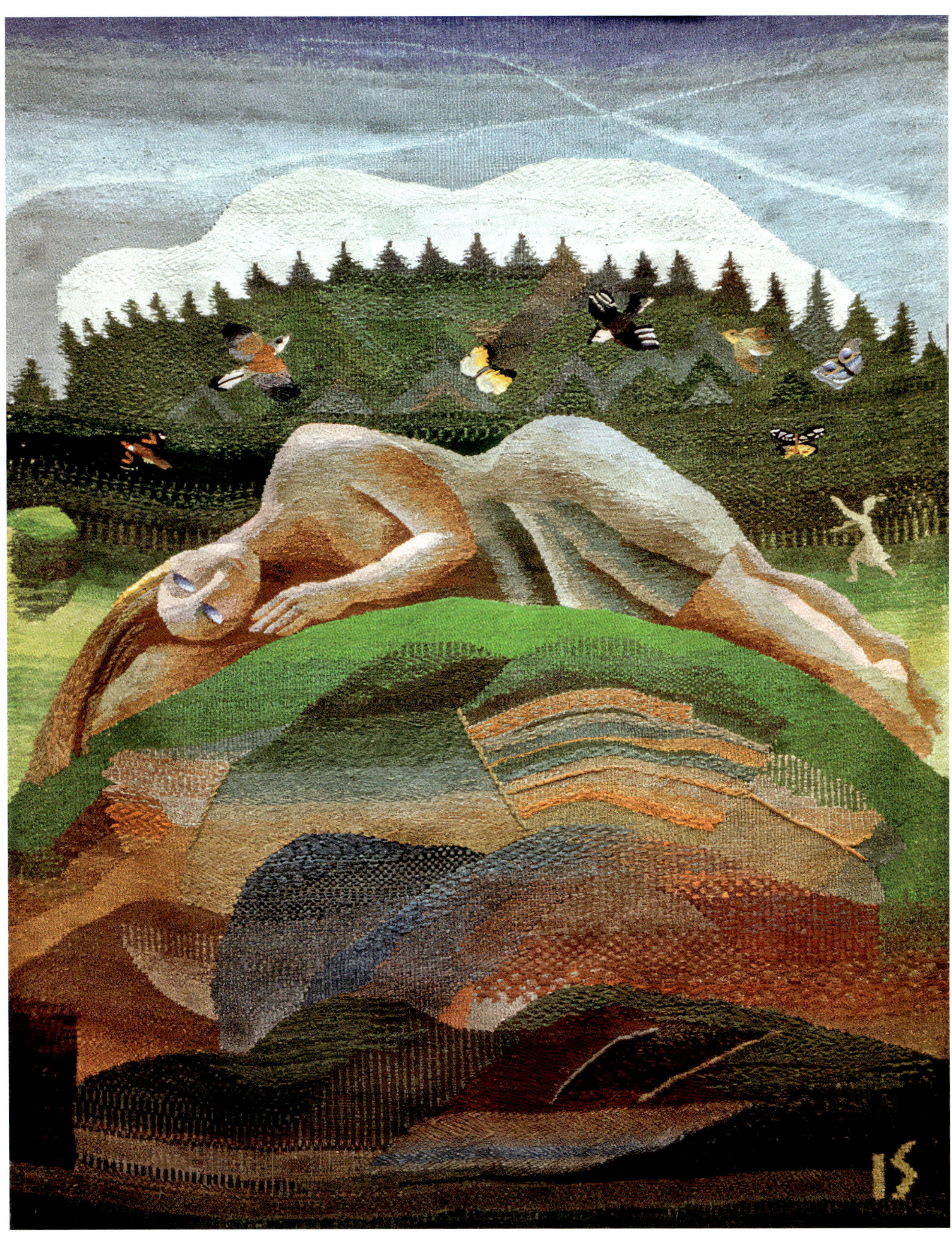

Vidzeme (Between)
Inga Skujina
1986 | 59" × 23.6" | wool, linen

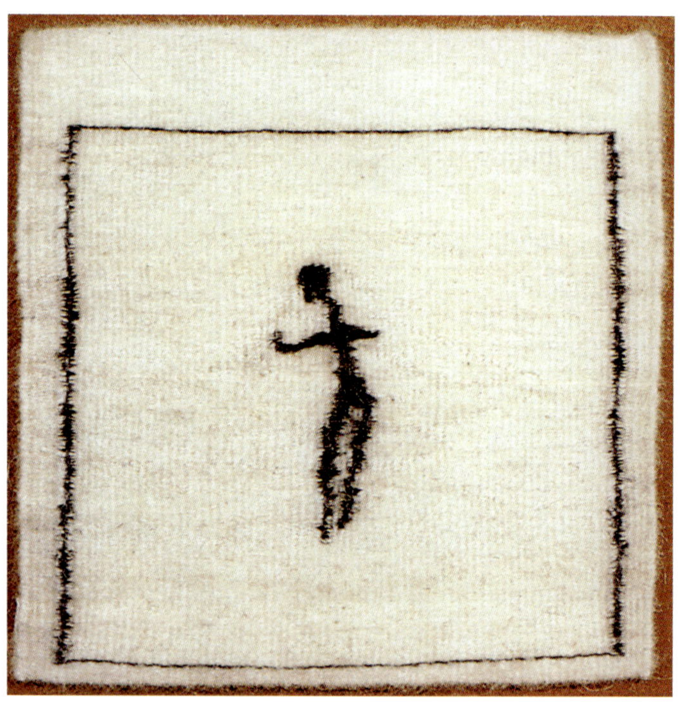

LEFT:
Dance of Life
Grażyna Brylewska
1996 | 7.9" × 7.9" | wool, cotton

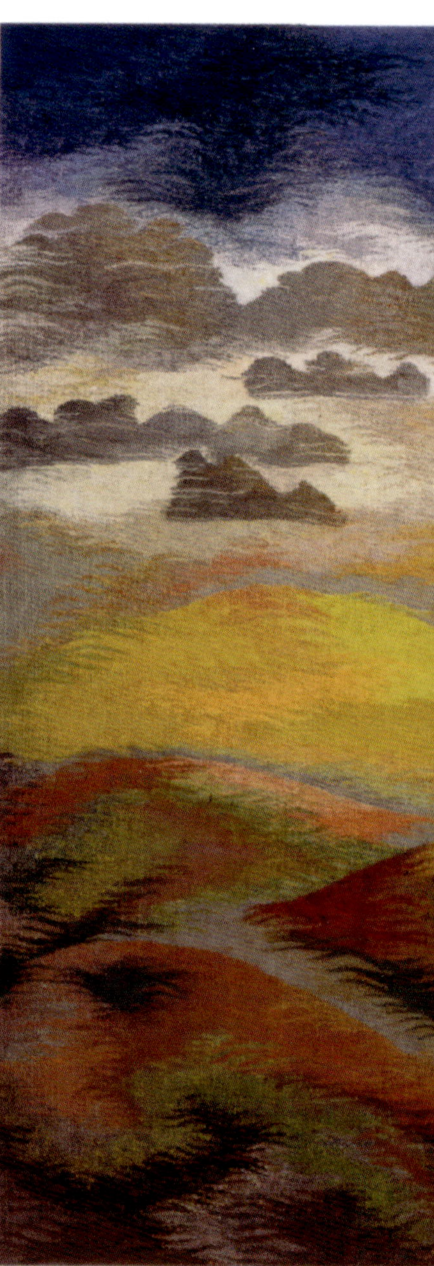

Something in this jittery minimalist tapestry that Grażyna Brylewska has woven speaks to the nature of the title—the figure dances and it looks delighted. The irregular edges of the lines add to the motion.

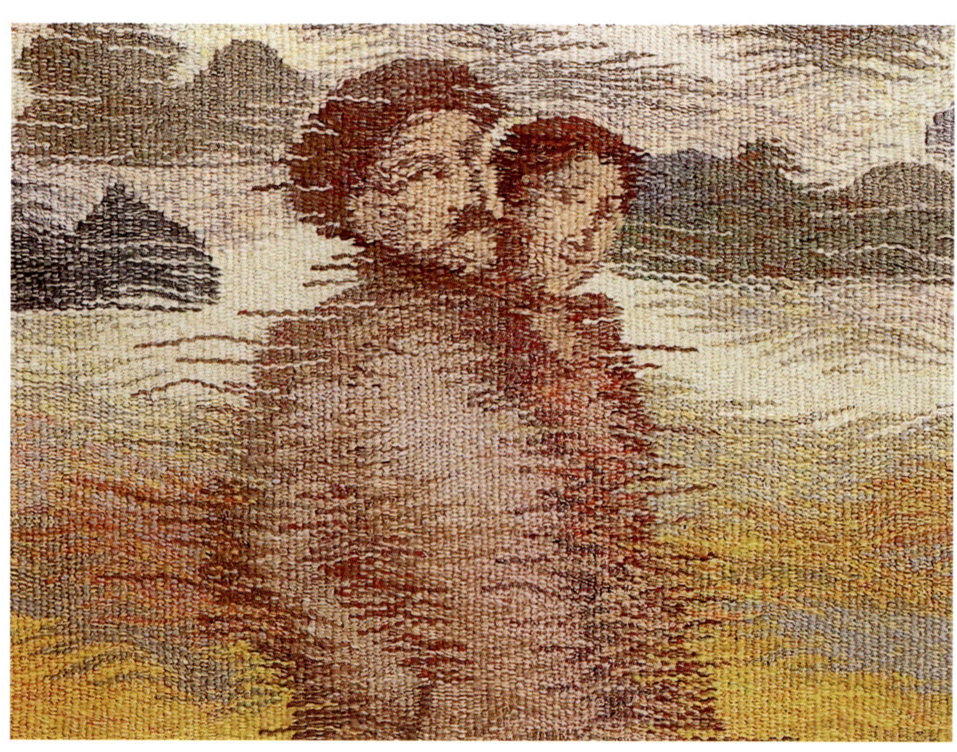

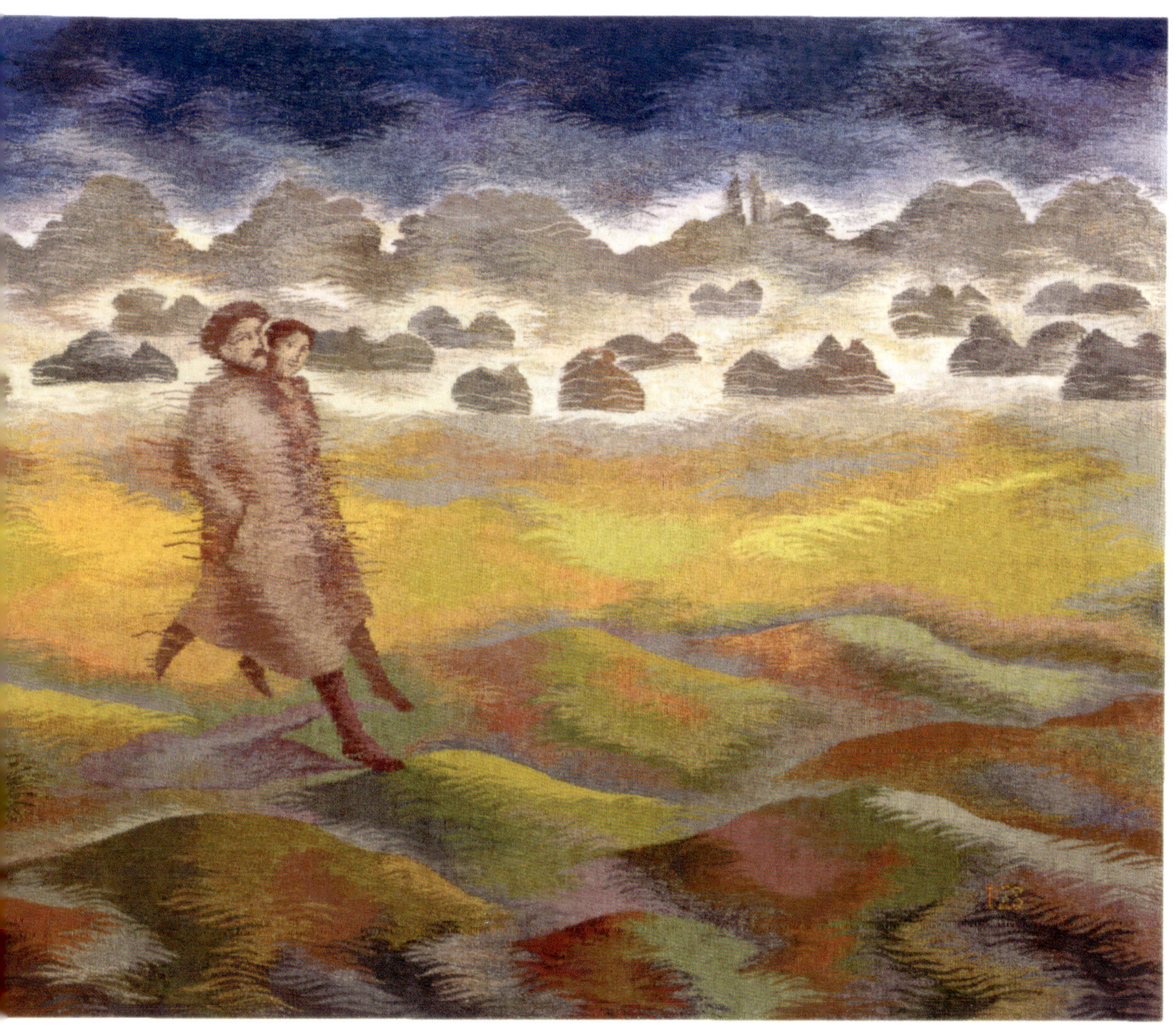

Skating on Mid-summer's Night
Zsuzsa Péreli
2003 | 43.3" × 66.9" | wool, silk

By contrast, Zsuzsa Péreli's couple are skating (almost floating) across the landscape; lines here also emphasize that impression of movement. In the detail opposite, you can see how well they work.

Ruth Manning employs wedge weave to create a series of triangles where we can see multicolored skin and clothing and a face looking straight out. Nothing (not even the vivid red stripe) is a single color. The scalloped edges along the vertical sides are typical of wedge weave.

Amanda Gizzi gives us a cook in a frenzy of making. In the cook's face, she incorporates vertical pale-orange lines to alternate with the off-white (pick and pick). She has outlined some of that wild ribbon. Is this pasta? She has devoted many pieces to food; they make me hungry.

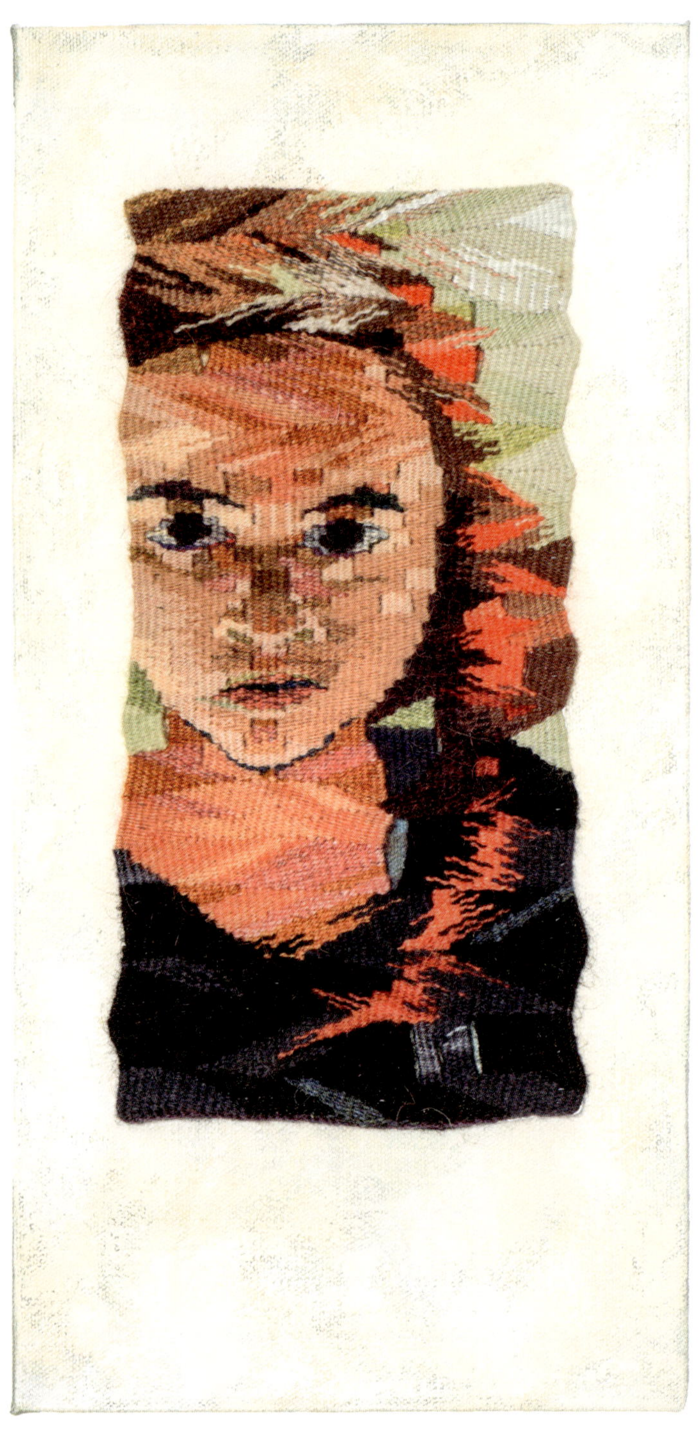

Red Stripe
Ruth Manning
2023 | 11" × 8" | wool; cotton warp

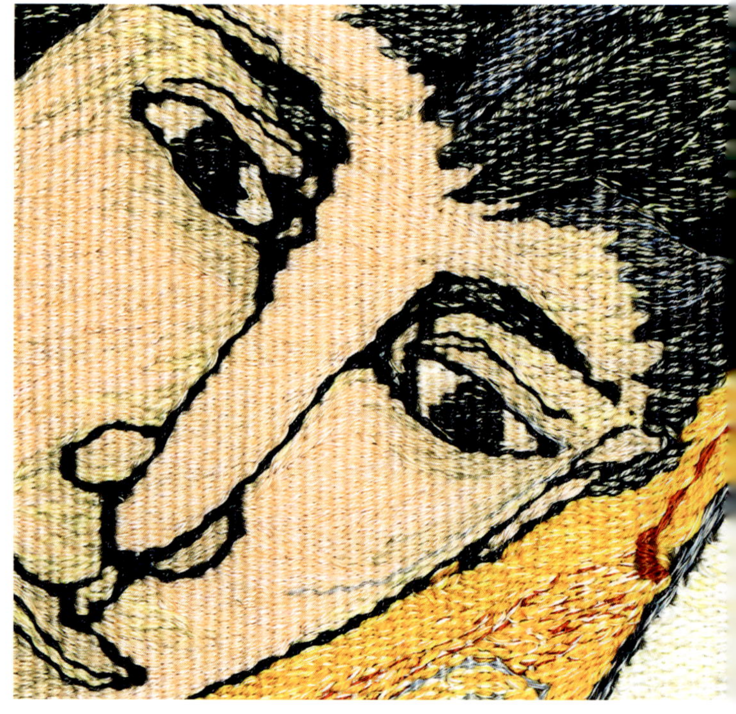

Sherbet Lemons, Sour Plooms (details)
Amanda Gizzi
2015 | 65" × 31.5" | linen, cotton, wool
Photographer: Joe Boyd

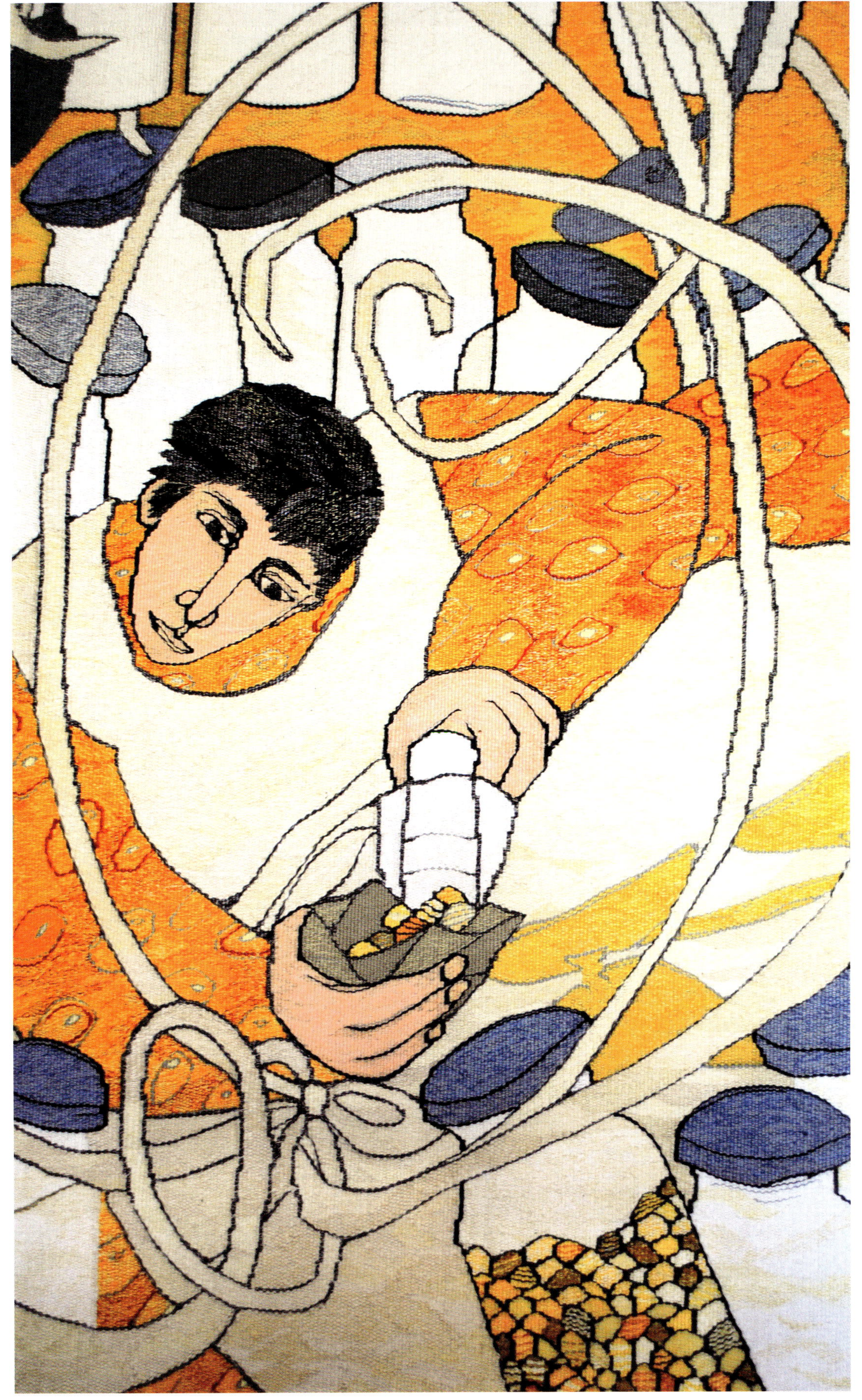

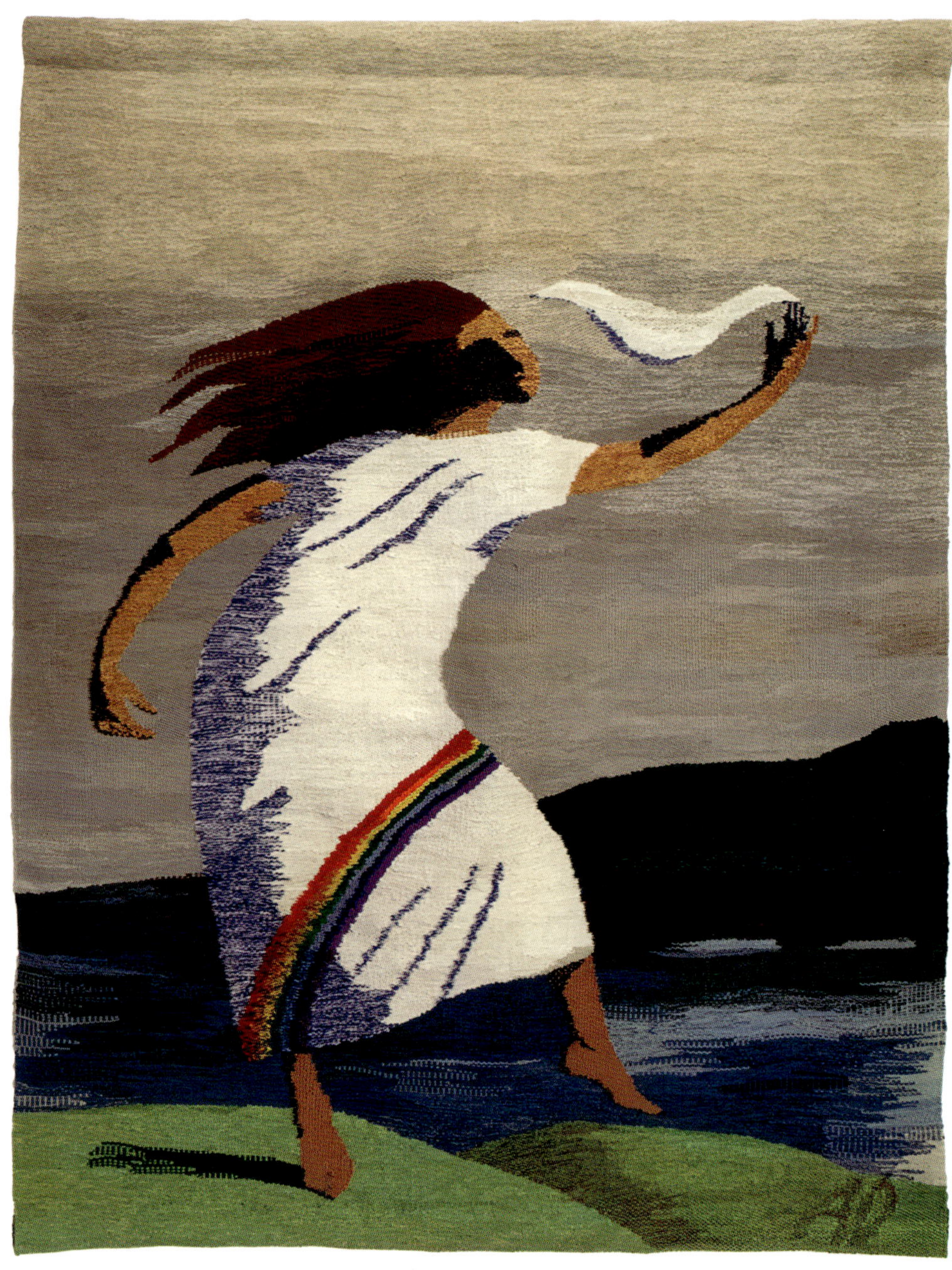

Light Dawned
Andra Dirina
2022 | 44" × 35.4" | wool, linen, synthetics

Andra Dirina's dark-blue lines in her figure's dress suggest shadows. The figure dances; a bird—or perhaps a handkerchief—flutters near her hand; the rainbow seems an image of peace. Against her motion, the landscape lies still.

Kate Derum's irregular thick lines give us several versions of an outlined sitting figure, like a series of sketches.

Julie Davies's frame around trees in a field in front of a gray sky is composed of irregular thick lines. She has woven what feel like pools of color.

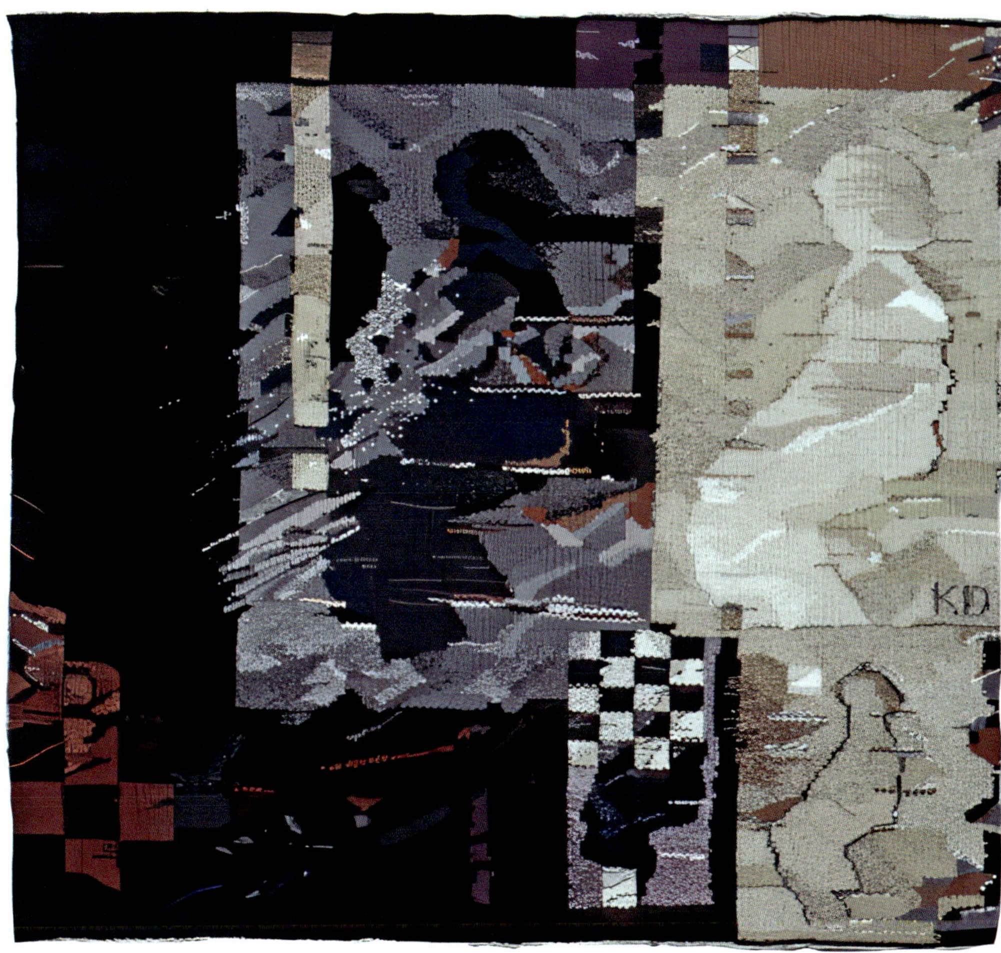

Waiting
Kate Derum
1993 | 30" × 33.1" |
wool, cotton, linen

BELOW: *The Clearing*
Julie Davies
2018 | 11.8" × 22" |
wool, linen; cotton warp

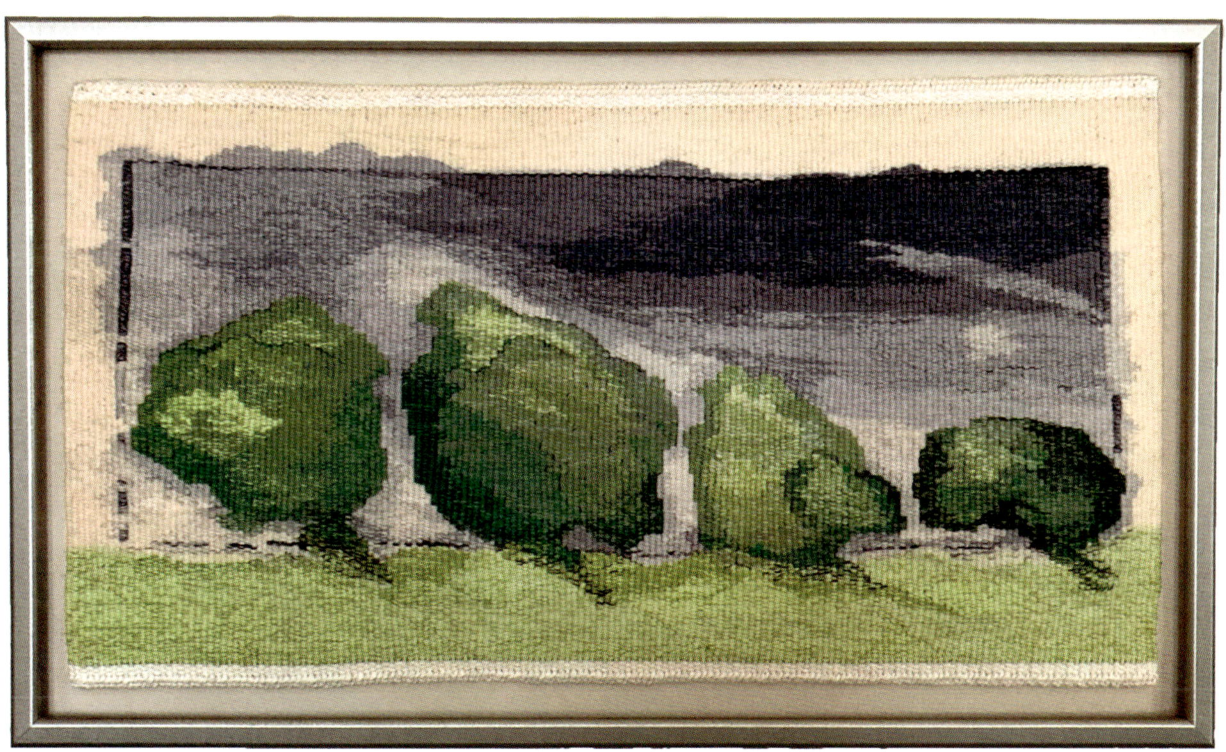

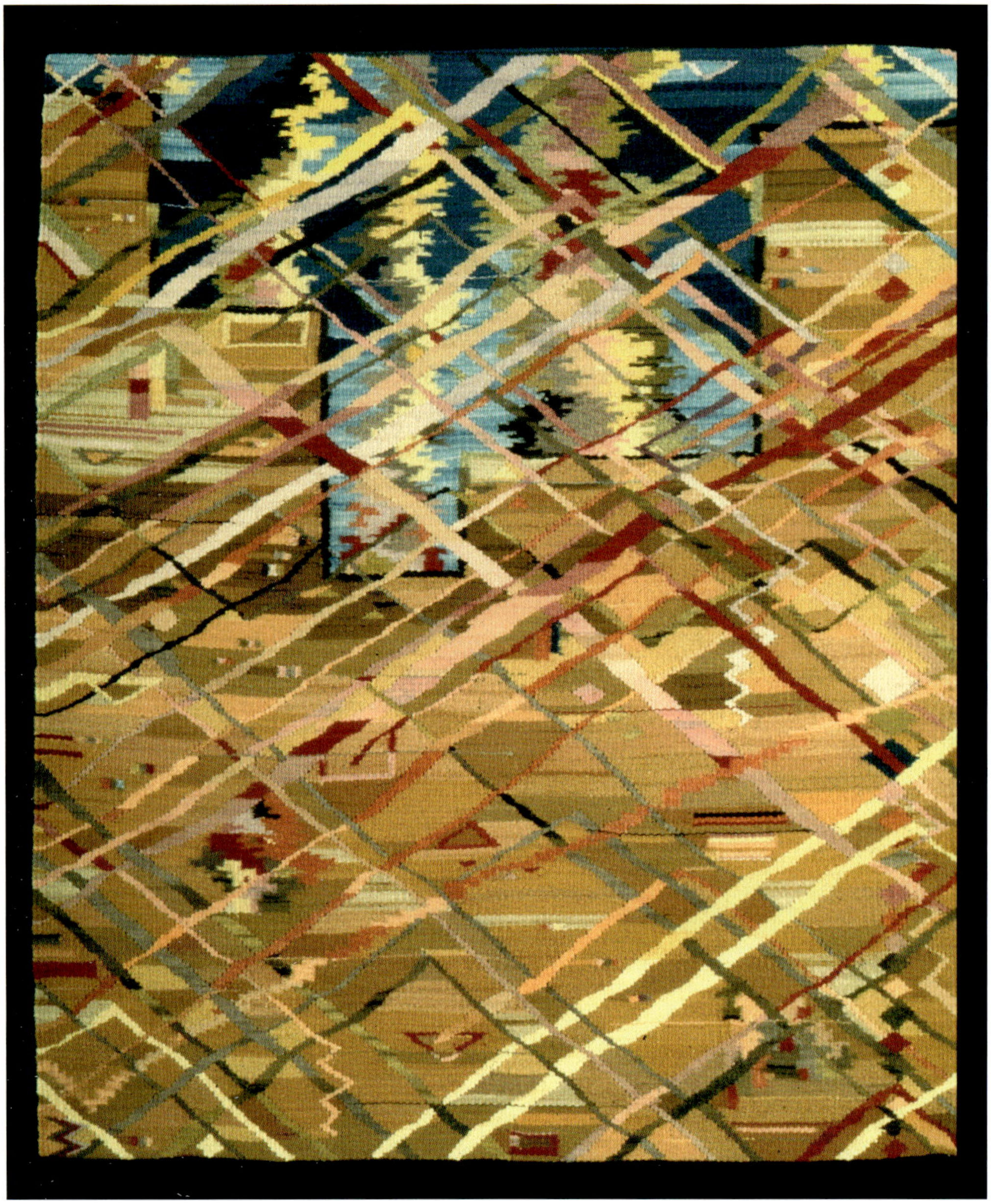

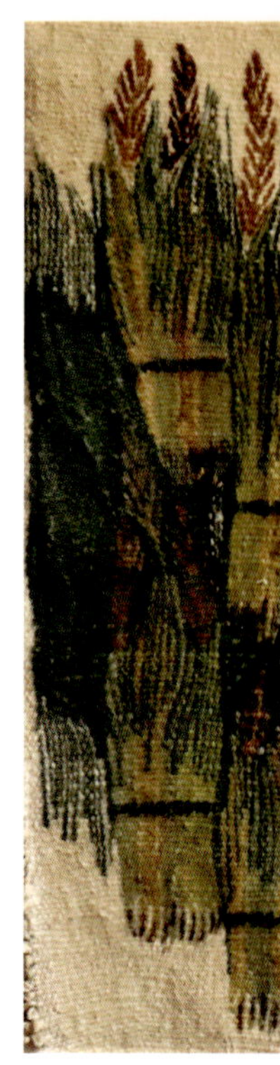

ABOVE: *Acoma Sky*
Donna Martin
1992 | 44"× 39" | wool, mohair

OPPOSITE, TOP: *Donkey in a Rice Field*
Ashour Meselhi
1971 | 18.5" × 42.5" | wool
Courtesy of Wissa Wassef Art Center, Egypt

OPPOSITE, BOTTOM: *Quetzalcoatl*
Marcelina Mendoza
2010 | 23.6" × 15.75" | silk; cotton warp

Donna Martin wove from bottom to top, line by line. She reincorporated the ends of her weft threads back into the weaving. You could never be sure which was the front of her work and which was the back. Her designs are always complex, lines crossing lines, sandy and brown and blues, colors she dyed herself.

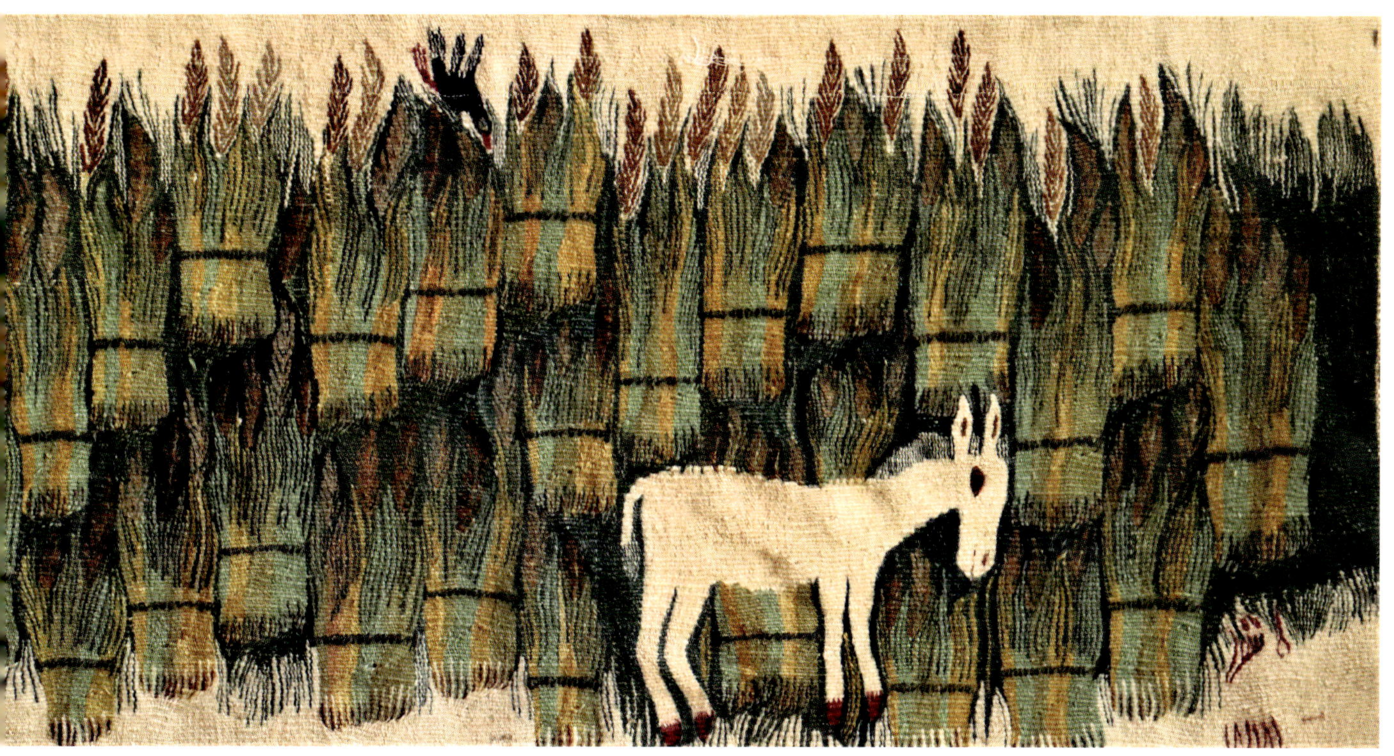

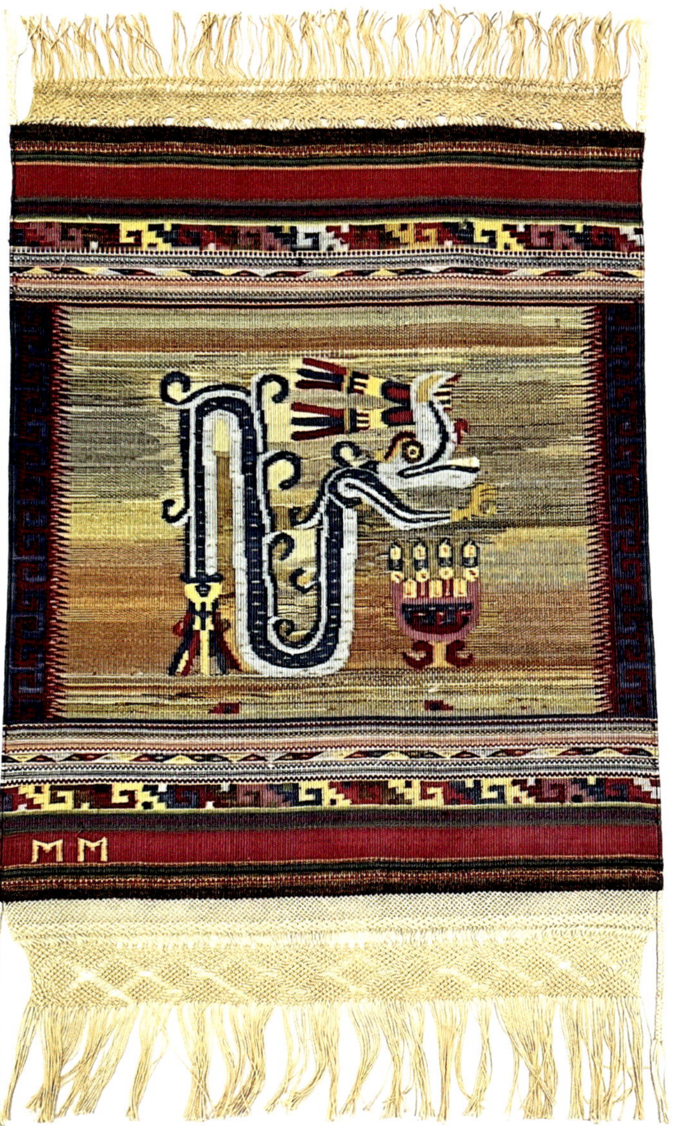

The Wissa Wassef studio in Egypt, first established by the architect Ramses Wissa Wassef in the 1950s, continues to contribute its locally-based weavers to the world. From the first, youngsters here learn the basics and do not use cartoons: before they begin, they do not have a written map for how and what they will weave. They work from their instincts. Ashour Meselhi's donkey is enveloped in the greenery, lines next to lines, of a rice field.

Marcelina Mendoza's marvelous god is embedded in horizontal lines and includes the elaborate finishing of the warp above and below the image. Mendoza has used vegetal dyes. Quetzalcoatl, the plumed serpent, has a major role in Zapotec mythology.

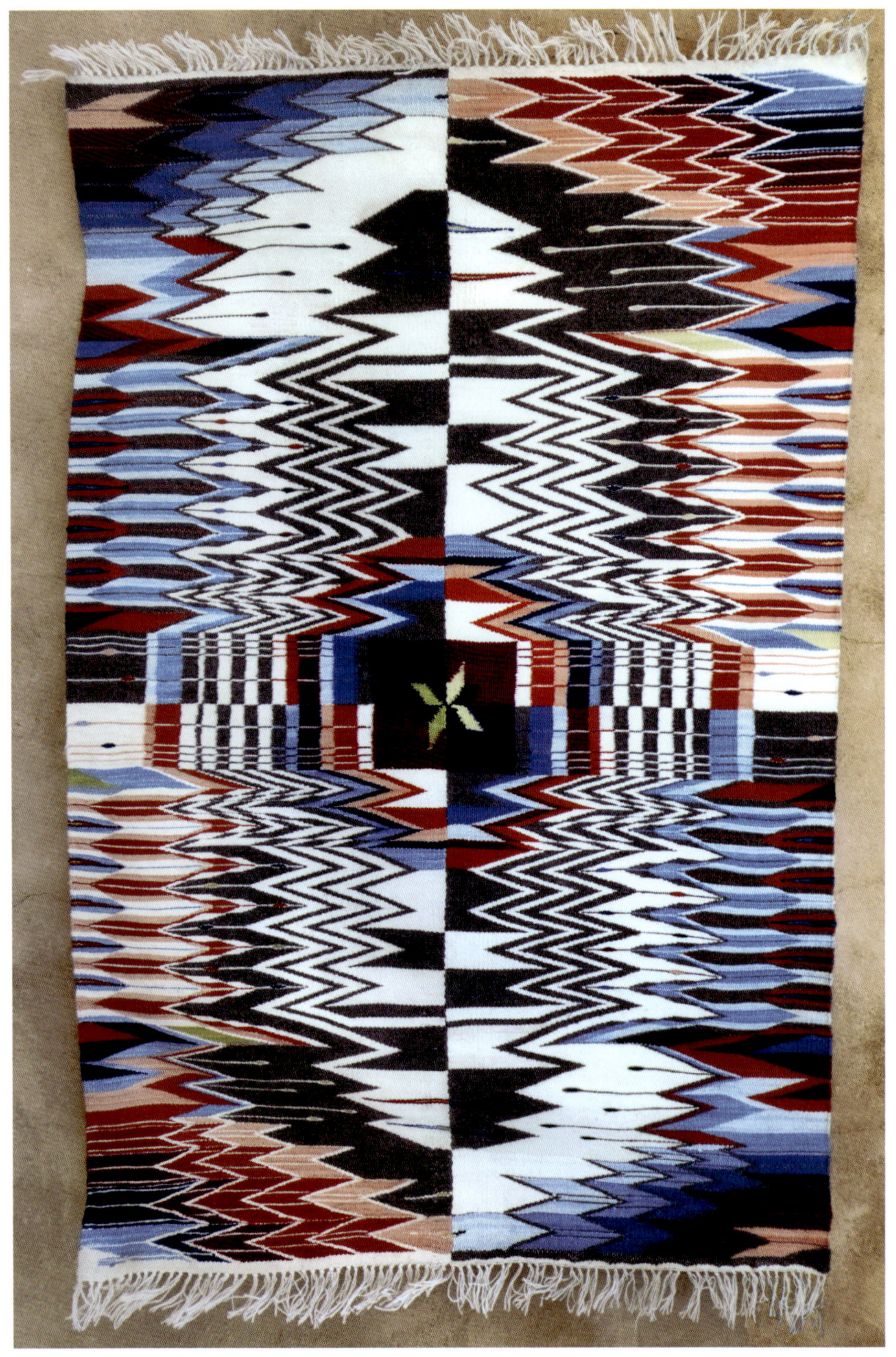

Taste the Tempest
Emily Trujillo
2023 | 2 pieces, 60" × 20" each section | wool, commercially and hand-dyed

Emily Trujillo, one of the latest generation of Chimayo weavers, uses line to make a series of bold diagonals in two pieces that she subsequently assembled into one. Shapes echo shapes; the lines meet each other exactly; the angles are handsome. For all their off-centered energy, the whole is in balance.

Johanna Schütz-Wolfe's woman has a body composed of vertical lines, almost as though she is a mummy, wrapped in layers of cloth.

Michelle Lester used similarly fine lines to delimit shapes, like boxes. Her landscape speaks of the Southwest, though she was born in Cleveland and lived most of her life in New York City.

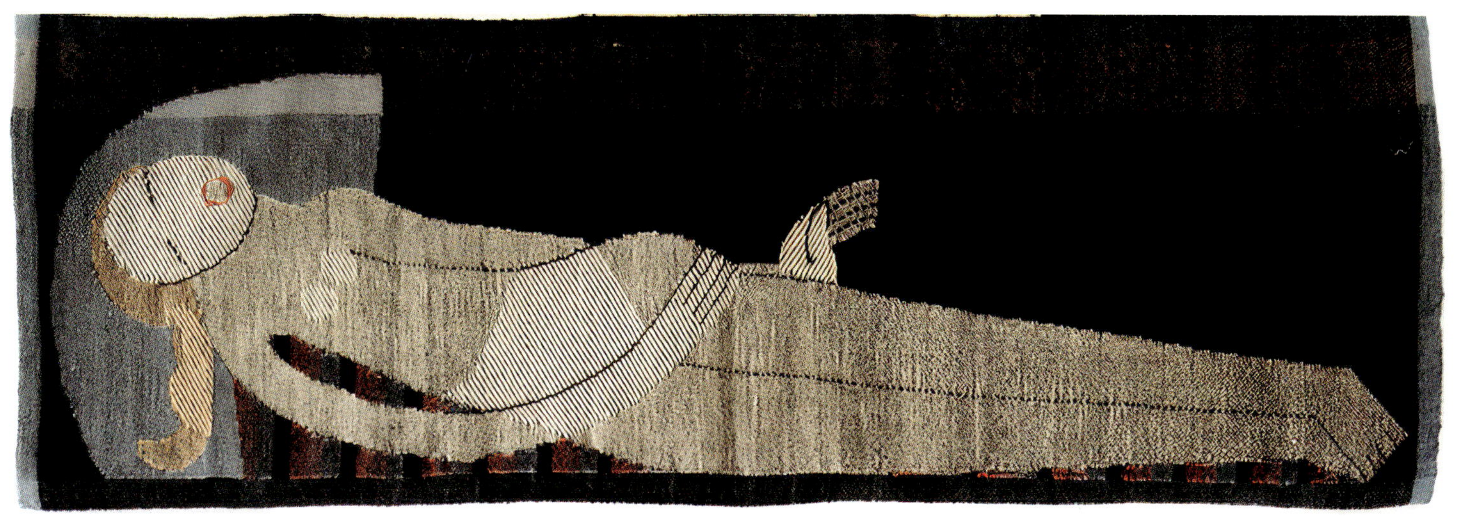

ABOVE: *Liegende* (Recumbent woman)
Johanna Schütz-Wolfe
1924 | 27.5" × 59" | wool

BELOW: *Yellow Boxes*
Michelle Lester
1977 | 53" × 72" | wool

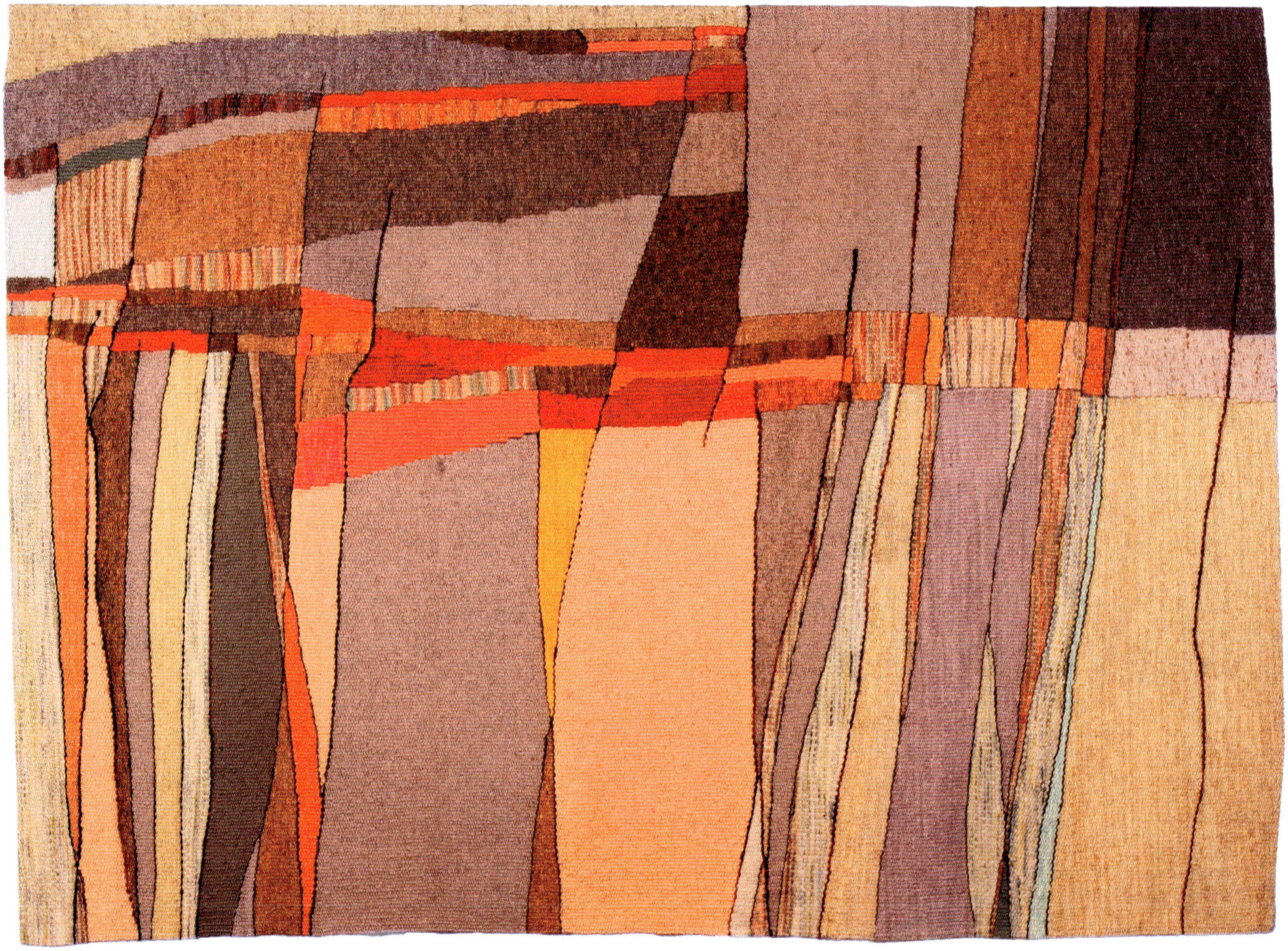

Jane Brunning connects her subject to the culture of the Mbuti tribe, one of the Indigenous Pygmy groups in Congo. Ituri is the name of their home, the rainforest. These repeated figures are very expressive, much more so than simple stick figures. Ultimately, the figures become marks of pure pattern. Having woven from the side, Brunning lets her warp drift off the left edge, almost like hair on a head.

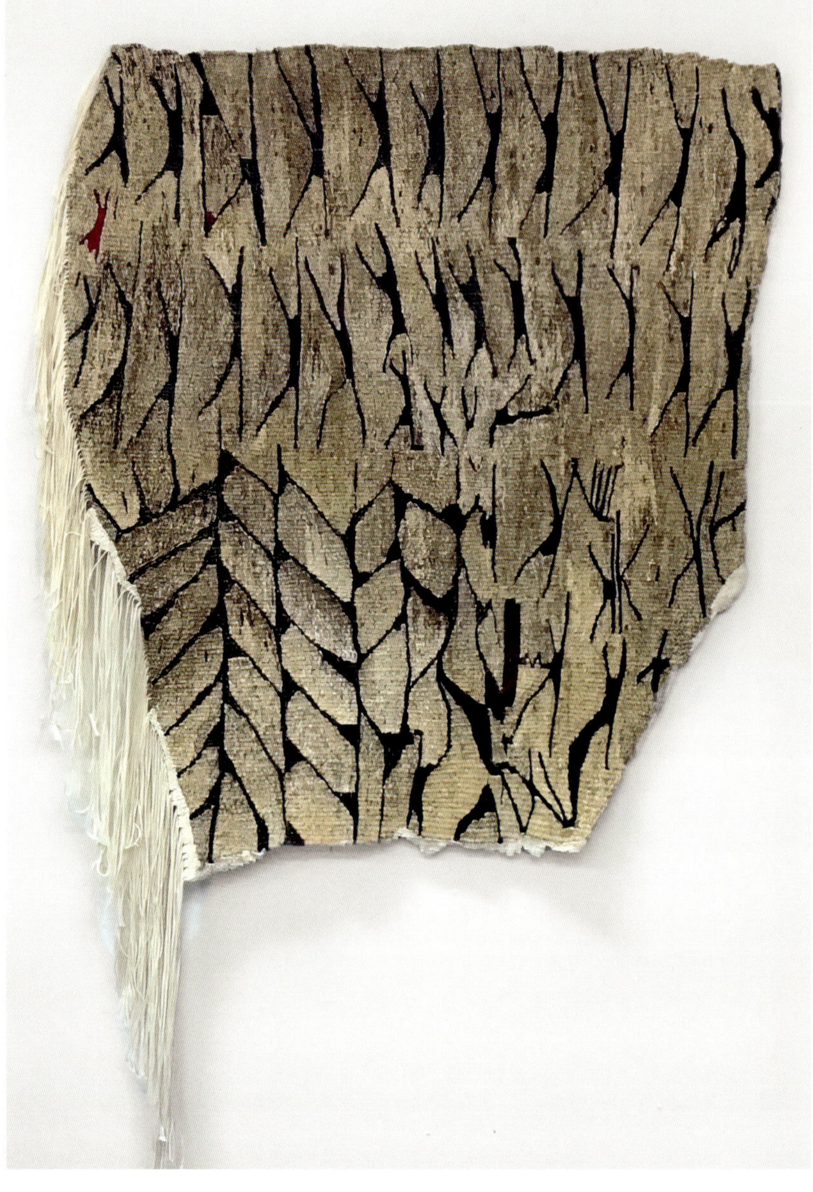

ABOVE: *Ituri*
Jane Brunning
2018 | 35.4" × 33.5" | hemp, nettle, rough silk, linen; cotton warp

Henrique Schucman's figures, in their limited palette of blacks and browns, are created by lines. They have facial tattoos, their hairstyle has wonderfully rendered bangs, and the back wall is covered with diamond shapes like some variety of twill.

Ieva Krumina's slender stick figures, composed of simple lines, walk up the sides of the moth wings. She says that she was inspired to weave the piece when "I once met a butterfly whose wing coloring resembled a map of the world."

OPPOSITE, TOP: *Los Indios* (The Indians)
Henrique Schucman
1998 | 39.4" × 47.25" | linen; cotton warp

OPPOSITE, BOTTOM: *We. They.*
Ieva Krumina
2006 | 50" × 83"

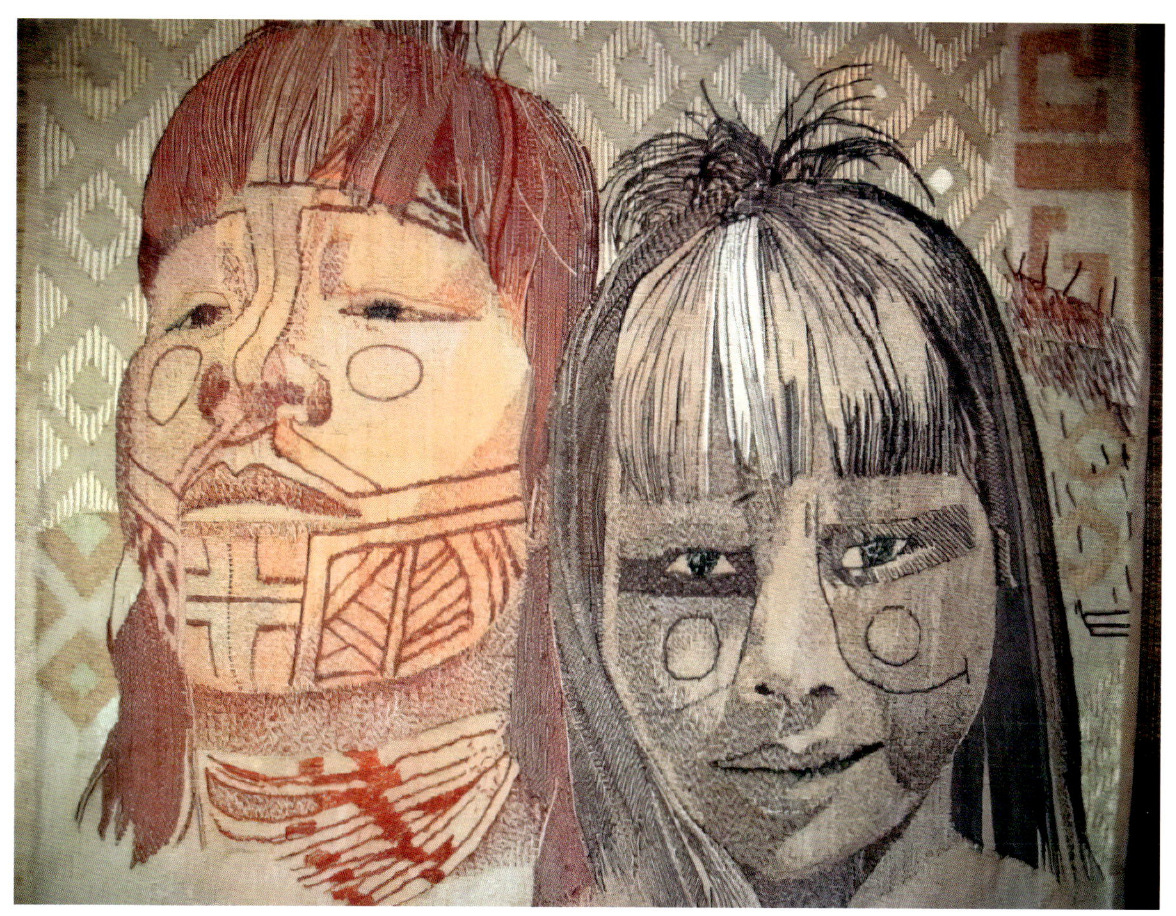

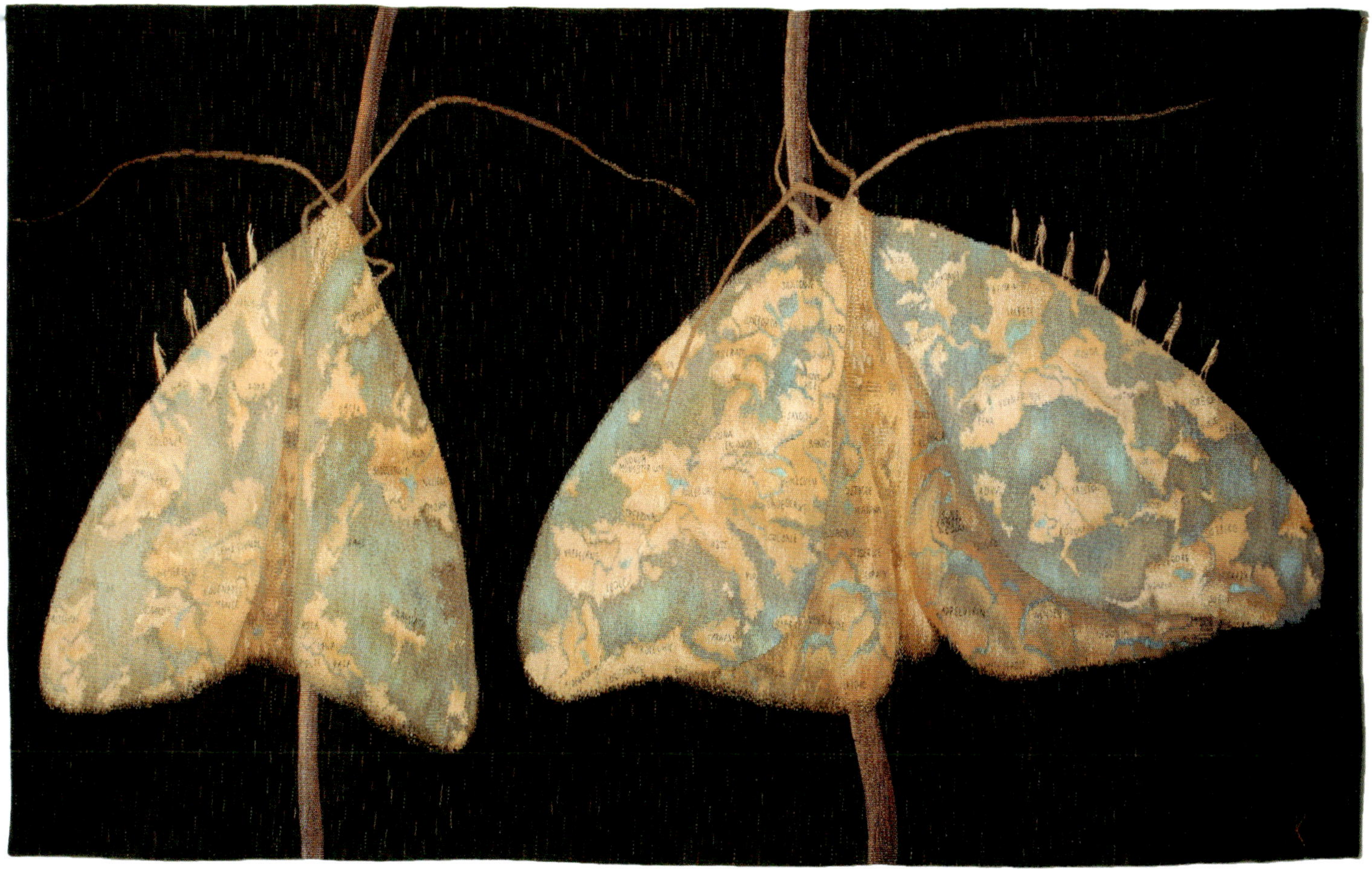

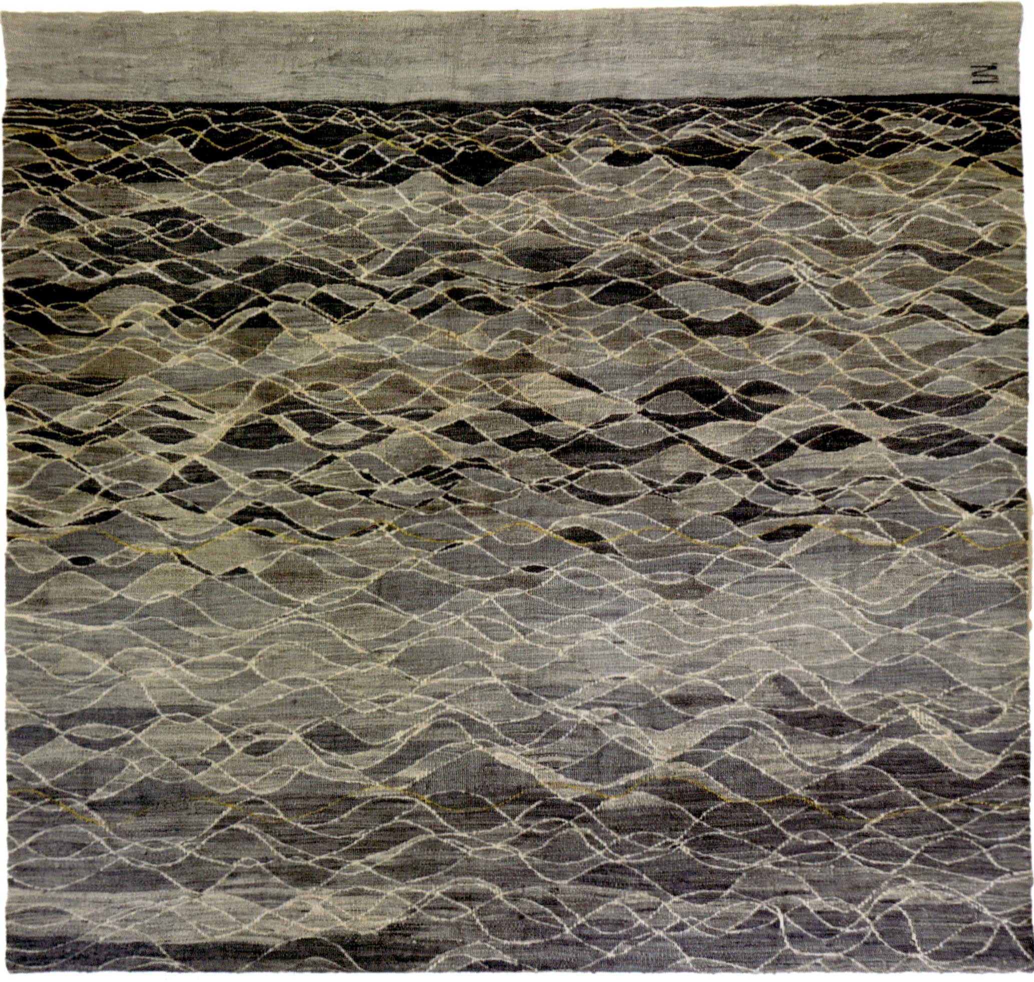

The Song of the Ocean
Inge Nørgaard
1999 | 53" × 58" | wool; cotton warp

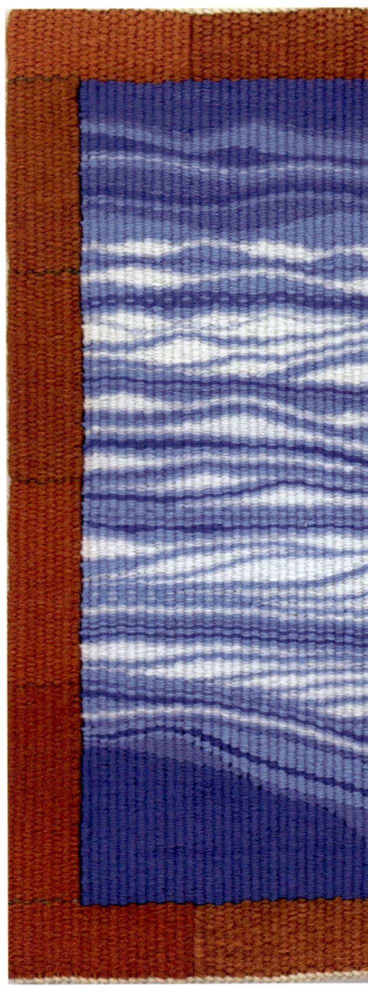

Wangaratta Water
Joy Smith
2020 | 7.9" × 7.9" |
cotton embroidery thread;
cotton seine twine warp

Inge Nørgaard's ocean has lines to define its marvelous curves, its waves and currents, as the colors shift from section to section.

The lines of Joy Smith's blue and white speak of the sea and the currents beneath the surface.

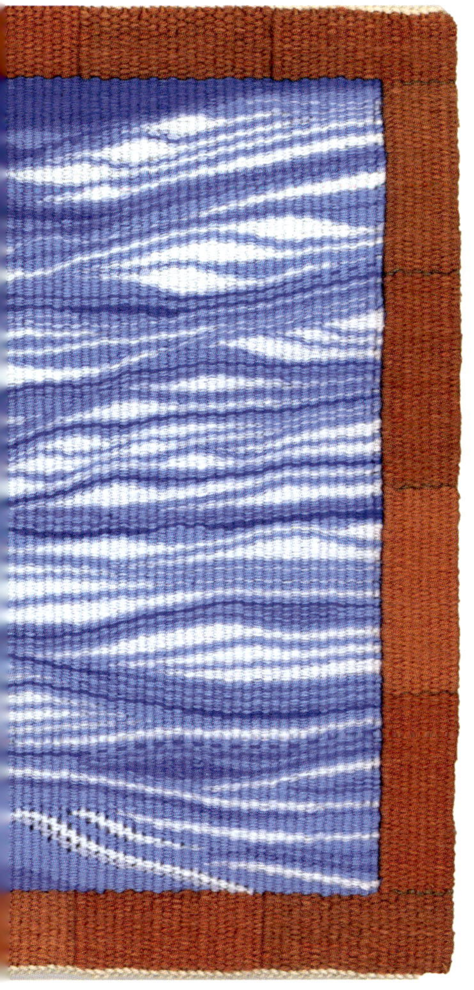

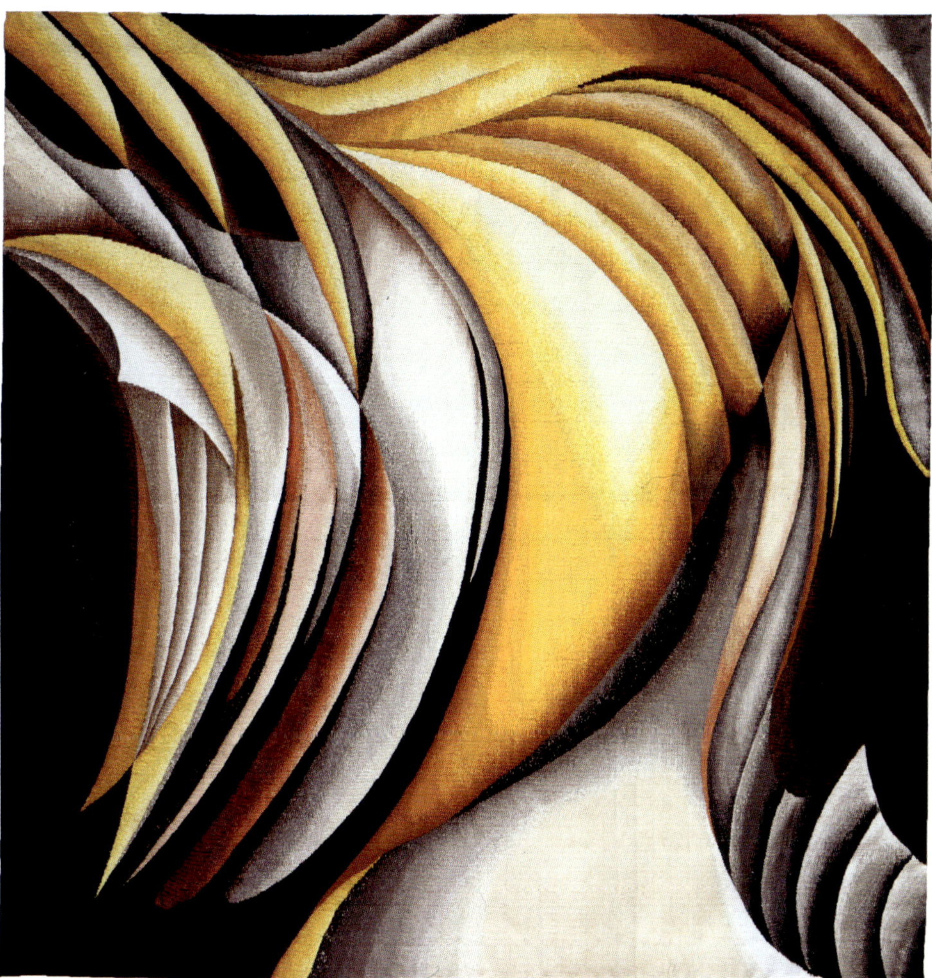

Spatial Extension
Stephen Thurston
1990 | 72" × 71" | wool, silk, rayon, cotton, metallic threads
Smithsonian Institution; gift of Joyce Thurston

The curved lines of Stephen Thurston offer twisting movement, almost like a spring, and give an illusion of compression and depth.

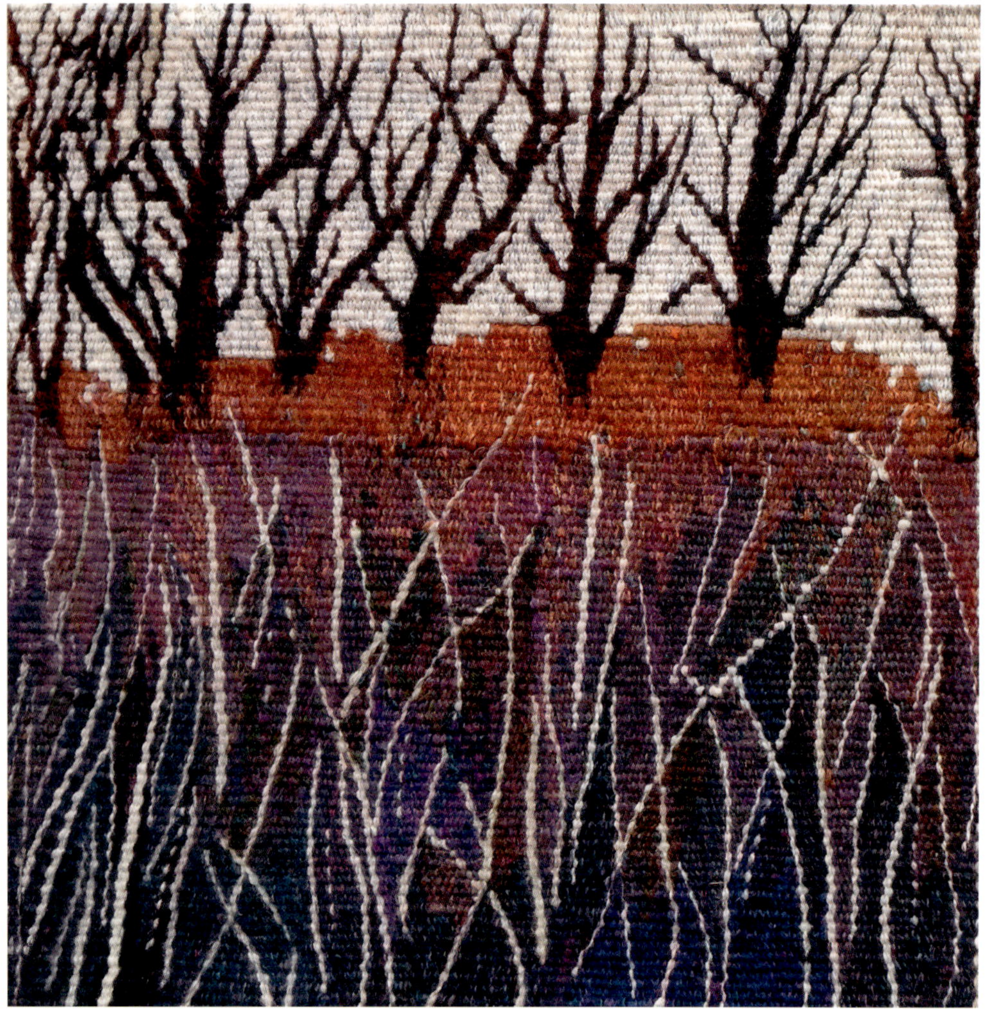

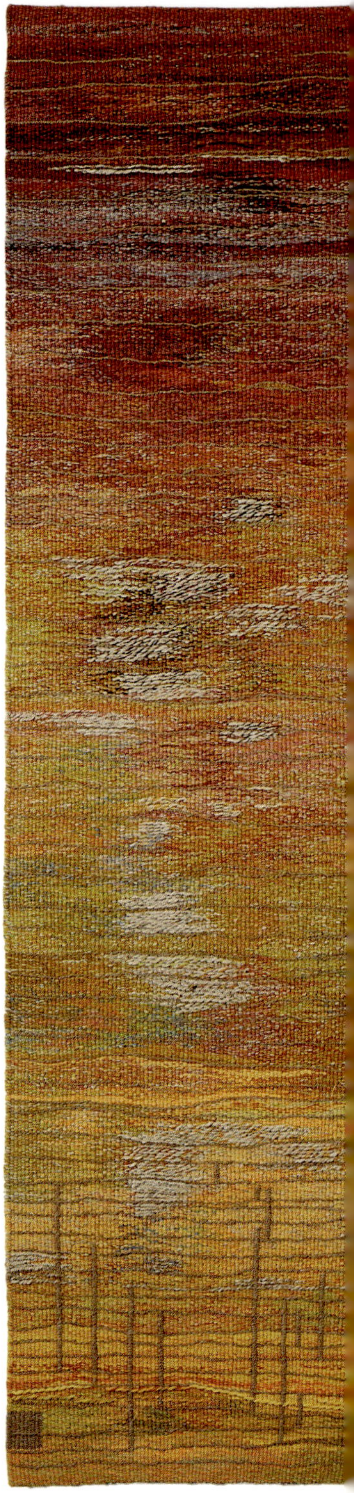

ABOVE: *Rustling Beech Hedges*
Clare Coyle
2018 | 13.4" × 13.4" | linen, wool, silk; cotton warp

RIGHT: *Spanish Caravan*
Anna Kocherovsky
2023 | 60" × 15", 60" × 12", 60" × 10" | wool, linen, metallic thread, cotton

OPPOSITE: *Versailles Orangerie*
Laura Foster Nicolson
1997 or 1998 | wool, cotton floss

Clare Coyle uses lines to suggest tree branches, grasses, and roots, and her title (*Rustling*) suggests sounds as well, and the likelihood that the wind is blowing. Woven from the side, her grasses are a tangle of oddly sorted lines.

Anna Kocherovsky's tall pieces are based on the contrast between the horizontal and vertical lines, which suggest a movement from bottom to top. In the left tapestry, the horizontal lines are barely evident but become more pronounced in the

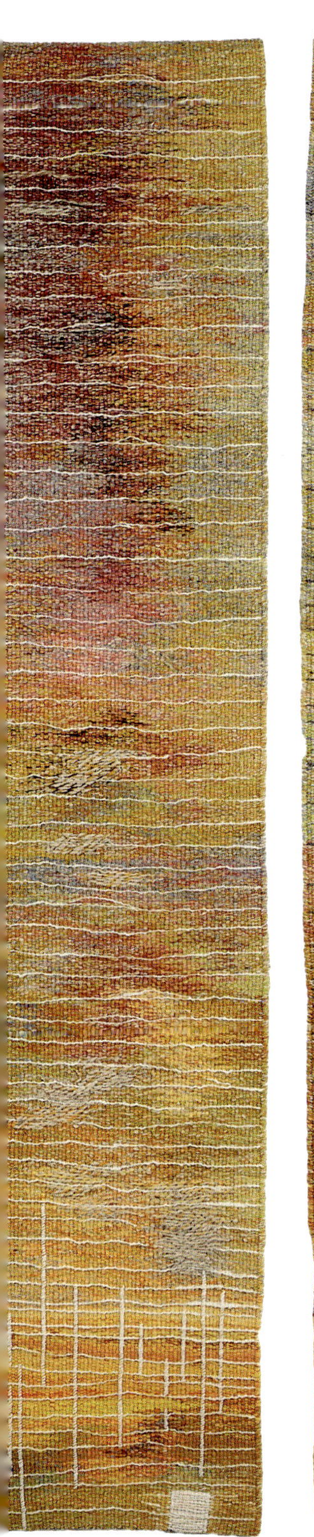

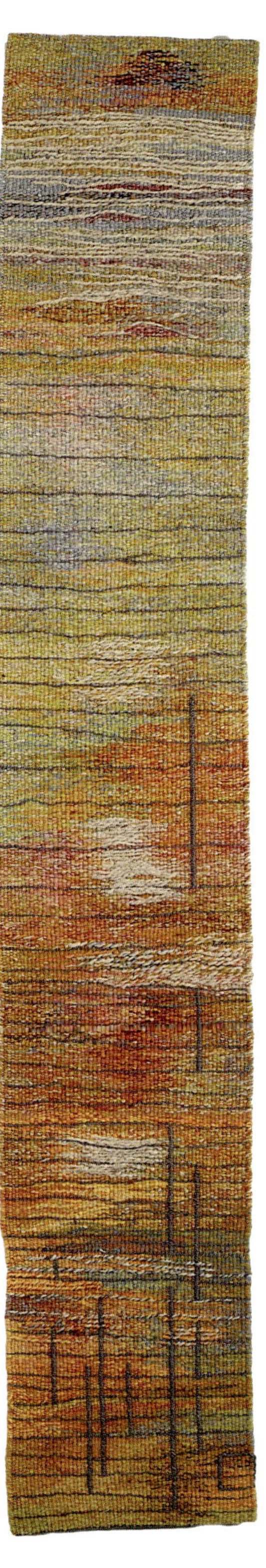

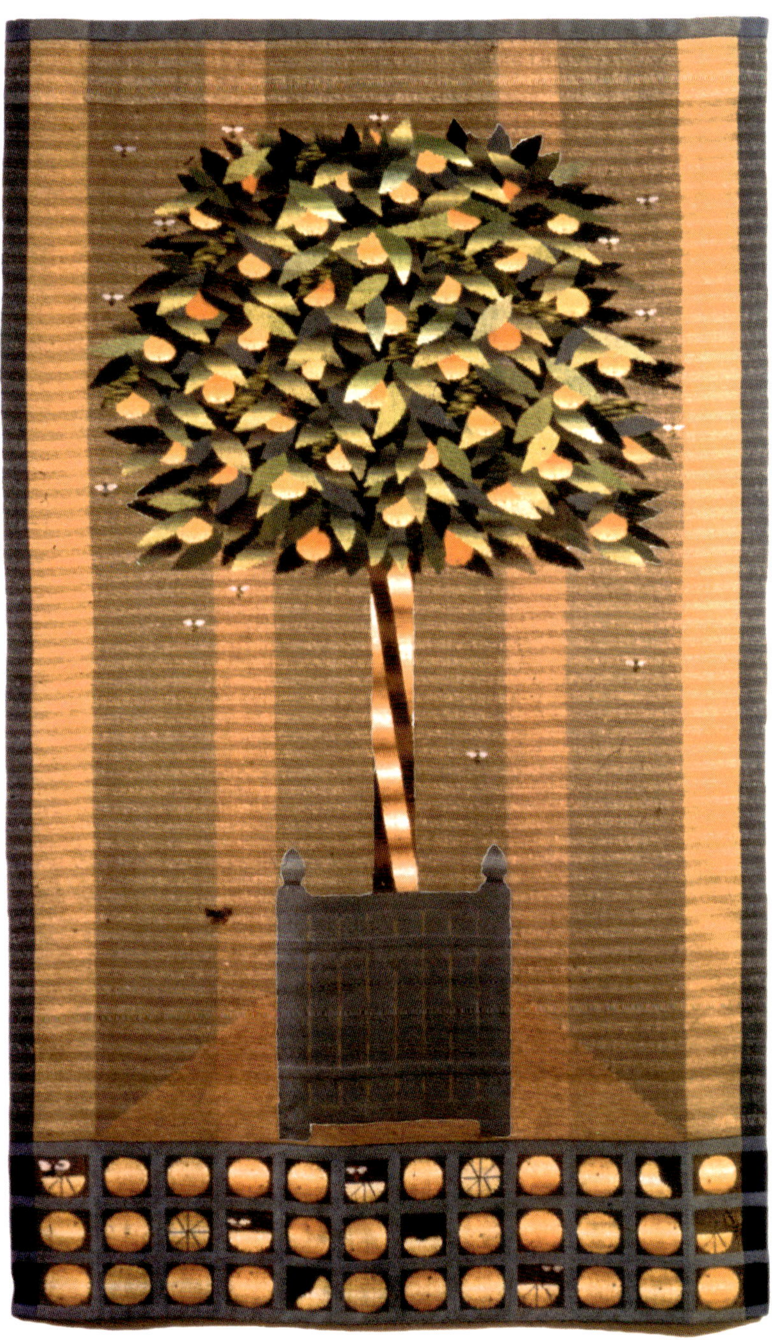

second and third parts. The progression from wider to narrower also suggests movement, as though we are moving farther away.

Laura Foster Nicolson builds her shapes, both the flat and the rounded ones, line by line. She took several photographs of the very stylized, precise Versailles gardens and produced many pieces of the carefully sculpted plants, trees, and grounds.

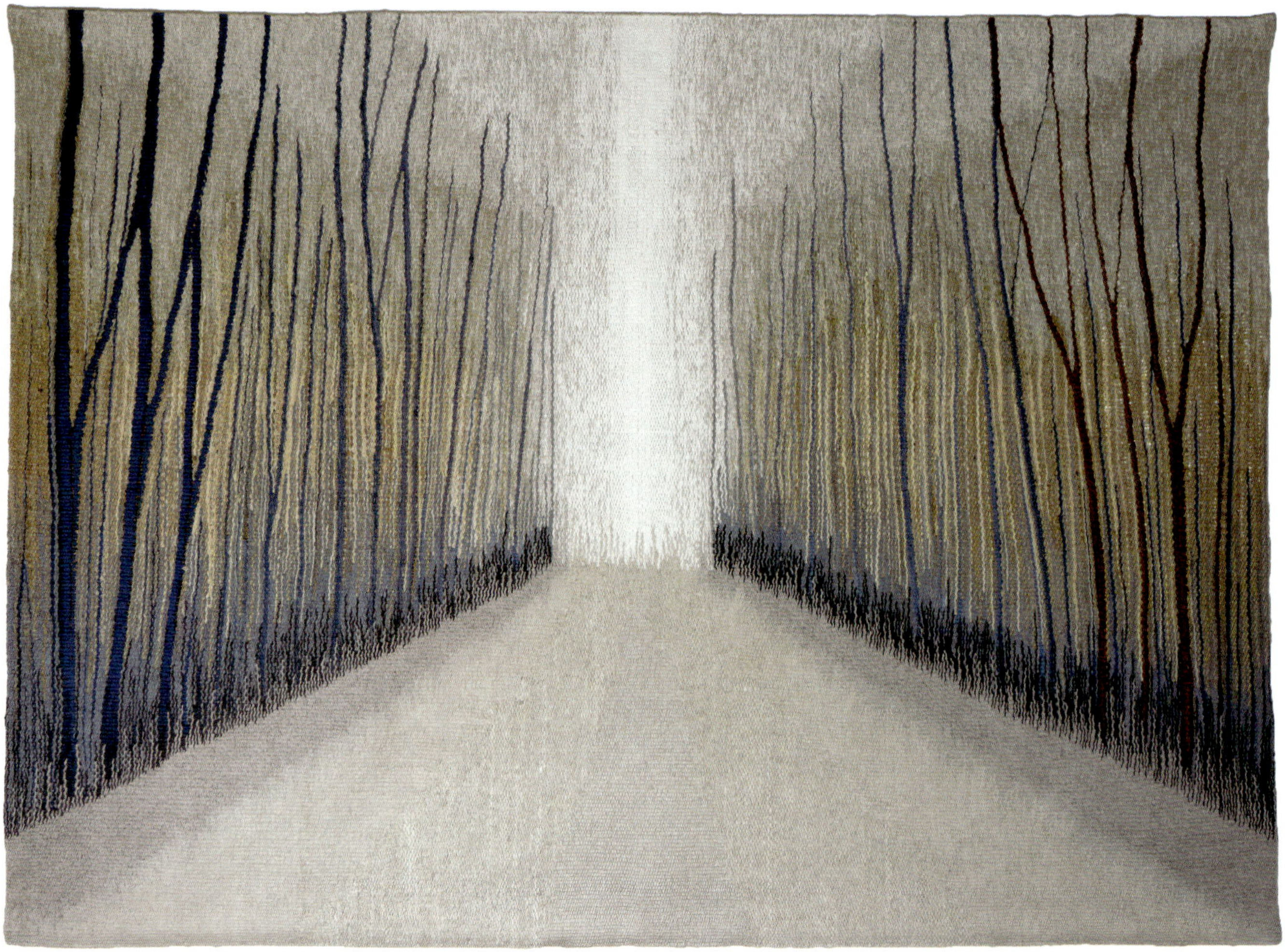

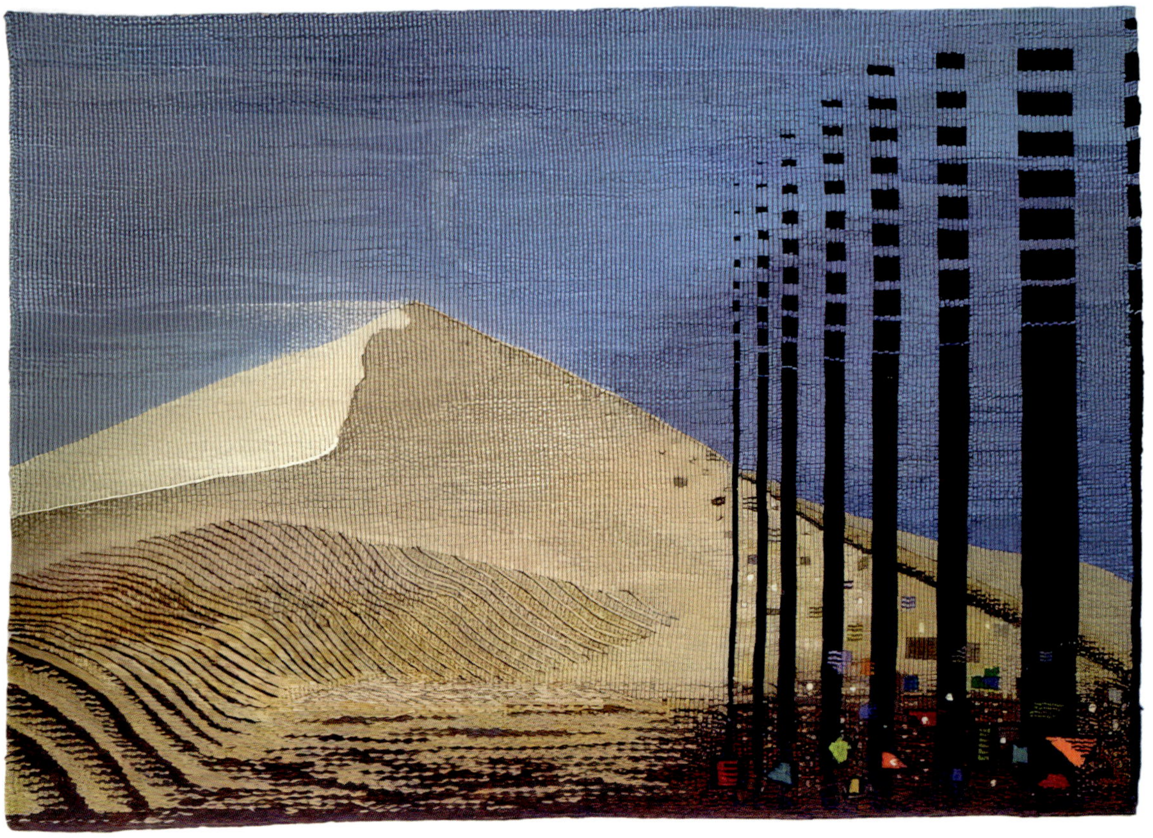

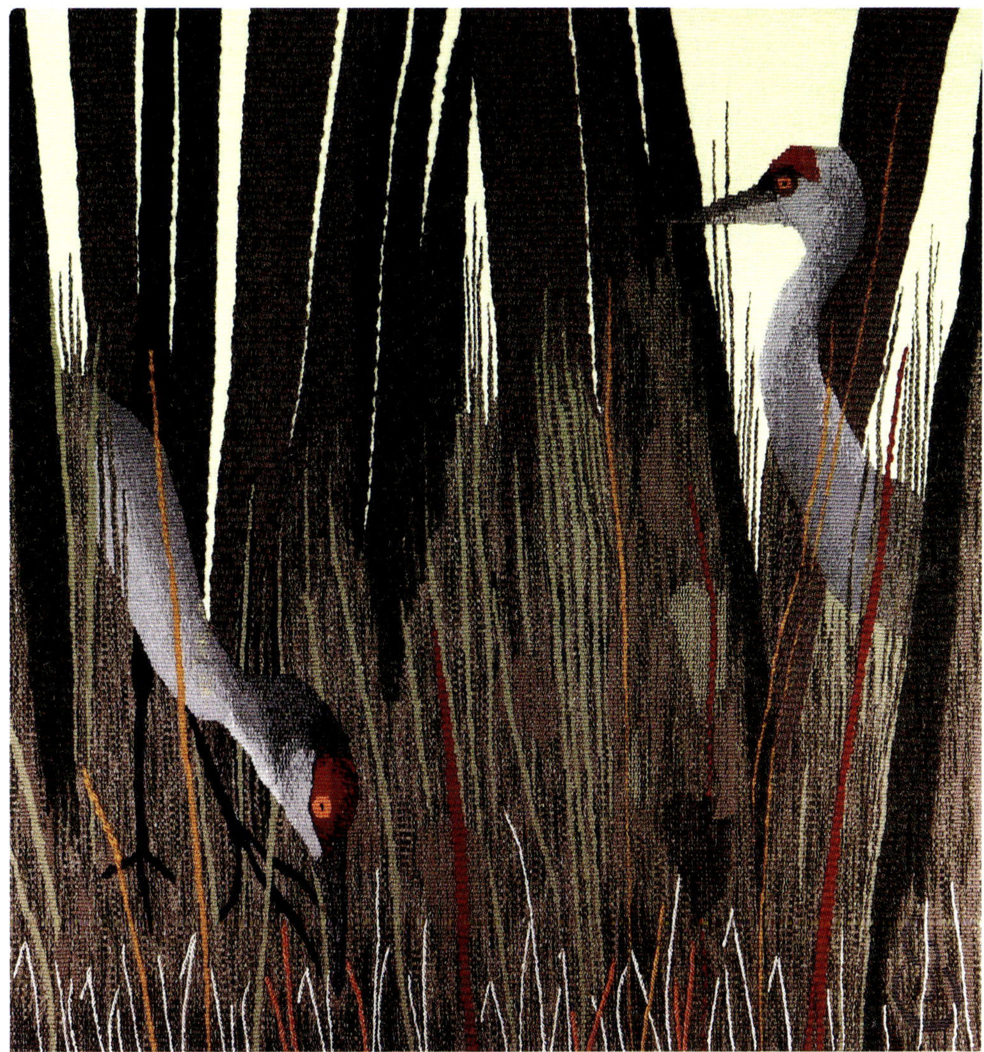

OPPOSITE, TOP: *Runaway*
Uisce A. Jakubczyk
2017 | 47.25" × 67" | paper fibers, yarns, metallic threads

OPPOSITE, BOTTOM: *Wind Doesn't Know for Borders*
from *Migration 2015* series
Minna Rothman
2015 | 27" × 38" | decorative thread, wool; linen warp

ABOVE: *November Light*
Elizabeth Buckley
2020 | 28" × 28" | wool (some hand-dyed)

Minna Rothman's landscape sets strong, dark, vertical poles against a massive pyramid. Rhythmic lines create the terraced dunes. The horizontal lines in the sky suggest a wind blowing sand from the peak of the pyramid. There is even a crescent moon.

Although *Runaway* looks as though you could walk from front to back, along a narrowing path, between lines that suggest blue and red trees, toward a white gateway, it is flat. Traditional tapestry weavers might shun perspective of this kind—but Uisce A. Jakubczyk's result is terrific.

Autumn permeates the world of Elizabeth Buckley's birds feeding. The dominant vertical lines of the plants and grasses are broken by the movement of the birds' heads and necks. The colors are right for this season of the year—both the browns and the grays and a sporadic dark red.

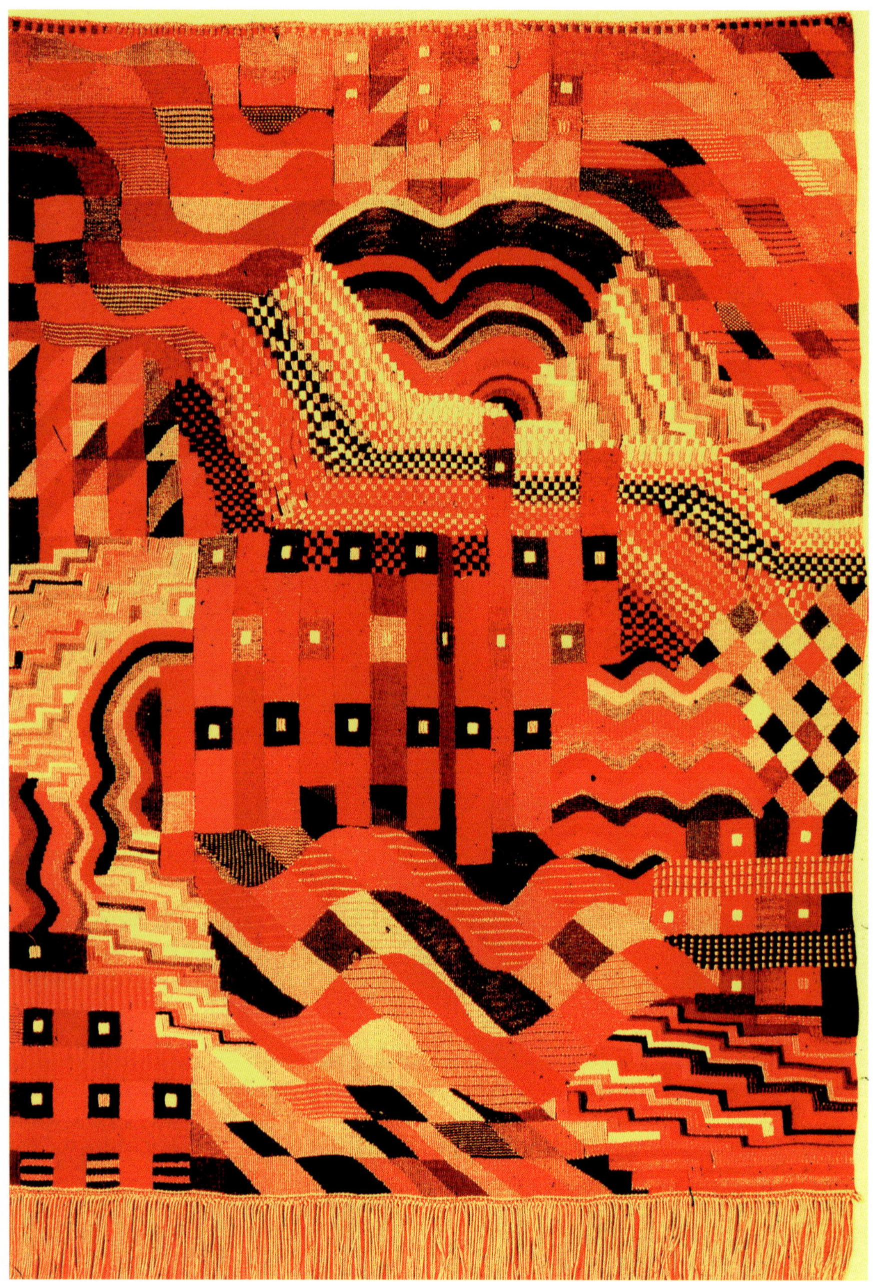

band

While bands are composed of lines, they look like a different element. So, let's look at them separately.

Schlitzgobelin, rot-grün Tapisserie (Slit tapestry, red-green)
Gunta Stölzl
1926–27 | 59" × 43.3" | cotton, wool, silk, linen

At the Bauhaus, Gunta Stölzl was especially accomplished. This tapestry embodies a glossary of colors and shapes, vertical columns, and curving bands, a radical experiment for the times. She might have been weaving a sampler, but the piece has real unity of vision, provided partly by the dominant colors and partly by the balance of forms. Weavers might study this to consider the possibilities of the medium.

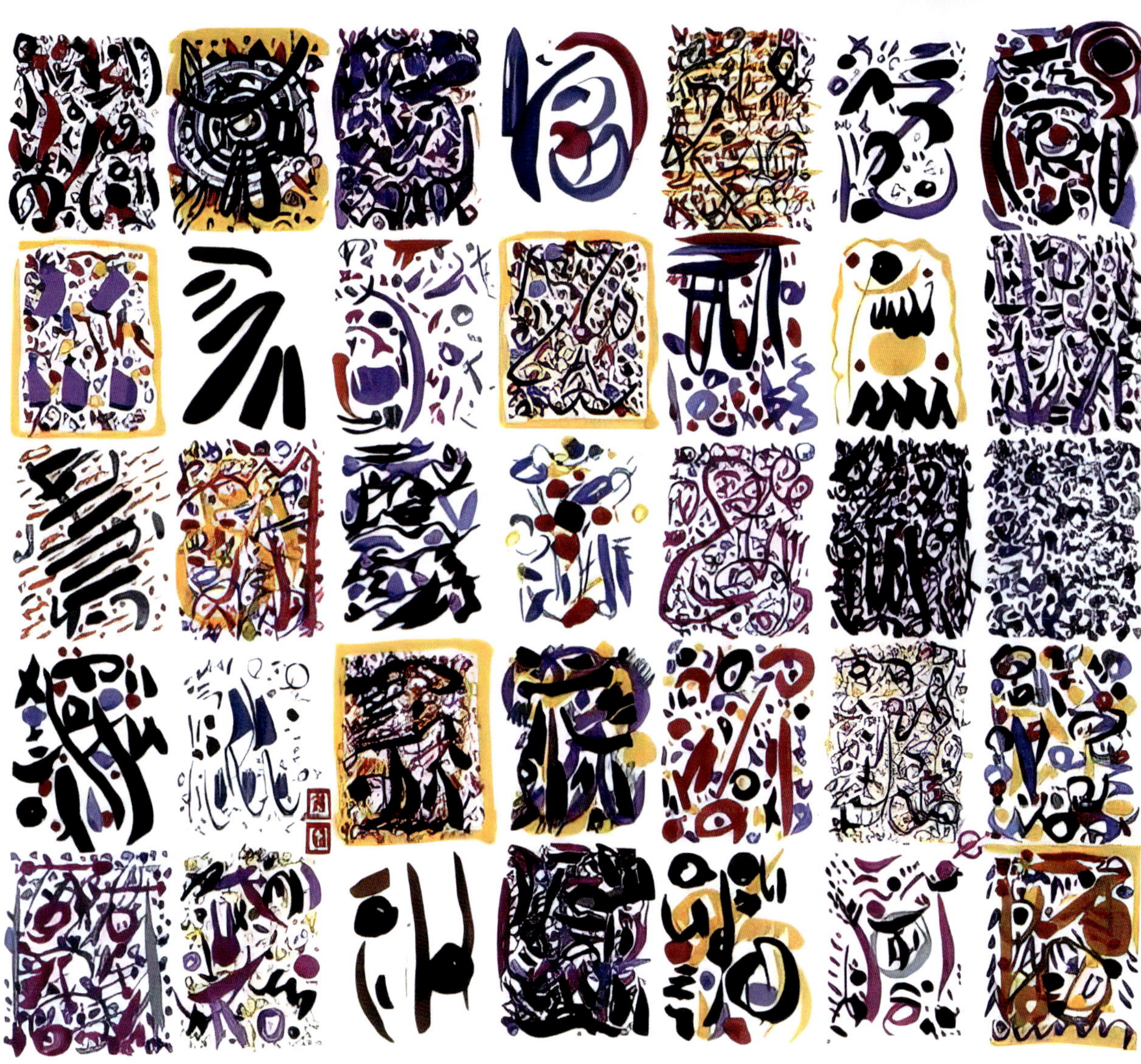

Dessins (Drawings)
Marcel Renesio
2002 | 61" × 68.9" | wool

Marcel Renesio also provides a glossary of shapes, even if his work does not break with tradition as dramatically as Stötzl's did. He has combined both sophisticated and simple forms, composed of lines and bands, thicker and thinner. The white separates it all into a grid.

Five tapestry weavers have chosen to consider the forest and tree trunks, the quintessential band. Each approaches the woods individually. Julia Mitchell focuses on tree trunks and an elaborate frame, which her trees occasionally disregard.

Trees
Julia Mitchell
2013 | 48" × 36" | wool, silk; linen warp

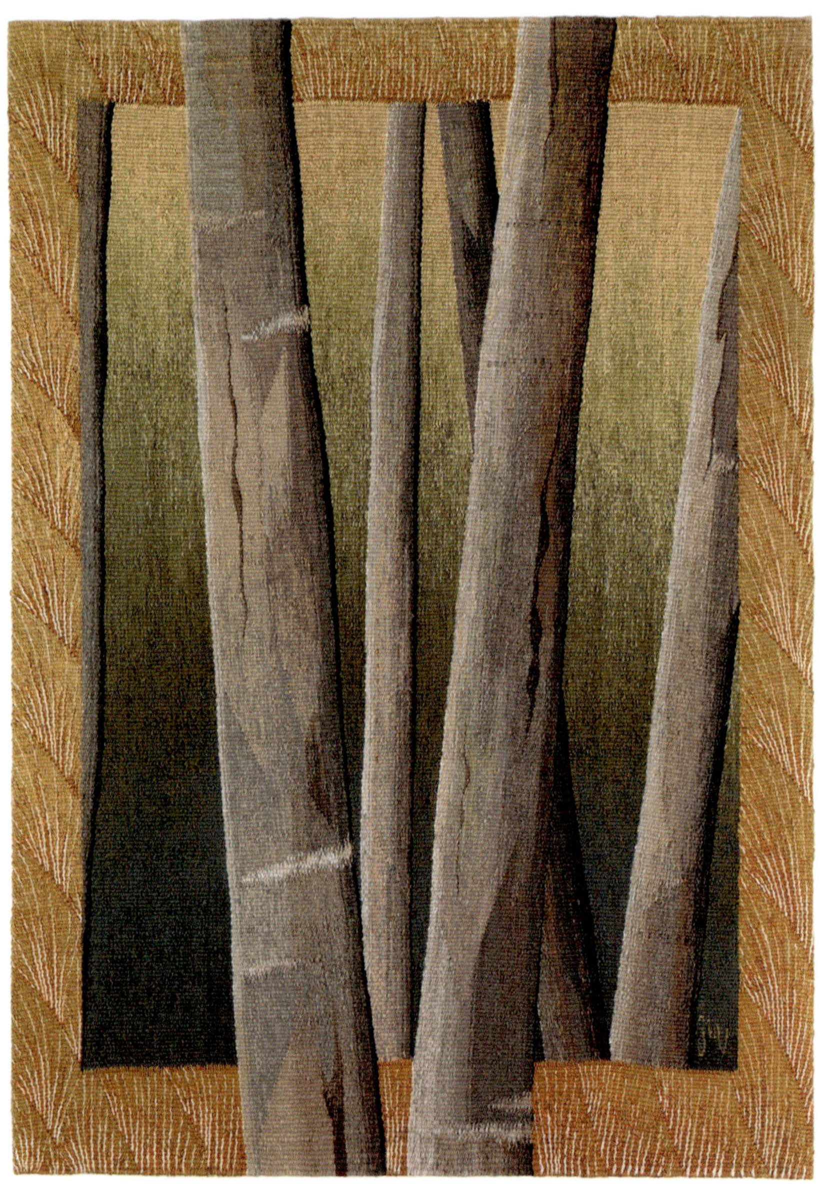

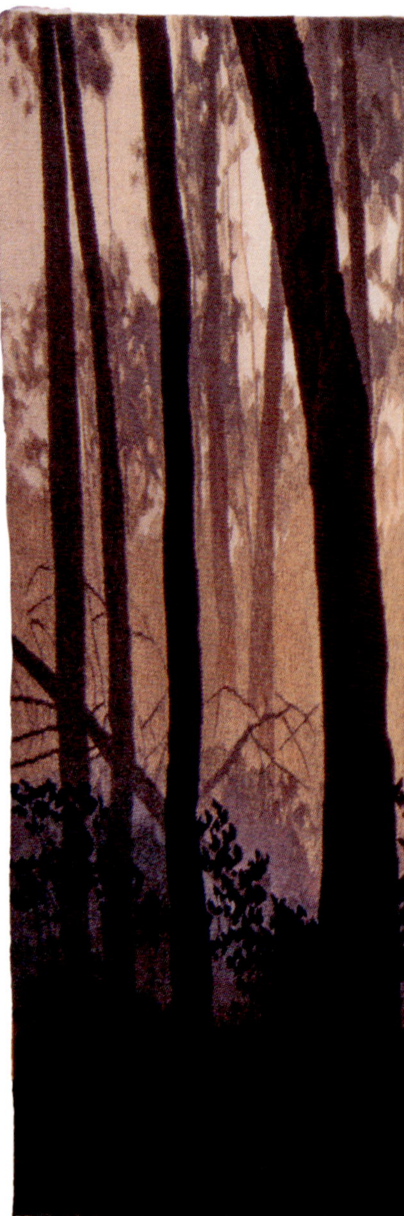

Baiba Ritere gives us the wide view of the woods, and an idea of how far back it reaches: black bands of trunks that grow fainter as they recede.

Harmony 01
Baiba Ritere
2011 | 5'8" × 9'10" | wool; linen warp
Museum of Decorative Art and Design, Latvia

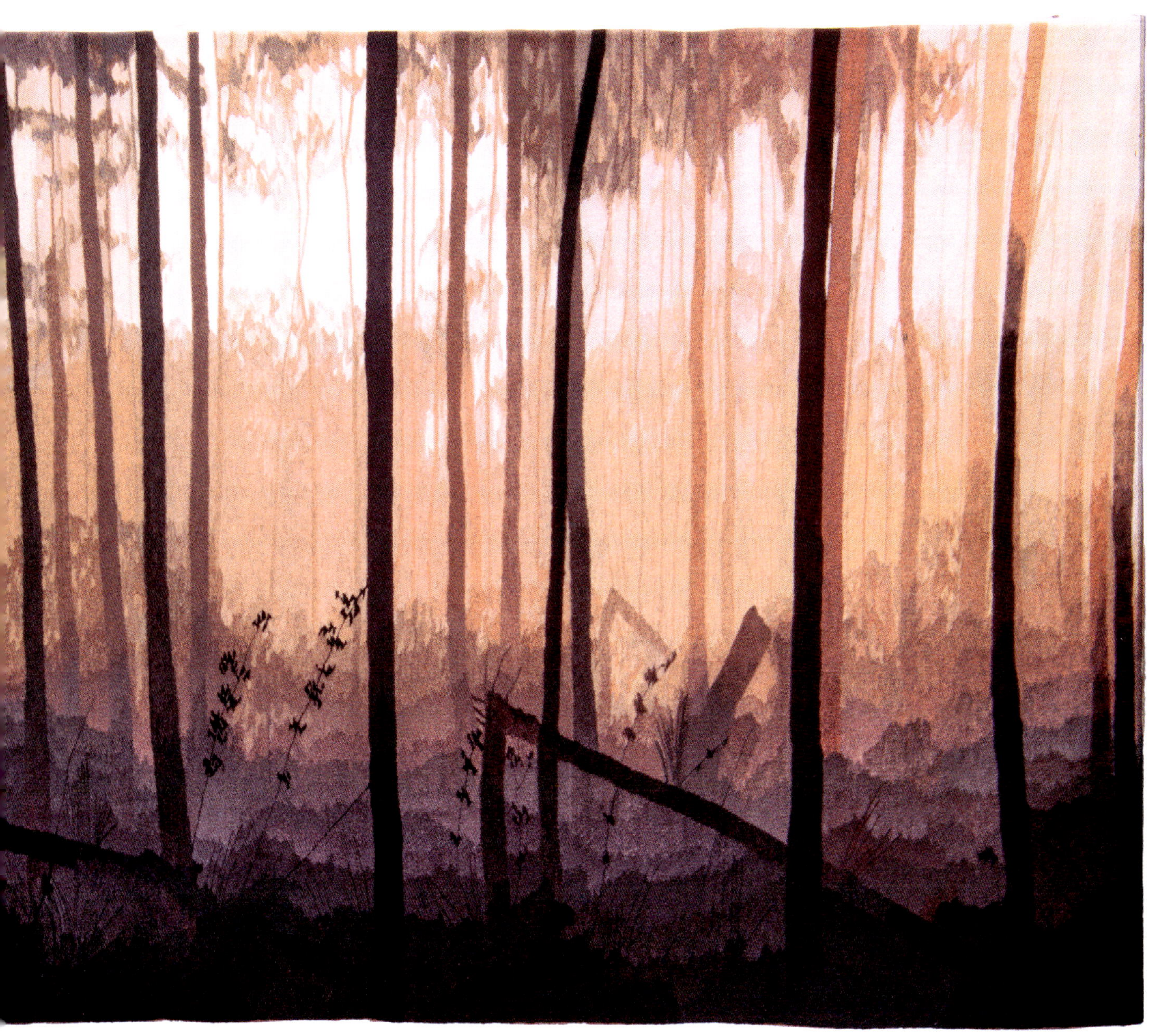

LEFT: *Birches*
Louise Oppenheimer
2008 | 67" × 39.4" | wool; cotton warp

RIGHT: *Waiting*
Ding Fang Wang
2014 | 38.6" × 27.5" | wool, synthetic fibers; cotton warp

Both Louise Oppenheimer and Ding Fang Wang are looking at birch trees, but in very distinct ways. Oppenheimer's trees, in bright whites and grays, reach out as though to touch each other, in solidarity, and Wang's, in a more subdued palette, try to reach the sky and show the branch structure we see when we look up.

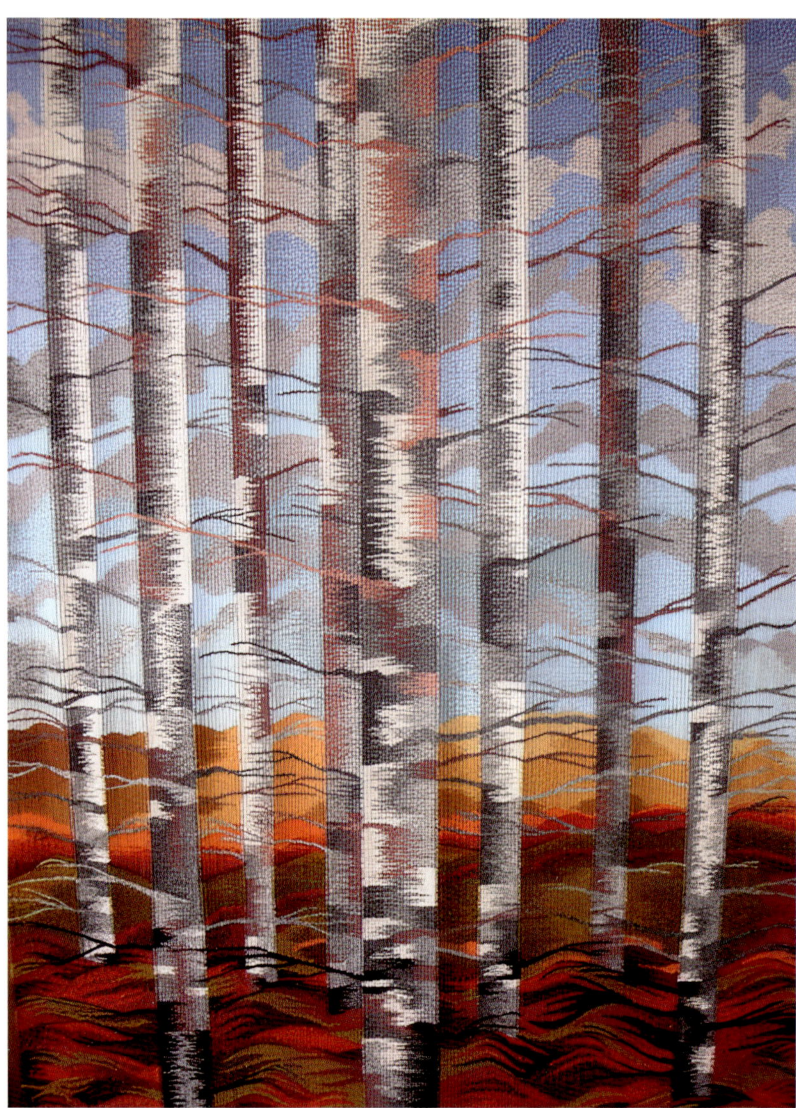

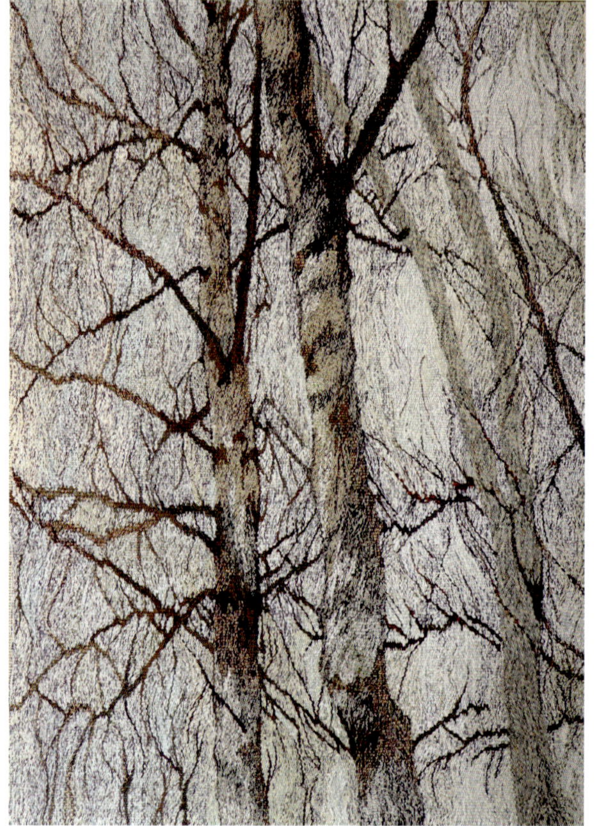

Rosemarie Rataiczyk's vegetation, like tree trunks, entices us to imagine magical woods, with colors and shapes we don't assume we know. The trunks, with their horizontal stripes, almost look like bamboo.

Vegetation
Rosemarie Rataiczyk
1988 | 47.25" × 59"
Courtesy of the Land Sachsen-Anhalt, Schloss Bemburg Museum

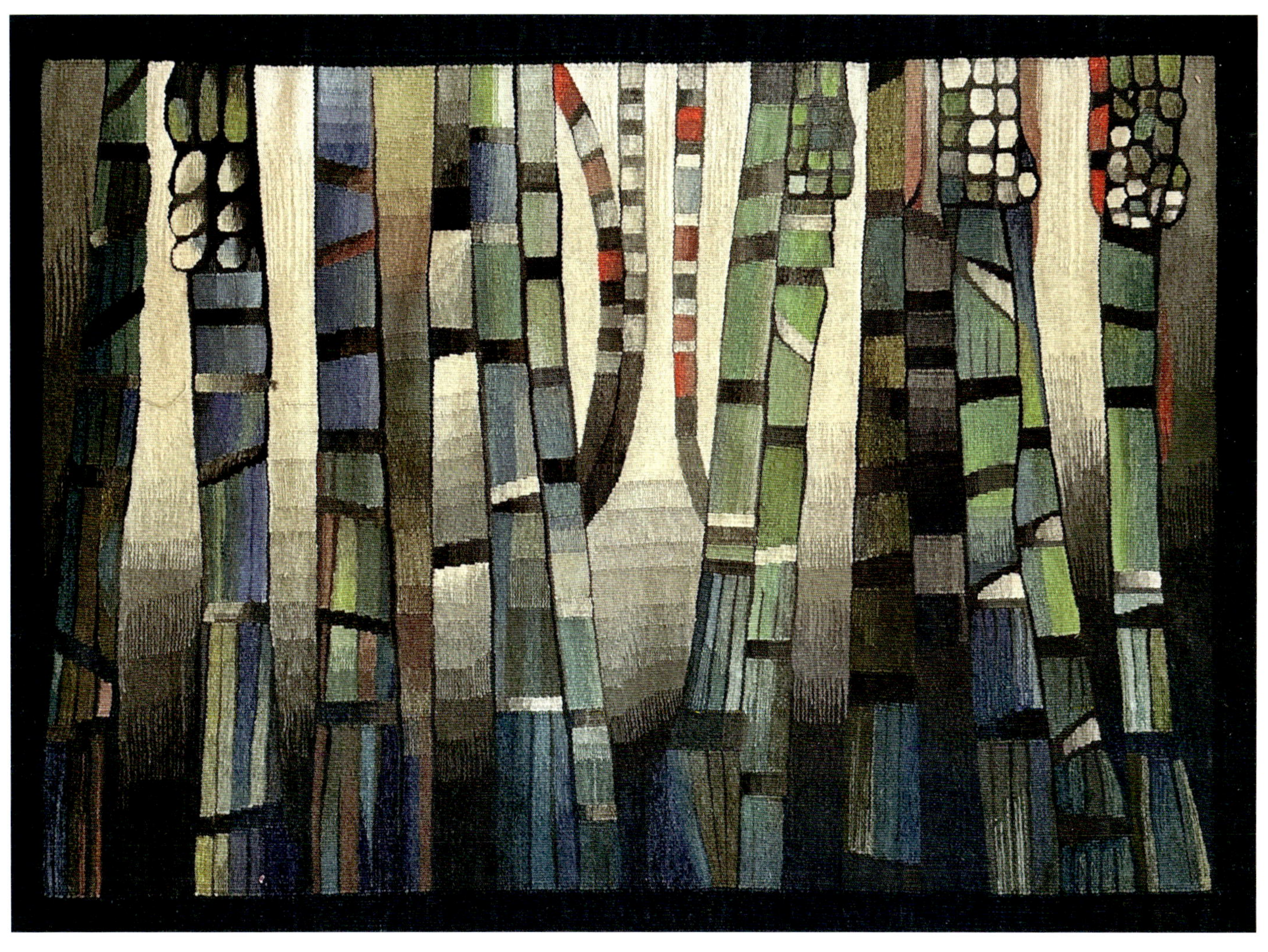

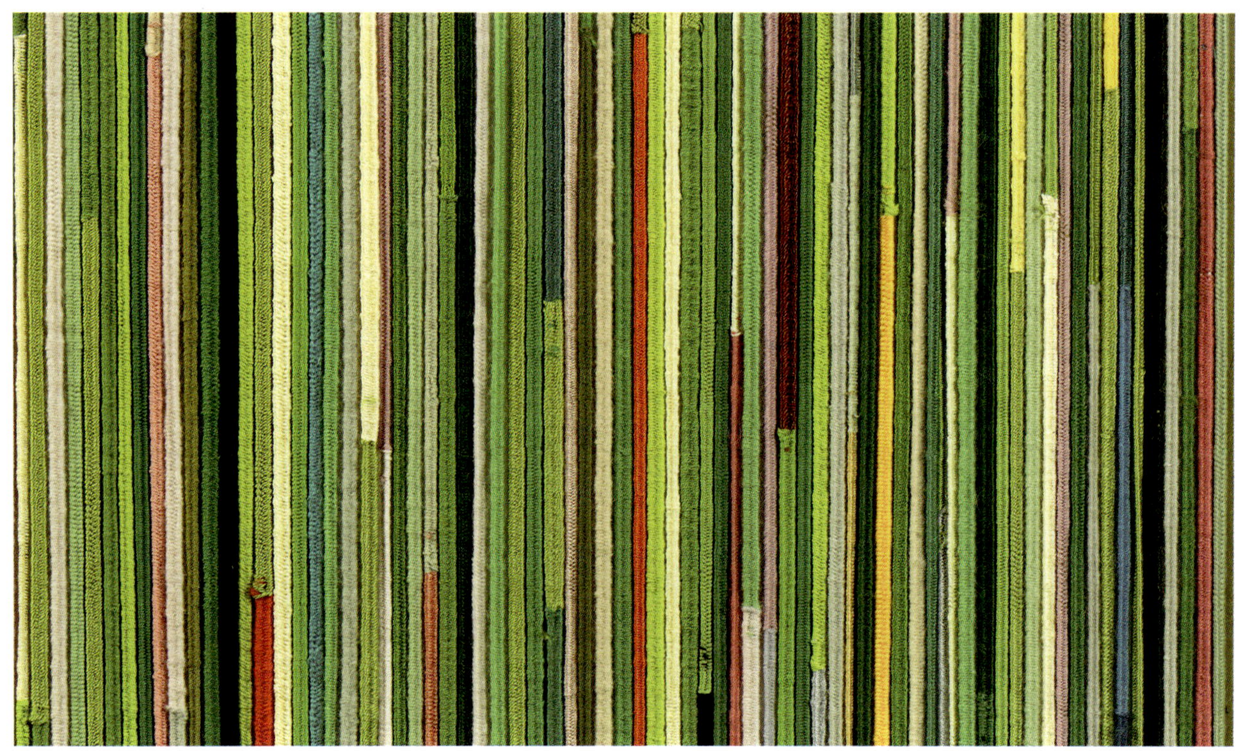

ABOVE: *Green Lines*
Susan Mowatt
2018 | 15.75" × 19.7" | wool, cotton, linen
Photographer: Shannon Tofts

BELOW: *At the Foot of the Alakau*
Malik Mykanov
2016 | 78.75" × 9'8.5" | wool, silk, acrylic; cotton warp

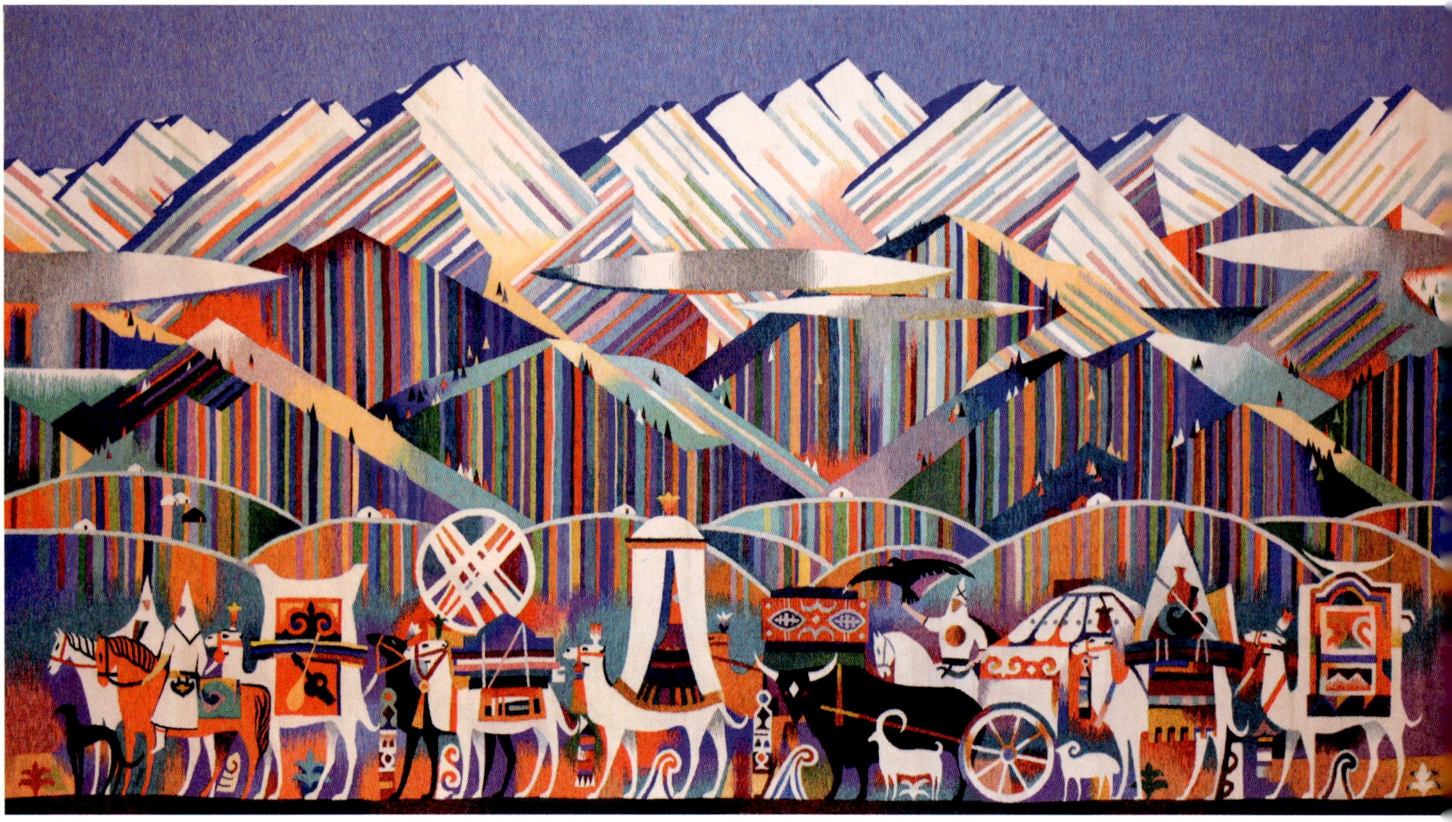

Susan Mowatt has woven narrow individual bands and then afterward assembled them into a single piece. Each section can sometimes be composed of more than one band. The verticality and the dominant green give both energy and unity.

Solveig Aalberg has combined five pieces into one, Her stripes meet very cleanly, although joins can be seen. Colors alternate with white. The thinning bands at the top give the illusion that the piece is receding. The size is immense—13 feet across.

Malik Mykanov has spoken about some of the origins for his approach to design and the importance of stripes in the culture of Kazakhstan. "The main visual motif is *alasha*, numerous colored lines different in width that fill almost the entire space of the composition." The round yurts contrast with the sharp mountains.

Passing Through
Solveig Aalberg
2012 | 79.5" × 13' | linen, cotton

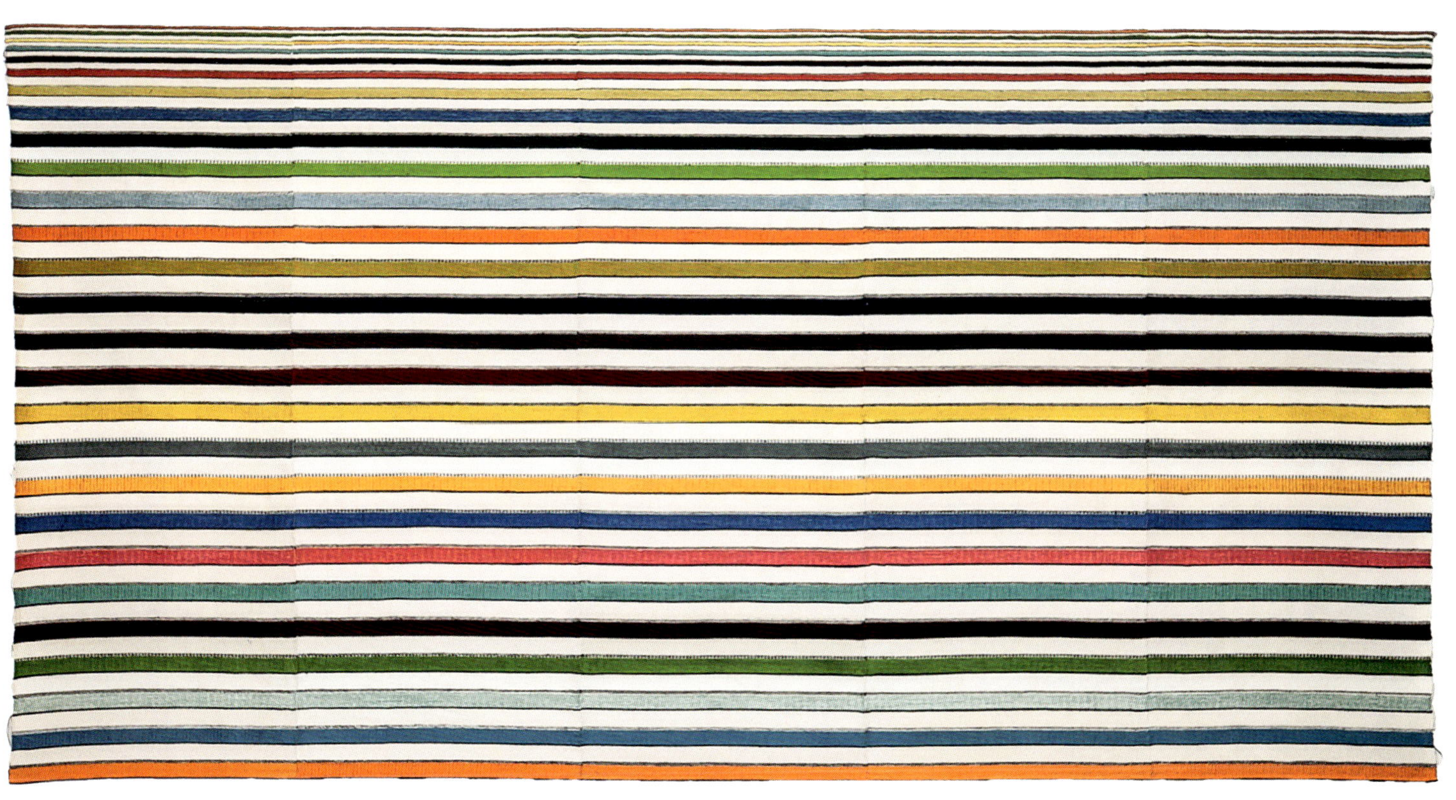

Using rough materials, Pilar Sala has constructed a whole piece of bands of natural colors, like tree bark. But the title suggests the disintegration of rocks and earth.

Bjørg Heggstad Jakhelln's graceful fluttering bands, both in solid colors and with stripes, float above a diamond, which might even suggest stained glass. Here the bands are distinct from one another, woven separately.

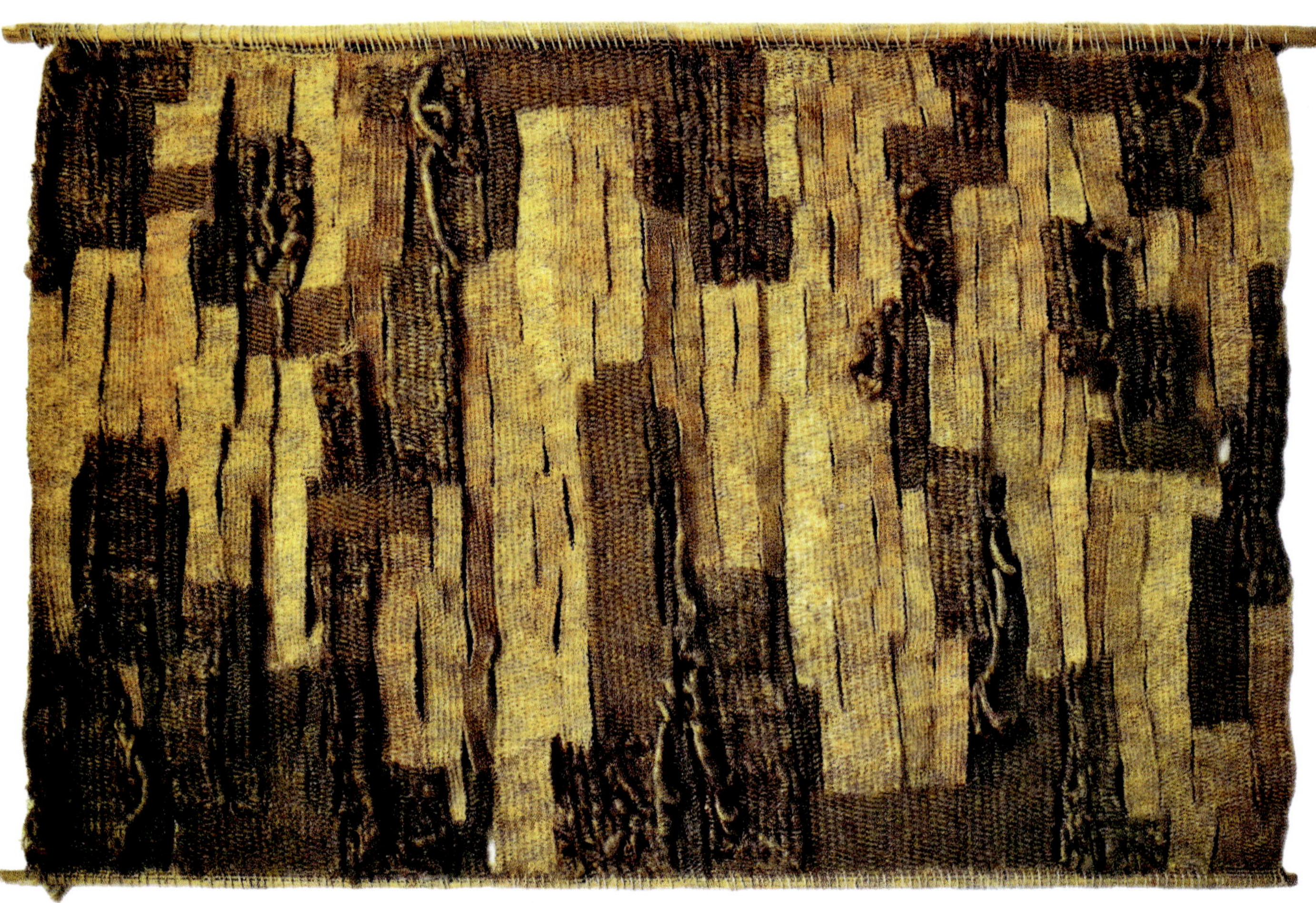

Erosion
Pilar Sala
1984 | 67" × 7'3" | sisal, hemp, jute

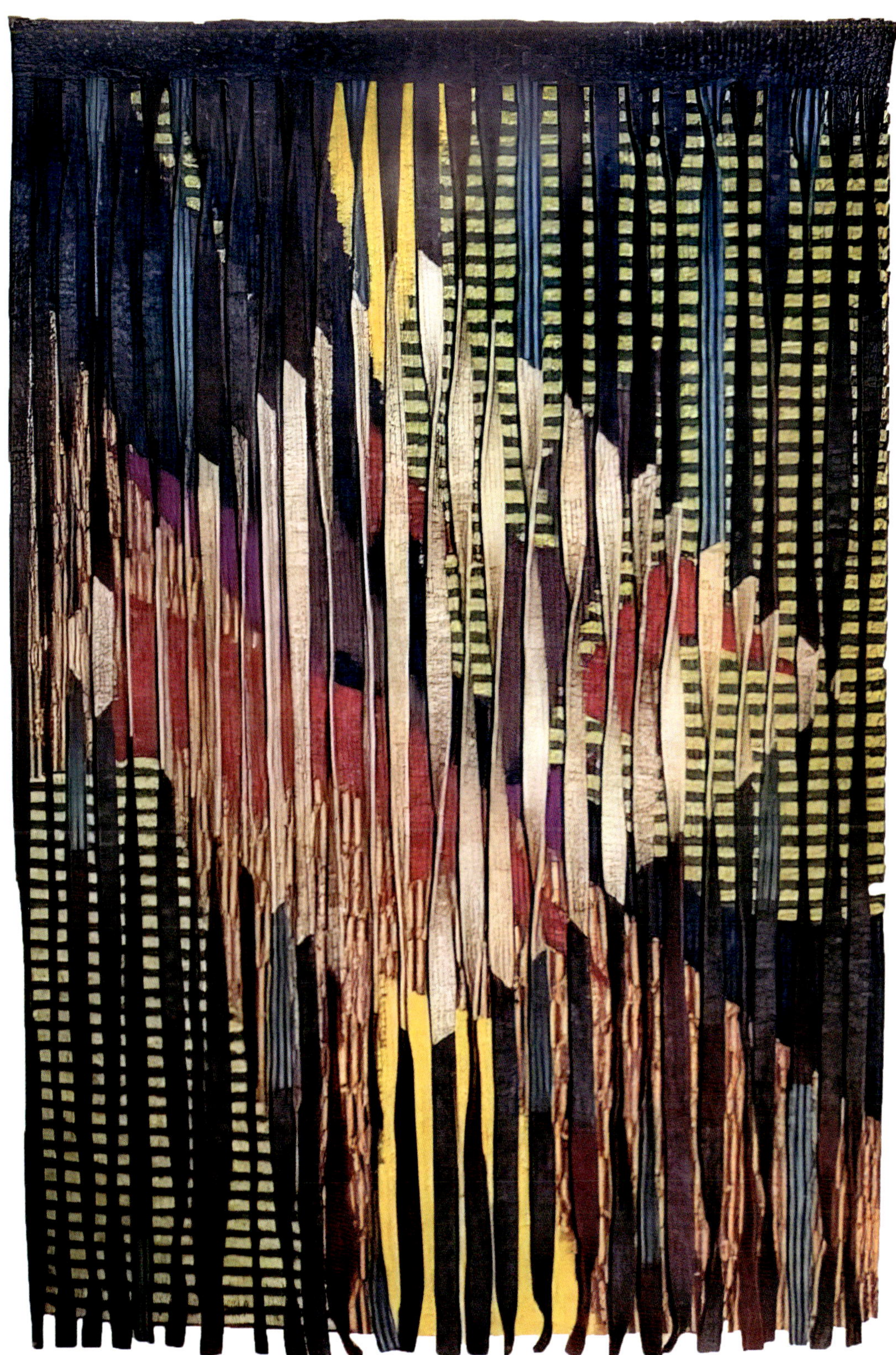

Mangfoldet Bakerfor (The variety beyond)
Bjørg Heggstad Jakhelln
1983 | 65" × 43.3" × 3.1"| wool, linen; hemp warp
Arctic University of Norway, Tromsø
Photographer: Cathrine Wang / KORO

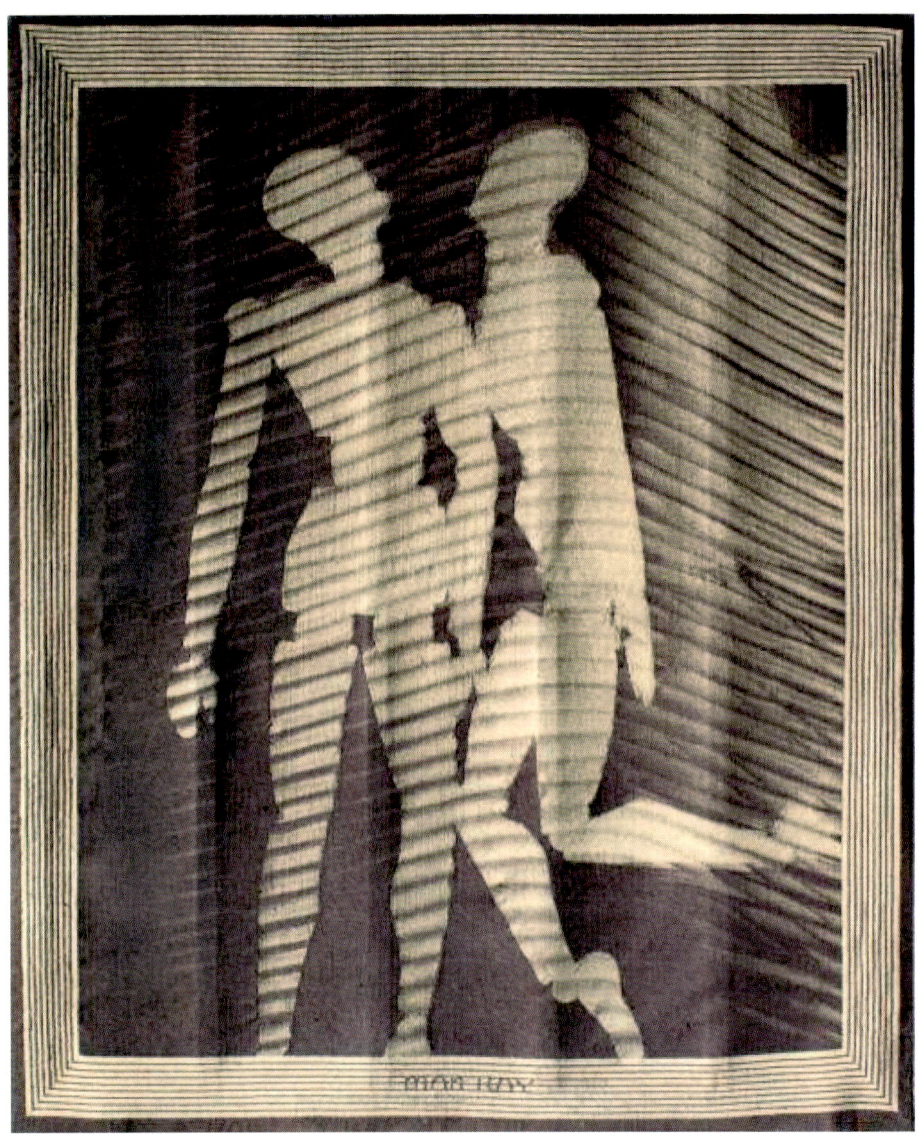

LEFT: *Shadows*
Man Ray
1938 | 77.5" × 65.5"
Atelier Legoueix

BELOW: *Silent*
Joan Baxter
2022 | 23.6" × 47.25" | wool, linen, cotton, foil

OPPOSITE: *Blue Sky*
Aija Baumane
2001 | 68.5" × 61" | linen, wool, synthetics, gold threads

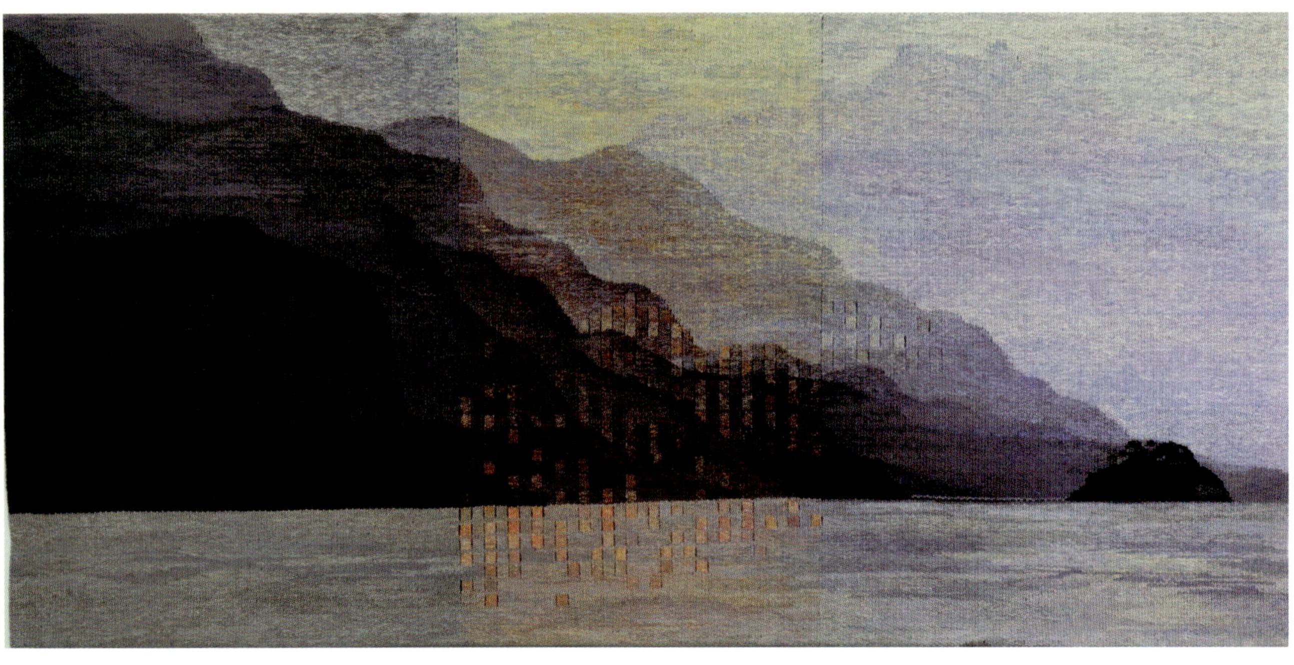

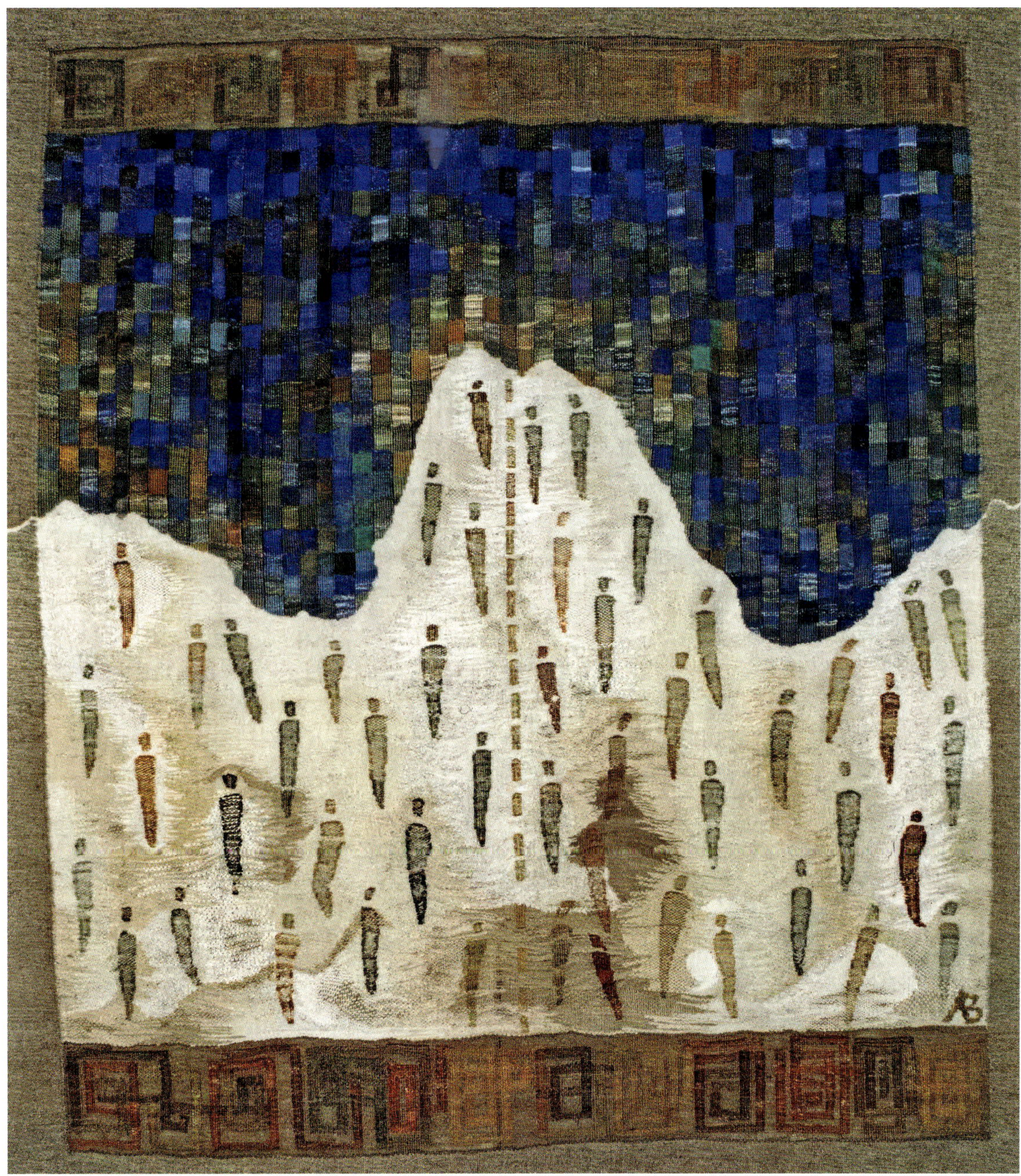

Man Ray, a well-known twentieth-century artist, designed this piece at the request of Marie Cuttoli, a French entrepreneur and patron of tapestry. Ray's silhouettes are defined by bands of light and shadow, as if cast by window blinds.

Aija Baumane has built her sky with columns of blues with a little green and yellow. The mountain shape below is constructed otherwise. Its white organic mass is full of bobbing figures.

Joan Baxter embellishes her landscape with mysterious interrupted vertical bands that work almost like rays of sun, emphasizing rain.

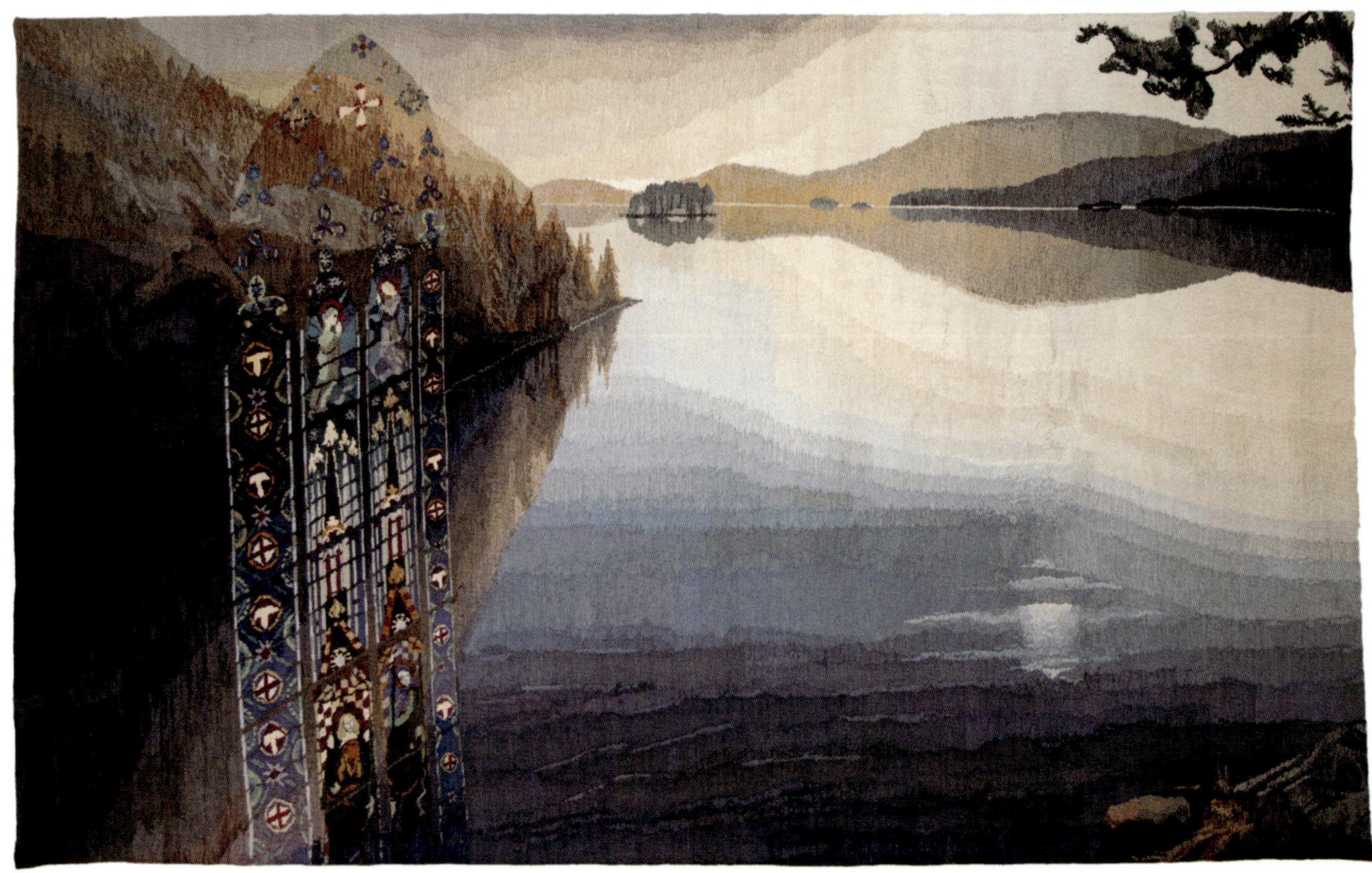

ABOVE: *Ataraxia* (middle section of triptych)
Soile Hovila
2020–23 | 67.7" × 9'3" | linen, wool, cotton, other fibers

OPPOSITE, TOP: *Around Haleakala*
Margo MacDonald
2022 | 34" × 30" | wool, cotton

OPPOSITE, BOTTOM: *Indivisible*
Chris E Minck Race
2021 | 10" × 17" | wool; cotton warp; cotton flag

Ataraxia (meaning tranquility of mind) varies colors in bands of water moving from front to back, and, *on the left*, the suggestion of a church's stained-glass window. Is this a holy scene?

Margo MacDonald helps us imagine a landscape intercutting land and sea. Her precise vertical bands each show something else at the national park known as Haleakala.

Chris E Minck Race connected her stripes of landscape together with the horizontal stripes of the US national flag.

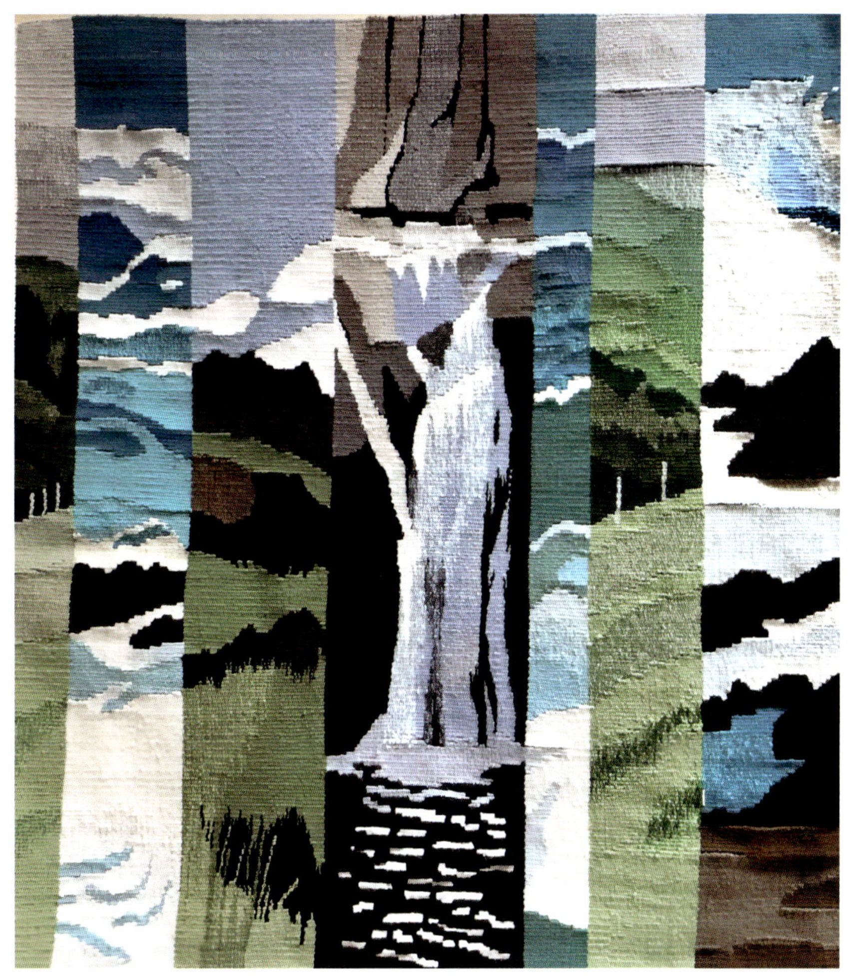

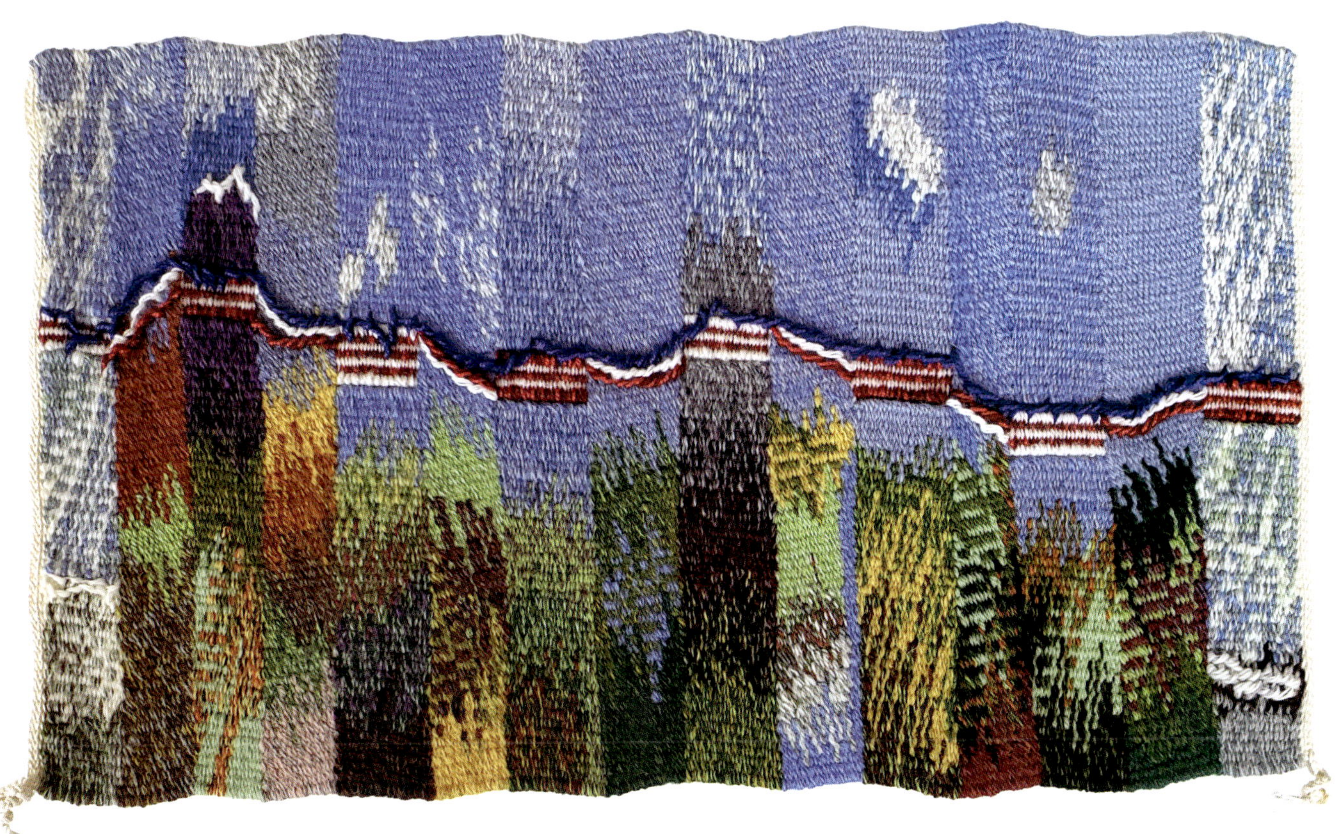

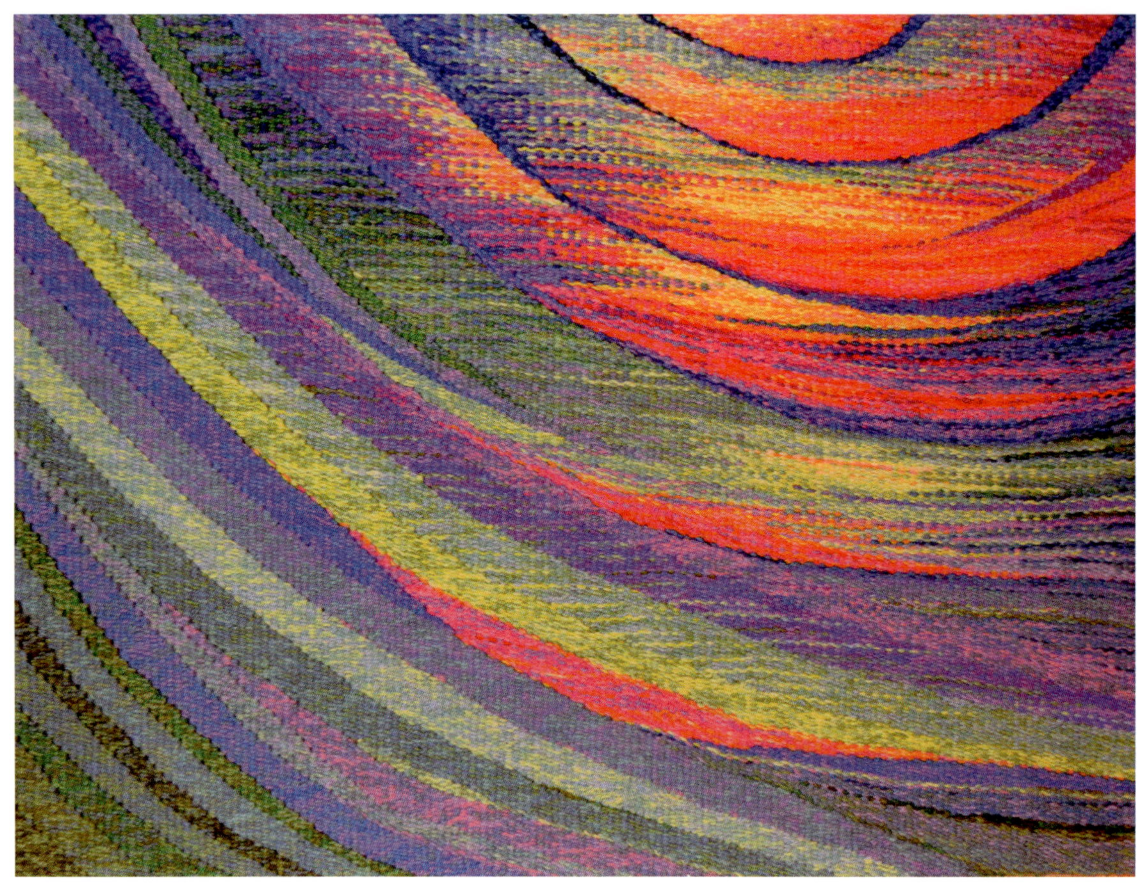

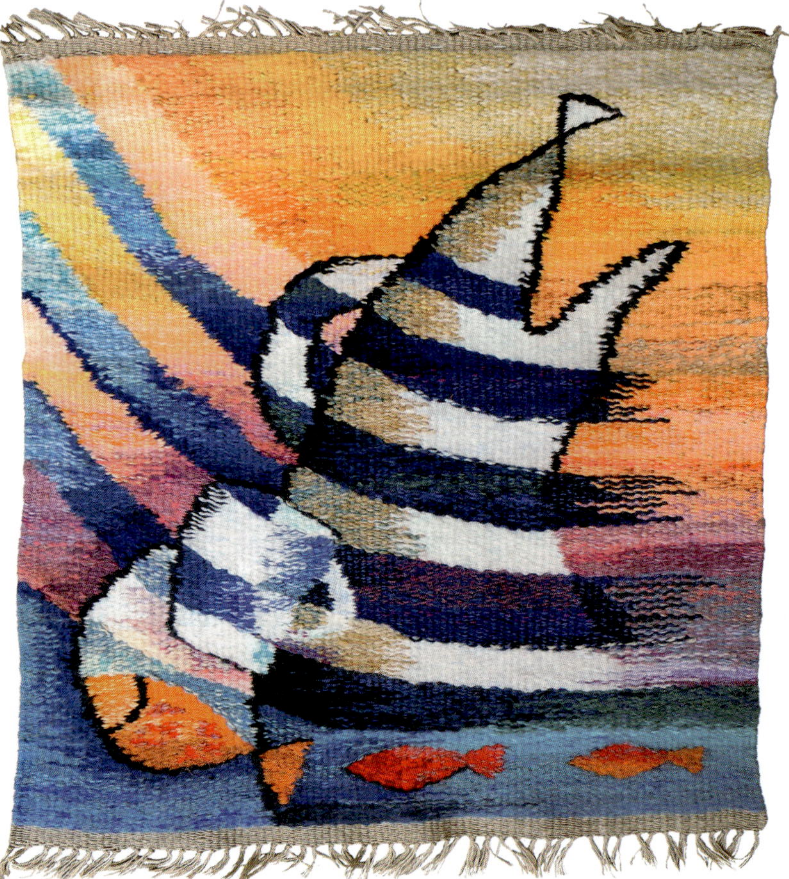

ABOVE: *Sky Streams*
Thoma Ewen
2013 | 2' × 3' | wool; cotton warp
Commission for private residence, Edmonton, Alberta

OPPOSITE: *Le Jardin des Étoiles*
(The starry garden)
Murray Gibson
1988 | 59" × 59" | wool, silk, metallic fibers
Collection of the Alberta Foundation for the Arts

LEFT:
Tea drinking of seawoman
Anastasia Schneider
2013 | 19.7" × 19.7" |
wool, rayon, linen

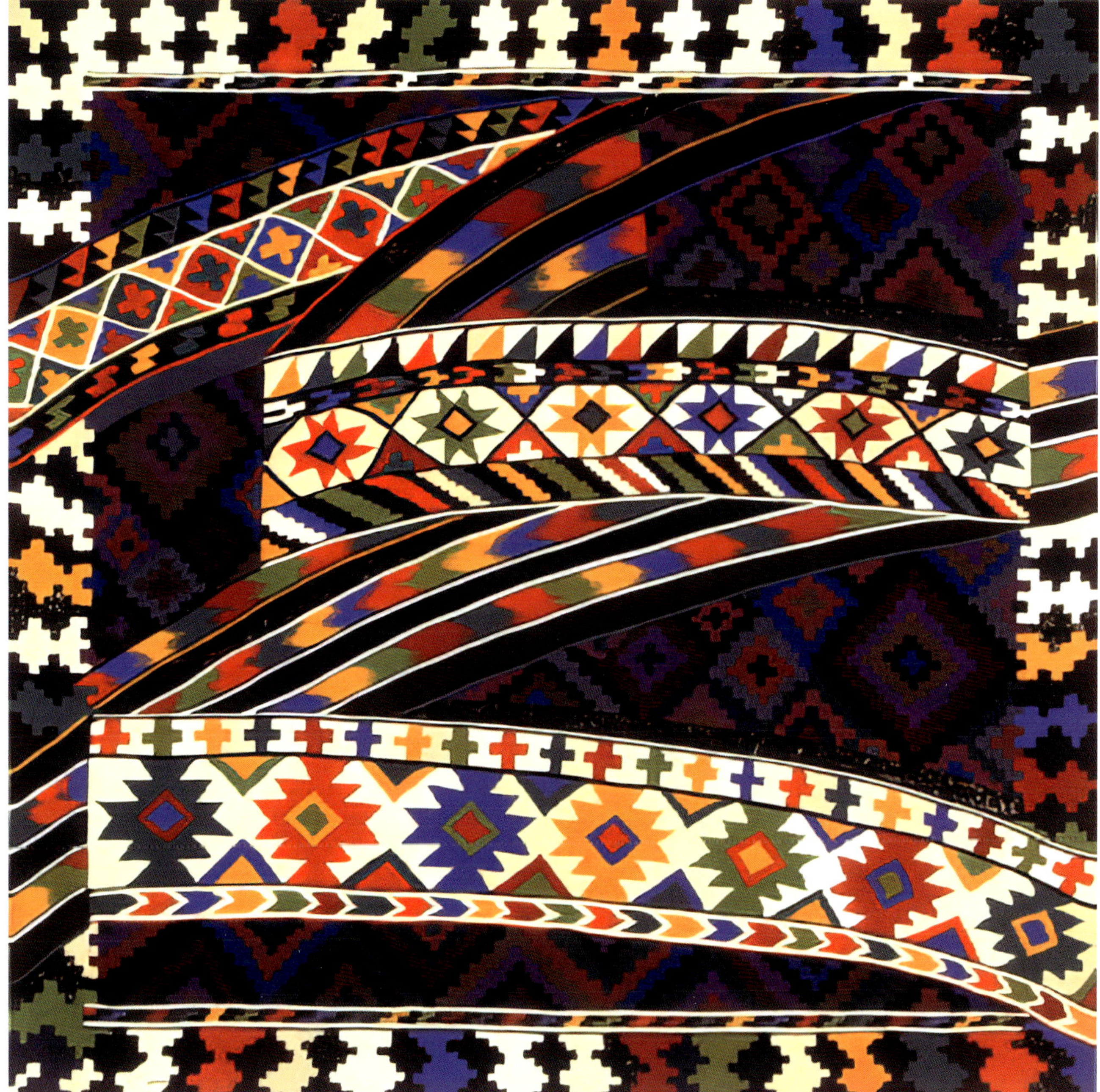

Thoma Ewen often fills her work with color and simple shapes. Here she has used curved bands in colors like a spiral. You can see particularly clearly how line creates these bands. Her hot red, top right, cools toward the bottom left.

Murray Gibson's richly patterned bands, like joyfully embellished belts, crisscross the field of the tapestry with immense energy, curving very slightly.

Anastasia Schneider's teapot looks like something alive, as though it will suddenly sprout legs and walk away. Her blue stripes fill the tapestry. The teapot might even be a creature with an open mouth.

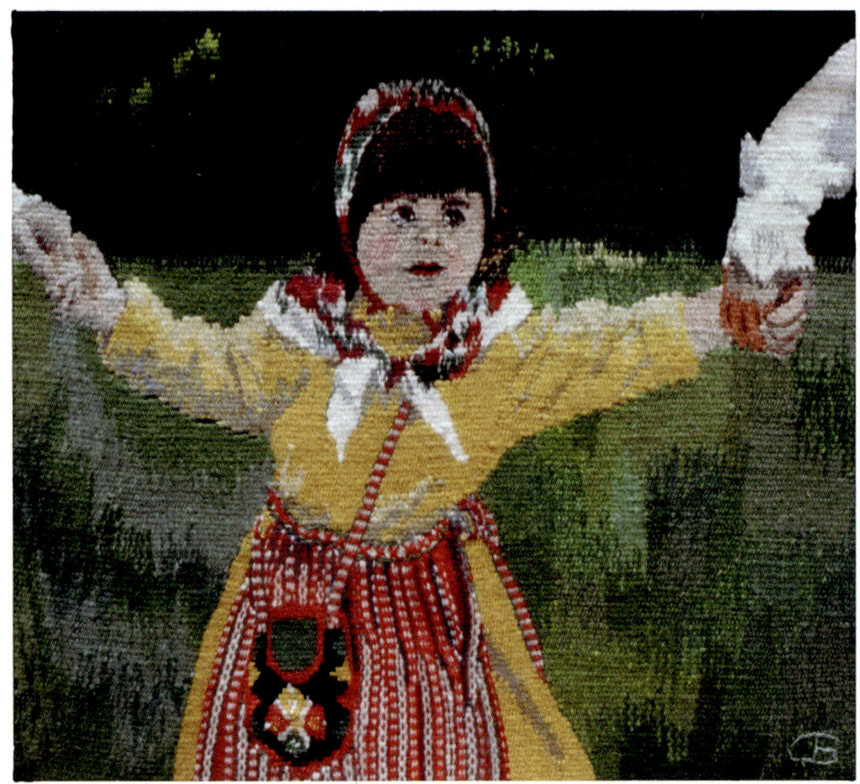

Cecilia Blomberg's *Emma* wears colors that reflect her ethnic roots, with the patterned bands of the apron showing these most clearly.

Ethnic roots are most obvious in the largest part of Zita Mateicha's exhilarating tapestry, with the belts that fall like a curtain, forming a background, or flags that wave in the wind or even threaten to overwhelm the small group of people at the bottom center.

ABOVE: *Emma*
Cecilia Blomberg
1993 | 18" × 21" | wool, linen

BELOW: *A Folklore Party*
Zita Mateicha
1987 | 65" × 11'6" × 3.1"–3.9" | linen, wool

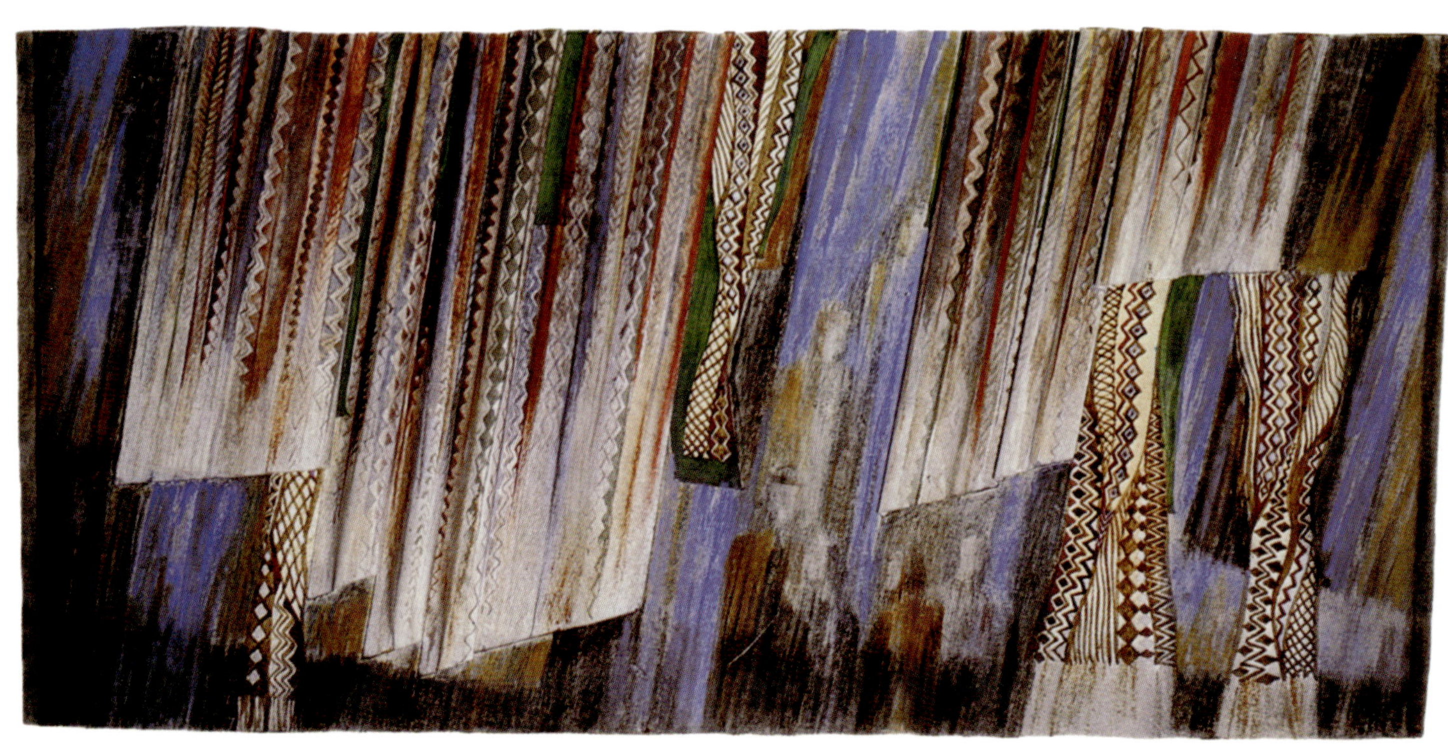

oh my! redux

What follows are some unexpected combinations of line and band.

Frances Crowe has combined many sorts of lines and stripes to give us the landscape where we might go walking.

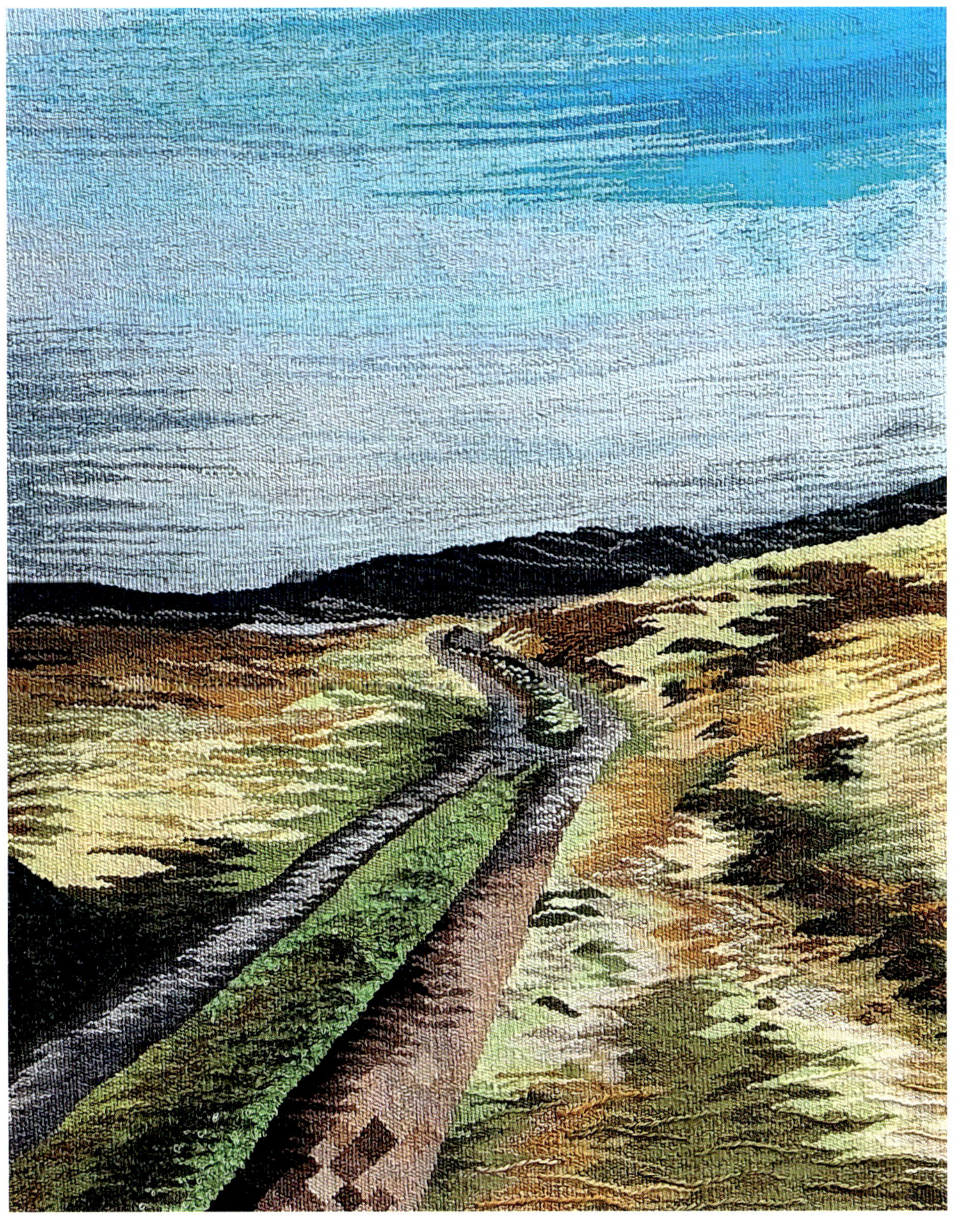

Track 1
Frances Crowe
2023 | 37.4" × 31.5"

Mette Handberg's cartoonlike piece just speaks of fun. The outlines show us a chicken's feathers and spreading wings. The colors seem to bleed through the outlines.

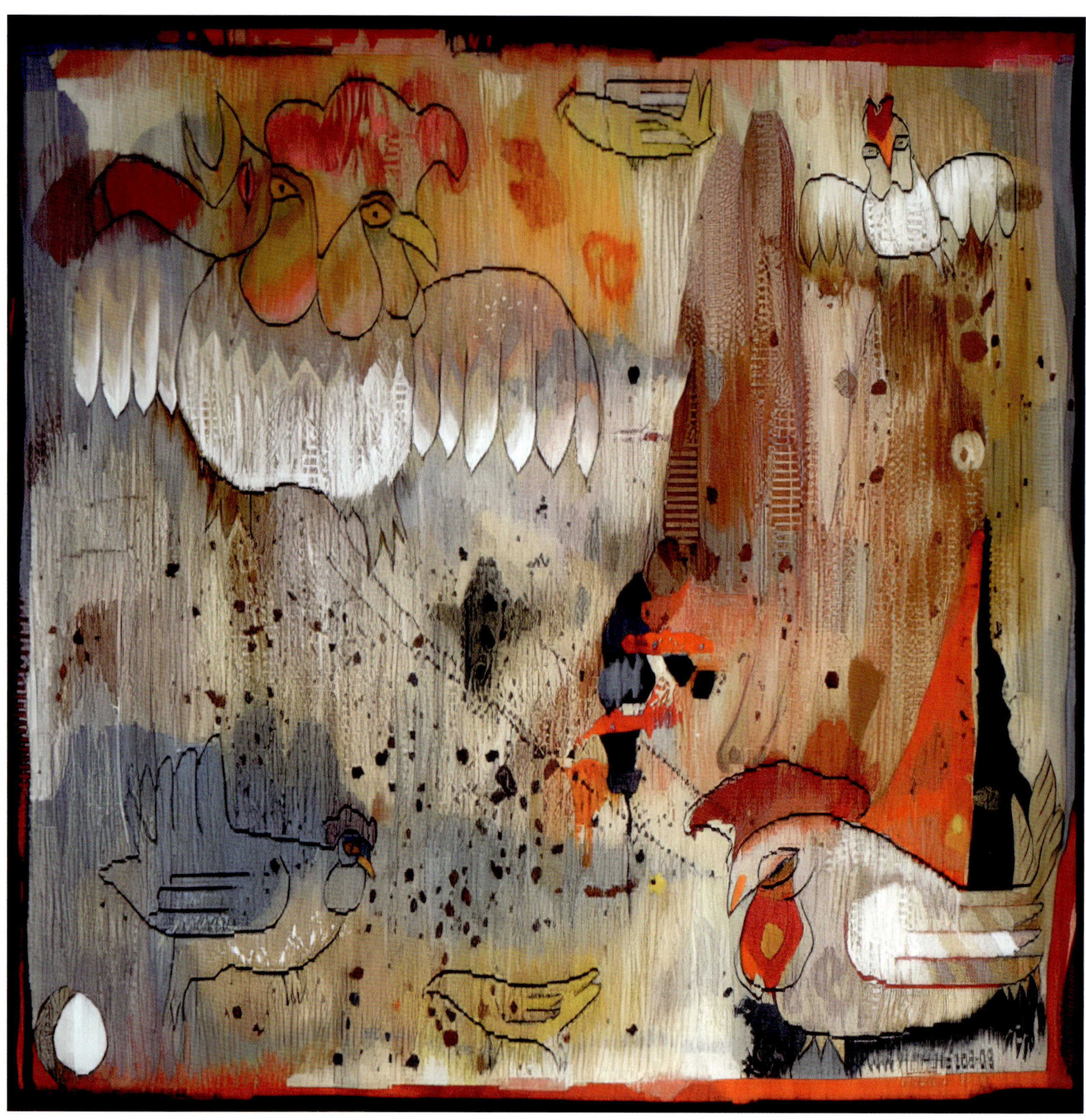

Chatbox
Mette Handberg
2008 | 57.5" × 57.9" | wool, cotton, linen, artificial fibers

Andrew Schneider's figures are looking at and reacting to the egg-like floating moon—or perhaps the moon is behind the dominant figure on the right. Curved stripes, bands, and lines in various permutations give us bodies defined by clothing with lovely designs.

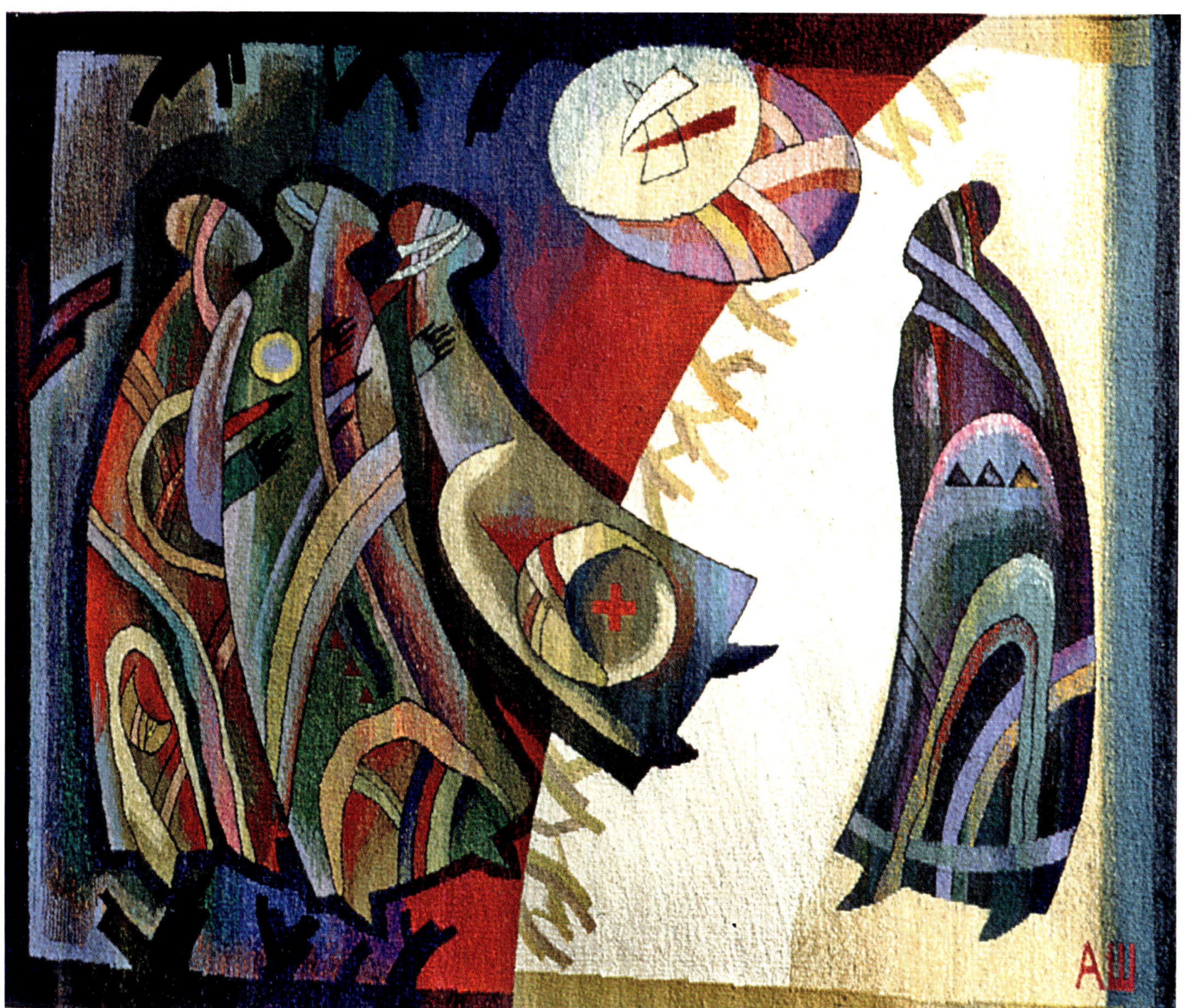

The Moon
Andrew Schneider
1995 | 47.25" × 76.75" | wool, linen

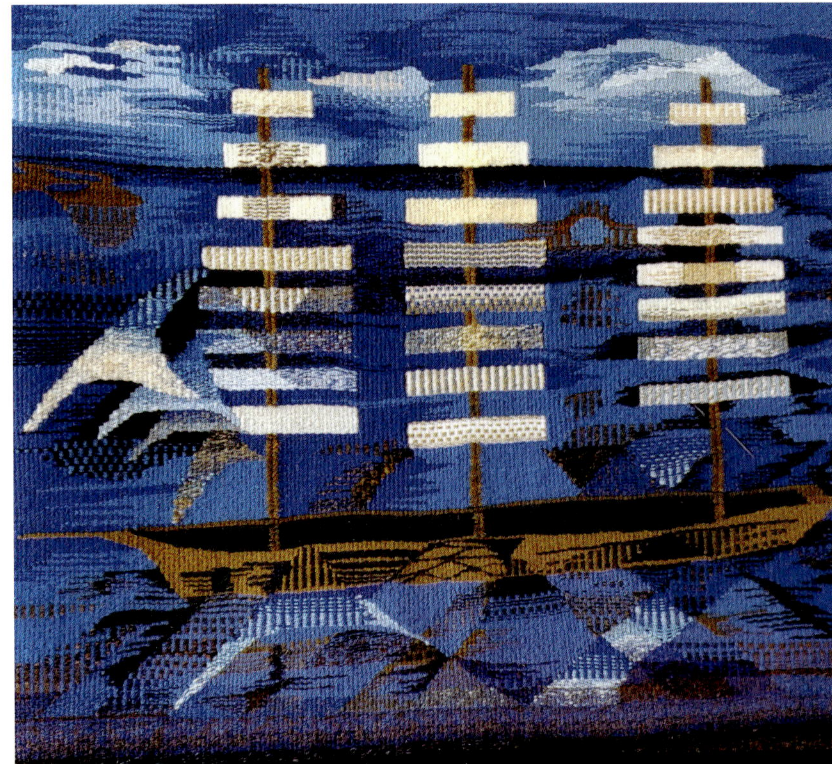

The Ghost Ship
Wendy Murray
1997 | 26" × 31" | wool

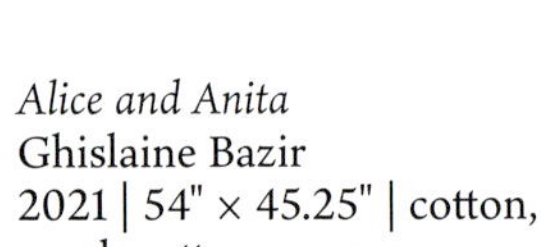

Alice and Anita
Ghislaine Bazir
2021 | 54" × 45.25" | cotton, wool; cotton warp

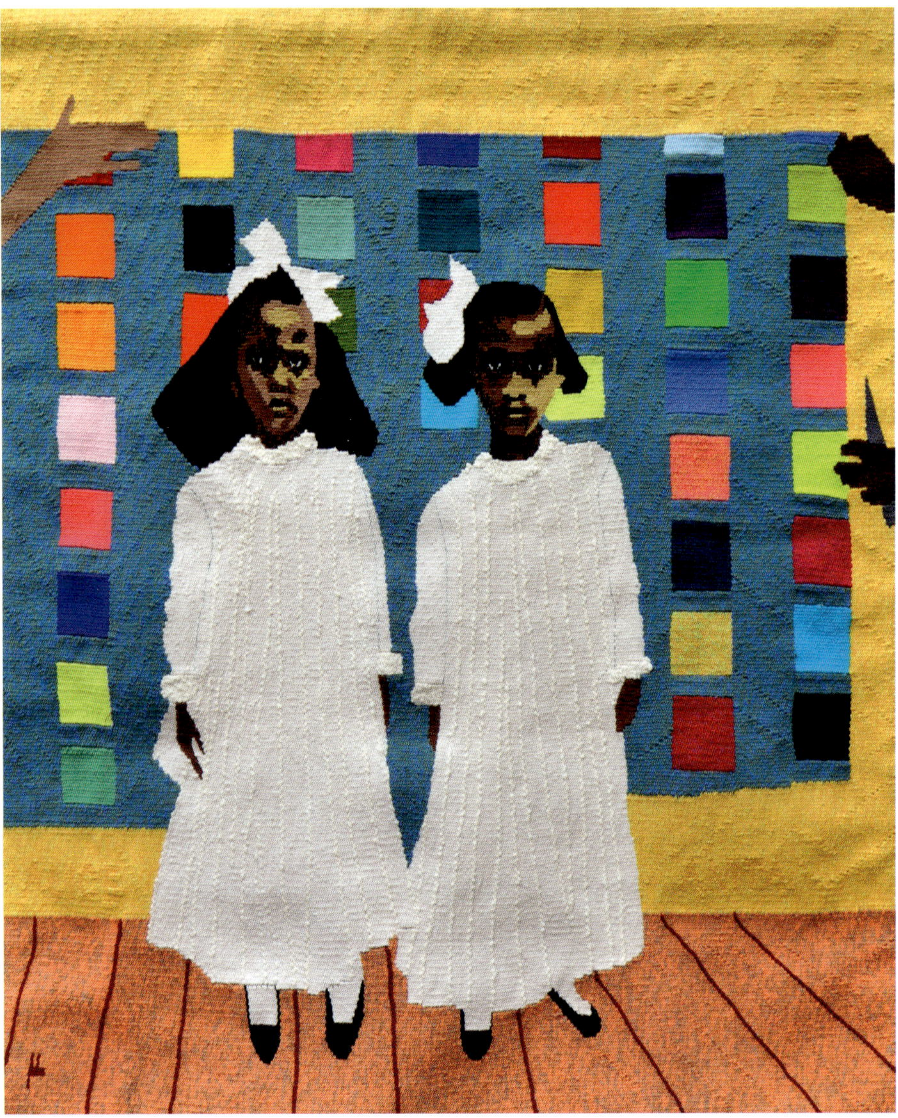

Wendy Murray has combined strong verticals and horizontals to construct her ship, in the middle of the sea, with the sails full of the wind; some billow. Note the comprehensive use of pick and pick.

Ghislaine Bazir's *Alice and Anita* are standing in front of a patchwork quilt with squares of colors building on top of each other. Their dresses contain subtle white stripes.

Tommye Scanlin often includes plants in her weavings. Here the central leaf is framed by checkerboards and lines. Her two sets of frames, light and dark, have similar but distinctive motifs.

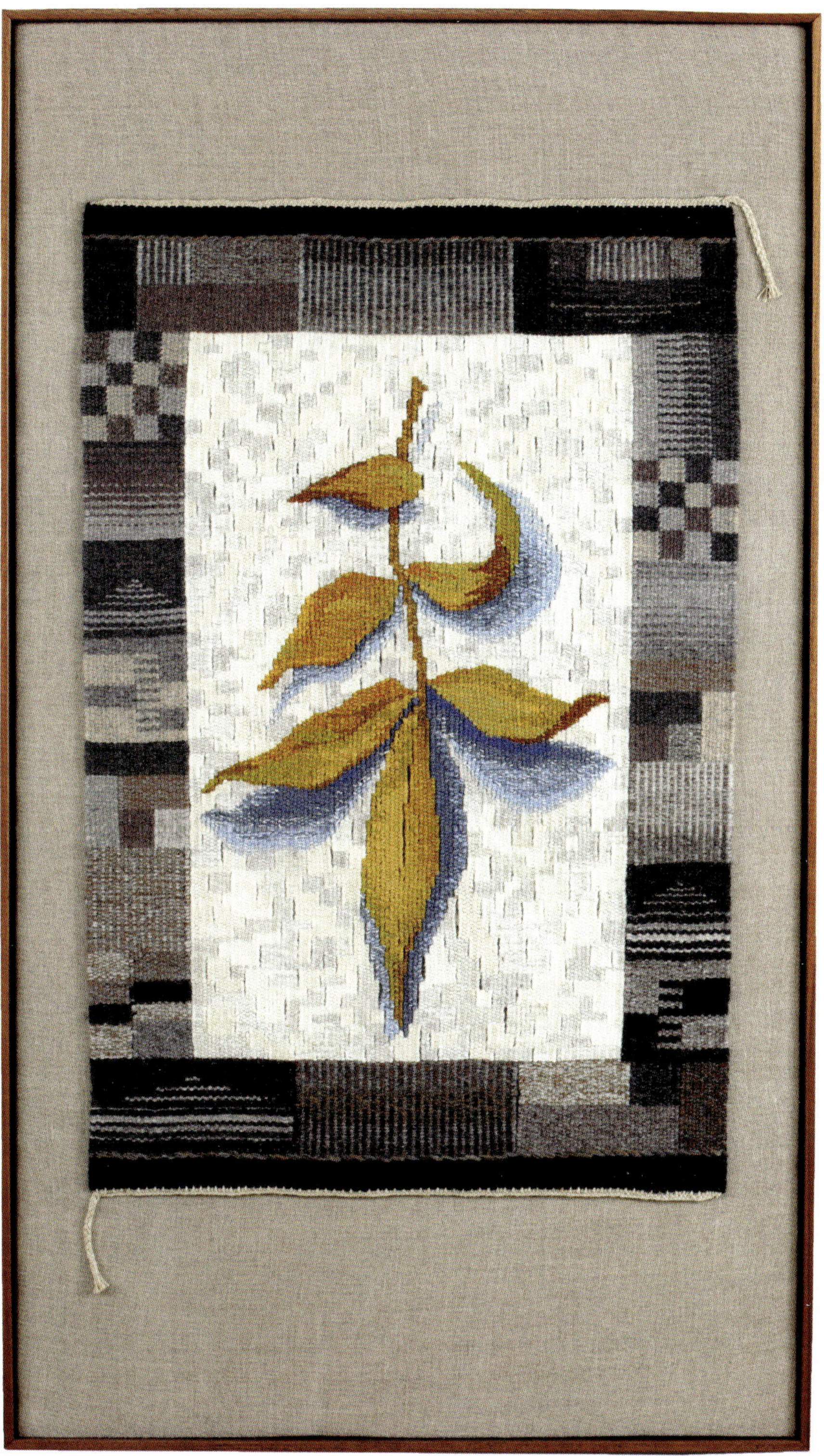

Hickory
Tommye Scanlin
2016 | 32" × 18" | wool, linen, cotton
Photographer: Tim Barnwell

Liliana Crespi here offers a visual interpretation of nonlinear bubble wrap or soap suds, with the colors of the rainbow. She has carefully orchestrated the changes of color, and the network itself that separates the colors.

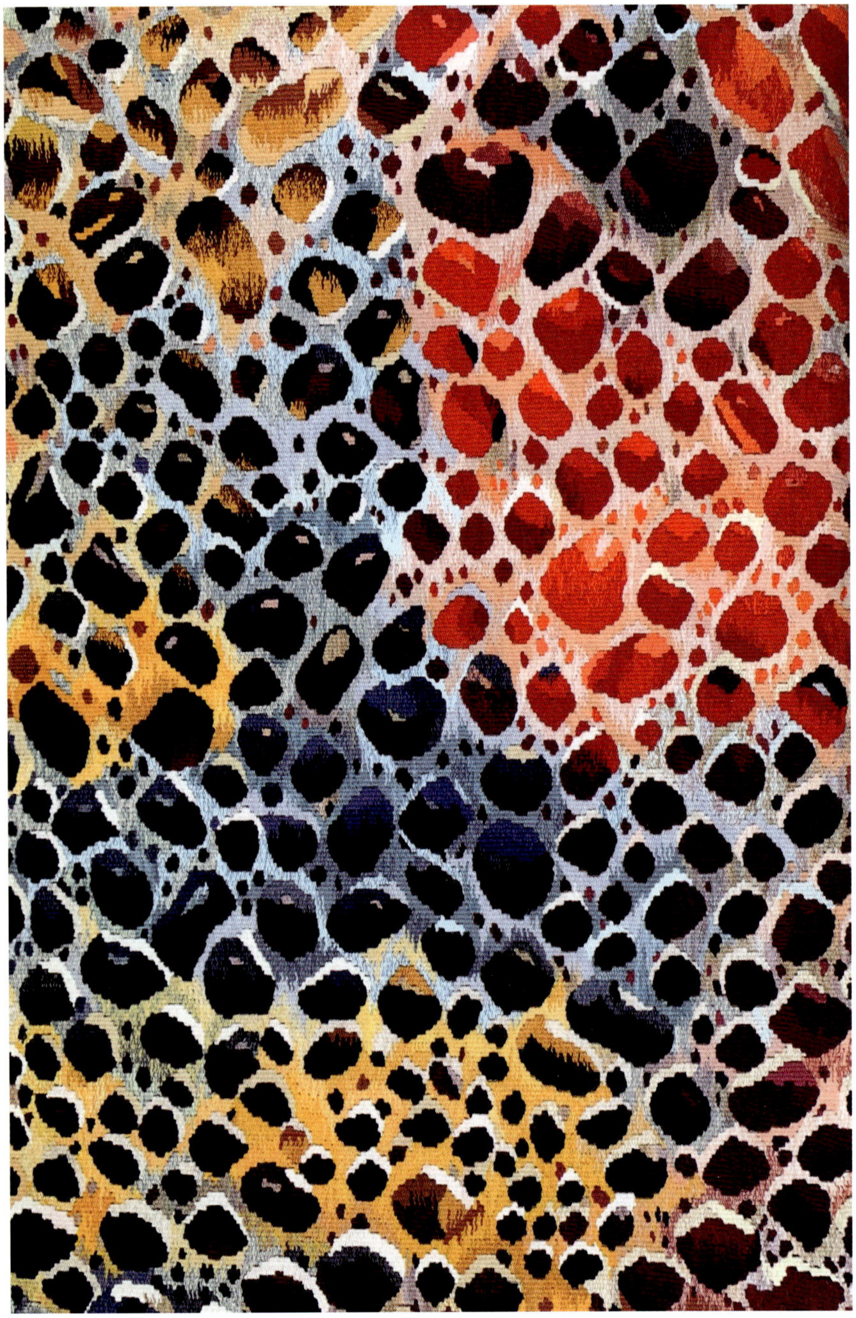

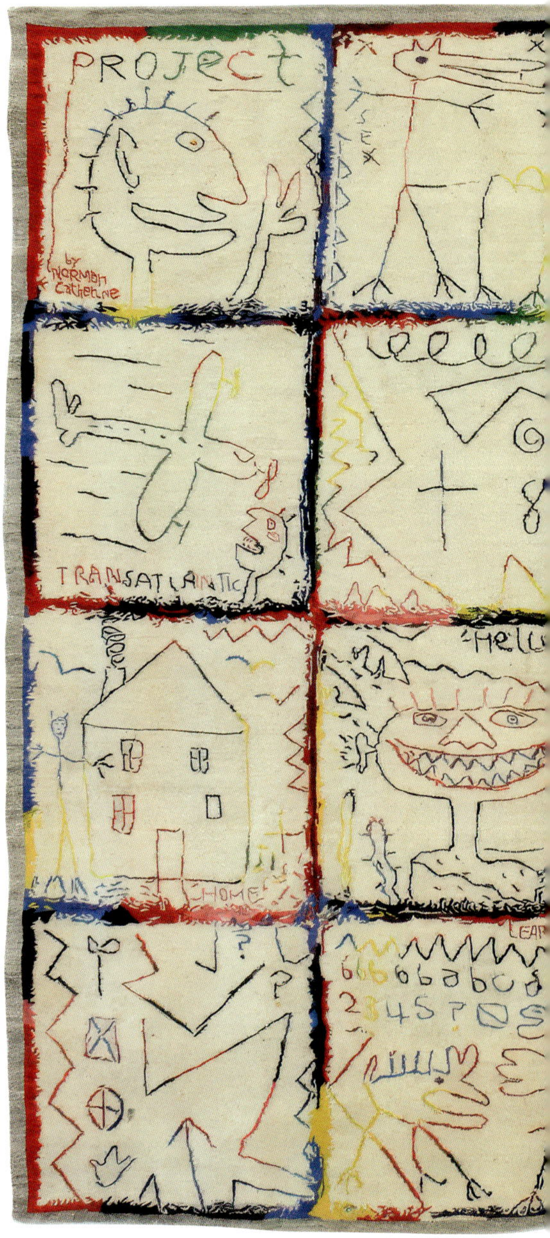

Norman Catherine designed sixteen squares filled with simple drawings, as though by a child, with bright colors that would appeal to a young person.

Bubbles
Liliana Crespi
2023 | 48" × 34" | wool, cotton; cotton warp

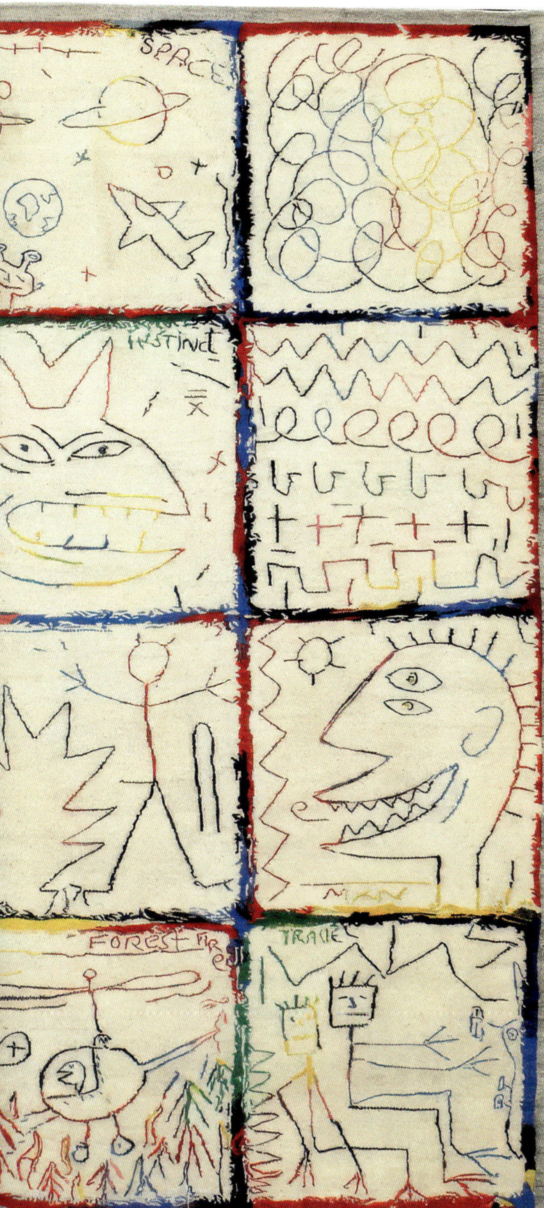

Project Board
Norman Catherine
Marguerite Stephens Tapestry Studio
1994 | 77" × 81.5" | mohair

In this mysterious tapestry, Suzanne Paquette combines lines, both vertical and horizontal, inside a field framed on three sides by small triangles. The central squarish shape, in brilliant reds and oranges, seemingly set on water, nonetheless sits in front of a dim cityscape.

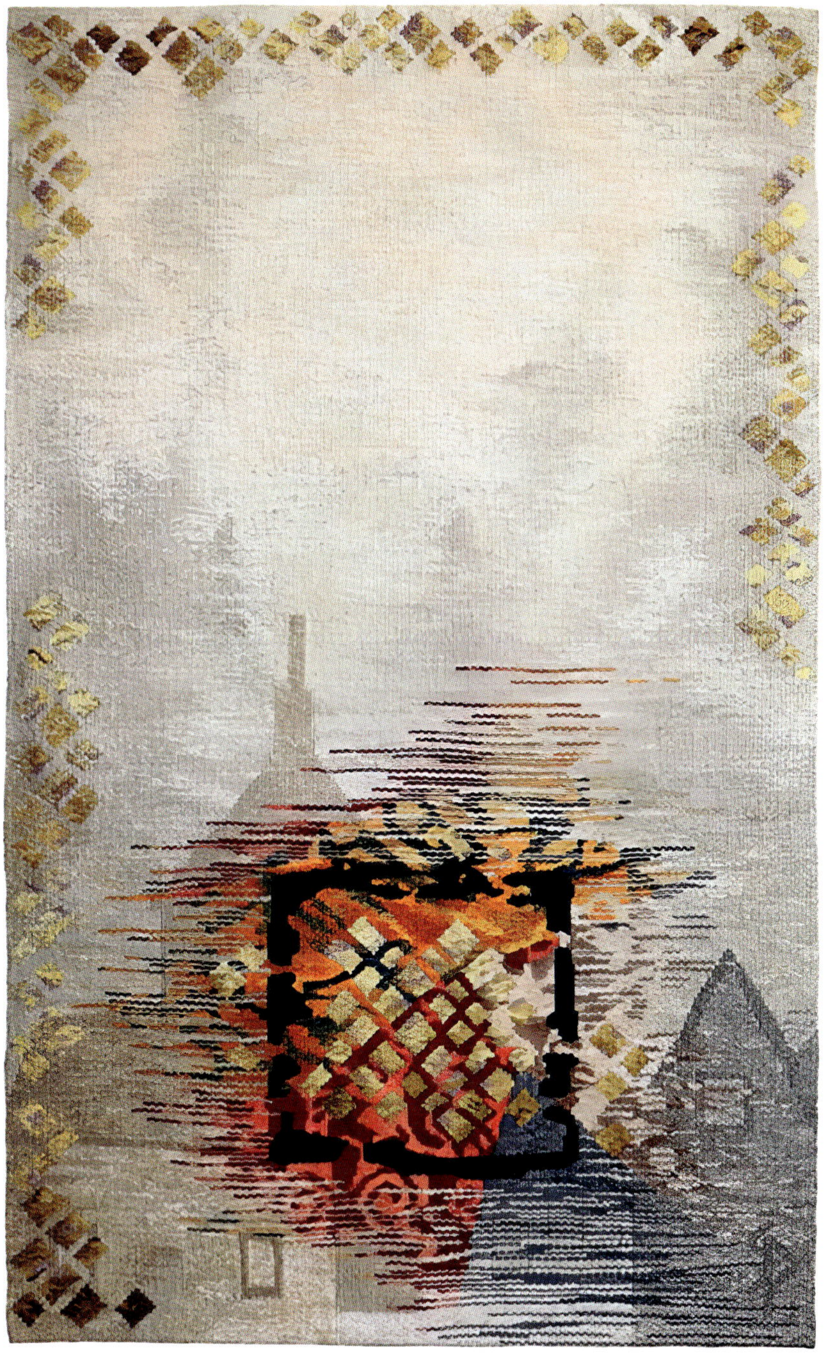

Oeuvres de femmes (Women's work)
Suzanne Paquette
2021 | 57.7" × 36.6" | cotton, wool, synthetic fibers

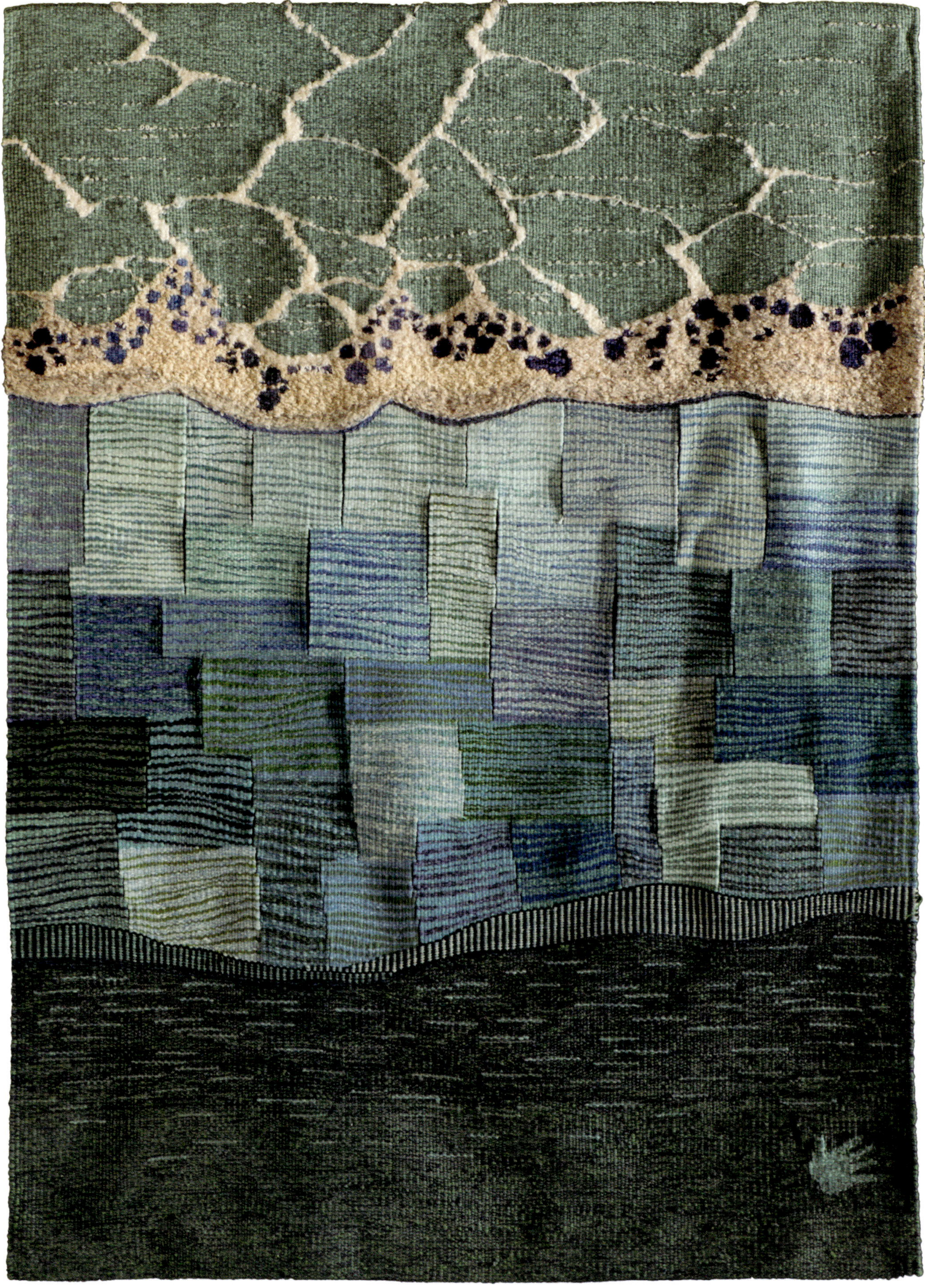

CHAPTER 8

slit

The space between warp threads disappears when interlaced by weft: The weaver has produced whole cloth. If, however, the weaver chooses *not* to weave across that space, they leave a slit, which is a technical term for the resulting gap between warps. Sometimes the slits permit the weaver to build up a shape—and sometimes slits can add subtlety and shadow or even suggest a line. During the Middle Ages, slit sewers had a well-established role in the weaving community. They made the cloth solid when, for design or ease of weaving, the weaver had purposely left a gap.

Slits can show up in the most surprising places. In a field of a single color, if the weaver does not weave across the entire area but goes to a certain point and then returns, then retreats as they weave only to the next warp thread over, and then returns, and so on, in time a visible diagonal slit will develop (the slit will look like a line). Inaccurately called a "lazy line," these can also add an element to what we see.

Flow 7: Seafoam
Alex Friedman
2016 | 48" × 34" | wool, wool bouclé, cotton, silk; cotton warp

Alex Friedman has here woven slits that make sections of cloth overlap each other slightly, creating shadows. The varied surface texture offers added visual interest. The vertical lines of slits contrast with what is above, a section that looks flat, with irregular shapes separated by off-white borders, the foam.

BELOW: *Facade*
Sharon Marcus
2003 | 23"–19" × 11.5"–15" | linen, wire; wool warp

OPPOSITE, TOP: *Witness Marks*
Liz Pulos
2019 | 36" × 38" | wool

OPPOSITE, BOTTOM: *Wehmut* (Melancholy)
from the *Heimweh* (Homesickness) series
Thomas Cronenberg
2015 | 40.3" × 59" | wool, cotton, linen; linen warp

Sharon Marcus includes a description of her process, which produces a rigid surface with slits, which she treats like holes, and which work like punctuation. To make this tapestry, it was "washed with regular laundry detergent in a washing machine, beat with [a] ball-peen hammer on an anvil, painted with a mixture of acrylic matte medium and Createx dry pigment, burnished on both sides with a jade burnishing tool." The piece becomes rigid. It is nonetheless cloth; it was woven.

In Liz Pulos's work, the slits punctuate the movement of the colors, creating visual interest. They slow the eye and vary the texture of her blue/purple ribbons as they unfurl across the triangle and the fiery oranges and reds.

The longest slits in Thomas Cronenberg's *Wehmut* appear in the yellow liquid in the middle of that pitcher.

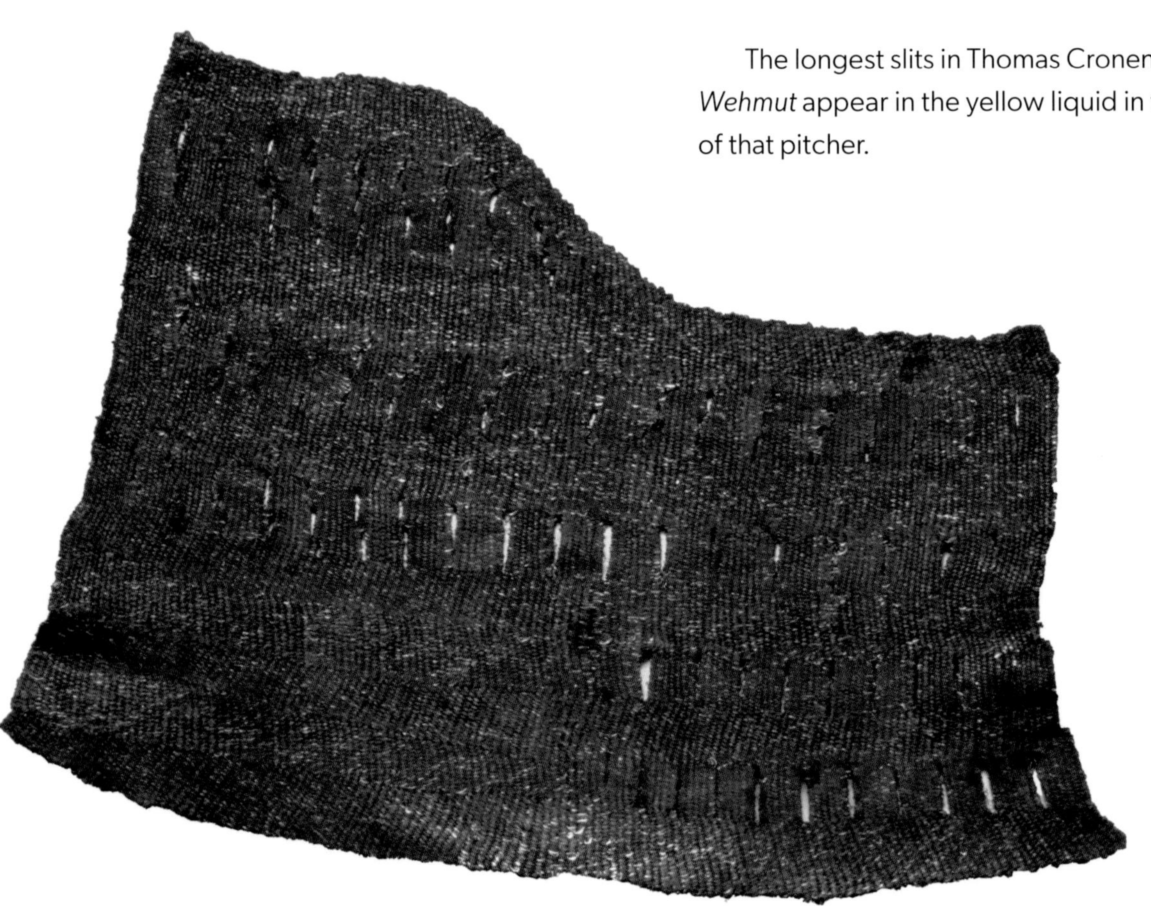

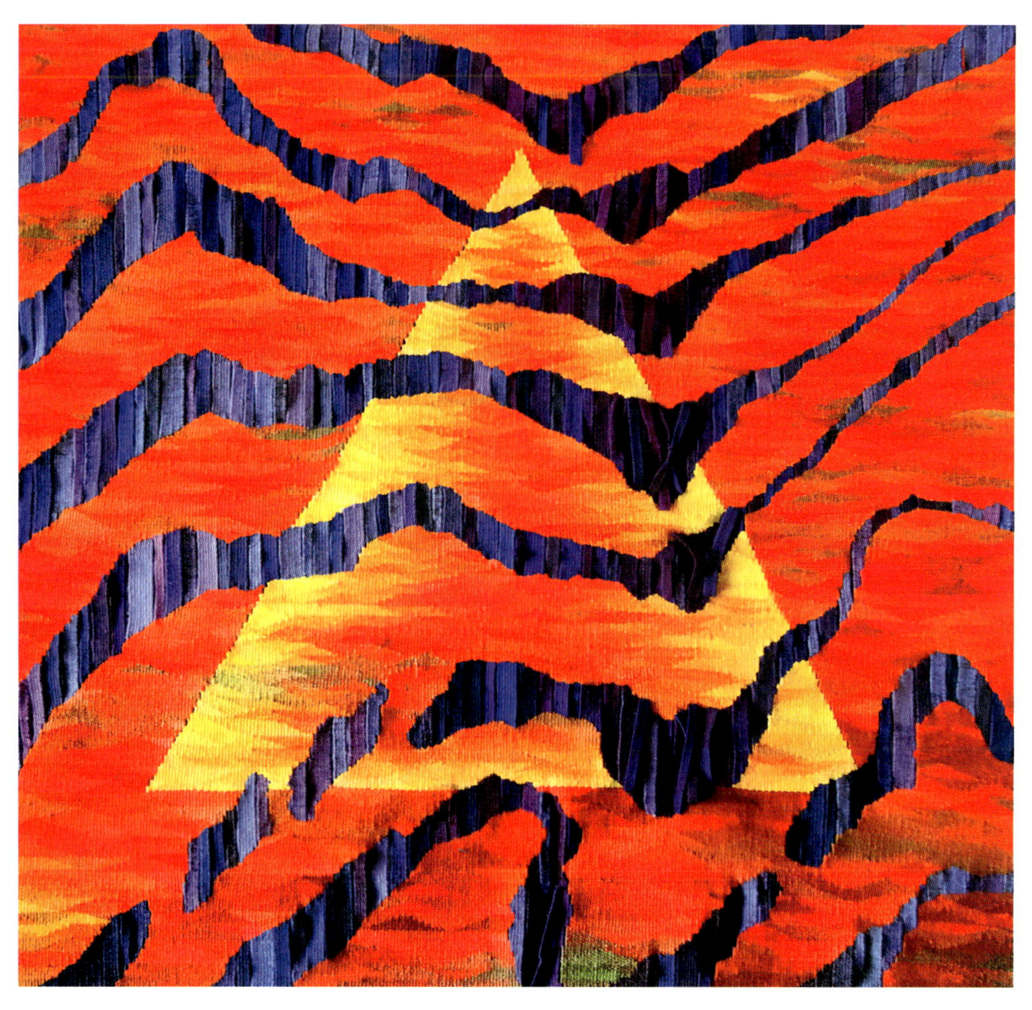

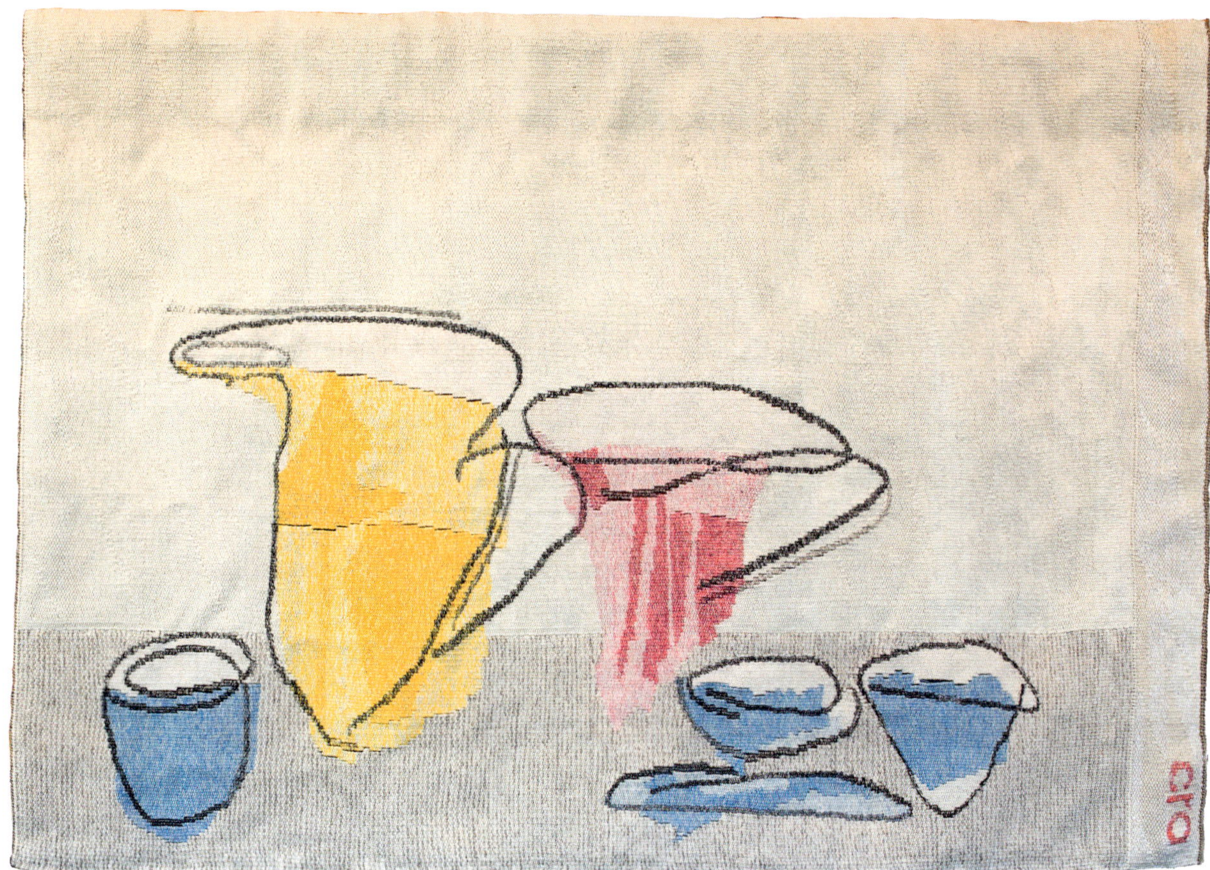

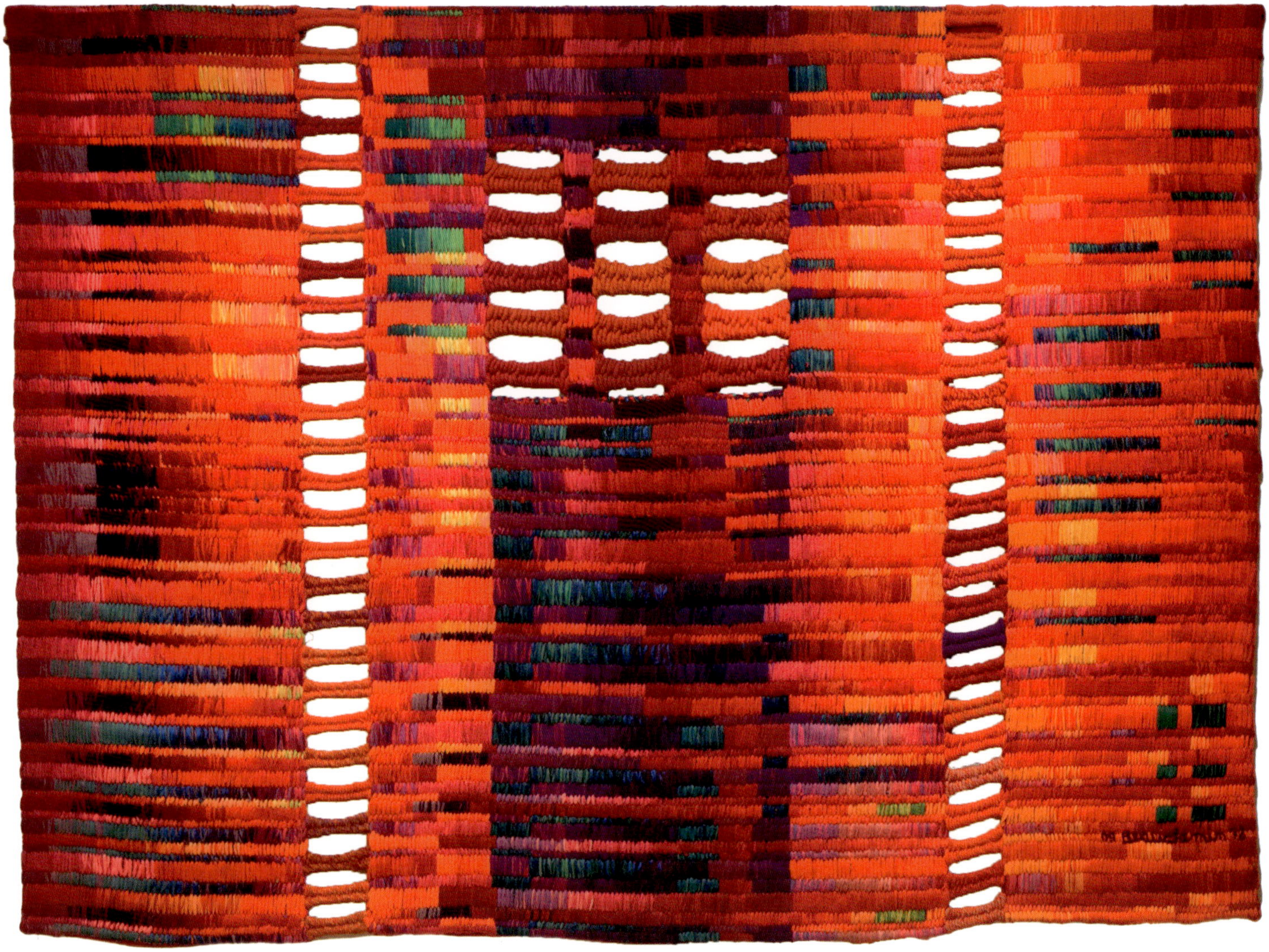

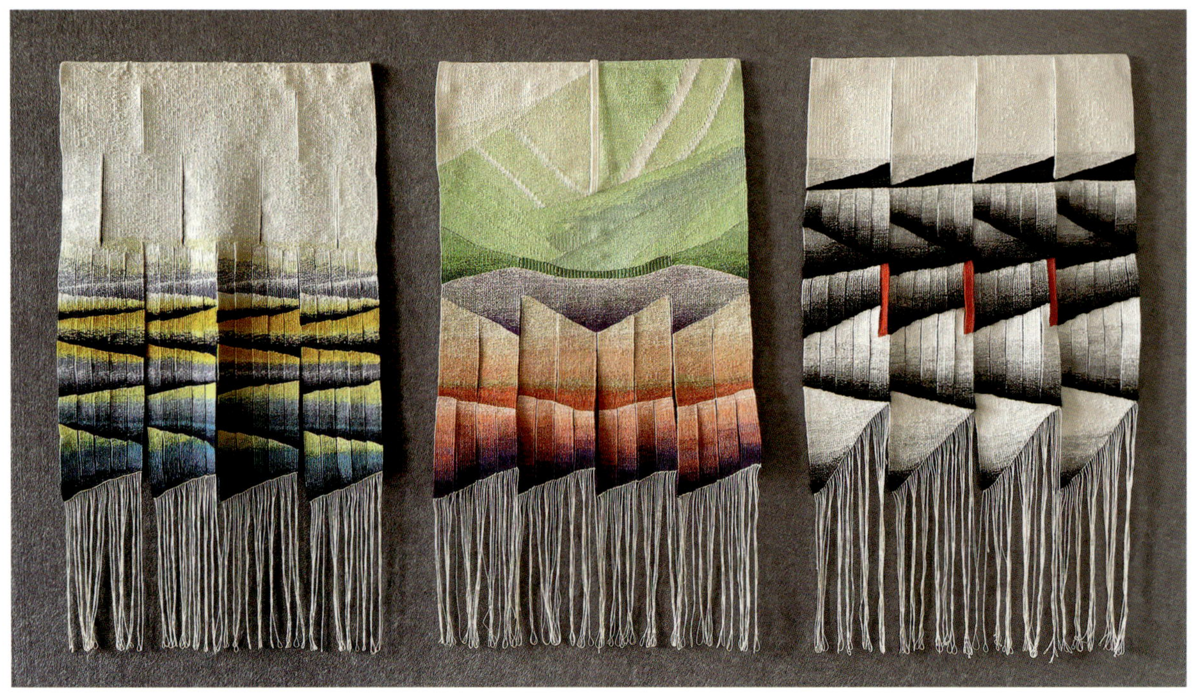

Micheline Beauchemin's slits are large and dramatic. A jig includes hops and jumps—and so does this tapestry.

Fannie Lee has made a three-part series with slits that suggest flaps, a banner, or even a flag. Note how often she incorporates very long slits. Each component looks as though it could work independently of the rest.

Emöke has made a sea of blues, its slits divided by the rays of a brilliant red-orange setting sun. These separate blocks of color make the water look rough.

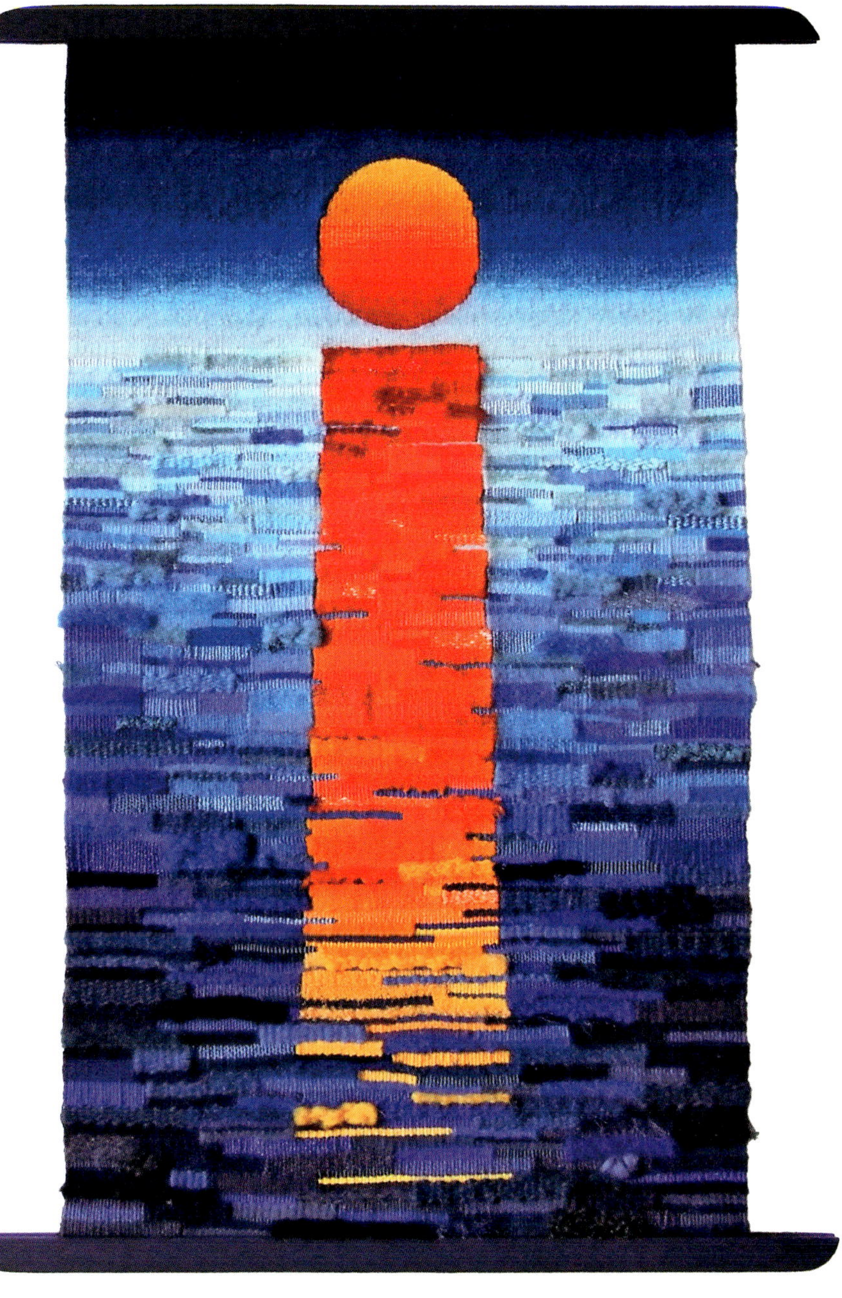

OPPOSITE, TOP: *3e Gigue* (3rd jig)
Micheline Beauchemin
1972 | 83.5" × 112.2" | wool
Musée National des Beaux-Arts du Québec
Photographer: Julie Bouffard

OPPOSITE, BOTTOM: *San Tien 1, 2, 3* (Mountain Sky)
Fannie Lee
2022–23 | 28" × 24" (each) | wool; cotton warp
Photographer: Richard Zampi

ABOVE: *Sol Lucet Omnibus* (The sun shines on all of us)
Emöke
2017 | 26" × 17.75"

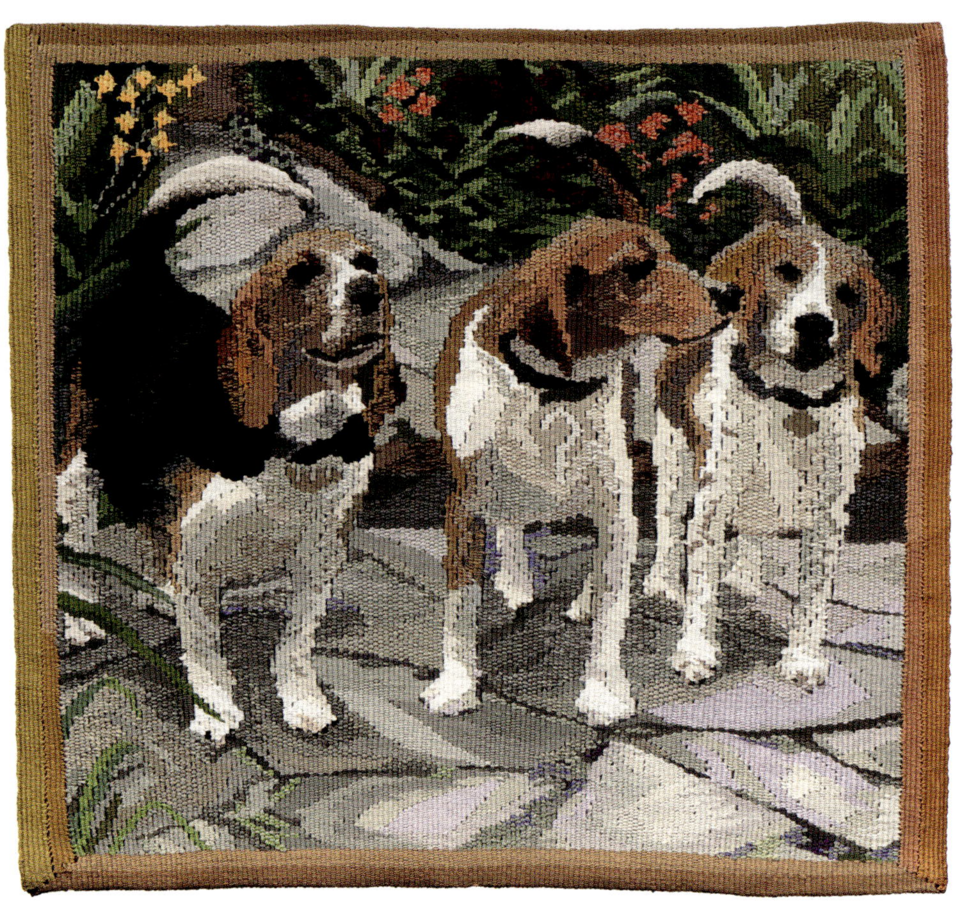

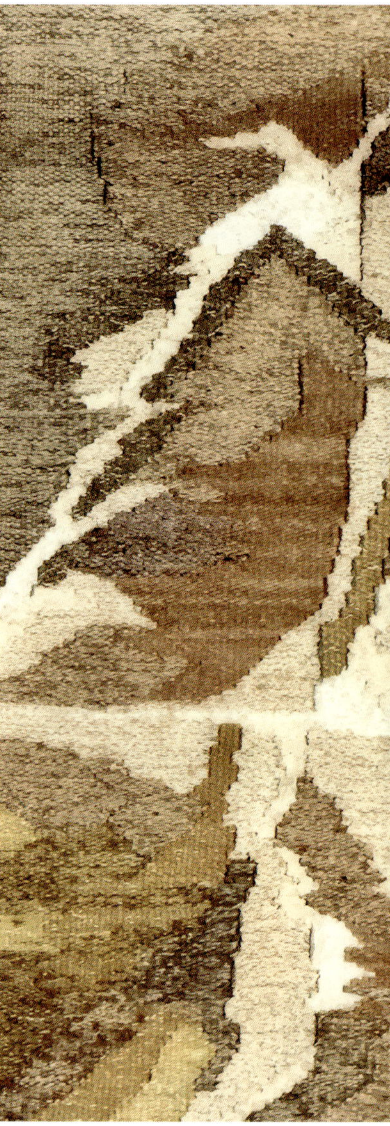

Beagles
Urban Jupena
2010 | 16" × 18" | cotton; linen warp

Urban Jupena has used slits to suggest bone structure and hair on the bodies and heads of these beagle puppies. (And what is that question mark on the center beagle?)

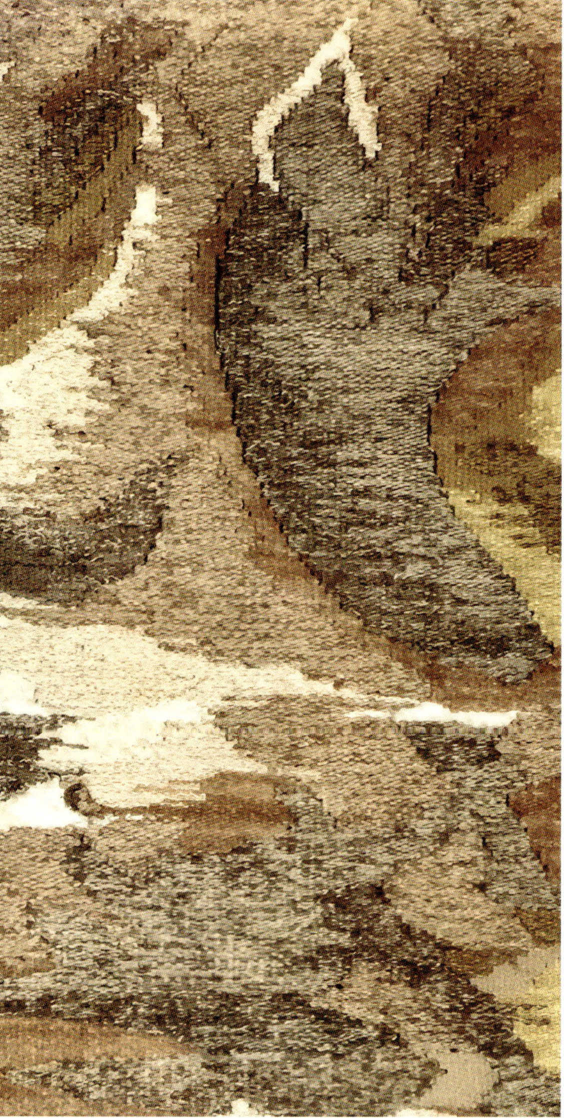

Flight
Esther Kolling
1985 | 29" × 29" | wool, cotton bouclé; cotton warp

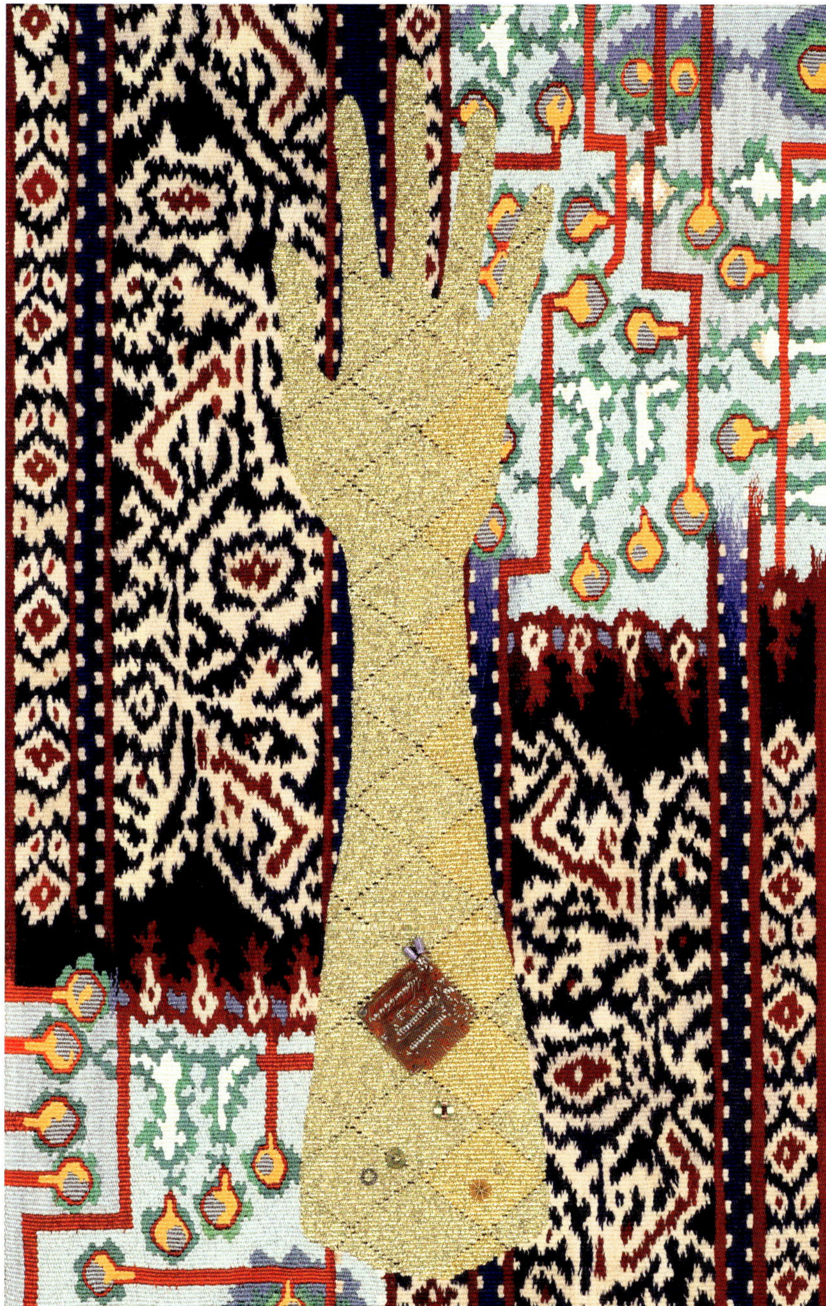

Ikat Algorithm
Barbara Heller
2008 | 37" × 24" | wool, rayon, metallic yarn, perle cotton, computer parts; linen warp

Esther Kolling's *Flight* suggests the air currents, and the wings in flight cutting their way through the sky. The slits mark the shift between colors.

Barbara Heller's tapestry includes unexpected slits in those crisscrossing lines that produce diamond patterning on the arm, like a tattoo.

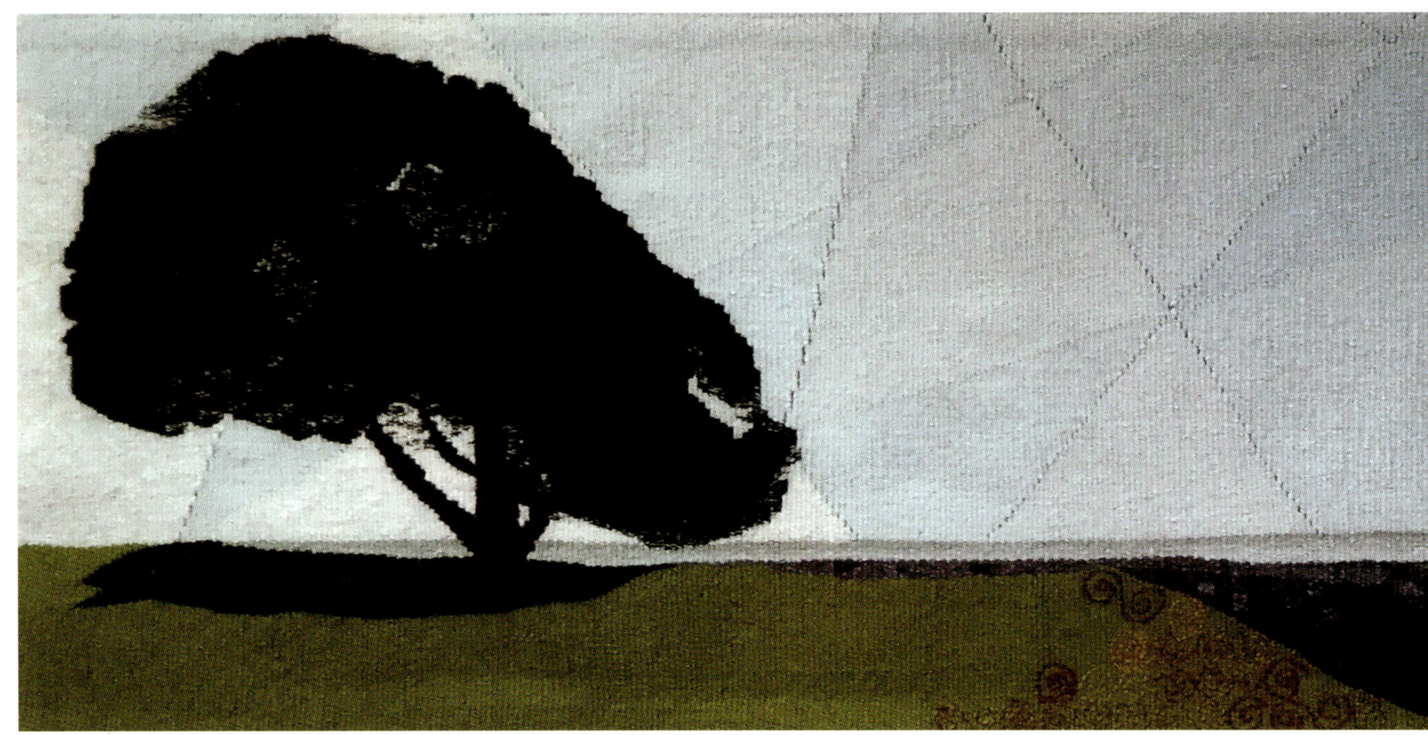

Matty Smith achieves a similar effect in *Adonis Rising*. She changes her blues, but her slits interrupt the expanse of sky, producing visible diagonals.

Susan Martin Maffei has long employed slits as a substitute for line. Her *Midnight Sunbathers* emphasizes bodies and the separation between body parts: Arms rest next to bodies; pairs of legs

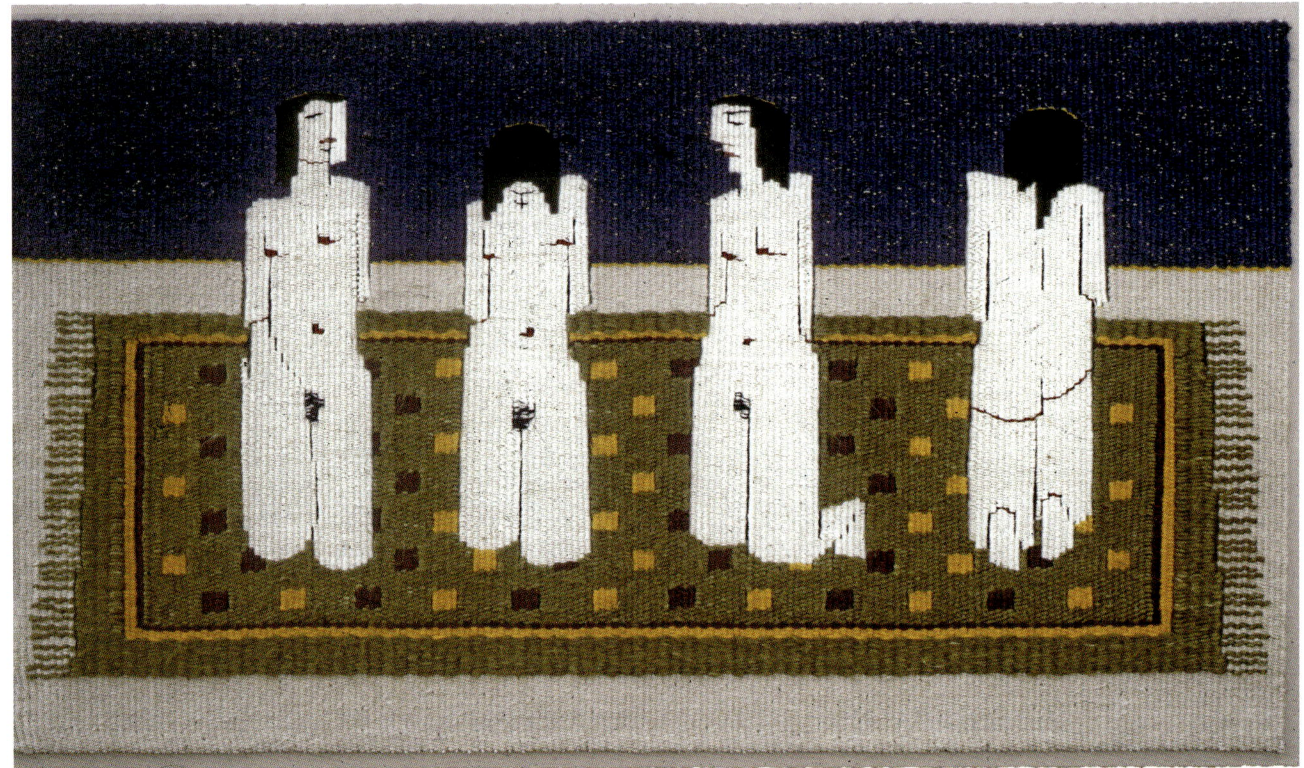

TOP: *Adonis Rising*
Matty Smith
2015 | 22.5" × 31" | wool; cotton warp

ABOVE: *Midnight Sunbathers*
Susan Martin Maffei
1990s | 18" × 28" | linen, cotton, wool, gold thread, silk; cotton warp

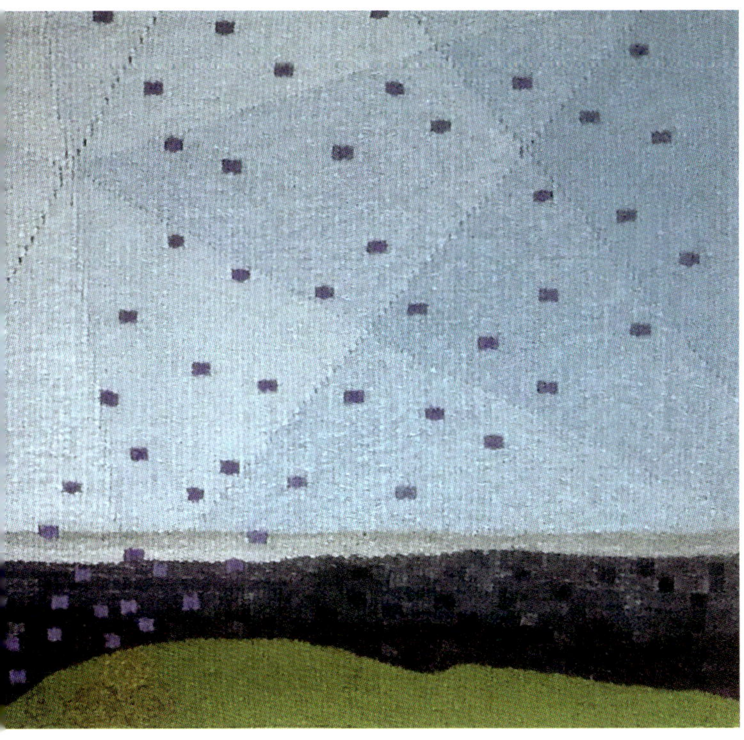

are divided; a face on the left is cut in two by a slit, as though seen from more than one angle.

Woven some thirty years later, Maffei's *Pandora Box: Honey Locust Tree* shows even greater ambition. She has inserted one major slit that is easy to see, near the top, between halves. But otherwise, she doesn't include any visible vertical separation between one warp and another. Rather, the slits mark the separation between the rounded forms, which look like pipes. Maffei knows how to control her weft yarn so precisely that she can make an edge look irregular, and powerfully dimensional, rather than just straight. It is a remarkable accomplishment.

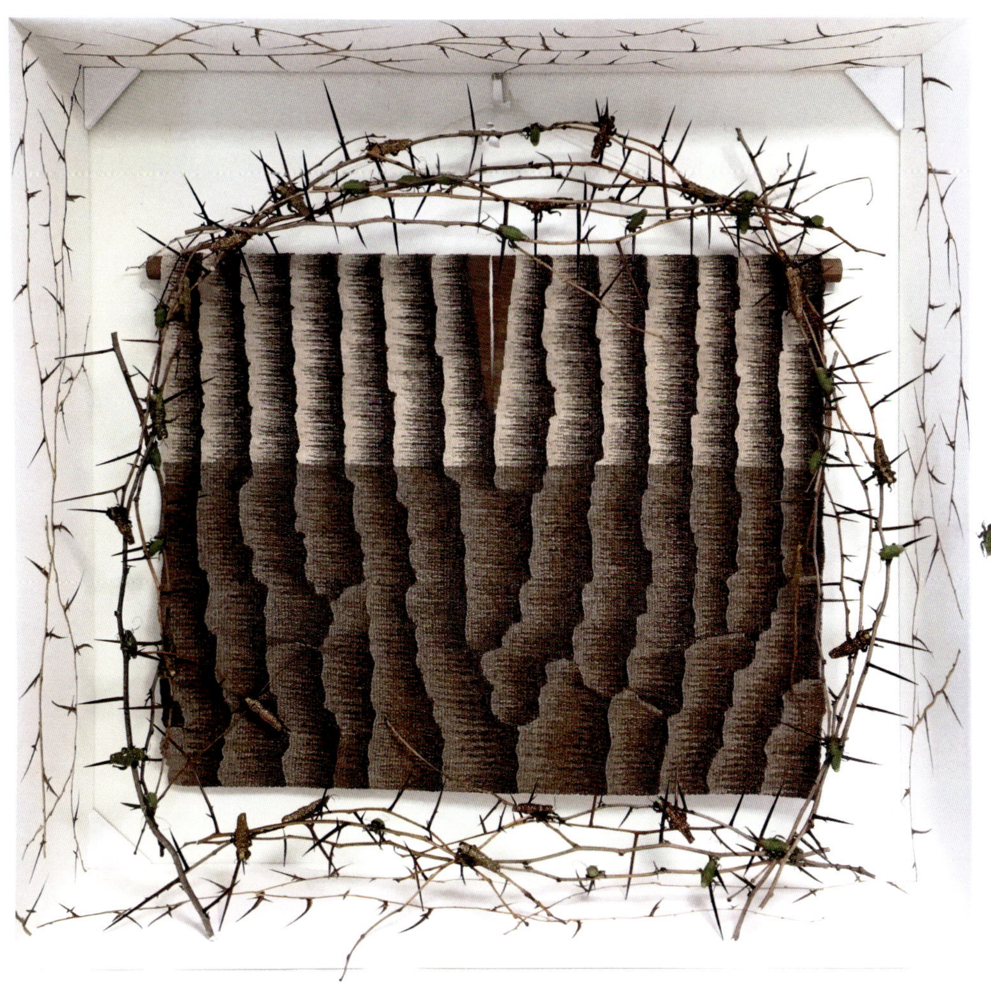

Pandora Box: Honey Locust Tree
Susan Martin Maffei
49.5" × 48" (with frame) | black walnut hand-dyed linen, ramie, hemp and wool, silk-covered stainless steel, rayon, silk, pine lumber, acrylic paints, conservation-sprayed thorns and branches of the honey locust, Velcro.

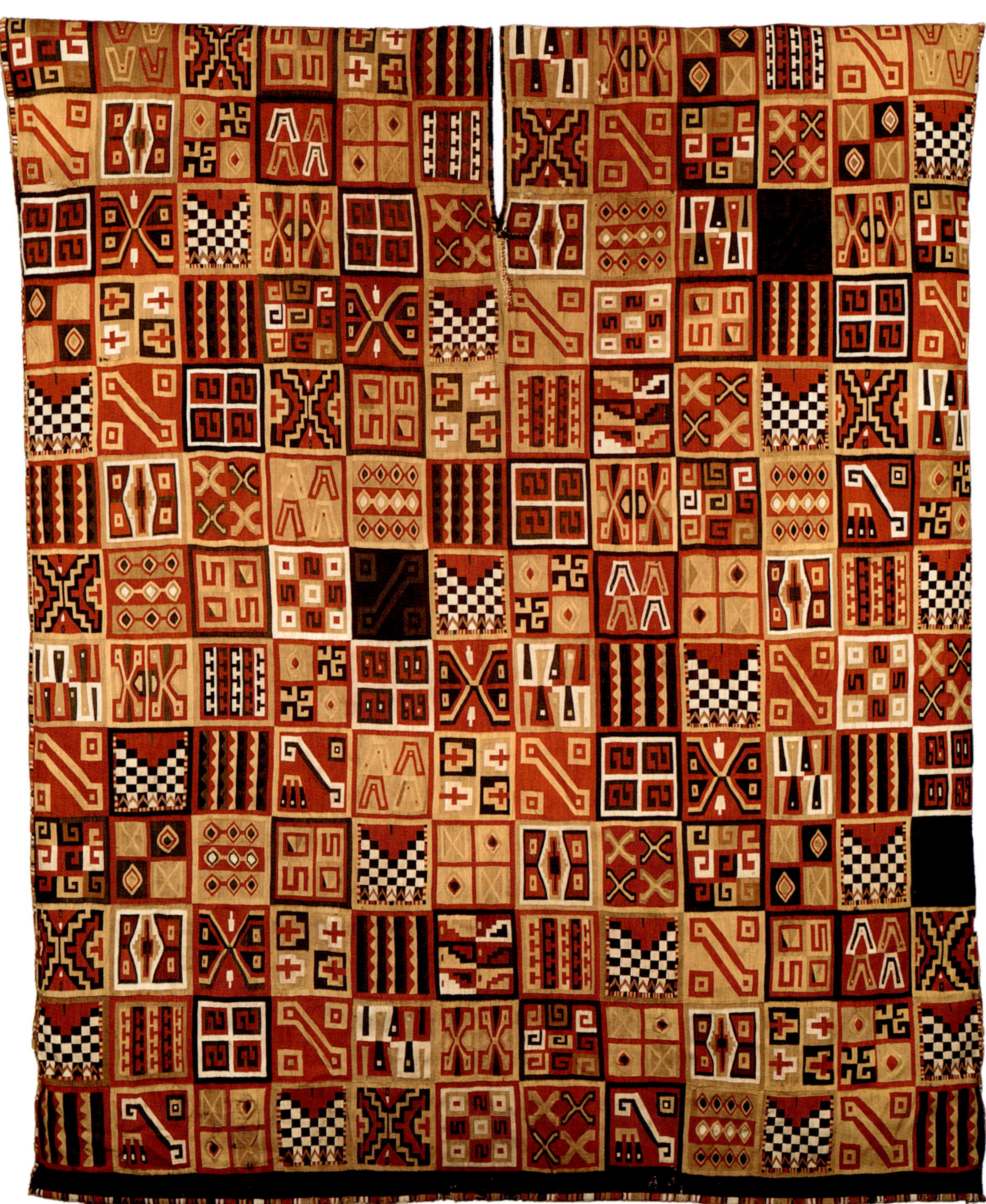

grid

Threads interlacing threads create a grid, a term that defines some of the most basic of weaving processes and patterns.

Many tapestry weavers echo the grid pattern in their imagery. The threads that divide the sections sometimes make strict vertical and horizontal lines and sometimes, more idiosyncratically, create wiggles and curves. A grid may develop a succession of images like a comic strip. (The technical term for a tapestry design is, after all, "cartoon.") While the weaver has a number of ways to tell a story, the grid pattern organizes the story more overtly: this and then this and then this.

All T'oqapu tunic
Unidentified Inka weaver
Late horizon Inka 1450–1540 CE | 35.5" × 30.4" | wool, cotton
Collection of Dumbarton Oaks

The design of this Inka tunic is familiar, the wide range of patterns mesmerizing. Each area shows something new and distinct, though now and again, there are repeats. The whole might even look like a game board. The limited palette (no blues, greens, or purples) adds to its elegantly hypnotic effect. Like all Inka textiles, it was valued for the time and effort that the weaver took to do it well.

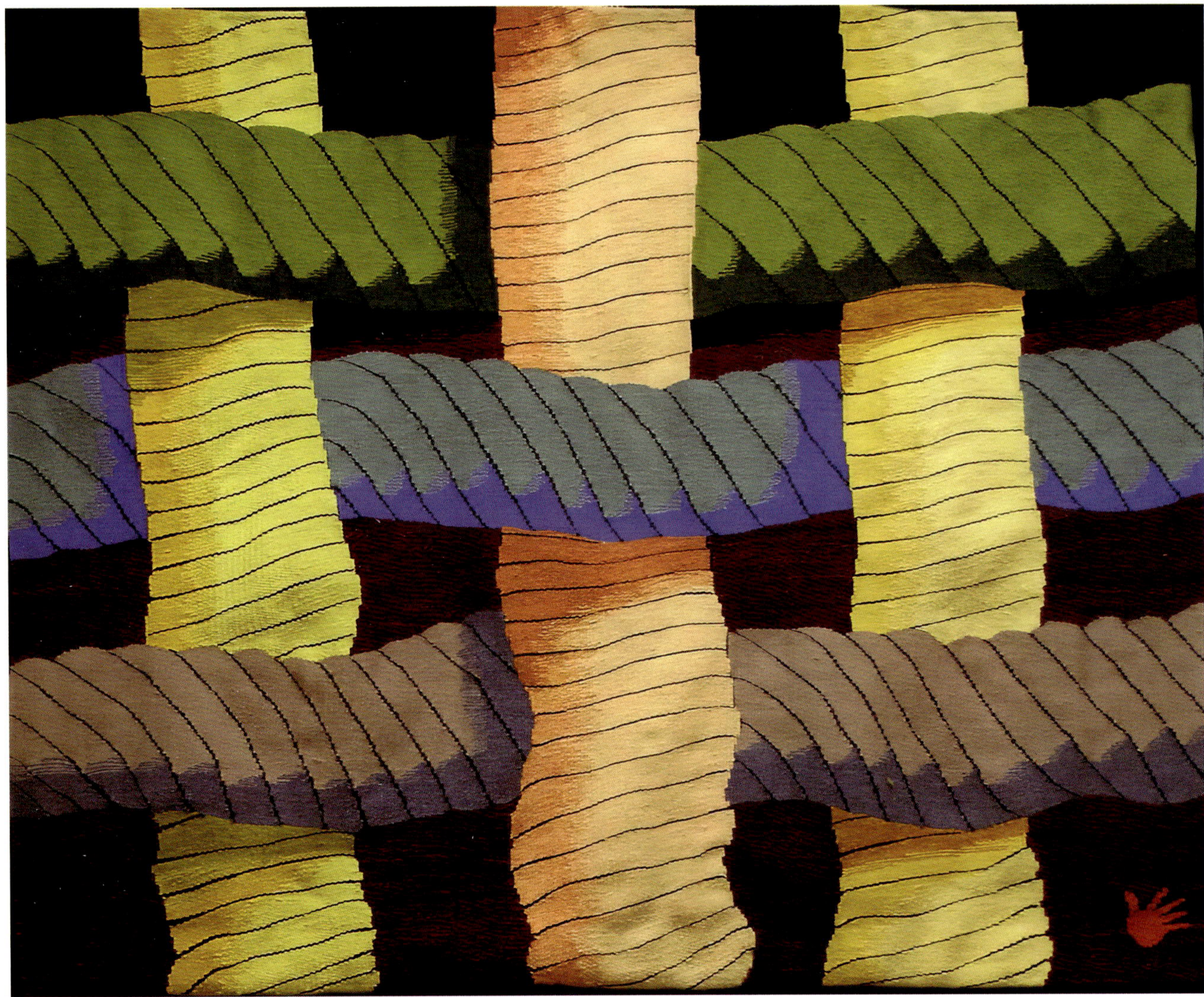

This playful tapestry by Alex Friedman, on the other hand, creates the quintessential visual of a grid, exaggerating the size of the threads so that they look as thick as a wrist, like rope.

Sara Lindsay has been working with gingham, in strips, for many years. It gives her pieces a particular texture, not flat like that created by a single thread, and no single color. It makes you want to count the squares. Here the large size of her squares (relative to the size of the whole, each 4 inches across) makes us look at the patterns more closely.

Sheila Hicks has assembled versions of the grid in *Quadrado Menos Obscuro*, where the thickness of the threads determines the visual result. Thinner threads form a frame; thicker threads take over the center.

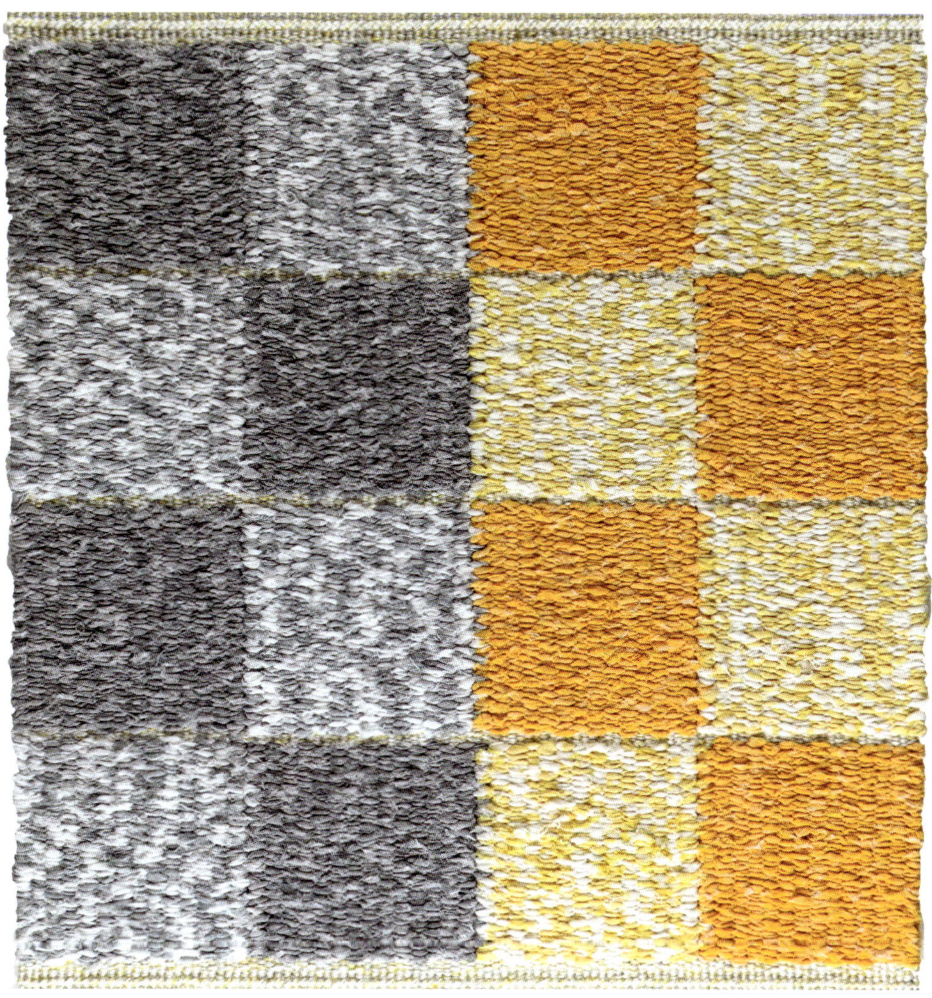

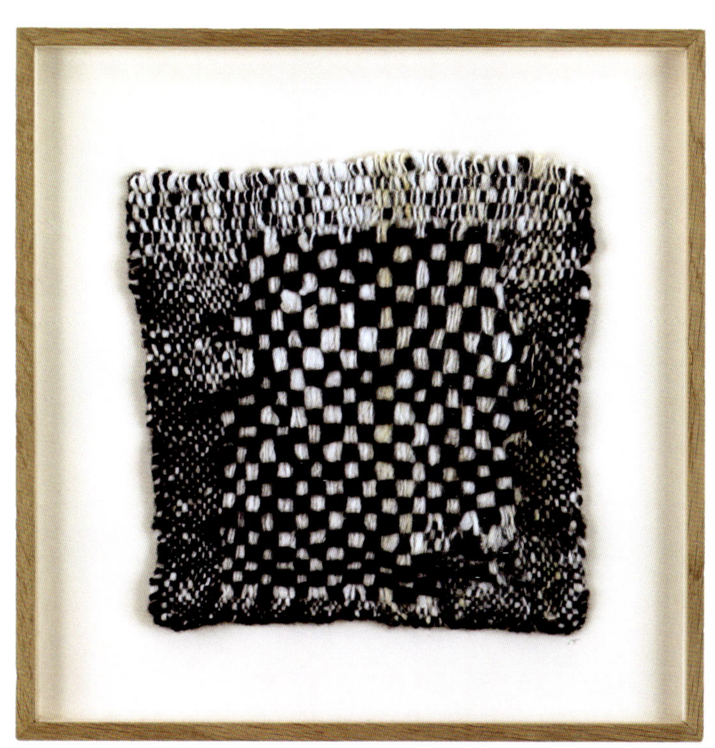

OPPOSITE: *Matrix*
Alex Friedman
2008 | 40.5" × 51" × 2" | wool; cotton warp

TOP:
Gingham Revisited (Lisbon)
Sara Lindsay
2023 | 15.3" × 15" | cotton, linen

RIGHT:
Quadrado Menos Obscuro
(The least obscure square)
Sheila Hicks
1961 | 11" × 11" | wool
Courtesy of Sikkema Jenkins & Co.

Ulrika Leander's jolly colors make the lively appeal of *A New Day*, a cityscape full of red roofs under a sky of squares. A few areas of gentle curves, a few rectangles, vary the dominant grid pattern.

A New Day
Ulrika Leander
2012 | 68" × 84" | wool; cotton warp

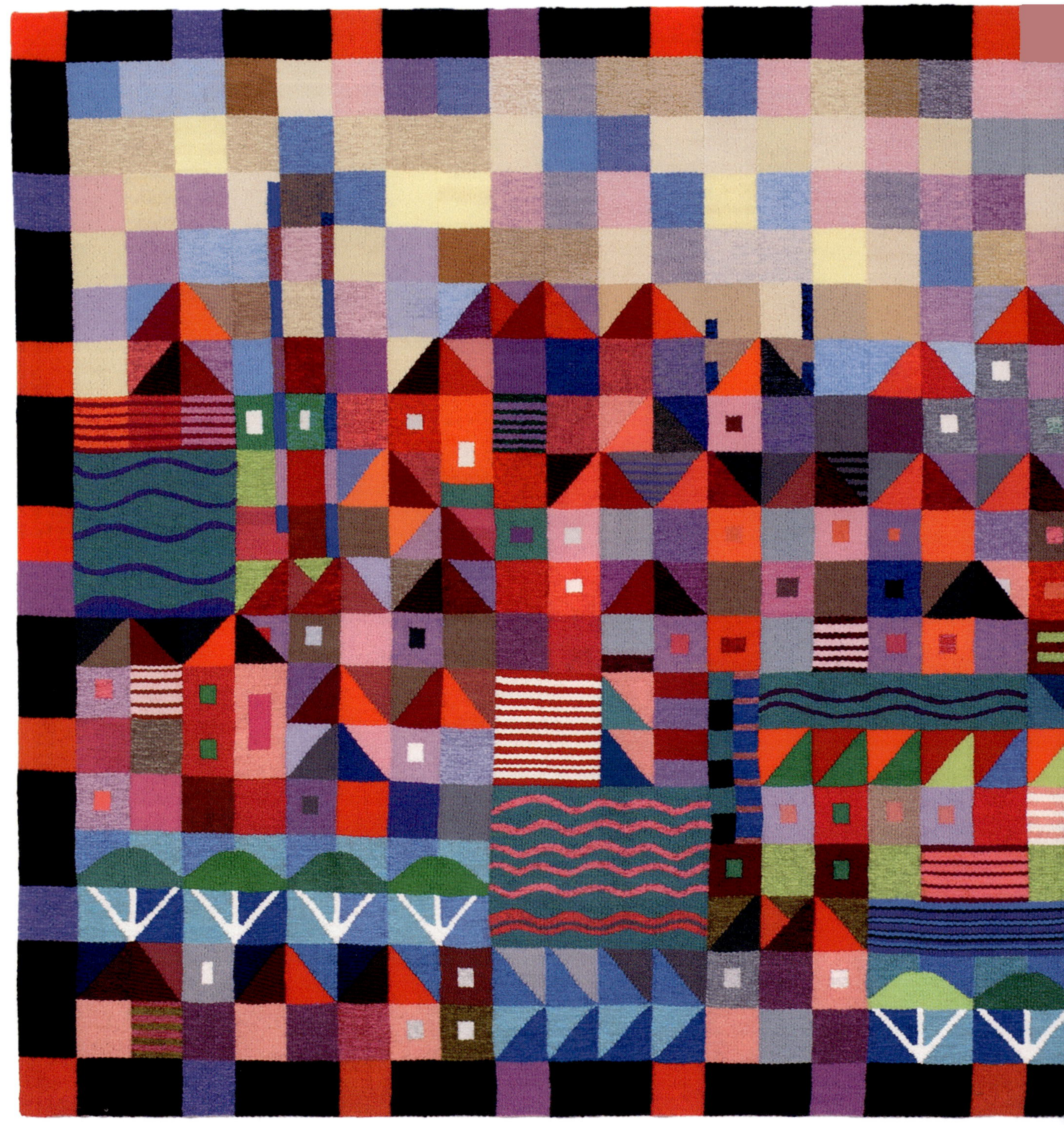

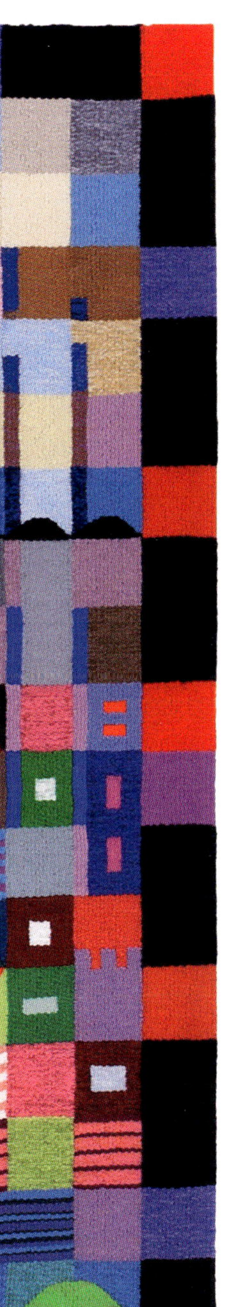

Barbara Setsu Pickett's *Plane and Perspective* was the first contemporary piece I remember that called my attention to the grid. Here it teases us with imagined spaces, by first appearing straight on, then as an optical illusion that draws us toward the rear, where the sun sets. We don't know what is actual vertical and what is actual horizontal.

Plane and Perspective
Barbara Setsu Pickett
1984 | 42.75" × 28.5" | wool

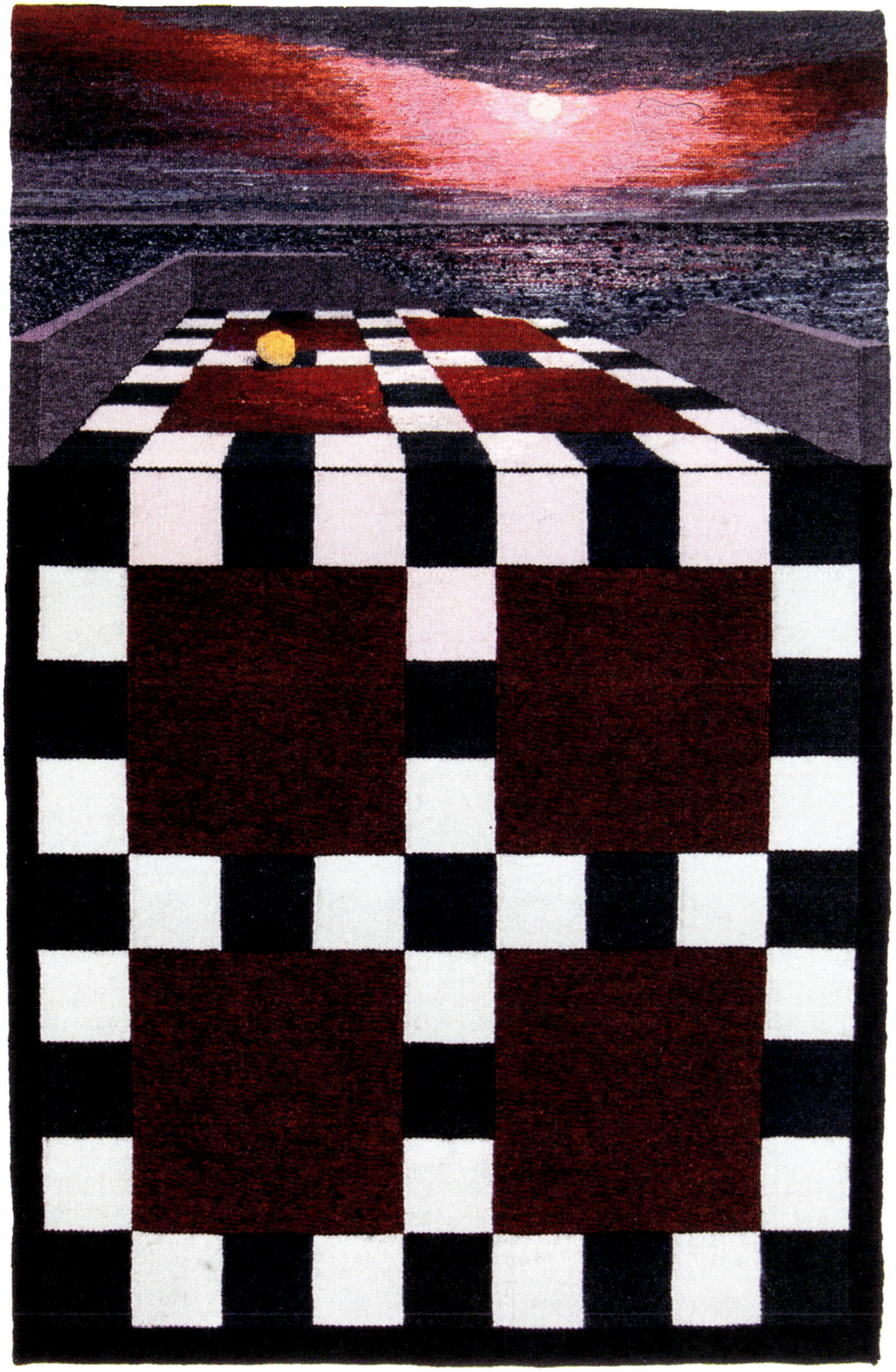

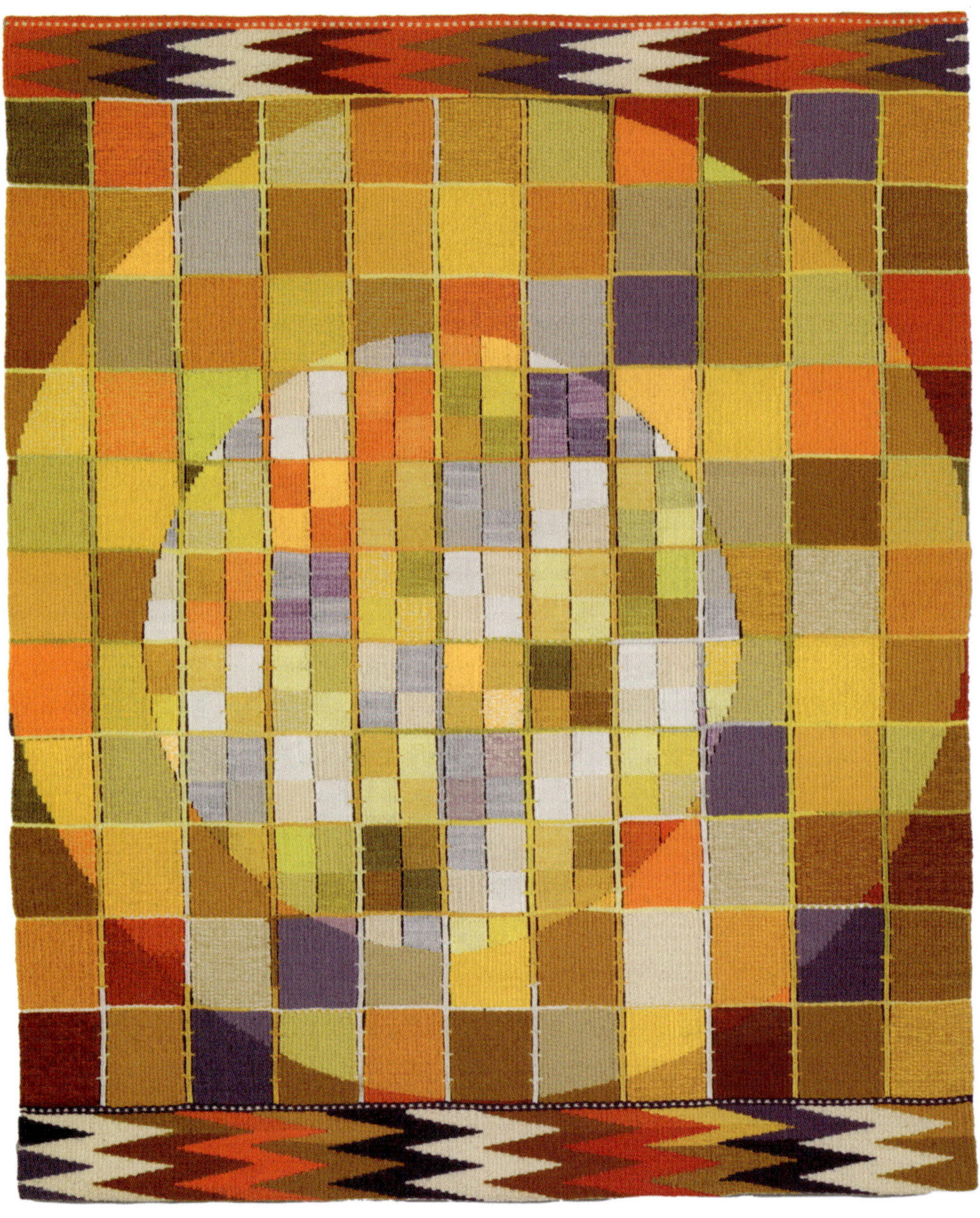

Åse Pedersen's *Energikilde*'s grid gives us circles set against squares. A smaller circle is defined by smaller squares. There are reminders here of Hicks's piece (page 175), but color makes the effect very different. At the bottom and top, lightning strikes. The whole sunlike effect speaks of energy being generated.

Energikilde (Energy source)
Åse Pedersen
1982 | 50.4" × 42.3" | wool, nylon, silk, hand-sewing; linen warp
Nasjonalmuseet, Oslo
Photographer: Annar Bjørgli

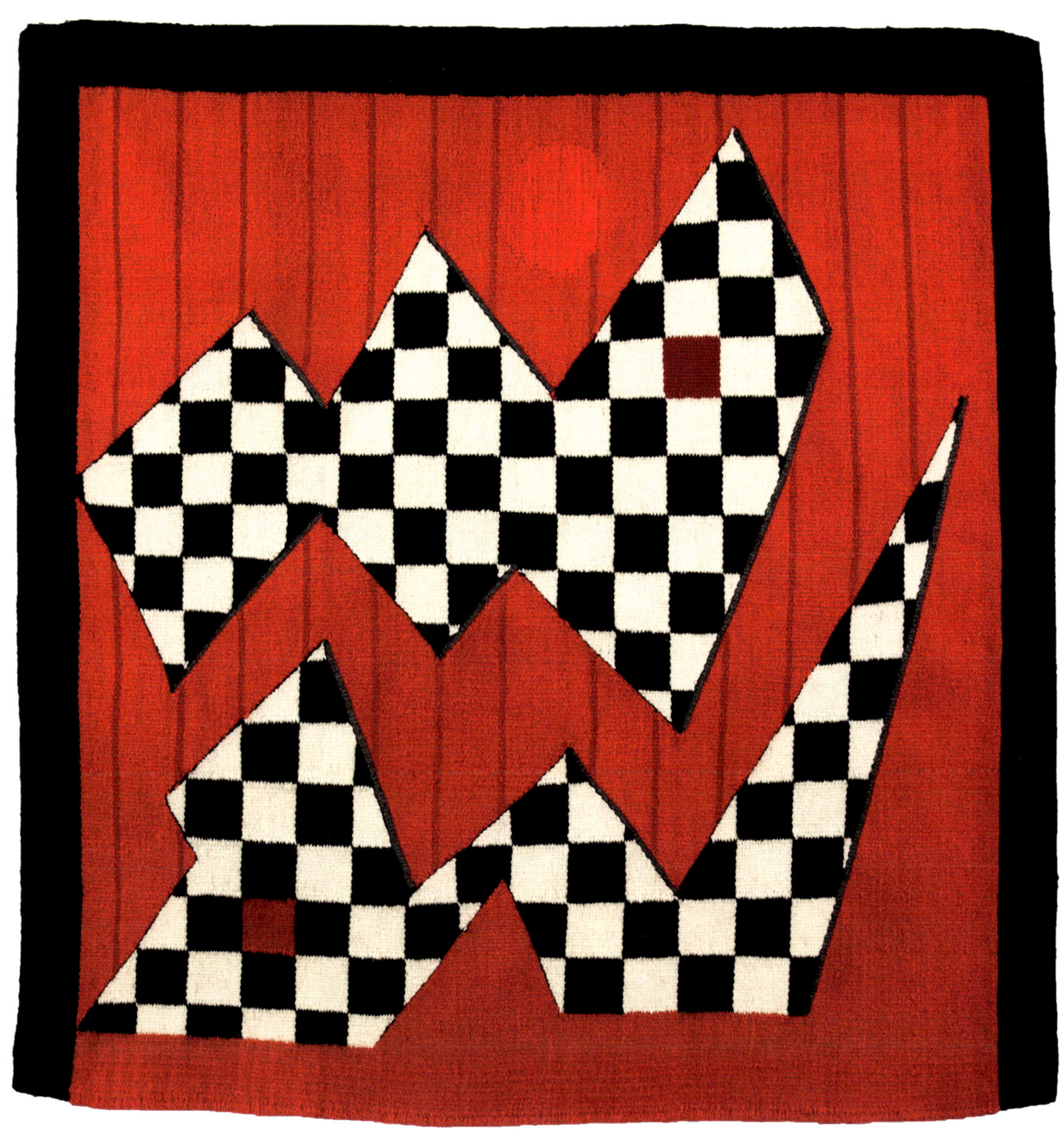

Origami
Klaus Anselm
2021 | 35" × 35" | wool; cotton warp
Photographer: Stacey Evans

Klaus Anselm inserts his black-and-white shards into a field of red columns. The black and white squares become part of a jagged intrusion. His title reminds us that origami is a system of folding paper to make shapes, such as animals and flowers, often with crisp points.

Forty-six Hungarian tapestry weavers, many of them members of the lively Hungarian Tapestry Weavers Association, worked together to make this tapestry. The image was taken from a 1772 map, designed by Miksa Hell, titled *The Carpathian Basin and Its Environs at the Time of the Conquest of Hungary*. The project marked the 1,100th anniversary of the arrival of the Magyar tribes in the land we know as Hungary. The grid design made their work simpler, since independent weavers could work on their section and not have to worry about what was going on to either side. Afterward, the whole was stitched together.

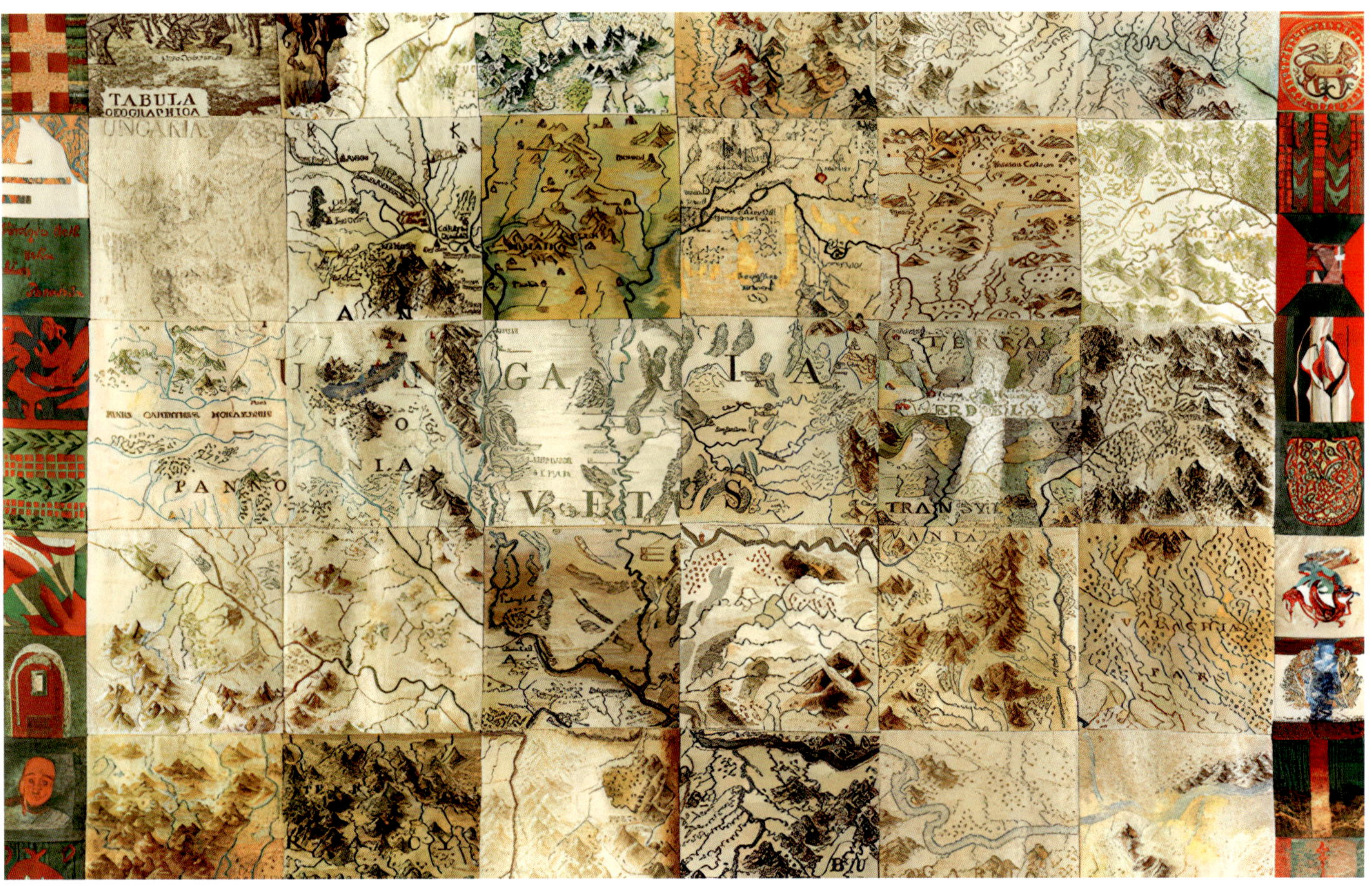

Tapestry without Borders
46 members of the Hungarian Association of Tapestry Artists
1995–96 | 9'10" × 11"5" | wool

Ken Done designed the iconic Sydney Opera House in twenty-eight possible permutations; the Australian Tapestry Workshop wove it. It looks like a roll of film, with its repeating images slightly different from each other.

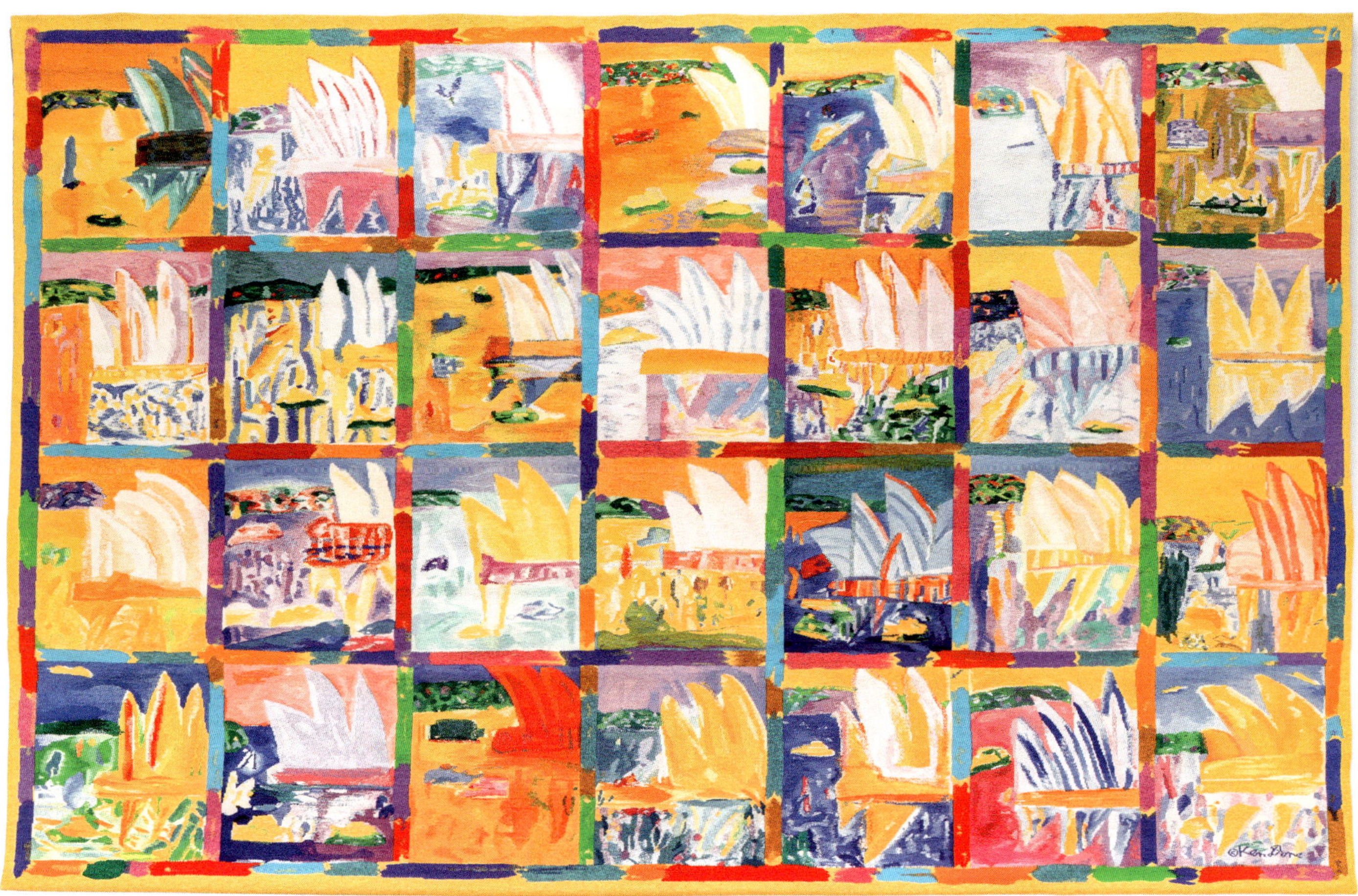

Twenty-Eight Views of the Opera House
Ken Done, designer
Australian Tapestry Workshop
1998–99 | 9'5" × 13' wool; cotton warp
Collection of the Powerhouse Museum

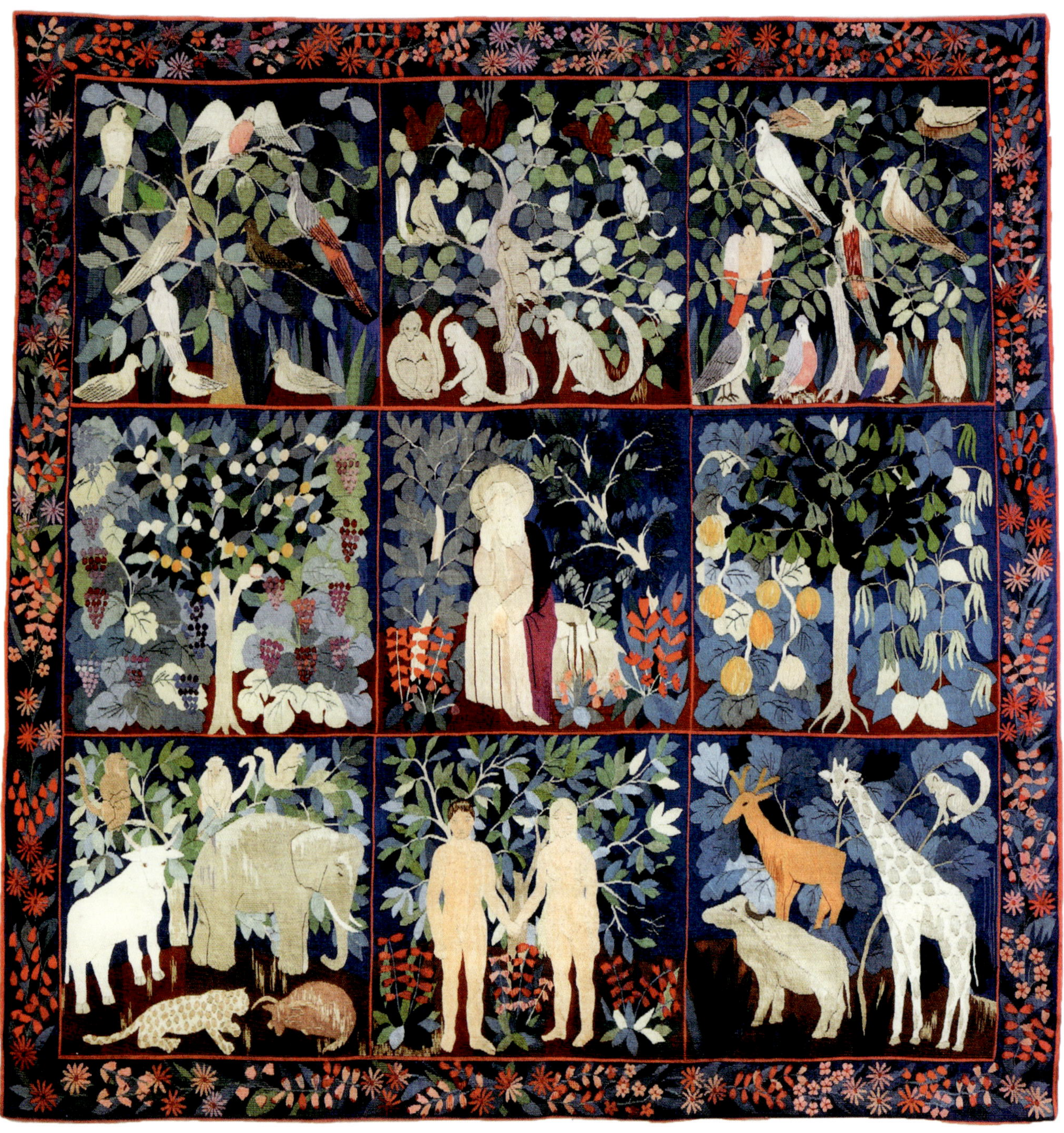

Creation
Noémi Ferenczy
Museum of Applied Arts, Budapest
1913 | 7'3.5" × 7'3.5" | wool

Noémi Ferenczy's title suggests the scenario, like something to be read, recounting episodes from the book of Genesis. God appears at the center, perhaps contemplating what he has done? Is it good news that there is no fall, no Eve eating an apple?

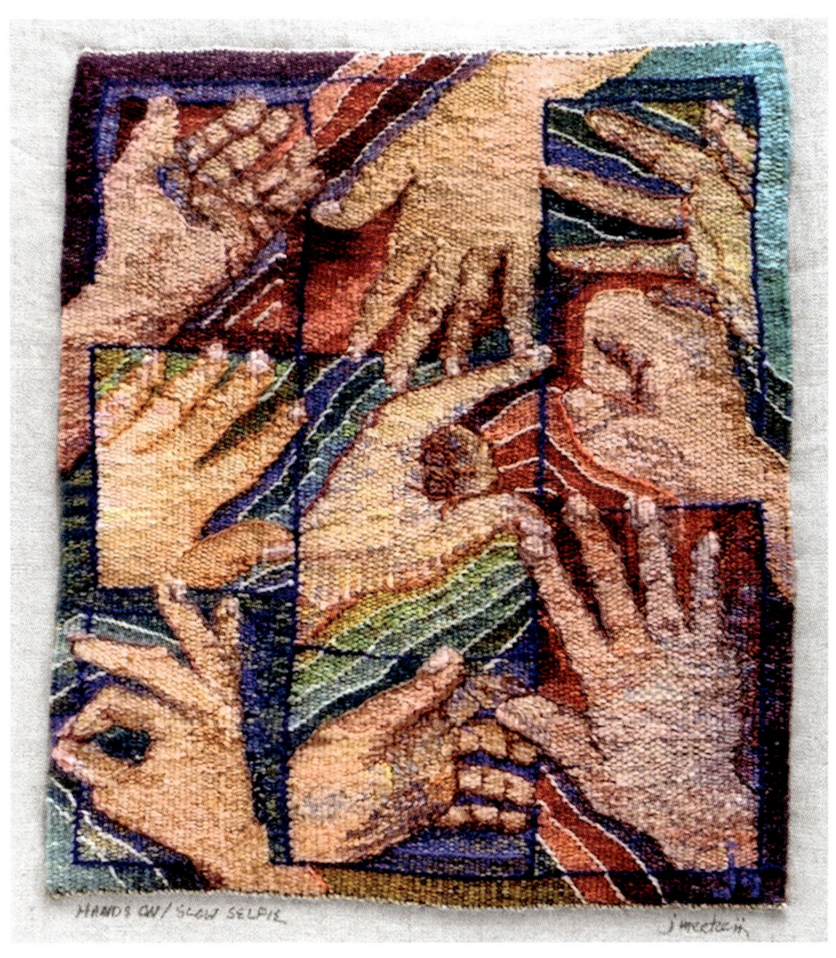

In this grid, Janette Meetze seems to imagine what hands need to do, hands that transgress the limits of the grid pattern.

Hands On
Janette Meetze
2015 | 14" × 12.5" | linen, cotton, silk, wool; linen warp

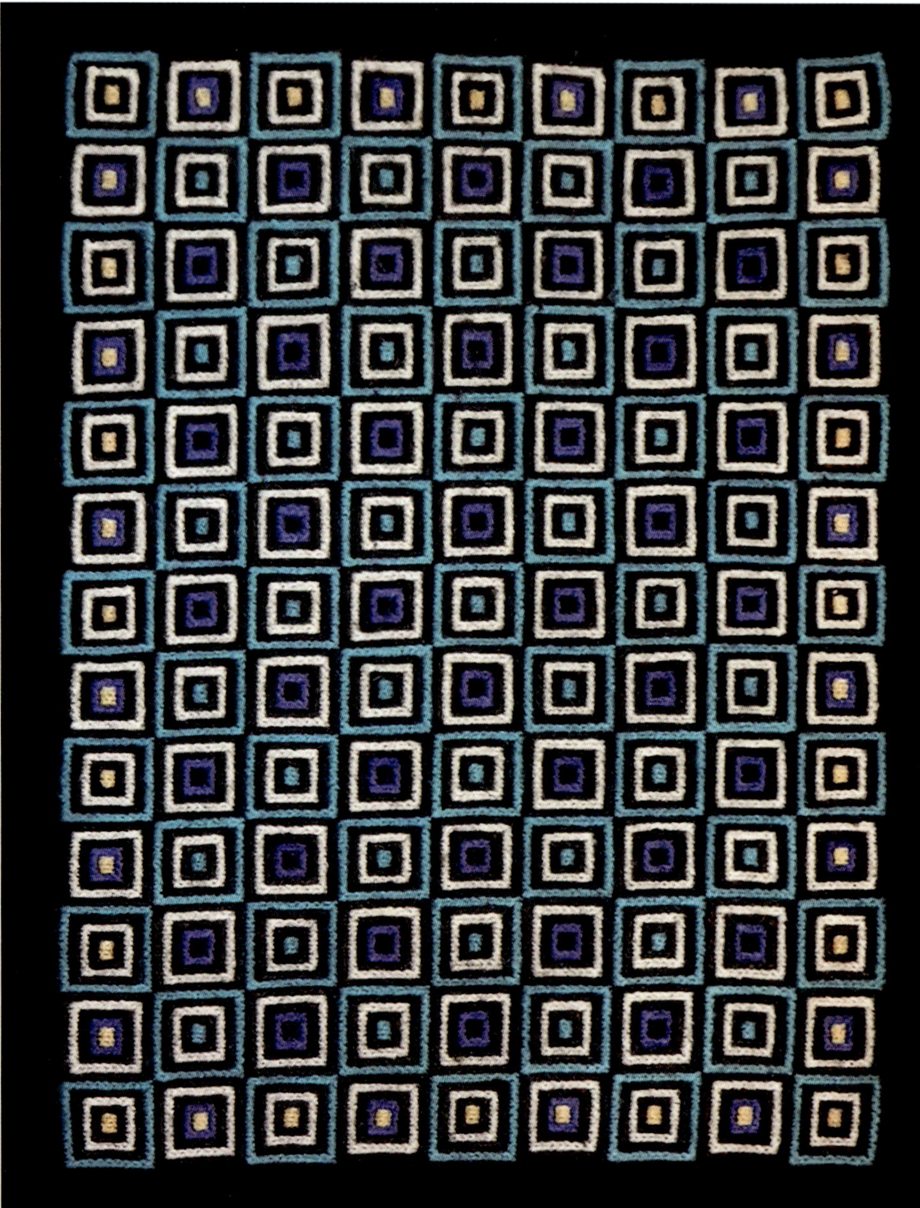

Cameron Kashani gives us squares inside squares inside an overall grid pattern. The colors make them bounce.

Hall of Images
Cameron Kashani
2019 | 19" × 15" | wool, silk, Tencel, cotton

Rosemary Whitehead has woven us diamonds, almost like a patchwork quilt. Hot colors emphasize the large diamond shapes.

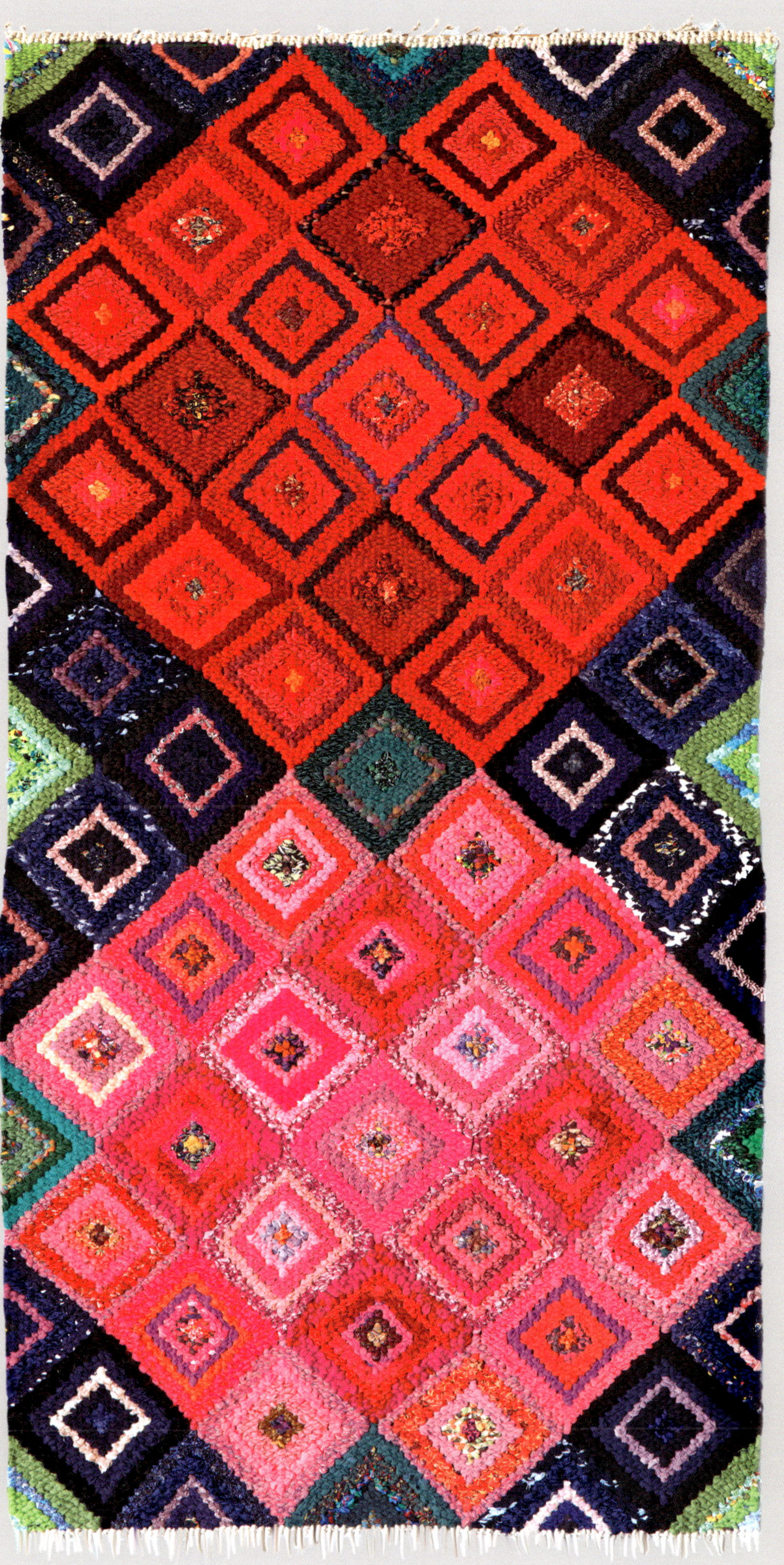

For Sister Phil
Rosemary Whitehead
2014 | 63.8" × 32.7" | natural and synthetic fibers; linen warp
Photographer: David Summerhayes

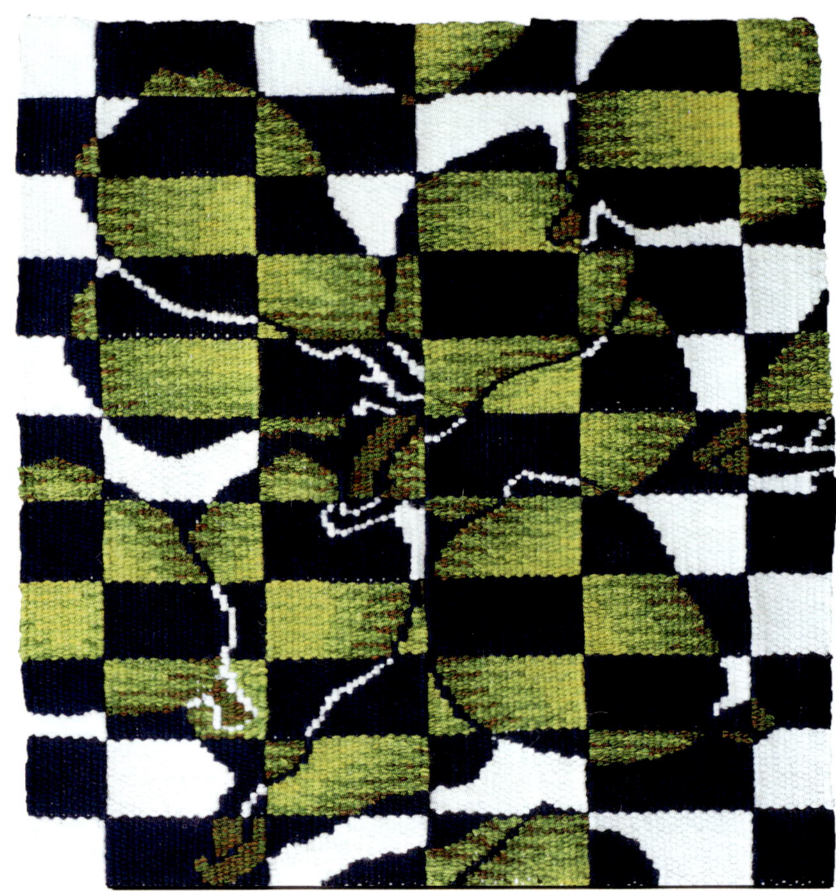

Green Pears
Mary Lane
2001 | 16" × 15" | wool; cotton warp

Mary Lane's pears have been embedded in the grid of blues and whites. Like the hands in Meetze's piece (page 183), the natural rounded shapes contrast with the straight lines of the grid.

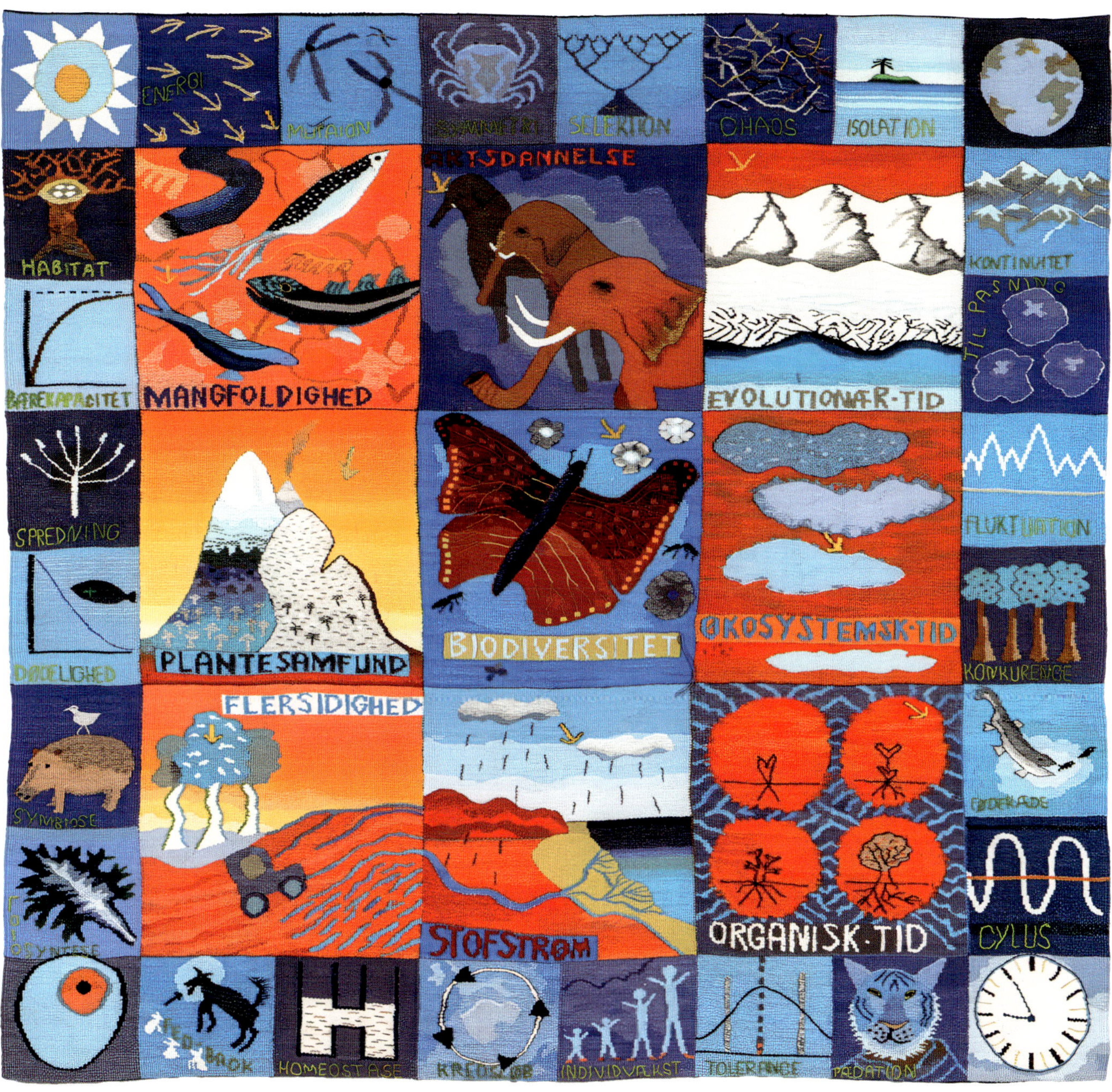

Margarethe Agger documents the world around us, showing us pictures of ecological change. She includes labels of what we are seeing and/or what we need to do.

Ecological Symphony
Margarethe Agger
2020 | 66.1" × 66.1" | Spælsau wool, cotton

The below title comes from a line in the Greek play *Agamemnon*. The protagonist has returned home from the Trojan War, bringing with him his concubine, the prophetess Cassandra, and his wife, Clytemnestra, throws a net around him and stabs him in his bath. Marshall's thin strips suggest the net.

Through the use of line and grid, Janet Brereton's huge knotted *Modern Woman* (about 6.5 feet square) offers hints of the programming with which women sometimes feel their lives are afflicted. The gaze is unflinching. Brereton was known for working with thick rope.

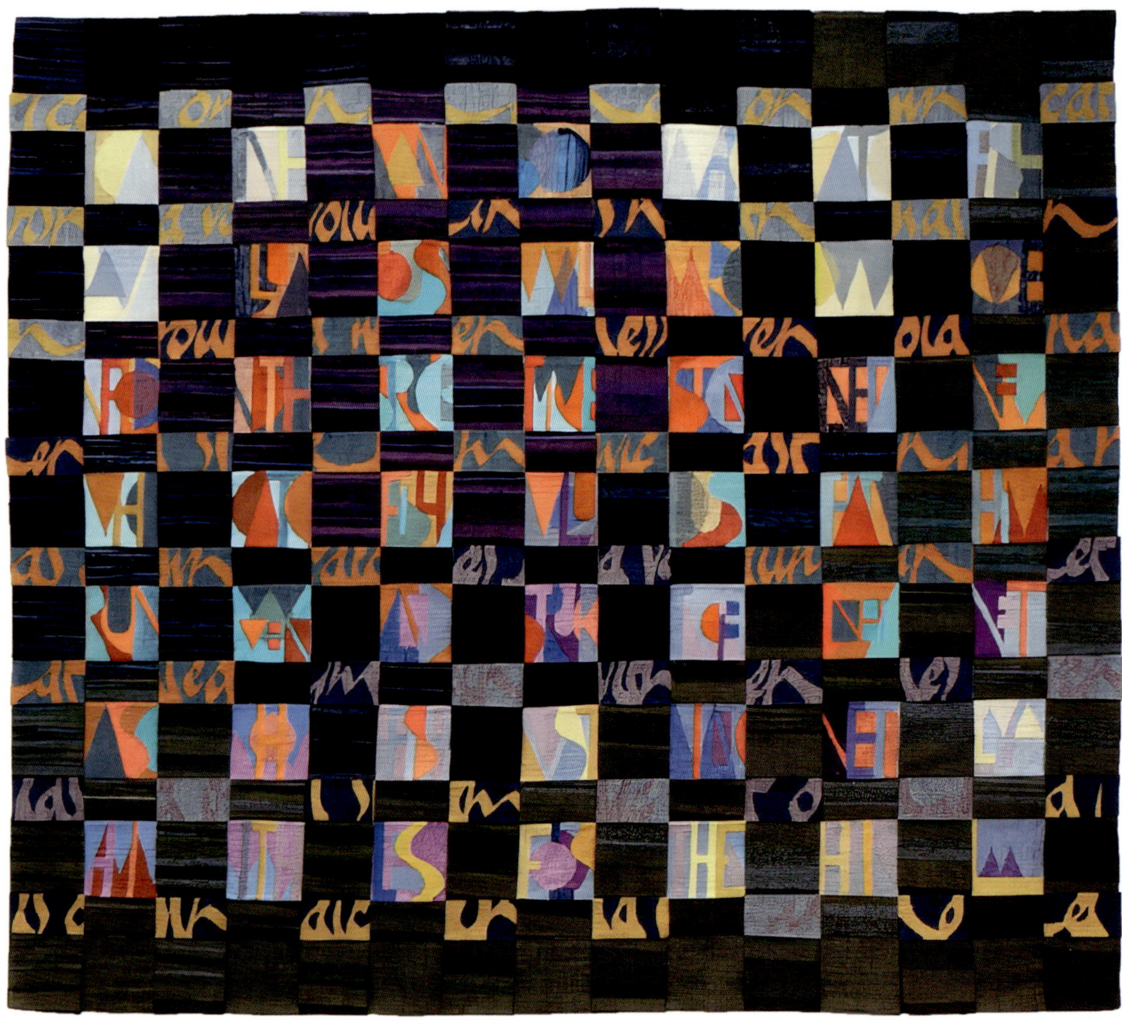

And then I struck him twice
Lindsey Marshall
2018 | 42" × 48" | cotton, linen, wool, synthetics

Modern Woman
Janet Brereton
1991 | 79.5" × 77.55" × 2" | cotton rope
Museum of Applied Arts and Sciences / Powerhouse

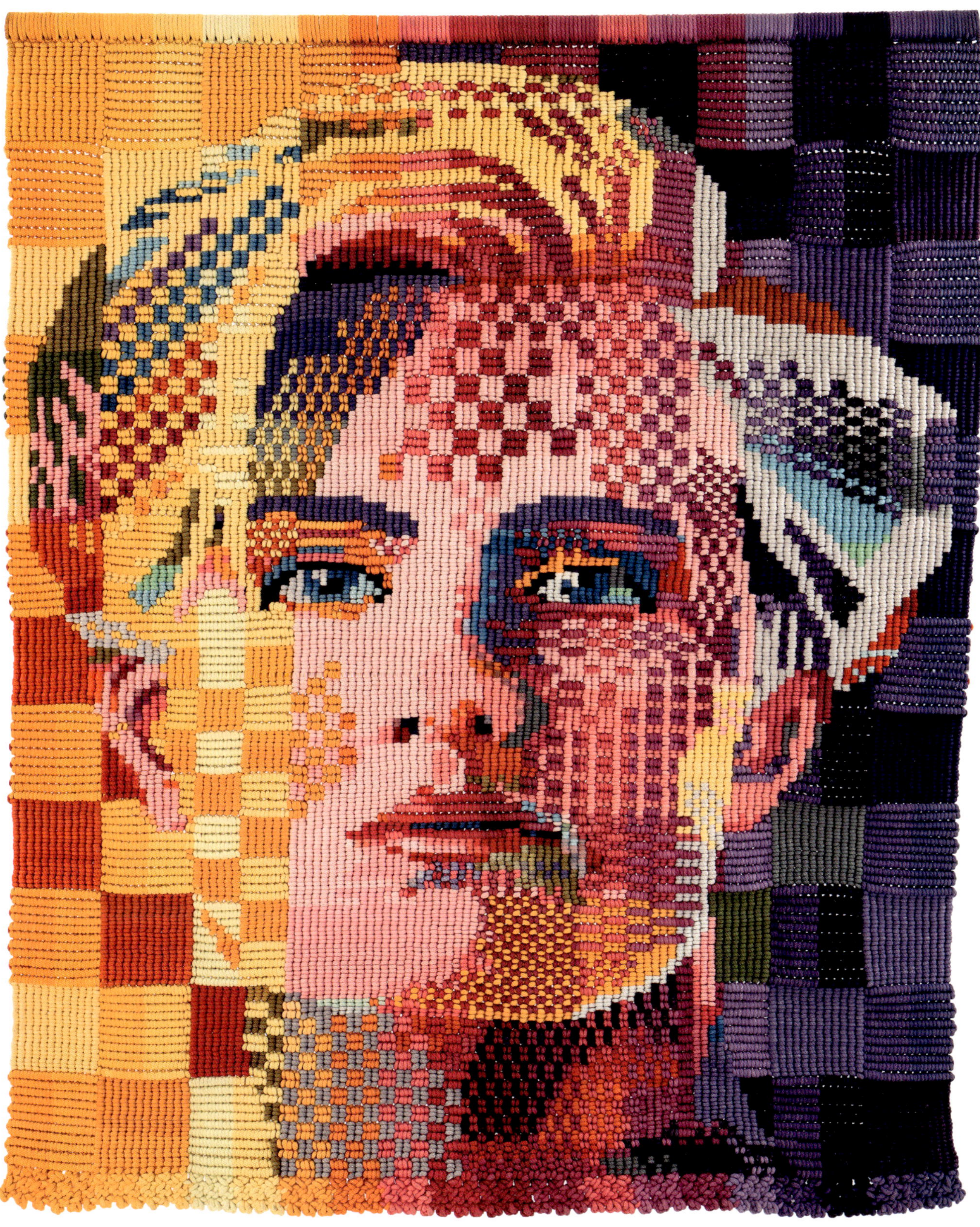

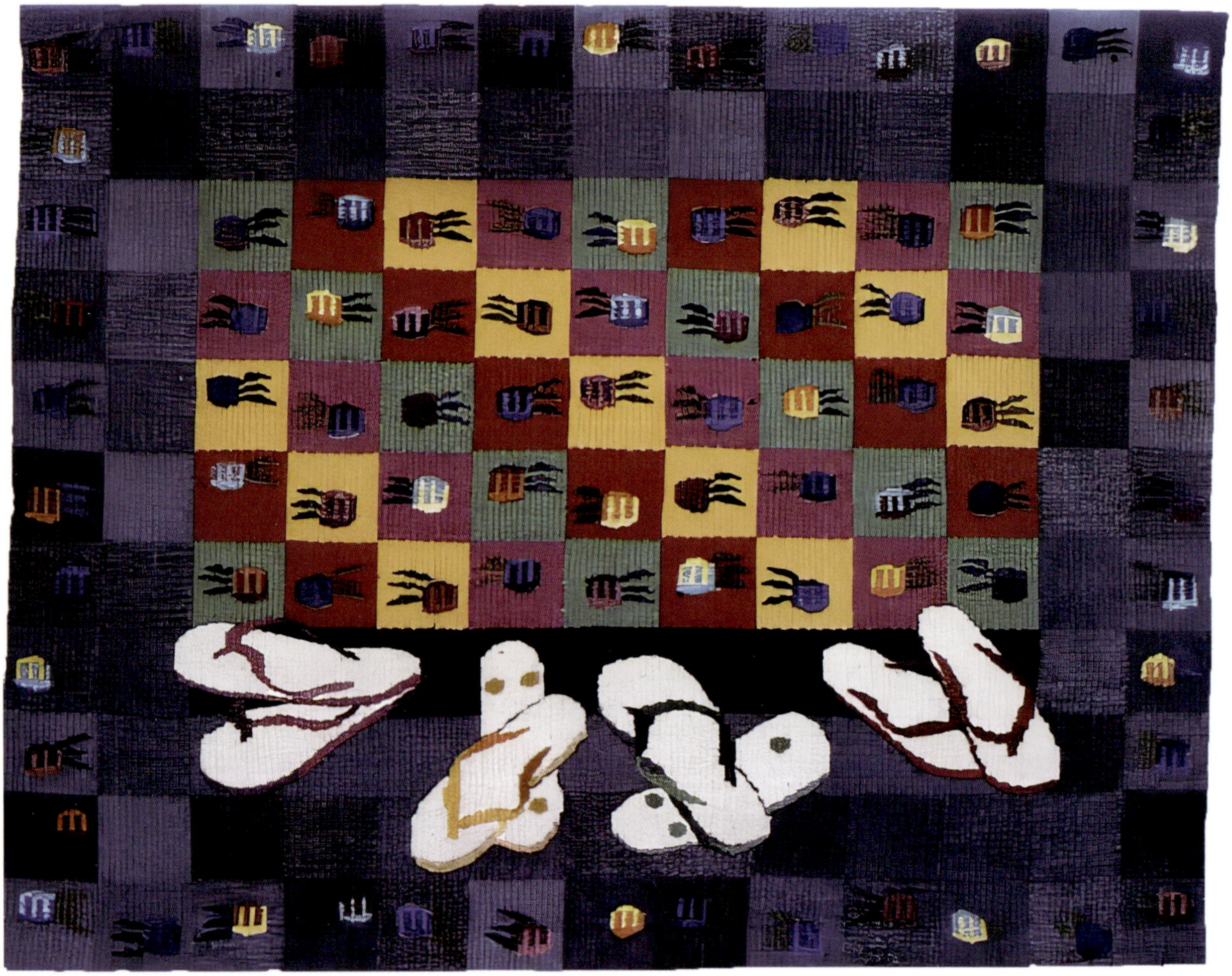

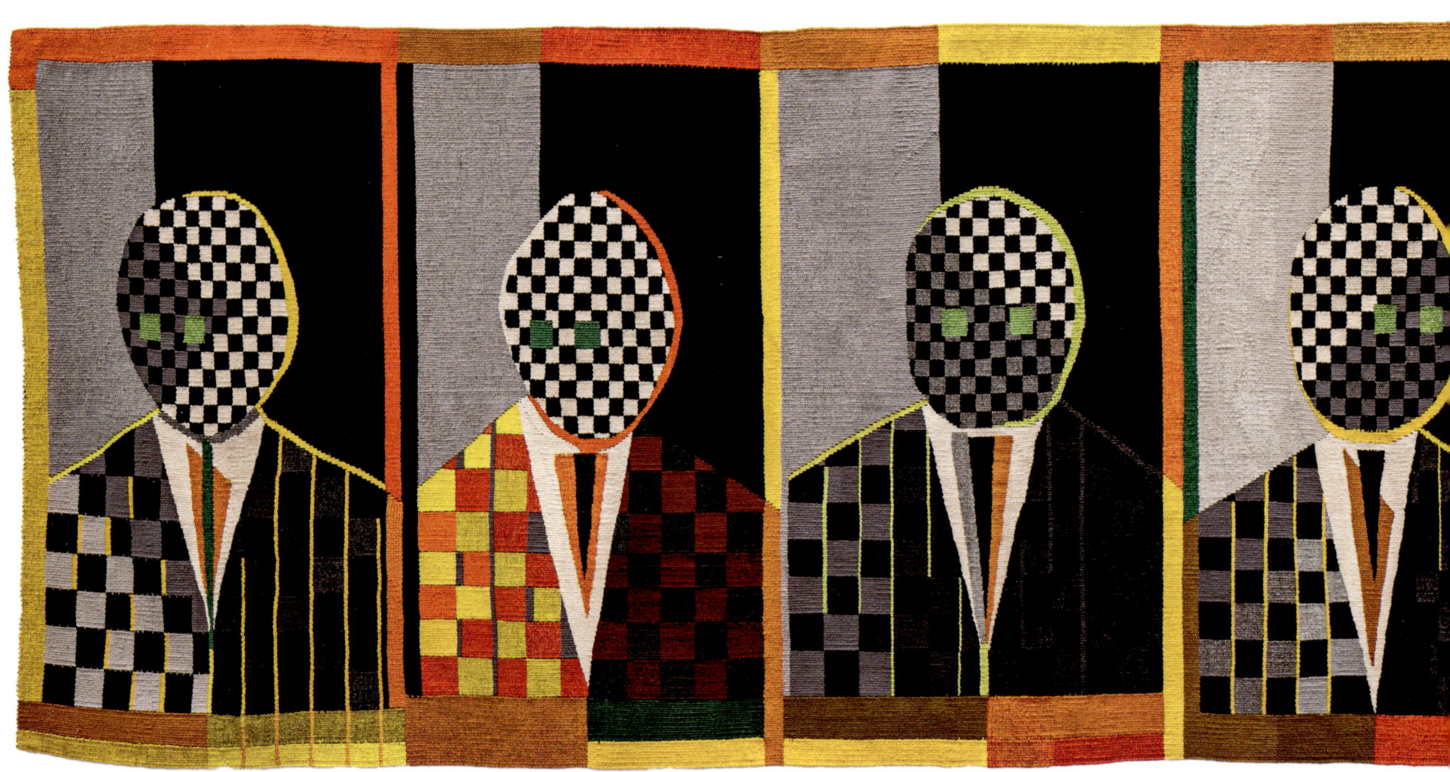

Women's Party
Grace Eckert
1985 | 33" × 41" | wool; linen warp

Grace Eckert lived for several years in the Middle East, where she obeyed the local clothing requirements for women—and covered up. But when she and her women friends got together and stepped over a threshold into someone's home, they could throw off the black outer garment and enjoy themselves. She says that all the women invariably wore brilliantly colored clothing underneath, so the mood was warm and full of life in the middle of the grays of their lives outside. Here the flip-flops across the bottom suggest relaxation, and the grid (the middle of the tapestry) shows growing plants.

Ende Flere Byråkrater (Even more bureaucrats)
Synnøve Anker Aurdal
1993 | 53" × 12'4" | wool, linen, viscose, silk cords

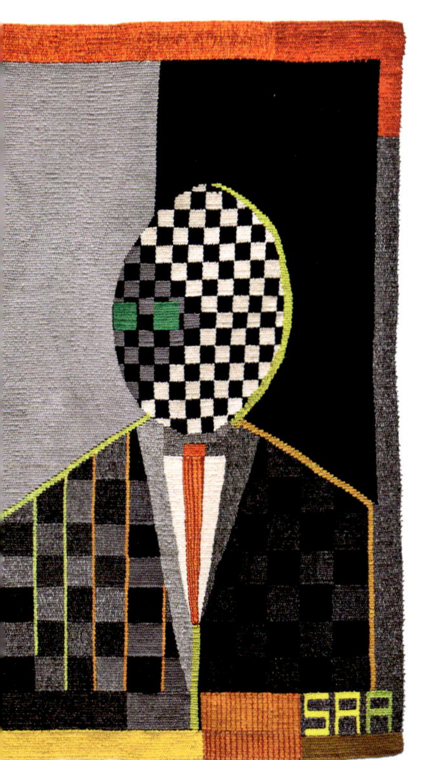

Synnøve Anker Aurdal has made use of checkerboard patterns and repetitions to satirize bureaucracy. Any individual can be exchanged with any other person in the organization and the results will be the same.

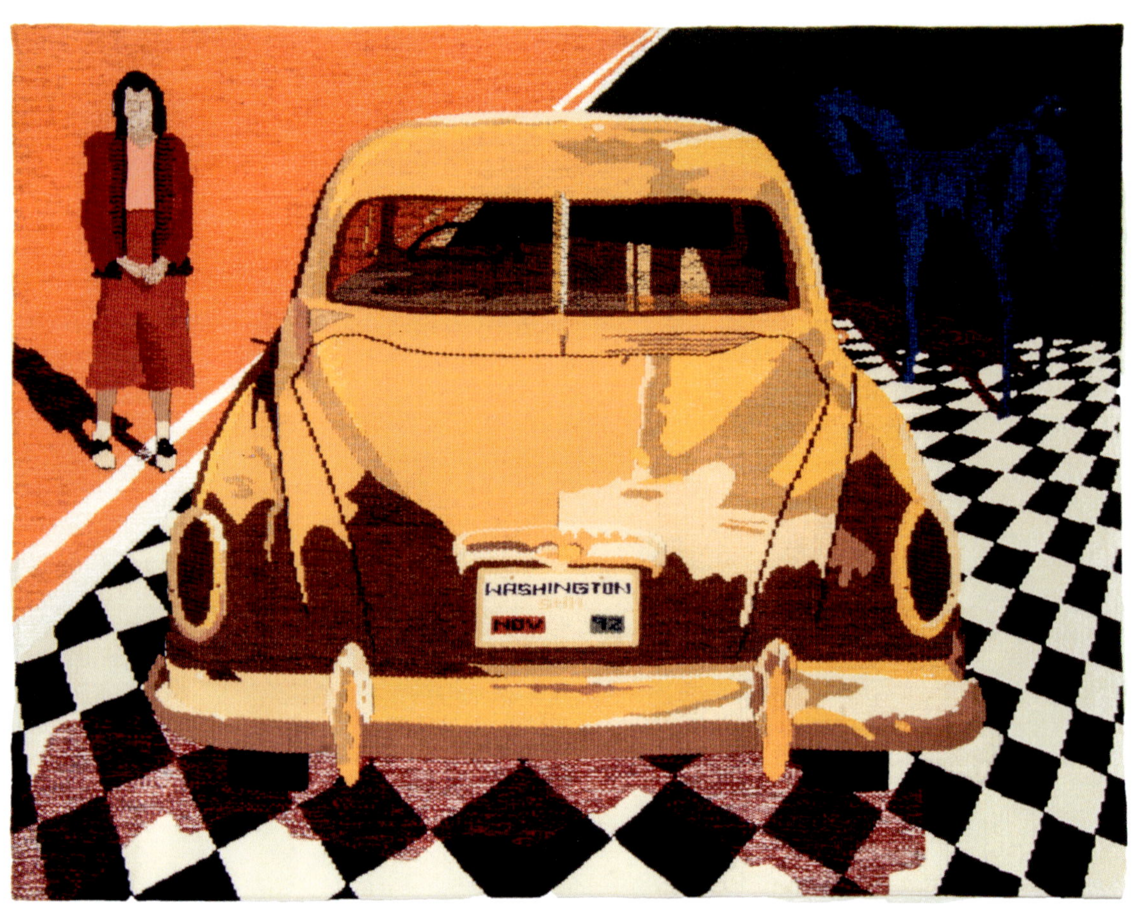
WASHINGTON

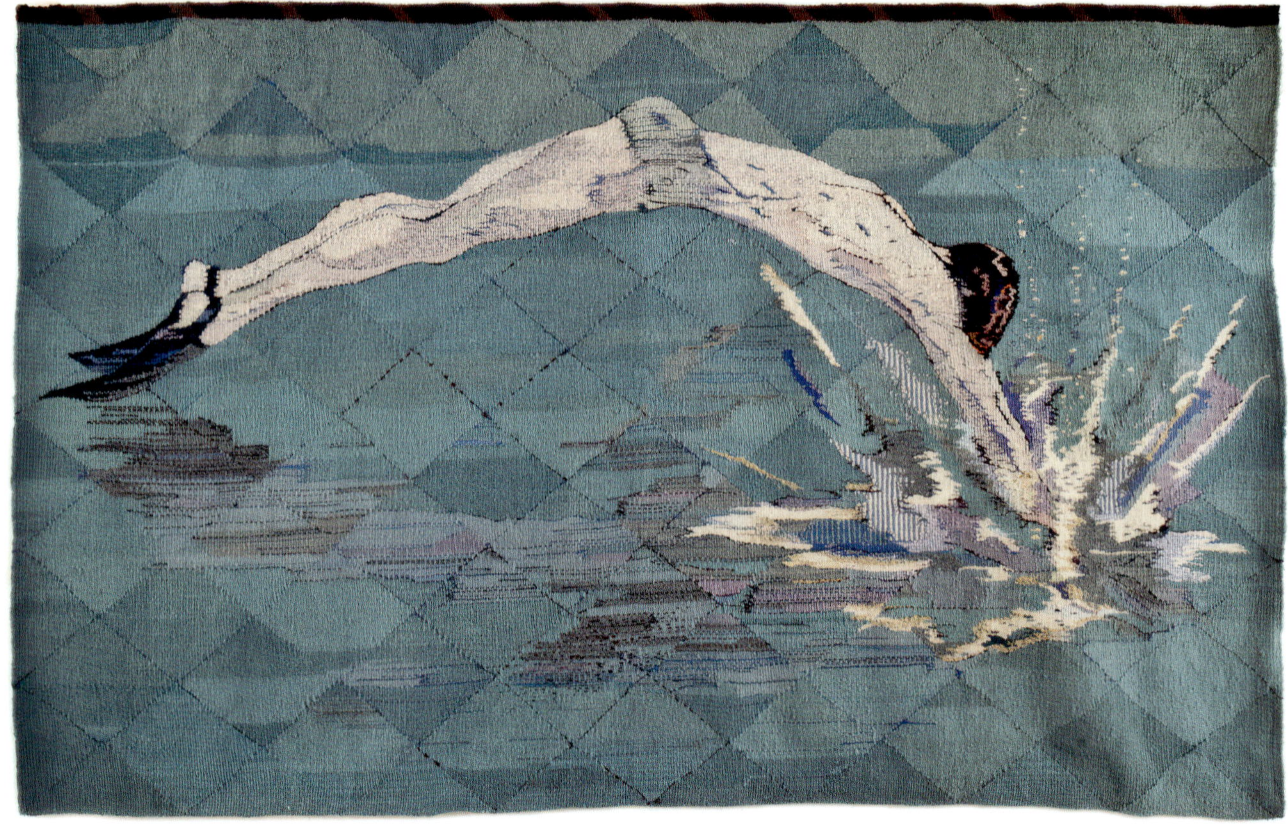

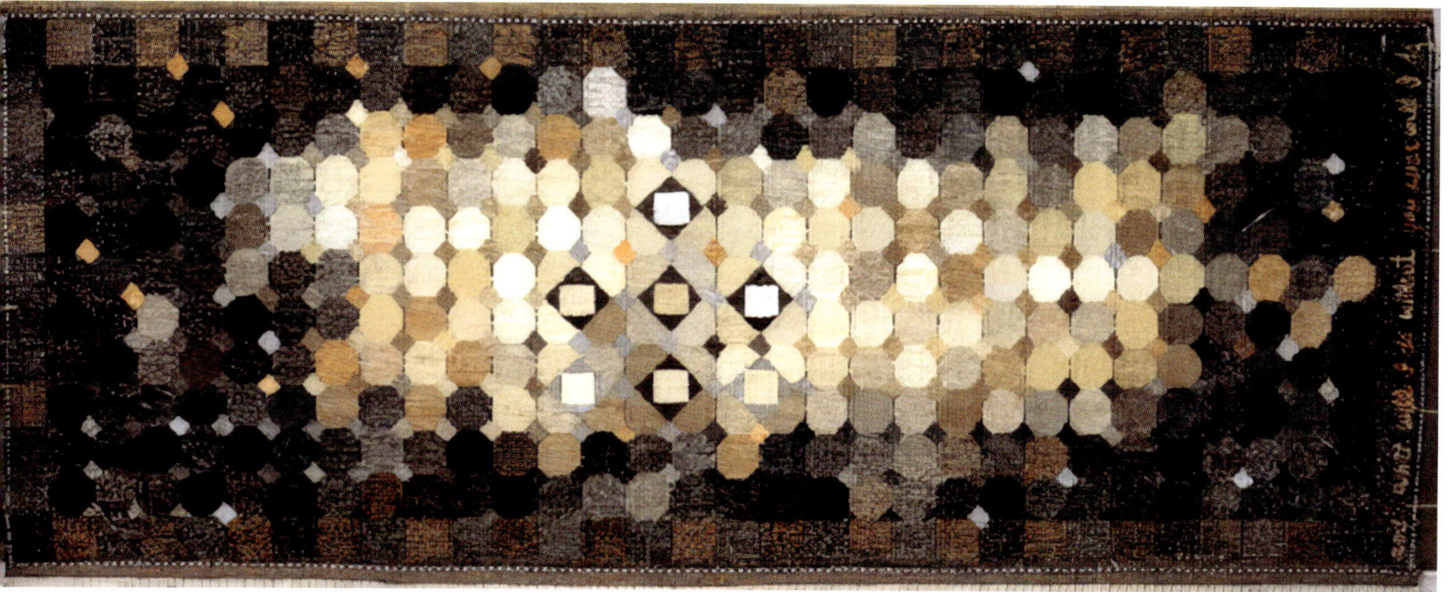

Susan Hart Henegar lays out her pavement in diamond patterns underneath the automobile. Unn Sonju does a similar thing with the patterns of the swimming pool as the diver descends into the water. In both of these tapestries, the weavers have included curved shapes—the automobile and the diver. The diver is a fully organic curve; the car is a wonderfully foreshadowed bright object.

Diana Wood Conroy has created a careful and precise group of shapes—she has long associated her work as a tapestry weaver with her work as an archeologist, where grids provide the structure for excavation. Here, most of the squares have been reshaped as octagons. They are inspired by fragments of a mosaic on a basilica floor in Soli, an ancient city in Cyprus.

OPPOSITE, TOP: *Primary Issues*
Susan Hart Henegar
1992 | 42" × 56" | wool, cotton; cotton warp

OPPOSITE, BOTTOM: *Aireborough Pool, Mikkel*
Unn Sonju
1985 | 47.25" × 76.75"

ABOVE: *Soli: Earth Archive 11 Without You*
Diana Wood Conroy
2017 | 23.6" × 64.2" | handspun wool, alpaca, silk dyed with pomegranate, metallic threads; cotton warp
Photographer: R. M. Conroy

Janet Moore gives us river currents as they crisscross each other. This produces grid shapes stretched to their limits. The body of water is not a sheet of glass; the currents also suggest weaving.

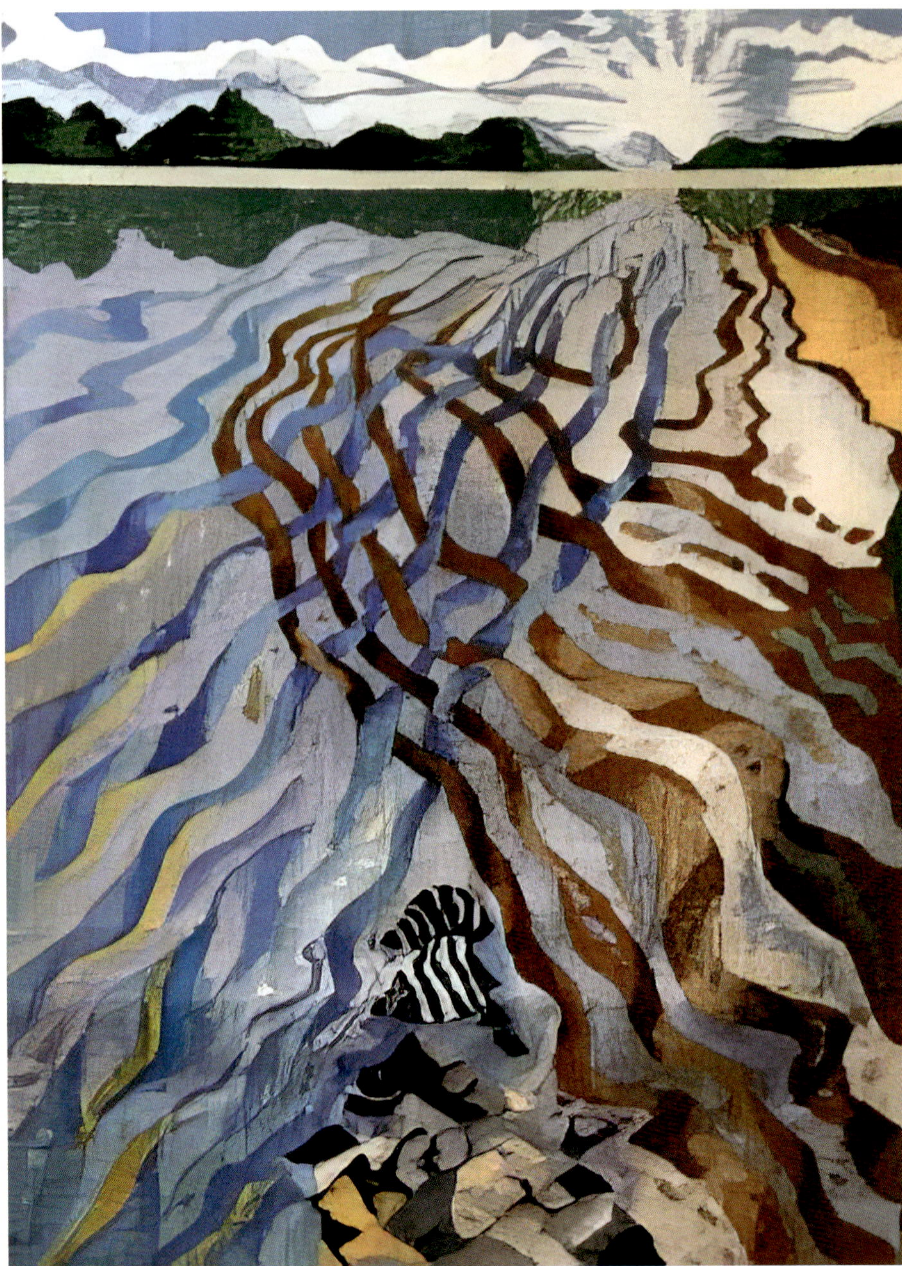

Confluence
Janet Moore
2022 | 27" × 23" | wool, lurex, silk; cotton warp

Both Sarah Swett and Joanne Soroka have embellished their work by including unexpected techniques; these add something more for us to see.

Swett's netting lies over the surface of a more traditional tapestry. She crocheted the net—a separate layer—several times, until she knew that the cloth beneath it could be read. (The knitting needles are real; the hands, woven.)

Soroka has always liked grids, seeing in them the connection among the threads, interdependent on each other, like the social network. She also adds unconventional materials—the painted ash keys, lotus leaves, and metallic thread—which alert the viewer: Here you will see something you don't expect.

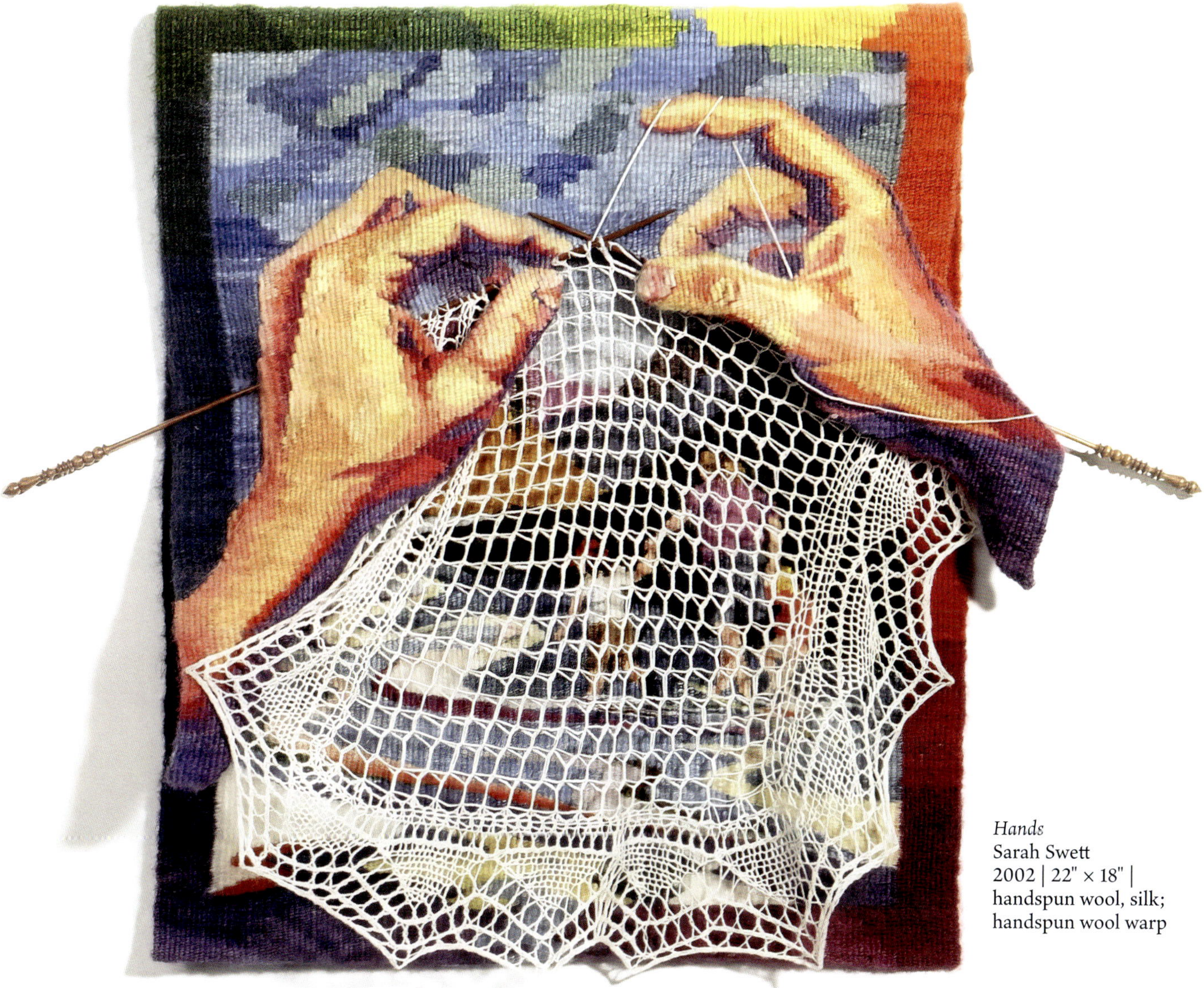

Hands
Sarah Swett
2002 | 22" × 18" | handspun wool, silk; handspun wool warp

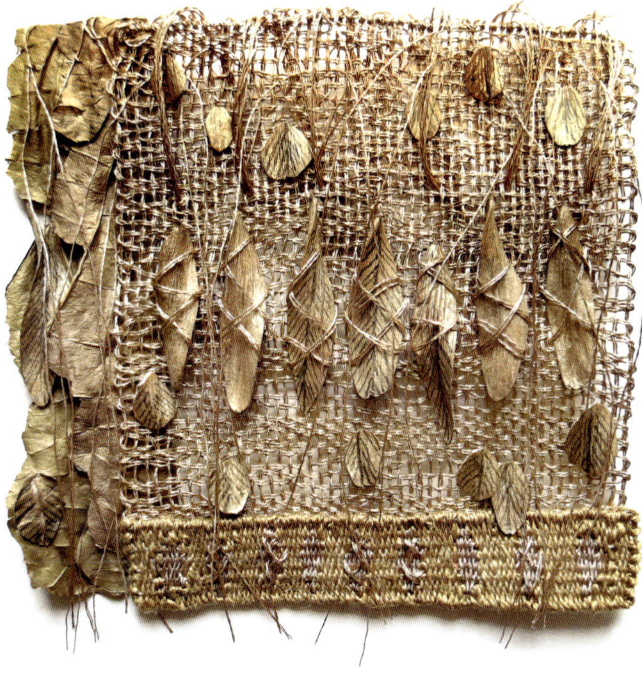

Captured
Joanne Soroka
2013 | 4" × 4" | painted ash keys and lotus leaves, metallic thread, linen

The following chapters fall into the category of theme rather than technique. We look at those themes that work especially well in tapestry, either because of the process of weaving, or because of historical precedent.

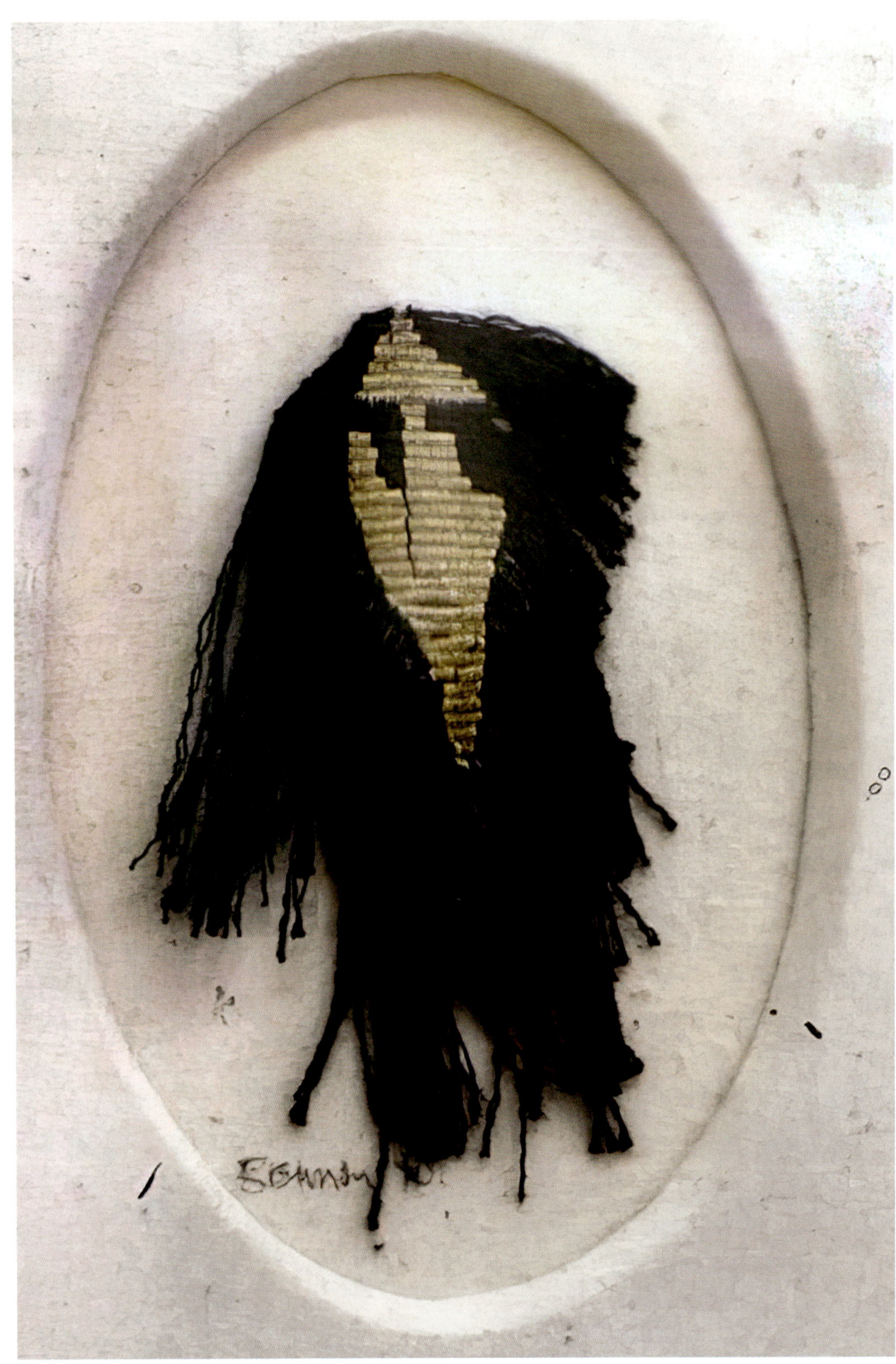

CHAPTER 10

size

Does size mean either big or small? Well, no. It might concern how dense the weave is. It might include one dimension, such as length, hugely out of proportion with the rest. It might even suggest the size of the materials.

We begin with small. While Coptic work from the first millennium CE is often quite small and woven with very fine threads, and while weavers in other cultures insert tapestry details into their clothing, most of the historical tapestries that come to mind are immense. Not any longer. Now there are many contemporary exhibitions of miniatures. Perhaps this is a way for contemporary tapestry weavers to work at a size that does not require years—even if it requires time, thought, and planning.

small

Archie Brennan's woman has one woven element—her face, which is about the size of a wide thumbnail. The threads of black warp form the rest of the tapestry, such as her hair.

Rachel Hine's little shy redhead seems worried as she looks up. Perhaps she feels small, and vulnerable.

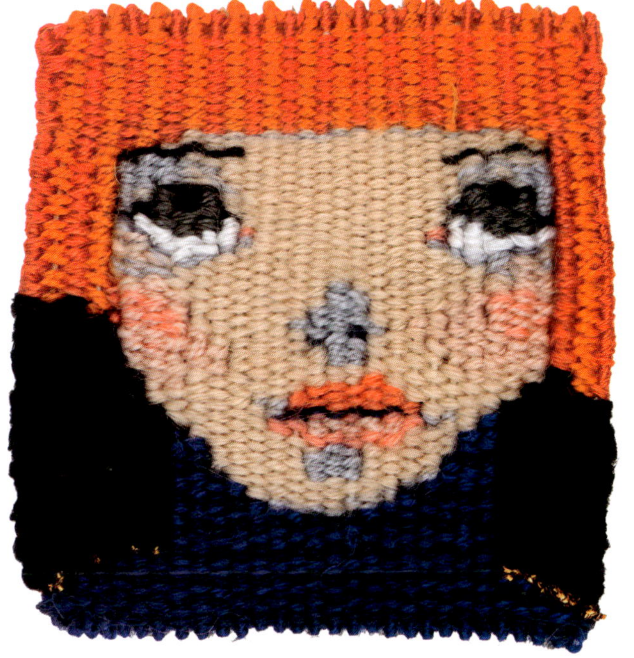

OPPOSITE: *woman with black hair*
Archie Brennan
size of wide thumbnail

RIGHT: *Lucy*
Rachel Hine
2019 | 2" × 2" | cotton, wool, metallic thread

The hand in Murray Gibson's piece, we imagine, is Penelope's. She is weaving and unweaving a tapestry, in order to put off insistent suitors, as she waits for Odysseus to return from the Trojan War. Part of the title, *Away: Return*, reminds us of the movement of the weft thread, over and under, back and forth.

For all the smallness of her piece, Pam Patrie's has a large impact. *Blue Sea Blue* feels like the ocean, with tides and white water. She has worked at a large number of warp threads—sixteen per inch—and that increases its detail and intensity.

Marilyn Rea-Menzies surrounds her largest lichen with thirteen bits and pieces of other lichen. Lichen is not one large object; she has captured its variations.

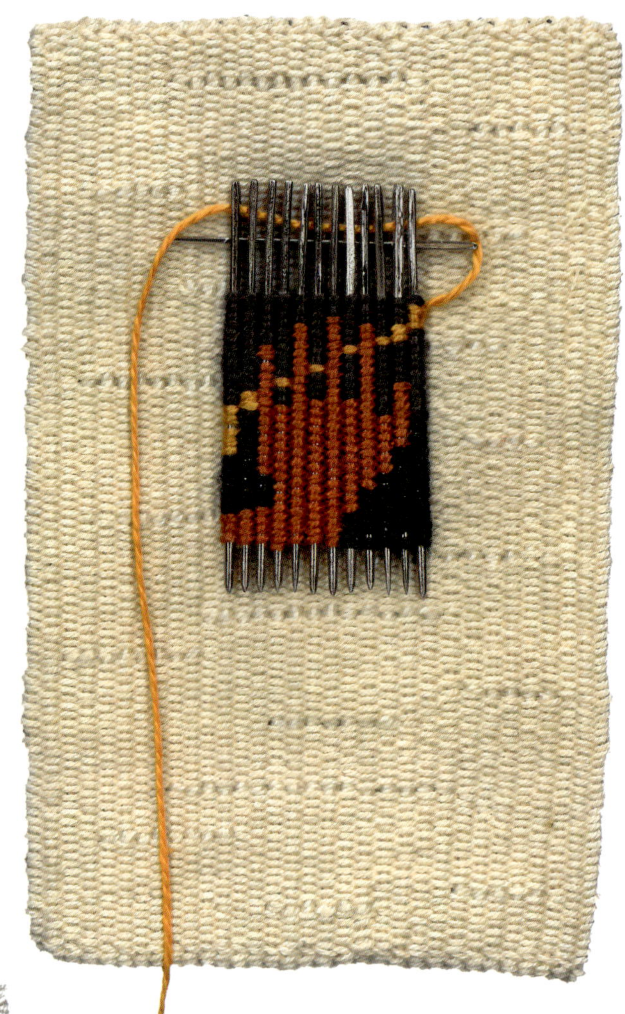

ABOVE: *Away: Return (Ulysses)*
Murray Gibson
2021 | 4.75" × 3" | darning needles, cotton seine twine, cotton embroidery thread

LEFT: *Blue Sea Blue*
Pam Patrie
2024 | 3" × 3" | Chinese silk twist, dyed with indigo

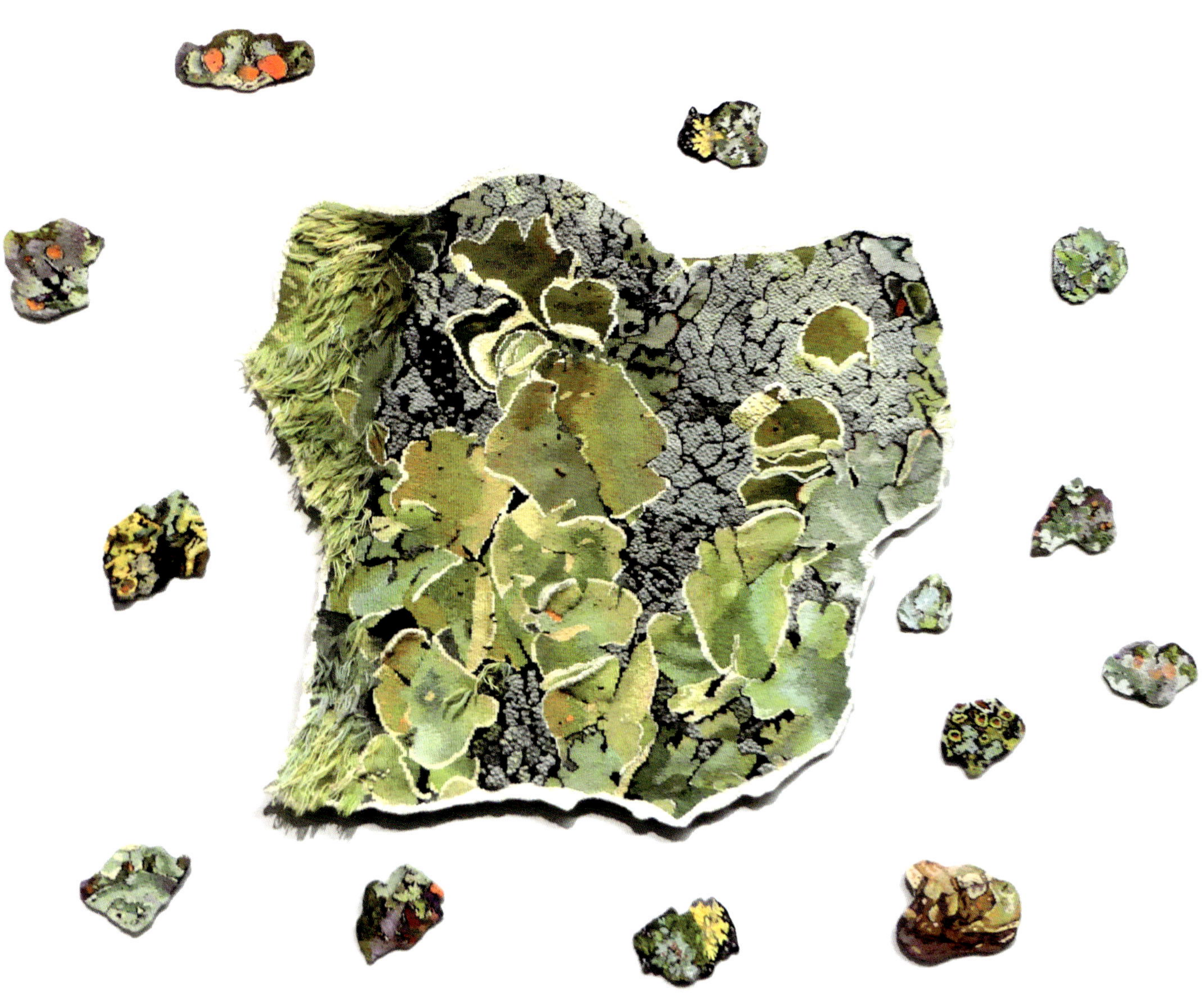

Lichen I
Marilyn Rea-Menzies
2021–22 | surrounding pieces 2.75" × 2" to 6" × 4.7", central piece 30.7" × 27" | wool; cotton warp

Linda Hutchins created these miniature tableaux, with chairs, cribs, stairs, tables, ladders—and even a door. She reduced each object to its essence, with details that she could weave using only black and yellow.

Tiny Tableau
Linda Hutchins
1996 | framed: 9" × 11", each piece 1.75" × 4.5" | cotton seine twine

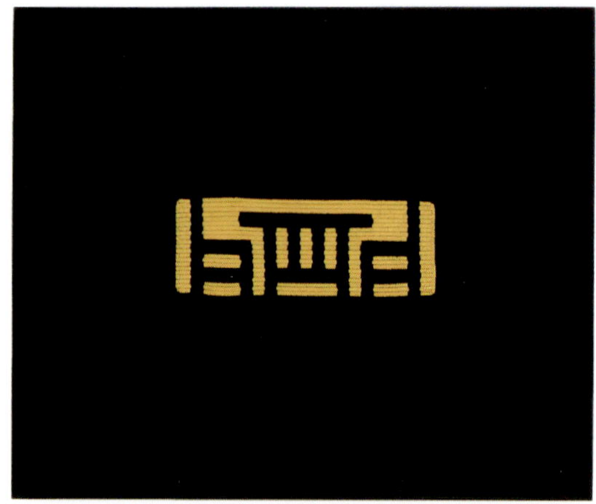

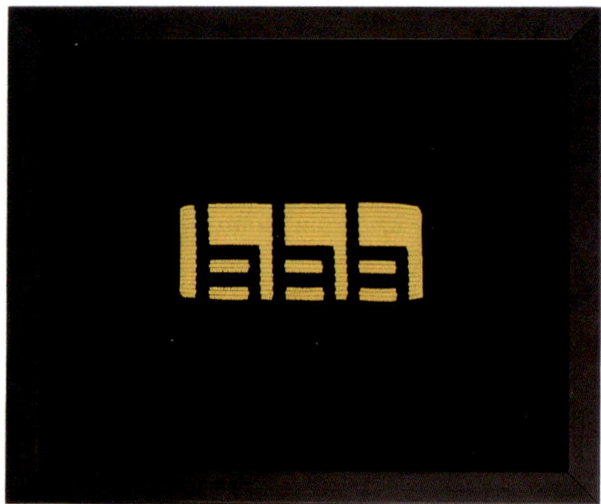

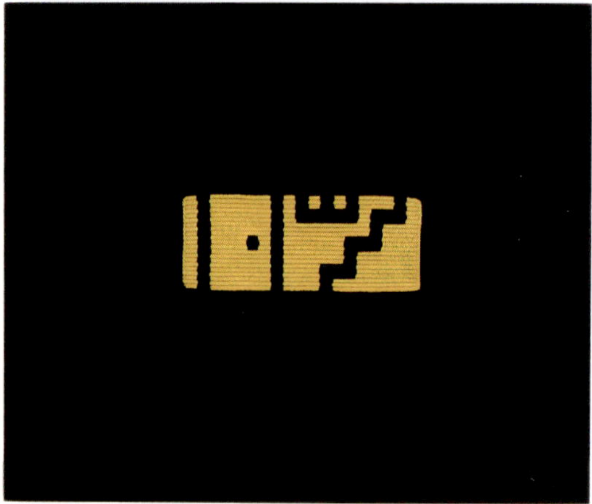

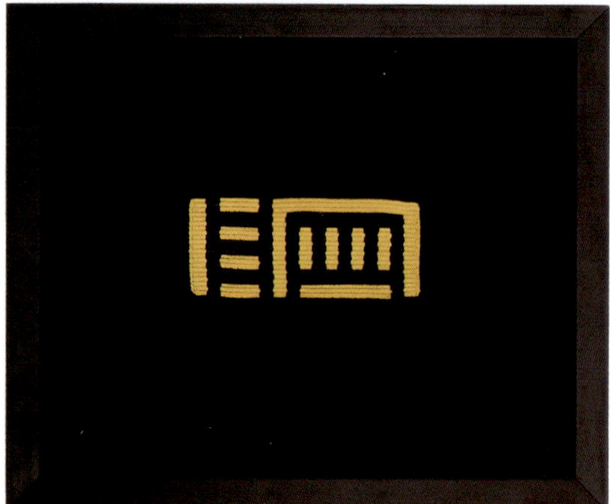

Olivier Mourgue's cartoon may be the smallest ever woven at la Manufacture Nationale des Gobelins, a studio otherwise known for the monumental. The white lines read like something someone wrote, with small details that might illustrate a point. (When the artist visited the studio to see what was happening, he wore the same colors as his piece.)

Les Oubliées (The forgotten ones)
Olivier Mourgue
La Manufacture Nationale des Gobelins, weaver: Jean Claude Lagrange
1984 | 19.7" × 22.45" | wool

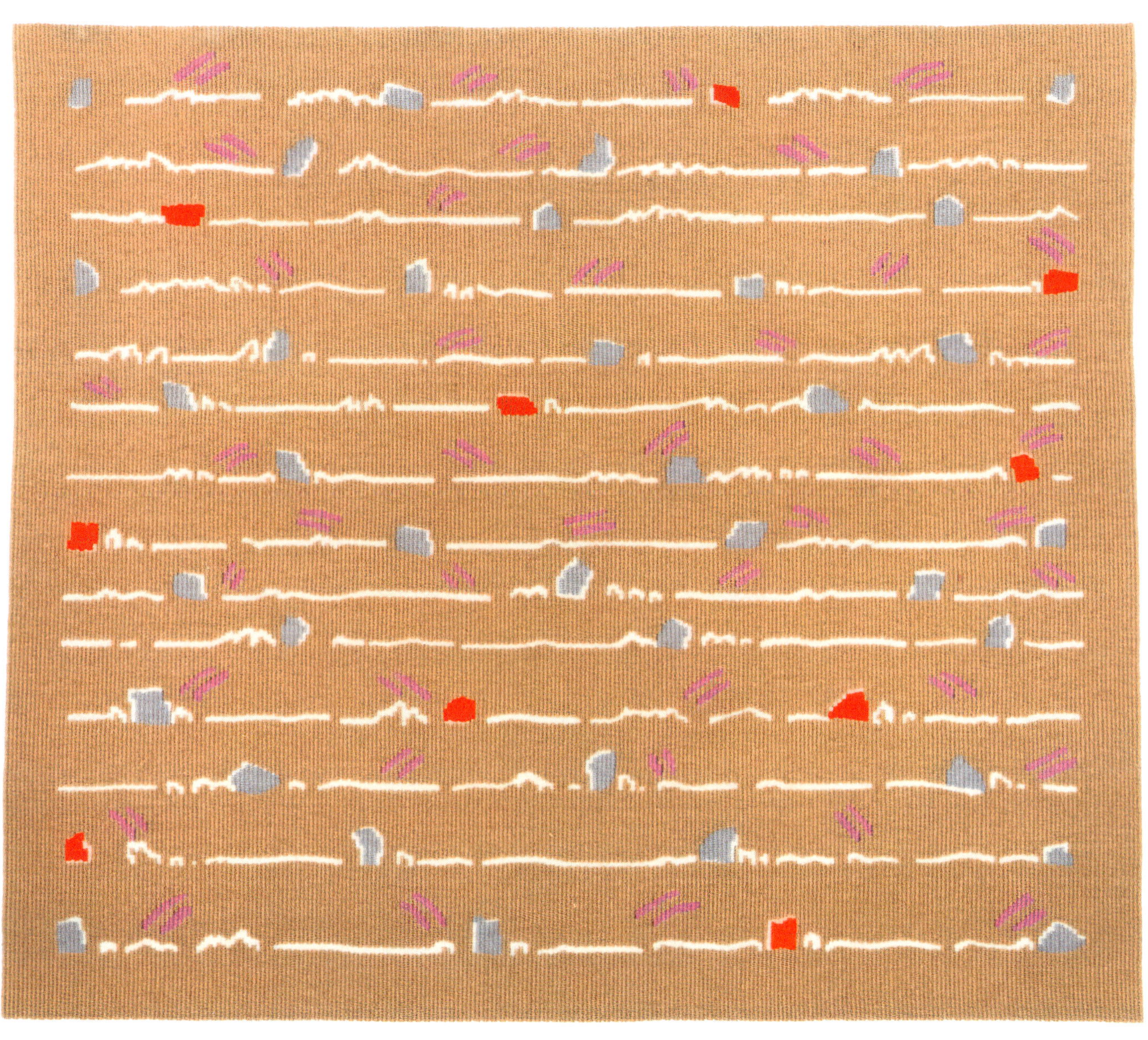

long

Kristin Tinsa Sæterdal decided to track the temperatures in Oslo, the highs and lows of every day, between 1937 and 2002. She assigned warmer colors to the daytime, when the temperature was apt to be higher. The final piece, stretching along one wall, turning a corner, and then going on, measures 46 feet.

Like many tapestries that were woven in series, *The Story of Saint Stephen* works in episodes, next to each other, much like a graphic novel. This piece hangs in the Medieval Museum / the Cluny in the middle of Paris. Ultimately, it runs 14'9". My favorite detail is the one I show here, *The Stoning of St. Stephen*. Note the stone on top of his head. The weavers focused on a sense of balance among the figures and landscape. God looks on approvingly while Saint Stephen submits to God's will.

BELOW AND OPPOSITE, BOTTOM: *Temperature Calendar*
Kristin Tinsa Sæterdal
2003 | 7.8" × 46' | wool, linen

OPPOSITE, TOP: *The Story of Saint Stephen*
Commissioned by Bishop Jean III Baillet, woven in Paris for Auxerre Cathedral; templates attributed to Gauthier de Campes
12 tapestries, 23 scenes. Episode here: Saint Stephen being stoned to death.
15th–16th century | 64"–70" × 14'9" | wool, silk

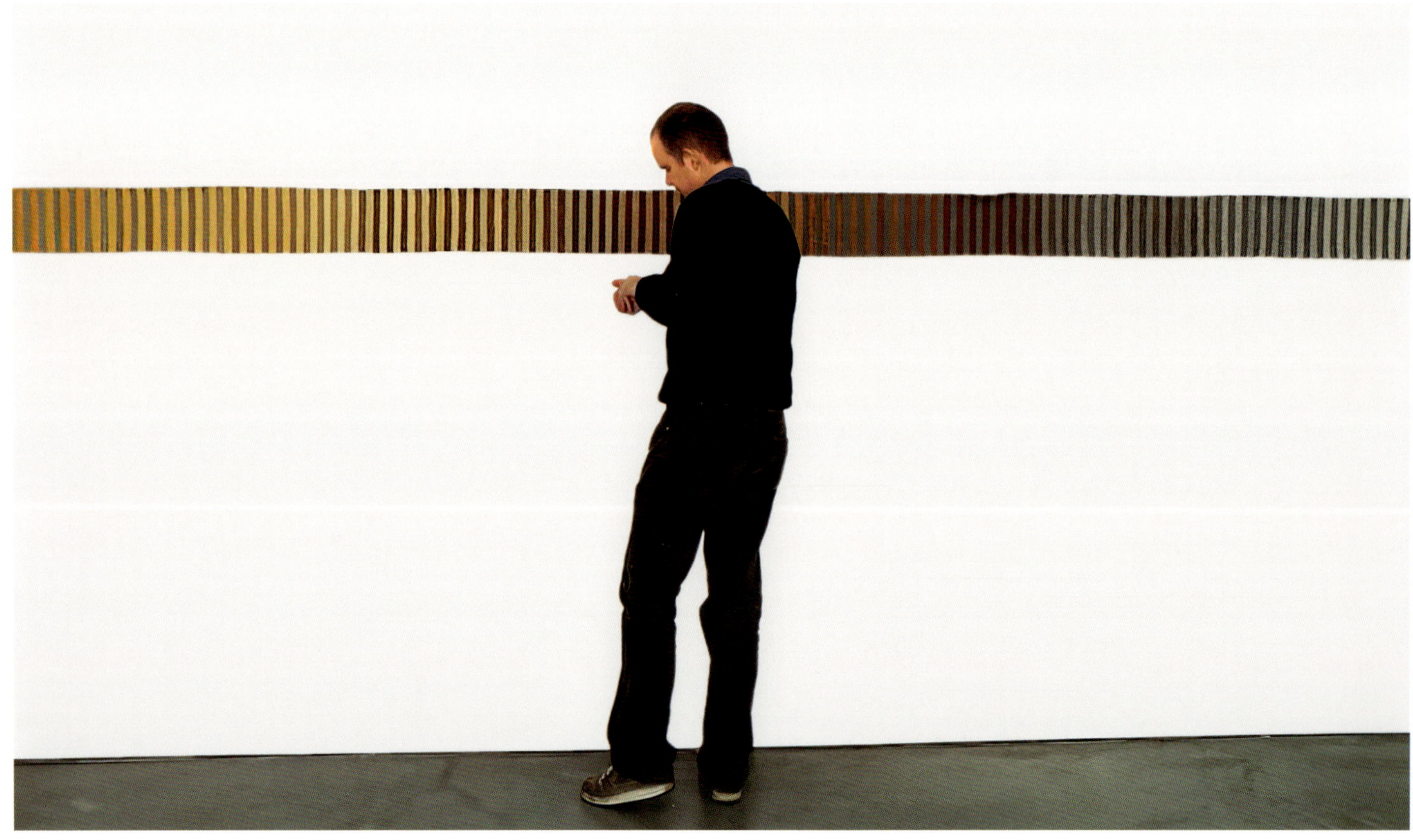

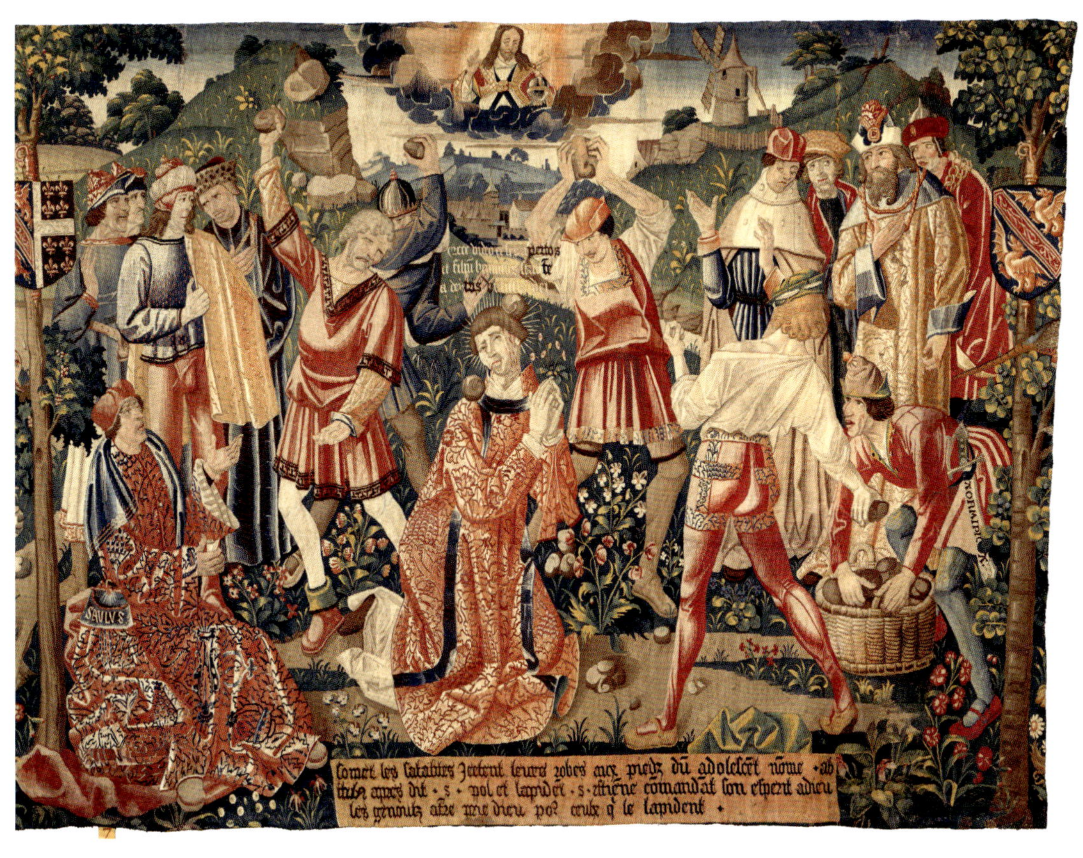

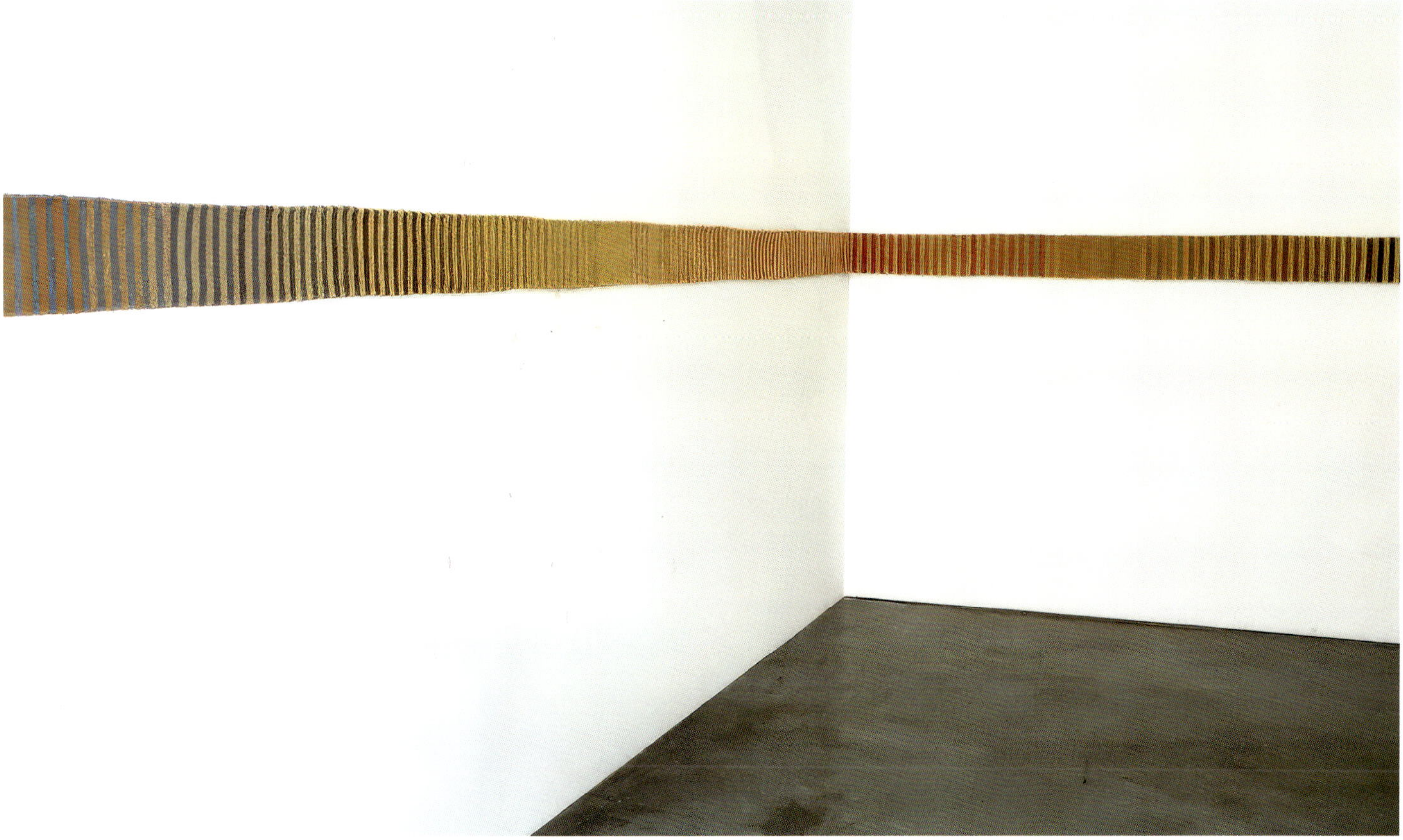

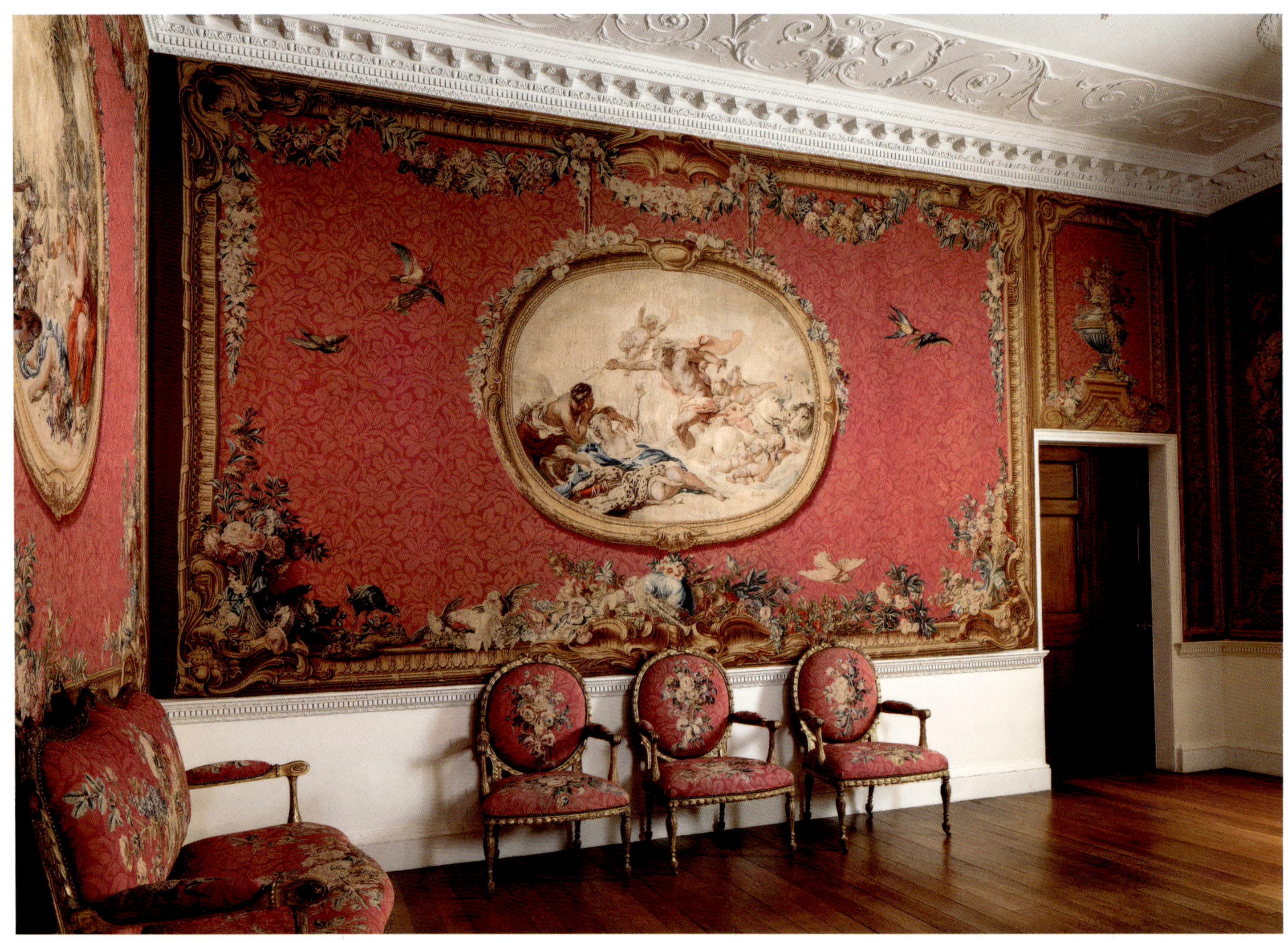

scale

Sporadically, the Metropolitan Museum of Art in New York City furnishes one of their galleries, all four walls, with this eighteenth-century tapestry. In this one, a single wall, the central image looks as though it might be a painting hanging on the wall. Looking at the whole, one can understand why one definition of the French word *tapisserie* can be "wallpaper." (The upholstery on the chairs, using the same palette, is also woven using tapestry technique.)

Croome Court
Commissioned by the 6th Earl of Coventry from Jacques Neilson Gobelins Workshop. Designed by Jacques Germain Soufflot, medallions by François Boucher.
1763–71 | 27'1" × 22'8" (one wall of the room) (entire piece is all four walls) | wool, silk

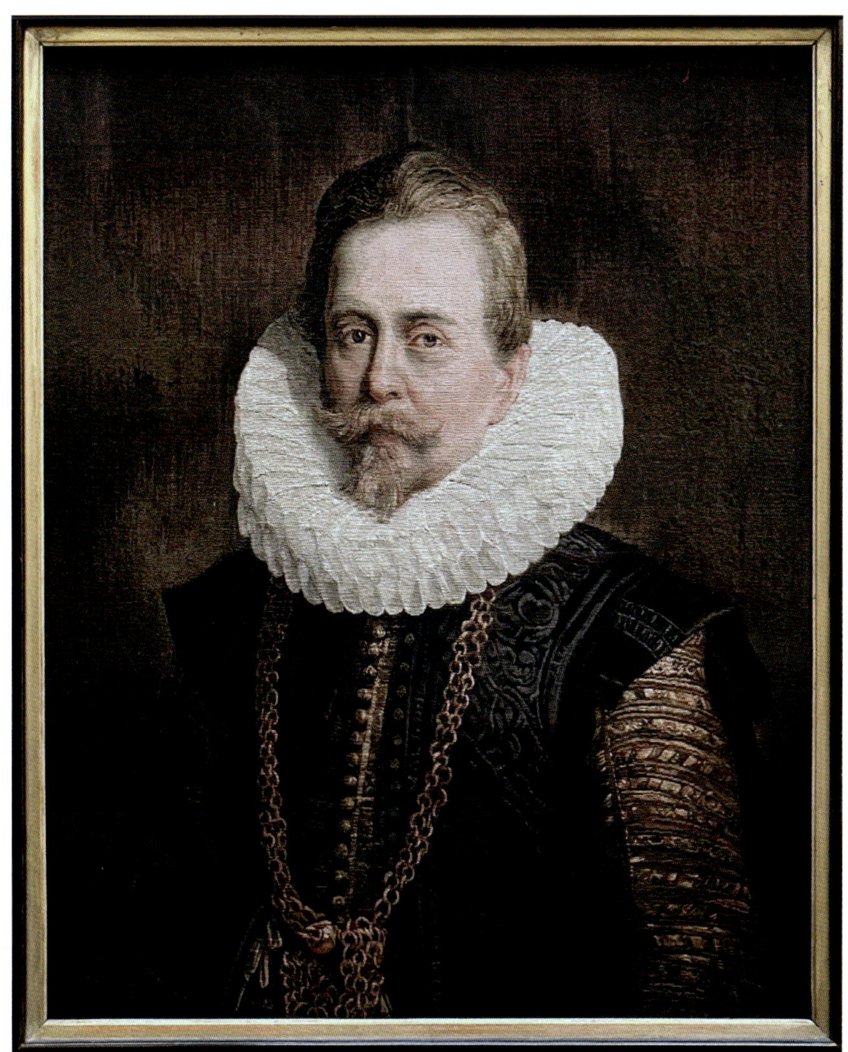

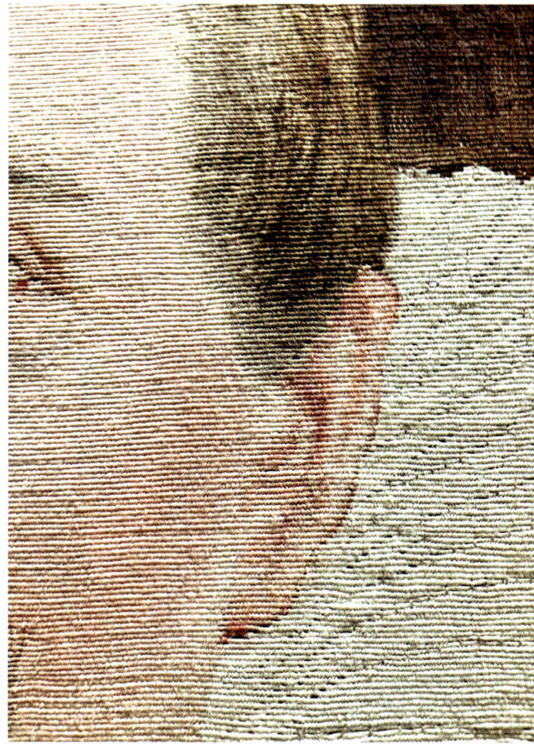

Portrait of Jean Charles de Cordes
1880 | 31.25" × 23.25" | ±28 epi
Manufacture Braquenié, Aubusson, France

dense weaving structures

Historically in Europe, between the seventeenth and nineteenth centuries, tapestry was supposed to replicate painting. As a result, the number of warp threads increased enormously so that the weaver could meticulously copy what the painter had done. Similarly, in Japan, weavers cut their fingernails into serrated edges so they could tamp weft threads into place—a style of weaving that speaks of the fineness of the warp, the large number of weft threads per inch.

This portrait was woven at eleven threads per centimeter—or about twenty-eight ends per inch. The density made such reproduction possible. In spite of what has faded, there remains something remarkable about what the weavers achieved. We can imagine real skin with a slight flush.

From the Kawashima Textile Factory in Kyoto, Japan, a small piece of a flower—where the leaves are woven at about forty-two warps per inch.

The Navajo value fineness in the weft. This *Two Grey Hills*, woven for a private collector, has 122 weft threads per inch. The spinner (Barbara Ornelas) is also the weaver of this remarkable piece.

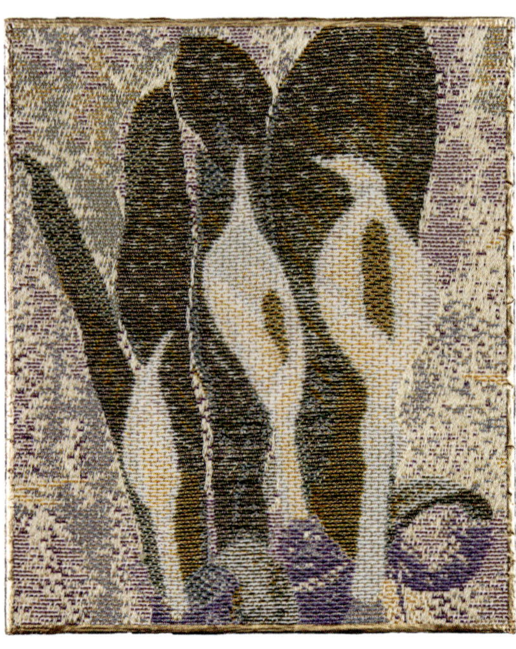

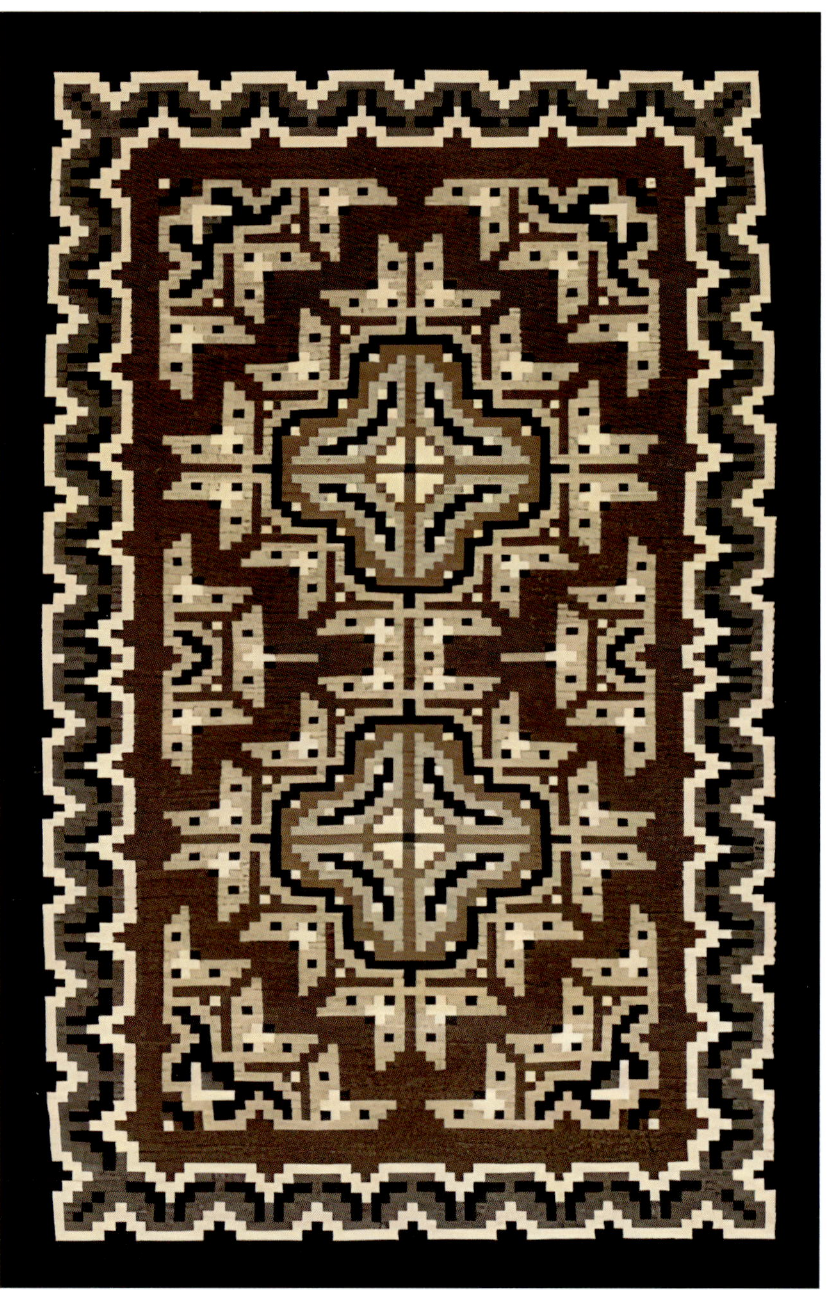

ABOVE: *Kawashima flower*
Kawashima Textile Factory
2000 | 5.5" × 4.5" | ±42 epi

RIGHT: *Two Grey Hills*
Barbara Ornelas
2019 | 44" × 30" | wool
122 wefts per inch; wool spun by Barbara Ornelas
Collection of Peter Goldman and Beverly Weber

OPPOSITE: *Children of the Dust*
Ann Shuttleworth
1996 | 57" × 53" | handspun wool, Karakul wool, unbleached and raw silk, raw and refined linen, mohair, sisal, rayon, handspun cotton; cotton seine twine double cotton warp

large materials

On the other end of this yarn size spectrum is Ann Shuttleworth's elephant. Yarns from all possible sources, the size of a pinkie, add to the massiveness of the animal. She says that she "always weave[s] with thick materials so the blind/vision-impaired viewer can 'see' them through touch. (Blindness runs in the family)."

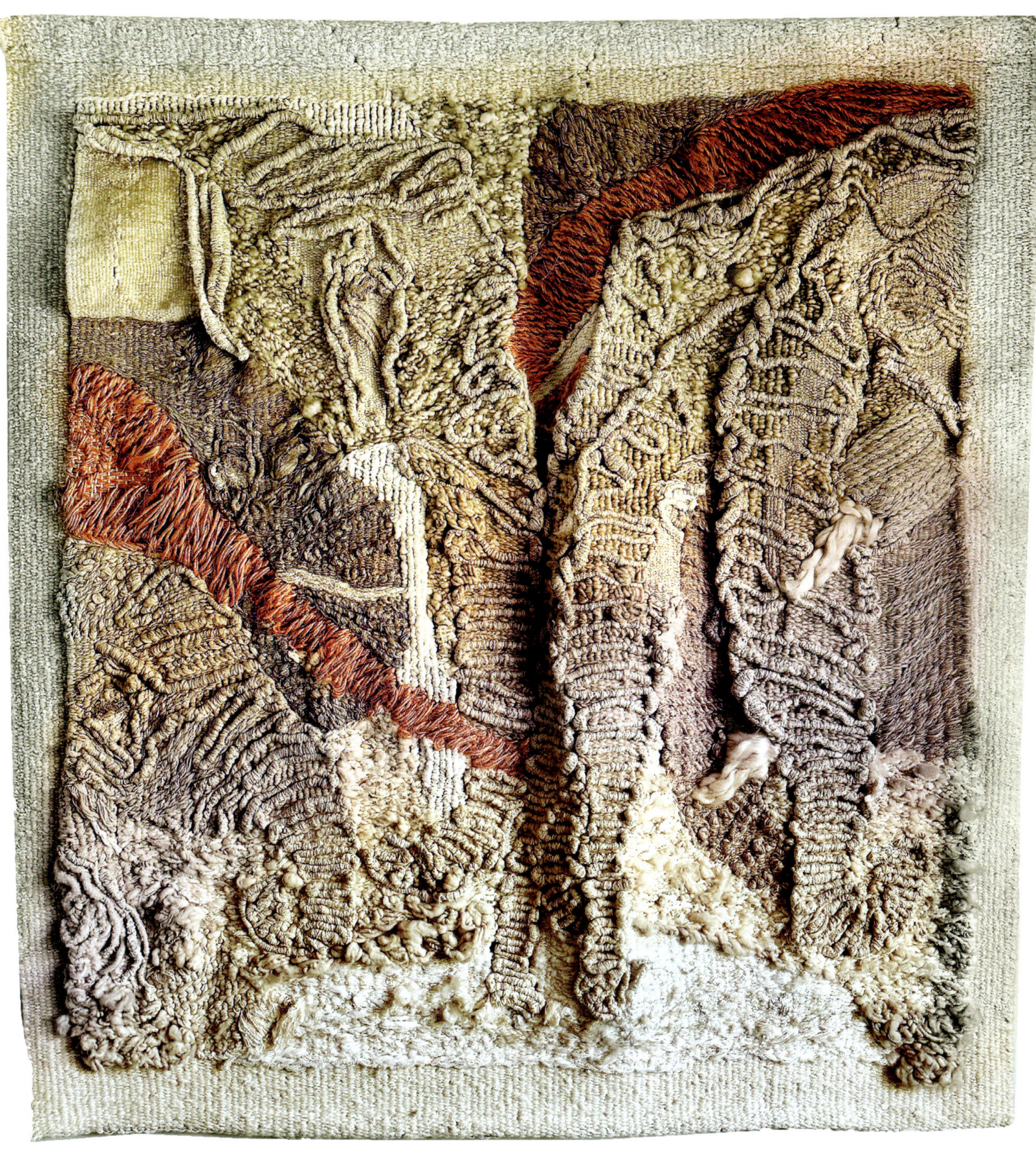

contemporary and immense

Here we see a cartoon, as used (in strips) for the process of weaving. Jacques Larochette worked for four years to get this tapestry woven. It hangs in the Basilica of Saint Francis in Buenos Aires—and his brother Jean Pierre wrote a book (*The Largest Tapestry in the World*) about the whole adventure. Actually, in the twentieth century, another tapestry of these dimensions was woven: Graham Sutherland's *Christ in His Glory* hangs in Coventry Cathedral in England. But the warp in Larochette's became horizontal when it was hung—and the result is a stable image. In England, where the warp is vertical as the piece hangs, the weft slides downward.

Turn the page: It took a team of sixteen—directed by Pedro Mendoza—weavers, spinners, dyers—to make this tapestry where it serves as a service to the community. As the team stands around it, the scale becomes clear.

OPPOSITE: Cartoon of tapestry, Basilica de San Francisco, Buenos Aires, Argentina
Horatio Butler, designer
Jacques Larochette, director of weaving
Woven by Isaias Cativa, Leonardo Delfer, Rafael Rivero, Rafael Alcar, and Antonio Falcon
1968–72 | 36' × 24' | wool, goat hair; cotton seine twine warp

FOLLOWING SPREAD: *Tequio* (Community work)
Carlos Zedillo Velasco, designer
Pedro Mendoza, project director
16-person team, including weavers Mario Mendoza Gutierrez, Abner Yair Mendoza Sosa, and Cesar Bautista; in charge of threads, bobbins, and finishing were Carmela Sosa Bautista, Diana Melisa Mendoza Sosa, and Raquel Gutierrez Martinez
2020 | 15' × 23' | wool, natural dyes

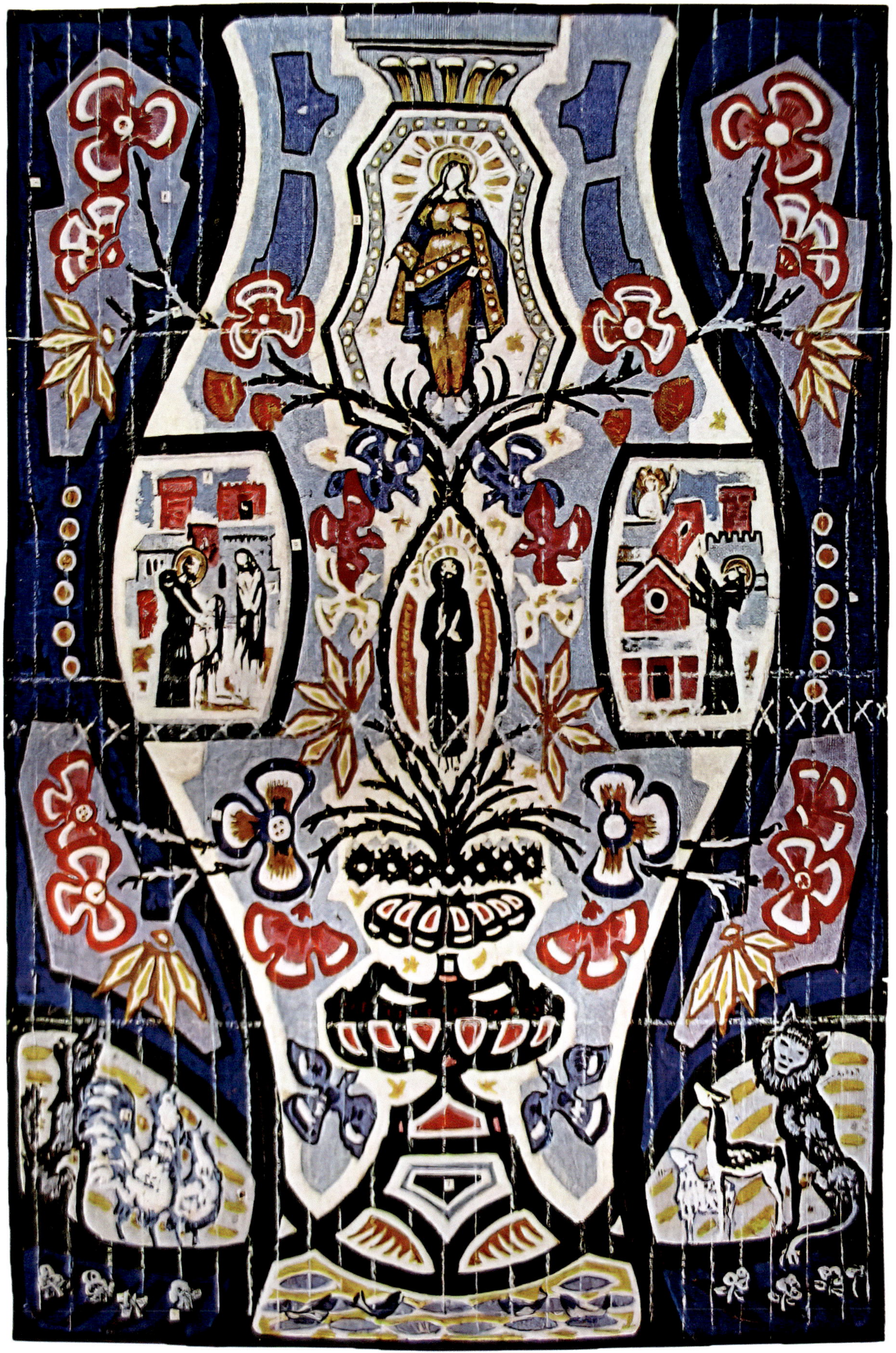

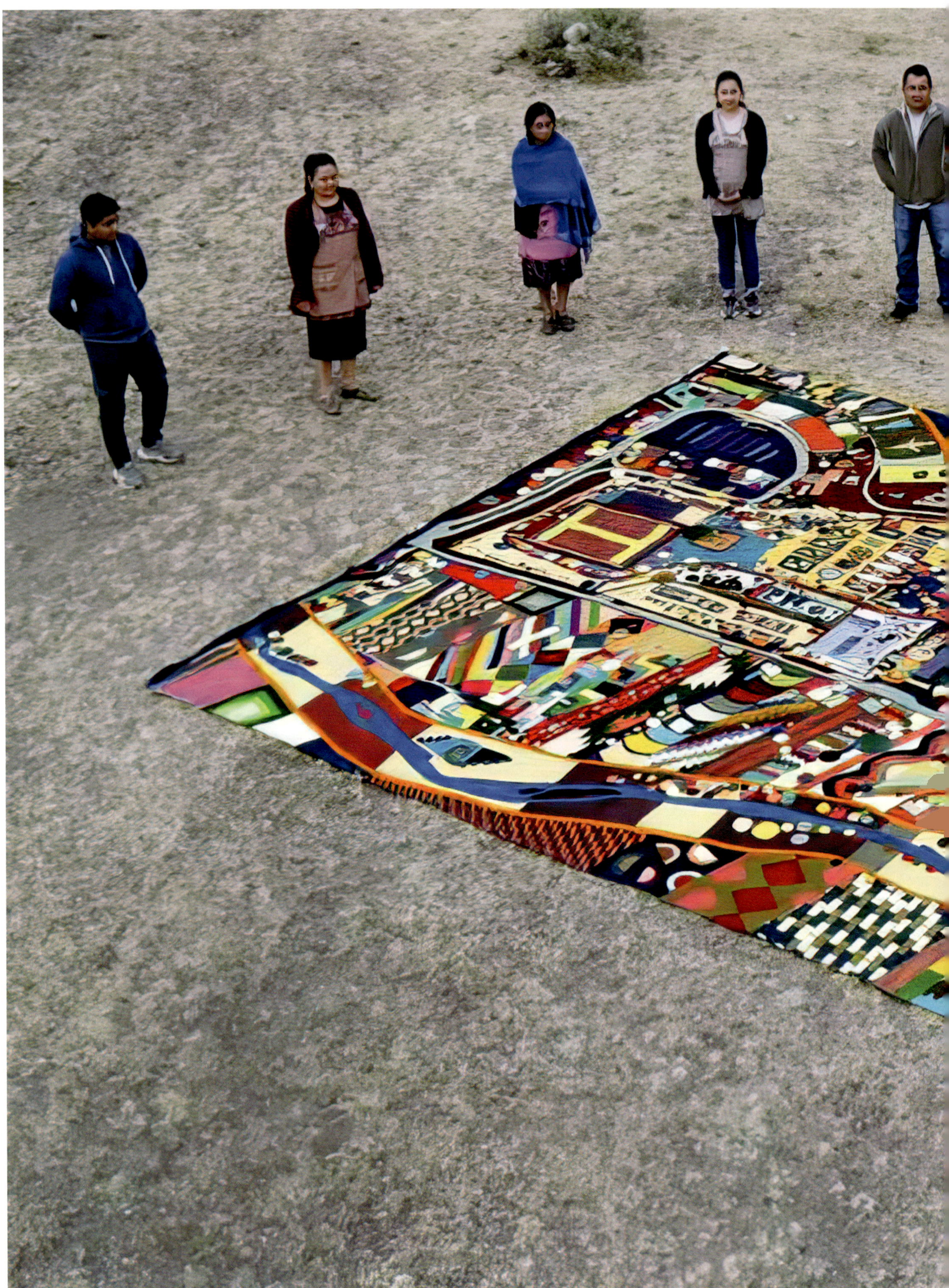

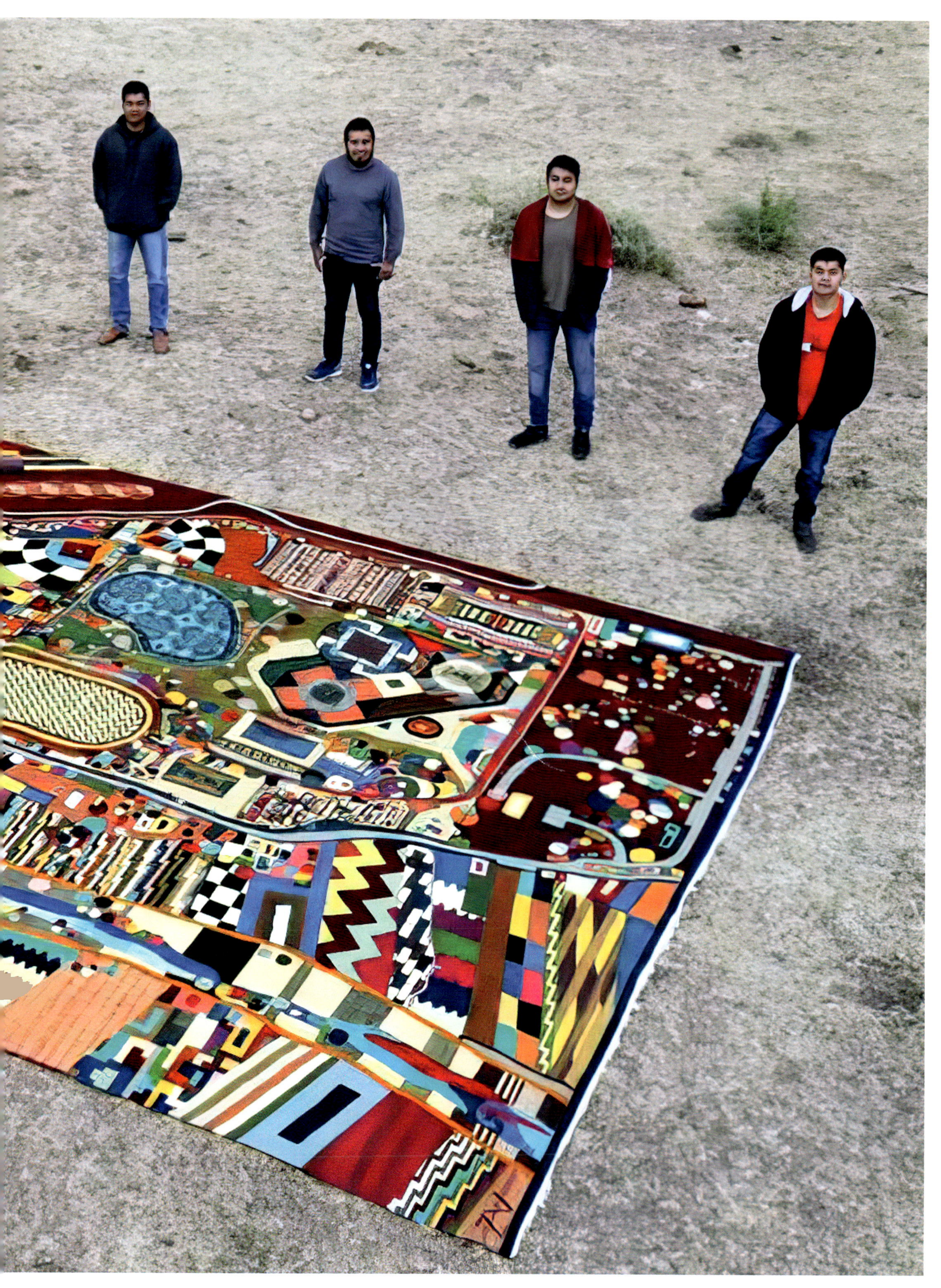

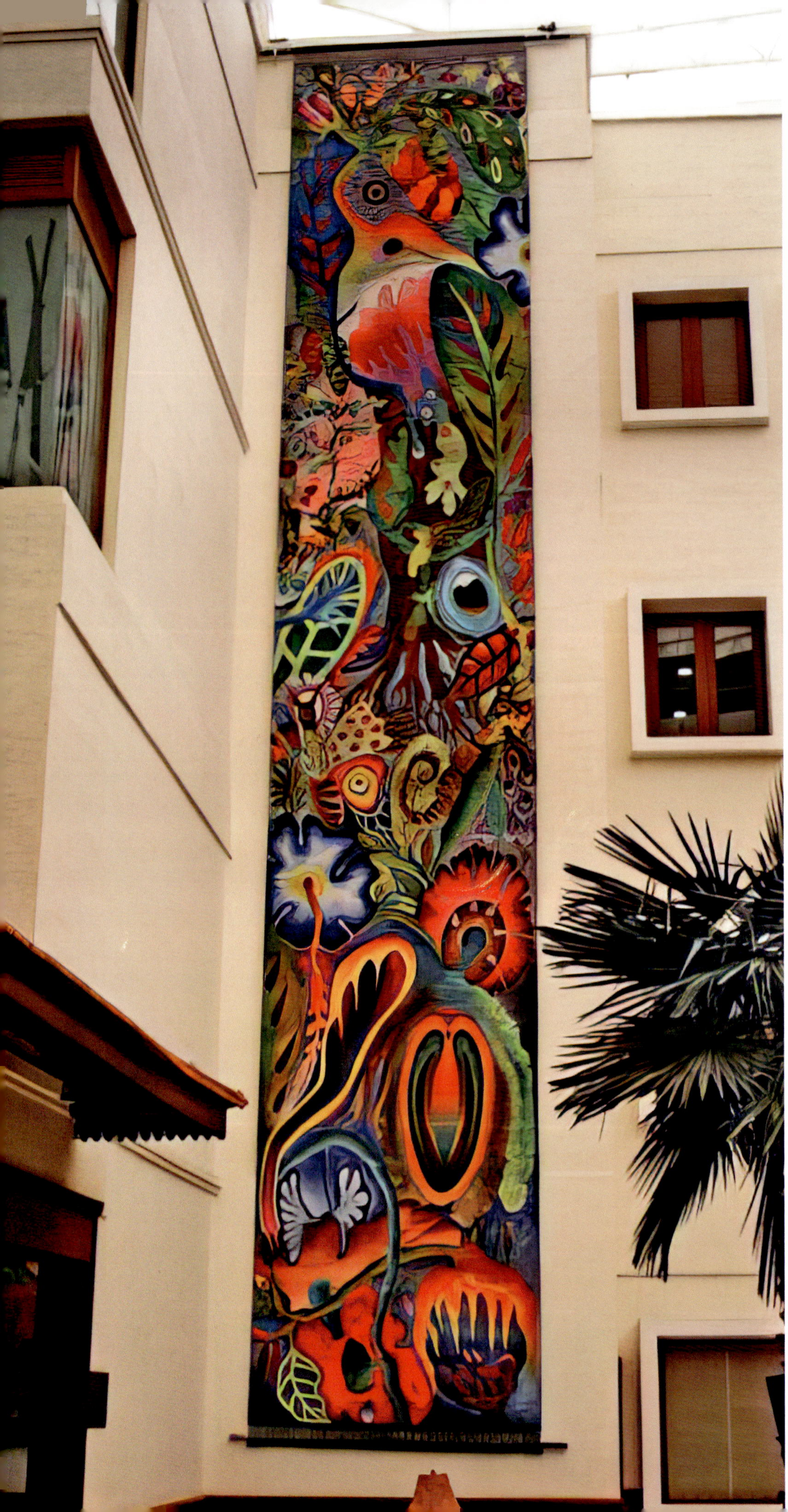

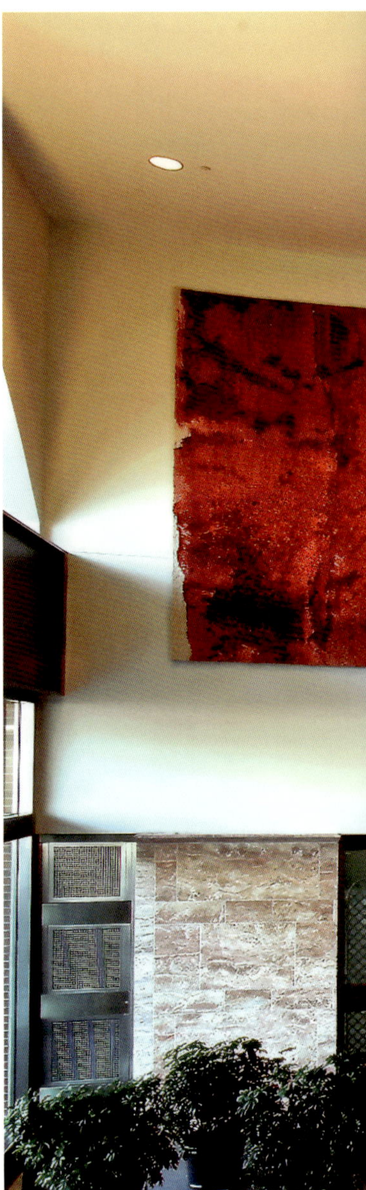

Commission for Paul Hotel, Bangalore, India
Tasara Weaving Center
Designers: Balakrishnan, Vasudevan
Weavers: Sabi, Sindhu, Sreeja
2008–09 | 18' × 47.3' | viscose; cotton warp

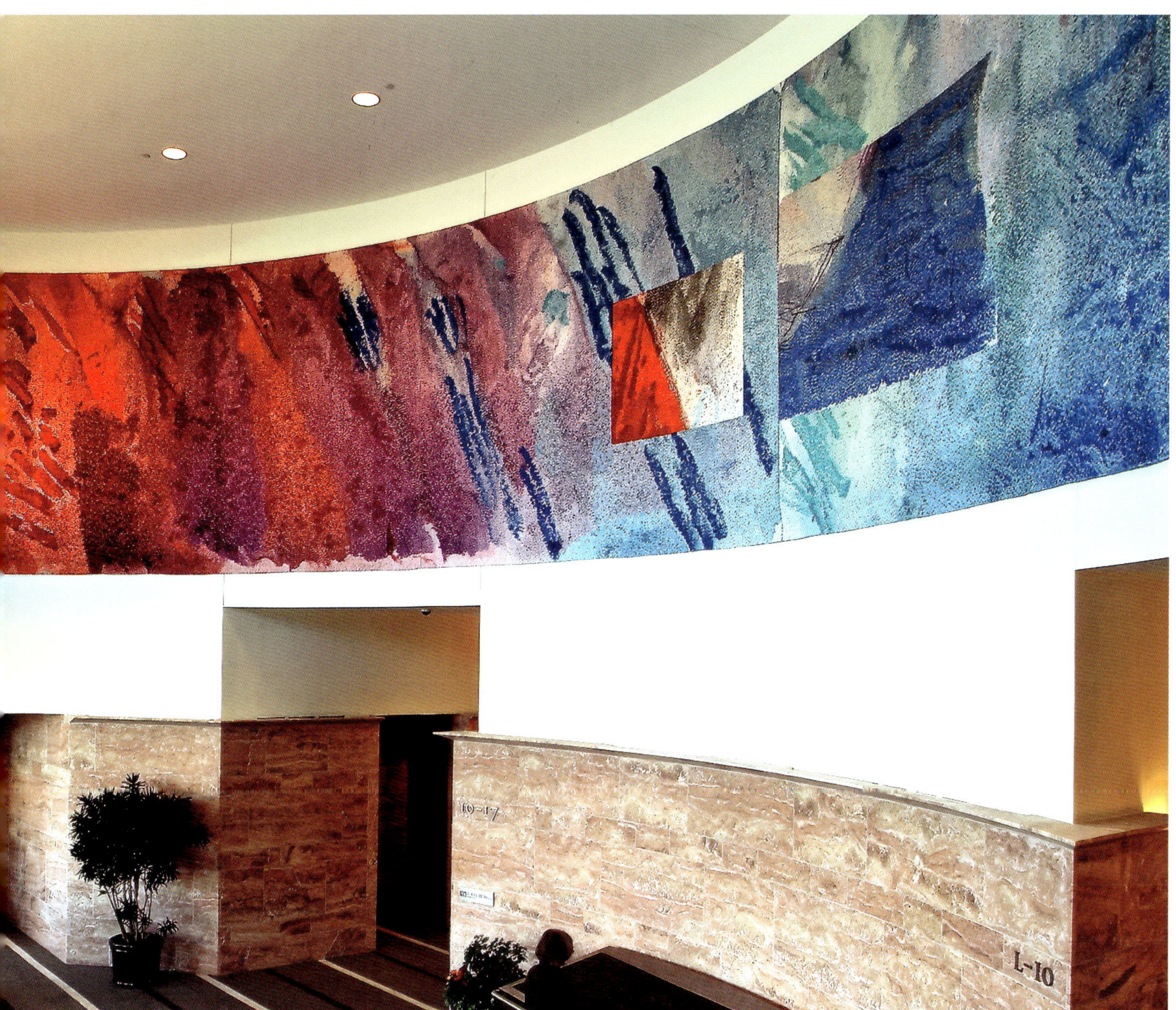

Signals
Helena Hernmarck
2002 | 11' × 80' | wool, linen, cotton
Commissioned by Michael McKinnell of Kallmann McKinnell & Wood
Architects for client Pembroke Real Estate, to hang in the World Trade Center West Lobby, 255 State Street, Boston, Massachusetts
Woven at Alice Lund Textiler, Borlänge, Sweden
Collection of Frida Lindberg, Stockholm, Sweden
Photographer: Andrew deLory
Courtesy of Helena Hernmarck

Another piece where scale communicates clearly—this 18-foot-tall tapestry, woven in India at the Tasara Weaving Center. The Tasara style of tapestry weaving shows both warp and weft, so there is less risk of weft slide. Indian textiles celebrate color, and this is no exception.

Helena Hernmarck has long established her reputation as a weaver of work that suits its environment. She works in collaboration, often with the builders and designers of the structures where her pieces are installed. This immense tapestry (880 square feet) follows the curve of the lobby. Her wool is sourced from Sweden's historic Rya sheep breed, and its luster adds immeasurably to the blues and reds.

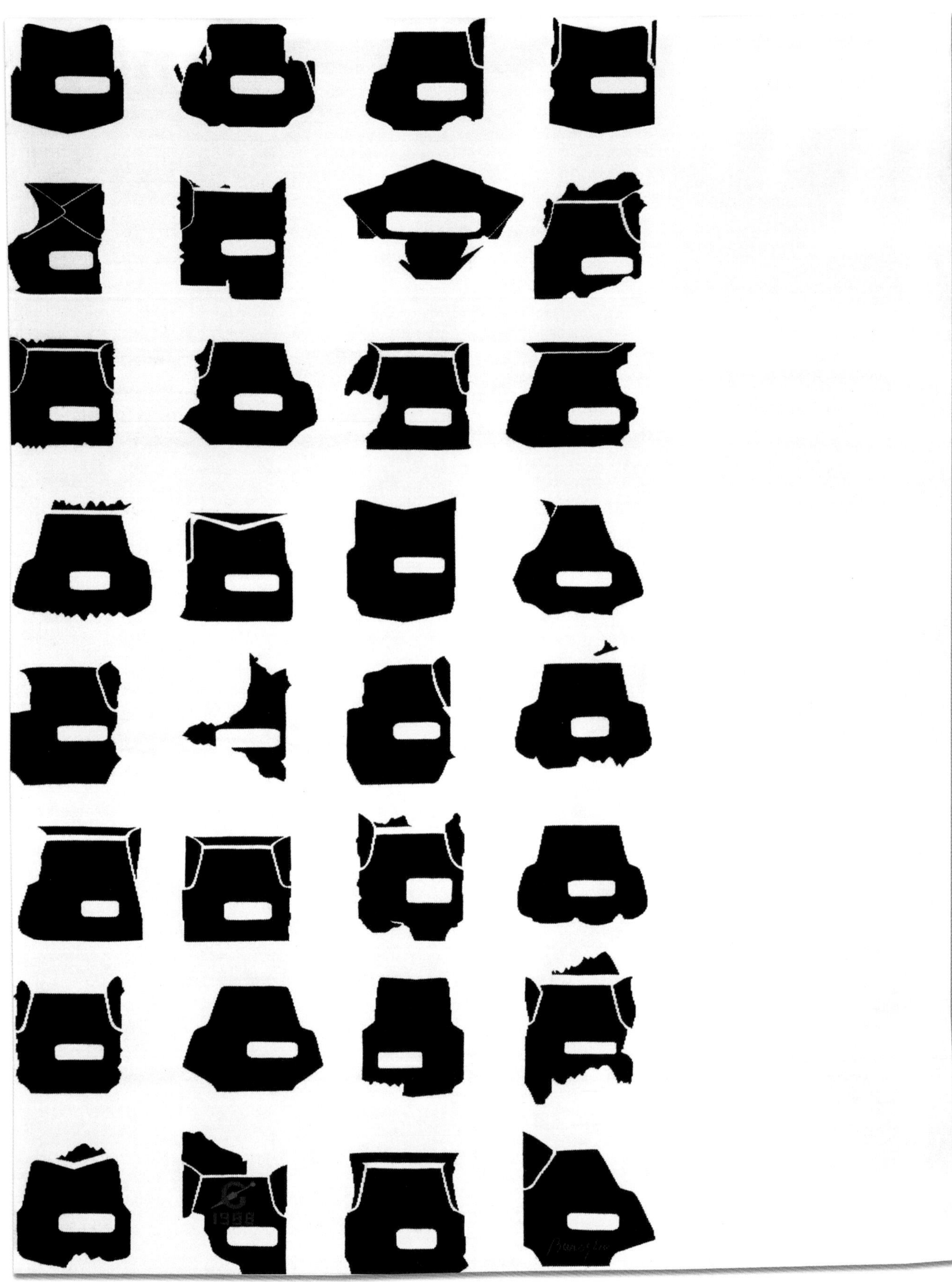

CHAPTER 11

mark

In the Middle Ages, European weaving guilds regulated the marks with which studios signed their tapestries. Those marks often included an image of the tool they worked with—a bobbin (*broche* in French) for the vertical warp weaving, and a different sort of bobbin (*flute* in French) for the horizontal warp weaving. Both of these tools held the weft yarn, and the *broche*, with a point at one end, further tamped that yarn into place.

In addition, marks included the official initials that specified the studios themselves. Some historical tapestry books have pages and pages of various marks; the British Tapestry Group is organizing an online database of weavers' marks.

This first piece is not a mark, but it could be. It was woven first at la Manufacture Nationale des Gobelins in the 1980s, and the weaver obtained permission from the designer to reduce the palette (originally various pastel blues) to a single color, the dark blue. It takes on the look of a group of Asian chops, which serve as signatures on legal and official documents, a tradition that goes back thousands of years. It signifies authorization by the person or company it represents.

OPPOSITE: *Dazibao*
(from the Chinese: a wall poster written in large letters)
Pierre Buraglio
Woven at la Manufacture Nationale des Gobelins
Head weaver: Elisabeth Rivaux; weaver: Jean Pierre Soyer
Photographer: Philippe Sébert. © ADAGP, Paris, 2025
1992 | 102.75" × 78.75" | wool

RIGHT: La Manufacture Nationale des Gobelins, ca. 2000

La Manufacture Nationale des Gobelins' mark is a *G* with a *broche* going through it. Over the years, the mark has evolved, from the highly stylized to the simple.

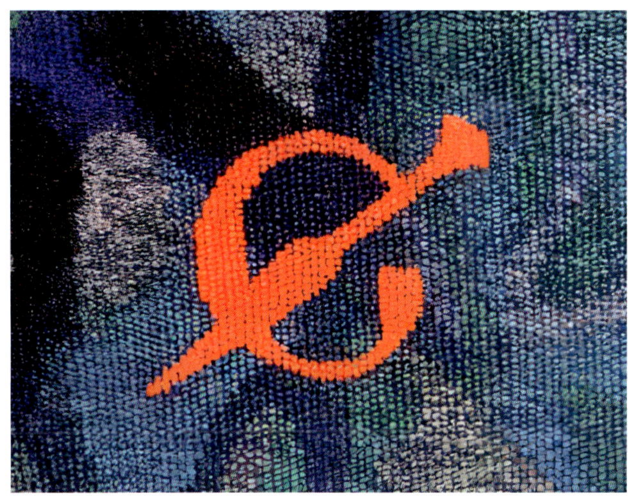

Weavers sign their work too.

Rothman, Heller, and Johns sign with their initials; Scanlin's *T* hugs her other initials. Cronenberg gives us the first three letters of his surname.

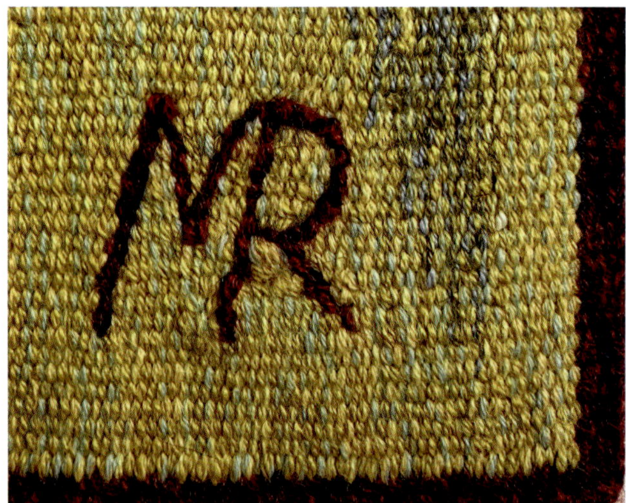

Minna Rothman

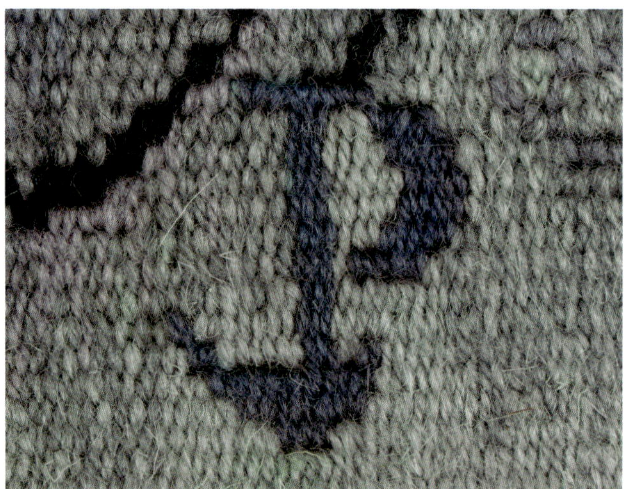

Pat Johns

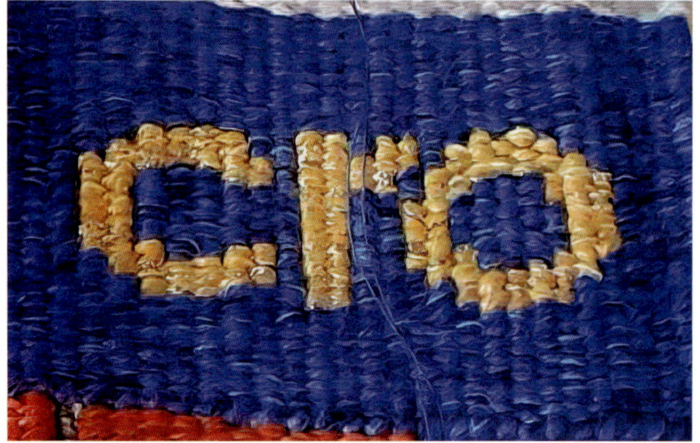

Thomas Cronenberg

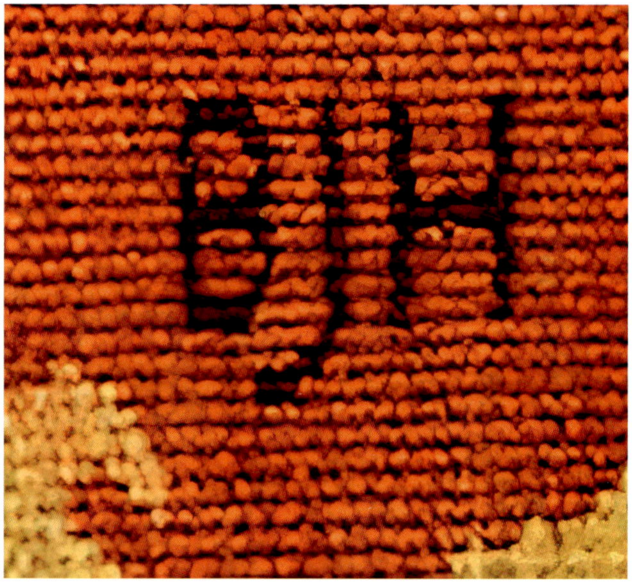

Barbara Juliet Heller

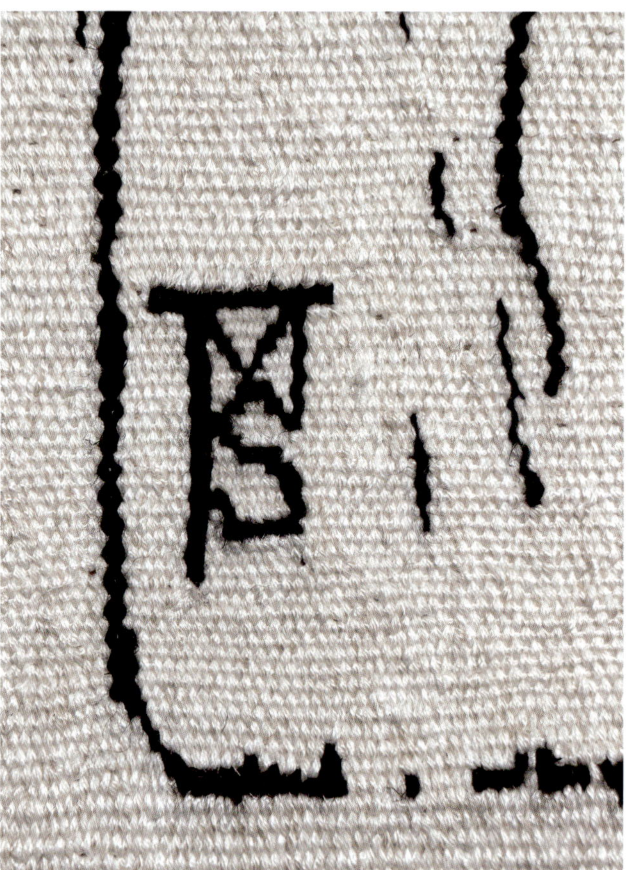

Tommye McClure Scanlin

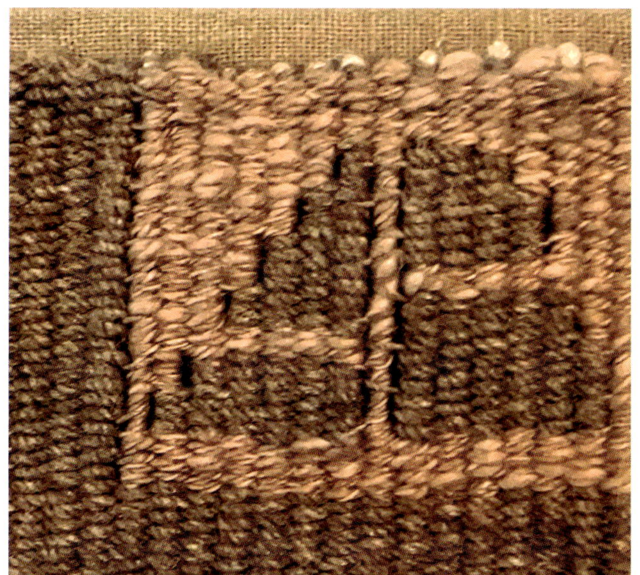

Archie Brennan

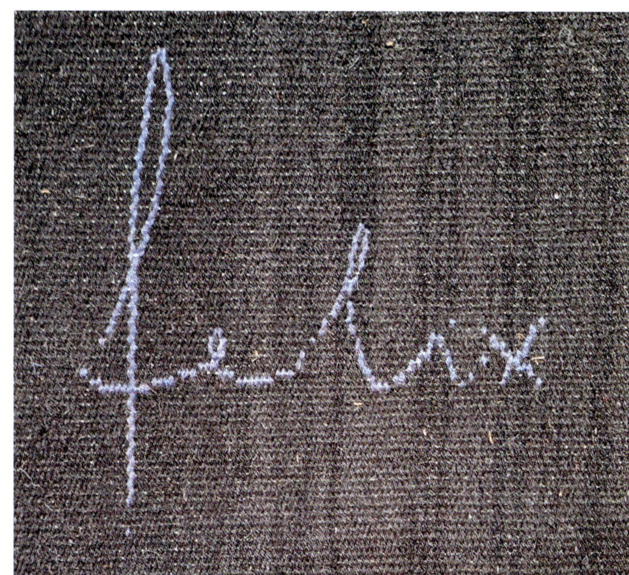

Feliksas Jakubauskas

Brennan emphasizes the woven quality of his letters, with the steps needed to construct the angles. The *A* and *B* are separated by a backbone of tan.

Jakubauskas writes his nickname. Perhaps it just adds to the fun that Felix is the Latin word for "happy."

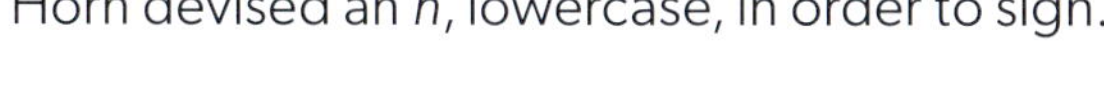

Horn devised an *h*, lowercase, in order to sign.

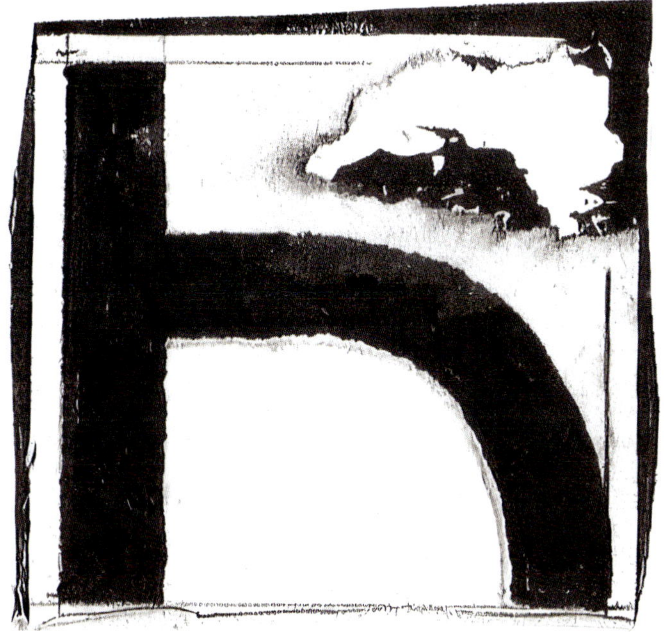

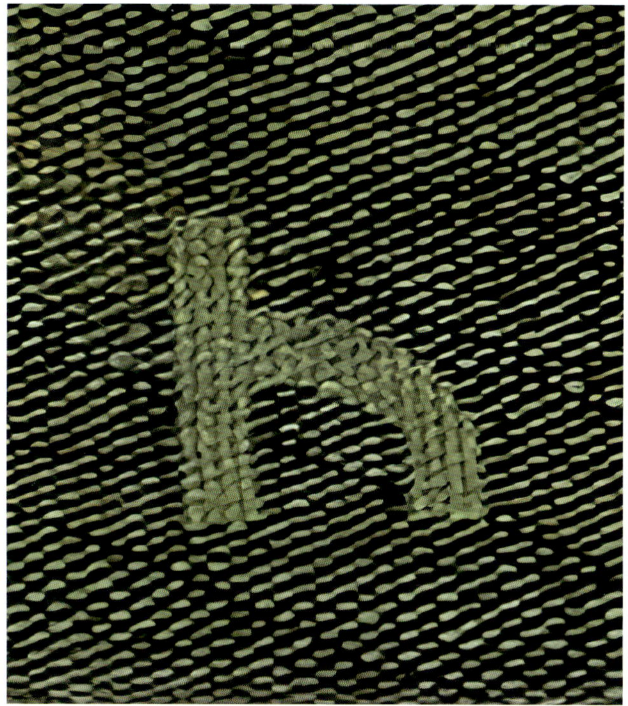

Peter Horn

V face series: Woman with braids
Victor Jacoby
1993 | 25" × 17" | wool

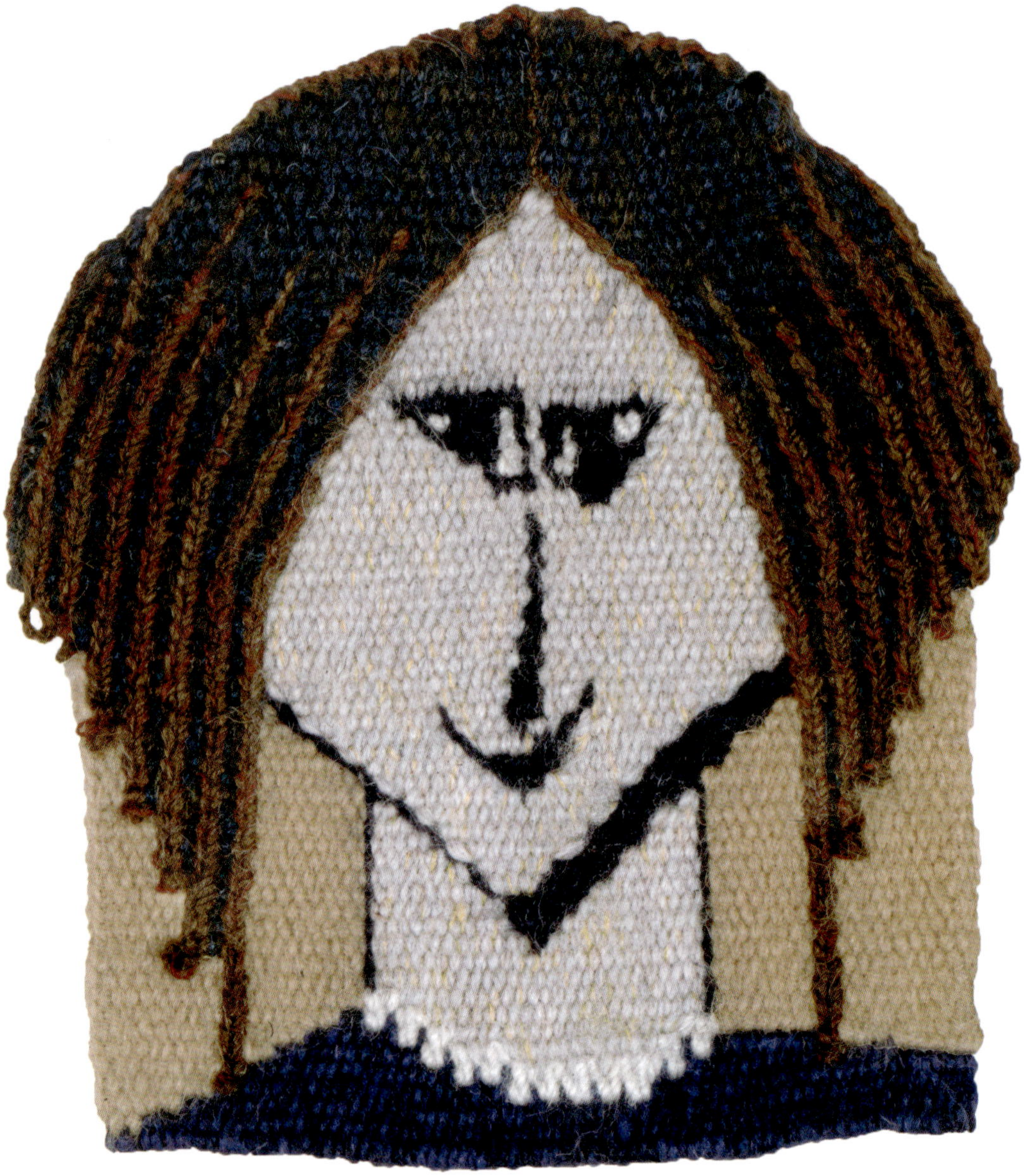

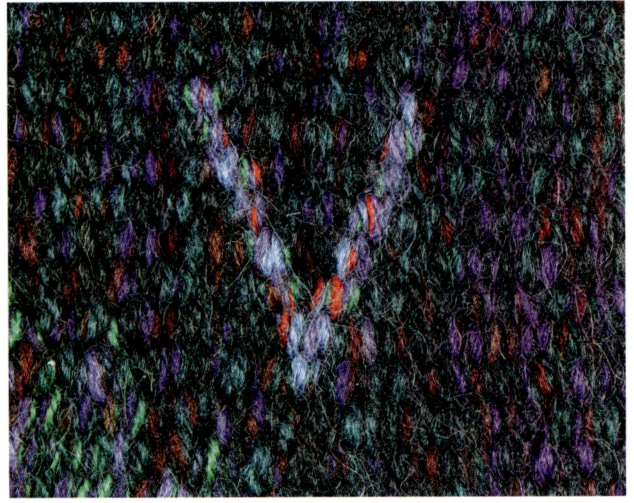

Victor Jacoby

Jacoby gives us the *V* of his first name and then later pursued that letter in a group of tapestries called *V face series*.

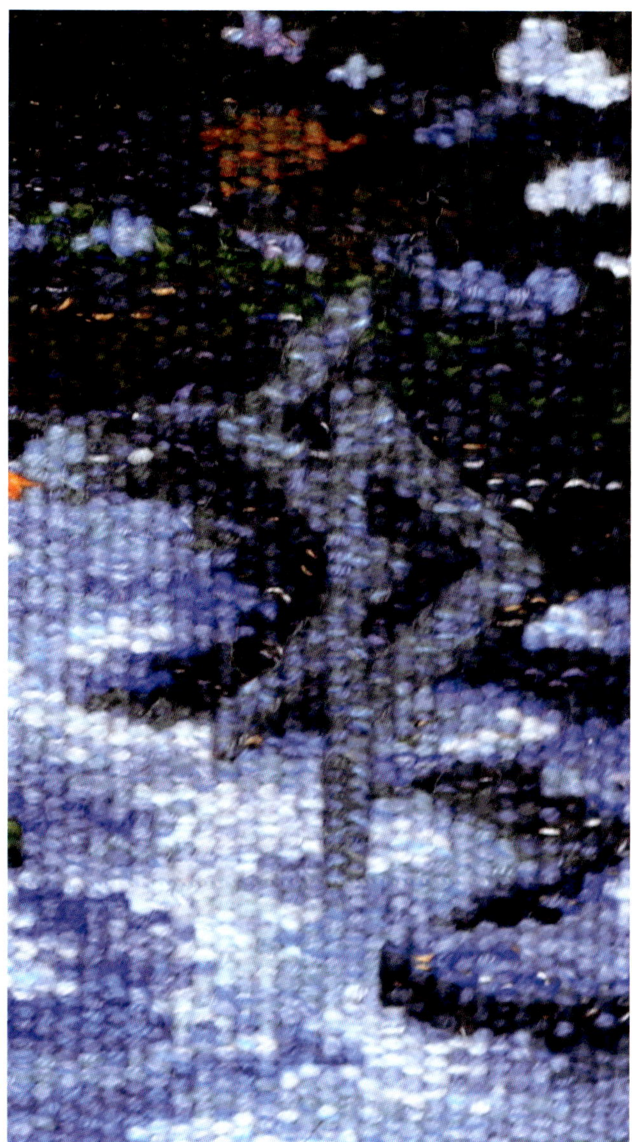

Suzanne Paquette

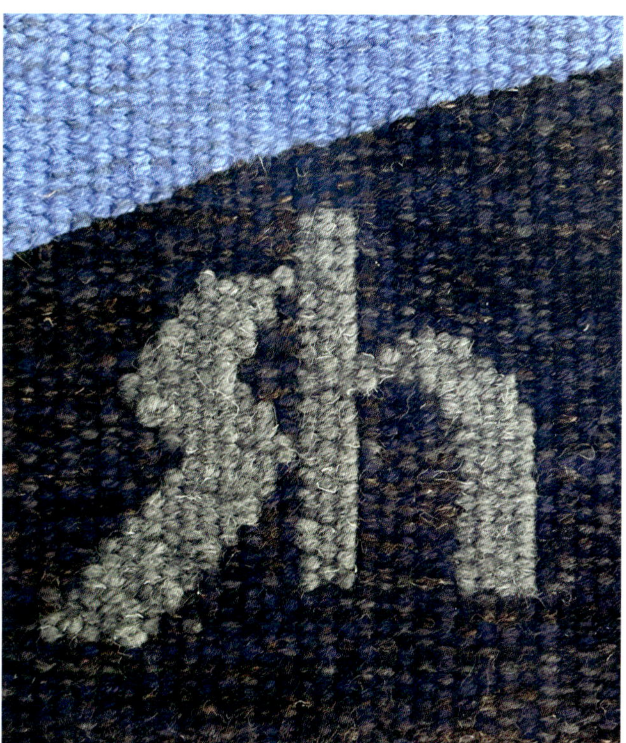

Susan Hart Henegar

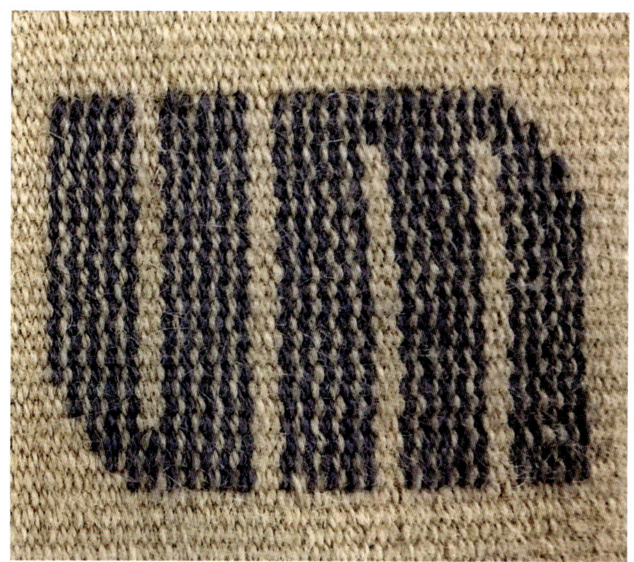

Ulrikka Mokdad

Paquette interlaces her two initials in blue. Hart Henegar designed her initials (first and last name) to succeed visually whether she was weaving from bottom to top or from side to side.

Mokdad uses carefully woven straight lines to produce *U* and *M*. These, by their spacing, the similarity of their vertical lines, and their opposed corners and curves, make an elegant unit.

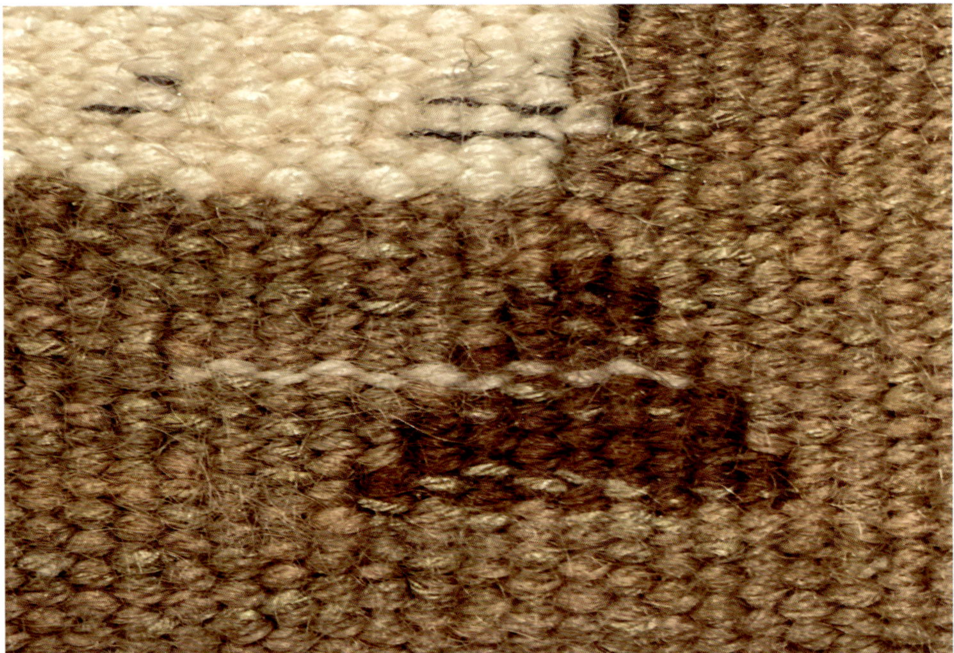

Jan Austin

Austin always makes sure there is a tail wandering off from the *A*.

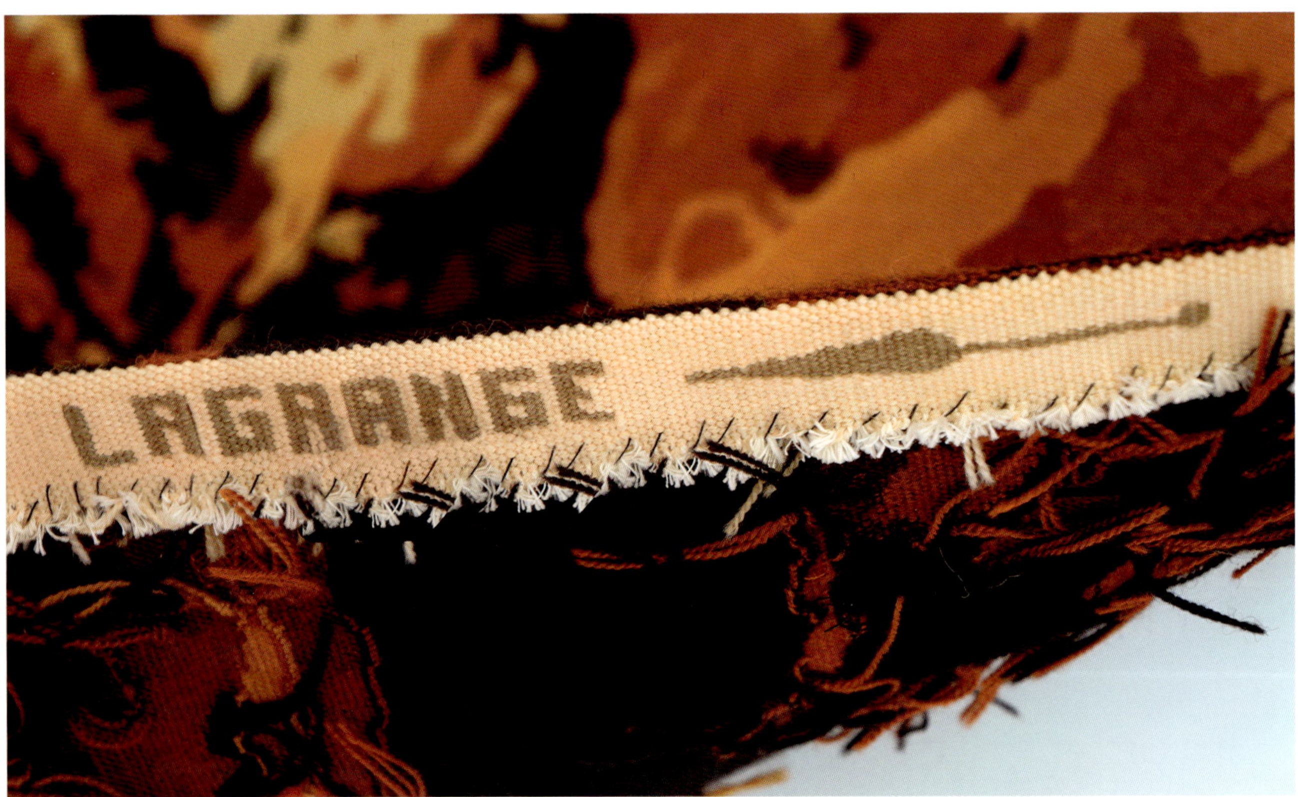

Jean Claude Lagrange

Lagrange signs in the hem on the rear of his tapestry, including the telltale *broche*.

When they began their careers, Larochette (weaver) and Lurie (designer) signed on the front of their pieces. In time, they felt that these interfered with the overall look of their tapestries, and so they wove them into the hem, then developed a label that is now sewn on the back.

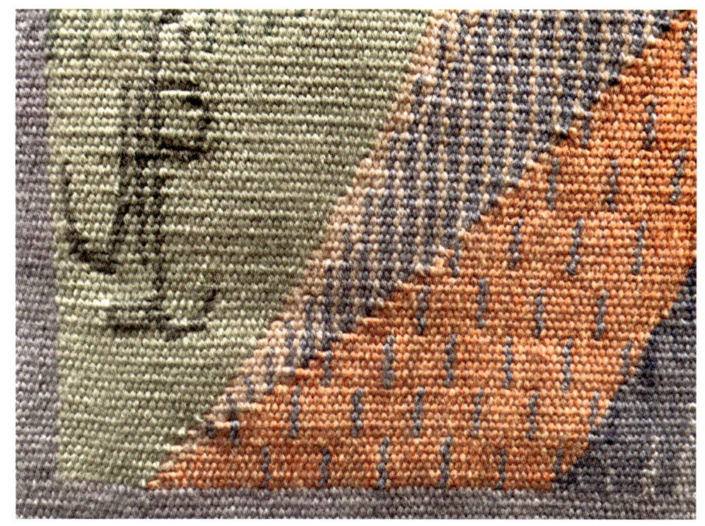

Jean Pierre Larochette and Yael Lurie

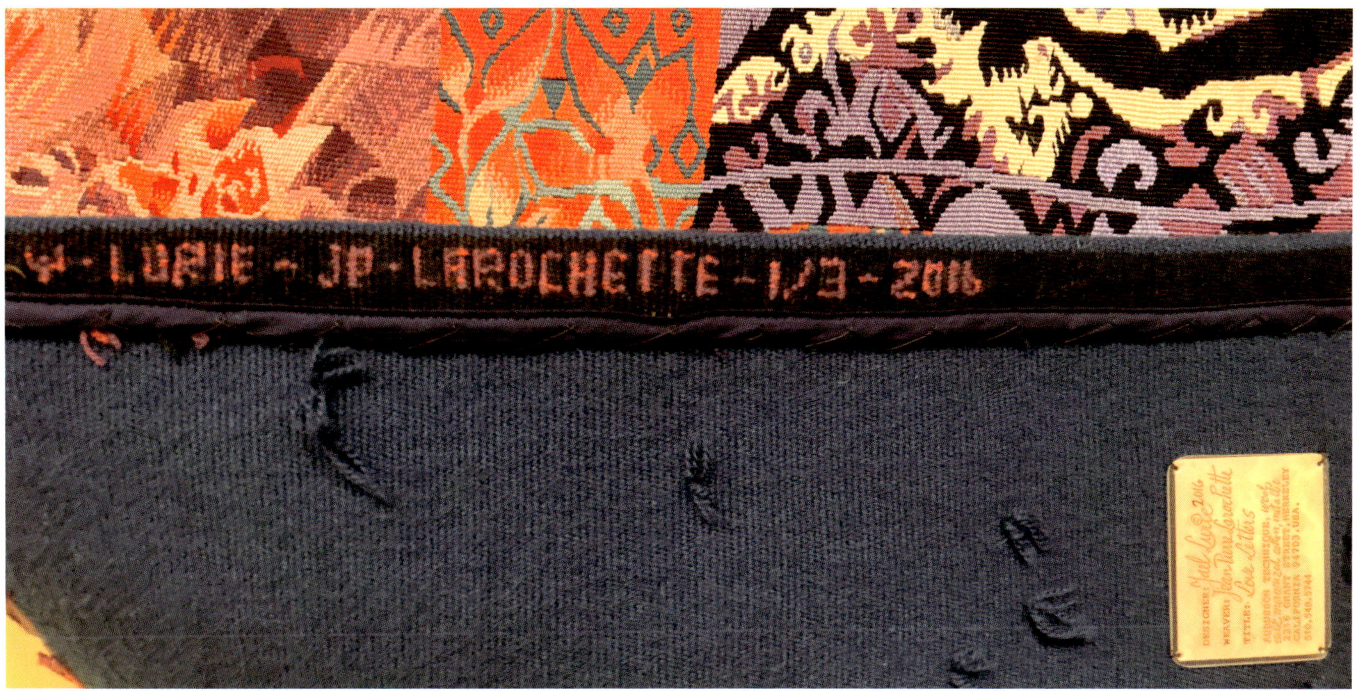

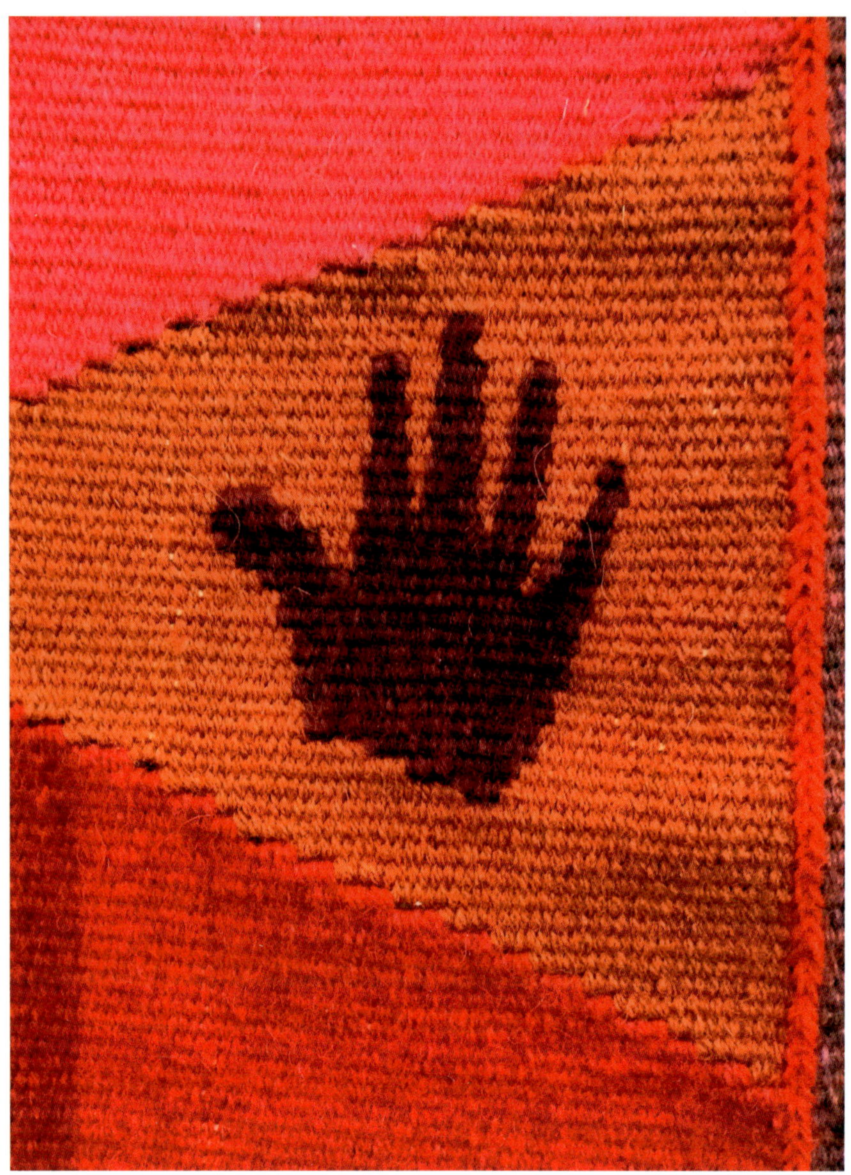

Alex Friedman

Friedman's hand reminds the viewer of the essential presence of the hand in the creation of the work.

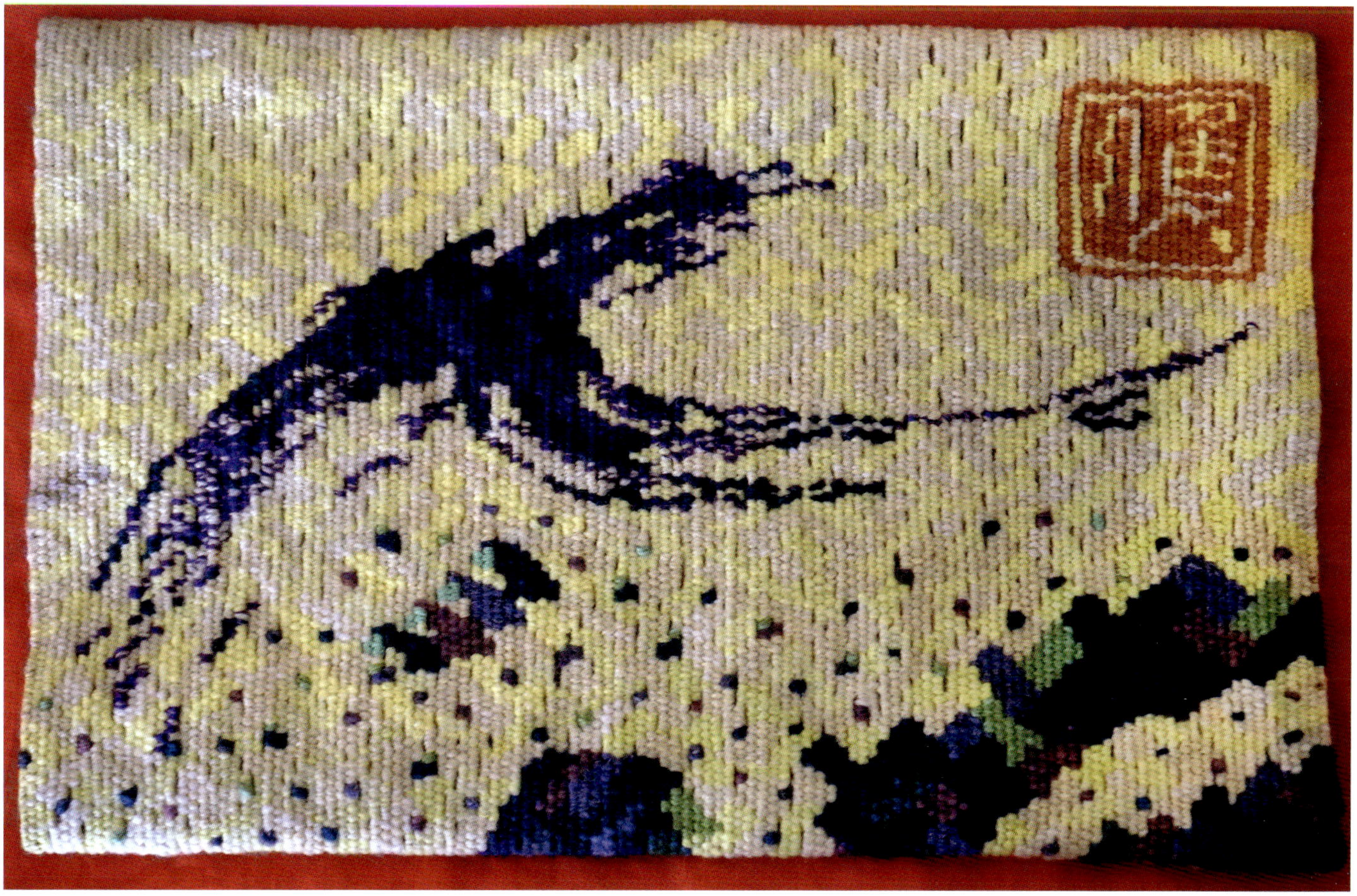

Mieko Konaka

Ah, at last—an actual signature chop, Mieko Konaka.

In contrast to the rest, Labhart's signature opens us up to another possibility for a mark: as an escape hatch. She says, "As a signature, most of my tapestries bear a small slit in the weave. This is my adaptation of a rule observed by Navajo weavers to ensure that the weaver's soul does not get trapped in the weave. With tapestry weaving being such a slow project, allowing for so much time to hang on to all kinds of thoughts, I am glad to rely on this emotional way out."

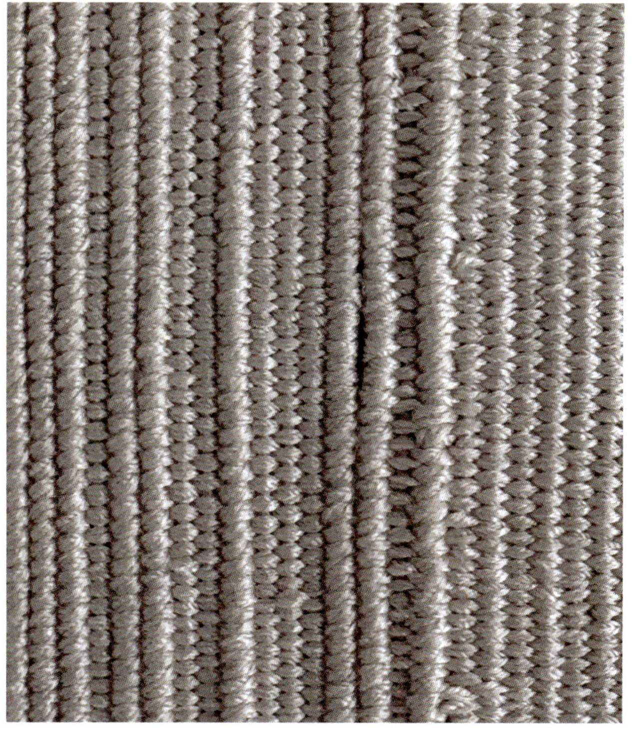

Catherine Labhart

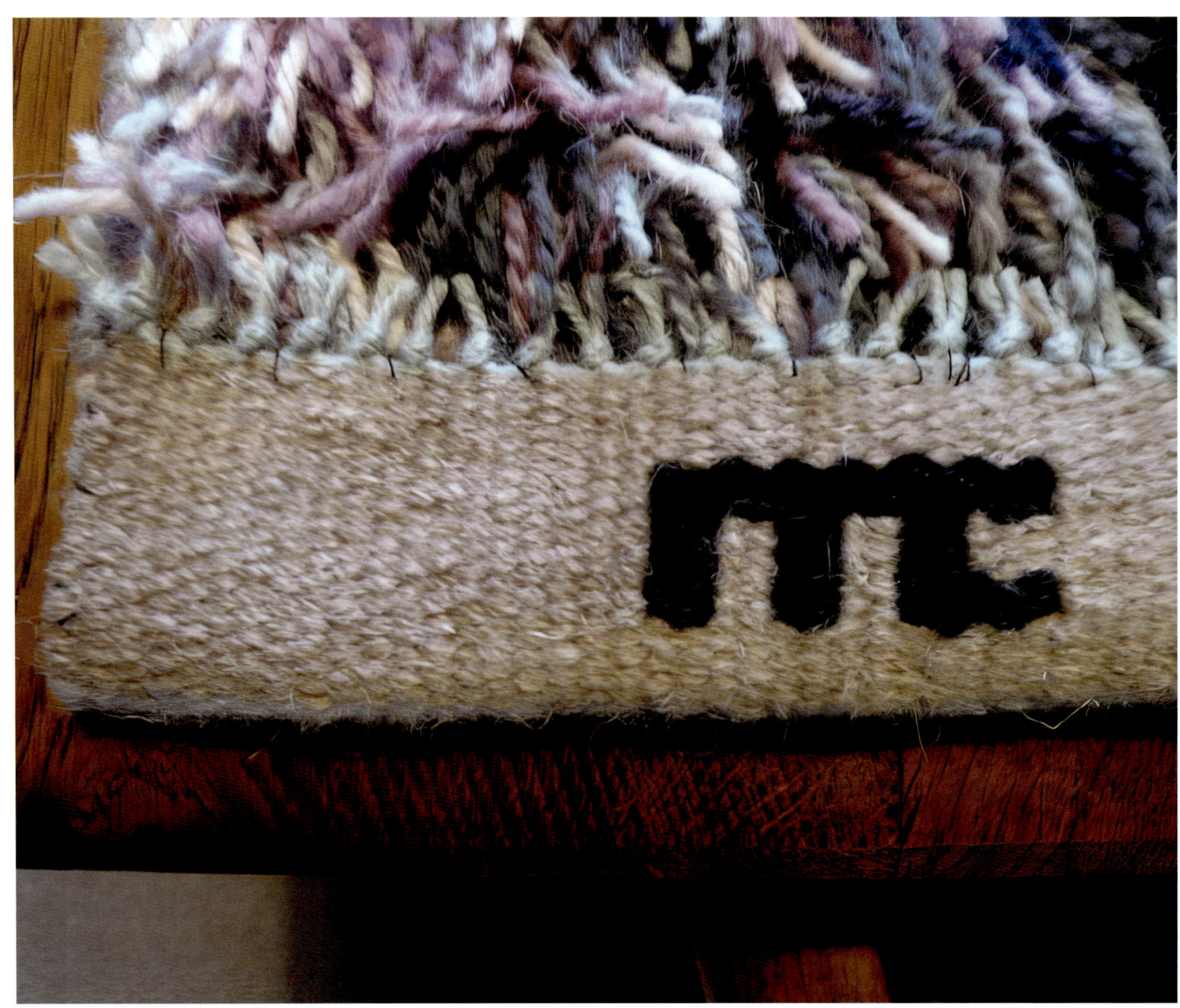

Michael Crompton marks time.

CHAPTER 12

time

If you go on a tour of a tapestry studio, either professional or amateur, you will likely say (or hear someone say), "Wow—that must take a lot of time. You must be very patient." And it is possible that the weaver might smile and offer an alternative: "Not patient, but passionate."

It is true that tapestry is labor intensive. A weaver begins with nothing but thread. There is at the beginning no surface (such as a canvas, such as paper) that a maker embellishes. There is only that which the maker makes, at the same time: both the field and the objects in the field. This presents challenges. Spontaneity takes on new meanings and requires different strategies.

The movement of time, and even the time needed in weaving, became subjects of tapestries. The pieces in this chapter display several approaches to a discussion of time.

self-awareness of time

Michael Crompton signs his pieces with his initials, mc, and inserts them into the hems of his pieces so that you can calculate the year he wove it. What follows is one aspect of the system: "From 2013 onwards my initials will begin from the edge of the tapestry, allowing one warp thread for each subsequent year [until you get to the mc of his initials]. 15 threads in from the edge will signify 2015."

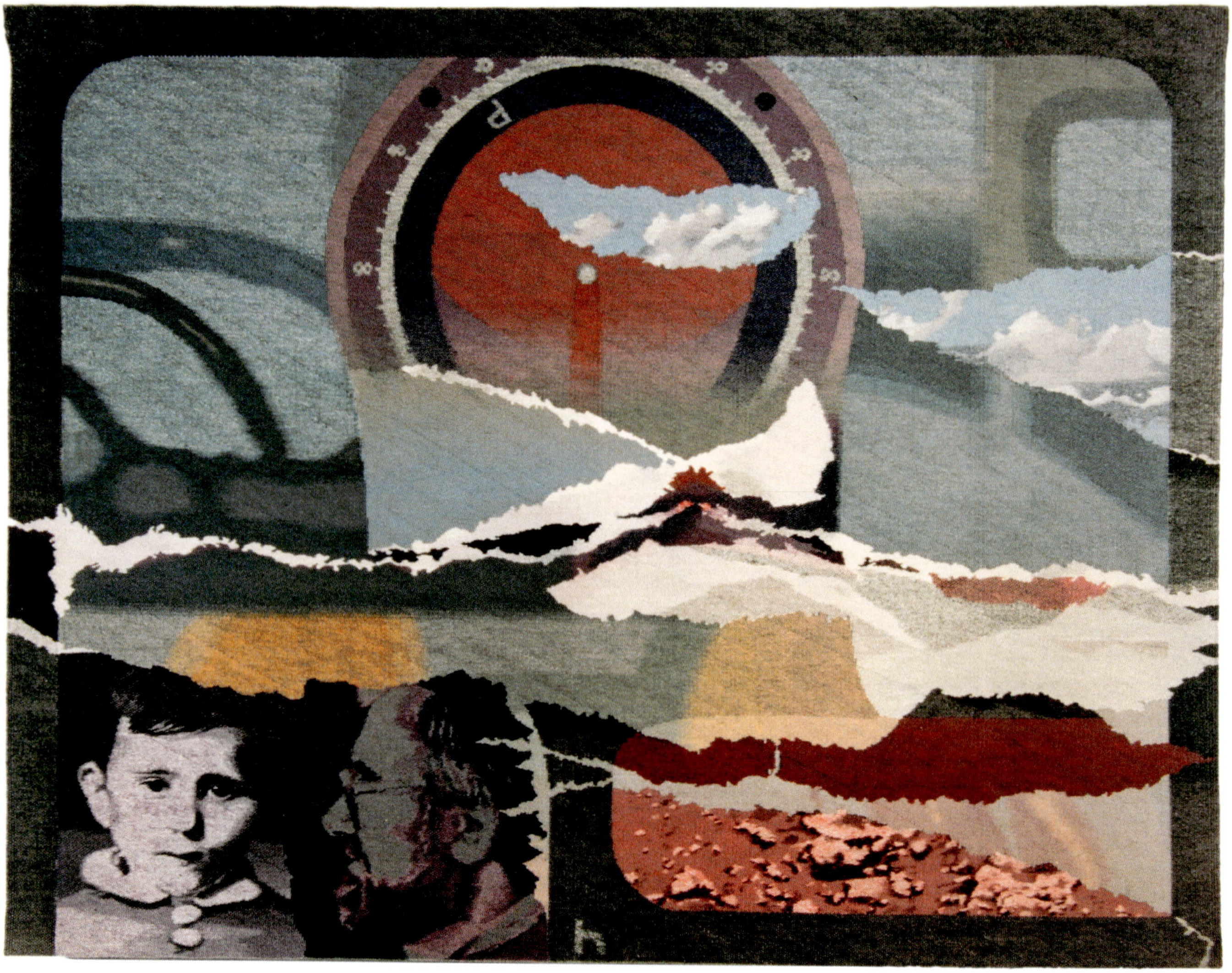

Peter Horn's *Dateline* features a child in the bottom left, looking out at us, and a profile of an adult male (Horn himself) looking at the child. In the rest, Horn has also inserted, as though constructing a collage, bits and pieces, some from his previous tapestries.

In her half-figurative, half-abstract tapestry, Karen Jackson made the left side of the piece her beginning point, marked the month and year she began, and then, on the right side, included the information about the month and year: She had finished.

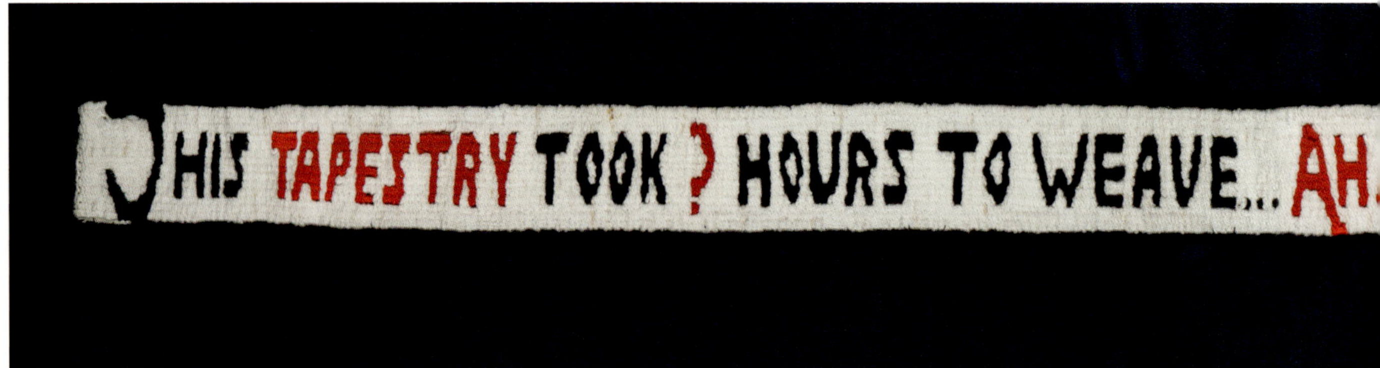

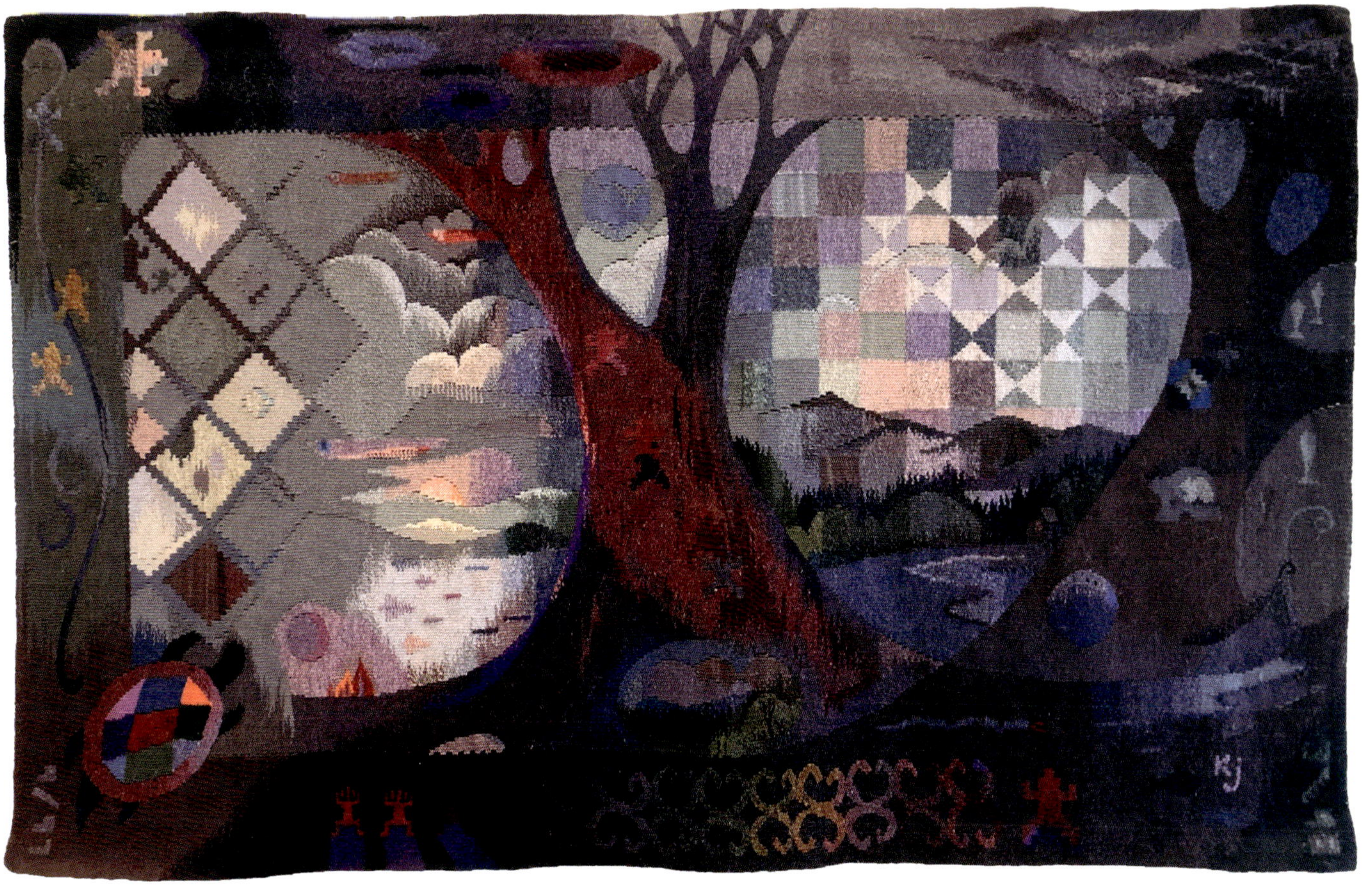

LEFT: *Datumsgrenze* (Dateline)
Peter Horn
1990 | 59" × 77.2" | wool; cotton warp

ABOVE AND RIGHT: *Time Quilt*
Karen Jackson
1997 | 24" × 46" | wool

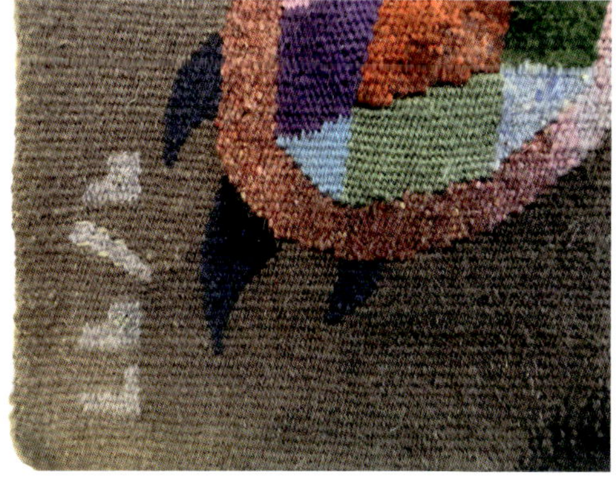

For a class, I wove a piece to see how self-referential I could be—and how long it would take. The last bit of information, at the end on the right, tells you the hours and minutes it took. I kept a chart with each day's work and added them up when I had finally finished (fourteen hours, thirty-seven minutes).

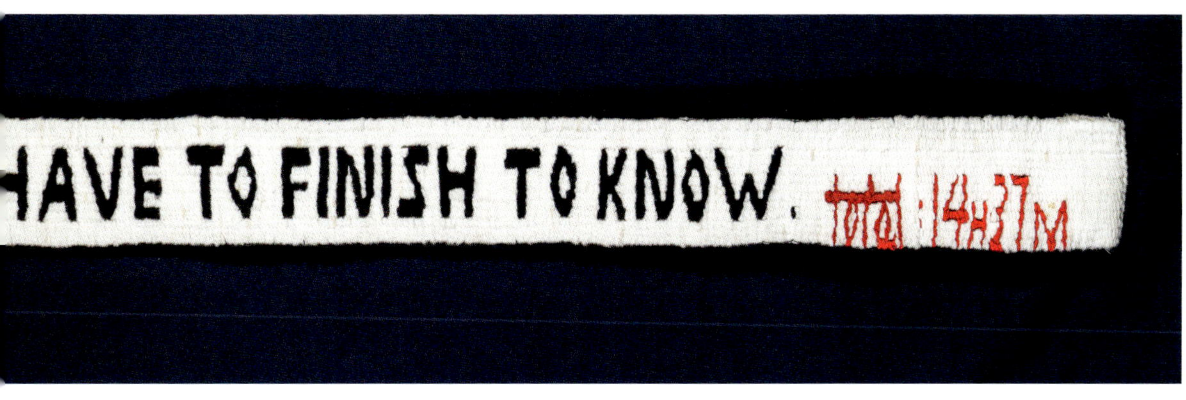

Black + White + Red All Over #65: how long
Micala Sidore
2020 | 6" × 46" | cotton

The red line in Janet Steer's piece shows where she walked. She embroidered her path on the cloth she wove out of the maps she used in making her trek.

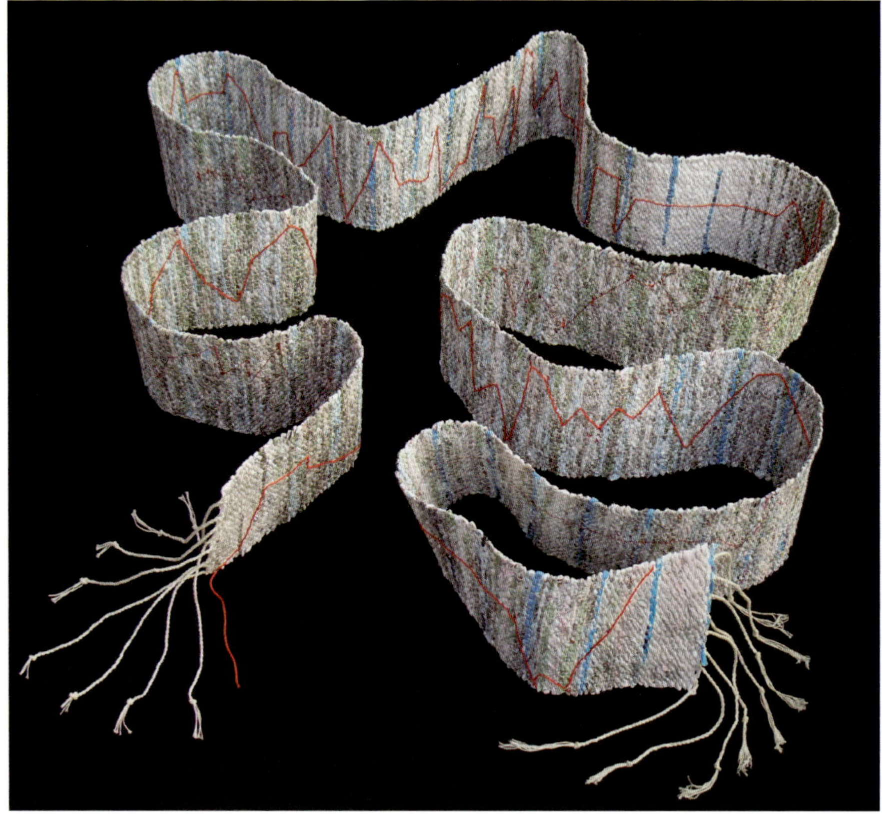

A Walk in the Mountains Arranged According to the Laws of Chance
Janet Steer
2019 | 4" × 78.75" | cotton yarn made from maps; cotton warp

seasons of the year (in increments)

A sixteenth-century group of four (two are shown here) shows the tasks and pleasures of those times of the year—fishing (spring) and skating (winter).

From the series *The Four Seasons* (spring and winter)
Cleveland Museum of Art
16th century | average size 8'5" × 8'8" | wool, silk, gold
Gift of Francis Ginn, Marian Ginn Jones, Barbara Ginn Griesinger, and Alexander Ginn in memory of Frank Hadley Ginn and Cornelia Root Ginn

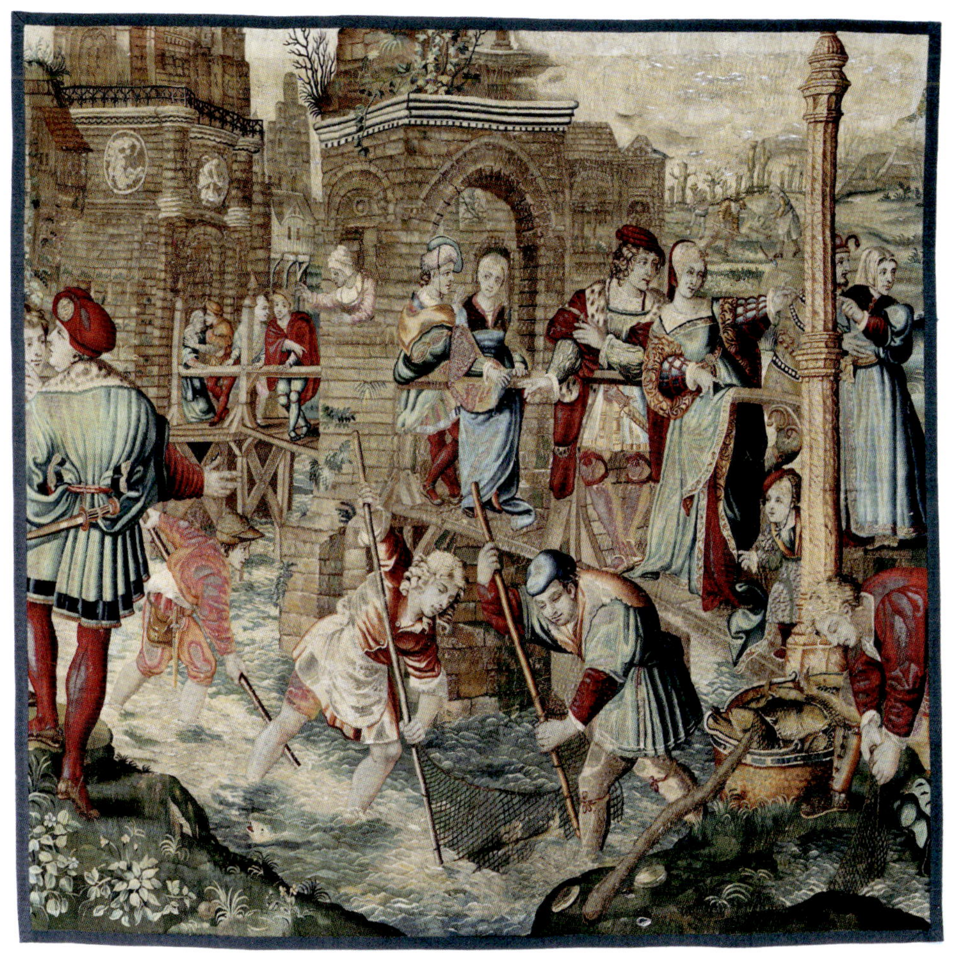

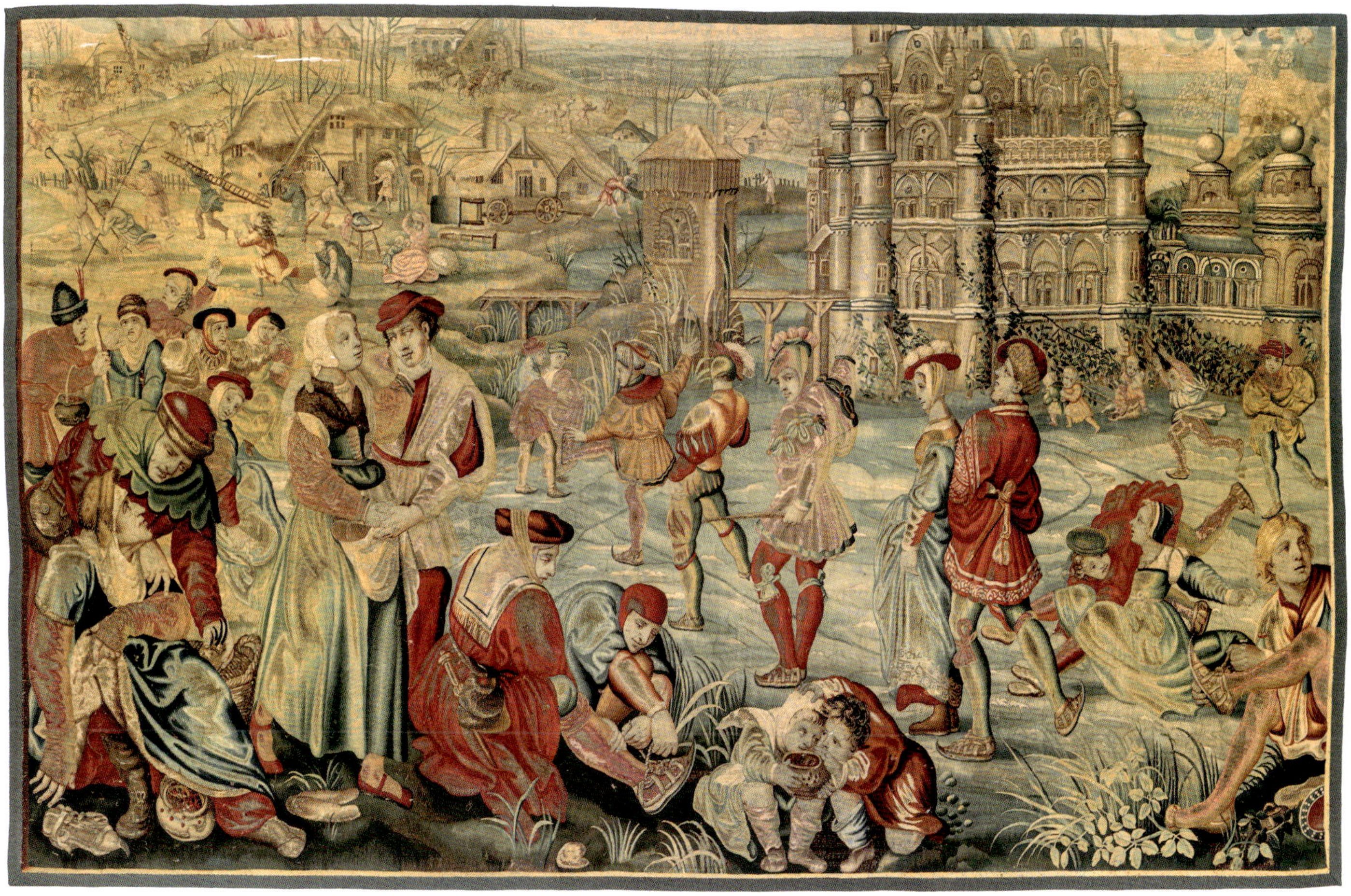

Audran's mid-eighteenth-century tapestry includes a few single columns in which details define the months.

January, February, March
Claude Audran le Jeune
Gobelins studio of M. Le Dauphin à Meudon
1710 | 9'10" × 16'5 | wool, silk, silver

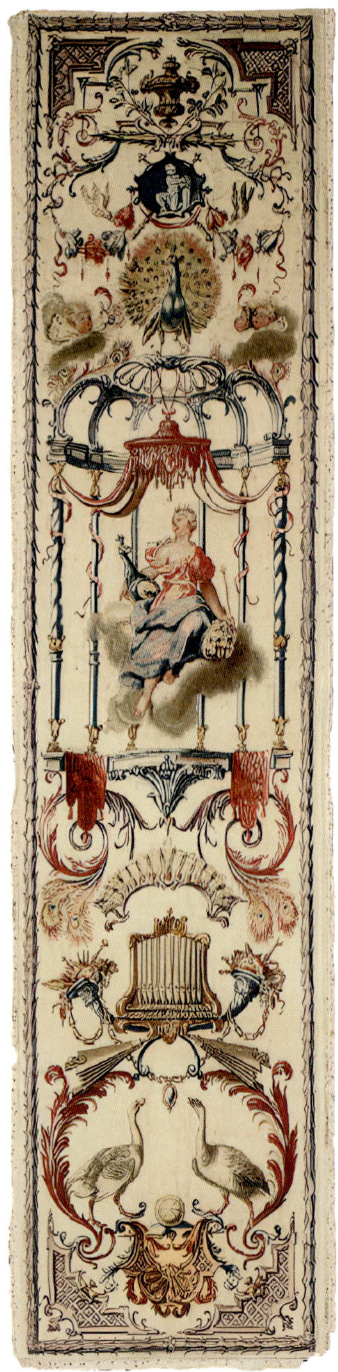

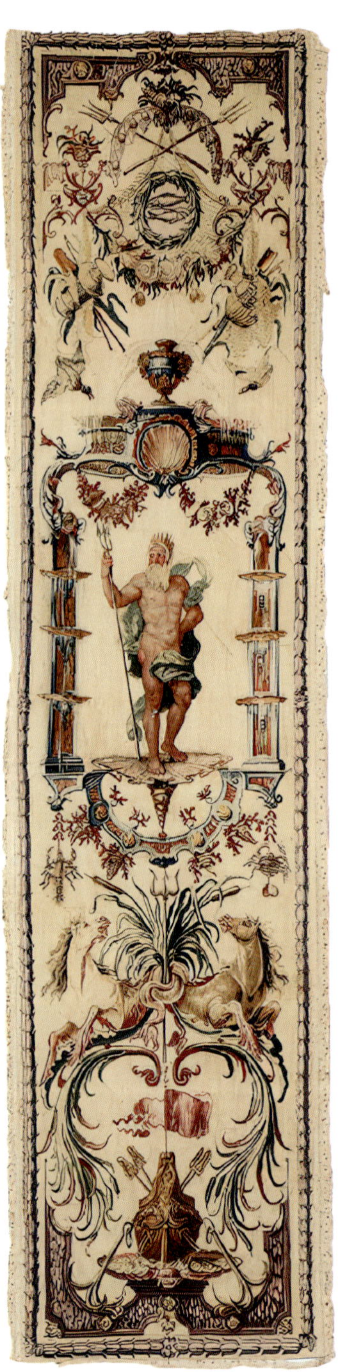

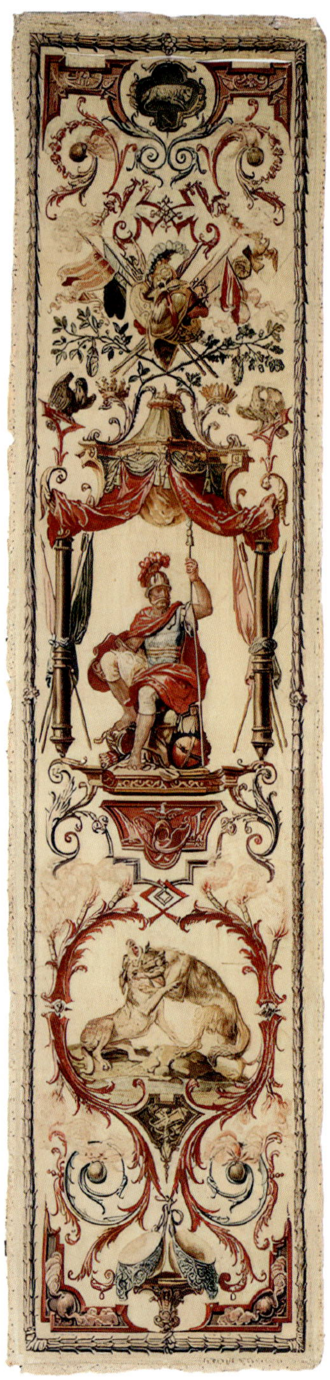

Marcel Gromaire made a twentieth-century series that pairs each time of year with a city and, in this case, energetic doves, horses, rabbits, and a cat.

Le Printemps, où Paris (Springtime, or Paris)
Marcel Gromaire
Woven at Manufacture Nationale des Gobelins
1967 | 9'11" × 14'4.5" | wool, synthetic dyes

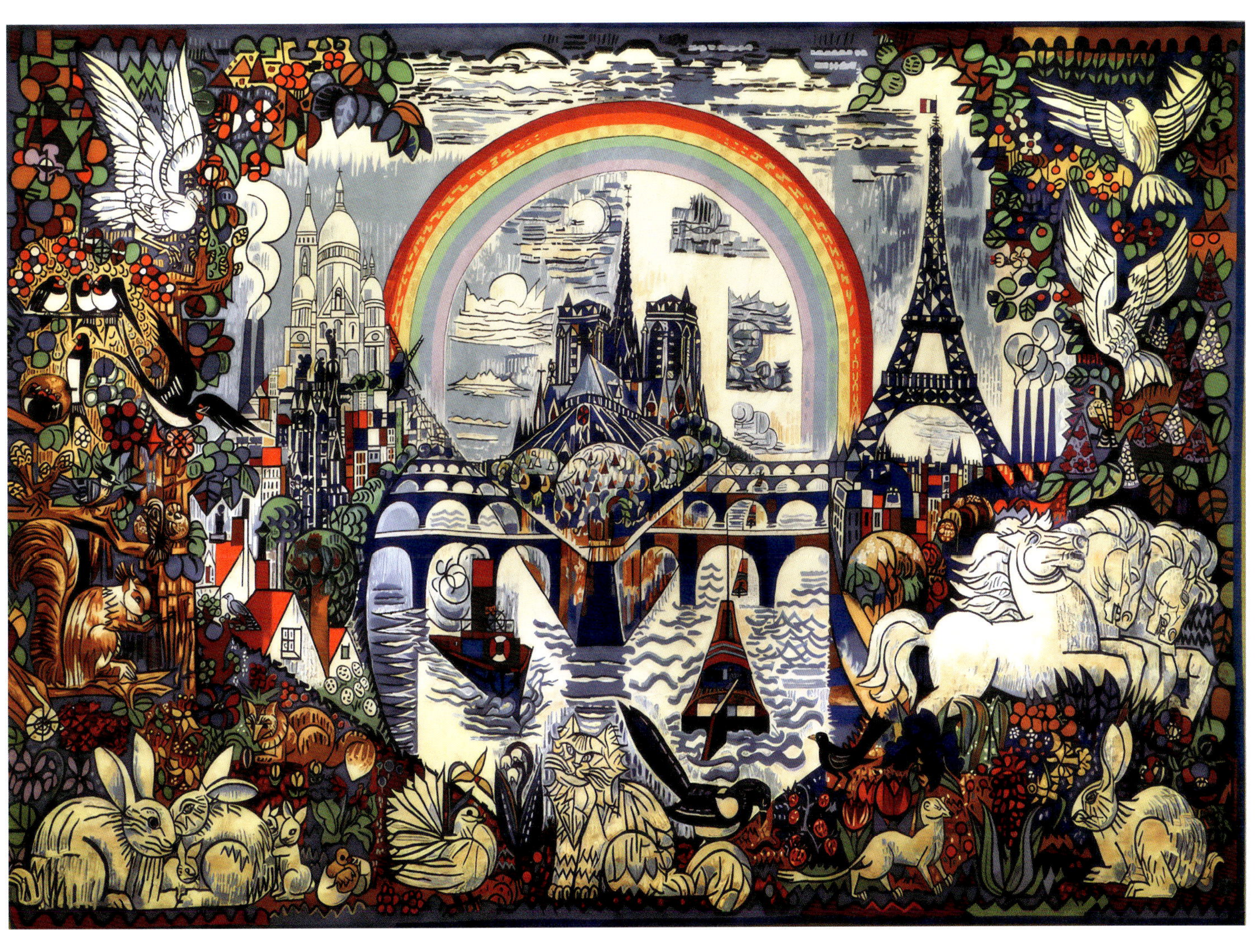

weavers marking times of the year

Susan Sargent, whose early work depicted an idealized rural New England, offers all four seasons here, a circular sequence of times passing, starting with the harvest (*upper left*) and proceeding clockwise.

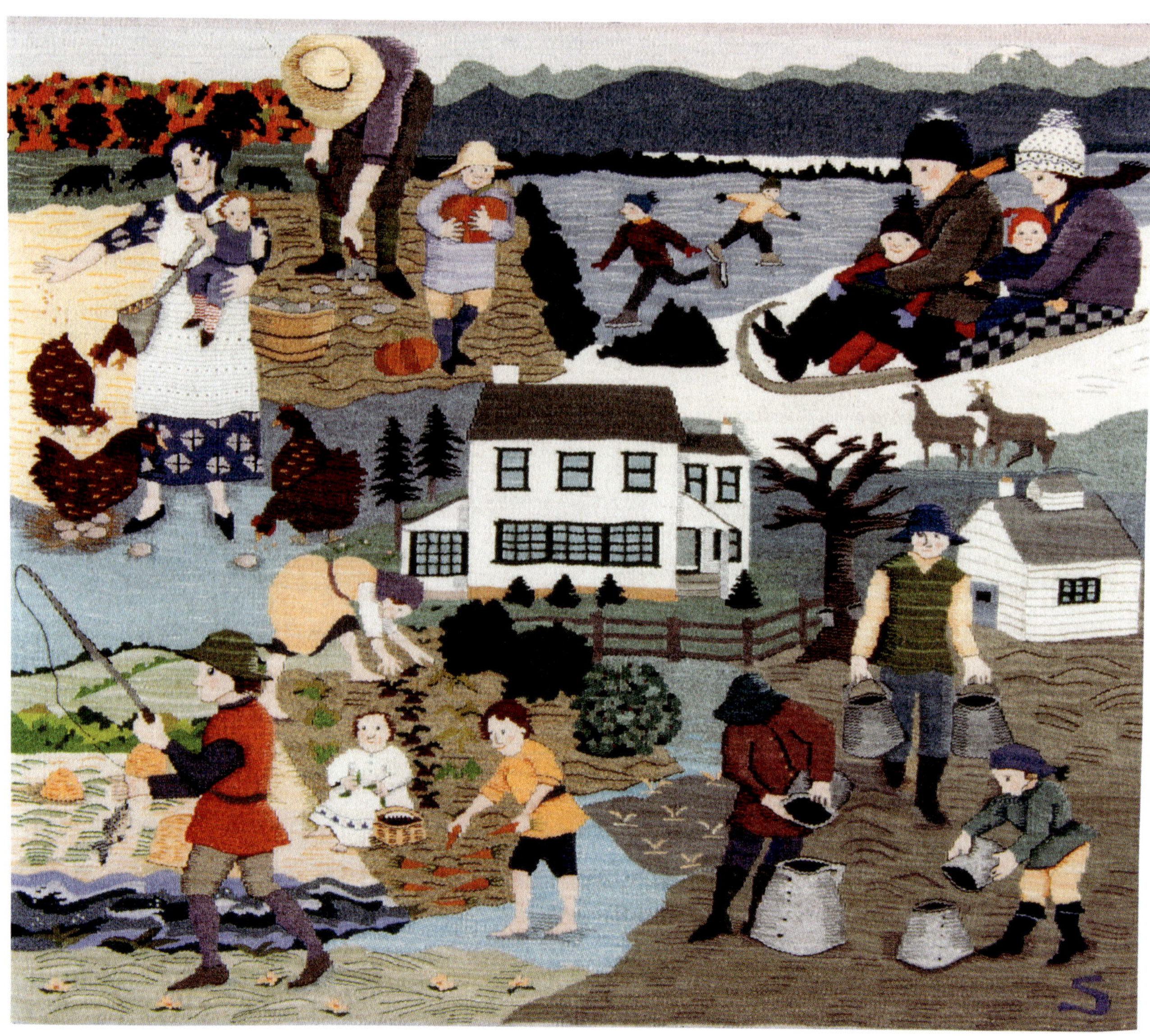

Four Seasons
Susan Sargent
ca. 1987 | 5' × 5' | wool

Jean Pierre Larochette and Yael Lurie give us a calendar of the twelve months, each one with the Hebrew name of the month, each including a symbol of the holiday that occurs in that month.

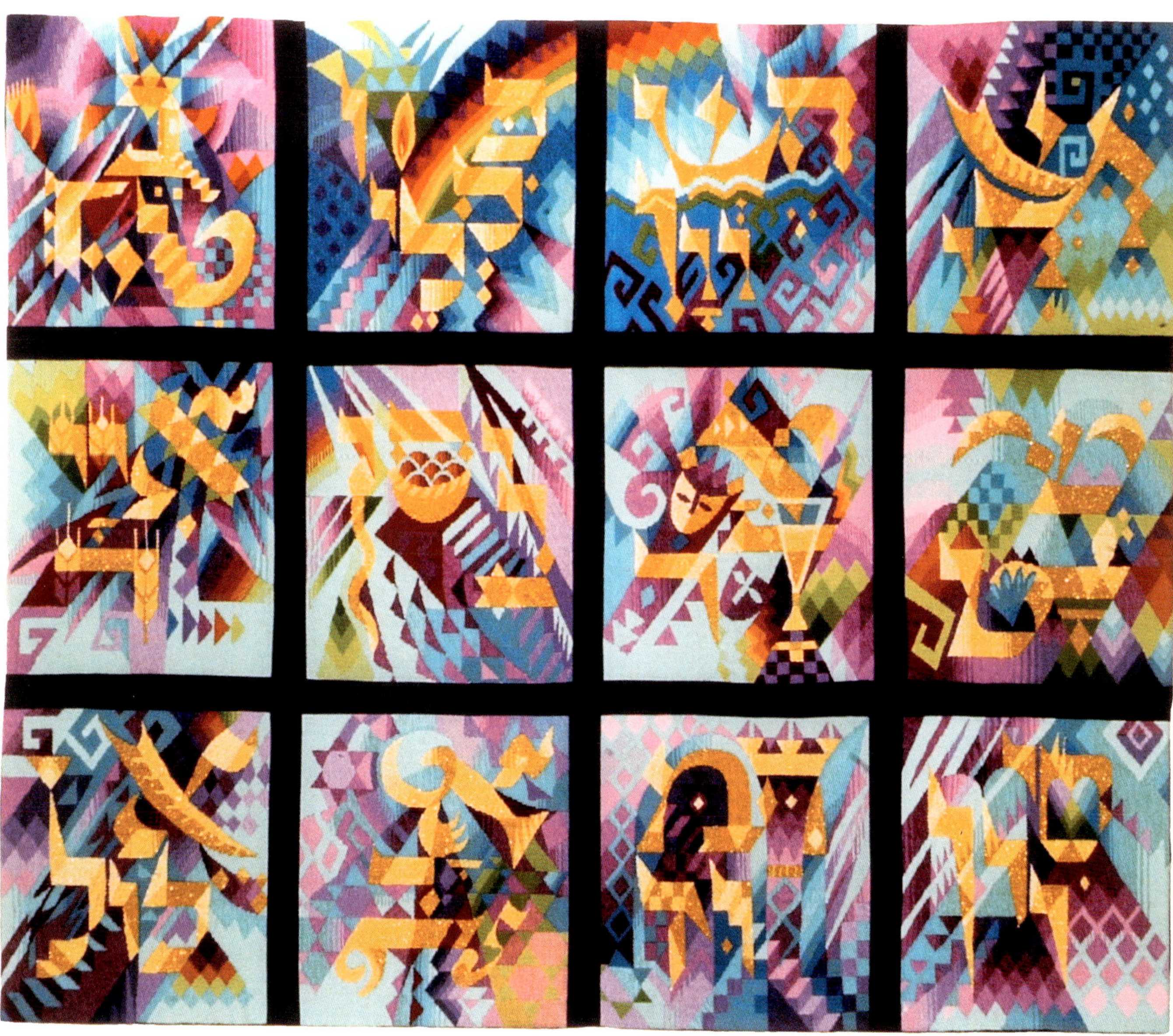

Twelve Months
Jean Pierre Larochette (weaver) and Yael Lurie (designer)
2005 | 46" × 60" | wool, DMC cotton, silk;
cotton seine twine warp

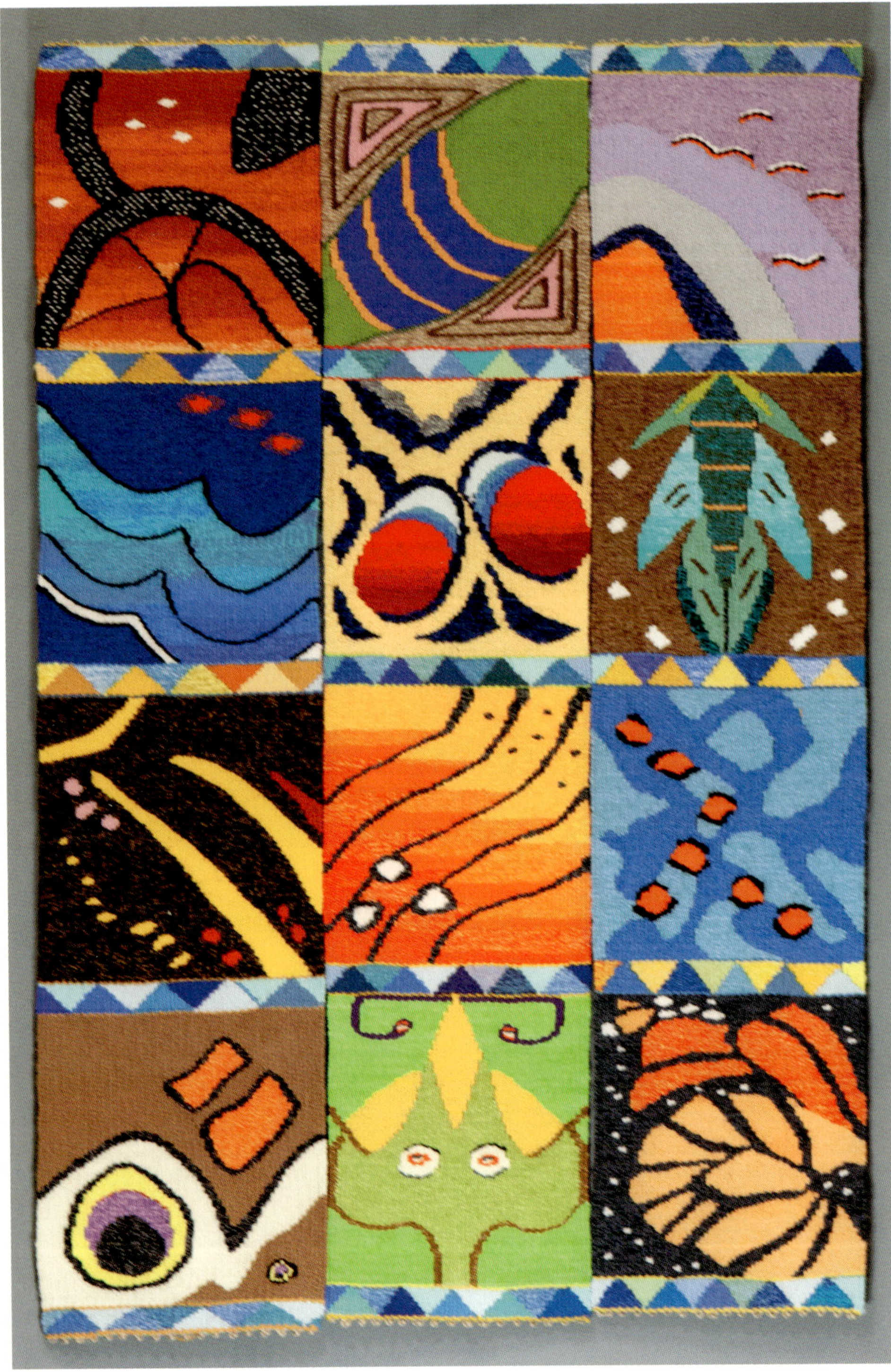

reams #5
Mary Jane Lord
2020 | 36" × 24" | cotton, cotton seine twine, wool

Mary Jane Lord extracted these details, an exercise in composition, from her woven calendars. The images are abstracted from natural forms, and experiment with color and pattern.

By contrast, Kathy Spoering has made realistic pieces for each of the months, what the world looks like from her home in Colorado. Here are January and September.

OPPOSITE: From a series of the months of the year—*January* and *September*
Kathy Spoering
2008–16 | each 18" × 18" | wool

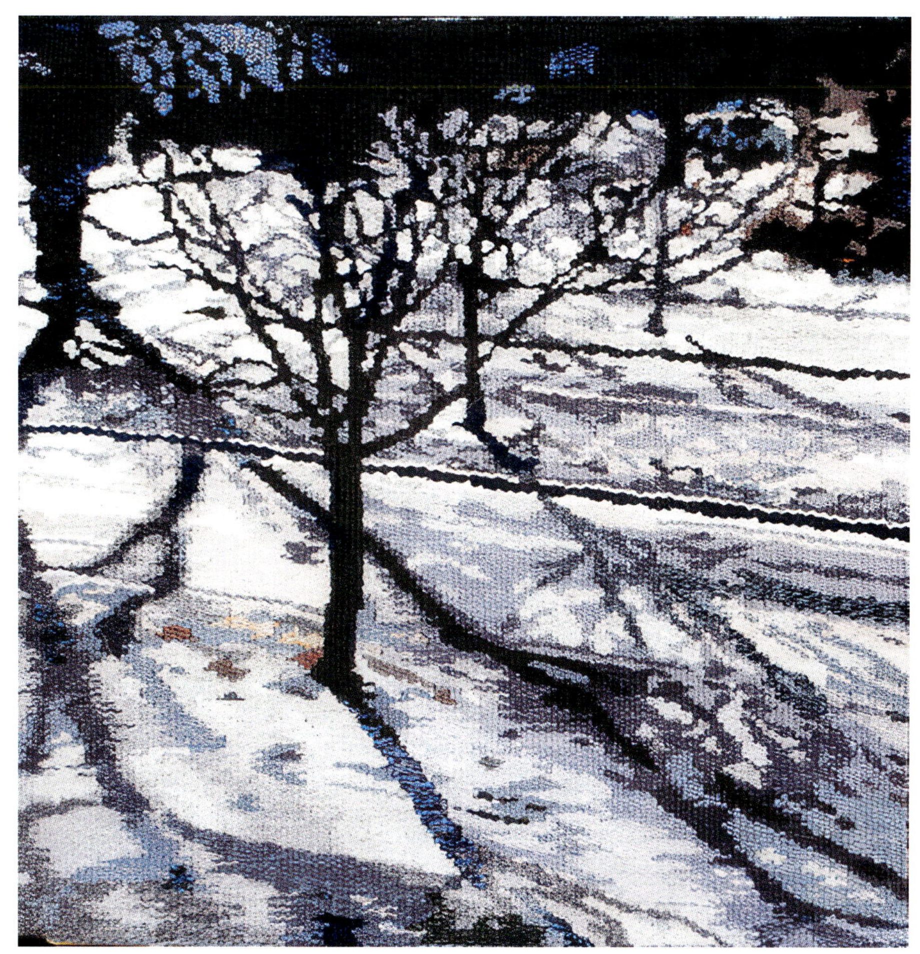

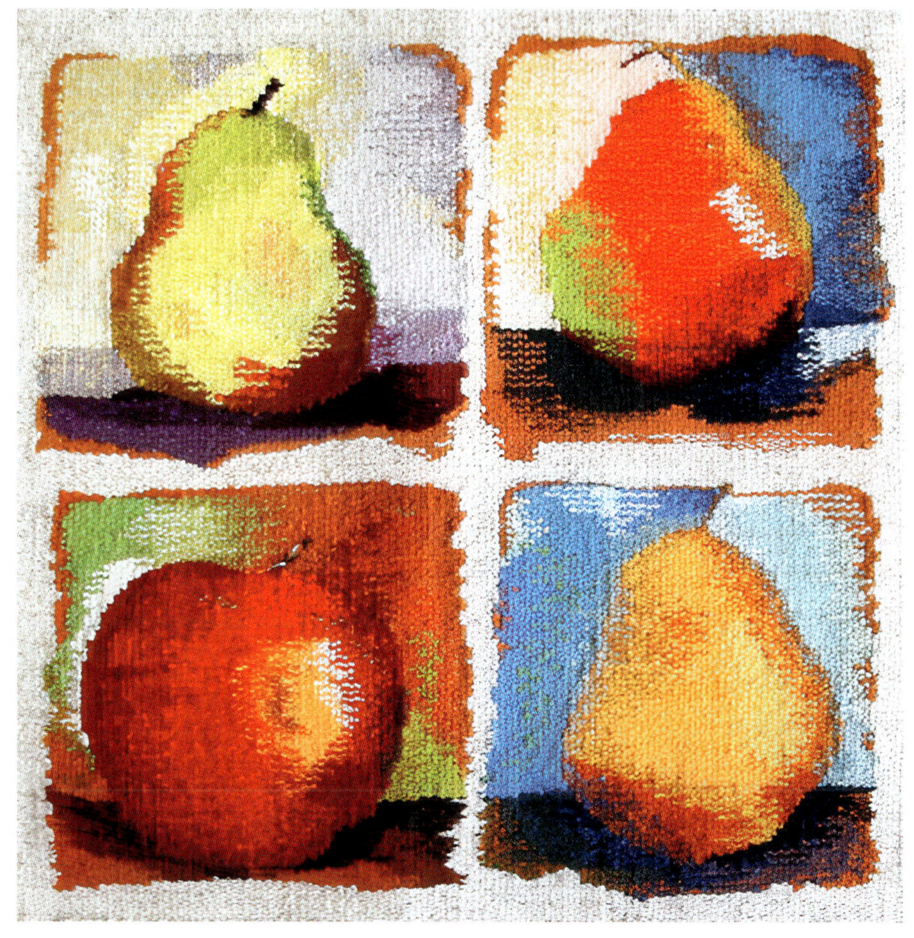

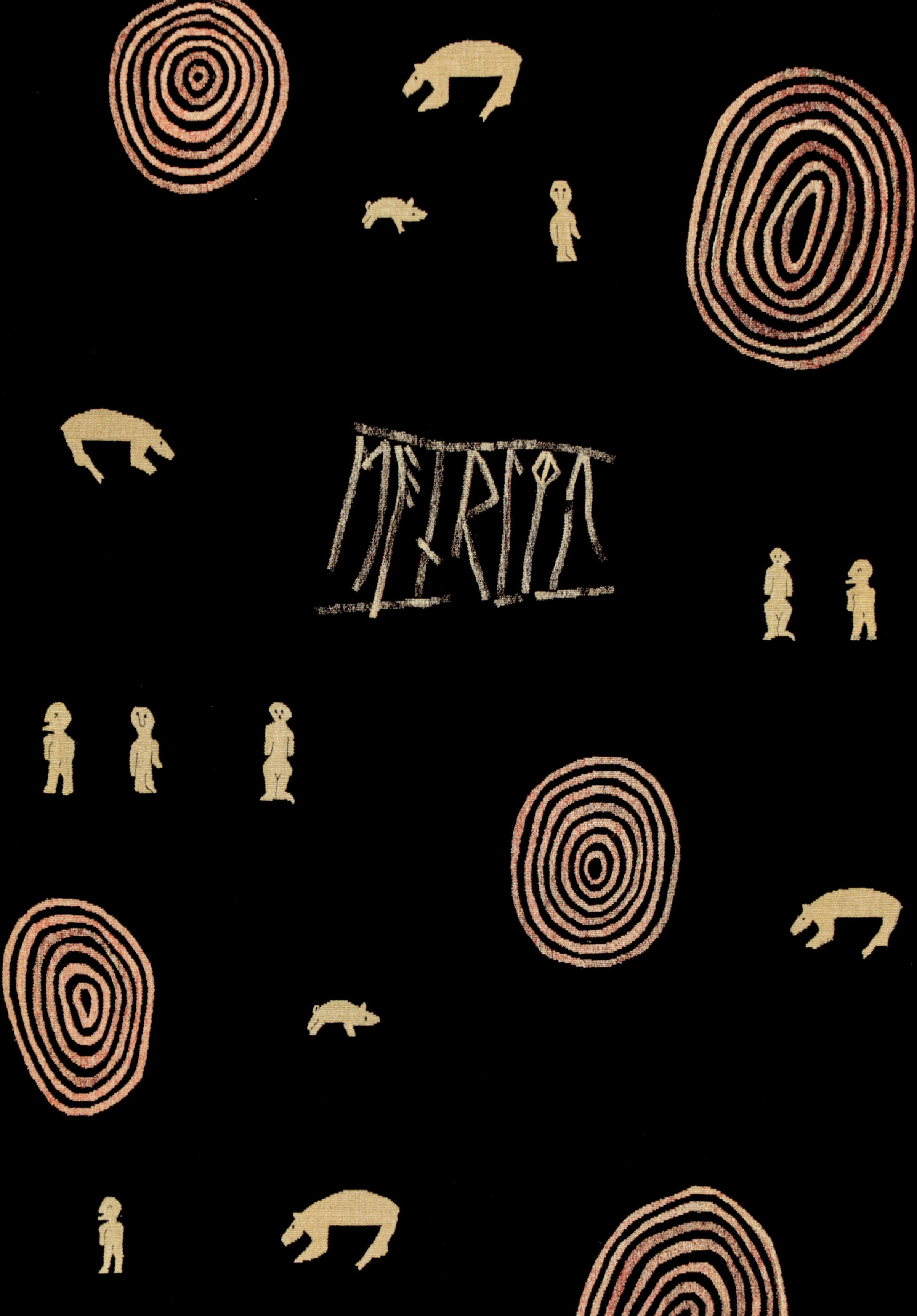

text

The word *text* has its roots in Latin *texere*, a verb meaning to weave. This chapter shows what the textiles have to say about themselves, sometimes by including words, and sometimes by playing with the forms of written language.

At the center of her tapestry, Anet Brusgaard, from Denmark, weaves runes, native to her culture. The runes are surrounded by a world of animallike fetishes, small figures, and concentric circles.

OPPOSITE: *Runer: Merling* (Runes: Merling [legendary aquatic creatures with the upper body of a human and the tail of a fish])
Anet Brusgaard
2017 | 19.7" × 15.75" | wool, gold; cotton warp

Lialia Kuchma's calligraphy gallops across the face of her weaving and incorporates a grand sense of gesture. At 4 by 7 feet, the effect is powerful.

BELOW: *Calligraphic Abstraction II*
Lialia Kuchma
1990 | 48" × 84" | wool; cotton warp

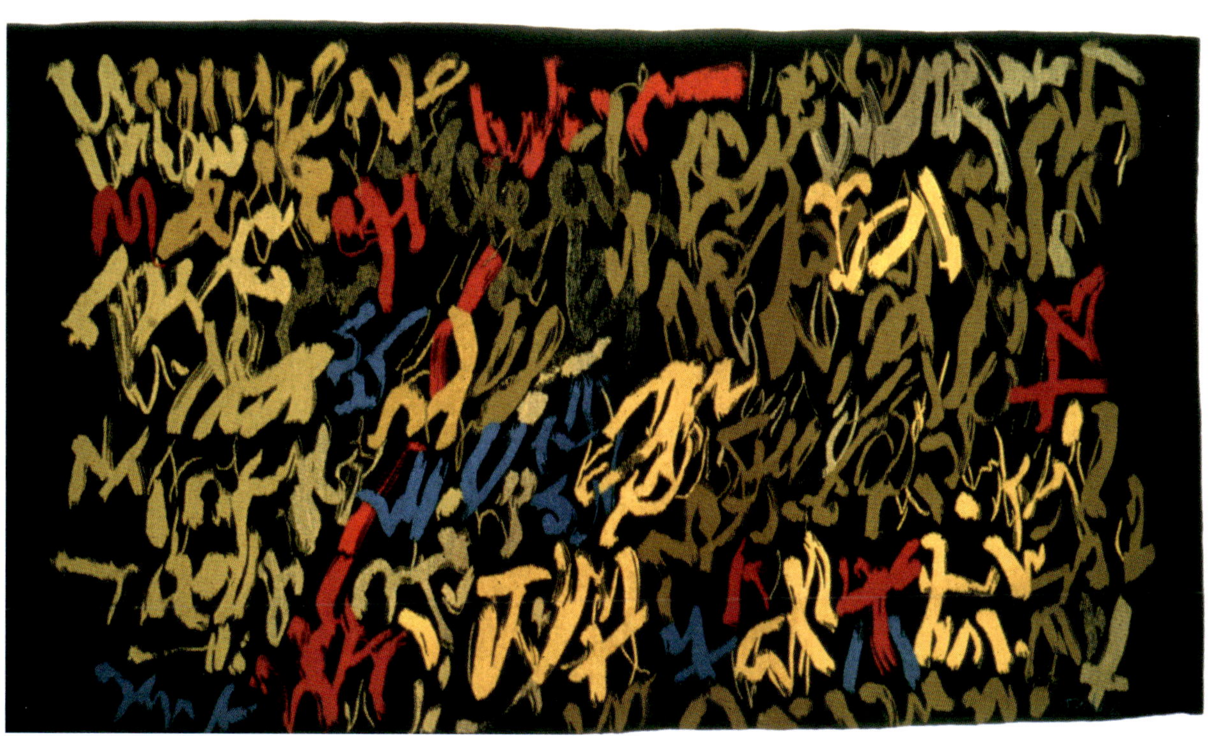

Ariadna Donner loves red, even if the dominant color here is blue. Her calligraphy works as exuberant decoration. At the same time, a landscape encircles us. There is a hint of cave paintings in these disparate forms.

The Long Red Year
Ariadna Donner
2002 | 12' × 7'10" | wool, cotton, linen, silk
Photographer: Ilkka Hietala

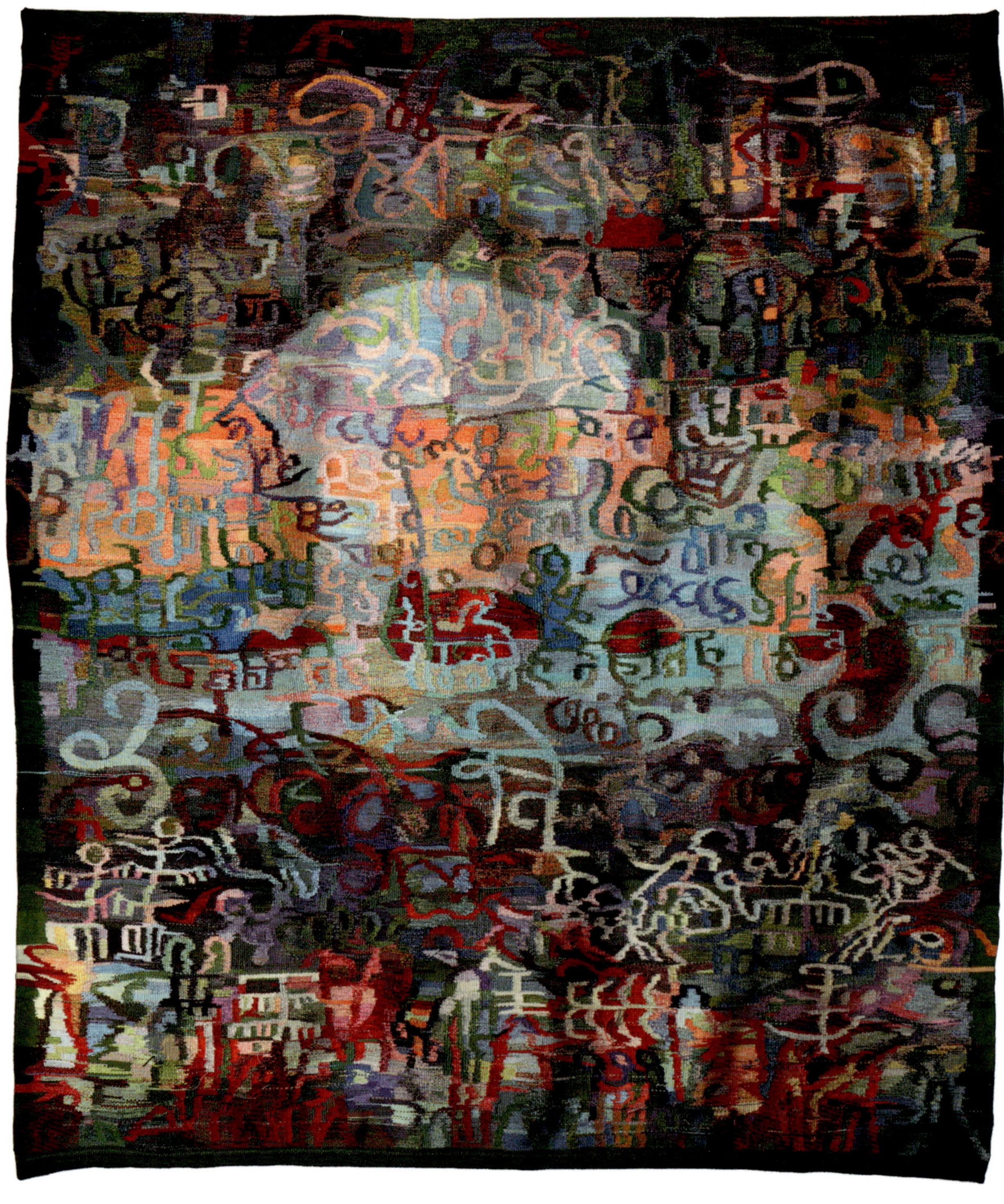

Erin Riley's tattoos are the subject of many of her tapestries, and they communicate their own stories and values.

Dress Too Short
Erin Riley
2023 | 43" × 48" | wool, cotton
Courtesy of Erin M. Riley and P·P·O·W New York
© Erin M. Riley
Photo: JSP Art Photography

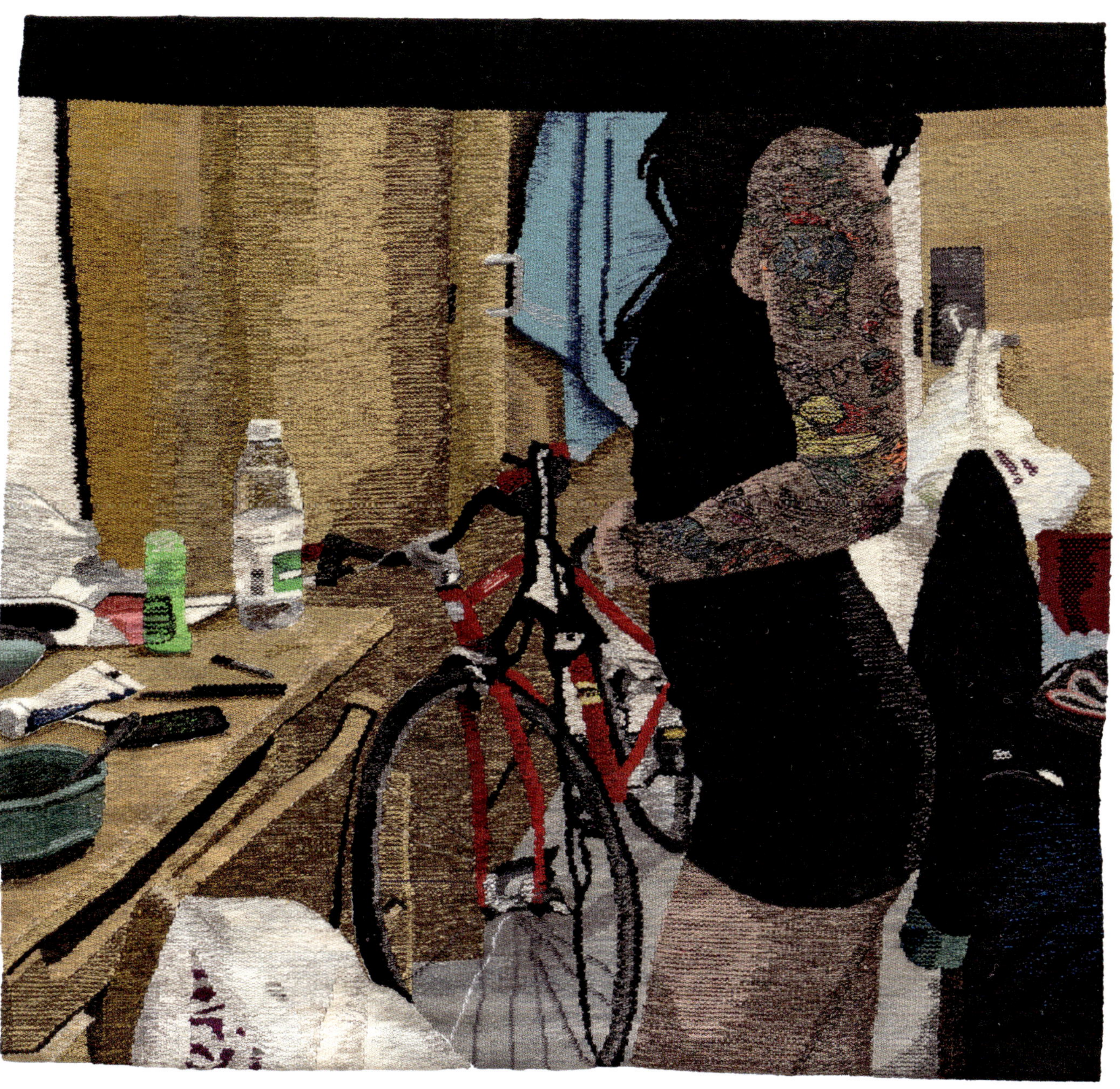

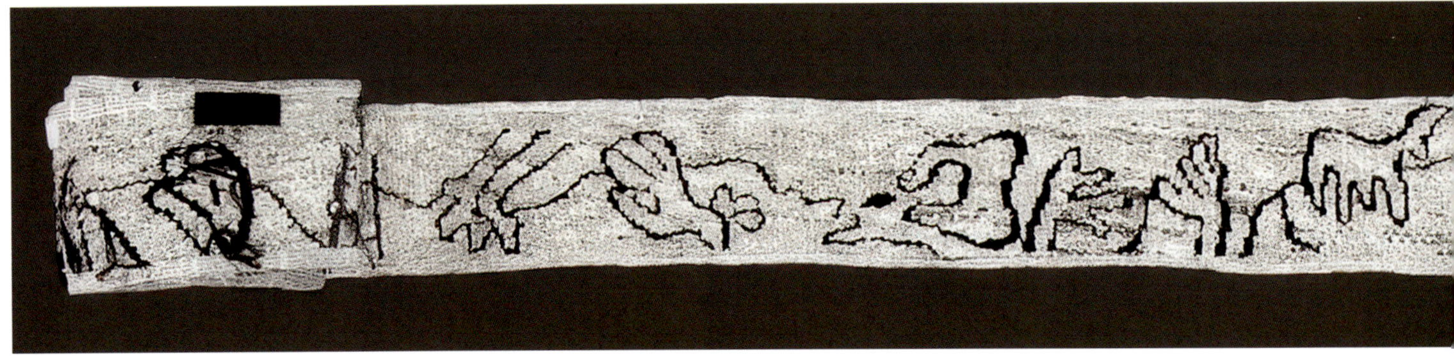

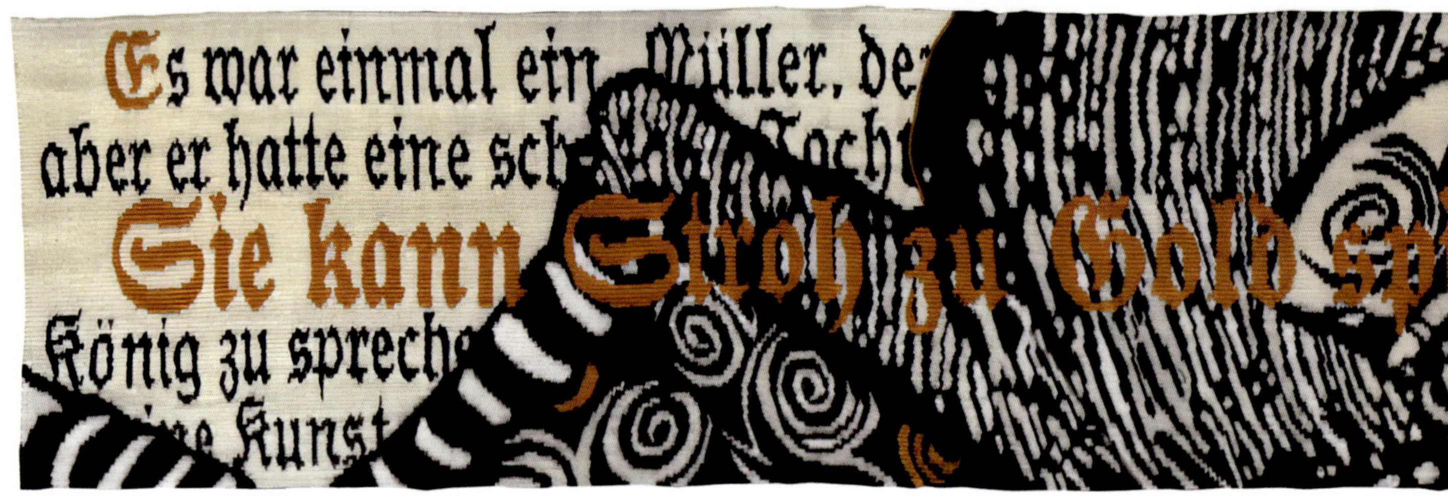

TOP: *des Mains* (About hands)
Catherine K
1995 | 4.75" × 47.25" | spun newsprint; cotton warp

ABOVE: *Rumpelstiltskin: Greed*
Murray Gibson
2020 | 9.4" × 39.4" | wool, cotton

OPPOSITE: *We Too Black Men Shall Rise*
Napoleon Jones-Henderson
1974–75 | 48" × 52" | wool, metallic yarns

Catherine K has often used newsprint, spun into thread, as the basis for what she makes. The sketchy images here seem like hieroglyphs, or maybe even sign language.

Murray Gibson weaves his words in Black Letter, a typeface, fitting for the nineteenth-century Grimm fairy tale of Rapunzel, which begins, "There once was a miller . . . " In the golden letters you can read (in German), "She can spin straw into gold."

Napoleon Jones-Henderson's profile is embedded into the lettering of the title, whose words are repeated several times. He is simultaneously constructing both an image and its meaning.

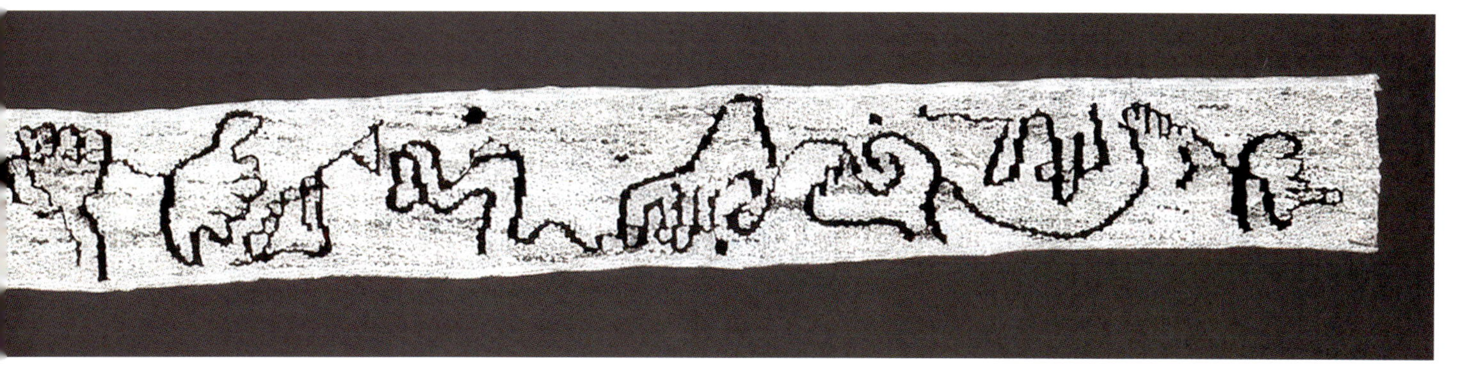

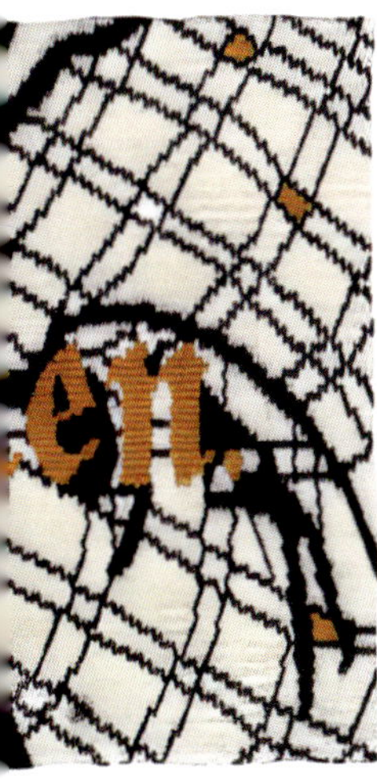

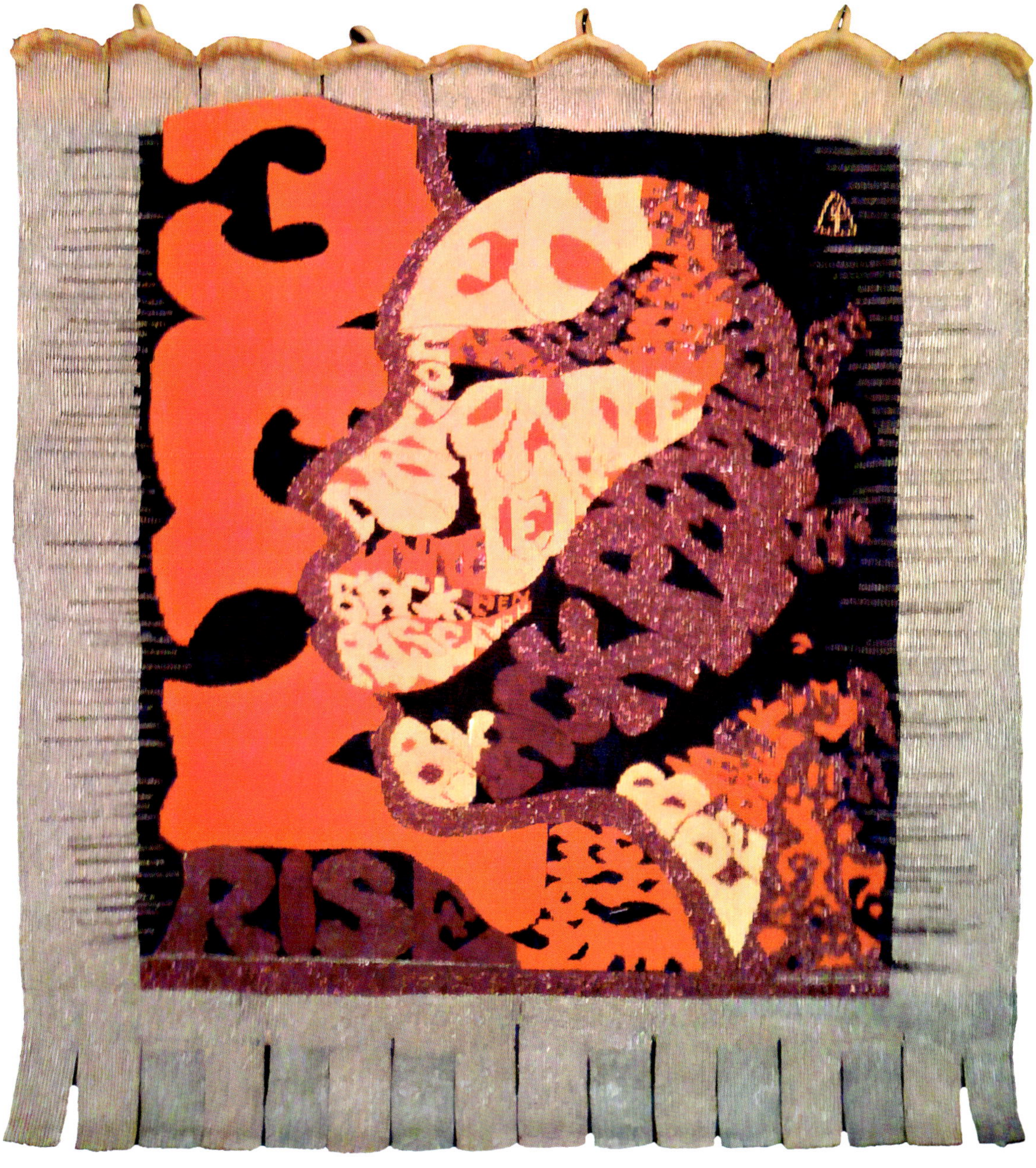

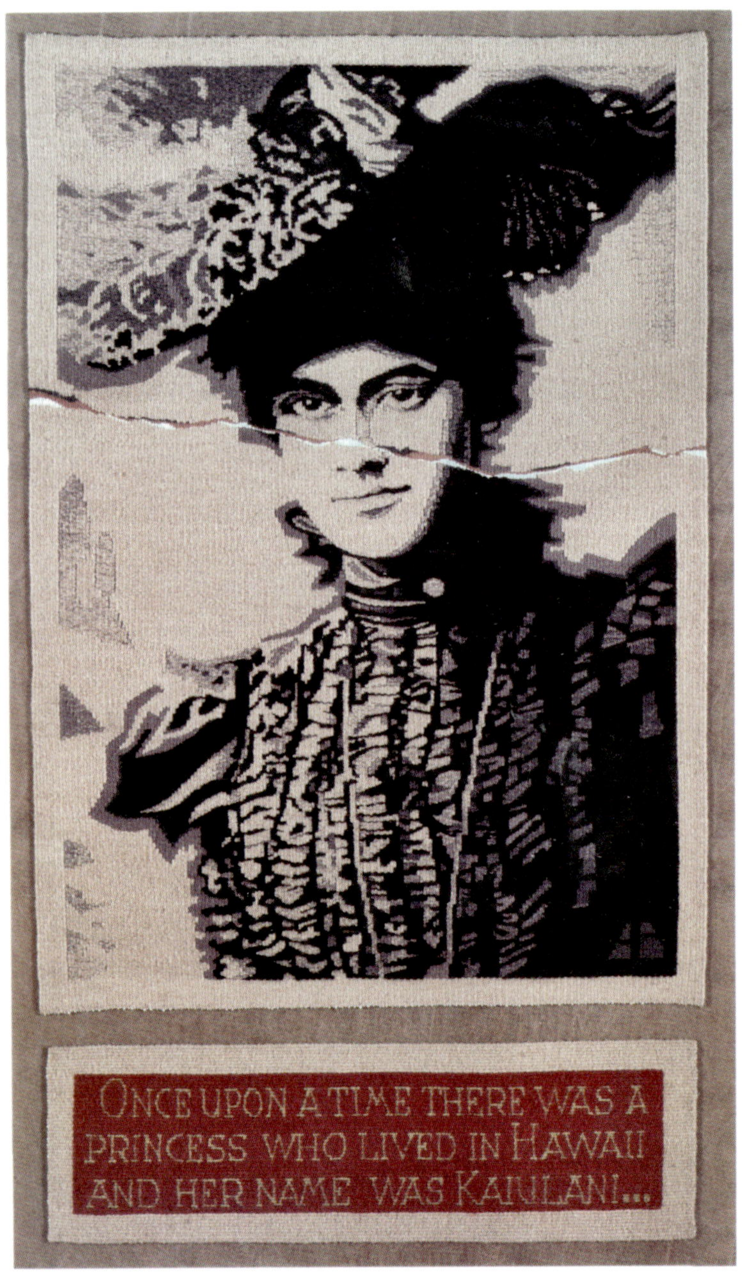

A Princess Ka'iulani (Once Upon a Time)
Archie Brennan
1993 | 42" × 25"

Archie Brennan included lettering of all sorts in his pieces, a primary characteristic of much that he wove. Here, he begins with what looks like a fairy tale about the princess pictured above. But he adds detail that makes us believe that the face, perhaps originally a photograph, has been torn in half. The weaving both reveals that tear—and fixes it by making the cloth whole again.

Pat Johns's tree includes her very handsome lettering (she has always said that she is a letterer, not a calligrapher). The word *Ceres* (the Roman goddess of agriculture) moves back and forth with the word *ceremony*, like leaves that flutter. The word *crescent* also appears. Colors are those of the harvest, ripe wheat, suggesting autumn.

Mieko Konaka's Japanese dominates a vertical space between two areas that might be trees or bushes. *Amida* might well refer to a sensual Buddha.

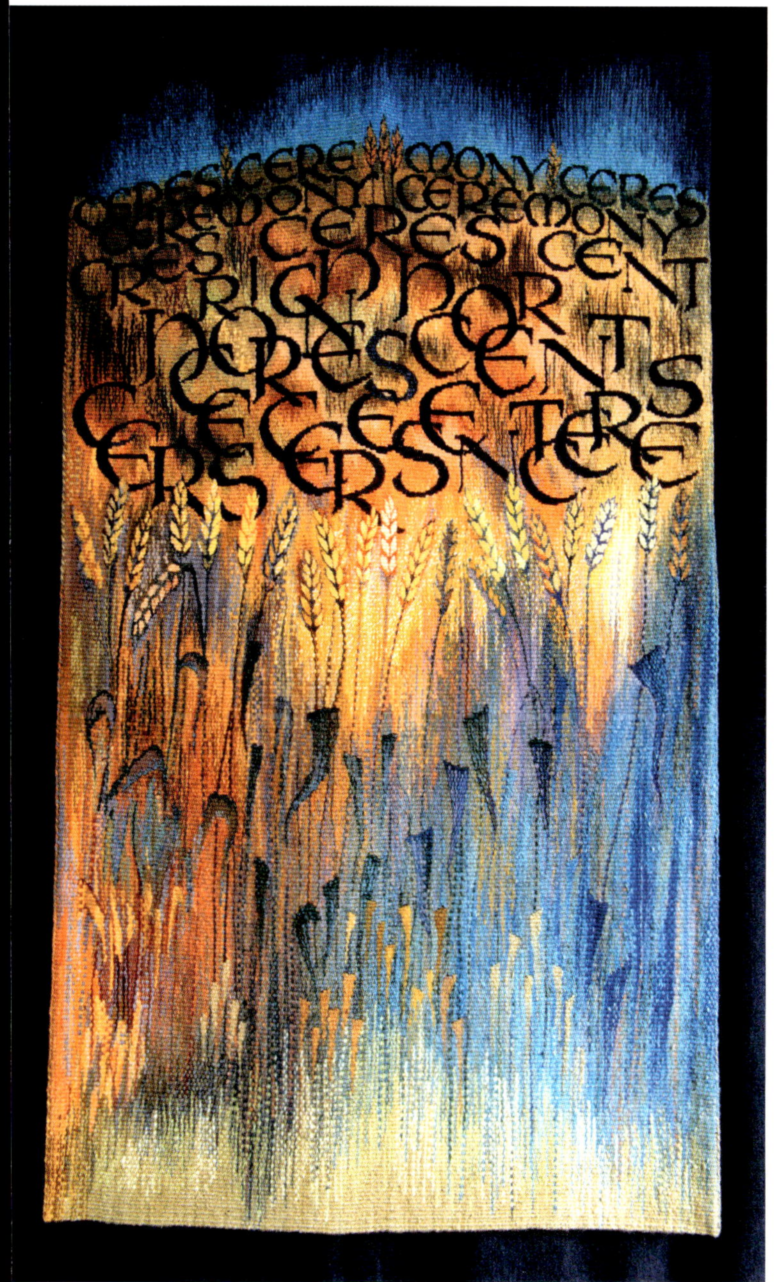

Ceres Ceremony
Pat Johns
1985 | 48" × 27" | wool

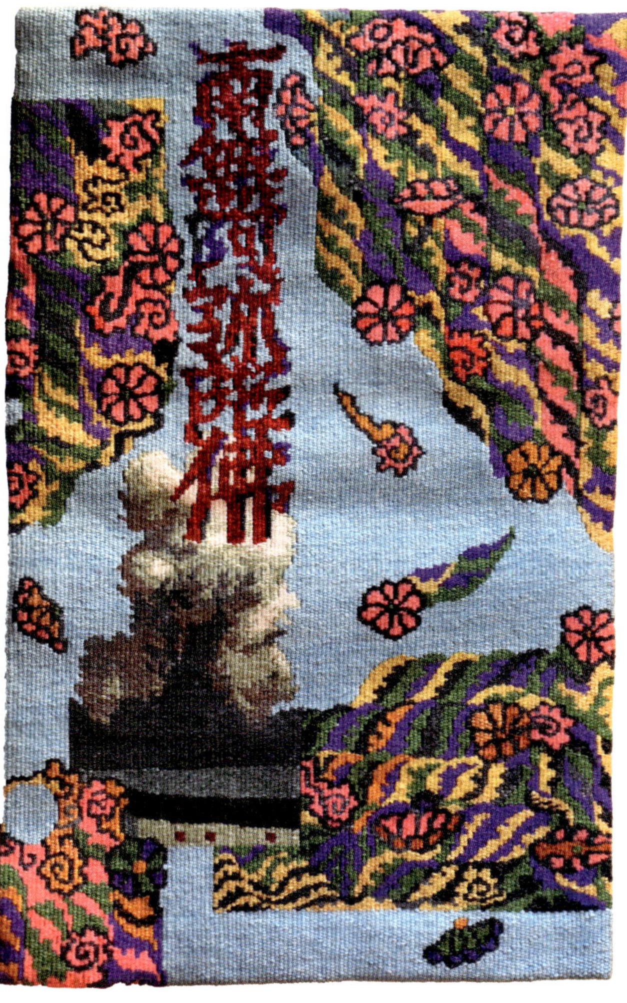

Namu Amida busto (I take refuge in Amida)
Mieko Konaka
2000 | 22" × 15" | wool; cotton warp

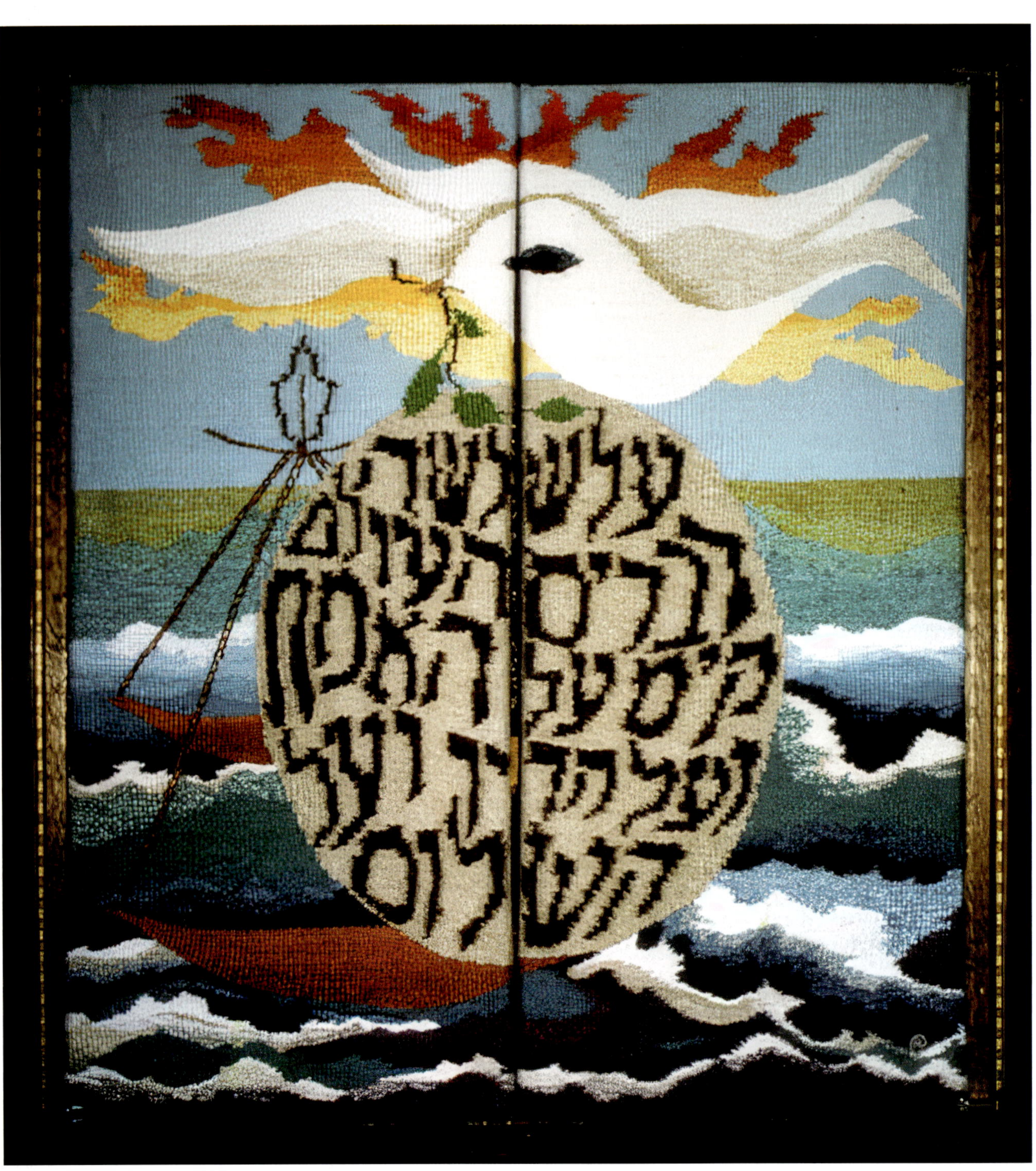

The ark curtain in a synagogue covers the entryway to the storage area for the Torah scrolls. Renate Chernoff's title translates what the Hebrew says. The curtain words guard the words within, with a stylized dove overseeing all.

OPPOSITE: *The World Is Based on Three Foundations: Truth, Justice and Peace*
Renate Chernoff
dimensions of each of two: 49" × 22.5" | wool, rayon

Jeyhan Rohani made several tapestries to honor his Islamic faith. *Āyat al-Kursī*, the throne verse of the Qur'an, is the one in which God introduces himself to mankind and says that nothing and no one is comparable to God.

BELOW: *Ayat Al Kursi*
Jeyhan Rohani
1989 | 42" × 54.5"

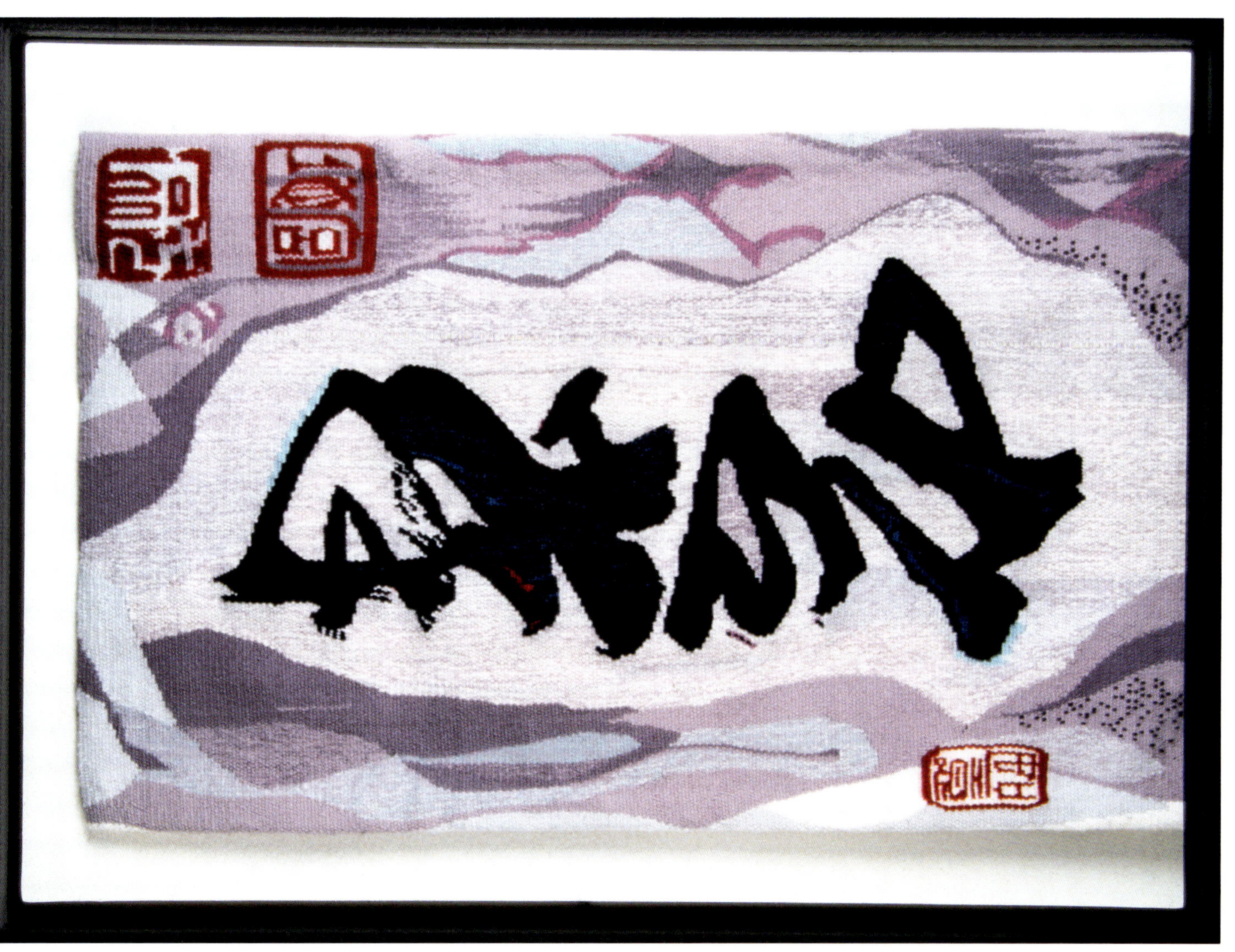

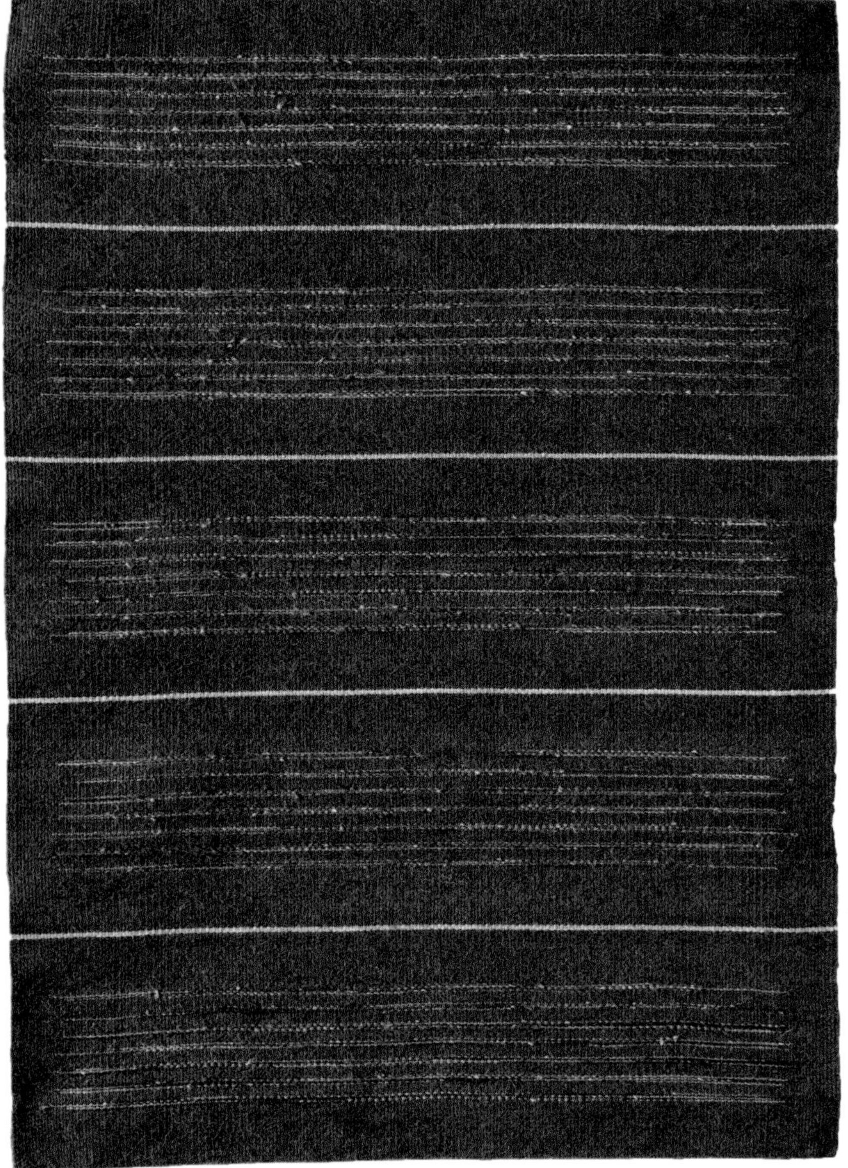

LEFT: *Prajnaparamita*
Michael Rohde
2024 | 41.5" × 30" | camel hair, wool, indigo
Photographer: W. Scott Miles

OPPOSITE, TOP: *The Color of No*
Susan Iverson
Photograph taken in gallery during exhibition
2022

OPPOSITE, BOTTOM: *Jonah*
Gabriella Hajnal
1968 | 58.25" × 94.5" | wool

Susan Iverson once filled several gallery rooms with her series of nos. She has explained that she chose the word "for its simplicity, its frequent use, its depth of meaning, and most importantly [that] it did not conjure up a specific image." She discovers that the colors she uses deepen how she understands the word and add to its meanings. The more she weaves them, the more she sees and hears in her mind's ear. And she continues to weave them.

Michael Rohde explains his *Prajnaparamita*: "It is the Sanskrit word conveying the idea of perfection of wisdom." The teaching centers on the empty nature of things and many thoughts. It "mirror[s] the shape of the written texts in the original format." What you read here is the suggestion of language, or perhaps the wisdom it articulates, not an actual text.

Gabriella Hajnal's text (in Hungarian) encircles the figure of Jonah, working like one of multiple frames; it comes from the biblical book of Jonah: "And he said: they cried to the Lord and He will hear me; from the throat of Sheol, and you will hear my words. For you cast me into the deep, into the midst of the sea, and the waters caught me; your eddies and foams have all passed over me." The entire image is rich with sea creatures (fish, octopi) and seaweed, with the colors of flames over and under—or are those red and yellow pointed shapes (another frame) teeth, fangs, or even ribs?

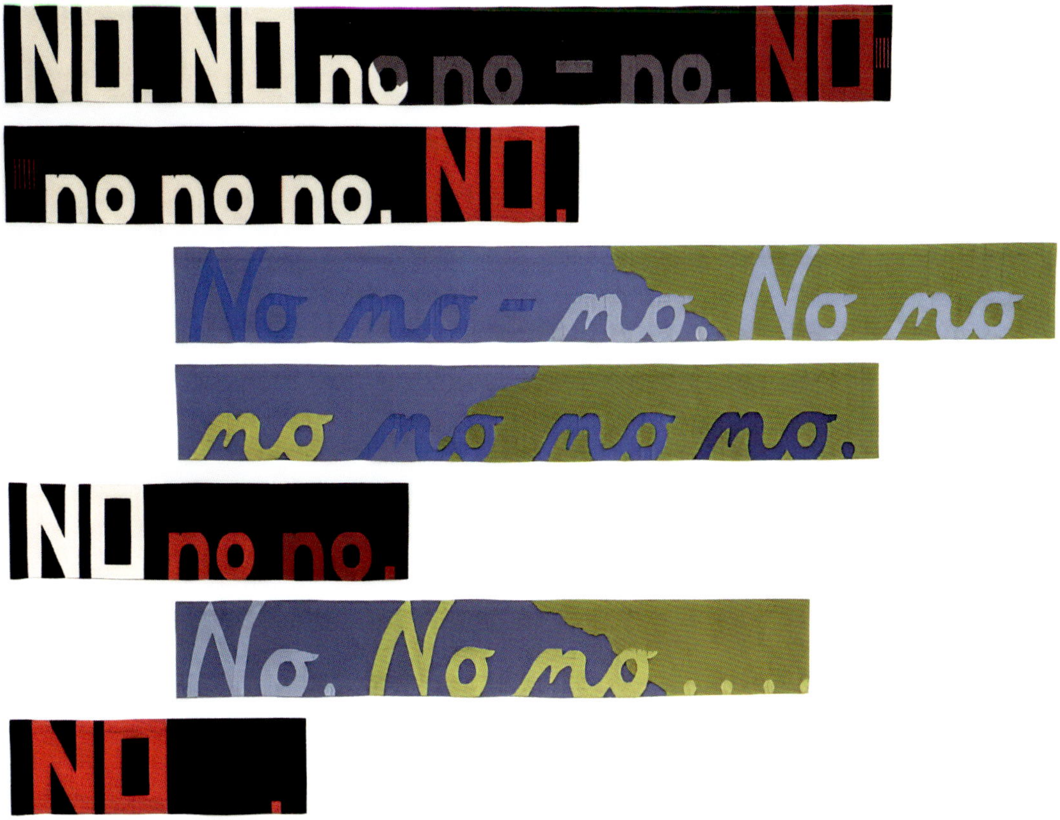

NO, NO no no – no. NO
no no no. NO.
No no – no. No no
no no no no.
NO no no.
No. No no....
NO .

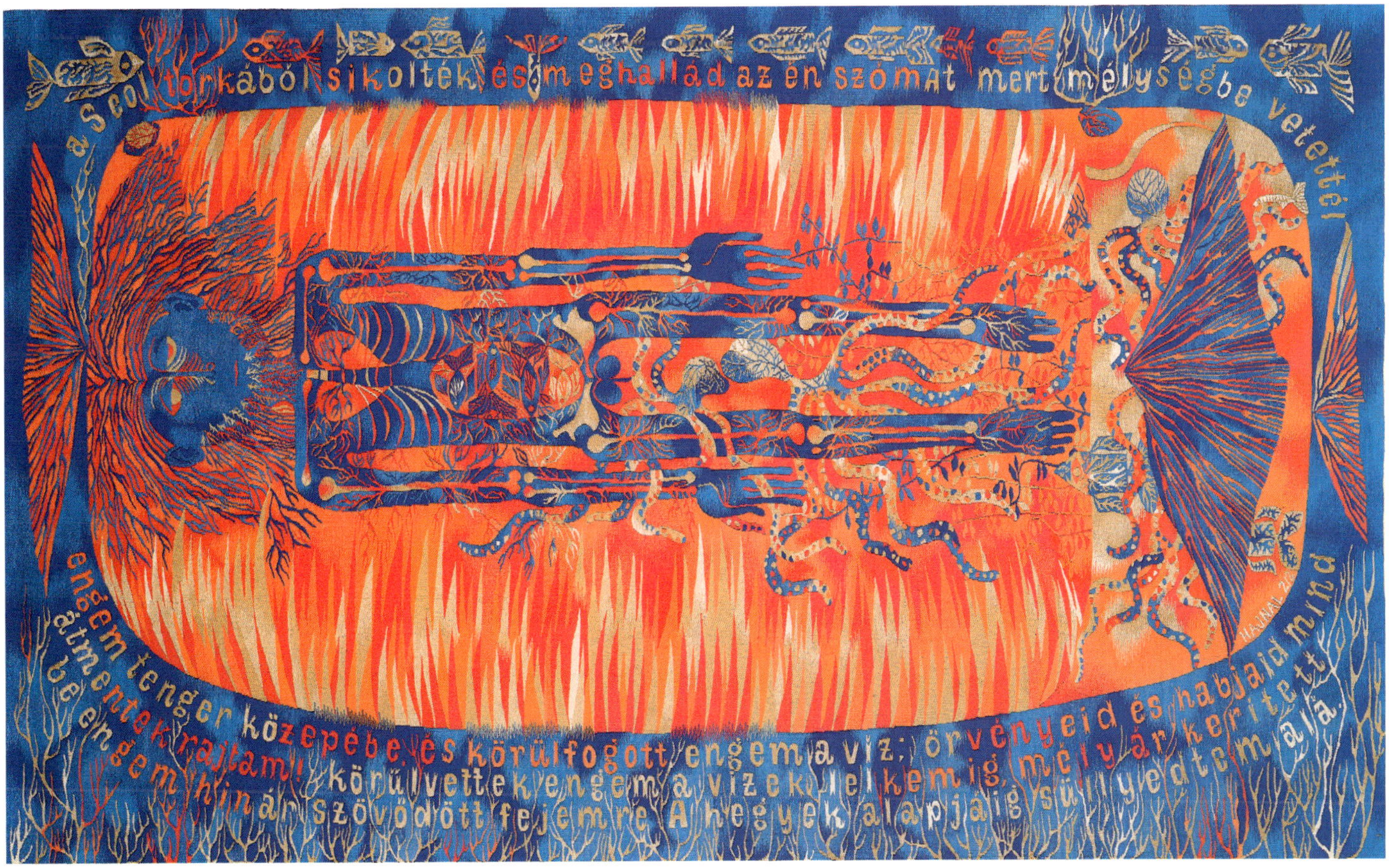

These final three pieces suggest stories without letters, what Andrea Heckman has named "non-alphabetic writing."

Sarah Paul Begay's *Navajo* has a backstory that tells what we may not be able to read, but includes a text even so. Part of what she has done is autobiographical. Amid the geometric shapes and forms of her weaving, she has inserted, in the middle, a line of dancers. The last of these, *to the far right*, is her father, who faces straight out as though to talk with those of us meeting him in this setting.

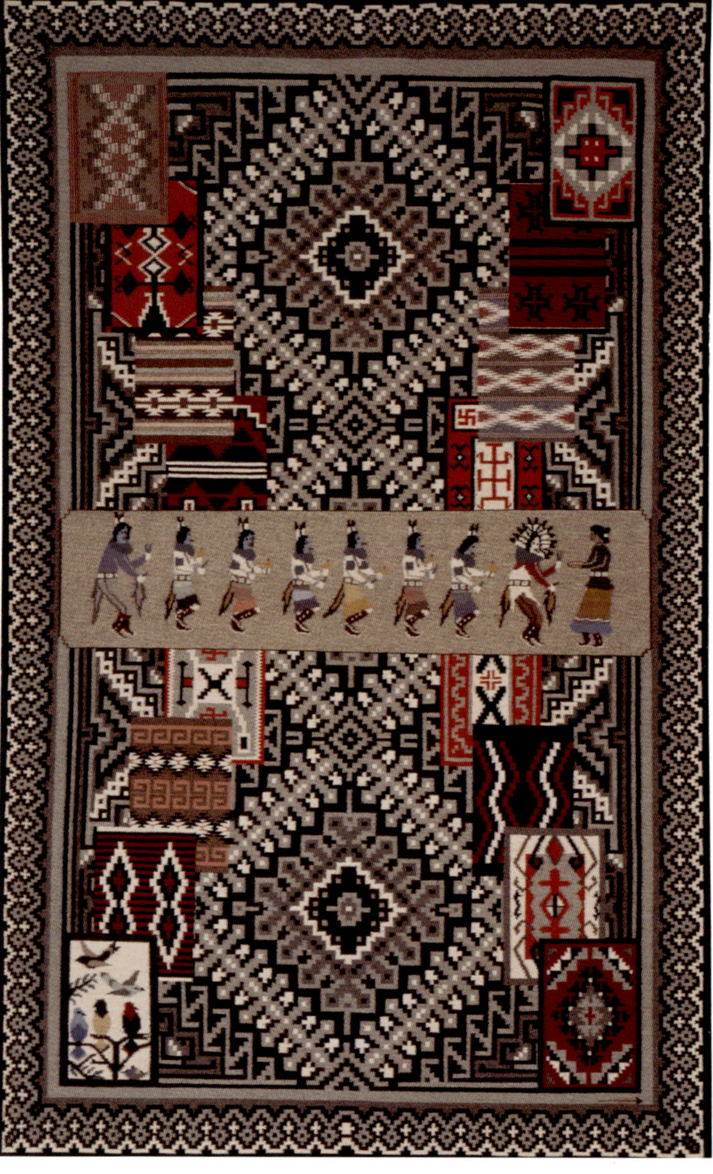

TOP: *The Navajo*
Sarah Paul Begay
1993 | 94.75" × 59.25" | wool
Donated to the Heard Museum by Dr. Charles and Linda Rimmer
Photographer: Craig Smith

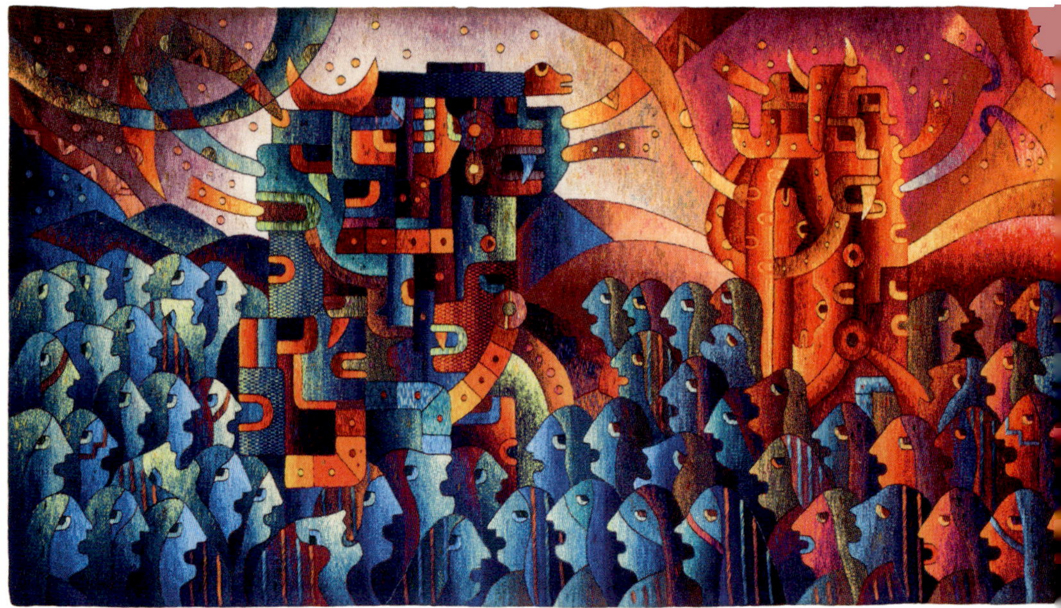

RIGHT: *Rituals and Visions in the Sacred Mountains*
Maximo Laura
Woven by Eloi Pariona for the Laura Tapestry Workshop
2009 | 47.4" × 18'2" | alpaca, synthetic fibers, cotton

Erasto (Tito) Mendoza Ruiz's animals fill the head, as local mythologies fill the lives and imaginations of the Zapotecs.

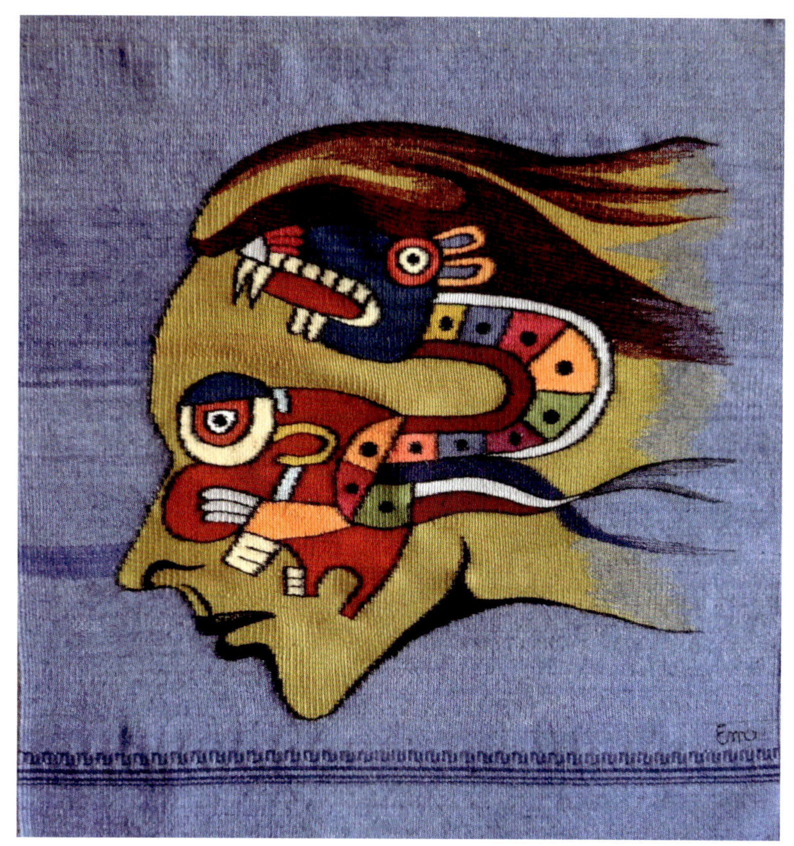

Nahual/Quetzalcoatl (Animal spirit / plumed serpent)
Erasto (Tito) Mendoza Ruiz
2015 | 17.8" × 17" | wool, silk, gold, silver, cotton warp

Maximo Laura is always showing us the history of where he lives (the Sierra of South America) and his ethnicity (Huari). A national treasure of Peru, he specifies in his designs how each symbol (for his cartoons, he draws simple shapes with lines) represents what he is communicating.

About this piece, he says, "According to the Andean worldview, the spirits rest within the mountains; from there, they help and protect their people in all activities of life."

He often uses red and blue—red as the earth (where we live) and blue as water (necessary for life).

Thus, he has given us an entire cosmos.

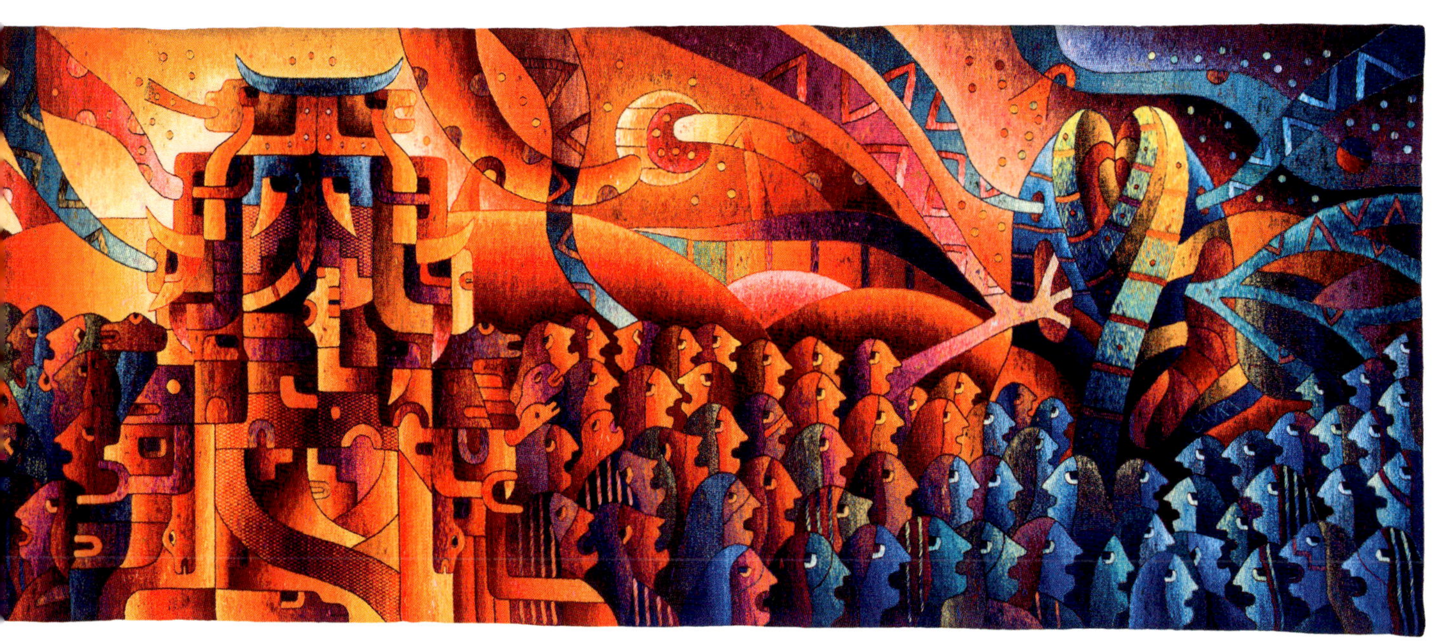

CONCLUSIONS

Laura fills his work with visual content that shows us his world—Huari history, myths, and metaphors. His goals are akin to what I wish to do in this book: share images from the worlds of tapestry and its traditions, stories, echoes, impressions. They tell us, as people who look at tapestries, what we can take into account when we study these images. As tapestry weavers, what we do with what we learn here will tell us the next steps we might take. And while I encourage the weavers out there to make something beautiful, something memorable, something that enables you to play with thread and the images in your mind, I also encourage the non-weavers to look carefully at the tapestries, both here and wherever else you encounter them. What do you see? What surprises you? What elements work especially well? How do they expand your idea of art?

I have written this book believing that the images (even more than what I write) will trigger ideas and, indeed, new places to go.

I wish you well.

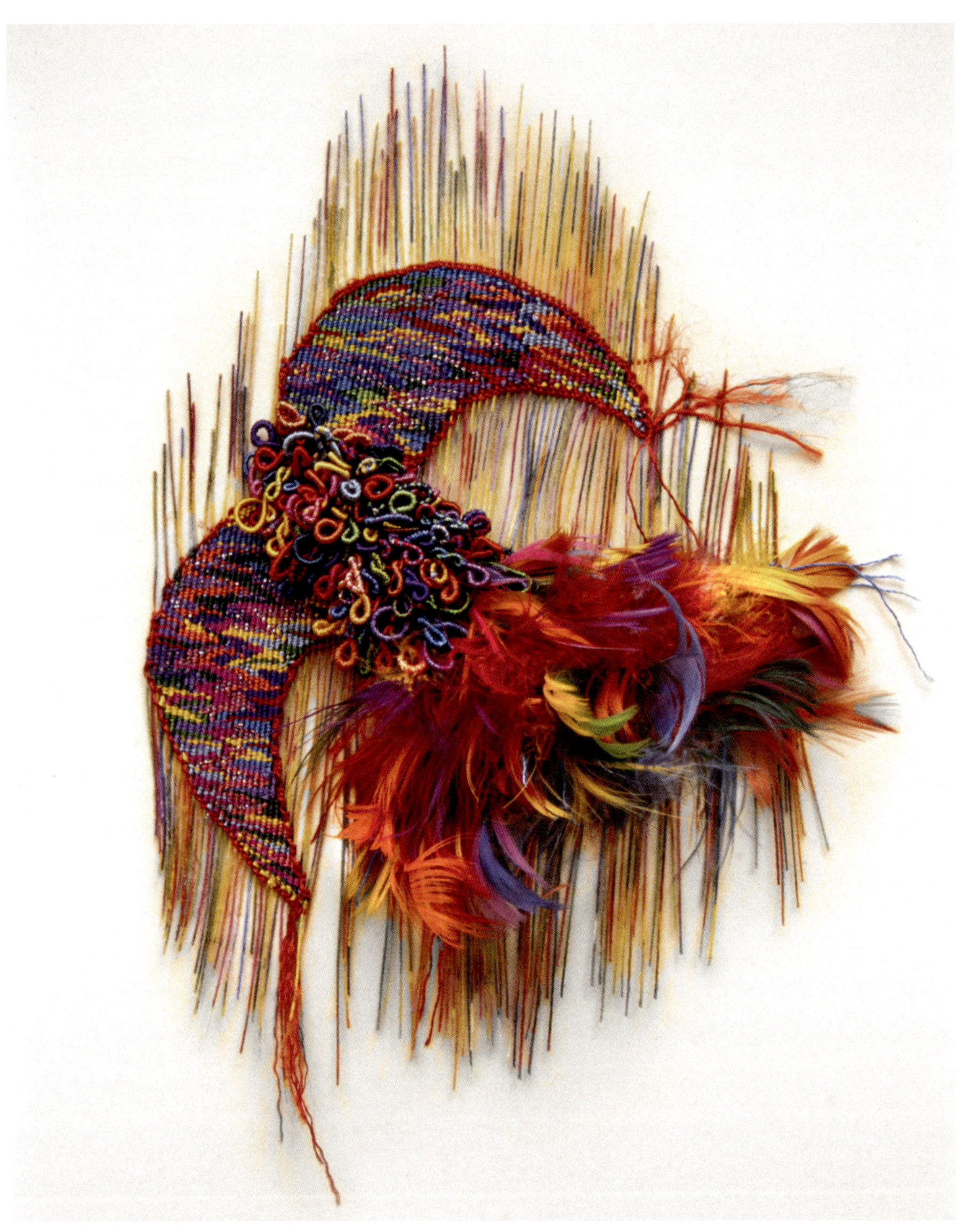

Homage to Bonaventura. Songbird
Anita Berman
1993 | 8" × 6" | rayon

INDEX of CONTRIBUTORS

Entries note birthplace and (if different) place of residence.

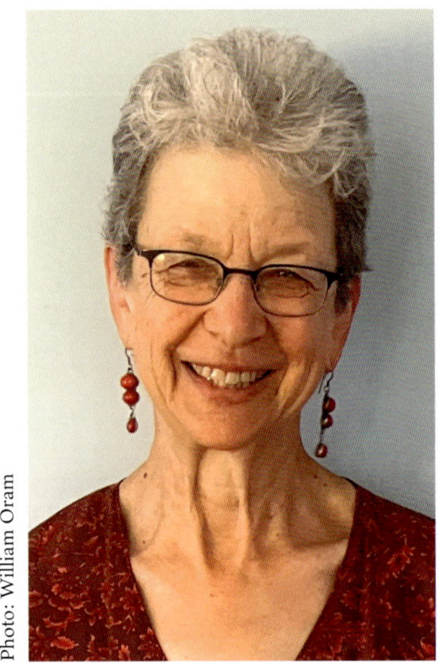

Photo: William Oram

Micala Sidore completed her first tapestry in 1979 and, between 1984 and 1987, interned at the renowned Manufacture Nationale des Gobelins in Paris, obtaining a rich foundation in the techniques and aesthetics of traditional French tapestry. At their request, she co-represented the studio at the International Tapestry Symposium in Melbourne, Australia in 1988. Her tapestries appear in museums and several private collections.

Micala runs Hawley Street Tapestry Studio in Northampton, Massachusetts, where she works out her cartoons, weaves tapestries, and gives workshops. She speaks four languages and travels extensively, conversing with weavers everywhere and sharing their work.

For more than 45 years, Micala has published articles and given talks and workshops throughout North America, Europe, Australia, and New Zealand. She exhibits her own work in individual and group shows in North America, Australia, and Poland. She is the author of over 45 articles as well as the book *The Art Is the Cloth: How to Look at and Understand Tapestries*. www.hawleystreet.com